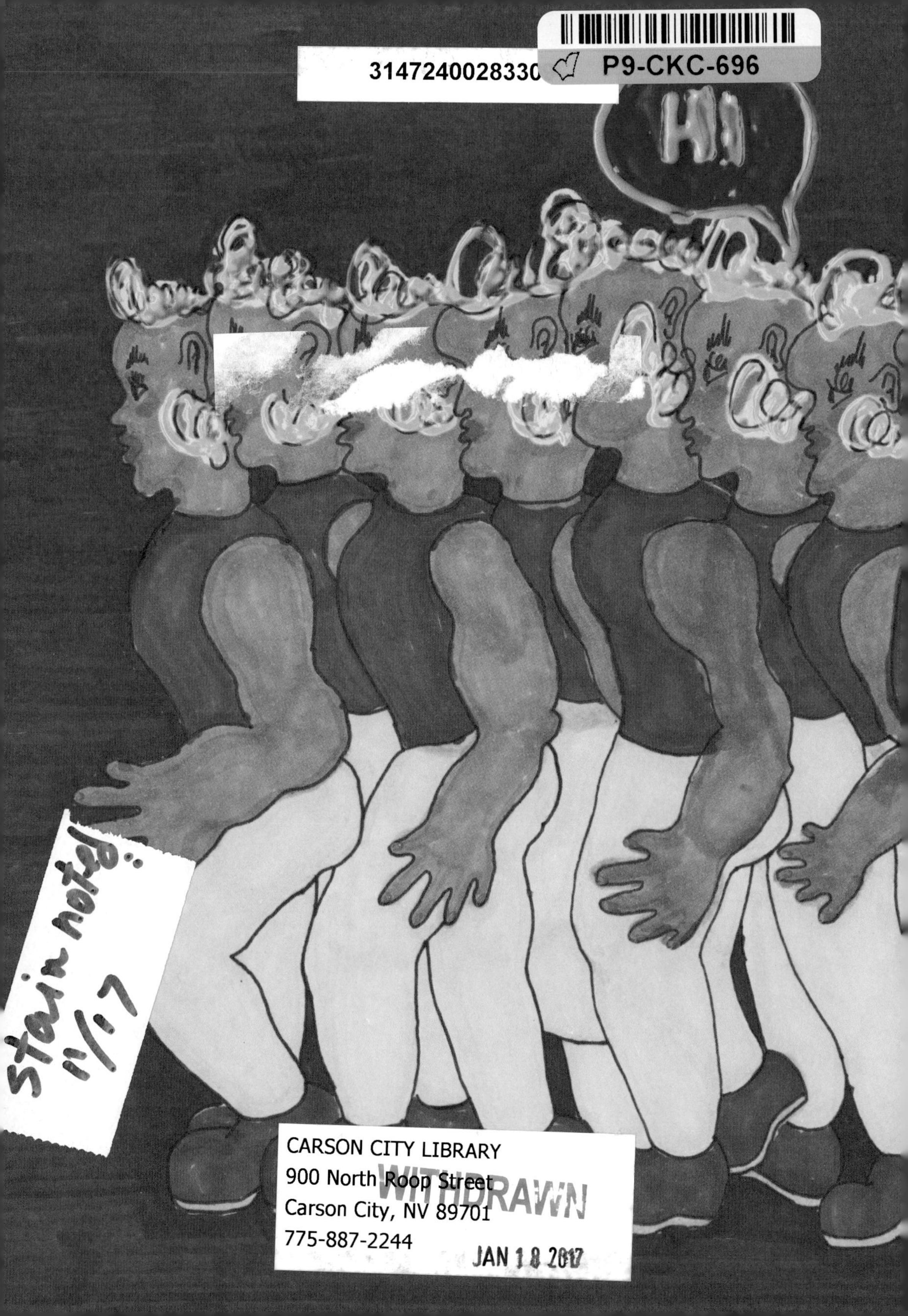
HI

THE BEST AMERICAN

# Comics 2016

GUEST EDITORS OF THE
BEST AMERICAN COMICS

2006 HARVEY PEKAR
2007 CHRIS WARE
2008 LYNDA BARRY
2009 CHARLES BURNS
2010 NEIL GAIMAN
2011 ALISON BECHDEL
2012 FRANÇOISE MOULY
2013 JEFF SMITH
2014 SCOTT McCLOUD
2015 JONATHAN LETHEM
2016 ROZ CHAST

THE BEST AMERICAN

# Comics

## 2016

EDITED *and* INTRODUCED

*by* Roz Chast

BILL KARTALOPOULOS,
*series editor*

HOUGHTON MIFFLIN HARCOURT

BOSTON · NEW YORK    2016

www.hmhco.com

*Library of Congress Cataloging-in-Publication Data is available.*

ISBN 978-0-544-75035-7

Book design: David Futato          Cover art: Marc Bell
Endpaper art: Char Esmé           Cover art direction: Christopher Moisan

PRINTED IN THE UNITED STATES OF AMERICA

DOC 10 9 8 7 6 5 4 3 2 1

Permissions credits are located on page 378.

# Contents

# Foreword

There is no "mainstream" in comics.

It's hard to conceive of there being a "mainstream" in comics for the simple reason that comics aren't a mass medium anymore. Not really. Not like they were in the early twentieth century, when the majority of American readers faithfully followed daily comic strips in the pages of newspapers, before radio became a fixture in the American home.

And comics aren't a mass medium like they were in the mid-twentieth century, when millions of copies of staple-bound "comic books" were bought at American newsstands and drugstores, before television became a part of daily life.

The larger book publishing industry still operates on a mass scale and can still be called a mass medium, but mainly by aggregating a large number of smaller audiences (including the audience for graphic novels). Relatively few individual books reach a truly mass audience.

Television and film remain mass media, though their delivery systems and platforms (and therefore their content) are rapidly changing in response to new digital networks and technology. Video games are certainly a highly inventive and lucrative mass medium. And the Internet is the biggest global mass medium ever invented by humans.

If there are any comics today that *are* mass media, and therefore "mainstream," they might be comics like these:

FFFFFFF
FFFFFFF
FFFFFF
FFFUU
UUUU
UUUU
UUUU
UUUU
UUUU-

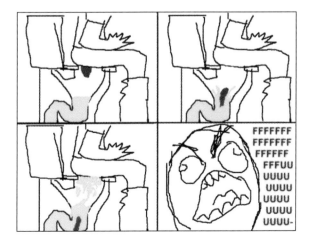

This is (according to online sources) the first of innumerable, anonymously produced "rage comics" that have proliferated virally on the Internet. The number of times that any of these comics have been seen may be unknowable, but the Know Your Meme page documenting the rage comics phenomenon has itself been viewed more than three million times.*

"Comics" is a constructed field, and it is, in some ways, a contested field. Best American Comics, by its very nature, participates in a critical dialogue about what the values and scope of that field might be as it constantly grows in complexity and diversity.

Beginning in the late nineteenth century, comics meant one thing in America: newspaper comic strips. Newspaper comic strips served a simple economic function: they encouraged the sale of newspapers. These comic strips were quite popular and served that function successfully, and as long as they observed broad editorial guidelines they could serve as the site for great aesthetic innovation by many artists including Winsor McCay (*Little Nemo in Slumberland*), George Herriman (*Krazy Kat*), Chester Gould (*Dick Tracy*), and countless others.

In the 1930s, the comics field bifurcated with the emergence of the comic book: a staple-bound pamphlet featuring comics stories. Some were published by established magazine publishers, others by new entrepreneurial outfits, and some were churned out by fly-by-night concerns. These comic books were distributed to newsstands, drugstores, and other outlets that served the periodical press.

The multipage comic book format allowed artists to experiment with new, sometimes innovative formal and narrative techniques while developing genres including superheroes, crime, horror, war, science fiction, parody, romance, and others. The lack of regulation or editorial oversight promoted great freedom that some artists and publishers seized to develop work that could satisfy a more mature readership. But this freedom also permitted slipshod quality, crass trend-hopping, and lurid, sensationalistic content in the hands of less scrupulous publishers, particularly in the 1950s as superhero comic books faded in popularity and crime and horror comics became more popular.

Comic books ran afoul of that decade's conservative culture wars. Comic books were perceived to be contributing factors to "juvenile delinquency," a mythical panic that nevertheless seized the public imagination (as memorialized in films like *Blackboard Jungle* and *The Wild One*). As a group, comic book publishers capitulated to political pressure

---

* In case it's unclear, I like rage comics. I used to tell my students that one day someone would adapt their aesthetics for expressive purposes; now I just show them *Best American Comics 2014* contributor Allie Brosh's work to prove that point.

and adopted the stringent, self-censorious "Comics Code" of 1954, which essentially guaranteed that comic books would only contain child-appropriate content.

This moral panic decimated the comic book industry. Many publishers went out of business, and countless artists, writers, and editors were out of work. Aesthetically, the Comics Code arrested much of the development within the comic book format, effectively banning entire genres, stalling the push toward a more a mature readership, and rendering the field less hospitable to artistic ambition. The superhero genre, which *specialized* in bloodless violence and simplistic morality, reemerged as a dominant genre, and as a result continues to be closely associated with the comics form in the US.

The Comics Code coincided with the new competition that all print media faced from television, a more powerful mass medium that could replace newspapers and magazines as a daily provider of information and entertainment. Even the well-established newspaper comic strips felt the squeeze. Comic strips were losing their primacy as circulation builders and were given less space in newspapers with each passing decade. Only rare sophisticated minimalists like Charles Schulz (*Peanuts*) could produce creatively successful work within these physical constraints.

The many constraints of conservative 1950s American culture were strongly challenged by the countercultural currents of the 1960s and '70s, and comics were no exception. Following the trail blazed by Robert Crumb, whose masterful and prolific comics art provided readers direct access to his subconscious id, a generation of young artists who'd been raised in the pre-Code era (including Art Spiegelman, Bill Griffith, Kim Deitch, Shary Flenniken, Robert Williams, Rory Hayes, Justin Green, Diane Noomin, Victor Moscoso, Spain Rodriguez, and many others) produced a body of so-called "underground comix": comic books that outwardly resembled more nominally "mainstream" comic books in their format, but were published outside of the Comics Code's purview to convey personal visions that often violated the social norms of the day.

Operating outside of the mainstream afforded underground cartoonists unprecedented freedom to experiment with form and content. The comics were not "underground" in the sense that they were illegal (though a few were busted for obscenity or trademark violation), but because they bypassed the mainstream distribution system that enforced the Comics Code. The underground comix, like any print media, needed their own distribution system to reach readers, and they found it in a loose network of "head shops" that had sprung up to sell hippie paraphernalia to a countercultural audience (psychedelic posters, beads, incense, rolling papers, water-pipes-for-tobacco-use-only, etc.). Through this alternative, non-mainstream channel, for the first time a generation of artists were able to use the comics form to express themselves freely and directly to an audience of peers. Issues of *Zap Comix*, founded by Crumb and featuring other contributors, enjoyed a combined circulation of more than a million copies.

But by the mid 1970s, the underground comix era ended. In part this had to do with changing sensibilities, as readers aged out of the hippie lifestyle. Politics and culture were changing, the Vietnam War had ended, and punks replaced hippies as the center of outsider culture. More directly, the 1973 *Miller v. California* Supreme Court ruling empowered local municipalities to enforce local standards of "obscenity," opening the door for zealous prosecutors to shut down undesirable head shops and other businesses, thus disrupting the alternative distribution network for countercultural material.

Meanwhile, the mass market newsstand-based channel for commercially driven comic books was also in decline. Comic books faced falling sales. The audience for superhero comic books was aging and shrinking but became more dedicated, sticking with titles longer, collecting back issues, and attending early fan conventions. The industry attracted fewer new readers, but adjusted its content to serve a new kind of older, long-term reader. An alternative distribution channel was created to serve the new subcultural audience for superhero comic books: a network of specialty comic book stores that has come to be known as the "direct market." With their cardboard boxes full of back issues, these were similar to stores carrying sports memorabilia, vintage magazines, coins, and stamps, but also offered up fresh weekly content delivered directly to a hardcore fan base from the commercial comic book publishers via new distributors. Specialty comic book stores serving a subcultural audience came to replace mass market newsstand distribution as the primary outlet for commercial comic books.

This new subcultural pipeline for comic book aficionados also became the distribution channel for the next wave of independent comics. Artists like Daniel Clowes, Peter Bagge, Julie Doucet, the Hernandez Brothers, Charles Burns, Chester Brown, and many more who came of age after the underground comix period were similarly dedicated to producing personal, artistic, expressive and innovative comic books. In the 1980s and '90s these artists began publishing their work, often through boutique publishers like Fantagraphics and Drawn and Quarterly. The comic book specialty stores that rose to meet the needs of a fan audience did not generally focus on this kind of material, but they did carry it and provided a natural conduit for the dedicated readers who sought out this work.

Outside of the increasingly conservative field of the newspaper comic strip, the subculture of the specialty comic book marketplace largely defined the "comics" field from the late '70s through the end of the millennium. Within this specialist microcosm, highly relative terminology began to acquire new semantic meaning. Superhero comics and other genre comics, clinging to their one-time mass market status and bolstered by their relatively large market share within the small specialty marketplace, were called "mainstream" comics. Anything else was "alternative."

Of course it was the "alternative" comics, with their wide range of human stories and diverse artistic styles, that eventually connected with a more general readership outside of the bubble world of the comic book store. Art Spiegelman's Pulitzer Prize–winning graphic novel *Maus* was an anomaly until it was followed several years later by other book-format "graphic novels," including Chris Ware's *Jimmy Corrigan—the Smartest Kid on Earth* and Daniel Clowes's *David Boring*. These and others (including an influx of popular manga) helped establish the graphic novel as a permanent category of mainstream publishing culture. A flood of book-format comics has poured into libraries and bookstores since then, creating a massive new structural (and cultural) bifurcation in the comics field. Genre-based comics continue to dominate the specialty marketplace; they have also traveled into the mainstream of culture, but most powerfully as adapted films and television programs (*The Avengers*, *Man of Steel*, *The Walking Dead*, etc.) rather than as *comics per se*.

So what kind of comic is the most "mainstream"? Is it the comic that sells best in comic book stores? Or the one that sells best in bookstores? The one that's been adapted into the most successful film? Or the comic that gets the most reviews from literary critics? Is it something like *Fun Home*, which has followed *Maus* into countless school curricula and was named *Time*'s book of the year when it debuted? Or Raina Telgemeier's middle-grade comics memoir *Smile*, which at the time of this writing has spent almost four years on the *New York Times*'s Paperback Graphic Books bestseller list? Do we measure sales, influence, or prestige? Or adherence to a cultural or national craft tradition? For a younger reader today, the most "mainstream" comic they encounter might be the comic with the most followers or reblogs on Tumblr, or the one with the most support on Kickstarter or Patreon. Different areas of comics can sometimes seem to be jockeying for "mainstream" status in the public eye, and they all have their partisans. But where does this leave the small, self-published work, seen only by dozens, that represents a real breakthrough for some artist? Or the excellent book without a publicist that fails to get substantial notice in the press? Or the incredible comic posted to a blog with only a handful of followers? Comics have gone in so many different directions that there is no baseline—no "normal"—anymore; not in terms of style, or form, or format, or narrative, or method of distribution. The most exciting comics artists today all understand that.

For the Best American Comics, questions of sales, popularity, convention, or even prestige are irrelevant. The Best American Comics is a critical project about comics, and the critical "mainstream" of comics is a deep, heterogeneous timeline of brilliant, singular works that each offer breathtaking new conceptions of what a comic might be.

We seek unique works that display fascinating aesthetic qualities, formal engagement, and innovation in the service of individual expression. All of the memorable works of comics history manifest these qualities—in totally different ways—as they express each artist's unique point of view on the world. The work we seek can be well known or under the radar; it can be highly successful or totally obscure. We are quite conscious that some of the great works of comics history emerged during the rapid churn of highly commercial eras, like the early newspaper comic strip or the mid-century comic book. But in the postwar years, most of the significant achievements in comics have happened outside the nominal mainstream, in the areas where artists enjoyed the most freedom. Regardless, comics, as a frequently marginalized and often commercialized medium, have a history of making art where no one expected it, so we try to remain mindful of every current branch of the comics family tree—even those that don't necessarily call themselves "comics."

Roz Chast is a case in point. As an artist who has been for years closely identified with the prestigious *New Yorker* magazine, she may be as "mainstream" as it gets. I have no doubt that she may be the favorite cartoonist of many people who don't identify as comics readers at all. Indeed, she's not someone who's generally been considered part of the "comics" field for most of her career. Her association with *The New Yorker* seems to overwhelm any other affiliations, but it shouldn't. She has been a cartoonist all along, blurring the lines between the single panel, illustrated texts, and sequence-based comics (her 1987 collection of straight-up comics, *Mondo Boxo*, was billed as a book of "cartoon stories"). The current phase of our ever-shifting context has created conditions that have encouraged the publication of her long-form visual memoir, *Can't We Talk About Something More Pleasant?* (excerpted in last year's Best American Comics). This perceptive, moving, and still funny book about the end of her parents' lives has met with an enormous response, and has, I suppose, brought her into the "graphic novel" club. But as Roz notes in her own introduction to this volume, underground comix including *Zap* and *The National Lampoon* were already formative for her. If she hadn't found a berth at *The New Yorker* so early in her own career, it's possible to imagine her charting a different course in the alternative press, alongside artists like Jules Feiffer, Lynda Barry, Matt Groening, Ben Katchor, Kaz, and others, forging a singular path outside of any nominal mainstream. Fortunately for us, the path she followed has brought her here.

*The Best American Comics 2016* represents a selection of outstanding work published between September 1, 2014, and August 31, 2015. Many of the works we considered came to us through our open submission process, which is open to any publisher or artist, including self-published and online work. Additionally, I sought out work for consideration at comic book stores, at comics festivals, online, and through recommendations from trusted colleagues. I amassed a large pool of comics and selected approximately 120 pieces to forward to our guest editor, who made the final selections that constitute the volume you're holding in your hands. In addition to the work we have reprinted here, I've assembled a lengthy list of additional Notable Comics that appears at the back of this book. If you have enjoyed any of the works in this book, the comics listed in our Notable Comics list are all also worth your time and attention. I have posted a version of this list to my website (on-panel.com) that includes links to sites where you can learn more about these works.

We are always seeking work to consider for the Best American Comics, and work can be sent at any time to our public postal address:

Bill Kartalopoulos
Series Editor
The Best American Comics
Houghton Mifflin Harcourt Publishing Company
3 Park Avenue, 19th Floor
New York, NY 10016

By the time this book is published, we will be seeking new, North American work published between September 1, 2016, and August 31, 2017, for consideration for *The Best American Comics 2018*. I can't recommend strongly enough that any artist or publisher send us any eligible material that they are willing to submit for consideration. If you have produced a comic that you feel good about, we want to see it. The continuing robust diversity of Best American Comics is greatly dependent upon your submissions.

Many thanks to Marc Bell for drawing a perfect cover for this volume. Marc has been drawing wonderful, artful, surreal, and funny comics with a strong, personal world-building component for a while now. It's perhaps appropriate that he follows Raymond Petition as a cover artist for this series, since Marc also has a foot in the world of contemporary art, making drawings and collages for a gallery context. Much has been made of the commonality between Robert Crumb and Philip Guston; Marc shares their influences, but also identifies and synthesizes their differences. Thanks as well to Char Esmé for crafting our excellent endpapers.

Thanks as always to our outstanding in-house editor at Houghton Mifflin Harcourt, Nicole Angeloro, who manages and coordinates the many swiftly moving parts behind this challenging annual book project with efficiency and grace. Thanks to art director Christopher Moisan, who works with our artists on the cover and endpapers for this volume. Thanks to David Futato, our interior designer, and Beth Burleigh Fuller, for managing the complex production behind this book. Thanks as well to Mary Dalton-Hoffman, who secures the crucial rights and permissions for this volume so efficiently every year. I thank all of my colleagues who offered suggestions, advice, and guidance as I worked on this volume.

Thanks, finally, to Roz Chast for her work on this volume. Working with Roz this past year has been a great pleasure. I truly appreciate the unique perspective and sheer enthusiasm she brought to the material we considered this year, and I'll always cherish my memories of sitting on the floor with her, eating PB&J and drinking coffee as we sifted through piles of comics together.

This year marks the tenth anniversary since The Best American Comics was launched in 2006. It is exciting to me to consider that comics is such a rich, diverse, and ever-changing field that I have no idea what the book's contents will look like in another ten years. We hope that you, the reader, will share our posture of openness toward the previously unimagined possibilities of what comics might be.

BILL KARTALOPOULOS

## Postscript

Just as we were preparing to send this book to press, one of our contributors, Geneviève Elverum, passed away on July 9, 2016, from pancreatic cancer. I had a chance to meet Geneviève a few times over the years, and like many who knew her I consider myself fortunate to have had any contact at all with this person who was so committed to the challenge of fully living a human life with integrity. Geneviève did not publish comics often, but as you'll see in the piece we're so happy to include here, her comics were always beautiful and unique, precisely because they were entirely expressive of who she was. I wish she could have lived to see this book, but that's the last reason I wish she was still alive.

# Introduction

I grew up in a small apartment in Brooklyn with an old, cranky couple (i.e., my parents) who liked things quiet. I had no siblings. Books were my main friends, along with crayons and paper and pencils, and my parents, who were schoolteachers, made sure that there was always an ample supply of those things around.

Luckily, I *liked* to draw and write and read. I didn't *like* going outside where it was always too hot or too cold. Also, I was clumsy and a hypochondriac. Reading and drawing and writing—indoors, by myself, in my bedroom—were a way to pass the time and avoid trouble in the form of children I disliked, getting yelled at by Mother, skinning my knees, gossiping old ladies who sat in folding chairs outside my building, bugs, creepy handymen, lockjaw, impetigo, splinters, the mumps, bullies, and so on.

I remember my first exposures to comics and cartoons. I had a friend in the building whose mother didn't care if she read *Archie* comics—unlike my mother, who believed that for every *Archie* you read, you lost an IQ point. I read about Archie and his pals whenever I played with this friend. I had a sense that Archie and Co. were citizens of Planet Duh, but I liked them anyway. My parents bought me Classic Comics, which I hated. I discovered a kindred spirit in Charles Addams one summer when I was eight or nine. When I was around twelve, I read through an older cousin's collection of *MAD* magazines. I especially adored Don Martin and all the parodies of popular culture, particularly the fake ads. And still later came the underground comics, like *Zap*, and *The National Lampoon*, with the Funnies section at the back: Gahan Wilson, Ed Subitzky, Rick Geary, Shary Flenniken, M. K. Brown, to name a few. It was great to know, as a child, that there were other people out there who thought the world was pretty weird.

I loved anything that made me laugh. I was over-serious and anxious, and anything that cracked me up—it was like magic.

As I mentioned before, I loved to draw. I especially liked to draw people, and I liked to draw things that made me laugh. One of my earliest memories of drawing something that really, really made me laugh happened when I was around ten. It was pretty much accidental.

My parents had gotten me a subscription to a quasi-educational magazine called *Highlights for Children*. I was obsessed with a feature it contained called "Our Own Page" that published poems and drawings submitted by kids, along with the kids' names, the cities and states where they were from, and their ages. I noticed that at least half of the drawings on that page that were done by girls were drawings of horses.

The problem was, I did not like horses. I did not ride horses, or read horse books, or watch horse TV shows. If someone had given me a pony, I would have been upset. To me, horses were large animals with enormous, frightening jaws filled with too many teeth, their back legs bent in a disturbing way, and worst of all, there was that eye that always seemed to be rolling around crazily in a gigantic, elongated head.

Nevertheless, I wanted to see my work on Our Own Page, and decided to teach myself how to draw a horse, since that's what was obviously required if that were to ever happen. I would draw horse after horse until I got it right. I got a pad of paper and a pen and got to work. I drew horses standing, horses rearing up, big horse heads with flowing manes and bulging veins. If Sally Sue Smithers, age 7½, from Nashville, Tennessee, could have a drawing on Our Own Page, then goddammit, so could and so *would* I.

I worked very diligently. I even named them: Brighty! Whitey! Flame! Prancer! Did I research these horses? No, I did not. I imagined what they looked like, and drew what I imagined.

When the sketchbook was full, I looked at it, and it made me laugh so hard that bad, loss-of-bodily-control things almost happened. I'd calm down and then look again and start laughing again.

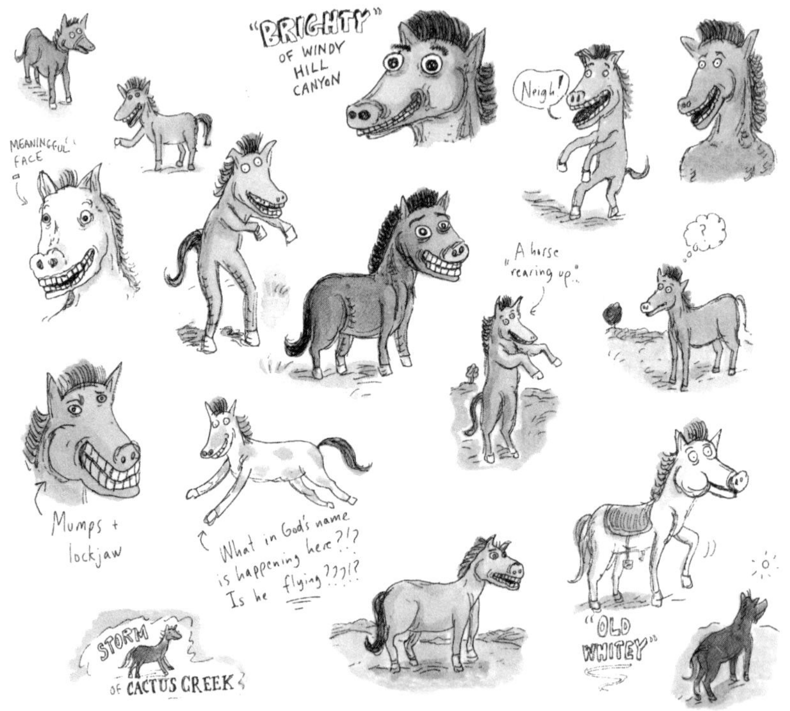
"BRIGHTY"
OF WINDY HILL CANYON
Neigh!
MEANINGFUL FACE
A horse "rearing up."
?
Mumps + lockjaw
What in God's name is happening here?!? Is he flying???!?
STORM OF CACTUS CREEK
"OLD WHITEY"

There was no eureka moment of "My horses came out wrong, but funny. Therefore, I'll be a cartoonist." No, no, no, no, no. But looking back, I might have thought that even if I couldn't draw a perfect horse, drawing a horse that could make me laugh that hard was not *nothing*.

Anyway, I never got a drawing onto Our Own Page, but they did publish a very corny poem I wrote about brotherhood, which I will not share with you.

Comics are a unique form of narrative. They combine words and pictures, but they are not simply illustrated books where the visual plays second fiddle to the verbal. Instead, the words and the pictures tell the story together. In the not-too-distant past, comics were thought of as the bastard child of drawing and writing: not a bonafide book, and definitely not Art with a capital *A*. They were reading material for people who were barely literate. Suitable for children who were just beginning to read, or people who were just learning the language, or folks who were just . . . blockheads.

But this has begun to change. We live in a golden age of comics. Not in the traditional newspaper sense, but often as graphic novels and memoirs. Readers (and publishers) are beginning to see what we cartoonists have known all along: that comics are the real thing. To paraphrase Marjane Satrapi, the creator of *Persepolis*, if you can both write and draw, why should you have to choose?

There are so many things I love about this form. I love that they are generally one-person creations. They are not made by committee, and there's no big budget involved. There are no "suits" looking over your shoulder, telling you that they love your work, but why don't you add a sassy talking dog or a wise alien?

No. You are alone in your comics world. All you need is paper and pen or a tablet and a stylus and, of course, an idea.

Another thing about this form that I love is that's it's very malleable. You can write and then do some simple drawings underneath. Or your comic can be almost completely wordless. You can have two or three panels. Or two or three hundred.

You can use whatever medium you want. Black and white, color, or a combination.

You can be funny, or serious, or both.

You can use photographs. Or drawings and photographs. Feel free to collage the two.

You can be an amazing draftsman, or use rudimentary stick figures.

If it's sequential art, it's a comic. And as long as you are telling your story in a compelling way, anything goes. To quote Popeye, form follows function.

When Bill asked me to be the guest editor for *The Best American Comics 2016*, I was flattered and also terrified. What made me so sure that I could decide who should be included and who should not? I wasn't even a "comics" artist. I was a *cartoonist*. And how did a person decide, anyway? I was no comics historian. I felt completely unqualified. But Bill reassured me that he "just" wanted me to be true to my taste. So, I started to read and reread and re-reread, and sort and select the comics for this volume, and in the process, I began to figure out what I thought about the work.

Last summer, Bill sent me the first carton of the four cartons of books I would receive over the next few months. Inside were everything from slickly produced work by famous names and published by major houses to the tiniest and humblest of self-published 'zines—a few pages folded and held together by a couple of staples. I knew who some of the cartoonists were. But most of them were completely new to me.

In addition to my anxiety about being unqualified, I had other worries: what if people disagreed with my taste and got angry? What if I didn't like enough stuff to fill a book?? What would happen then??? But it turned out I had the opposite problem: I liked too much and had to whittle stuff down.

I made three piles: YES, NO, and MAYBE. There were comics that grabbed me right off the bat, and comics that did whatever the opposite of being grabbed right off the bat was. And comics I wasn't sure what I thought of.

As I read, I saw that I had some definite preferences and aversions: narrative was always extremely important. The story had to keep me wanting to turn the page. Visual delight alone wasn't enough. I liked things that were funny, but not jokey, especially if the writer/artist had a dark, absurd sense of humor. I didn't care if something was sexually explicit, but if it was misogynistic, I got too sad and had to bail. I loved real-life medical narratives. In the end, what is more dramatic than the struggle between illness and health? Or life and death?

I tried to be open to things that I didn't like right away. Not everything reveals itself on first reading. Some selections that I had put in the NO pile became my strongest YES-SES. Others I wanted to like, but I felt like I'd come into the theater in the middle of a movie and didn't know what the hell was going on. And some graphic novels or memoirs were impossible to excerpt—the story resonated only in its entirety.

What you are about to read is a selection of my favorite pieces. There are stories by people you'll probably know, and people that I hope you will discover, as I did. There is traditional storytelling, and also comics that are unlike anything I'd ever seen, but that still work. I've included a mix of visual and narrative styles. I like variety. Also, there's something thrilling about seeing people invent new ways to tell their story. To me, it's proof that the art form of comics is healthy: it lives and grows and reinvents itself. It's alive!

ROZ CHAST

THE BEST AMERICAN

# Comics 2016

# Killing and Dying

## ADRIAN TOMINE

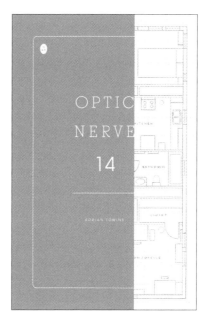

*originally published in*

Optic Nerve #14

DRAWN AND QUARTERLY

6.6 × 10.1 inches • 40 pages

OPTIC
NERVE
14
ADRIAN TOMINE

## Biography

Adrian Tomine was born in 1974 in Sacramento, California. He is the writer/artist of the comic book series *Optic Nerve,* as well as the books *Shortcomings*, *Summer Blonde*, and *Scenes from an Impending Marriage*. His most recent book is *Killing and Dying*. He is also a frequent contributor to *The New Yorker*, with over a dozen cover illustrations to his name. Tomine lives in Brooklyn, New York, with his wife and two daughters.
adrian-tomine.com

## Statement

This story was originally published in issue 14 of *Optic Nerve*, published by Drawn and Quarterly.

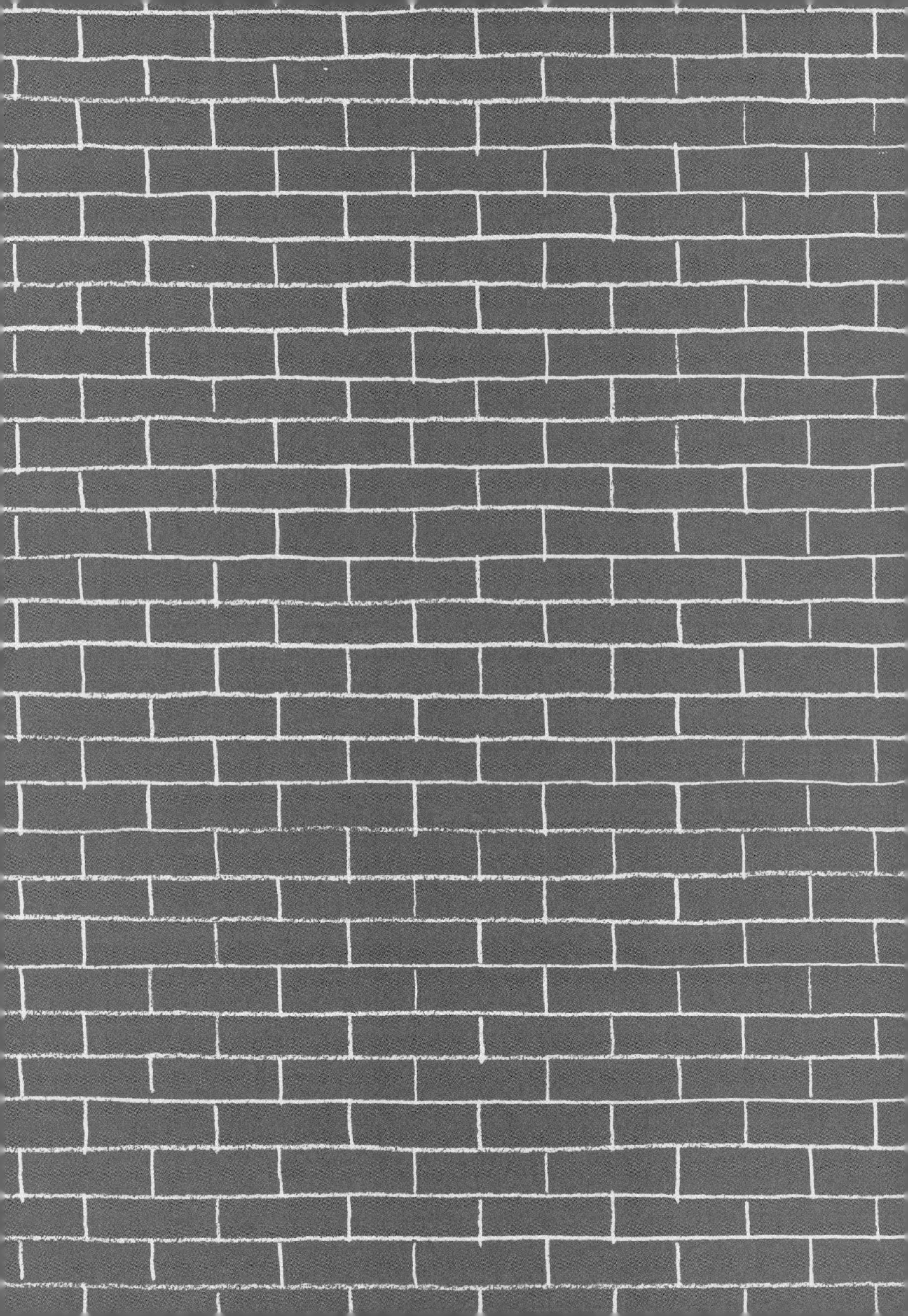

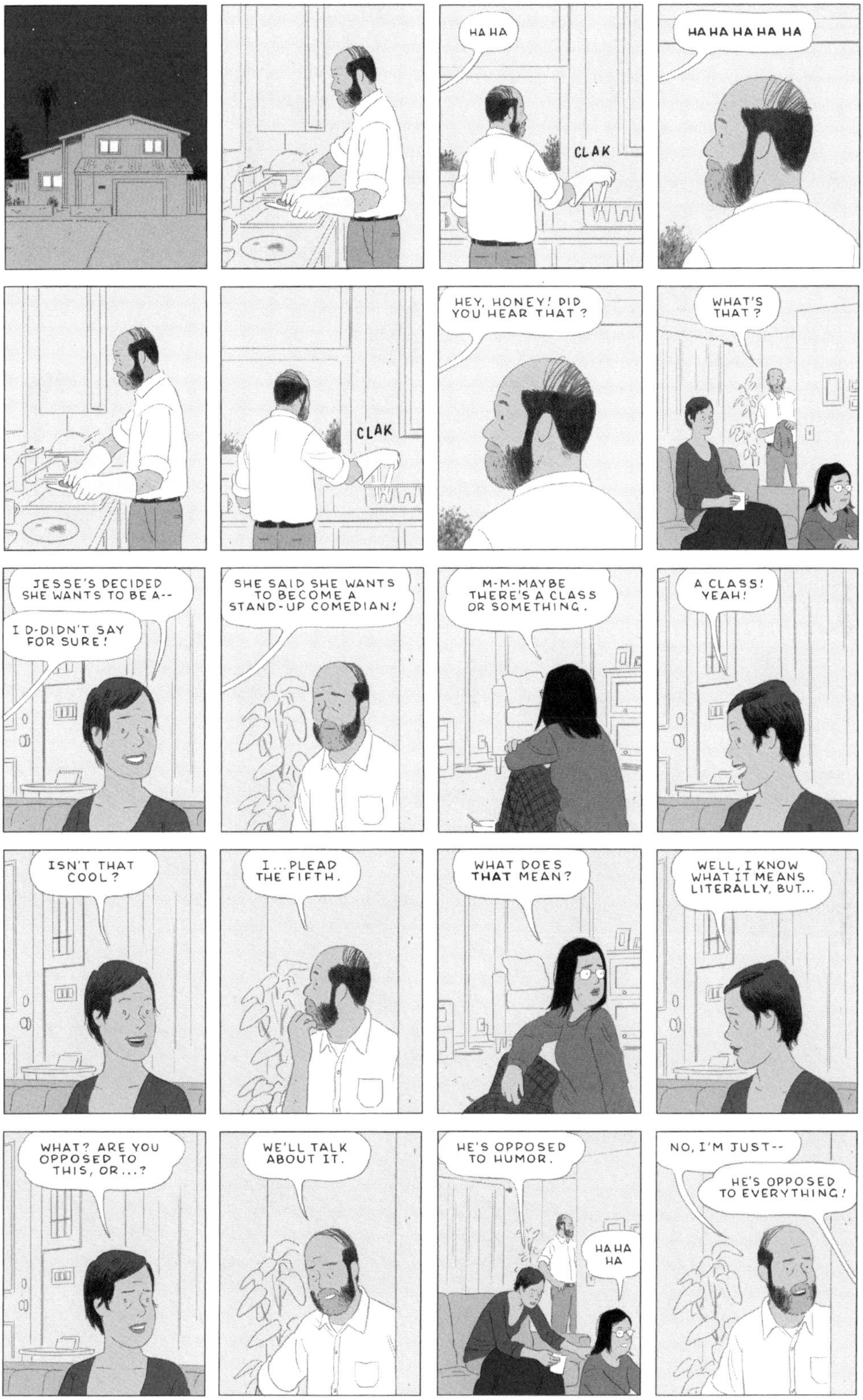
HA HA
HA HA HA HA HA
CLAK
CLAK
HEY, HONEY! DID YOU HEAR THAT?
WHAT'S THAT?
JESSE'S DECIDED SHE WANTS TO BE A--
I D-DIDN'T SAY FOR SURE!
SHE SAID SHE WANTS TO BECOME A STAND-UP COMEDIAN!
M-M-MAYBE THERE'S A CLASS OR SOMETHING.
A CLASS! YEAH!
ISN'T THAT COOL?
I...PLEAD THE FIFTH.
WHAT DOES THAT MEAN?
WELL, I KNOW WHAT IT MEANS LITERALLY, BUT...
WHAT? ARE YOU OPPOSED TO THIS, OR...?
WE'LL TALK ABOUT IT.
HE'S OPPOSED TO HUMOR.
HA HA HA
NO, I'M JUST--
HE'S OPPOSED TO EVERYTHING!

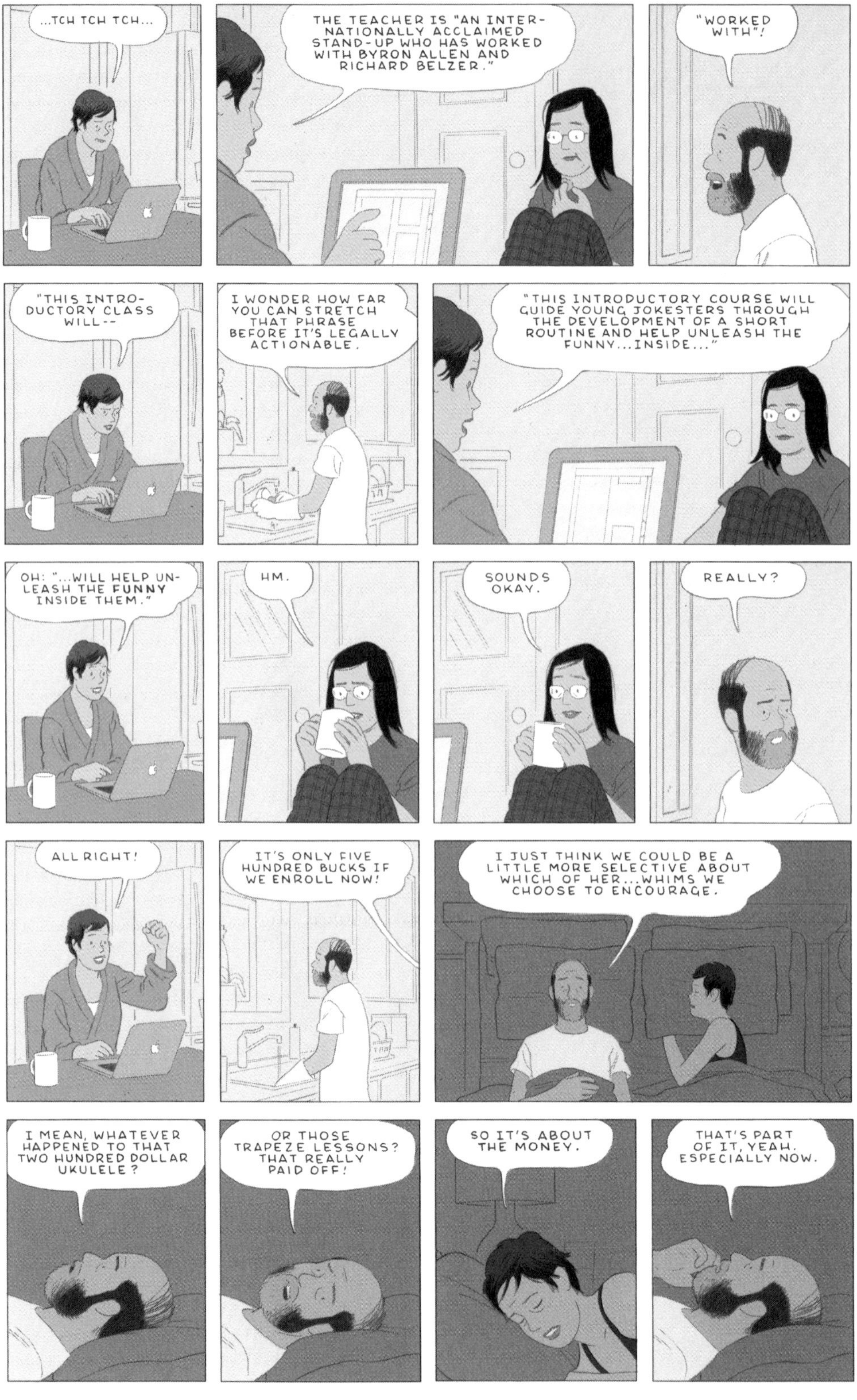
...TCH TCH TCH...
THE TEACHER IS "AN INTERNATIONALLY ACCLAIMED STAND-UP WHO HAS WORKED WITH BYRON ALLEN AND RICHARD BELZER."
"WORKED WITH"!
"THIS INTRODUCTORY CLASS WILL--
I WONDER HOW FAR YOU CAN STRETCH THAT PHRASE BEFORE IT'S LEGALLY ACTIONABLE.
"THIS INTRODUCTORY COURSE WILL GUIDE YOUNG JOKESTERS THROUGH THE DEVELOPMENT OF A SHORT ROUTINE AND HELP UNLEASH THE FUNNY...INSIDE..."
OH: "...WILL HELP UNLEASH THE **FUNNY** INSIDE THEM."
HM.
SOUNDS OKAY.
REALLY?
ALL RIGHT!
IT'S ONLY FIVE HUNDRED BUCKS IF WE ENROLL NOW!
I JUST THINK WE COULD BE A LITTLE MORE SELECTIVE ABOUT WHICH OF HER...WHIMS WE CHOOSE TO ENCOURAGE.
I MEAN, WHATEVER HAPPENED TO THAT TWO HUNDRED DOLLAR UKULELE?
OR THOSE TRAPEZE LESSONS? THAT REALLY PAID OFF!
SO IT'S ABOUT THE MONEY.
THAT'S PART OF IT, YEAH. ESPECIALLY NOW.

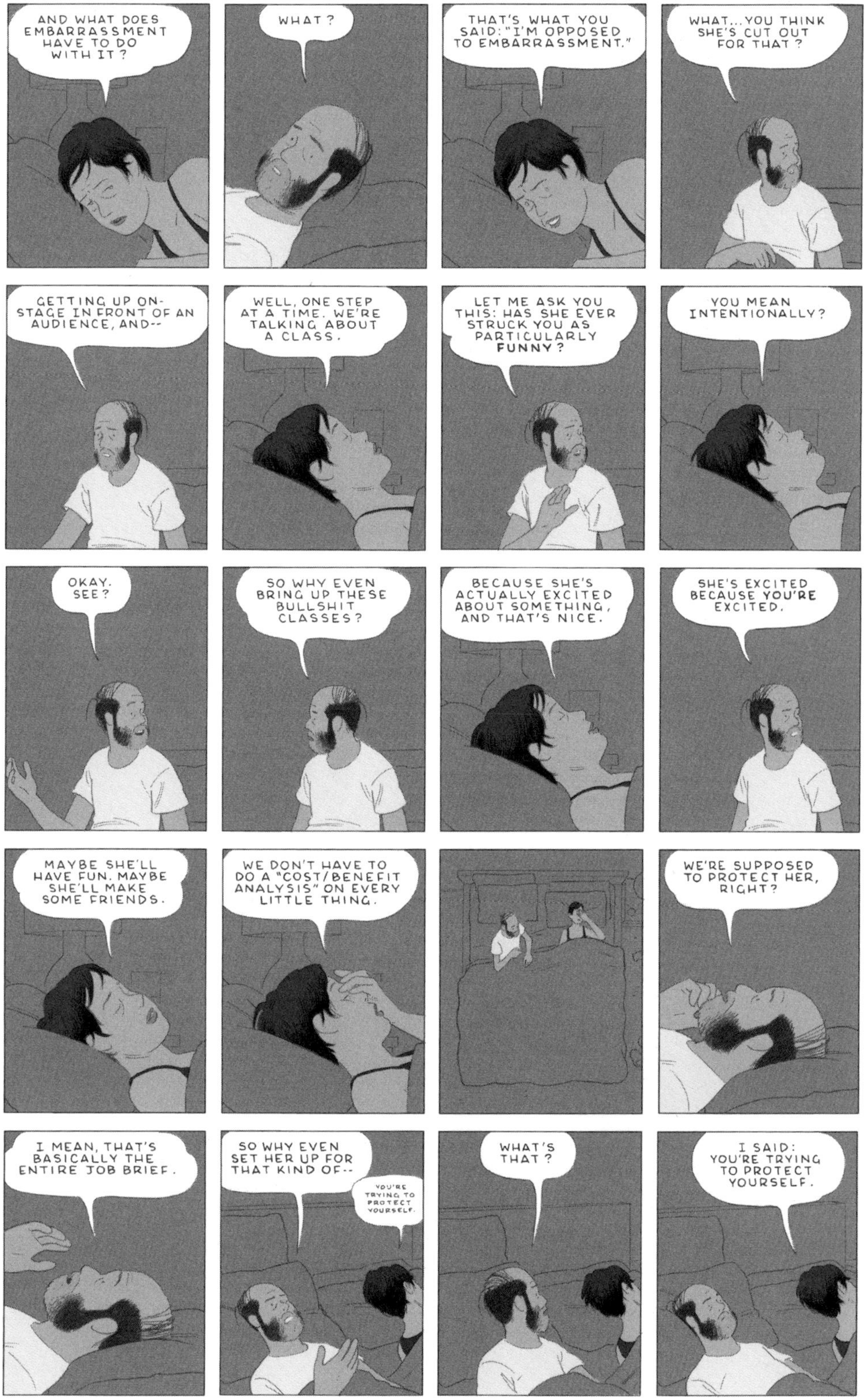
AND WHAT DOES EMBARRASSMENT HAVE TO DO WITH IT?
WHAT?
THAT'S WHAT YOU SAID: "I'M OPPOSED TO EMBARRASSMENT."
WHAT... YOU THINK SHE'S CUT OUT FOR THAT?
GETTING UP ON-STAGE IN FRONT OF AN AUDIENCE, AND--
WELL, ONE STEP AT A TIME. WE'RE TALKING ABOUT A CLASS.
LET ME ASK YOU THIS: HAS SHE EVER STRUCK YOU AS PARTICULARLY **FUNNY**?
YOU MEAN INTENTIONALLY?
OKAY. SEE?
SO WHY EVEN BRING UP THESE BULLSHIT CLASSES?
BECAUSE SHE'S ACTUALLY EXCITED ABOUT SOMETHING, AND THAT'S NICE.
SHE'S EXCITED BECAUSE **YOU'RE** EXCITED.
MAYBE SHE'LL HAVE FUN. MAYBE SHE'LL MAKE SOME FRIENDS.
WE DON'T HAVE TO DO A "COST/BENEFIT ANALYSIS" ON EVERY LITTLE THING.
WE'RE SUPPOSED TO PROTECT HER, RIGHT?
I MEAN, THAT'S BASICALLY THE ENTIRE JOB BRIEF.
SO WHY EVEN SET HER UP FOR THAT KIND OF--
YOU'RE TRYING TO PROTECT YOURSELF.
WHAT'S THAT?
I SAID: YOU'RE TRYING TO PROTECT YOURSELF.

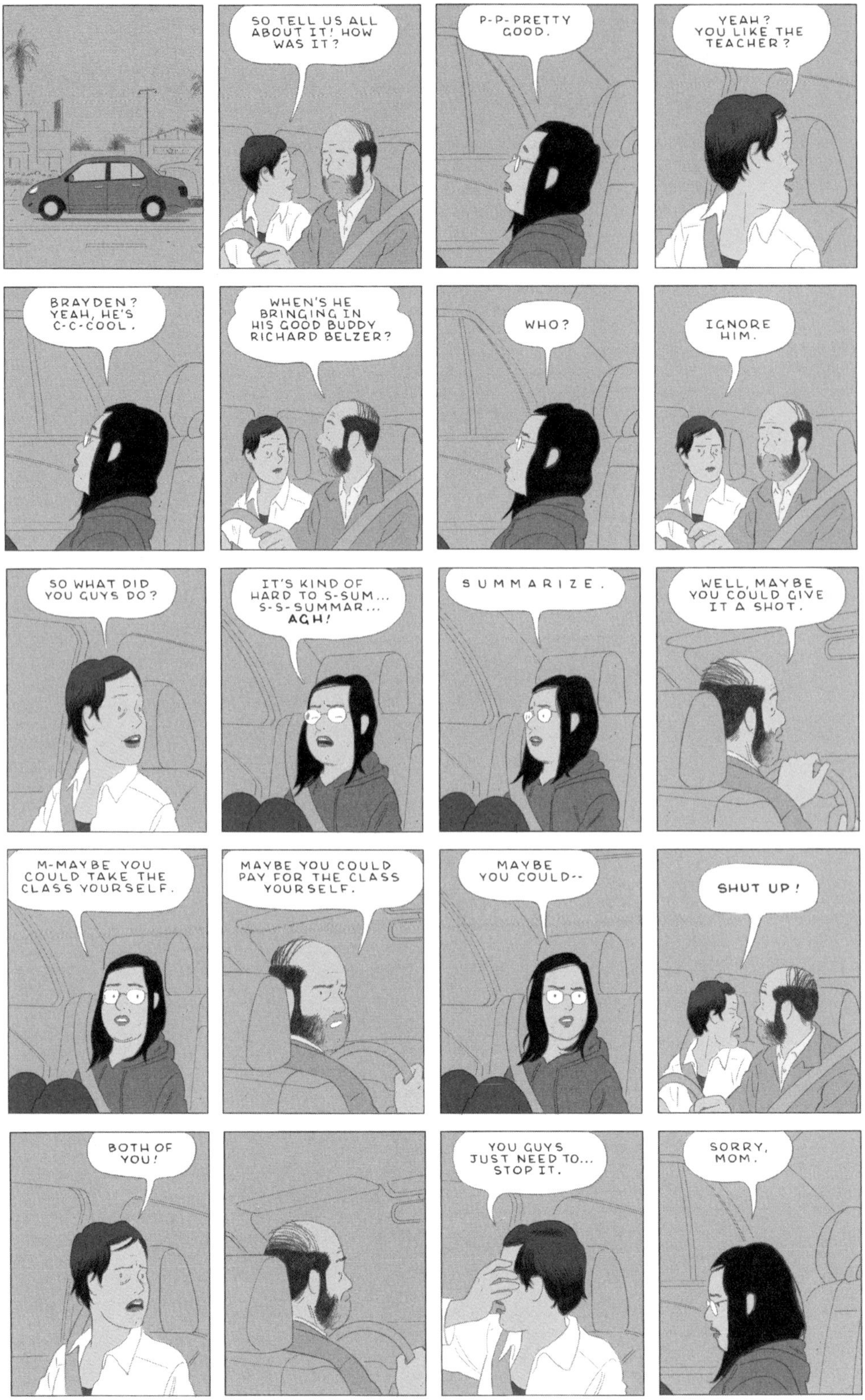
SO TELL US ALL ABOUT IT! HOW WAS IT?
P-P-PRETTY GOOD.
YEAH? YOU LIKE THE TEACHER?
BRAYDEN? YEAH, HE'S C-C-COOL.
WHEN'S HE BRINGING IN HIS GOOD BUDDY RICHARD BELZER?
WHO?
IGNORE HIM.
SO WHAT DID YOU GUYS DO?
IT'S KIND OF HARD TO S-SUM... S-S-SUMMAR... AGH!
SUMMARIZE.
WELL, MAYBE YOU COULD GIVE IT A SHOT.
M-MAYBE YOU COULD TAKE THE CLASS YOURSELF.
MAYBE YOU COULD PAY FOR THE CLASS YOURSELF.
MAYBE YOU COULD--
SHUT UP!
BOTH OF YOU!
YOU GUYS JUST NEED TO... STOP IT.
SORRY, MOM.

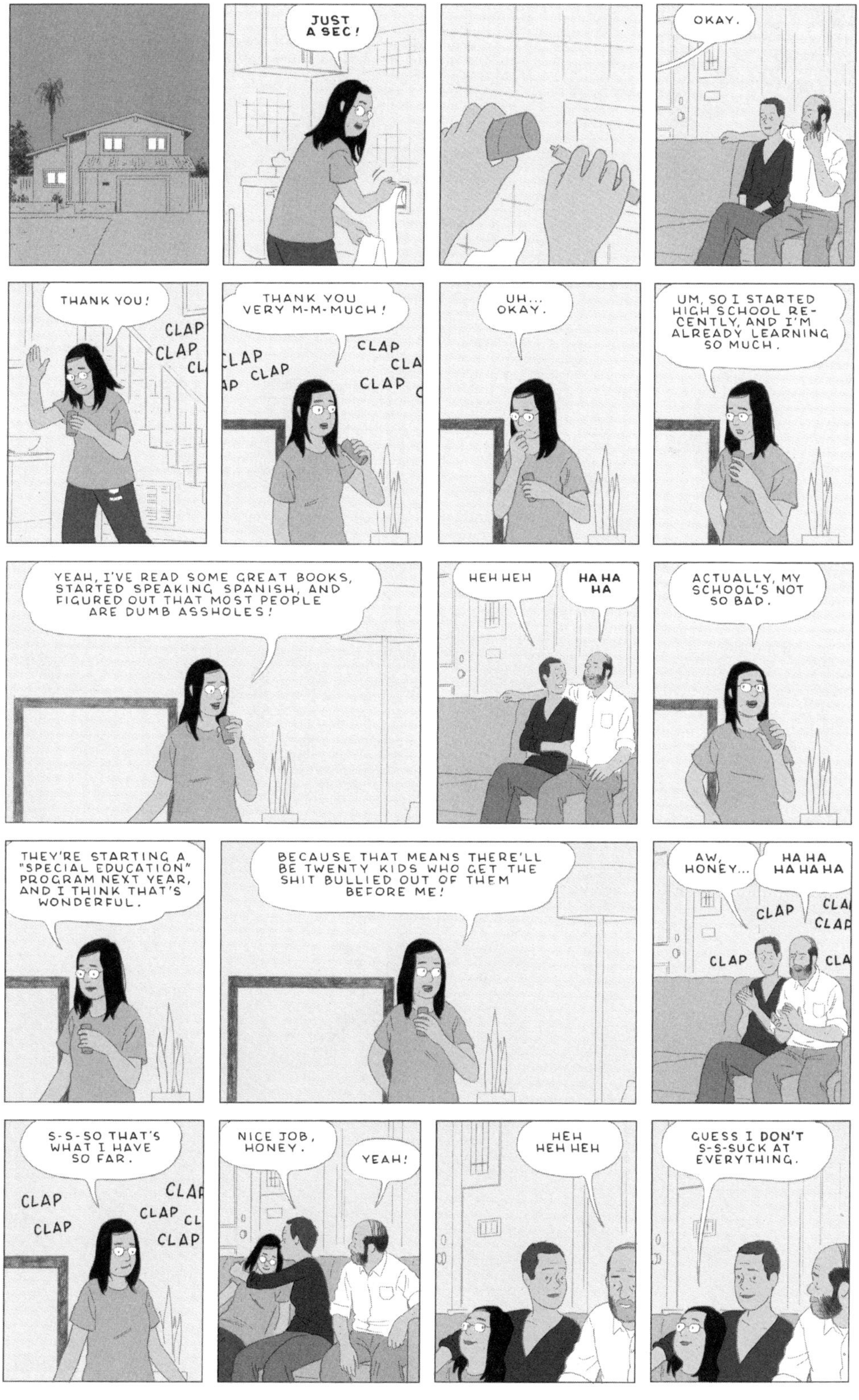
JUST A SEC!
OKAY.
THANK YOU!
CLAP
CLAP
THANK YOU VERY M-M-MUCH!
CLAP
CLAP
CLAP
UH... OKAY.
UM, SO I STARTED HIGH SCHOOL RE-CENTLY, AND I'M ALREADY LEARNING SO MUCH.
YEAH, I'VE READ SOME GREAT BOOKS, STARTED SPEAKING SPANISH, AND FIGURED OUT THAT MOST PEOPLE ARE DUMB ASSHOLES!
HEH HEH
HA HA HA
ACTUALLY, MY SCHOOL'S NOT SO BAD.
THEY'RE STARTING A "SPECIAL EDUCATION" PROGRAM NEXT YEAR, AND I THINK THAT'S WONDERFUL.
BECAUSE THAT MEANS THERE'LL BE TWENTY KIDS WHO GET THE SHIT BULLIED OUT OF THEM BEFORE ME!
AW, HONEY...
HA HA HA HA HA
CLAP
CLAP
S-S-SO THAT'S WHAT I HAVE SO FAR.
CLAP
CLAP
CLAP
CLAP
NICE JOB, HONEY.
YEAH!
HEH HEH HEH
GUESS I DON'T S-S-SUCK AT EVERYTHING.

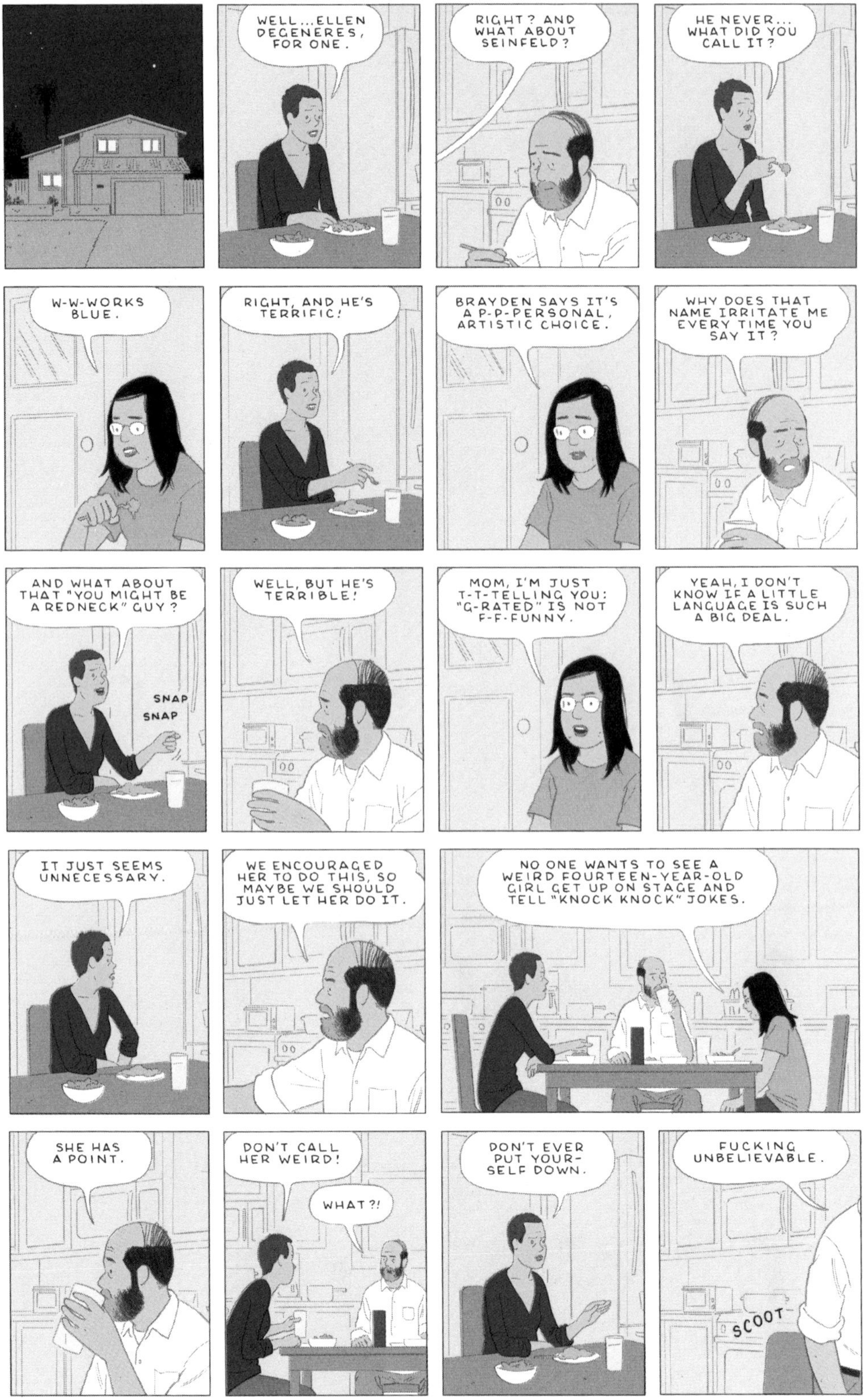
WELL...ELLEN DEGENERES, FOR ONE.
RIGHT? AND WHAT ABOUT SEINFELD?
HE NEVER... WHAT DID YOU CALL IT?
W-W-WORKS BLUE.
RIGHT, AND HE'S TERRIFIC!
BRAYDEN SAYS IT'S A P-P-PERSONAL, ARTISTIC CHOICE.
WHY DOES THAT NAME IRRITATE ME EVERY TIME YOU SAY IT?
AND WHAT ABOUT THAT "YOU MIGHT BE A REDNECK" GUY?
SNAP
SNAP
WELL, BUT HE'S TERRIBLE!
MOM, I'M JUST T-T-TELLING YOU: "G-RATED" IS NOT F-F-FUNNY.
YEAH, I DON'T KNOW IF A LITTLE LANGUAGE IS SUCH A BIG DEAL.
IT JUST SEEMS UNNECESSARY.
WE ENCOURAGED HER TO DO THIS, SO MAYBE WE SHOULD JUST LET HER DO IT.
NO ONE WANTS TO SEE A WEIRD FOURTEEN-YEAR-OLD GIRL GET UP ON STAGE AND TELL "KNOCK KNOCK" JOKES.
SHE HAS A POINT.
DON'T CALL HER WEIRD!
WHAT?!
DON'T EVER PUT YOURSELF DOWN.
FUCKING UNBELIEVABLE.
SCOOT

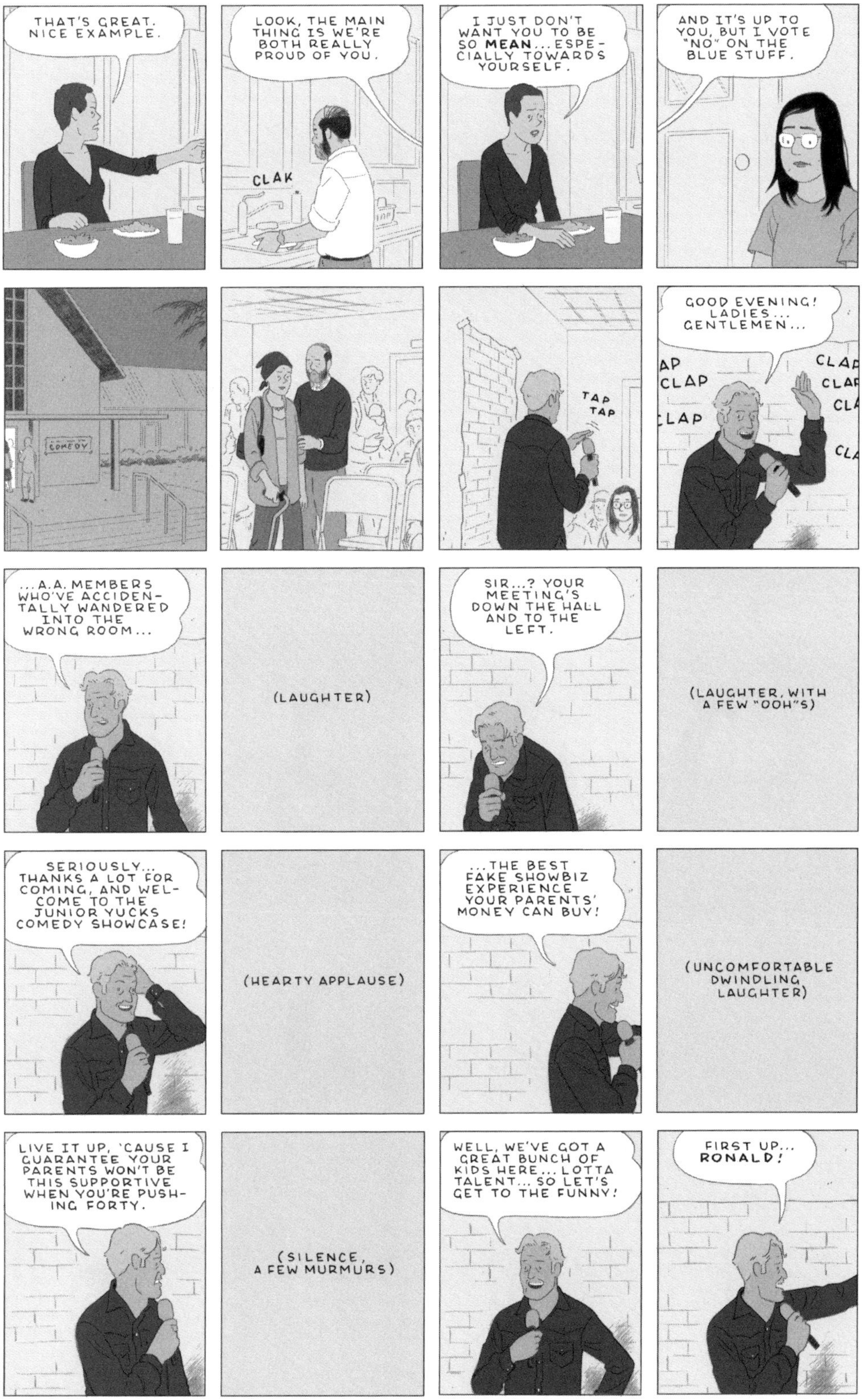
THAT'S GREAT. NICE EXAMPLE.
LOOK, THE MAIN THING IS WE'RE BOTH REALLY PROUD OF YOU.
CLAK
I JUST DON'T WANT YOU TO BE SO MEAN... ESPECIALLY TOWARDS YOURSELF.
AND IT'S UP TO YOU, BUT I VOTE "NO" ON THE BLUE STUFF.
COMEDY
TAP TAP
GOOD EVENING! LADIES... GENTLEMEN...
CLAP CLAP CLAP CLAP
...A.A. MEMBERS WHO'VE ACCIDENTALLY WANDERED INTO THE WRONG ROOM...
(LAUGHTER)
SIR...? YOUR MEETING'S DOWN THE HALL AND TO THE LEFT.
(LAUGHTER, WITH A FEW "OOH"S)
SERIOUSLY... THANKS A LOT FOR COMING, AND WELCOME TO THE JUNIOR YUCKS COMEDY SHOWCASE!
(HEARTY APPLAUSE)
...THE BEST FAKE SHOWBIZ EXPERIENCE YOUR PARENTS' MONEY CAN BUY!
(UNCOMFORTABLE DWINDLING LAUGHTER)
LIVE IT UP, 'CAUSE I GUARANTEE YOUR PARENTS WON'T BE THIS SUPPORTIVE WHEN YOU'RE PUSHING FORTY.
(SILENCE, A FEW MURMURS)
WELL, WE'VE GOT A GREAT BUNCH OF KIDS HERE... LOTTA TALENT... SO LET'S GET TO THE FUNNY!
FIRST UP... RONALD!

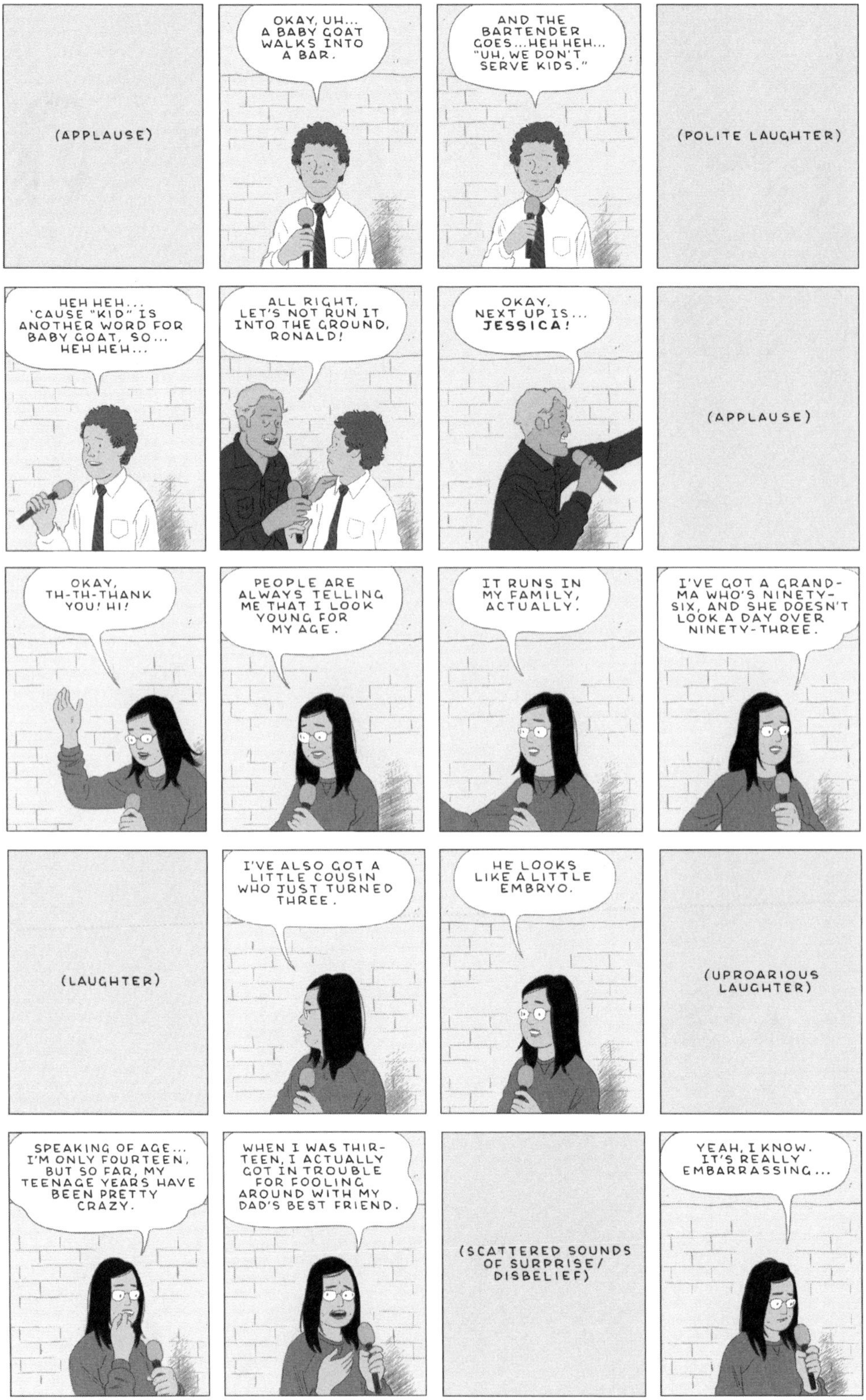
(APPLAUSE)
OKAY, UH... A BABY GOAT WALKS INTO A BAR.
AND THE BARTENDER GOES... HEH HEH... "UH, WE DON'T SERVE KIDS."
(POLITE LAUGHTER)
HEH HEH... 'CAUSE "KID" IS ANOTHER WORD FOR BABY GOAT, SO... HEH HEH...
ALL RIGHT, LET'S NOT RUN IT INTO THE GROUND, RONALD!
OKAY, NEXT UP IS... **JESSICA!**
(APPLAUSE)
OKAY, TH-TH-THANK YOU! HI!
PEOPLE ARE ALWAYS TELLING ME THAT I LOOK YOUNG FOR MY AGE.
IT RUNS IN MY FAMILY, ACTUALLY.
I'VE GOT A GRAND-MA WHO'S NINETY-SIX, AND SHE DOESN'T LOOK A DAY OVER NINETY-THREE.
(LAUGHTER)
I'VE ALSO GOT A LITTLE COUSIN WHO JUST TURNED THREE.
HE LOOKS LIKE A LITTLE EMBRYO.
(UPROARIOUS LAUGHTER)
SPEAKING OF AGE... I'M ONLY FOURTEEN, BUT SO FAR, MY TEENAGE YEARS HAVE BEEN PRETTY CRAZY.
WHEN I WAS THIR-TEEN, I ACTUALLY GOT IN TROUBLE FOR FOOLING AROUND WITH MY DAD'S BEST FRIEND.
(SCATTERED SOUNDS OF SURPRISE/ DISBELIEF)
YEAH, I KNOW. IT'S REALLY EMBARRASSING...

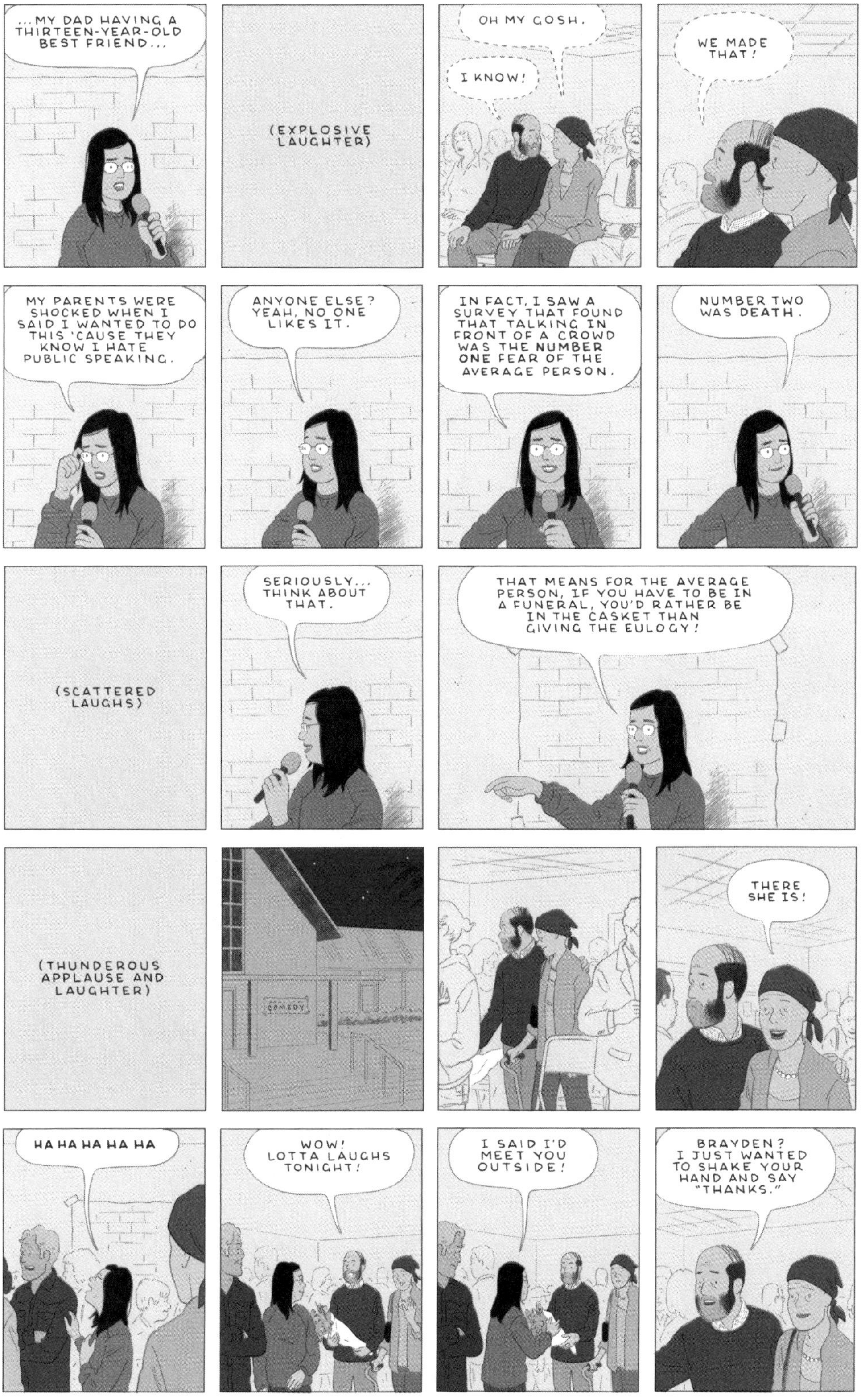

...MY DAD HAVING A THIRTEEN-YEAR-OLD BEST FRIEND...
(EXPLOSIVE LAUGHTER)
OH MY GOSH.
I KNOW!
WE MADE THAT!
MY PARENTS WERE SHOCKED WHEN I SAID I WANTED TO DO THIS 'CAUSE THEY KNOW I HATE PUBLIC SPEAKING.
ANYONE ELSE? YEAH, NO ONE LIKES IT.
IN FACT, I SAW A SURVEY THAT FOUND THAT TALKING IN FRONT OF A CROWD WAS THE NUMBER ONE FEAR OF THE AVERAGE PERSON.
NUMBER TWO WAS DEATH.
(SCATTERED LAUGHS)
SERIOUSLY... THINK ABOUT THAT.
THAT MEANS FOR THE AVERAGE PERSON, IF YOU HAVE TO BE IN A FUNERAL, YOU'D RATHER BE IN THE CASKET THAN GIVING THE EULOGY!
(THUNDEROUS APPLAUSE AND LAUGHTER)
COMEDY
THERE SHE IS!
HA HA HA HA HA
WOW! LOTTA LAUGHS TONIGHT!
I SAID I'D MEET YOU OUTSIDE!
BRAYDEN? I JUST WANTED TO SHAKE YOUR HAND AND SAY "THANKS."

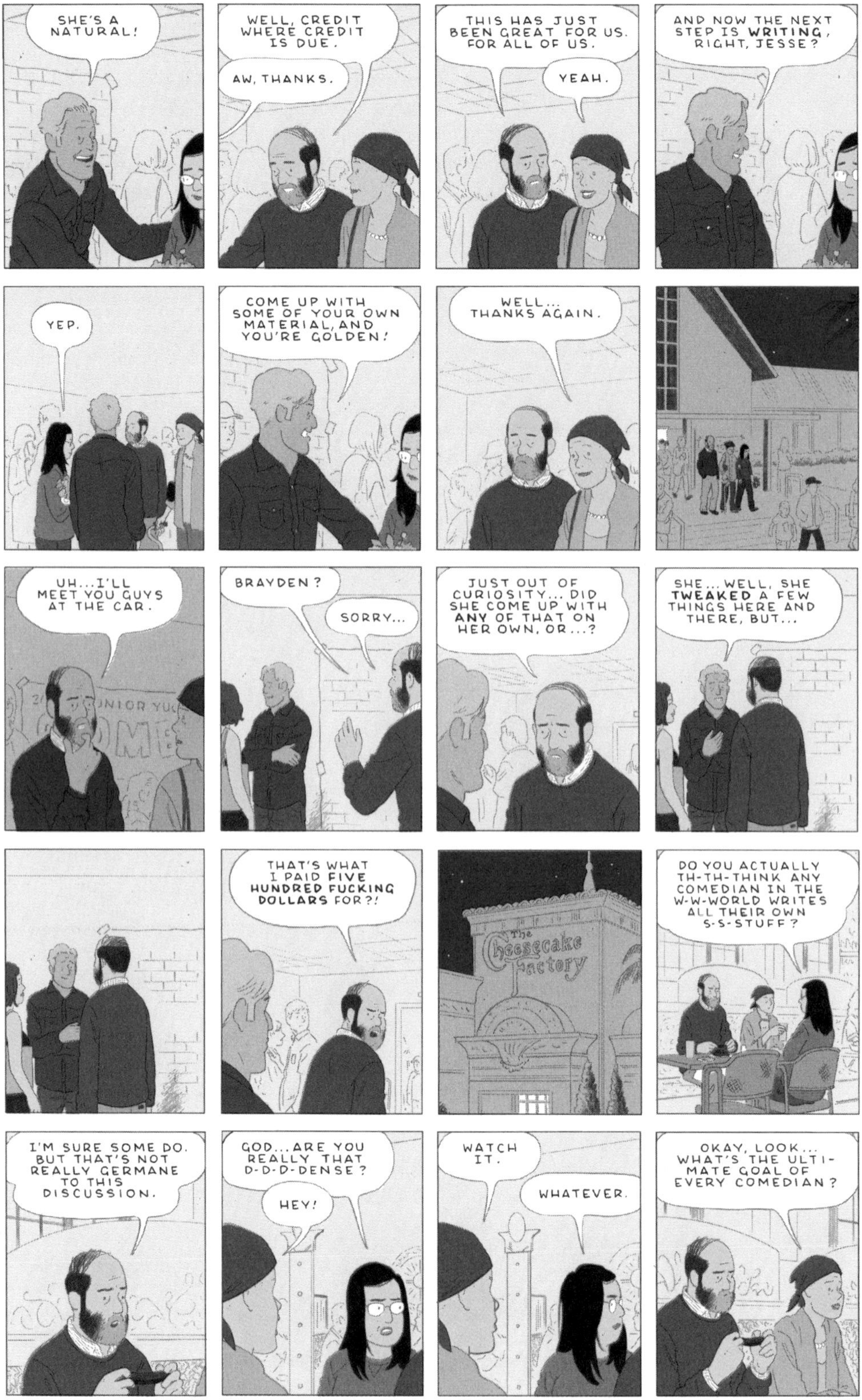
SHE'S A NATURAL!
WELL, CREDIT WHERE CREDIT IS DUE.
AW, THANKS.
THIS HAS JUST BEEN GREAT FOR US. FOR ALL OF US.
YEAH.
AND NOW THE NEXT STEP IS **WRITING**, RIGHT, JESSE?
YEP.
COME UP WITH SOME OF YOUR OWN MATERIAL, AND YOU'RE GOLDEN!
WELL... THANKS AGAIN.
UH...I'LL MEET YOU GUYS AT THE CAR.
BRAYDEN?
SORRY...
JUST OUT OF CURIOSITY... DID SHE COME UP WITH **ANY** OF THAT ON HER OWN, OR...?
SHE... WELL, SHE **TWEAKED** A FEW THINGS HERE AND THERE, BUT...
THAT'S WHAT I PAID **FIVE HUNDRED FUCKING DOLLARS** FOR?!
The Cheesecake Factory
DO YOU ACTUALLY TH-TH-THINK ANY COMEDIAN IN THE W-W-WORLD WRITES ALL THEIR OWN S-S-STUFF?
I'M SURE SOME DO. BUT THAT'S NOT REALLY GERMANE TO THIS DISCUSSION.
GOD... ARE YOU REALLY THAT D-D-D-DENSE?
HEY!
WATCH IT.
WHATEVER.
OKAY, LOOK... WHAT'S THE ULTI-MATE GOAL OF EVERY COMEDIAN?

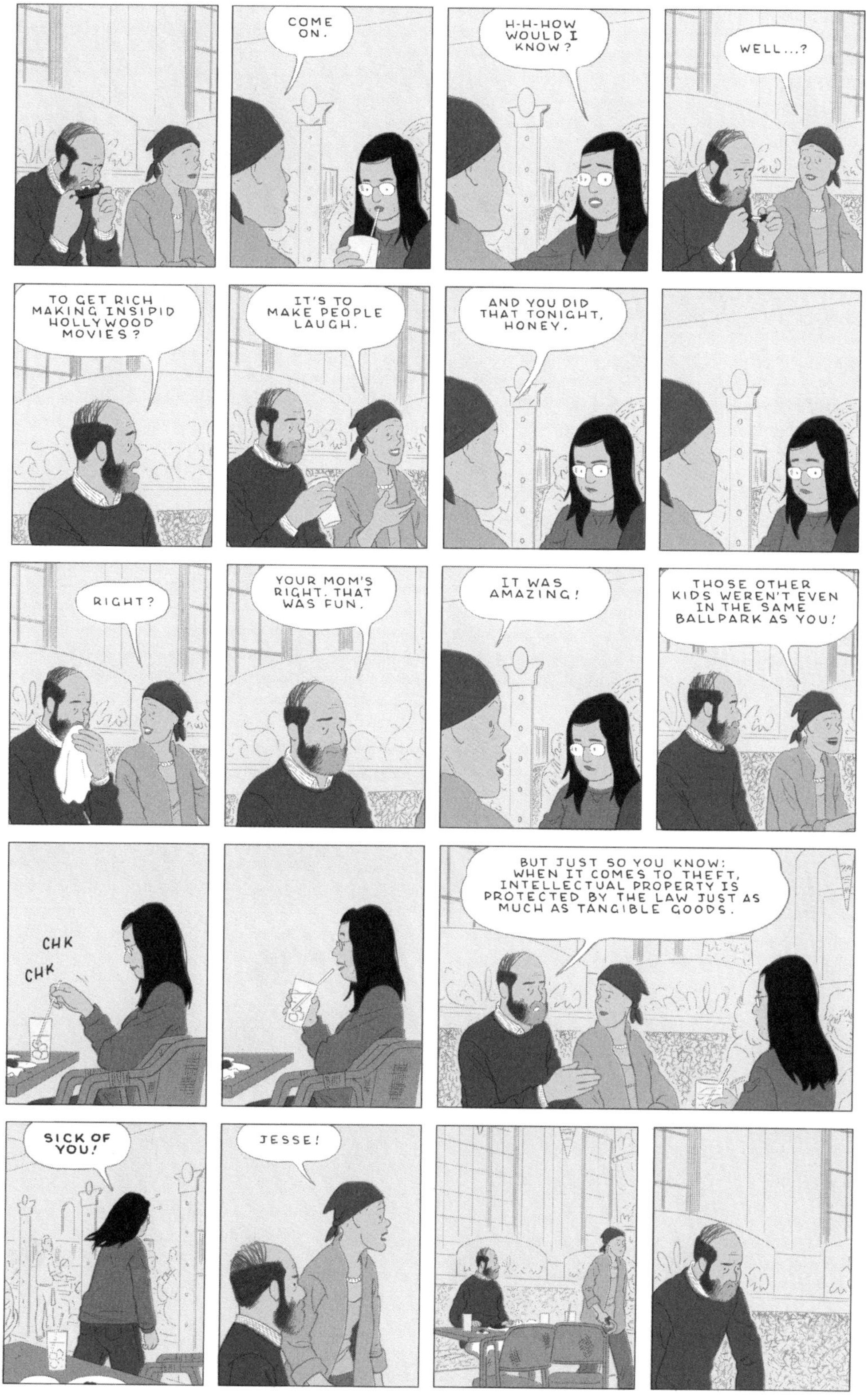
COME ON.
H-H-HOW WOULD I KNOW?
WELL...?
TO GET RICH MAKING INSIPID HOLLYWOOD MOVIES?
IT'S TO MAKE PEOPLE LAUGH.
AND YOU DID THAT TONIGHT, HONEY.
RIGHT?
YOUR MOM'S RIGHT. THAT WAS FUN.
IT WAS AMAZING!
THOSE OTHER KIDS WEREN'T EVEN IN THE SAME BALLPARK AS YOU!
CHK
CHK
BUT JUST SO YOU KNOW: WHEN IT COMES TO THEFT, INTELLECTUAL PROPERTY IS PROTECTED BY THE LAW JUST AS MUCH AS TANGIBLE GOODS.
SICK OF YOU!
JESSE!

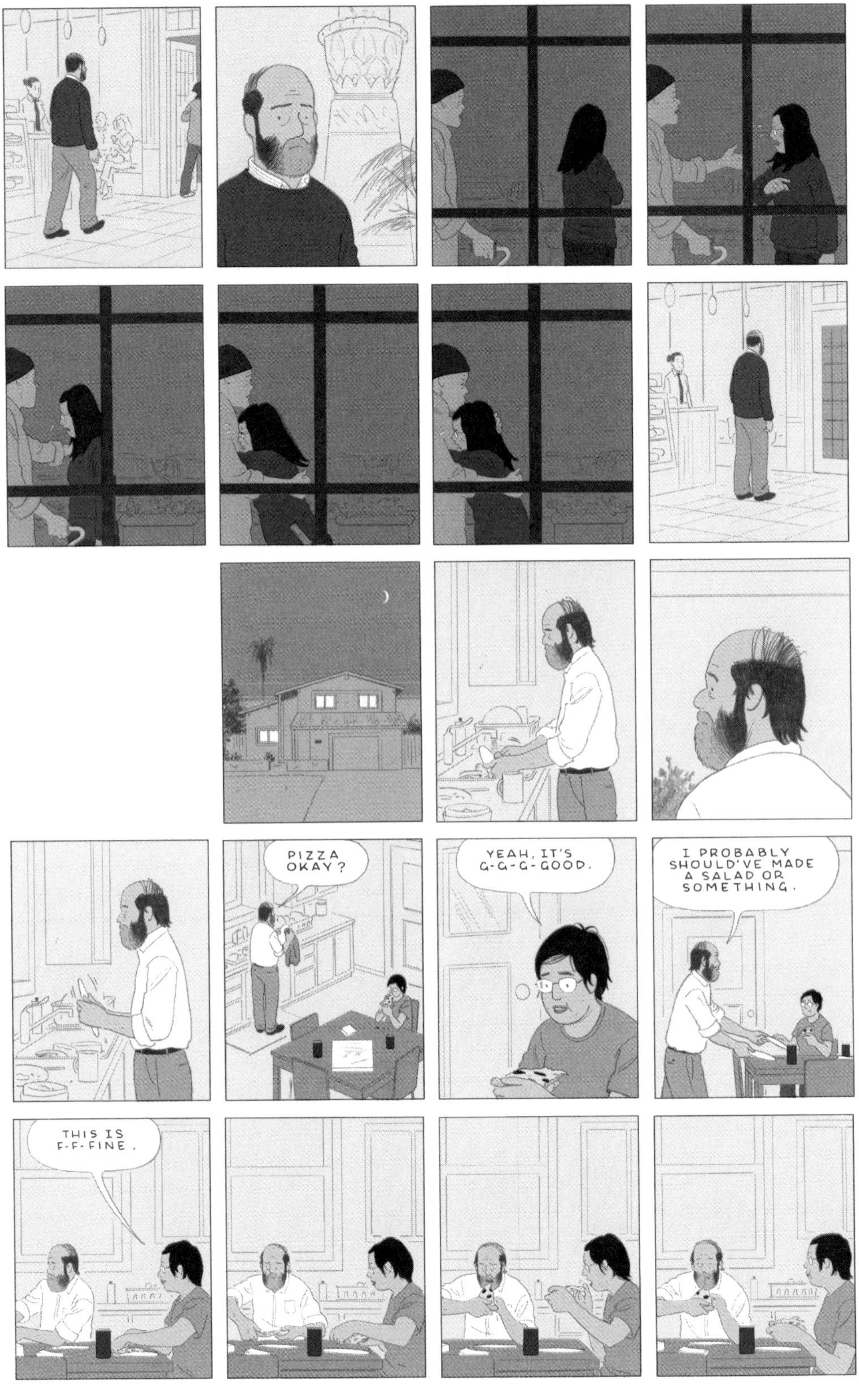
PIZZA OKAY?
YEAH, IT'S G-G-G-GOOD.
I PROBABLY SHOULD'VE MADE A SALAD OR SOMETHING.
THIS IS F-F-FINE.

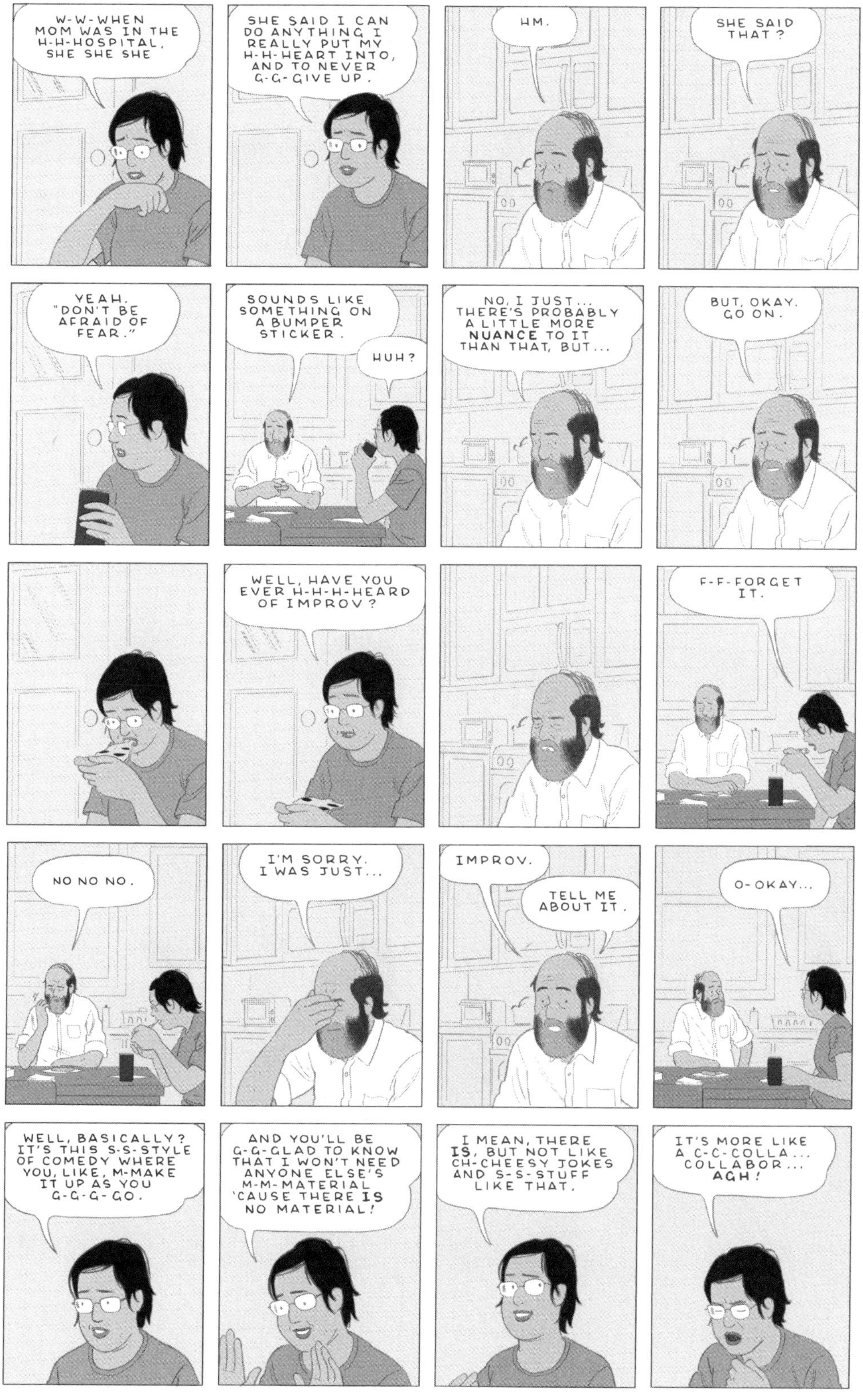
W-W-WHEN MOM WAS IN THE H-H-HOSPITAL, SHE SHE SHE
SHE SAID I CAN DO ANYTHING I REALLY PUT MY H-H-HEART INTO, AND TO NEVER G-G-GIVE UP.
HM.
SHE SAID THAT?
YEAH. "DON'T BE AFRAID OF FEAR."
SOUNDS LIKE SOMETHING ON A BUMPER STICKER.
HUH?
NO, I JUST... THERE'S PROBABLY A LITTLE MORE **NUANCE** TO IT THAN THAT, BUT...
BUT, OKAY. GO ON.
WELL, HAVE YOU EVER H-H-H-HEARD OF IMPROV?
F-F-FORGET IT.
NO NO NO.
I'M SORRY. I WAS JUST...
IMPROV.
TELL ME ABOUT **IT**.
O-OKAY...
WELL, BASICALLY? IT'S THIS S-S-STYLE OF COMEDY WHERE YOU, LIKE, M-MAKE IT UP AS YOU G-G-G-GO.
AND YOU'LL BE G-G-GLAD TO KNOW THAT I WON'T NEED ANYONE ELSE'S M-M-MATERIAL 'CAUSE THERE **IS** NO MATERIAL!
I MEAN, THERE **IS**, BUT NOT LIKE CH-CHEESY JOKES AND S-S-STUFF LIKE THAT.
IT'S MORE LIKE A C-C-COLLA... COLLABOR... **AGH!**

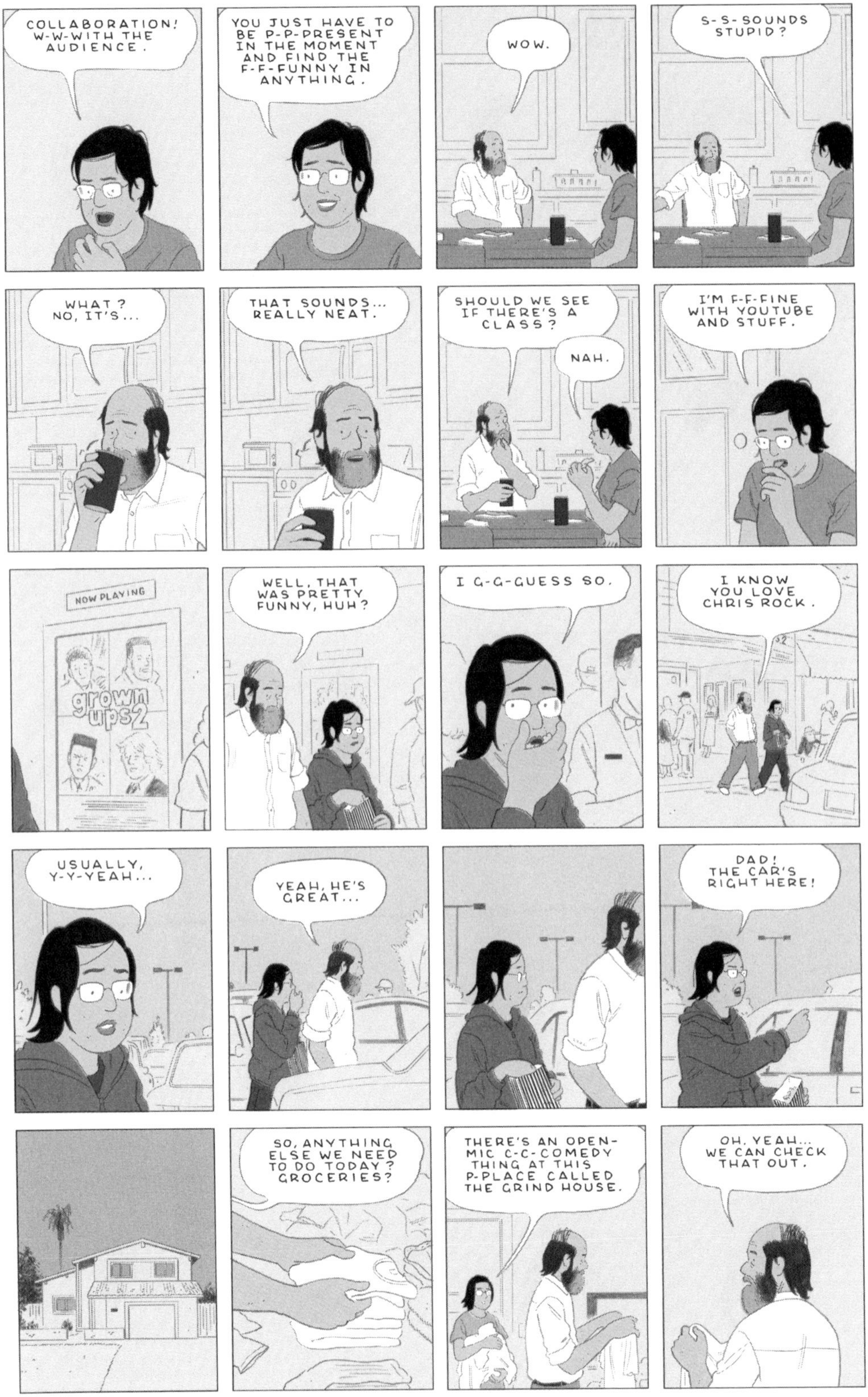
COLLABORATION! W-W-WITH THE AUDIENCE.
YOU JUST HAVE TO BE P-P-PRESENT IN THE MOMENT AND FIND THE F-F-FUNNY IN ANYTHING.
WOW.
S-S-SOUNDS STUPID?
WHAT? NO, IT'S...
THAT SOUNDS... REALLY NEAT.
SHOULD WE SEE IF THERE'S A CLASS?
NAH.
I'M F-F-FINE WITH YOUTUBE AND STUFF.
NOW PLAYING
grown ups2
WELL, THAT WAS PRETTY FUNNY, HUH?
I G-G-GUESS SO.
I KNOW YOU LOVE CHRIS ROCK.
USUALLY, Y-Y-YEAH...
YEAH, HE'S GREAT...
DAD! THE CAR'S RIGHT HERE!
SO, ANYTHING ELSE WE NEED TO DO TODAY? GROCERIES?
THERE'S AN OPEN-MIC C-C-COMEDY THING AT THIS P-PLACE CALLED THE GRIND HOUSE.
OH. YEAH... WE CAN CHECK THAT OUT.

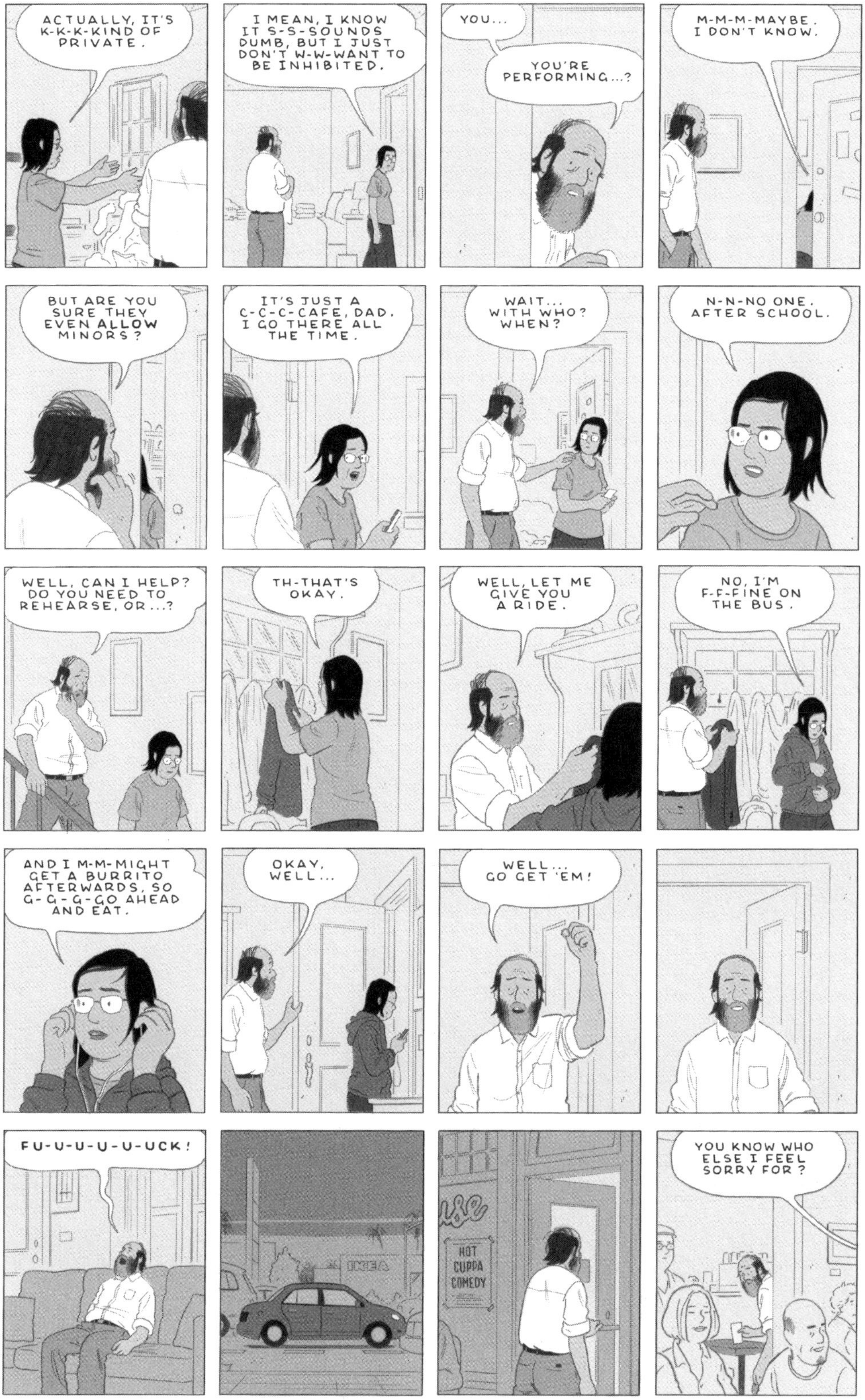
ACTUALLY, IT'S K-K-K-KIND OF PRIVATE.
I MEAN, I KNOW IT S-S-SOUNDS DUMB, BUT I JUST DON'T W-W-WANT TO BE INHIBITED.
YOU...
YOU'RE PERFORMING...?
M-M-M-MAYBE. I DON'T KNOW.
BUT ARE YOU SURE THEY EVEN ALLOW MINORS?
IT'S JUST A C-C-C-CAFE, DAD. I GO THERE ALL THE TIME.
WAIT... WITH WHO? WHEN?
N-N-NO ONE. AFTER SCHOOL.
WELL, CAN I HELP? DO YOU NEED TO REHEARSE, OR...?
TH-THAT'S OKAY.
WELL, LET ME GIVE YOU A RIDE.
NO, I'M F-F-FINE ON THE BUS.
AND I M-M-MIGHT GET A BURRITO AFTERWARDS, SO G-G-G-GO AHEAD AND EAT.
OKAY. WELL...
WELL... GO GET 'EM!
FU-U-U-U-U-UCK!
IKEA
HOT CUPPA COMEDY
YOU KNOW WHO ELSE I FEEL SORRY FOR?

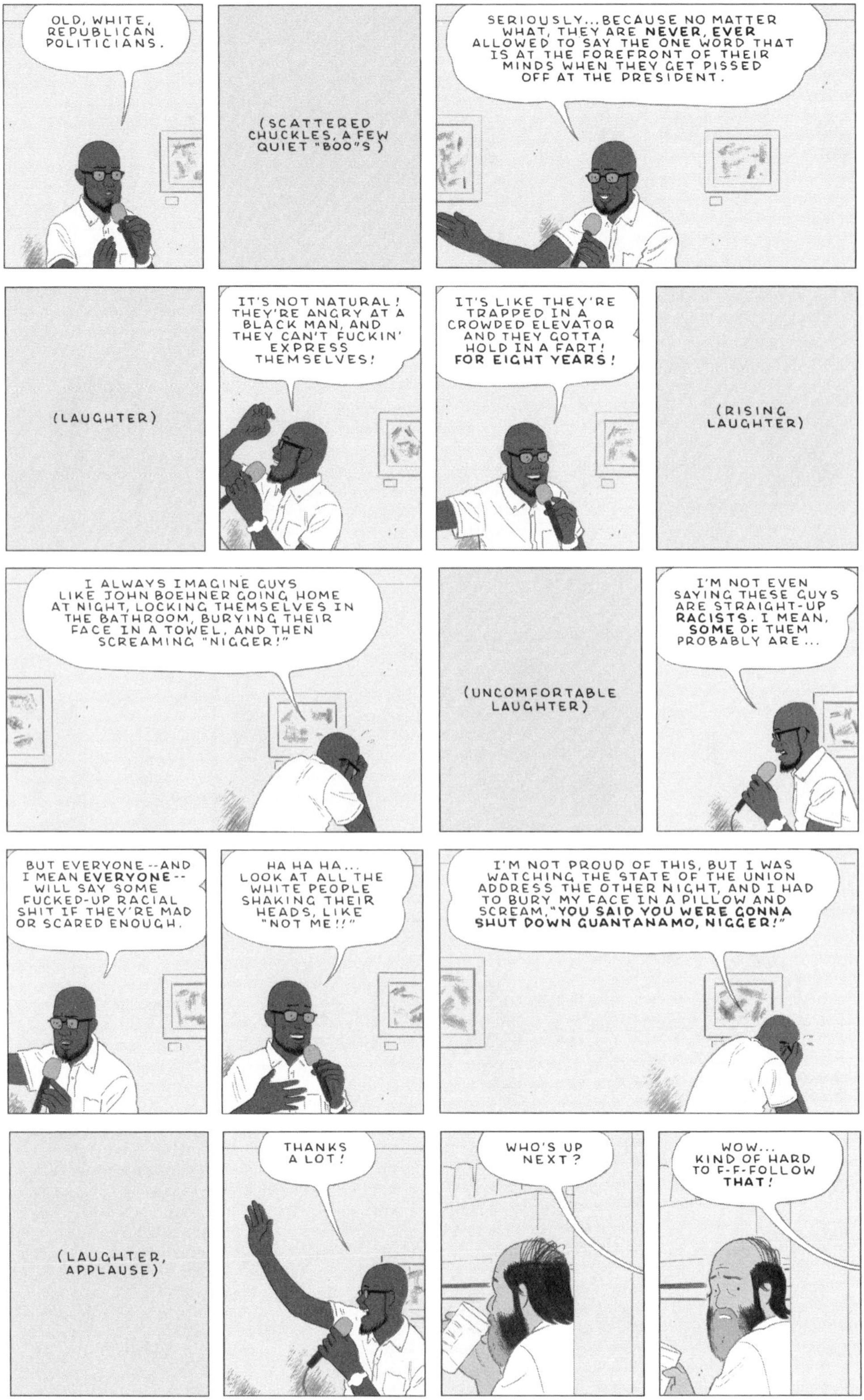
OLD, WHITE, REPUBLICAN POLITICIANS.
(SCATTERED CHUCKLES, A FEW QUIET "BOO"S)
SERIOUSLY... BECAUSE NO MATTER WHAT, THEY ARE **NEVER, EVER** ALLOWED TO SAY THE ONE WORD THAT IS AT THE FOREFRONT OF THEIR MINDS WHEN THEY GET PISSED OFF AT THE PRESIDENT.
(LAUGHTER)
IT'S NOT NATURAL! THEY'RE ANGRY AT A BLACK MAN, AND THEY CAN'T FUCKIN' EXPRESS THEMSELVES!
IT'S LIKE THEY'RE TRAPPED IN A CROWDED ELEVATOR AND THEY GOTTA HOLD IN A FART! **FOR EIGHT YEARS!**
(RISING LAUGHTER)
I ALWAYS IMAGINE GUYS LIKE JOHN BOEHNER GOING HOME AT NIGHT, LOCKING THEMSELVES IN THE BATHROOM, BURYING THEIR FACE IN A TOWEL, AND THEN SCREAMING "NIGGER!"
(UNCOMFORTABLE LAUGHTER)
I'M NOT EVEN SAYING THESE GUYS ARE STRAIGHT-UP **RACISTS**. I MEAN, **SOME** OF THEM PROBABLY ARE...
BUT EVERYONE--AND I MEAN **EVERYONE**--WILL SAY SOME FUCKED-UP RACIAL SHIT IF THEY'RE MAD OR SCARED ENOUGH.
HA HA HA... LOOK AT ALL THE WHITE PEOPLE SHAKING THEIR HEADS, LIKE "NOT ME!!"
I'M NOT PROUD OF THIS, BUT I WAS WATCHING THE STATE OF THE UNION ADDRESS THE OTHER NIGHT, AND I HAD TO BURY MY FACE IN A PILLOW AND SCREAM, **"YOU SAID YOU WERE GONNA SHUT DOWN GUANTANAMO, NIGGER!"**
(LAUGHTER, APPLAUSE)
THANKS A LOT!
WHO'S UP NEXT?
WOW... KIND OF HARD TO F-F-FOLLOW **THAT!**

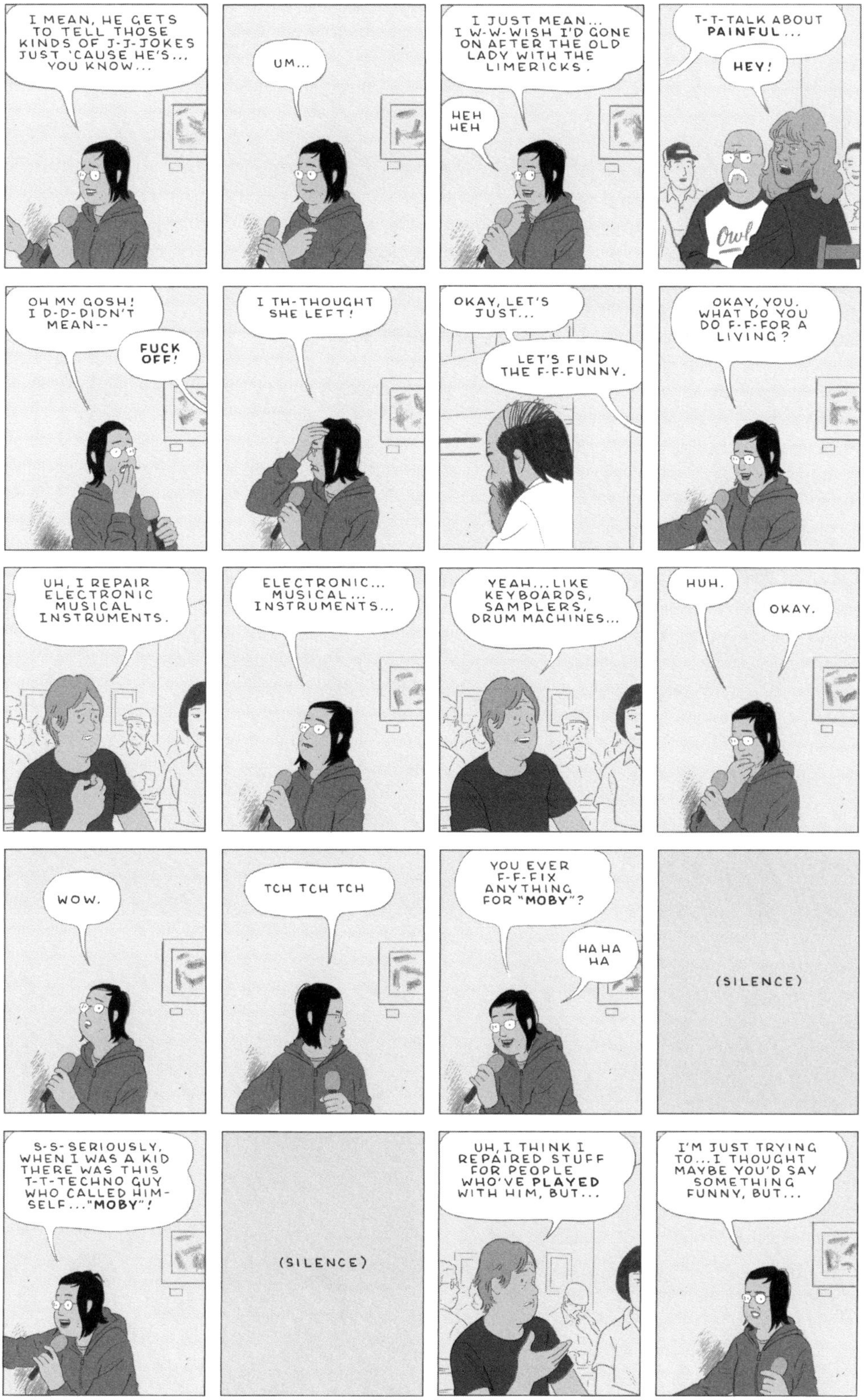
I MEAN, HE GETS TO TELL THOSE KINDS OF J-J-JOKES JUST 'CAUSE HE'S... YOU KNOW...
UM...
I JUST MEAN... I W-W-WISH I'D GONE ON AFTER THE OLD LADY WITH THE LIMERICKS.
HEH HEH
T-T-TALK ABOUT **PAINFUL**...
**HEY!**
Owl
OH MY GOSH! I D-D-DIDN'T MEAN--
**FUCK OFF!**
I TH-THOUGHT SHE LEFT!
OKAY, LET'S JUST...
LET'S FIND THE F-F-FUNNY.
OKAY, YOU. WHAT DO YOU DO F-F-FOR A LIVING?
UH, I REPAIR ELECTRONIC MUSICAL INSTRUMENTS.
ELECTRONIC... MUSICAL... INSTRUMENTS...
YEAH... LIKE KEYBOARDS, SAMPLERS, DRUM MACHINES...
HUH.
OKAY.
WOW.
TCH TCH TCH
YOU EVER F-F-FIX ANYTHING FOR "**MOBY**"?
HA HA HA
(SILENCE)
S-S-SERIOUSLY, WHEN I WAS A KID THERE WAS THIS T-T-TECHNO GUY WHO CALLED HIM-SELF..."**MOBY**"!
(SILENCE)
UH, I THINK I REPAIRED STUFF FOR PEOPLE WHO'VE **PLAYED** WITH HIM, BUT...
I'M JUST TRYING TO... I THOUGHT MAYBE YOU'D SAY SOMETHING FUNNY, BUT...

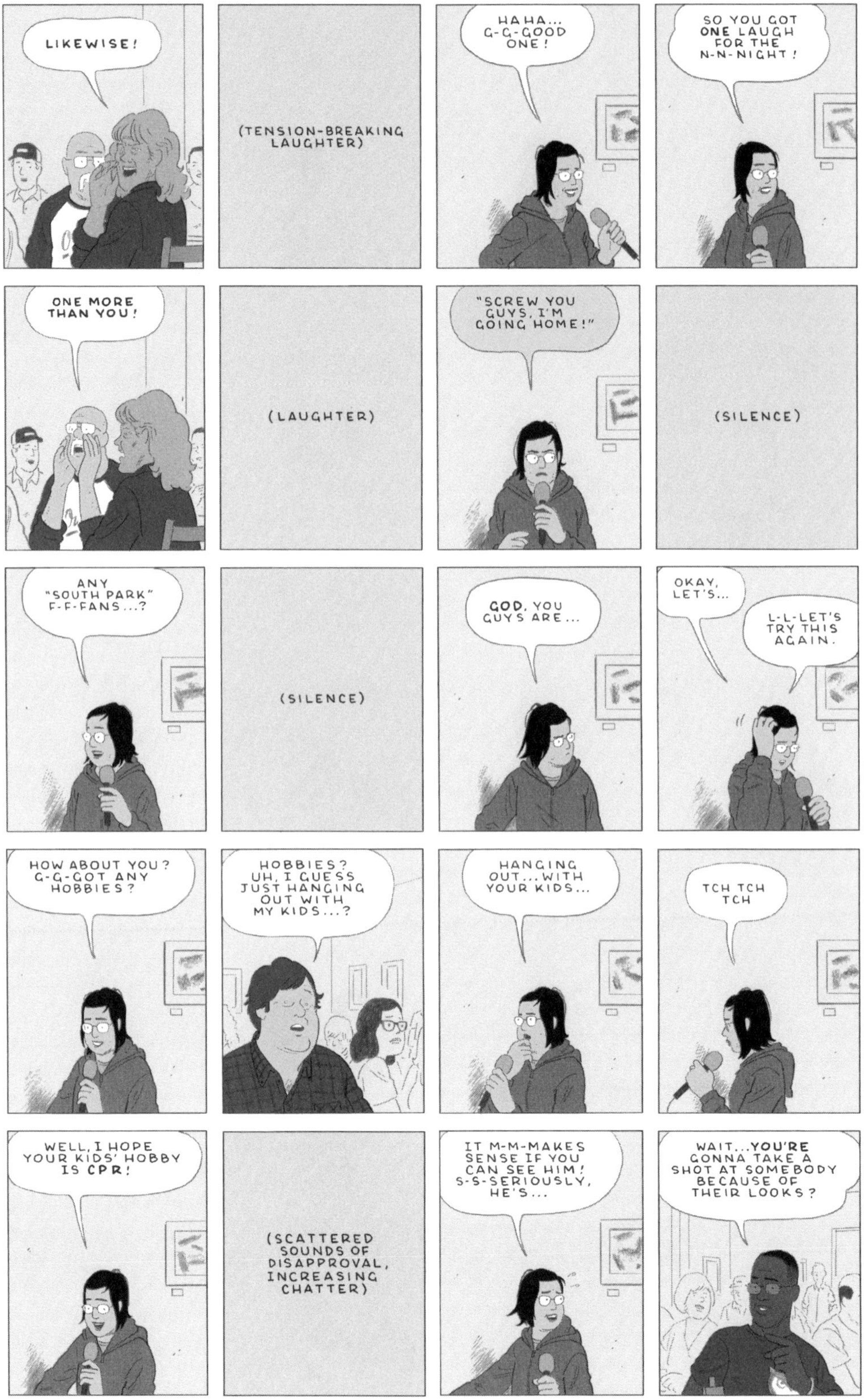

LIKEWISE!
(TENSION-BREAKING LAUGHTER)
HA HA... G-G-GOOD ONE!
SO YOU GOT **ONE** LAUGH FOR THE N-N-NIGHT!
**ONE MORE THAN YOU!**
(LAUGHTER)
"SCREW YOU GUYS, I'M GOING HOME!"
(SILENCE)
ANY "SOUTH PARK" F-F-FANS...?
(SILENCE)
**GOD**, YOU GUYS ARE...
OKAY, LET'S...
L-L-LET'S TRY THIS AGAIN.
HOW ABOUT YOU? G-G-GOT ANY HOBBIES?
HOBBIES? UH, I GUESS JUST HANGING OUT WITH MY KIDS...?
HANGING OUT... WITH YOUR KIDS...
TCH TCH TCH
WELL, I HOPE YOUR KIDS' HOBBY IS **CPR**!
(SCATTERED SOUNDS OF DISAPPROVAL, INCREASING CHATTER)
IT M-M-MAKES SENSE IF YOU CAN SEE HIM! S-S-SERIOUSLY, HE'S...
WAIT... **YOU'RE** GONNA TAKE A SHOT AT SOMEBODY BECAUSE OF THEIR LOOKS?

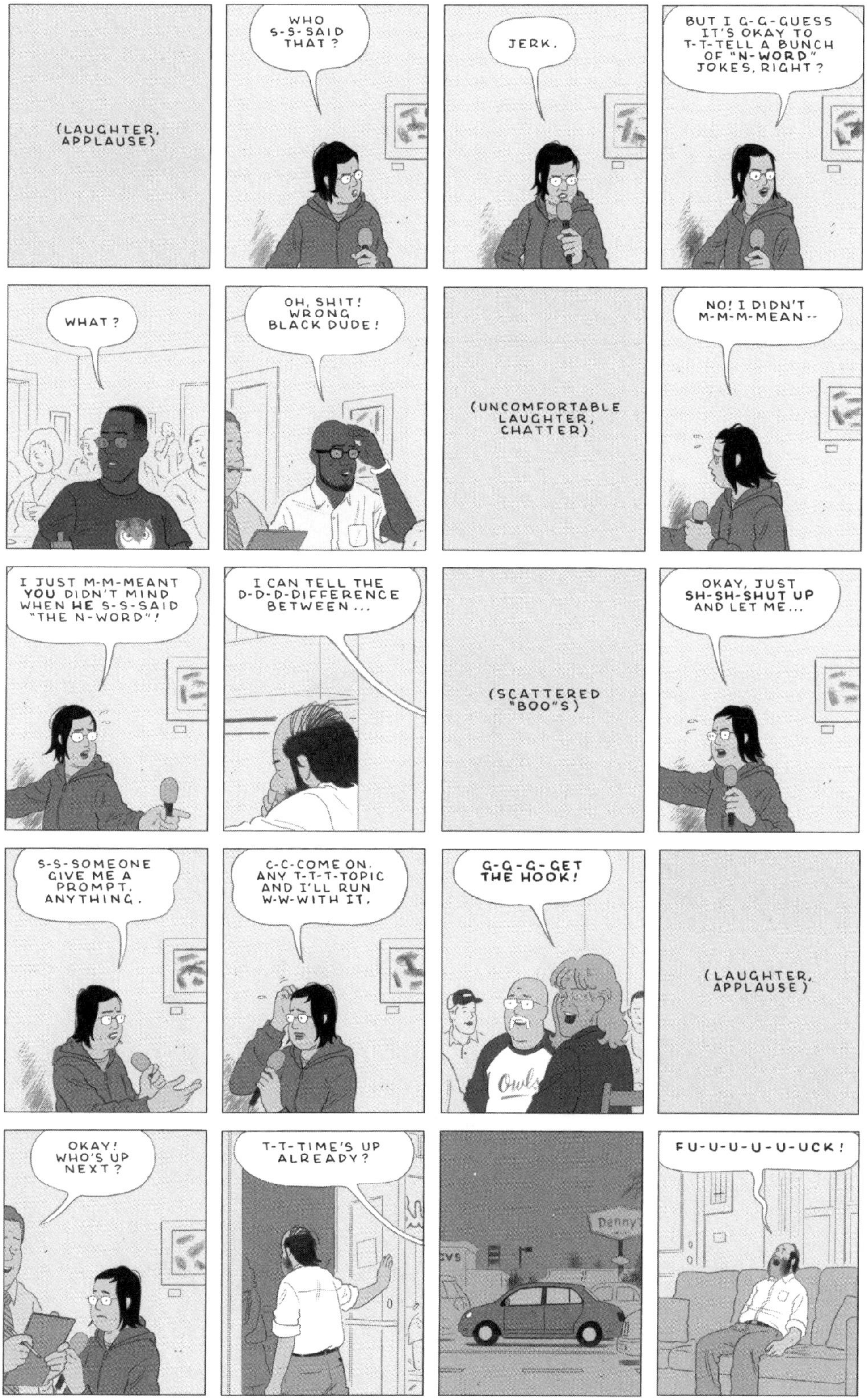
(LAUGHTER, APPLAUSE)
WHO S-S-SAID THAT?
JERK.
BUT I G-G-GUESS IT'S OKAY TO T-T-TELL A BUNCH OF "N-WORD" JOKES, RIGHT?
WHAT?
OH, SHIT! WRONG BLACK DUDE!
(UNCOMFORTABLE LAUGHTER, CHATTER)
NO! I DIDN'T M-M-M-MEAN--
I JUST M-M-MEANT YOU DIDN'T MIND WHEN HE S-S-SAID "THE N-WORD"!
I CAN TELL THE D-D-D-DIFFERENCE BETWEEN...
(SCATTERED "BOO"S)
OKAY, JUST SH-SH-SHUT UP AND LET ME...
S-S-SOMEONE GIVE ME A PROMPT. ANYTHING.
C-C-COME ON. ANY T-T-T-TOPIC AND I'LL RUN W-W-WITH IT.
G-G-G-GET THE HOOK!
Owls
(LAUGHTER, APPLAUSE)
OKAY! WHO'S UP NEXT?
T-T-TIME'S UP ALREADY?
Denny's
CVS
FU-U-U-U-U-UCK!

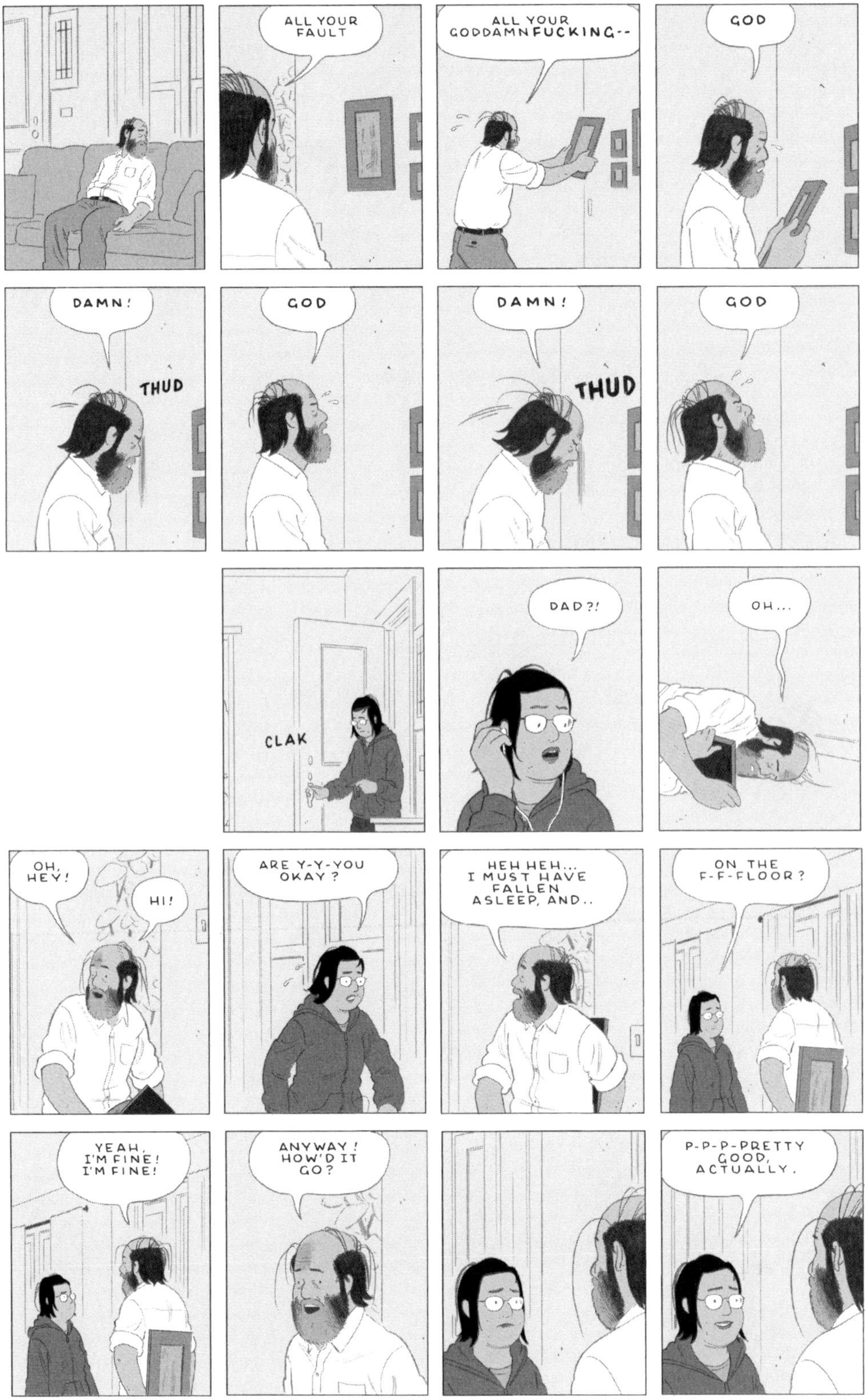
ALL YOUR FAULT
ALL YOUR GODDAMN FUCKING--
GOD
DAMN!
THUD
GOD
DAMN!
THUD
GOD
CLAK
DAD?!
OH...
OH, HEY!
HI!
ARE Y-Y-YOU OKAY?
HEH HEH... I MUST HAVE FALLEN ASLEEP, AND..
ON THE F-F-FLOOR?
YEAH, I'M FINE! I'M FINE!
ANYWAY! HOW'D IT GO?
P-P-P-PRETTY GOOD, ACTUALLY.

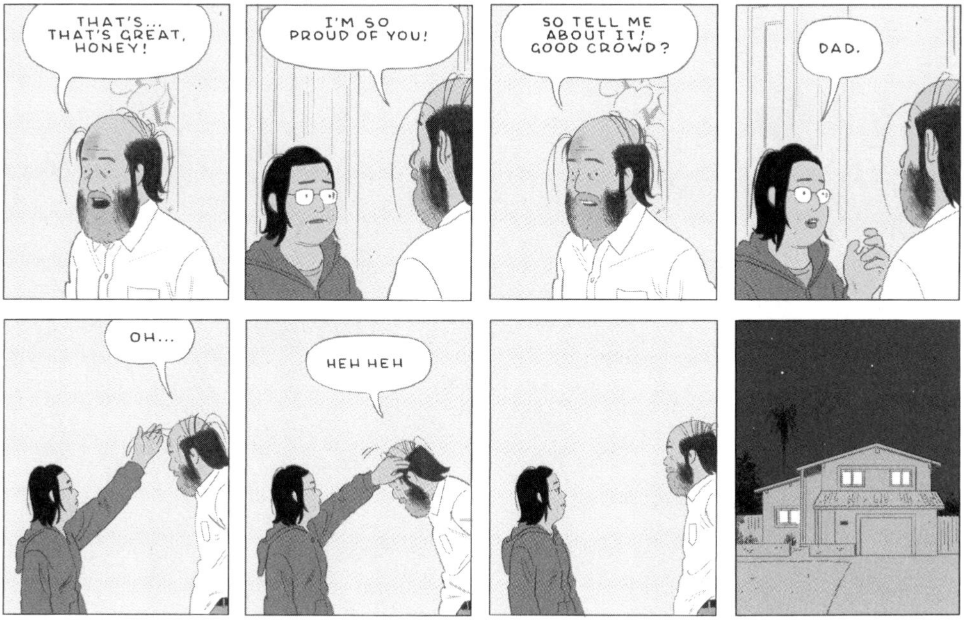
THAT'S... THAT'S GREAT, HONEY!
I'M SO PROUD OF YOU!
SO TELL ME ABOUT IT! GOOD CROWD?
DAD.
OH...
HEH HEH

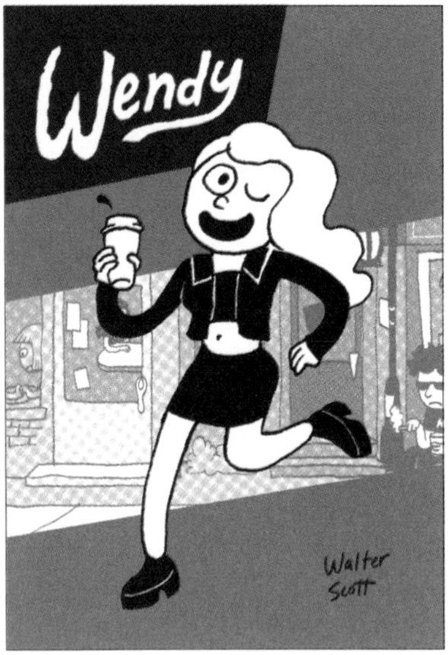
Wendy
Walter Scott

# Wendy (*Excerpt*)

WALTER SCOTT

*excerpted from*

Wendy

KOYAMA PRESS

6.5 × 9 inches • 216 pages

## Biography

Walter Scott is an interdisciplinary artist from the Mohawk community of Kahnawake, near Montreal. He now lives between Montreal, Toronto, and elsewhere, working across writing, illustration, performance, and sculpture. You can find Wendy as a book, and online, on Random House's web magazine *Hazlitt*, and *The Hairpin*. Scott has also exhibited sculptures, drawings, and performance work in Canada, the United States, and Japan. *Wendy's Revenge*, the second anthology, will be published by Koyama Press in Fall 2016. wwalterscott.com

## Statement

The first Wendy I ever drew (seen in this book as "Wendy on a Bendy") was scribbled on a placemat in the Saint-Henri neighborhood of Montreal, where I was living at the time. It was an offhand gesture, later Photoshopped into a comic format and posted online. Encouraged by friends, I continued to make Wendy stories for small 'zines and as posters. Soon, an entire Wendy-verse began to take shape. This excerpt is especially reflective of my existence at the time—living in the lower-rent part of town, feeling a bit aimless, going to punk shows in dingy track-side lofts, getting involved with sketchy dudes with sketchy band names, and spending long underemployed afternoons doodling on placemats in cafés. Since then, Wendy has more of less left the punk scene; on the journey to find out who she really is, she has found herself immersed in the locations and characters of the contemporary art world—the galleries, the parties, the curators, writers, activists, wannabes, drunks, her parents, the frenemies, and the friendship.

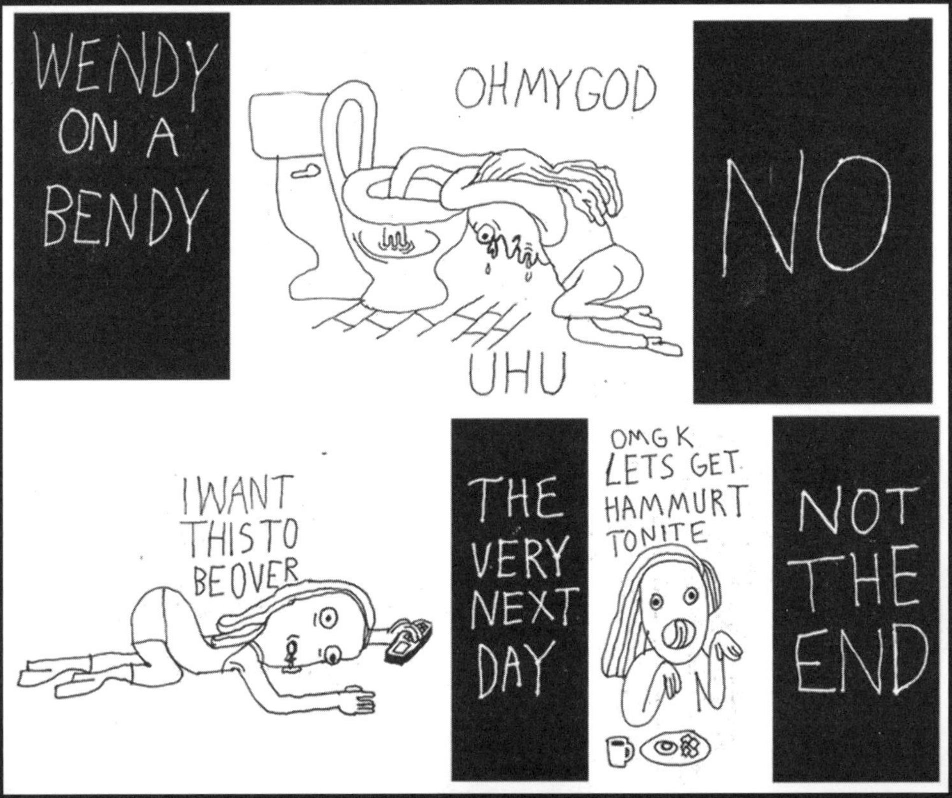
WENDY ON A BENDY
OHMYGOD
UHU
NO
I WANT THIS TO BE OVER
THE VERY NEXT DAY
OMG K LETS GET HAMMURT TONITE
NOT THE END

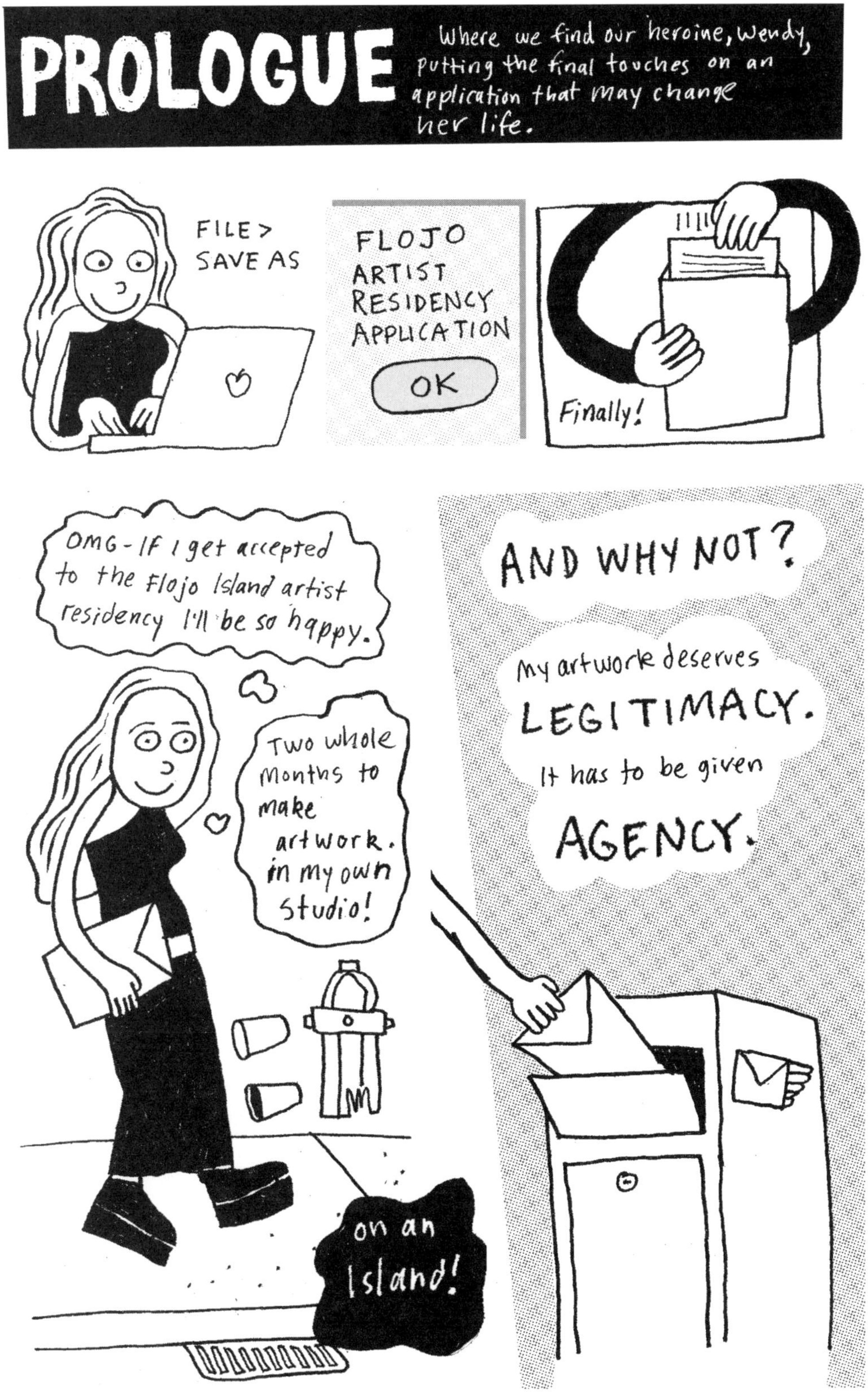
PROLOGUE
Where we find our heroine, Wendy, putting the final touches on an application that may change her life.
FILE > SAVE AS
FLOJO ARTIST RESIDENCY APPLICATION
OK
Finally!
OMG - If I get accepted to the Flojo Island artist residency I'll be so happy.
Two whole Months to make artwork. in my own studio!
on an Island!
AND WHY NOT?
My artwork deserves LEGITIMACY.
It has to be given AGENCY.

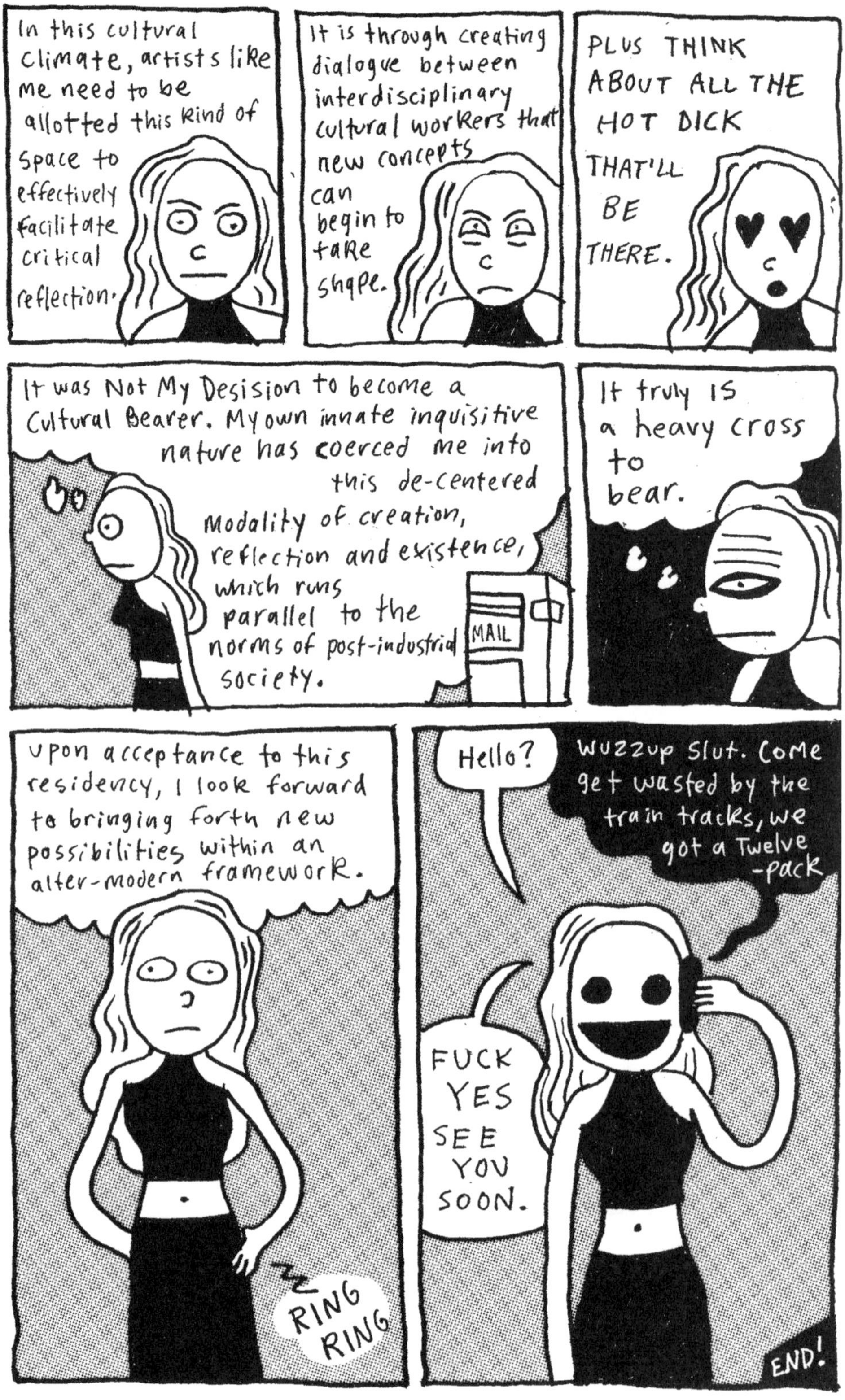
In this cultural climate, artists like me need to be allotted this kind of space to effectively facilitate critical reflection.
It is through creating dialogue between interdisciplinary cultural workers that new concepts can begin to take shape.
PLUS THINK ABOUT ALL THE HOT DICK THAT'LL BE THERE.
It was Not My Desision to become a Cultural Bearer. My own innate inquisitive nature has coerced me into this de-centered modality of creation, reflection and existence, which runs parallel to the norms of post-industrial society.
MAIL
It truly is a heavy cross to bear.
Upon acceptance to this residency, I look forward to bringing forth new possibilities within an alter-modern framework.
RING RING
Hello?
WUZZUP Slut. Come get wasted by the train tracks, we got a Twelve -pack
FUCK YES SEE YOU SOON.
END!

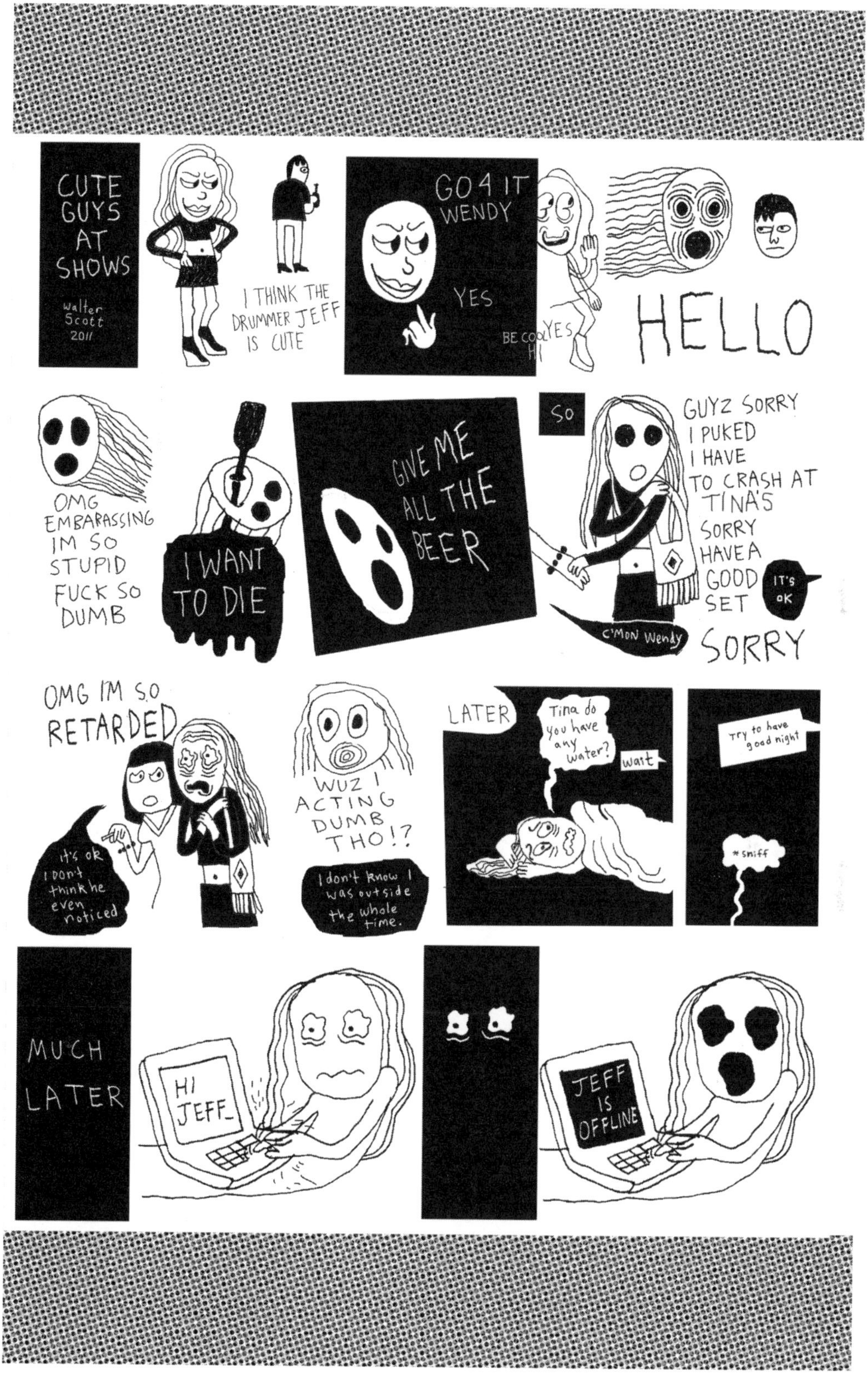
CUTE GUYS AT SHOWS
walter Scott 2011
I THINK THE DRUMMER JEFF IS CUTE
GO 4 IT WENDY
YES
BE COOL
YES
HI
HELLO
OMG EMBARASSING IM SO STUPID FUCK SO DUMB
I WANT TO DIE
GIVE ME ALL THE BEER
SO
GUYZ SORRY I PUKED I HAVE TO CRASH AT TINA'S SORRY HAVE A GOOD SET
IT'S OK
C'MON Wendy
SORRY
OMG IM SO RETARDED
it's ok I don't think he even noticed
WUZ I ACTING DUMB THO!?
I don't know I was outside the whole time.
LATER
Tina do you have any water?
wait
Try to have good night
*sniff
MUCH LATER
HI JEFF_
JEFF IS OFFLINE

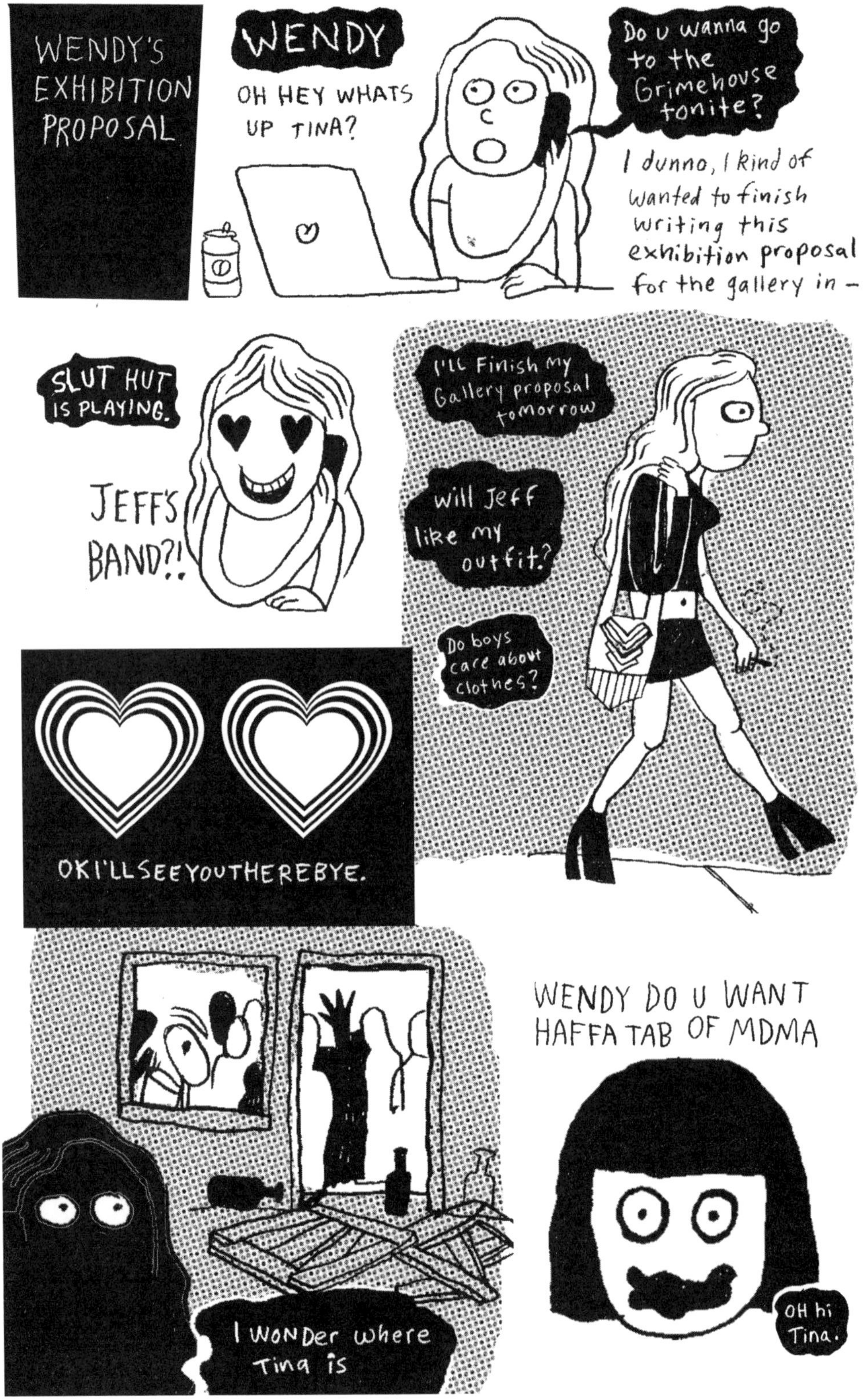
WENDY'S EXHIBITION PROPOSAL
WENDY
OH HEY WHATS UP TINA?
Do u wanna go to the Grimehouse tonite?
I dunno, I kind of wanted to finish writing this exhibition proposal for the gallery in –
SLUT HUT IS PLAYING.
JEFF'S BAND?!
I'll Finish my Gallery proposal tomorrow
will Jeff like my outfit?
Do boys care about clothes?
OKI'LLSEEYOUTHEREBYE.
I WONDER where Tina is
WENDY DO U WANT HAFFA TAB OF MDMA
OH hi Tina.

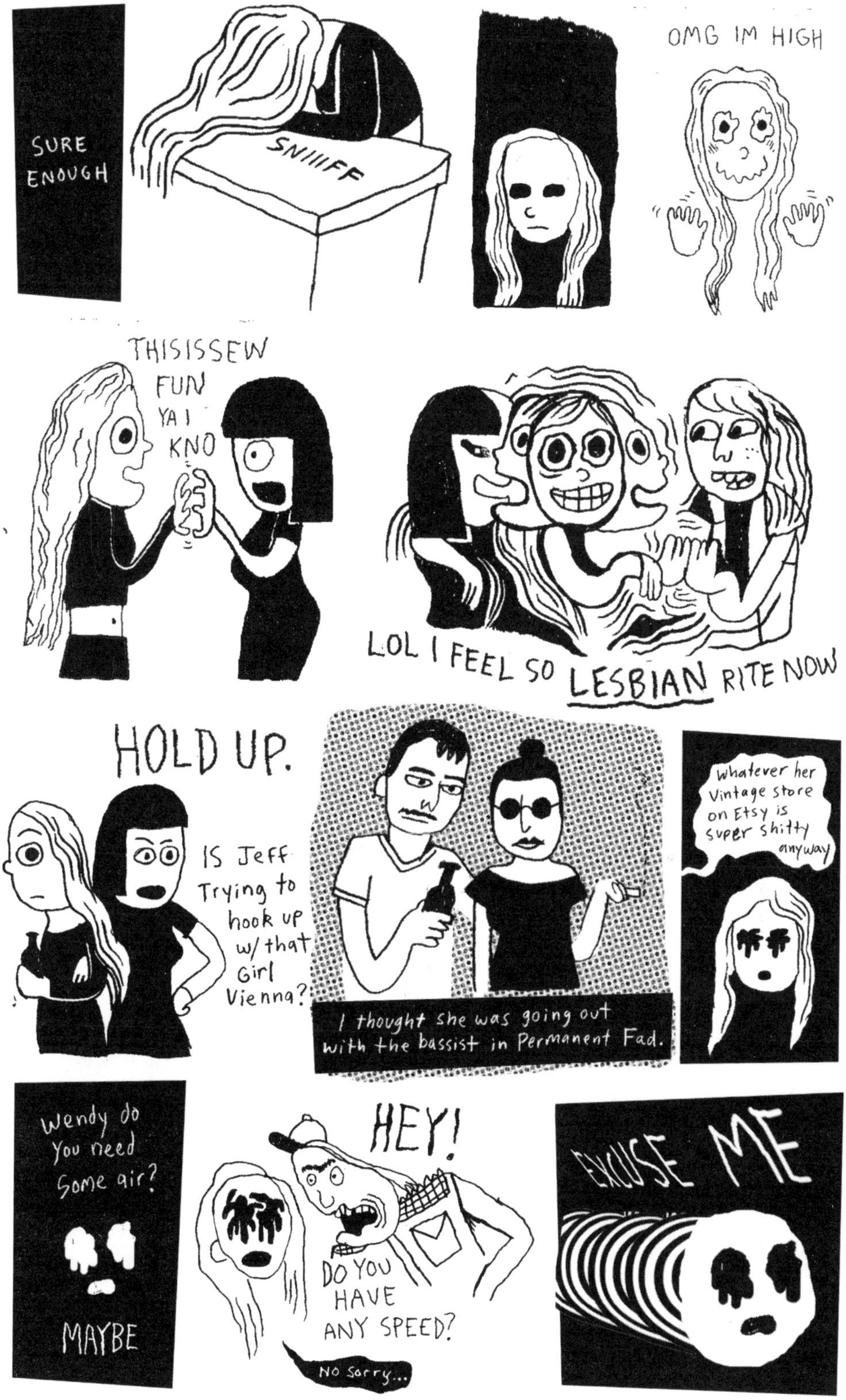
SURE ENOUGH
SNIIIFF
OMG IM HIGH
THISISSEW FUN YA I KNO
LOL I FEEL SO LESBIAN RITE NOW
HOLD UP.
IS Jeff Trying to hook up w/ that Girl Vienna?
I thought she was going out with the bassist in Permanent Fad.
whatever her Vintage store on Etsy is super shitty anyway
Wendy do you need Some air?
MAYBE
HEY!
DO YOU HAVE ANY SPEED?
No sorry...
EXCUSE ME

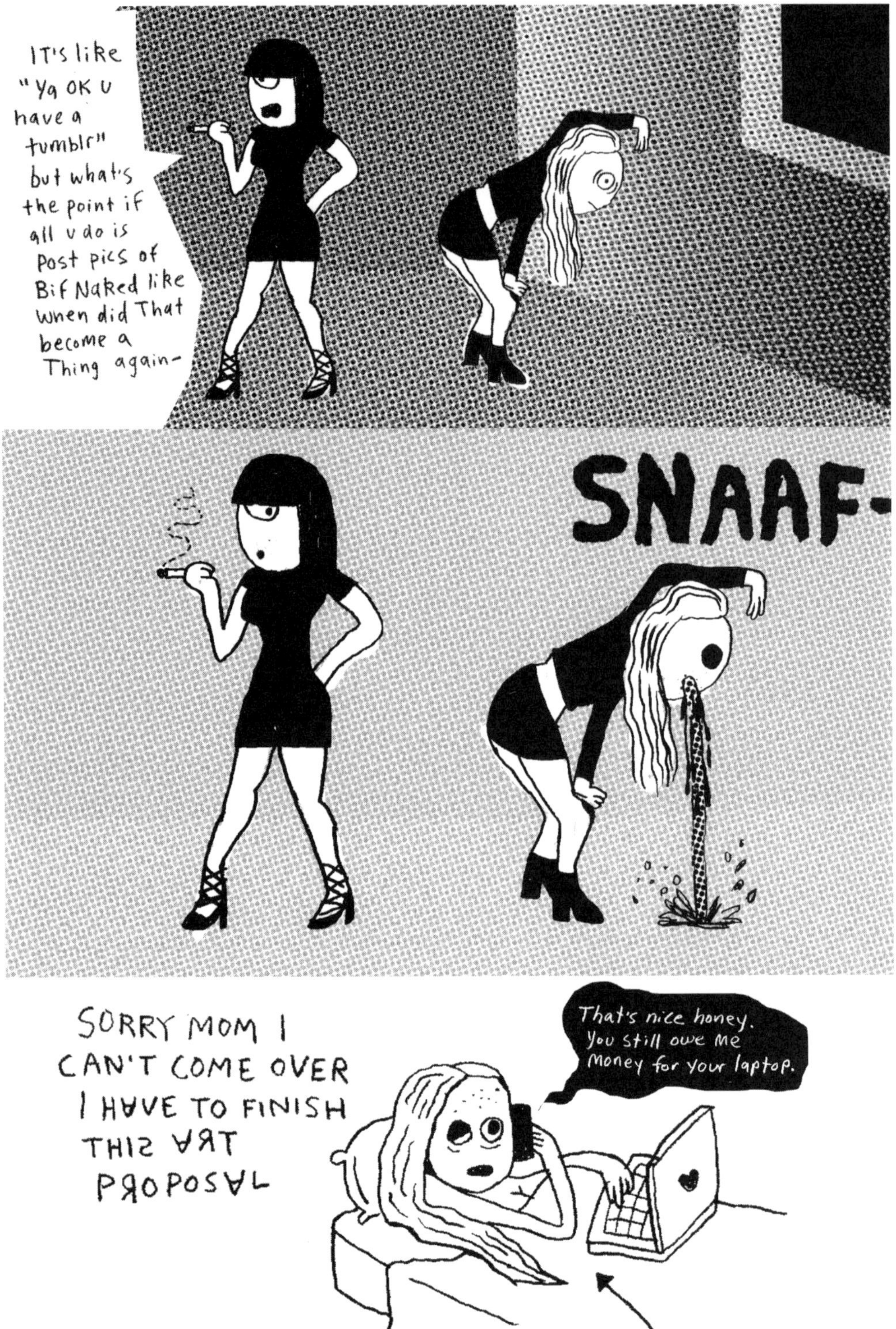

IT's like "Ya OK U have a tumblr" but what's the point if all u do is Post pics of Bif Naked like when did That become a Thing again-
SNAAF-
SORRY MOM I CAN'T COME OVER I HAVE TO FINISH THIS ART PROPOSAL
That's nice honey. You still owe me money for your laptop.
Slept one hour

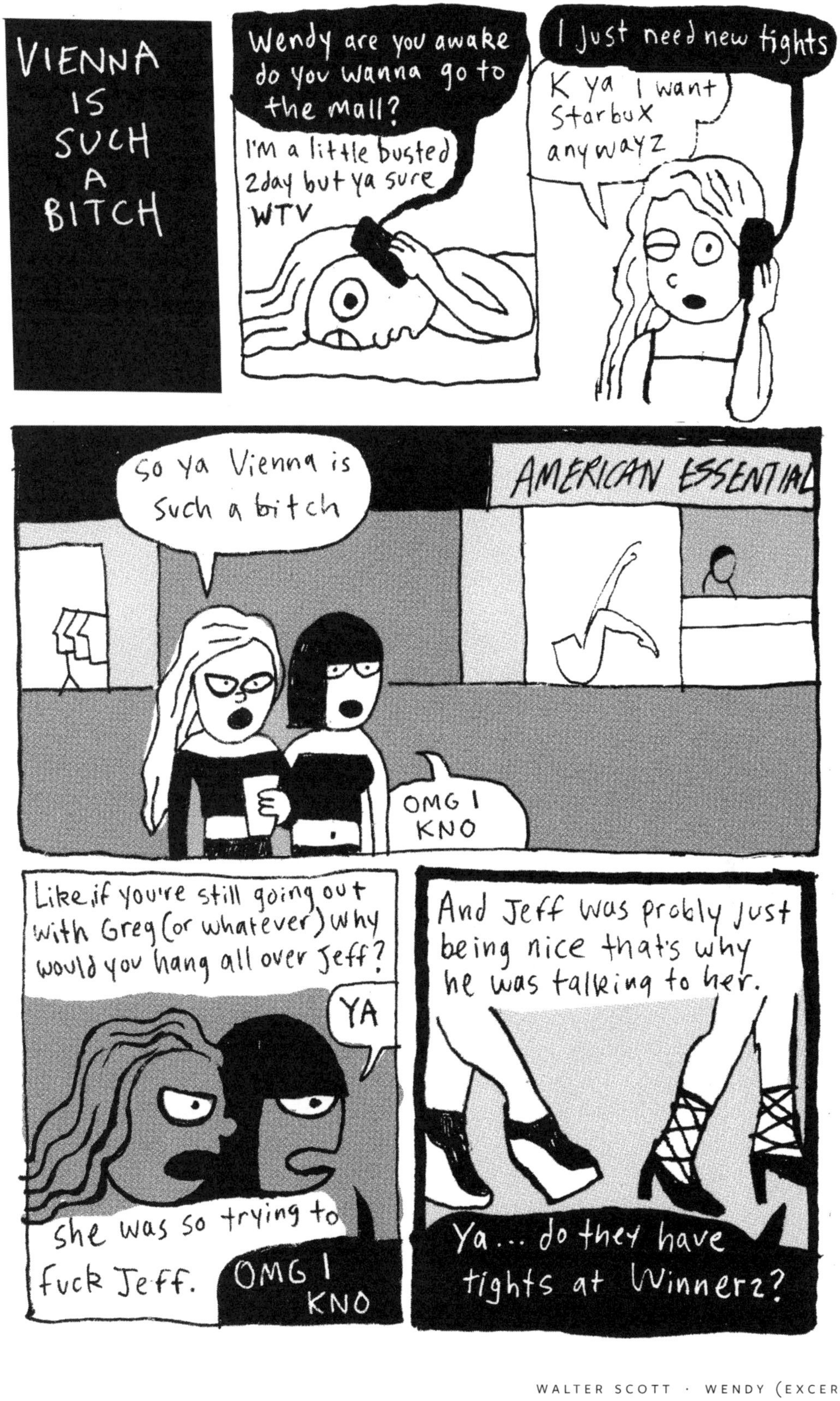
VIENNA IS SUCH A BITCH
Wendy are you awake do you wanna go to the mall?
I'm a little busted 2day but ya sure WTV
I just need new tights
K ya I want Starbux anywayz
So ya Vienna is such a bitch
AMERICAN ESSENTIAL
OMG I KNO
Like, if you're still going out with Greg (or whatever) why would you hang all over Jeff?
YA
she was so trying to fuck Jeff.
OMG I KNO
And Jeff was probly just being nice that's why he was talking to her.
Ya... do they have tights at Winnerz?

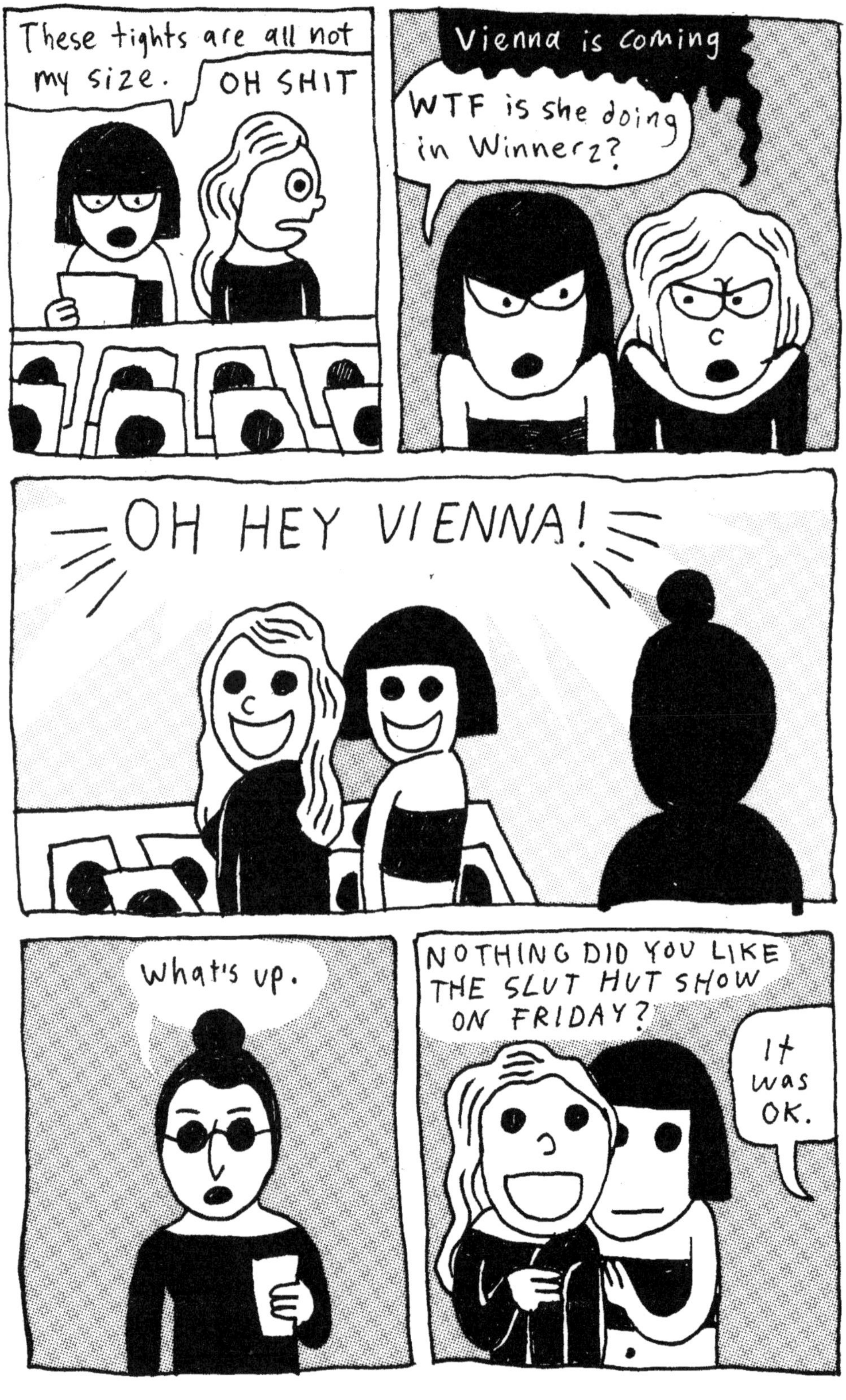
These tights are all not my size.
OH SHIT
Vienna is coming
WTF is she doing in Winnerz?
OH HEY VIENNA!
What's up.
NOTHING DID YOU LIKE THE SLUT HUT SHOW ON FRIDAY?
It was OK.

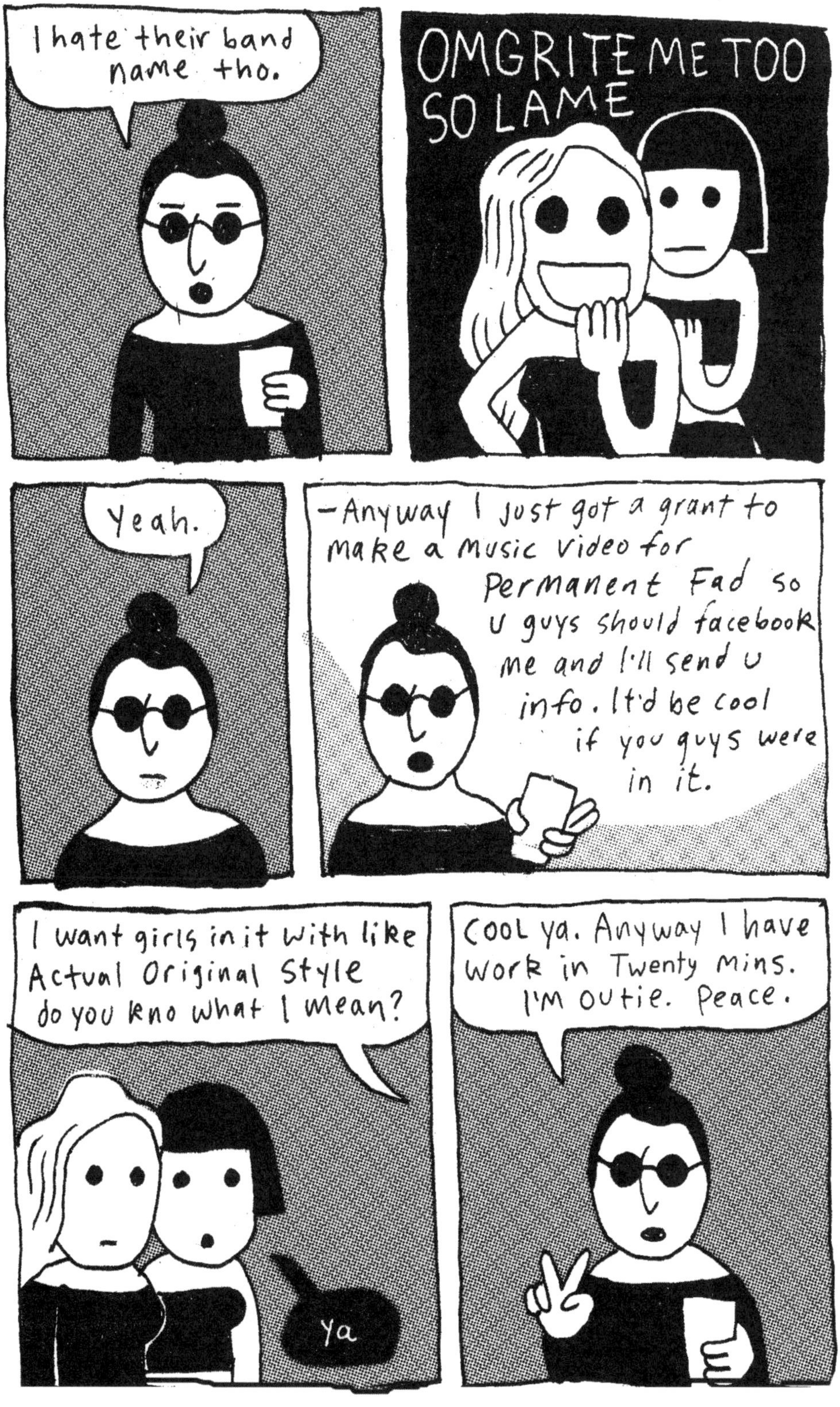
I hate their band name tho.
OMGRITE ME TOO SO LAME
Yeah.
–Anyway I just got a grant to make a music video for Permanent Fad so u guys should facebook me and I'll send u info. It'd be cool if you guys were in it.
I want girls in it with like Actual Original Style do you kno what I mean?
ya
COOL ya. Anyway I have work in Twenty mins. I'M outie. Peace.

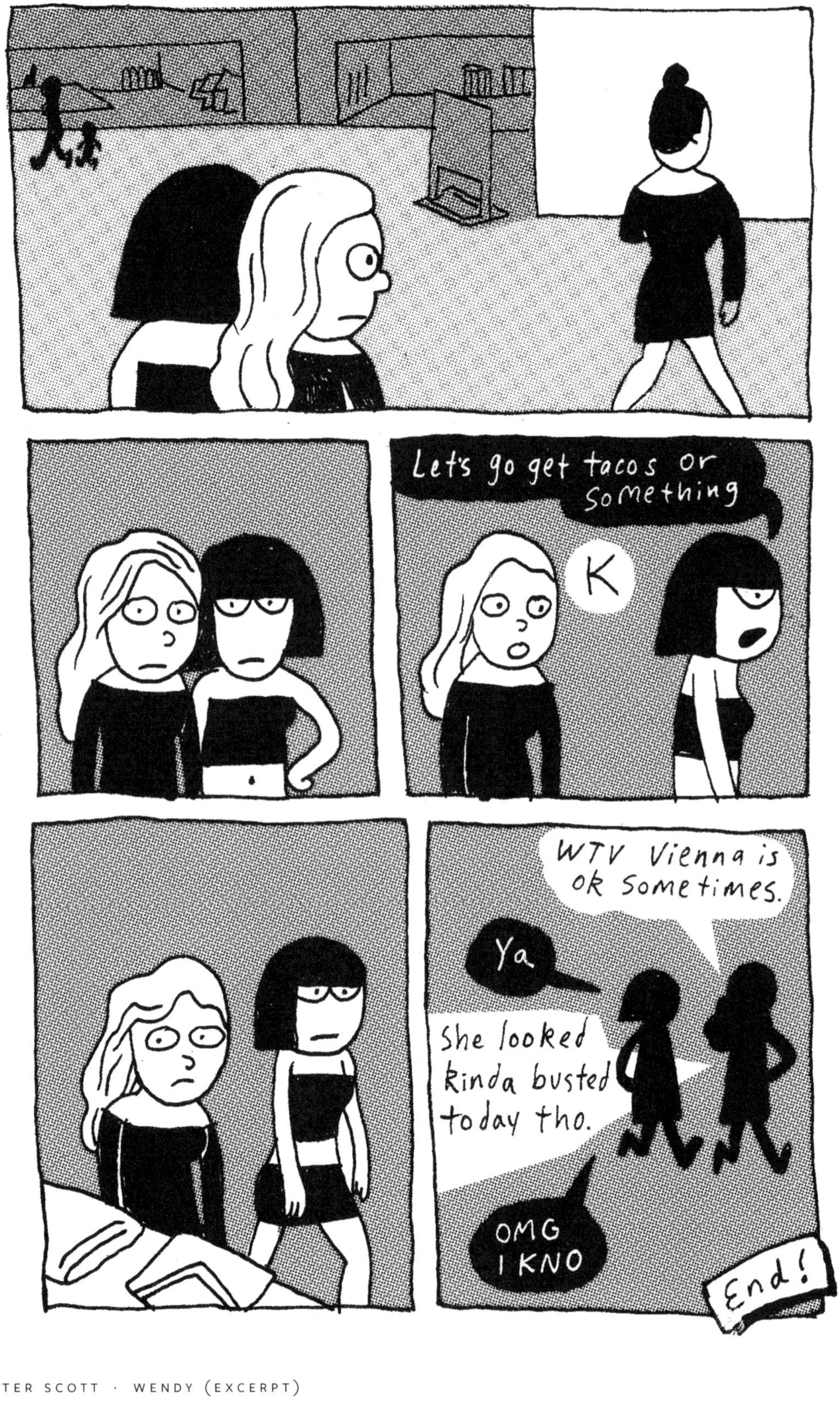
Let's go get tacos or something
K
WTV Vienna is ok sometimes.
Ya
She looked kinda busted today tho.
OMG I KNO
End!

# The Last Saturday (*Excerpt*)

## CHRIS WARE

*originally published in*

### www.theguardian.com

GUARDIAN NEWS AND MEDIA

digital

## Biography

Chris Ware is the author of *Jimmy Corrigan—the Smartest Kid on Earth* and *Building Stories*, which was deemed a Top Ten Fiction Book of 2012 by the *New York Times* and *Time*. A contributor to *The New Yorker*, his work has been exhibited at the MoCa Los Angeles, the MCA Chicago, and the Whitney Museum of American Art.

## Statement

"The Last Saturday" offered up my usual experiments on reader tolerance as well as the usual comics-specific "space versus time" test, which print newspapers are still especially well-positioned to catalyze (i.e., how, exactly, limited page size compresses the chronology and musicality of a visual story until everything, including legibility, can no longer escape). Fortunately, the chapter of the story serialized in the *Guardian*'s Saturday Magazine, from which this excerpt is selected, also tried to capture the main character's abbreviated if not unreliable childhood memories, to say nothing of his emotionally constipated inner life, so maybe everything sort of worked out in the end. The pages have been substantially enlarged here, somewhat exceeding my preferred ratio of texture of consciousness to paper—but in anthologies one almost always has to make some sort of friendly concession.

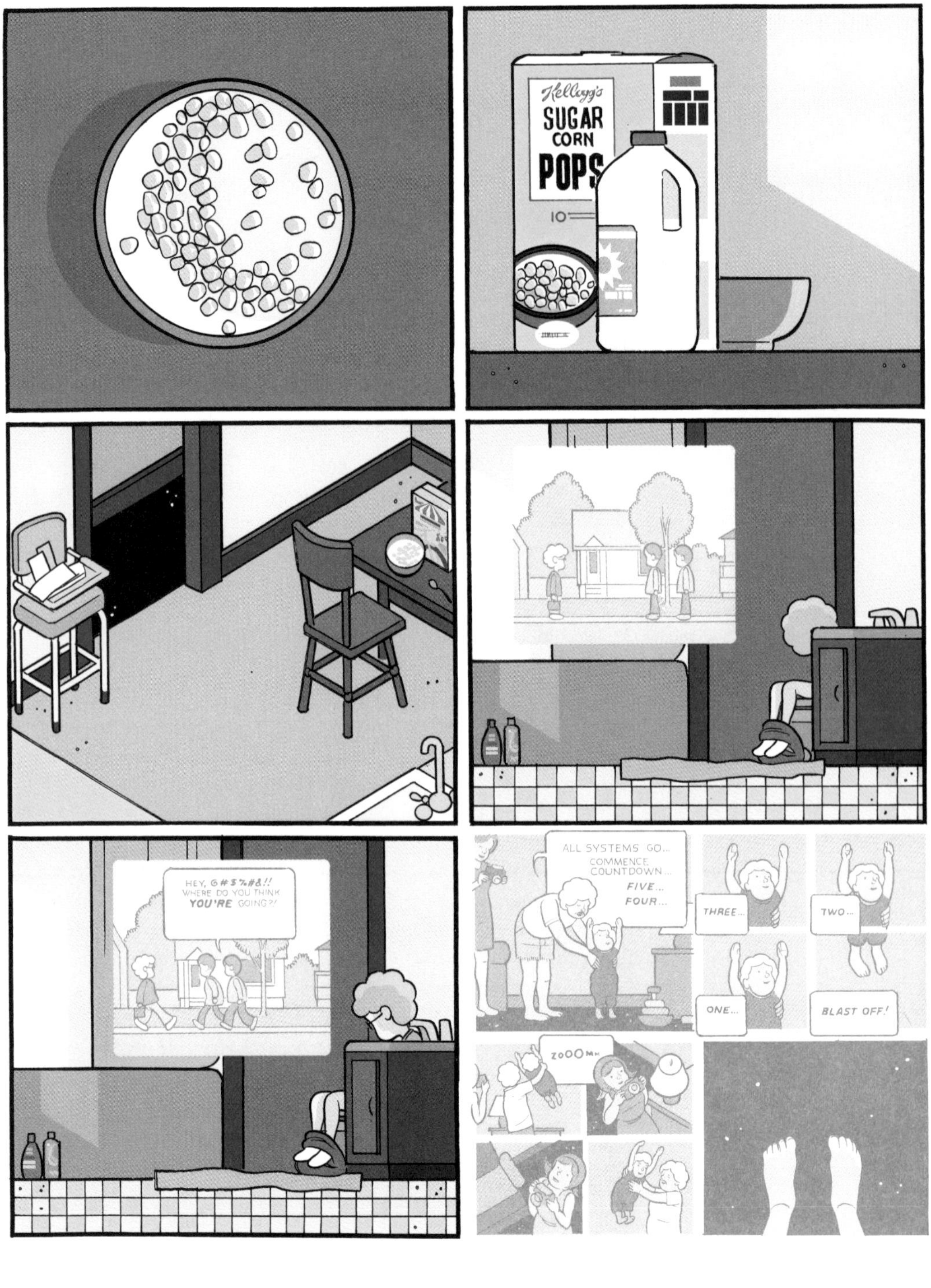
Kellogg's
SUGAR CORN POPS
10¢
HEY, G#$%#&!!
WHERE DO YOU THINK YOU'RE GOING?!
ALL SYSTEMS GO...
COMMENCE COUNTDOWN...
FIVE...
FOUR...
THREE...
TWO...
ONE...
BLAST OFF!
ZOOOMM

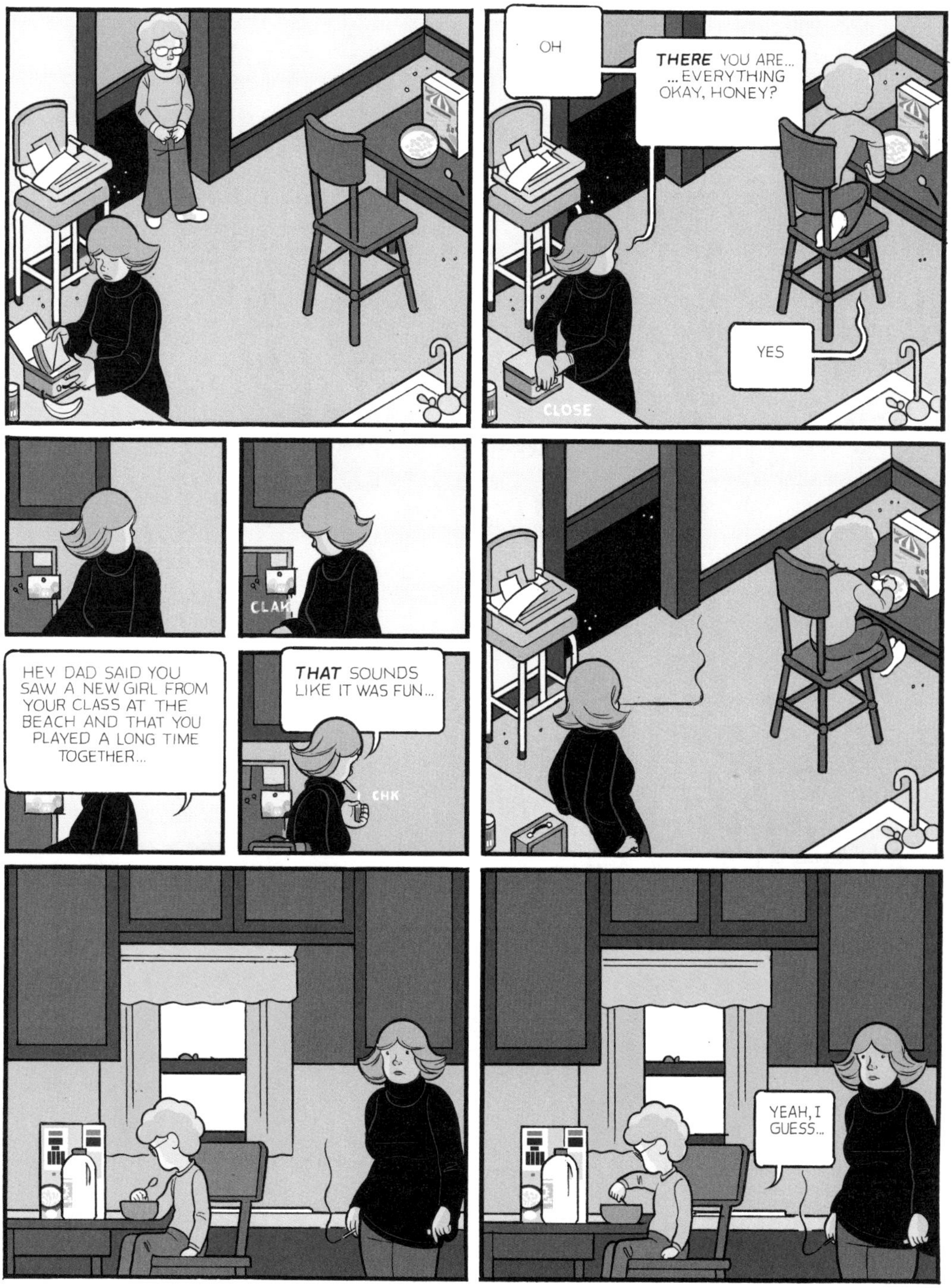
OH
THERE YOU ARE... ...EVERYTHING OKAY, HONEY?
YES
CLOSE
CLAK
HEY DAD SAID YOU SAW A NEW GIRL FROM YOUR CLASS AT THE BEACH AND THAT YOU PLAYED A LONG TIME TOGETHER...
THAT SOUNDS LIKE IT WAS FUN...
CHK
YEAH, I GUESS...

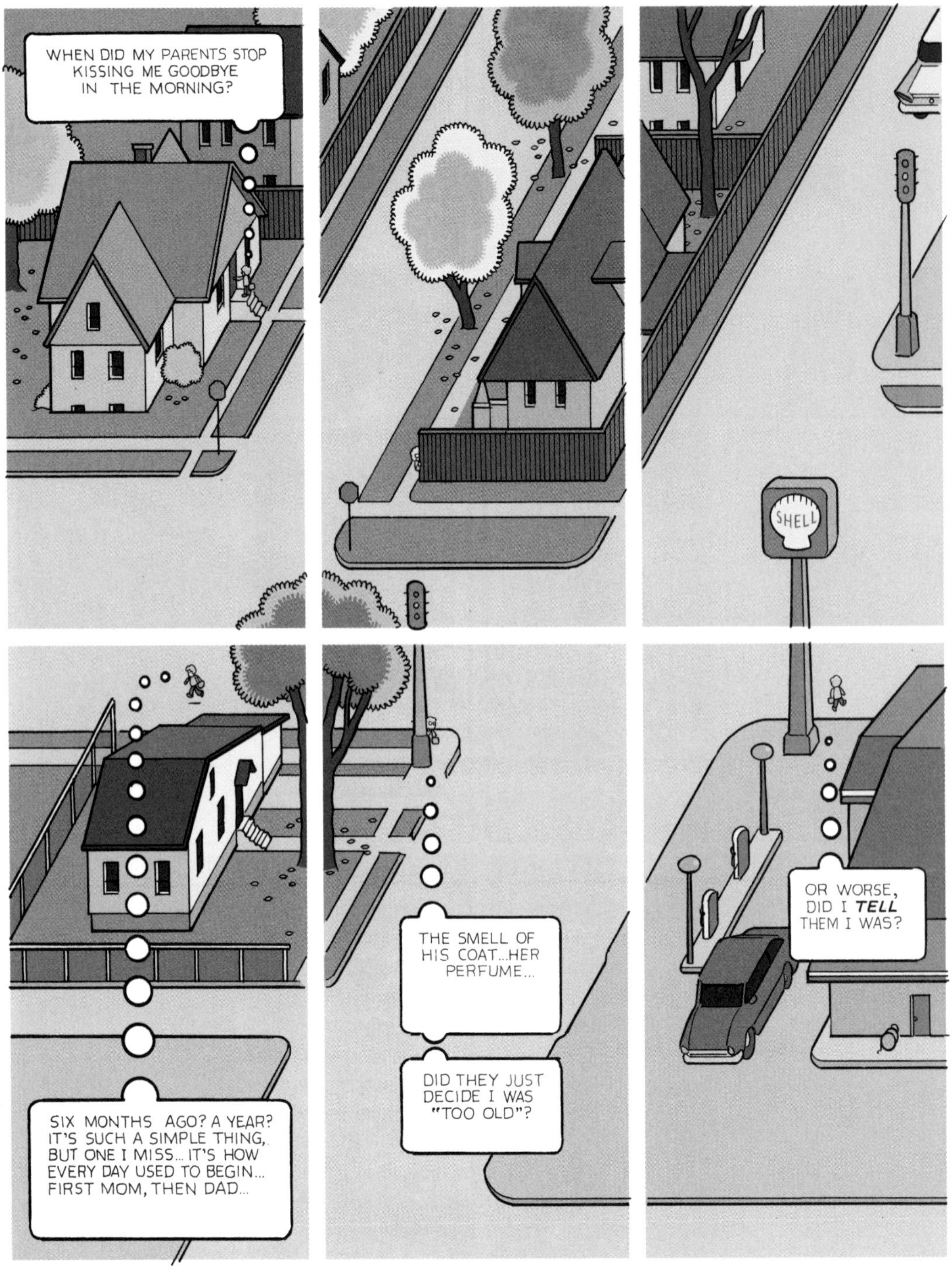
WHEN DID MY PARENTS STOP KISSING ME GOODBYE IN THE MORNING?
SHELL
SIX MONTHS AGO? A YEAR? IT'S SUCH A SIMPLE THING, BUT ONE I MISS... IT'S HOW EVERY DAY USED TO BEGIN... FIRST MOM, THEN DAD...
THE SMELL OF HIS COAT...HER PERFUME...
DID THEY JUST DECIDE I WAS "TOO OLD"?
OR WORSE, DID I **TELL** THEM I WAS?

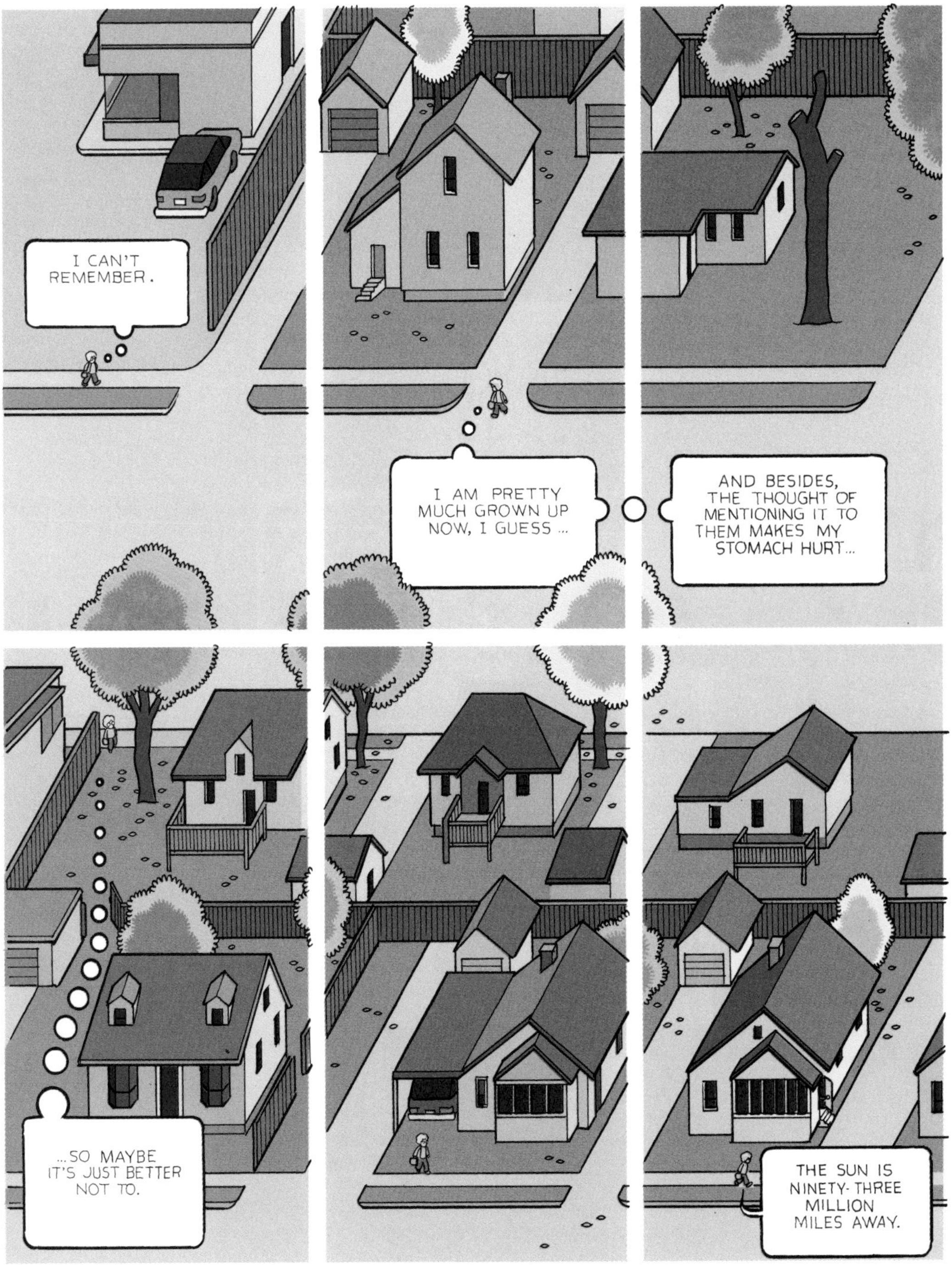
I CAN'T REMEMBER.
I AM PRETTY MUCH GROWN UP NOW, I GUESS ...
AND BESIDES, THE THOUGHT OF MENTIONING IT TO THEM MAKES MY STOMACH HURT...
...SO MAYBE IT'S JUST BETTER NOT TO.
THE SUN IS NINETY-THREE MILLION MILES AWAY.

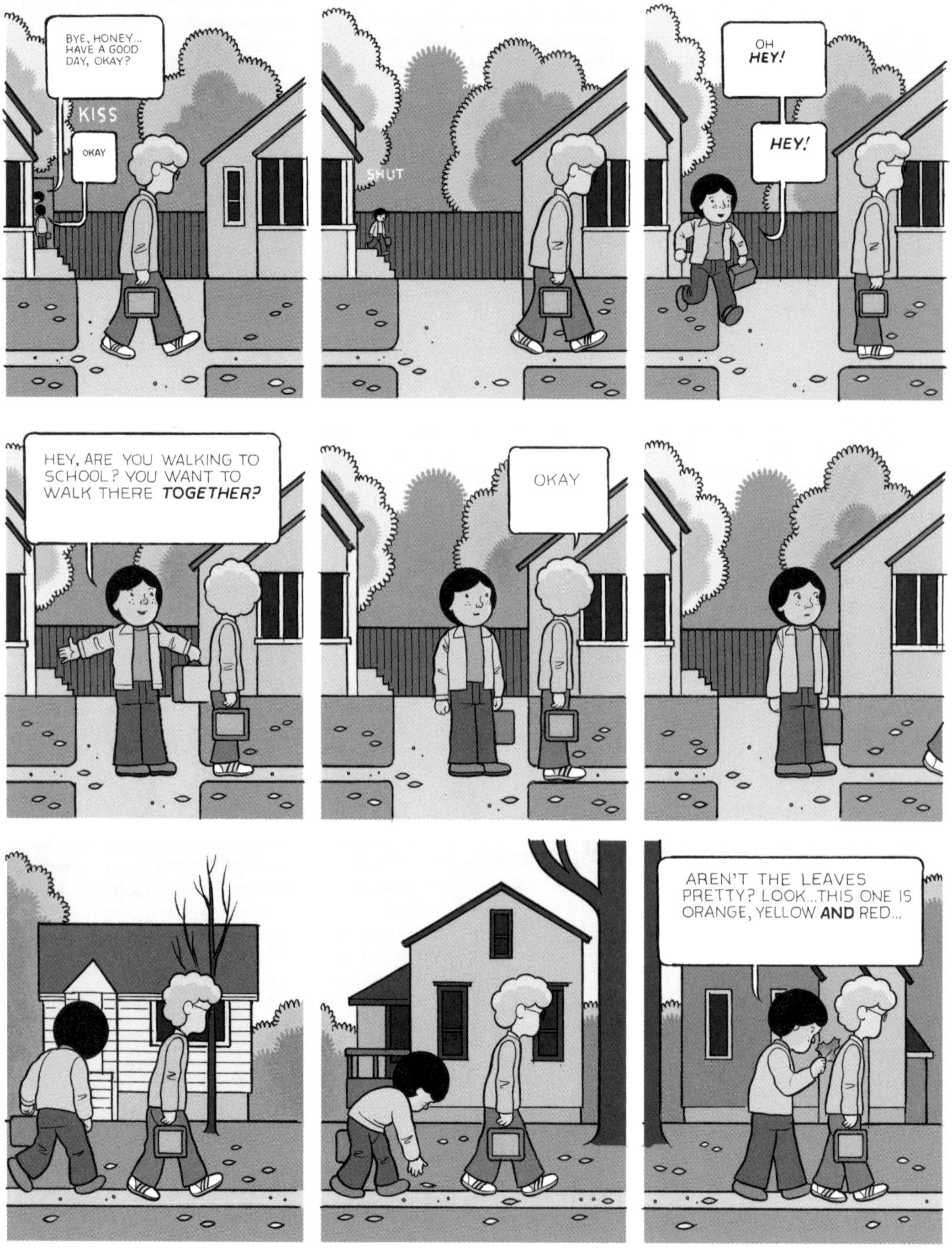
BYE, HONEY... HAVE A GOOD DAY, OKAY?
KISS
OKAY
SHUT
OH **HEY!**
**HEY!**
HEY, ARE YOU WALKING TO SCHOOL? YOU WANT TO WALK THERE **TOGETHER?**
OKAY
AREN'T THE LEAVES PRETTY? LOOK...THIS ONE IS ORANGE, YELLOW **AND** RED...

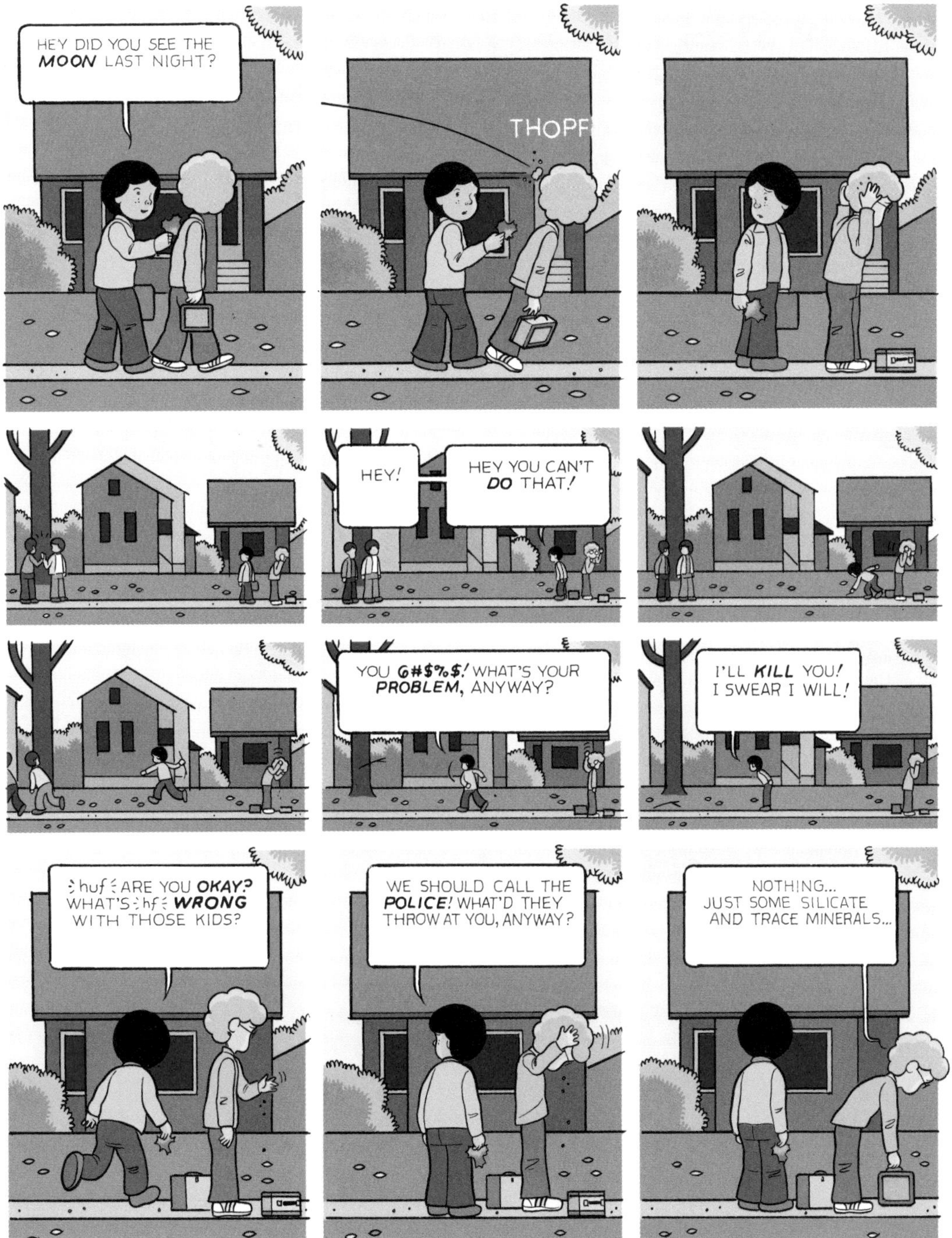
HEY DID YOU SEE THE MOON LAST NIGHT?
THOPF
HEY!
HEY YOU CAN'T DO THAT!
YOU G#$%$! WHAT'S YOUR PROBLEM, ANYWAY?
I'LL KILL YOU! I SWEAR I WILL!
huf ARE YOU OKAY? WHAT'S hf WRONG WITH THOSE KIDS?
WE SHOULD CALL THE POLICE! WHAT'D THEY THROW AT YOU, ANYWAY?
NOTHING... JUST SOME SILICATE AND TRACE MINERALS...

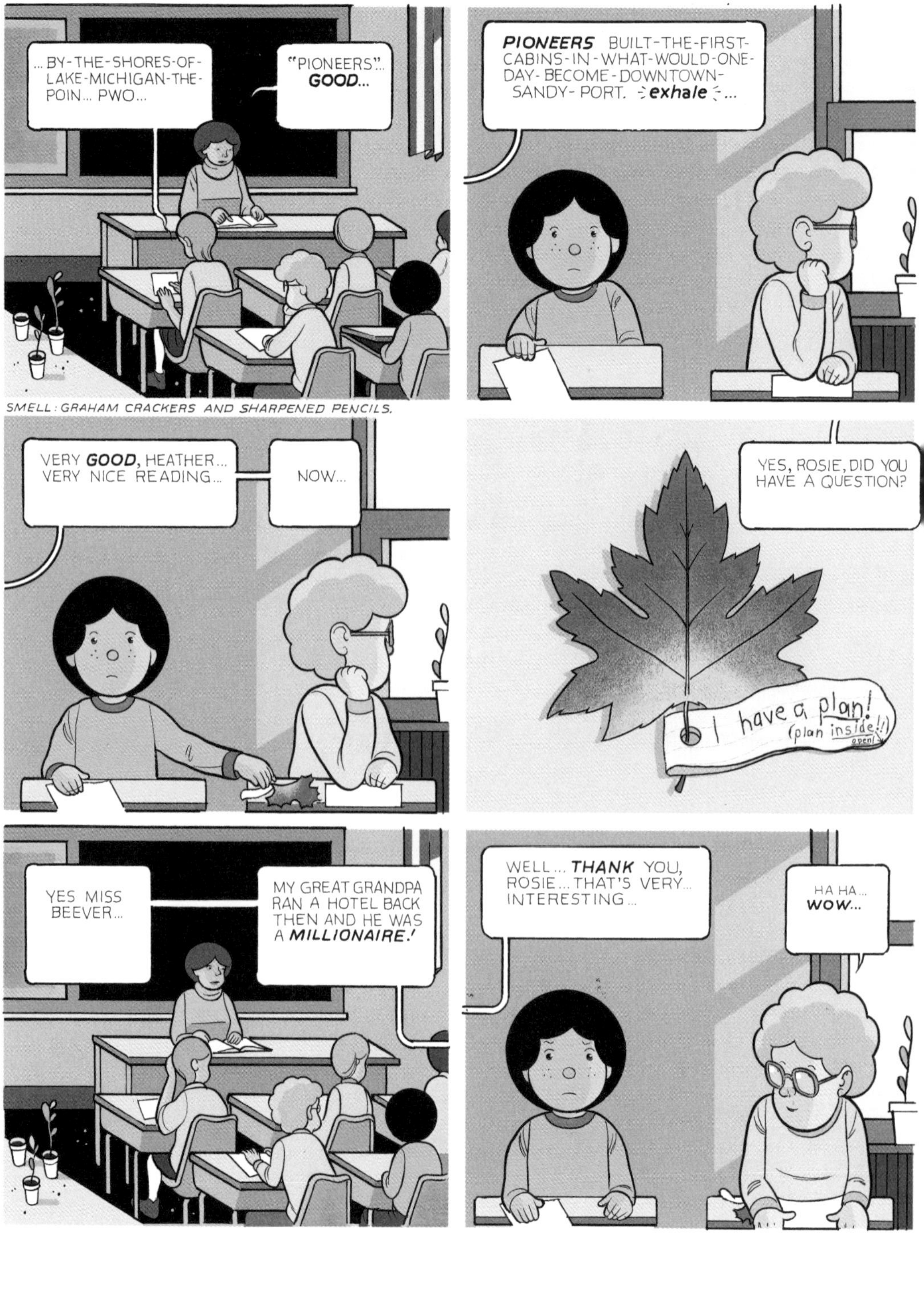
...BY-THE-SHORES-OF-LAKE-MICHIGAN-THE-POIN... PWO...
"PIONEERS"... **GOOD...**
SMELL: GRAHAM CRACKERS AND SHARPENED PENCILS.
**PIONEERS** BUILT-THE-FIRST-CABINS-IN-WHAT-WOULD-ONE-DAY-BECOME-DOWNTOWN-SANDY-PORT. **exhale**...
VERY **GOOD**, HEATHER... VERY NICE READING...
NOW...
YES, ROSIE, DID YOU HAVE A QUESTION?
I have a plan! (plan inside!!) open!
YES MISS BEEVER...
MY GREAT GRANDPA RAN A HOTEL BACK THEN AND HE WAS A **MILLIONAIRE!**
WELL... **THANK** YOU, ROSIE... THAT'S VERY... INTERESTING...
HA HA... **WOW...**

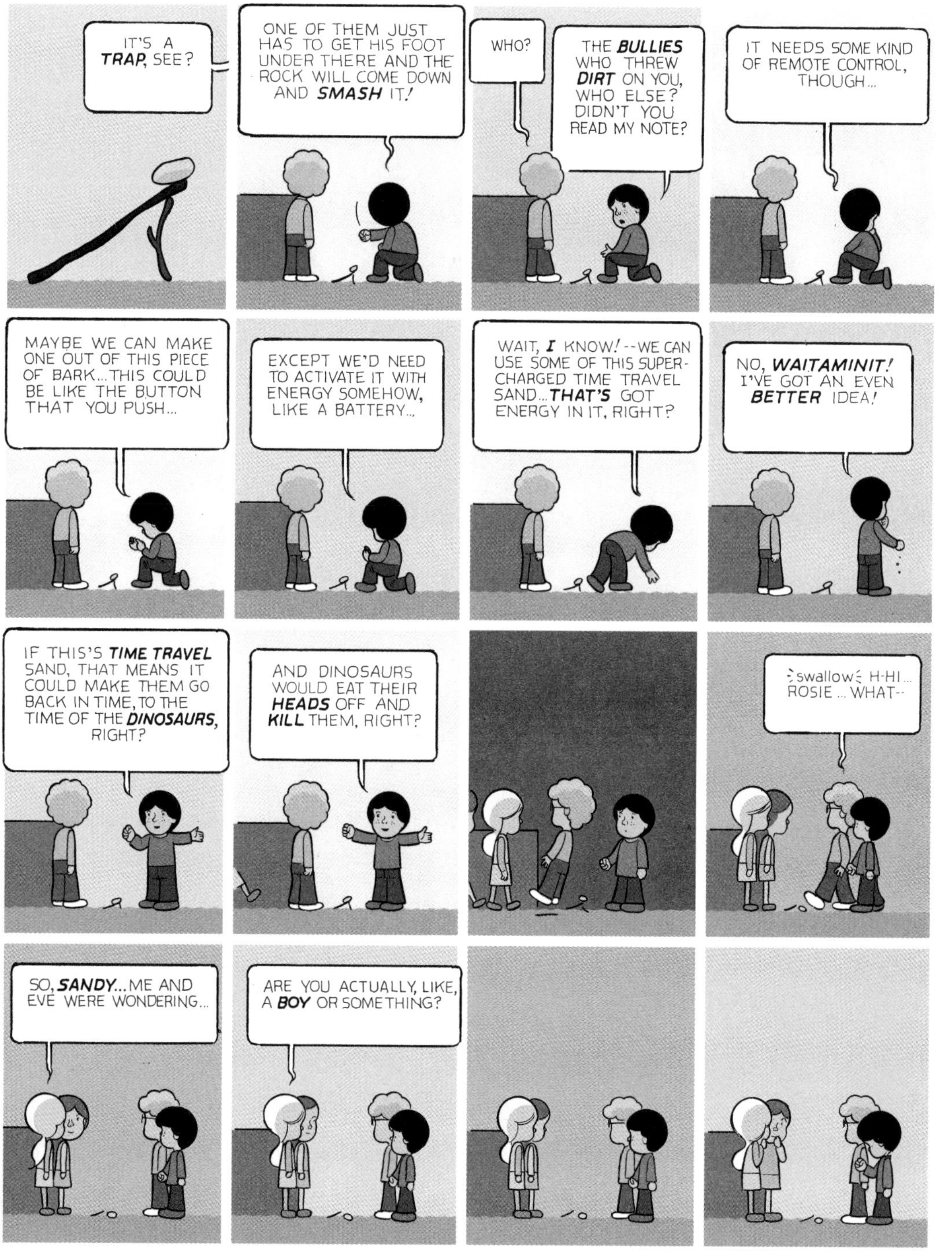
IT'S A TRAP, SEE?
ONE OF THEM JUST HAS TO GET HIS FOOT UNDER THERE AND THE ROCK WILL COME DOWN AND SMASH IT!
WHO?
THE BULLIES WHO THREW DIRT ON YOU, WHO ELSE? DIDN'T YOU READ MY NOTE?
IT NEEDS SOME KIND OF REMOTE CONTROL, THOUGH...
MAYBE WE CAN MAKE ONE OUT OF THIS PIECE OF BARK... THIS COULD BE LIKE THE BUTTON THAT YOU PUSH...
EXCEPT WE'D NEED TO ACTIVATE IT WITH ENERGY SOMEHOW, LIKE A BATTERY...
WAIT, I KNOW! --WE CAN USE SOME OF THIS SUPER-CHARGED TIME TRAVEL SAND... THAT'S GOT ENERGY IN IT, RIGHT?
NO, WAITAMINIT! I'VE GOT AN EVEN BETTER IDEA!
IF THIS'S TIME TRAVEL SAND, THAT MEANS IT COULD MAKE THEM GO BACK IN TIME, TO THE TIME OF THE DINOSAURS, RIGHT?
AND DINOSAURS WOULD EAT THEIR HEADS OFF AND KILL THEM, RIGHT?
swallow H-HI... ROSIE... WHAT--
SO, SANDY... ME AND EVE WERE WONDERING...
ARE YOU ACTUALLY, LIKE, A BOY OR SOMETHING?

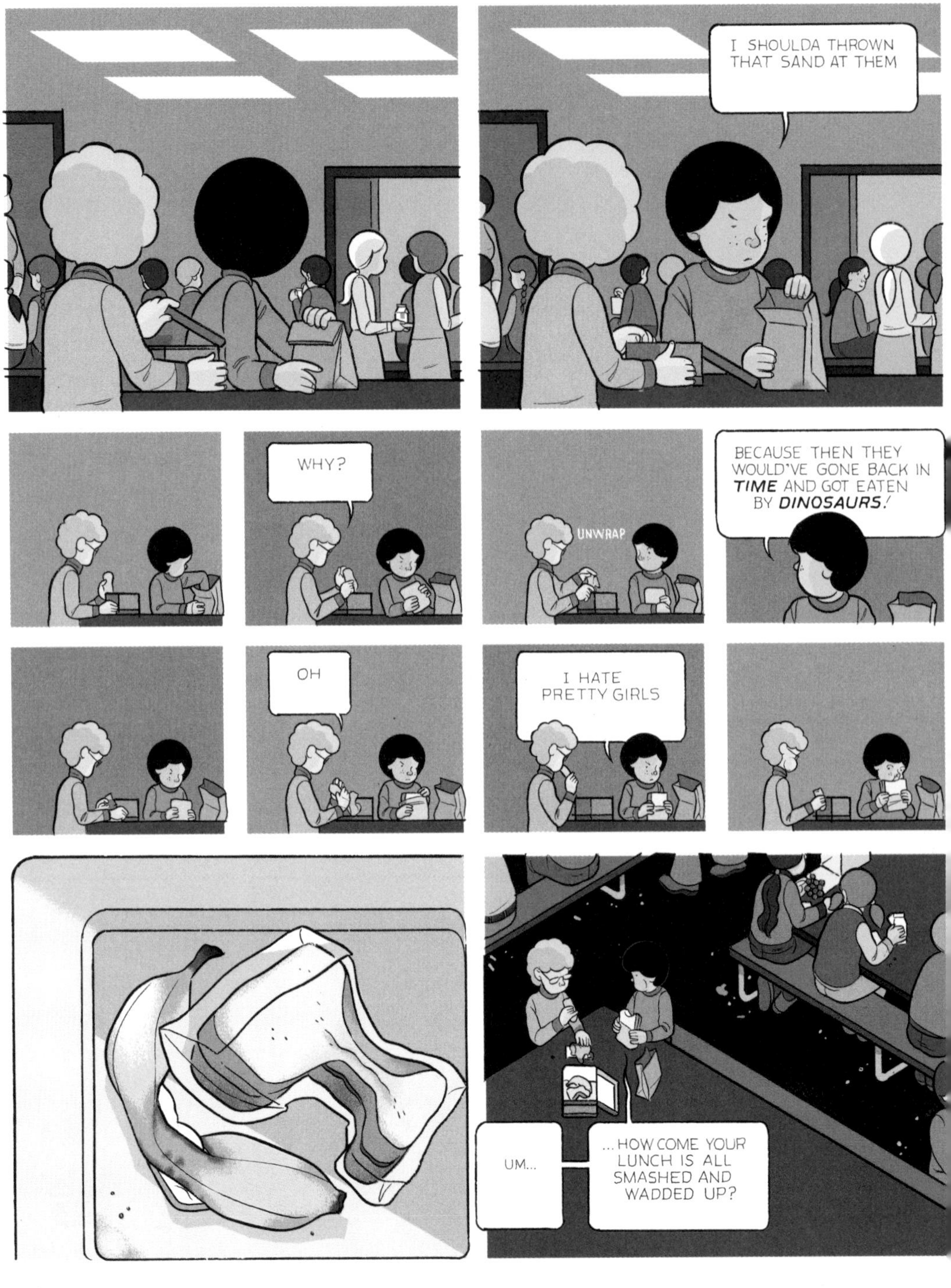
I SHOULDA THROWN THAT SAND AT THEM
WHY?
UNWRAP
BECAUSE THEN THEY WOULD'VE GONE BACK IN TIME AND GOT EATEN BY DINOSAURS!
OH
I HATE PRETTY GIRLS
UM...
...HOW COME YOUR LUNCH IS ALL SMASHED AND WADDED UP?

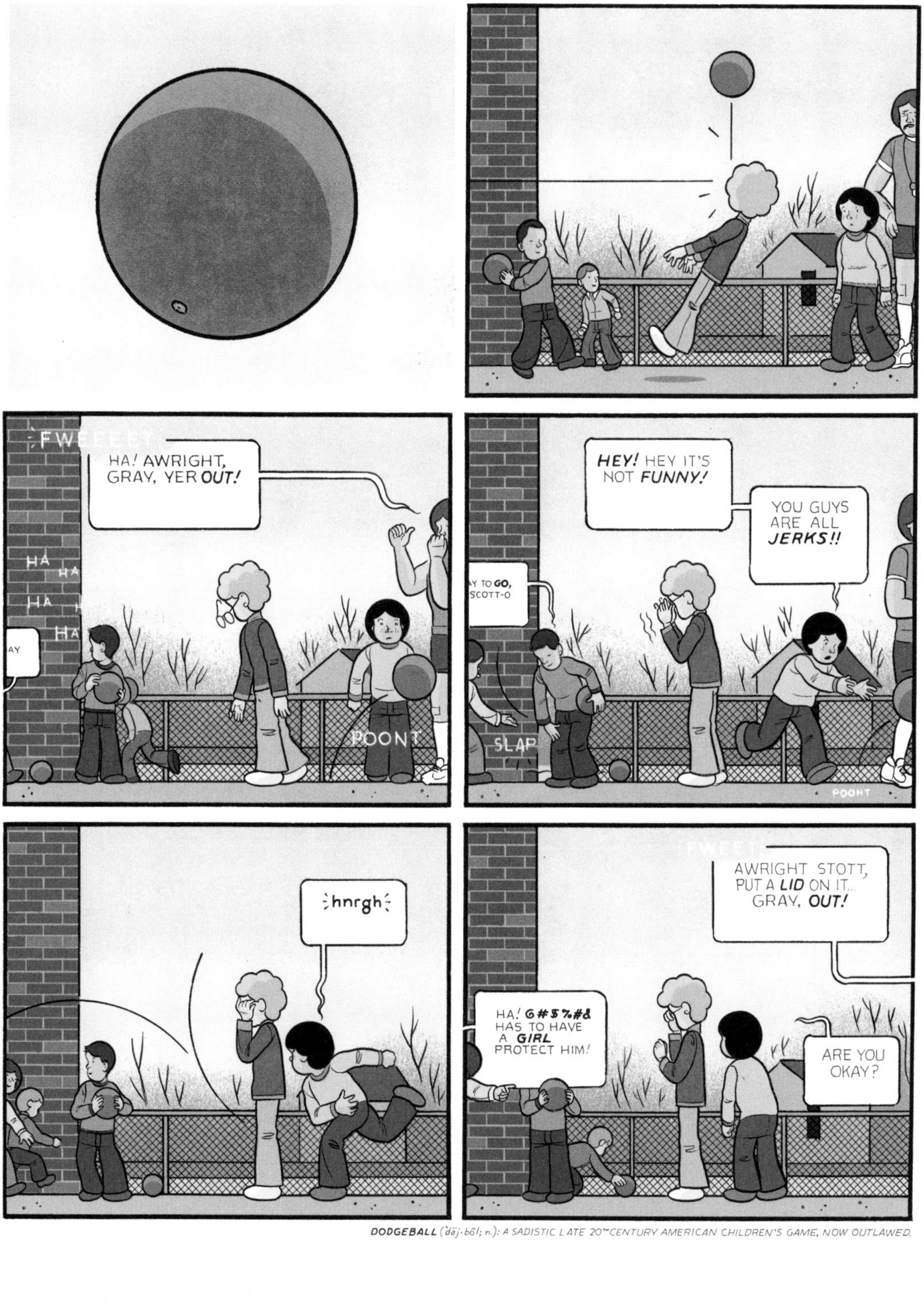
FWEEEEET
HA! AWRIGHT, GRAY, YER OUT!
HA HA HA HA
AY
POONT
HEY! HEY IT'S NOT FUNNY!
YOU GUYS ARE ALL JERKS!!
AY TO GO, SCOTT-O
SLAP
POONT
hnrgh
FWEET
AWRIGHT STOTT, PUT A LID ON IT... GRAY, OUT!
HA! G#$%#& HAS TO HAVE A GIRL PROTECT HIM!
ARE YOU OKAY?

DODGEBALL (ˈdäj·bôl; n.): A SADISTIC LATE 20TH CENTURY AMERICAN CHILDREN'S GAME, NOW OUTLAWED.

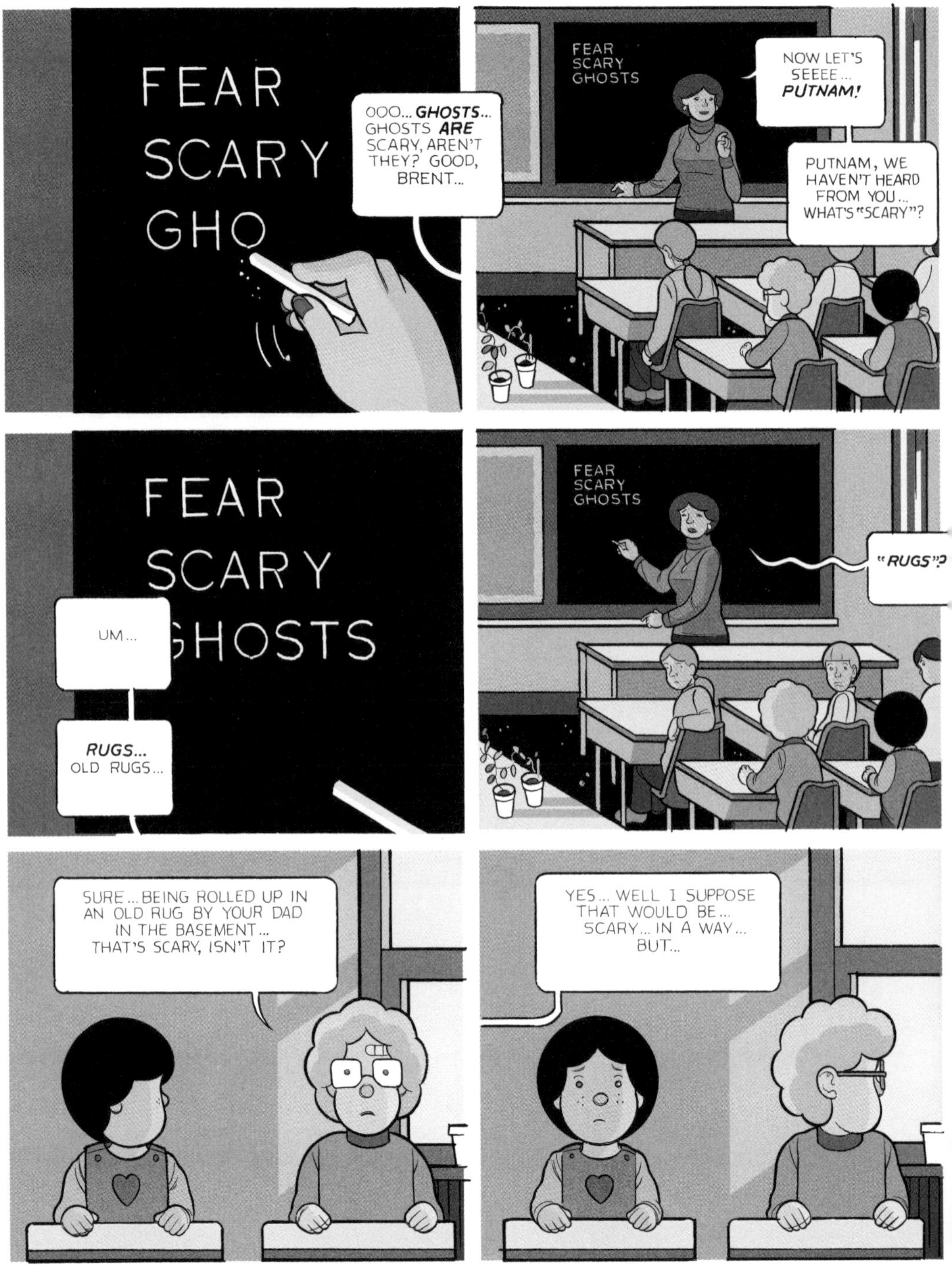
FEAR
SCARY
GHO
OOO... GHOSTS... GHOSTS ARE SCARY, AREN'T THEY? GOOD, BRENT...
FEAR SCARY GHOSTS
NOW LET'S SEEEE... PUTNAM!
PUTNAM, WE HAVEN'T HEARD FROM YOU... WHAT'S "SCARY"?
FEAR
SCARY
GHOSTS
UM...
RUGS... OLD RUGS...
FEAR SCARY GHOSTS
"RUGS"?
SURE... BEING ROLLED UP IN AN OLD RUG BY YOUR DAD IN THE BASEMENT... THAT'S SCARY, ISN'T IT?
YES... WELL I SUPPOSE THAT WOULD BE... SCARY... IN A WAY... BUT...

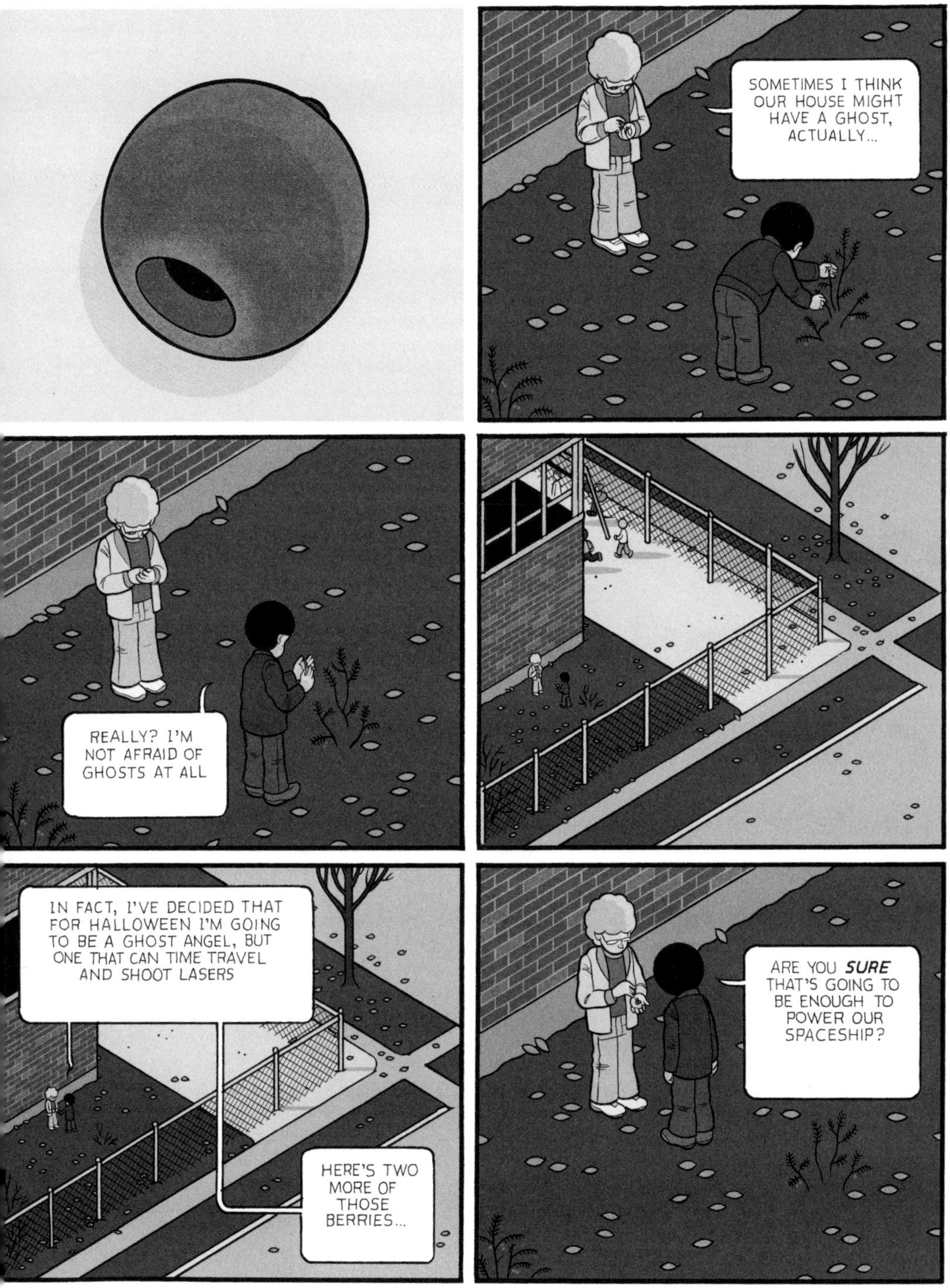
SOMETIMES I THINK OUR HOUSE MIGHT HAVE A GHOST, ACTUALLY...
REALLY? I'M NOT AFRAID OF GHOSTS AT ALL
IN FACT, I'VE DECIDED THAT FOR HALLOWEEN I'M GOING TO BE A GHOST ANGEL, BUT ONE THAT CAN TIME TRAVEL AND SHOOT LASERS
HERE'S TWO MORE OF THOSE BERRIES...
ARE YOU **SURE** THAT'S GOING TO BE ENOUGH TO POWER OUR SPACESHIP?

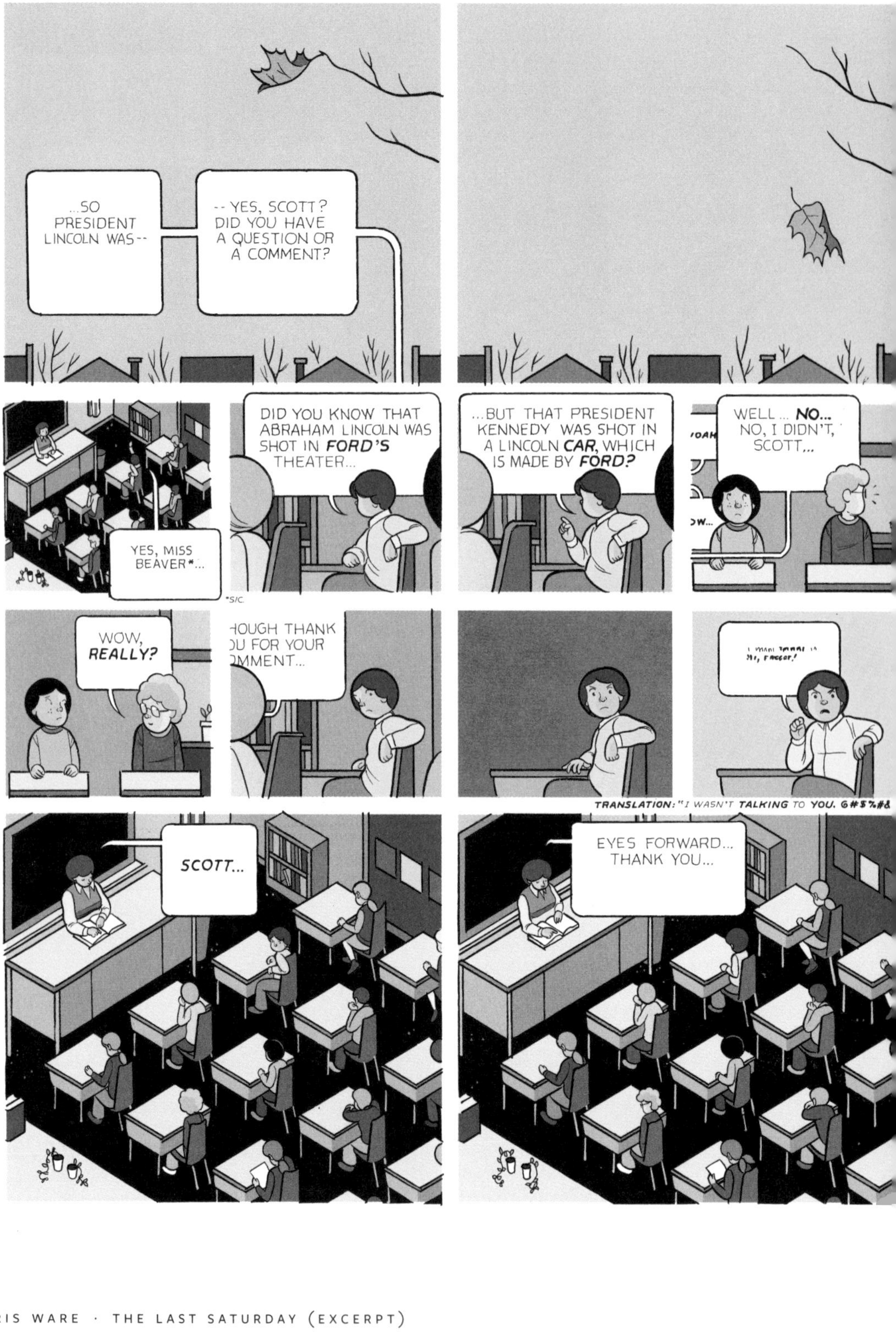
...SO PRESIDENT LINCOLN WAS--
-- YES, SCOTT? DID YOU HAVE A QUESTION OR A COMMENT?
YES, MISS BEAVER*...
*SIC.
DID YOU KNOW THAT ABRAHAM LINCOLN WAS SHOT IN **FORD'S** THEATER...
...BUT THAT PRESIDENT KENNEDY WAS SHOT IN A LINCOLN **CAR**, WHICH IS MADE BY **FORD?**
WELL... **NO...** NO, I DIDN'T, SCOTT...
WOW, **REALLY?**
HOUGH THANK
OU FOR YOUR
OMMENT...
**TRANSLATION:** "I WASN'T **TALKING** TO **YOU.** G#$%#&
**SCOTT...**
EYES FORWARD... THANK YOU...

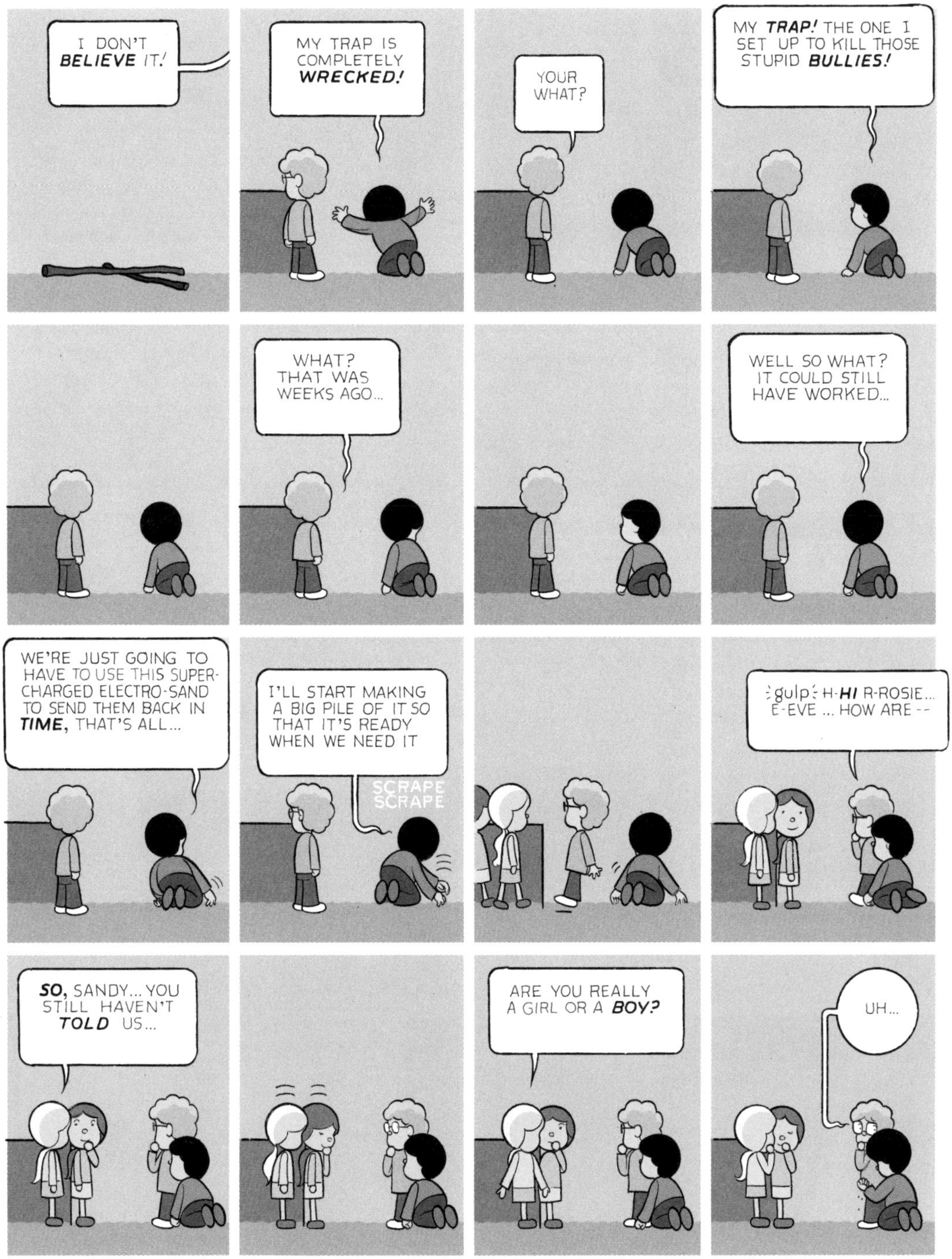
I DON'T BELIEVE IT!
MY TRAP IS COMPLETELY WRECKED!
YOUR WHAT?
MY TRAP! THE ONE I SET UP TO KILL THOSE STUPID BULLIES!
WHAT? THAT WAS WEEKS AGO...
WELL SO WHAT? IT COULD STILL HAVE WORKED...
WE'RE JUST GOING TO HAVE TO USE THIS SUPER-CHARGED ELECTRO-SAND TO SEND THEM BACK IN TIME, THAT'S ALL...
I'LL START MAKING A BIG PILE OF IT SO THAT IT'S READY WHEN WE NEED IT
SCRAPE SCRAPE
:gulp: H-HI R-ROSIE... E-EVE ... HOW ARE --
SO, SANDY... YOU STILL HAVEN'T TOLD US...
ARE YOU REALLY A GIRL OR A BOY?
UH...

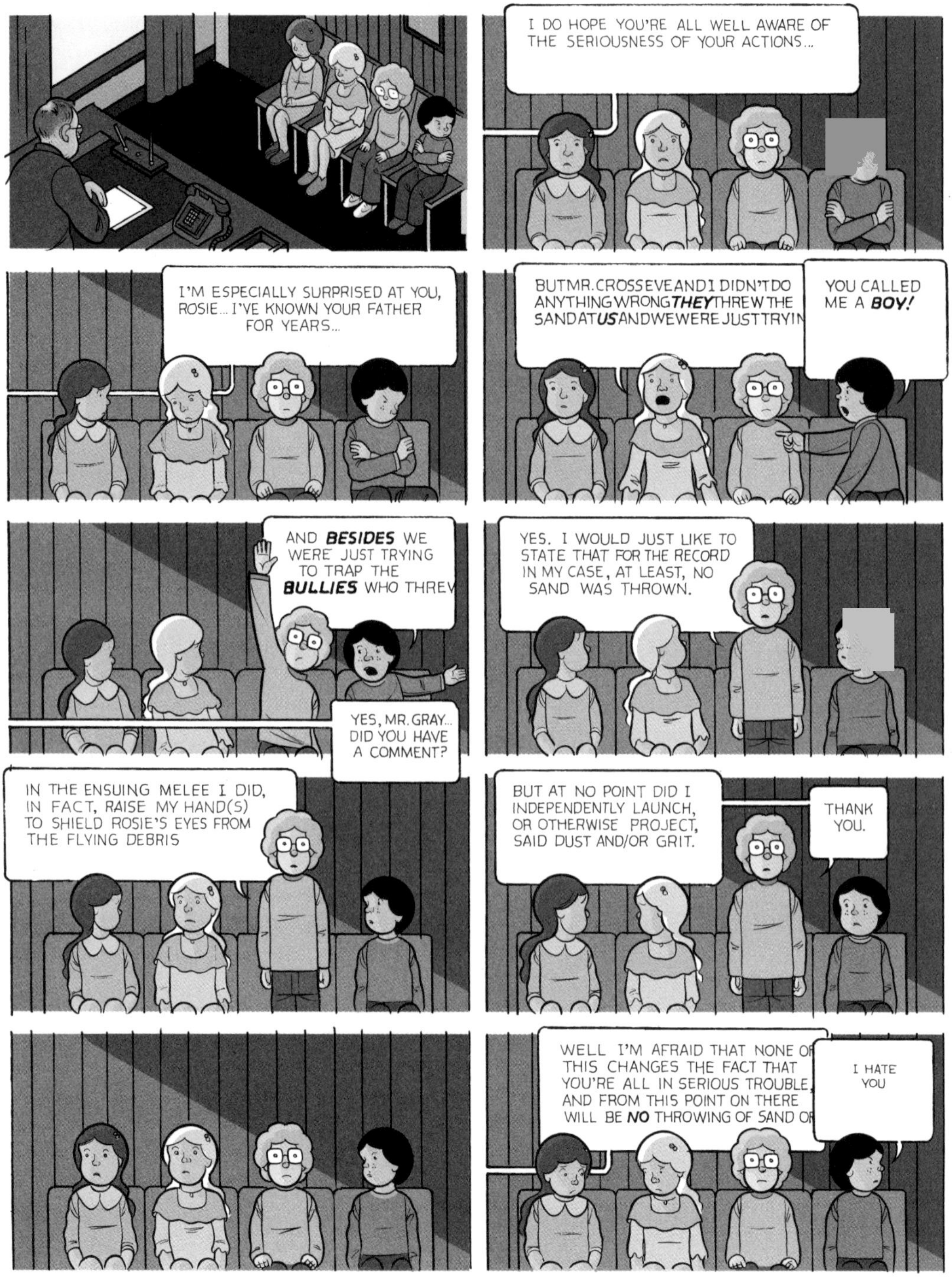

I DO HOPE YOU'RE ALL WELL AWARE OF THE SERIOUSNESS OF YOUR ACTIONS...
I'M ESPECIALLY SURPRISED AT YOU, ROSIE... I'VE KNOWN YOUR FATHER FOR YEARS...
BUT MR. CROSSEVE AND I DIDN'T DO ANYTHING WRONG **THEY** THREW THE SAND AT **US** AND WE WERE JUST TRYIN
YOU CALLED ME A **BOY!**
AND **BESIDES** WE WERE JUST TRYING TO TRAP THE **BULLIES** WHO THREV
YES, MR. GRAY... DID YOU HAVE A COMMENT?
YES. I WOULD JUST LIKE TO STATE THAT FOR THE RECORD IN MY CASE, AT LEAST, NO SAND WAS THROWN.
IN THE ENSUING MELEE I DID, IN FACT, RAISE MY HAND(S) TO SHIELD ROSIE'S EYES FROM THE FLYING DEBRIS
BUT AT NO POINT DID I INDEPENDENTLY LAUNCH, OR OTHERWISE PROJECT, SAID DUST AND/OR GRIT.
THANK YOU.
WELL I'M AFRAID THAT NONE OF THIS CHANGES THE FACT THAT YOU'RE ALL IN SERIOUS TROUBLE, AND FROM THIS POINT ON THERE WILL BE **NO** THROWING OF SAND OR
I HATE YOU

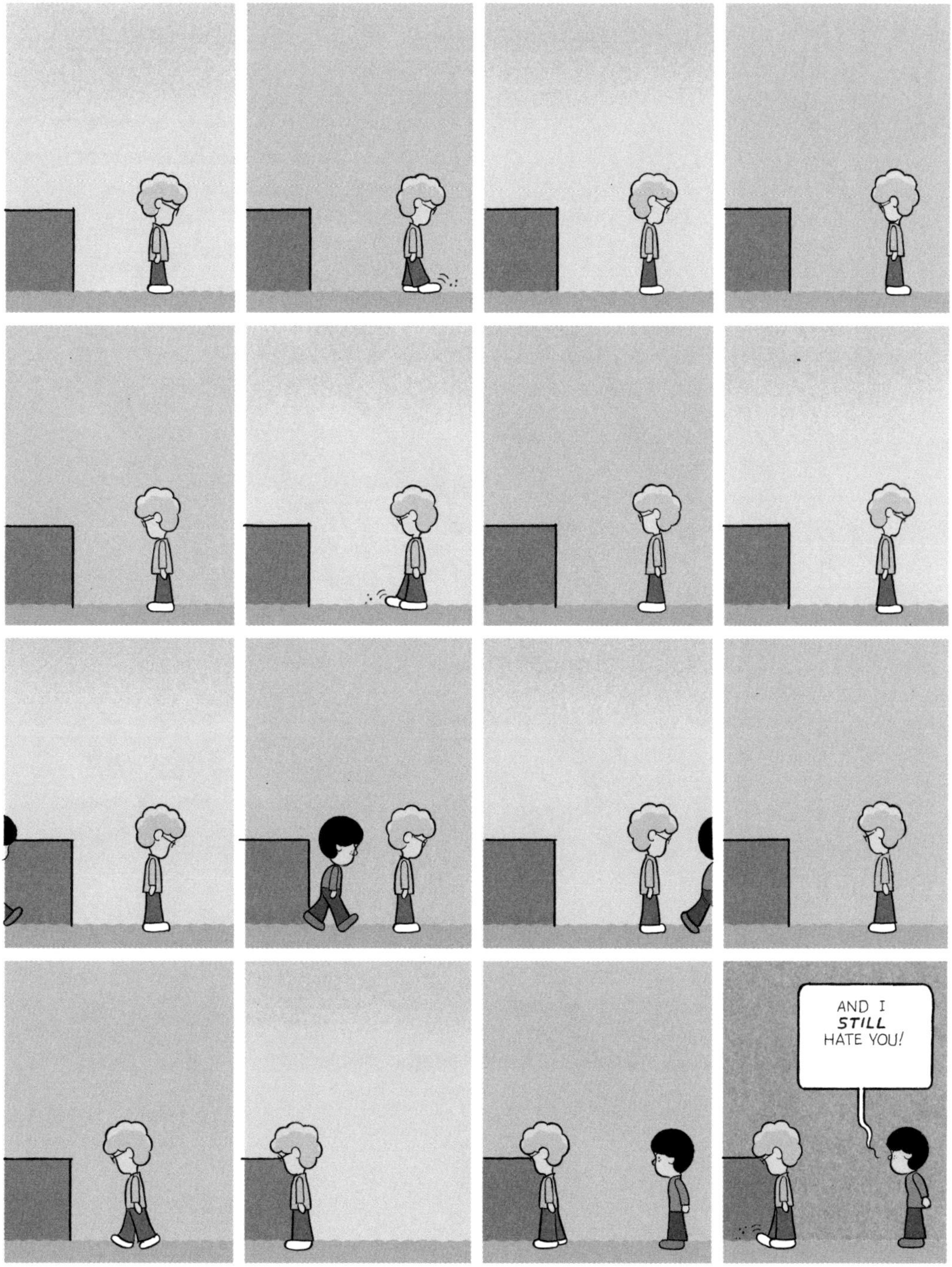
AND I STILL HATE YOU!

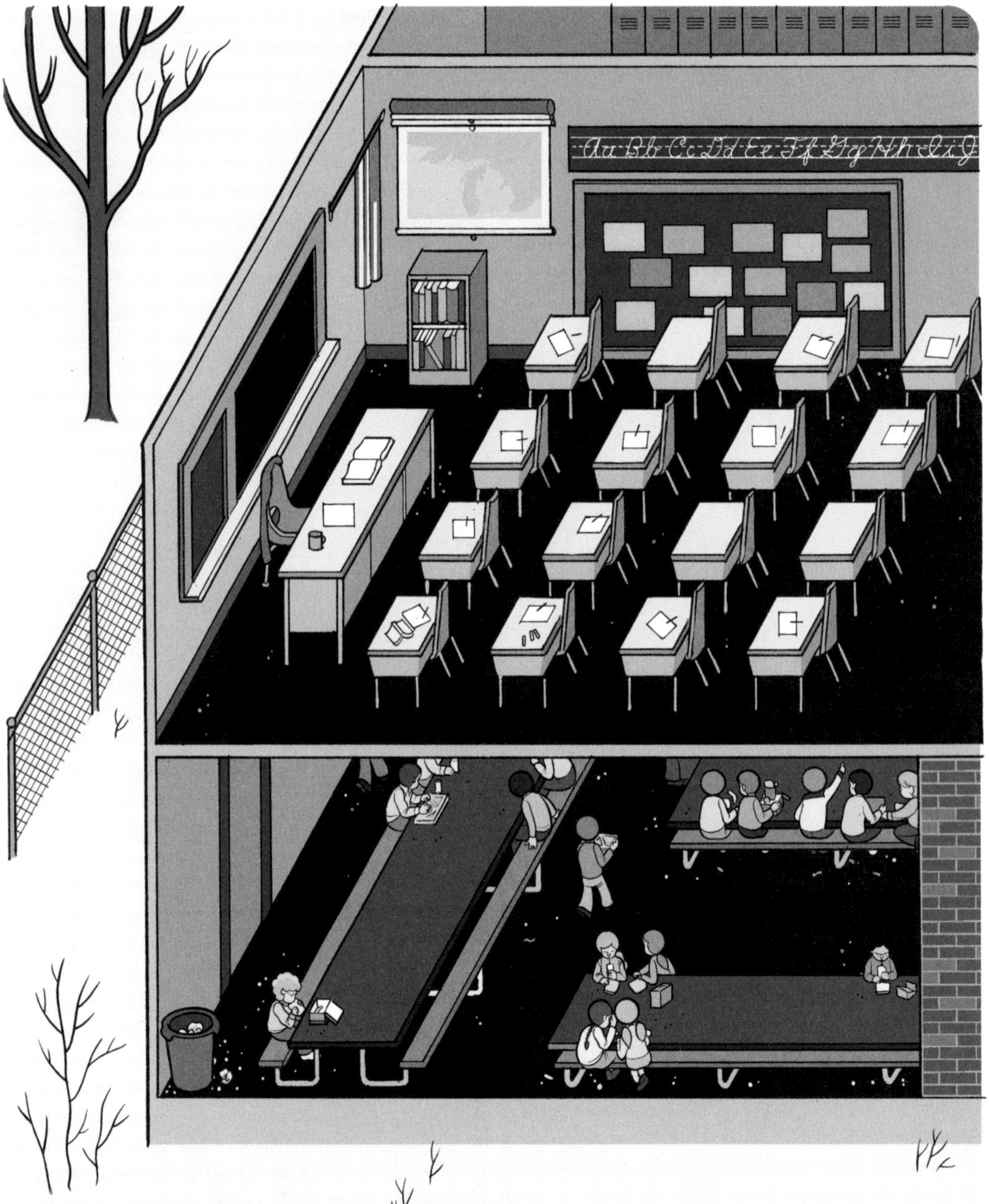
Aa Bb Cc Dd Ee Ff Gg Hh Ii Jj

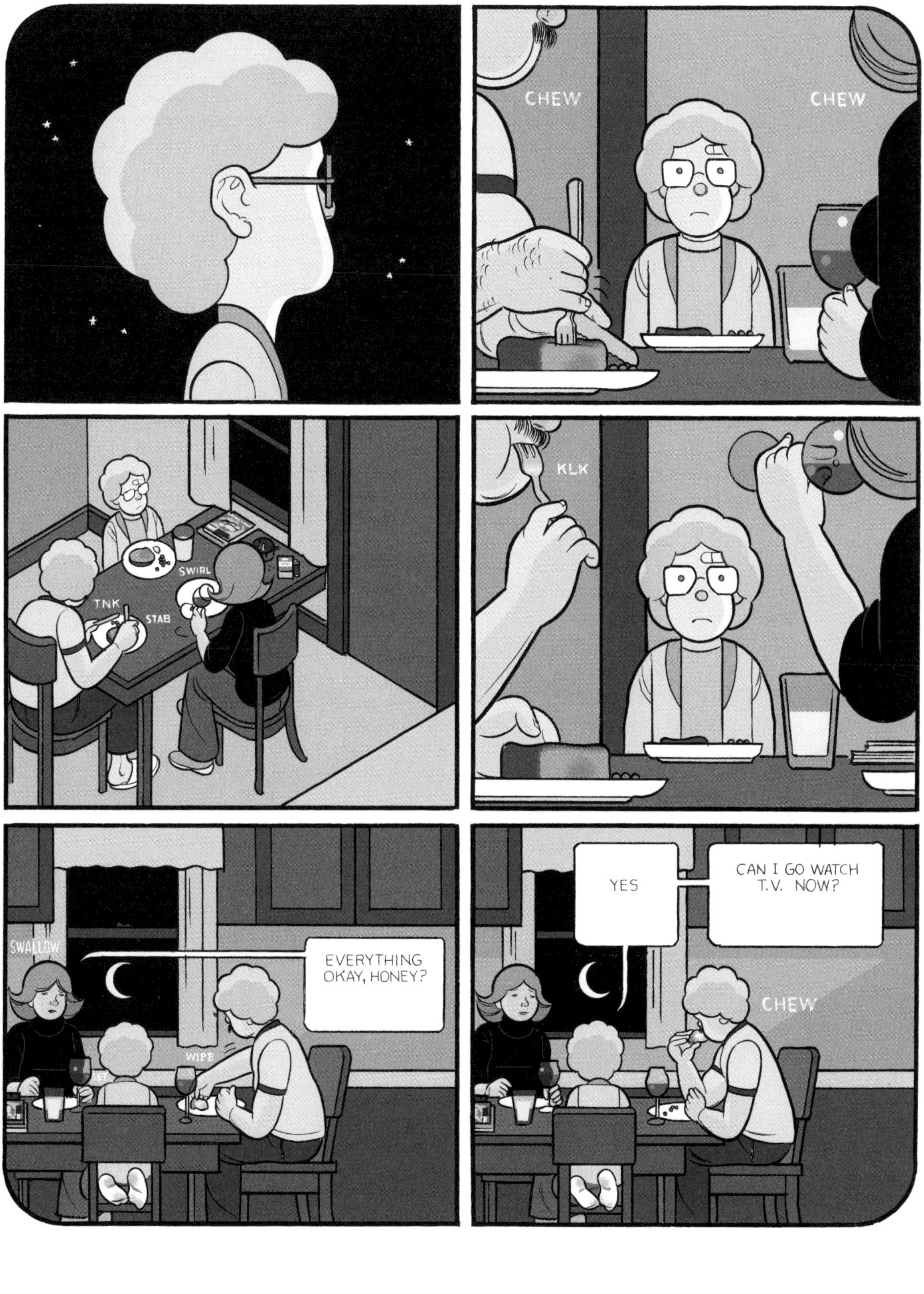
CHEW
CHEW
TNK
STAB
SWIRL
KLK
SWALLOW
EVERYTHING OKAY, HONEY?
WIPE
CAN I GO WATCH T.V. NOW?
YES
CHEW

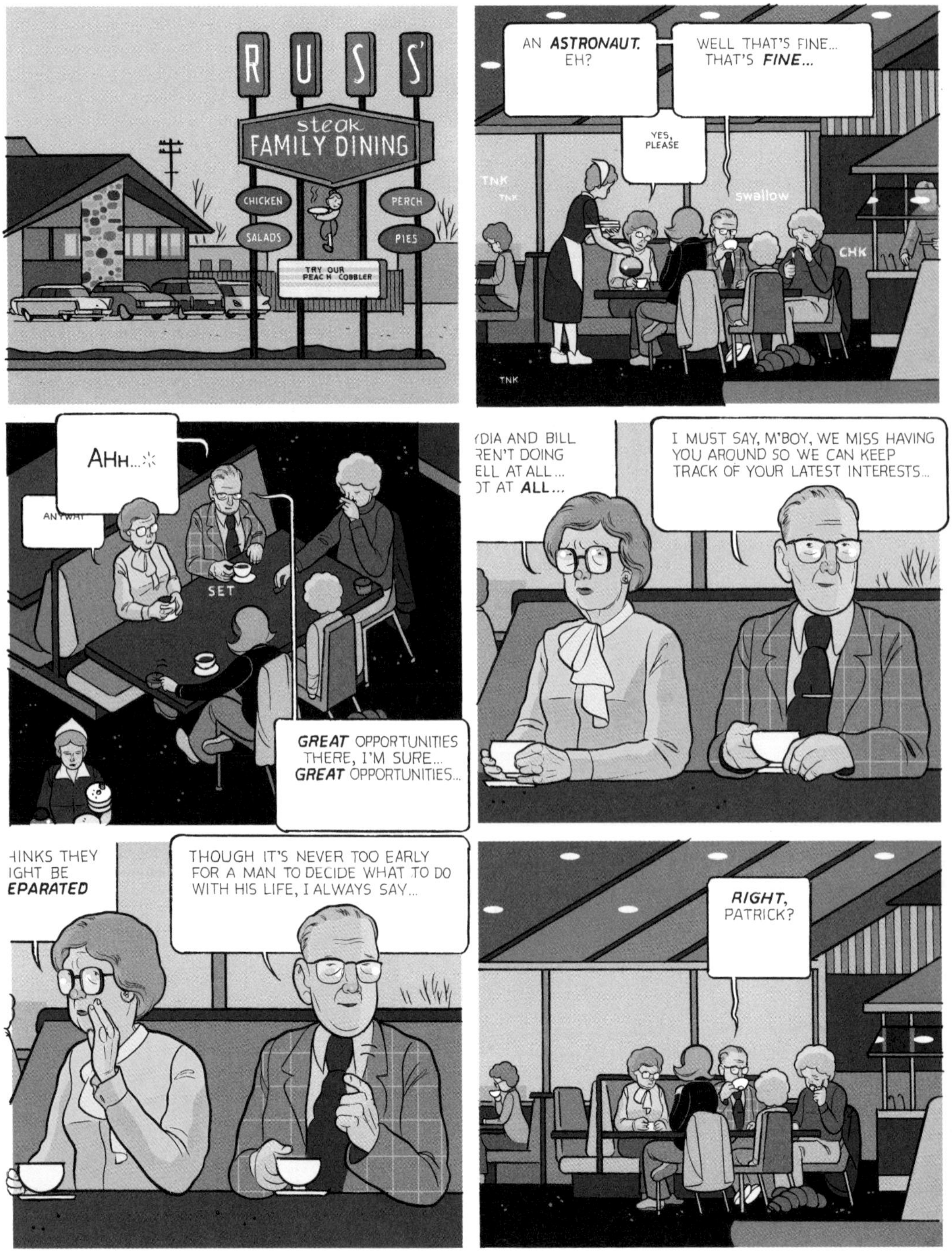
RUSS'
steak
FAMILY DINING
CHICKEN
SALADS
PERCH
PIES
TRY OUR PEACH COBBLER
AN **ASTRONAUT.** EH?
WELL THAT'S FINE... THAT'S ***FINE...***
YES, PLEASE
TNK
TNK
swallow
CHK
TNK
AHH...
SET
**GREAT** OPPORTUNITIES THERE, I'M SURE... **GREAT** OPPORTUNITIES...
YDIA AND BILL
REN'T DOING
ELL AT ALL...
OT AT ***ALL...***
I MUST SAY, M'BOY, WE MISS HAVING YOU AROUND SO WE CAN KEEP TRACK OF YOUR LATEST INTERESTS...
HINKS THEY
IGHT BE
***EPARATED***
THOUGH IT'S NEVER TOO EARLY FOR A MAN TO DECIDE WHAT TO DO WITH HIS LIFE, I ALWAYS SAY...
***RIGHT,*** PATRICK?

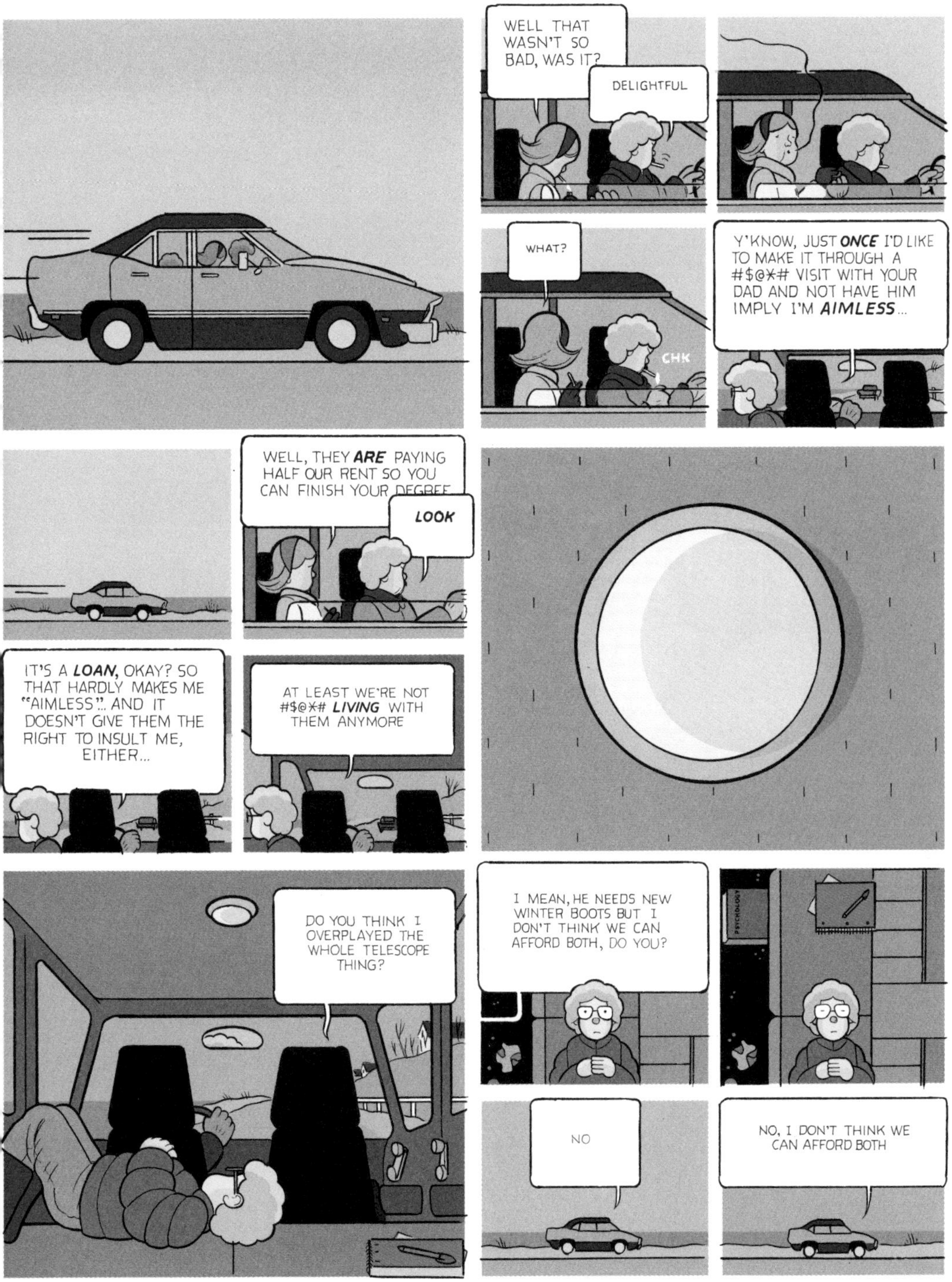
WELL THAT WASN'T SO BAD, WAS IT?
DELIGHTFUL
WHAT?
CHK
Y'KNOW, JUST **ONCE** I'D LIKE TO MAKE IT THROUGH A #$@*# VISIT WITH YOUR DAD AND NOT HAVE HIM IMPLY I'M ***AIMLESS***...
WELL, THEY ***ARE*** PAYING HALF OUR RENT SO YOU CAN FINISH YOUR DEGREE
***LOOK***
IT'S A ***LOAN,*** OKAY? SO THAT HARDLY MAKES ME "AIMLESS"... AND IT DOESN'T GIVE THEM THE RIGHT TO INSULT ME, EITHER...
AT LEAST WE'RE NOT #$@*# ***LIVING*** WITH THEM ANYMORE
DO YOU THINK I OVERPLAYED THE WHOLE TELESCOPE THING?
I MEAN, HE NEEDS NEW WINTER BOOTS BUT I DON'T THINK WE CAN AFFORD BOTH, DO YOU?
PSYCHOLOGY
NO
NO, I DON'T THINK WE CAN AFFORD BOTH

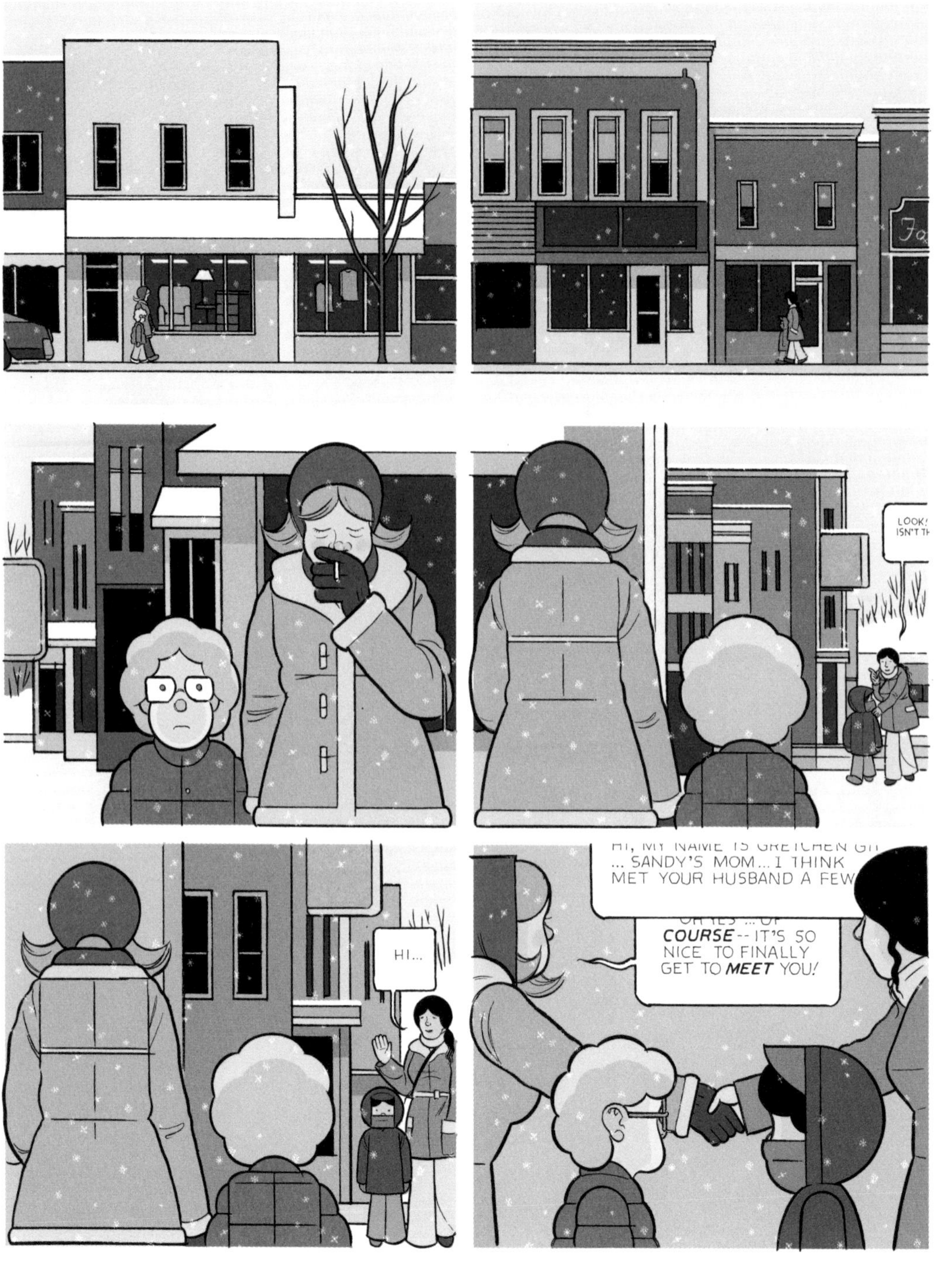
LOOK!
ISN'T
HI...
... SANDY'S MOM... I THINK
MET YOUR HUSBAND A FEW
COURSE -- IT'S SO NICE TO FINALLY GET TO MEET YOU!

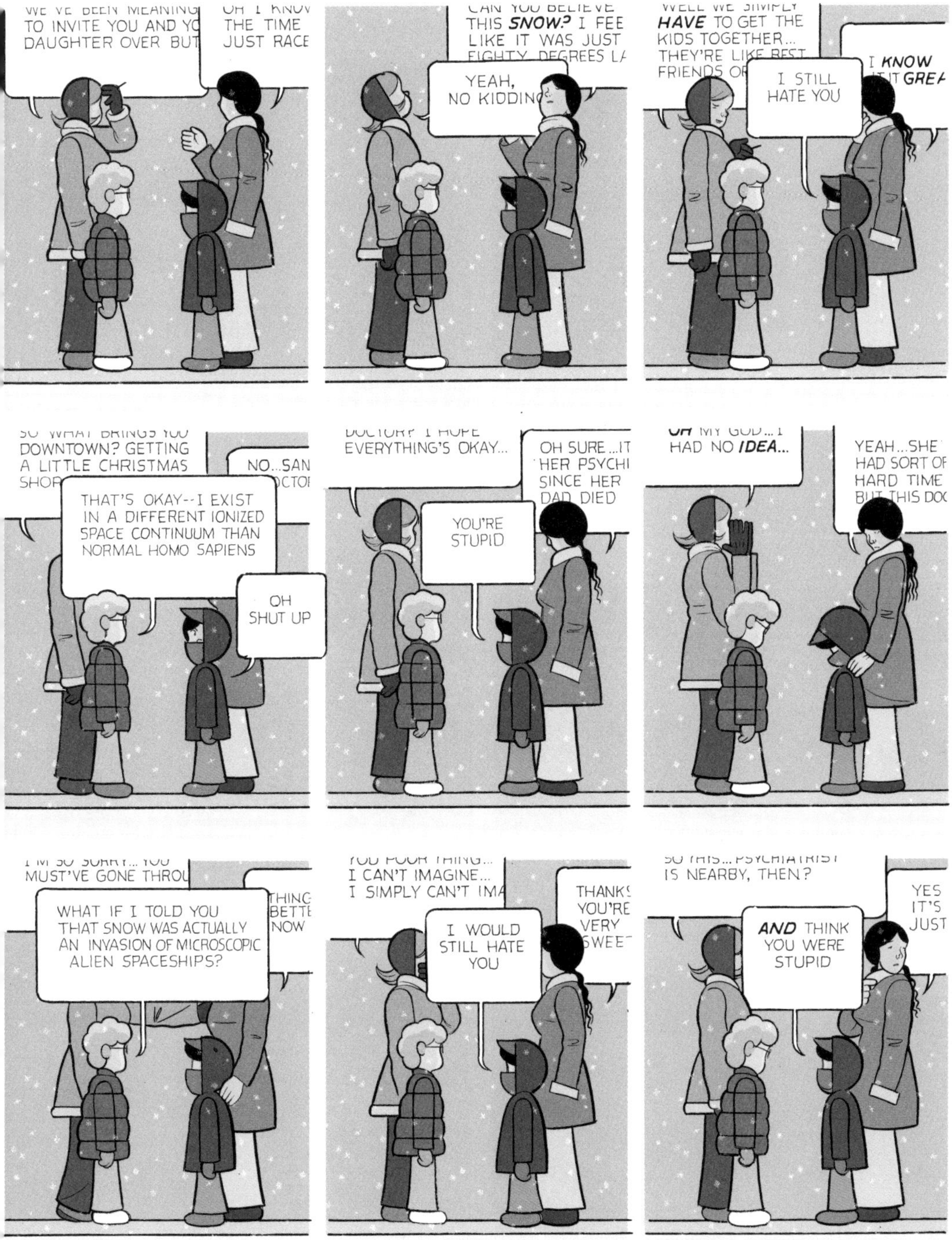
TO INVITE YOU AND YO
DAUGHTER OVER BUT
THE TIME
JUST RACE
THIS SNOW? I FEE
LIKE IT WAS JUST
YEAH, NO KIDDIN
HAVE TO GET THE KIDS TOGETHER... THEY'RE LIKE BEST FRIENDS OR
I STILL HATE YOU
I KNOW
DOWNTOWN? GETTING A LITTLE CHRISTMAS
NO...SAN
THAT'S OKAY--I EXIST IN A DIFFERENT IONIZED SPACE CONTINUUM THAN NORMAL HOMO SAPIENS
OH SHUT UP
EVERYTHING'S OKAY...
OH SURE ...IT
HER PSYCHI
SINCE HER
DAD DIED
YOU'RE STUPID
HAD NO IDEA...
YEAH...SHE
HAD SORT OF
HARD TIME
MUST'VE GONE THROU
WHAT IF I TOLD YOU THAT SNOW WAS ACTUALLY AN INVASION OF MICROSCOPIC ALIEN SPACESHIPS?
I CAN'T IMAGINE...
I SIMPLY CAN'T IMA
I WOULD STILL HATE YOU
IS NEARBY, THEN?
AND THINK YOU WERE STUPID
YES
IT'S
JUST

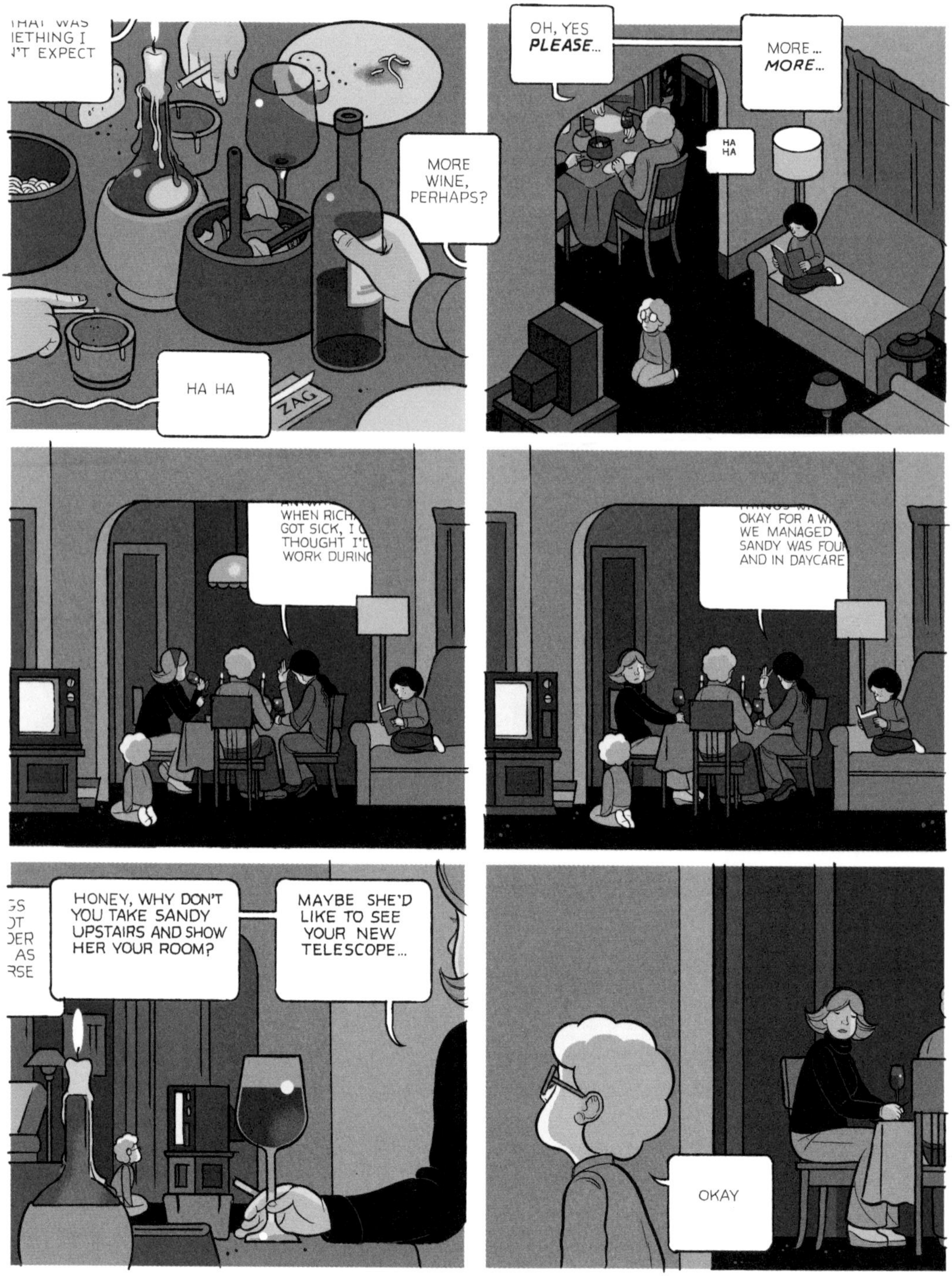
IETHING I
'T EXPECT
MORE WINE, PERHAPS?
HA HA
OH, YES PLEASE...
MORE... MORE...
HA HA
WHEN RICH
GOT SICK, I
THOUGHT I'
WORK DURIN
OKAY FOR A W
WE MANAGED
SANDY WAS FOU
AND IN DAYCARE
HONEY, WHY DON'T YOU TAKE SANDY UPSTAIRS AND SHOW HER YOUR ROOM?
MAYBE SHE'D LIKE TO SEE YOUR NEW TELESCOPE...
OKAY

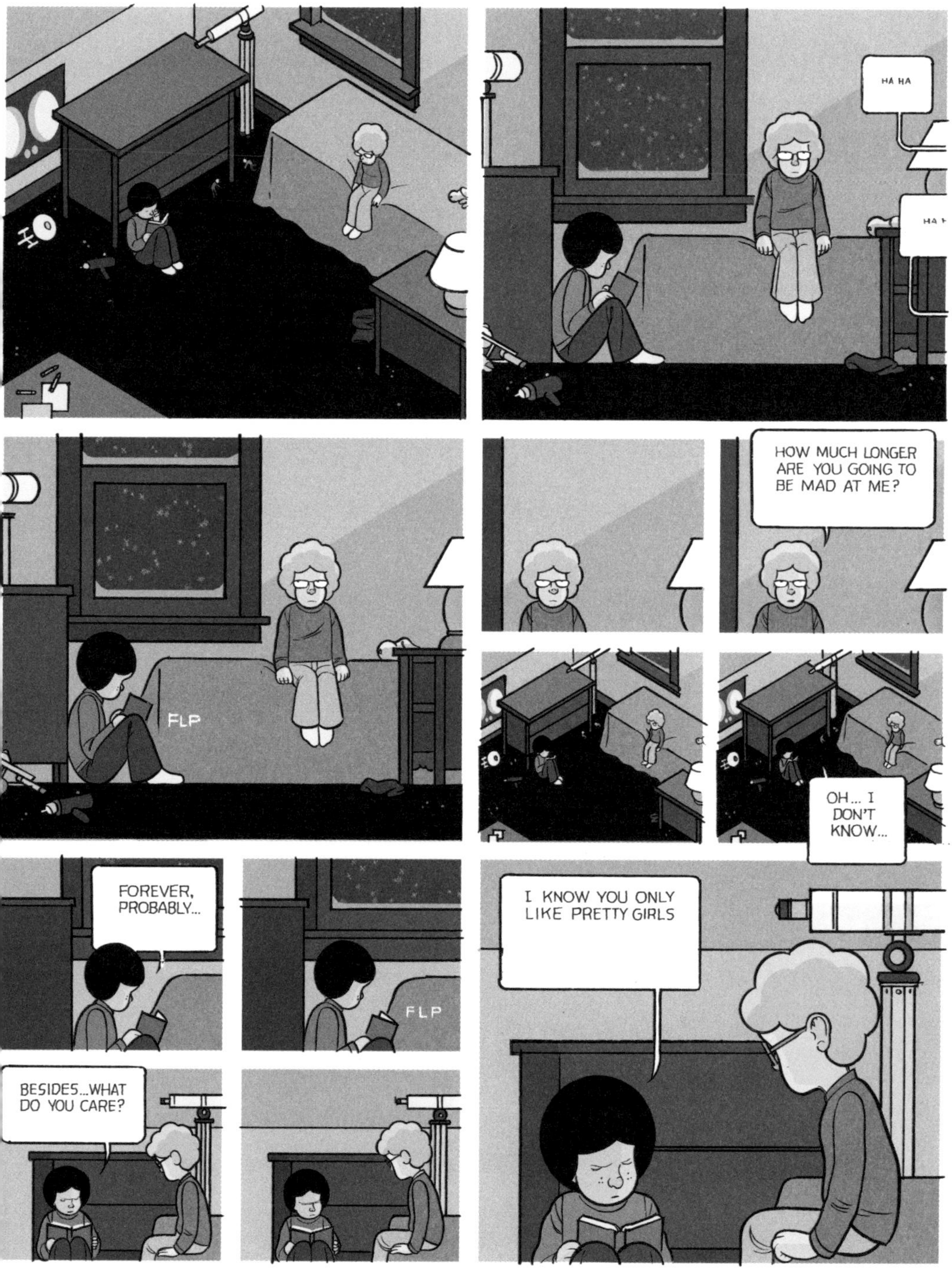
HA HA
FLP
HOW MUCH LONGER ARE YOU GOING TO BE MAD AT ME?
OH... I DON'T KNOW...
FOREVER, PROBABLY...
FLP
BESIDES...WHAT DO YOU CARE?
I KNOW YOU ONLY LIKE PRETTY GIRLS

# The Swim AND Today

## ANNE EMOND

*originally published at*

okey-panky.com AND comiques.tumblr.com
ELECTRIC LITERATURE and SELF-PUBLISHED
digital

## Biography

Anne Emond is a Brooklyn-based writer, illustrator, and comics artist. She graduated in 2010 with an MFA in Illustration from the School of Visual Arts. For the past five years she has drawn a semi-autobiographical webcomic at comiques.tumblr.com called *Comiques*, for which she was awarded a gold medal in 2014 from the Society of Illustrators. Her first full-length comic book, *Debbie's Inferno*, was published by the small comics press Retrofit in September 2014. She is currently working on an illustrated children's novel about a ghost and a girl detective.   anneemond.com

## Statement

"The Swim" originally appeared on Electric Literature's *Okey-Panky* site. I had sketched out a comic many years ago of a little old lady going swimming alone at night but had never resolved what would happen to her (I originally thought she would meet her undersea doppelgänger). I was halfway through inking the final comic when I thought of having a fish come to greet her. "Today," originally posted on comiques.tumblr.com, was inspired by my own laziness.

# THE SWIM

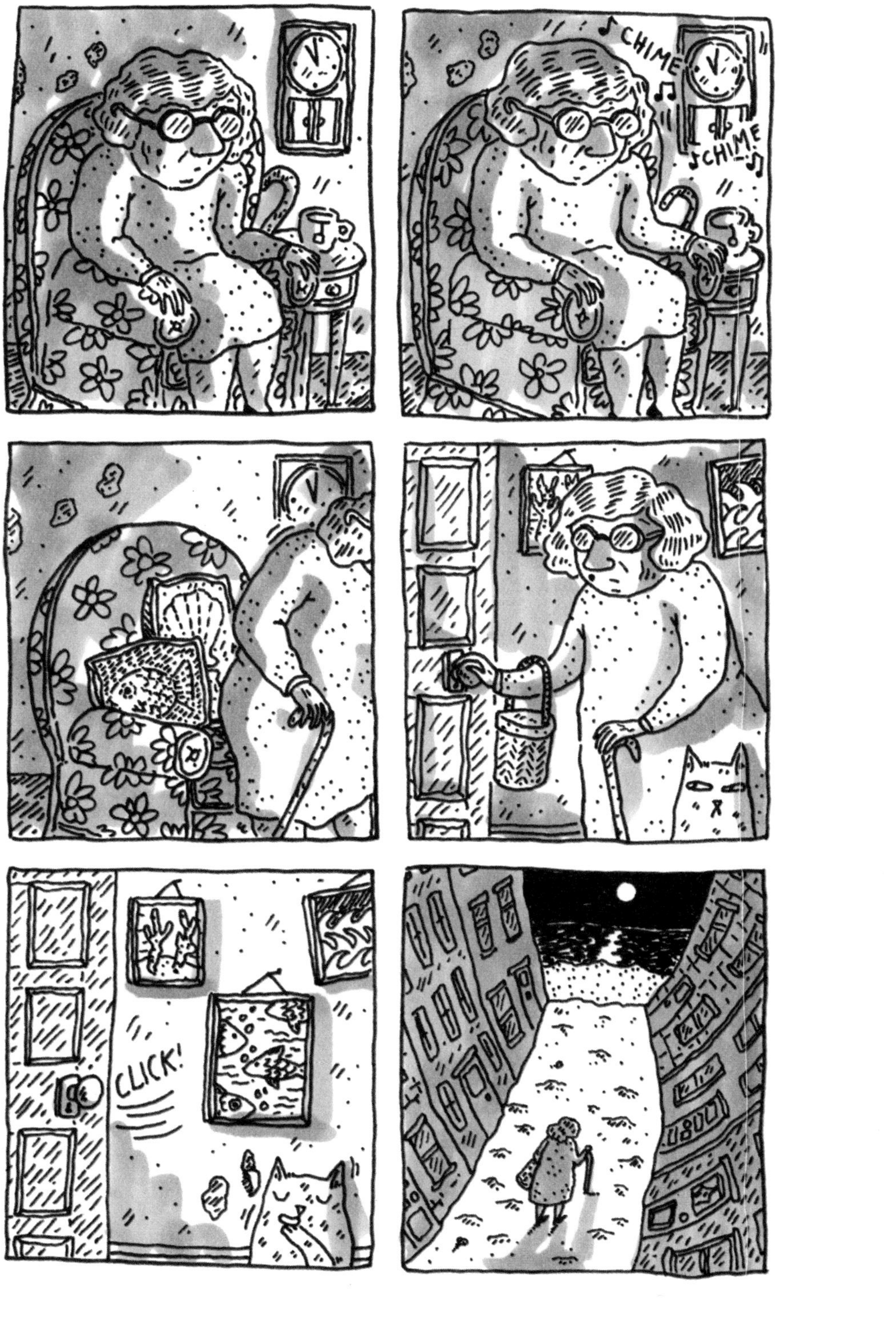
CHIME
CHIME
CLICK!

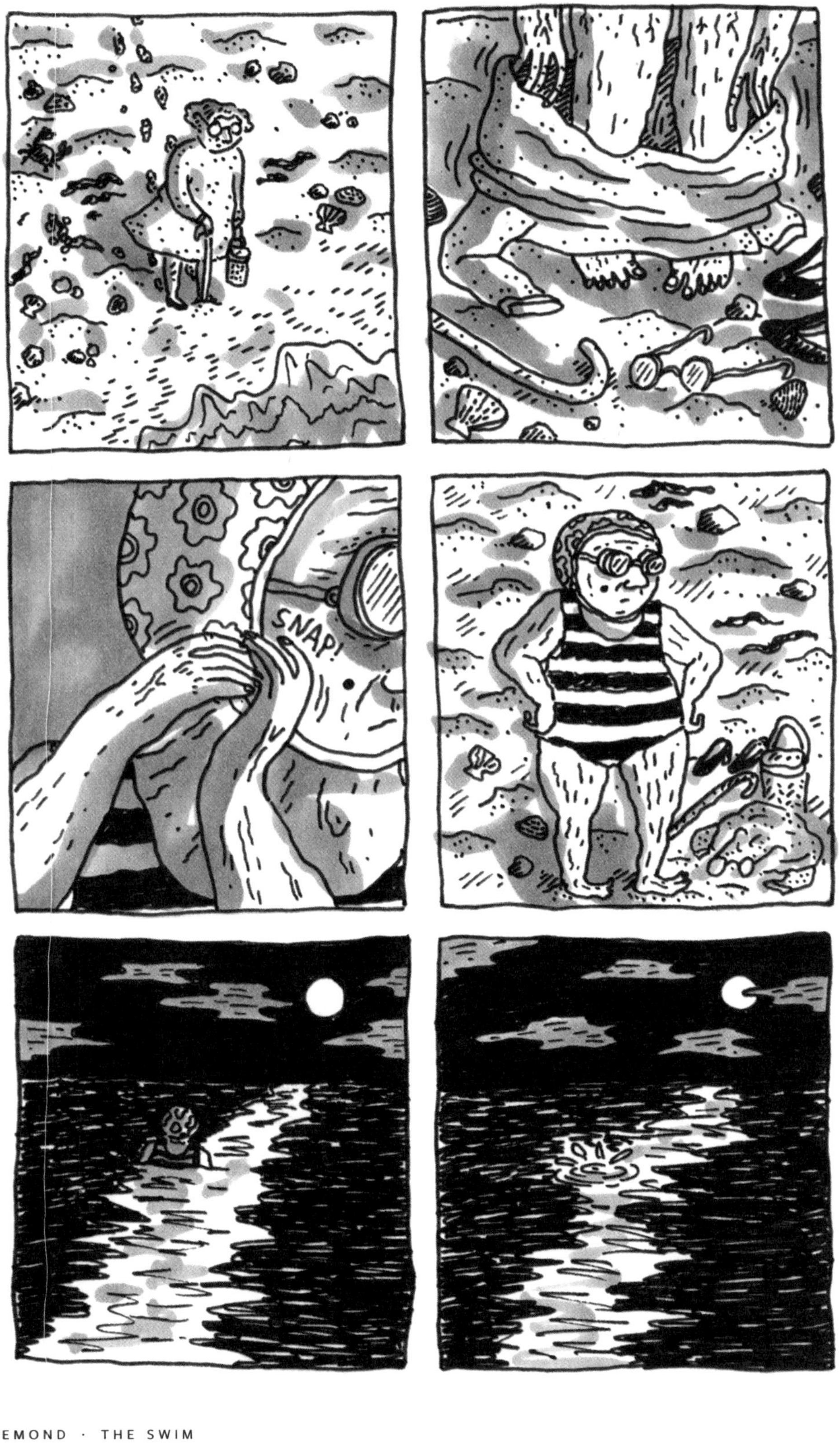
SNAP!

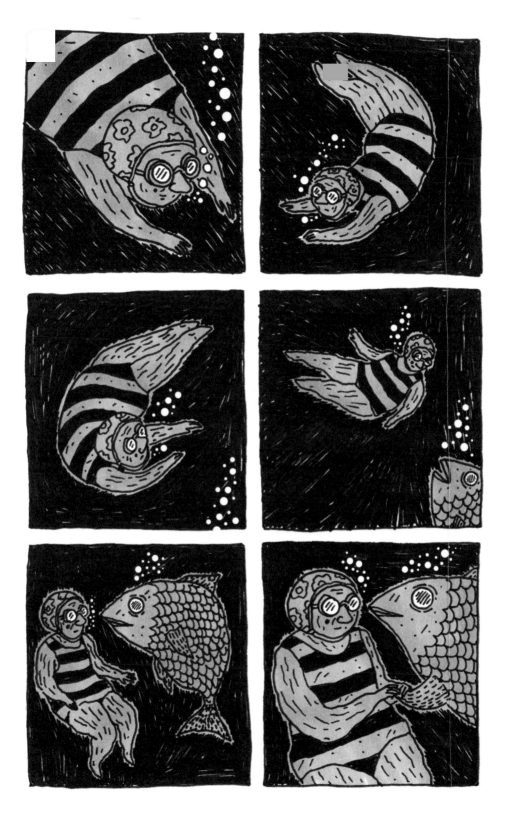

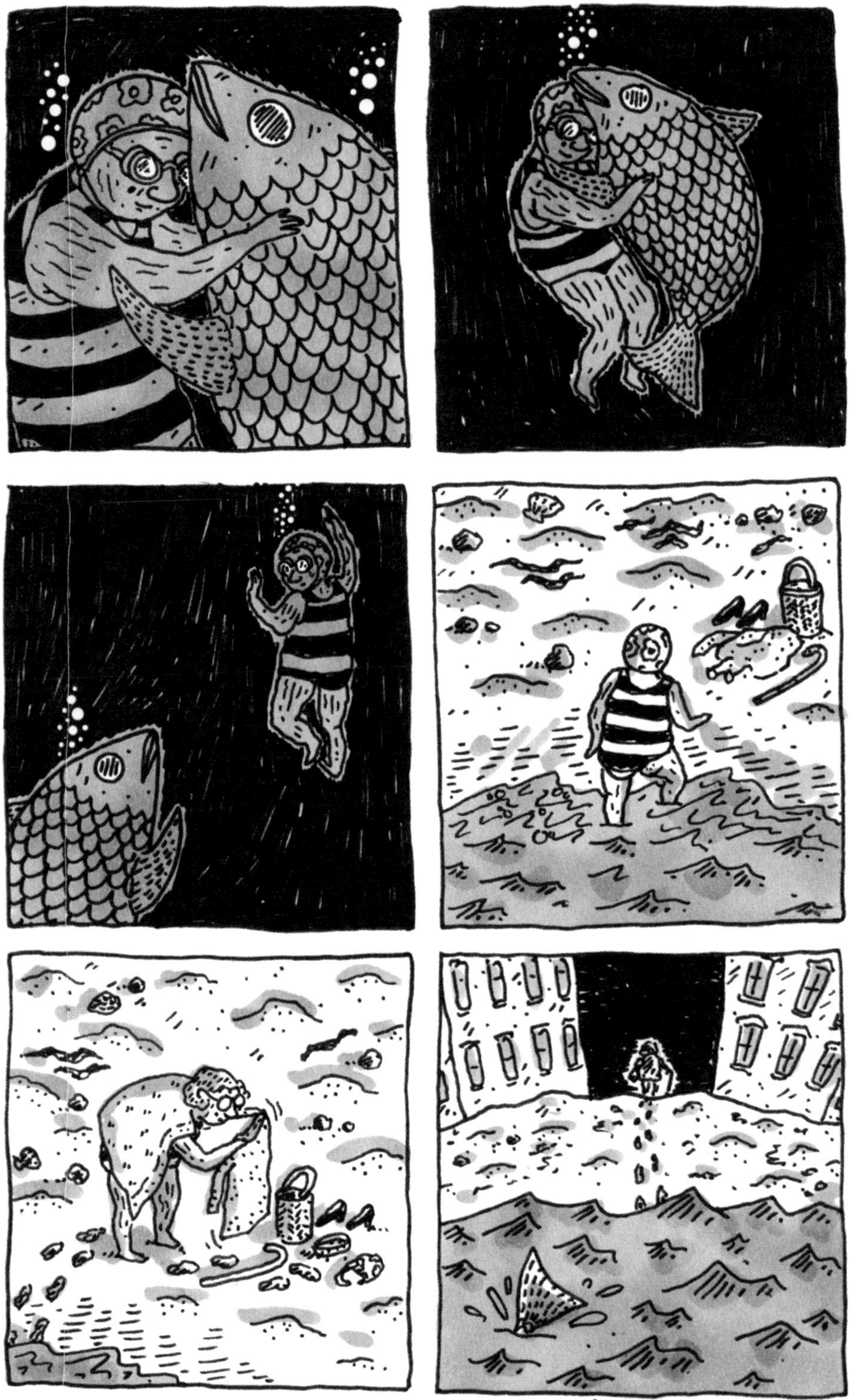
ANNE EMOND, 2015

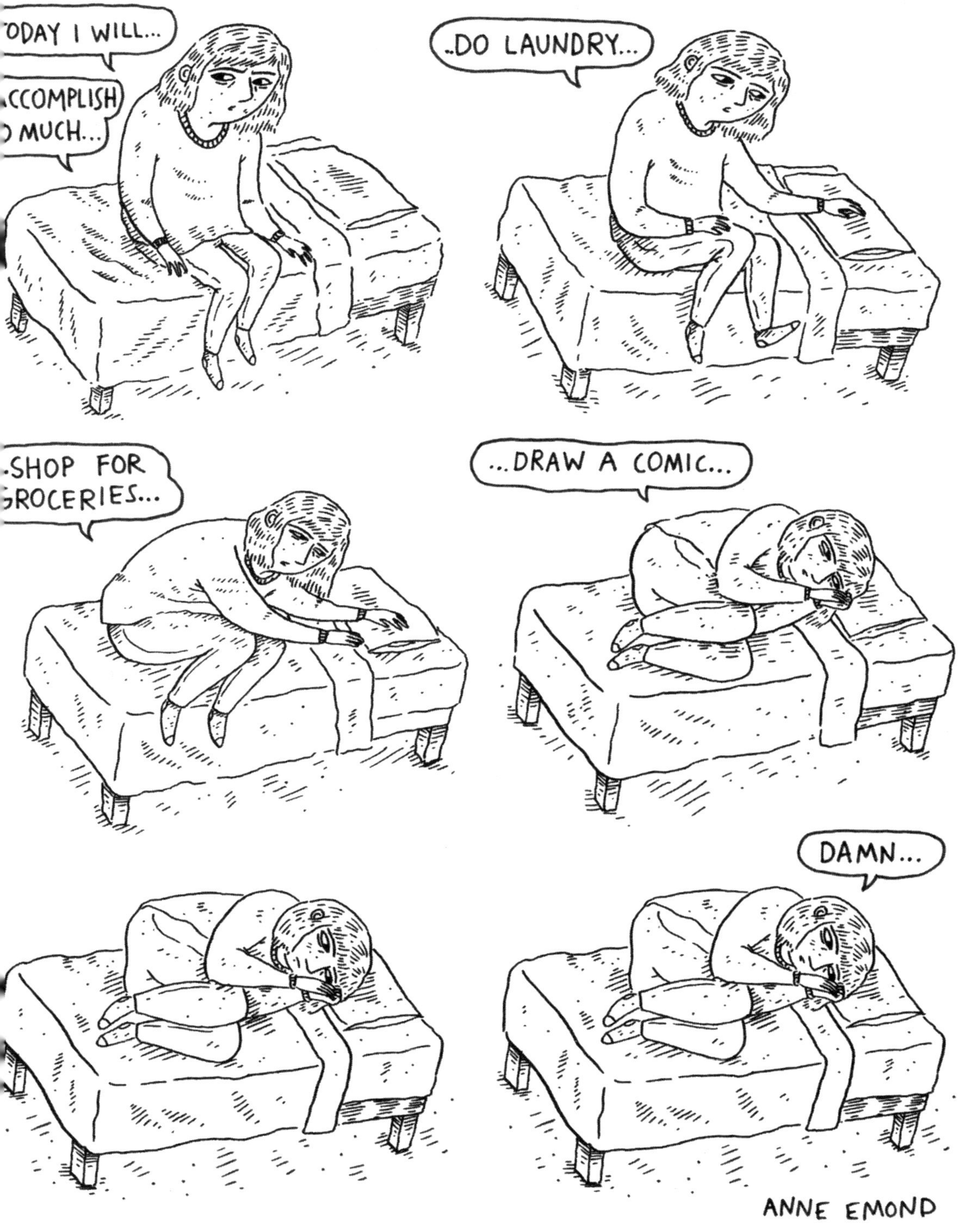
ODAY I WILL...
CCOMPLISH
MUCH...
..DO LAUNDRY...
SHOP FOR
ROCERIES...
...DRAW A COMIC...
DAMN...
ANNE EMOND

MONTE BEAUCHAMP
MASTERFUL MARKS
CARTOONISTS WHO CHANGED THE WORLD
16 GRAPHIC BIOGRAPHIES

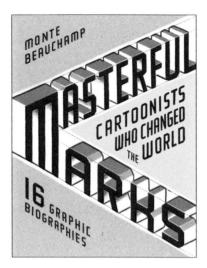

# R. Crumb and Me

DREW FRIEDMAN

*originally published in*

Masterful Marks

SIMON & SCHUSTER

8.4 × 10.9 inches • 128 pages

## Biography

Drew Friedman's comics and illustrations have appeared in Art Spiegelman's *RAW*, R. Crumb's *Weirdo*, *American Splendor*, *Heavy Metal*, *National Lampoon*, *SPY*, *MAD*, *The New Yorker*, the *New York Times*, the *New York Observer*, etc., as well as creating numerous book, CD, and DVD covers. His work has been collected in five anthologies. Drew Friedman's *Sideshow Freaks* was published in 2011. Steven Heller in the *New York Times* wrote of his three volumes of portraiture of Old Jewish Comedians: "A festival of drawing virtuosity and fabulous craggy faces. Friedman might very well be the Vermeer of the Borscht Belt." The Society of Illustrators hosted a showing of his Old Jewish Comedians artwork in 2014. His latest book of portraits, *Heroes of the Comics*, was published by Fantagraphics with a foreword by Al Jaffee. The sequel *More Heroes of the Comics* is due out in 2016. Friedman lives in Pennsylvania with his wife and frequent collaborator, K. Bidus.

## Statement

I was commissioned to create this eight-page comic by Monte Beauchamp for his publication *Masterful Marks*, contemporary comics artists creating illustrated comic biographies of legendary cartoonists. I chose Robert Crumb, but rather than create a standard biography (he's already presented his entire life and dirty laundry in his work over the years), I chose to show how he influenced me, how I eventually would create work for his publication, *Weirdo*, and how we became friends.

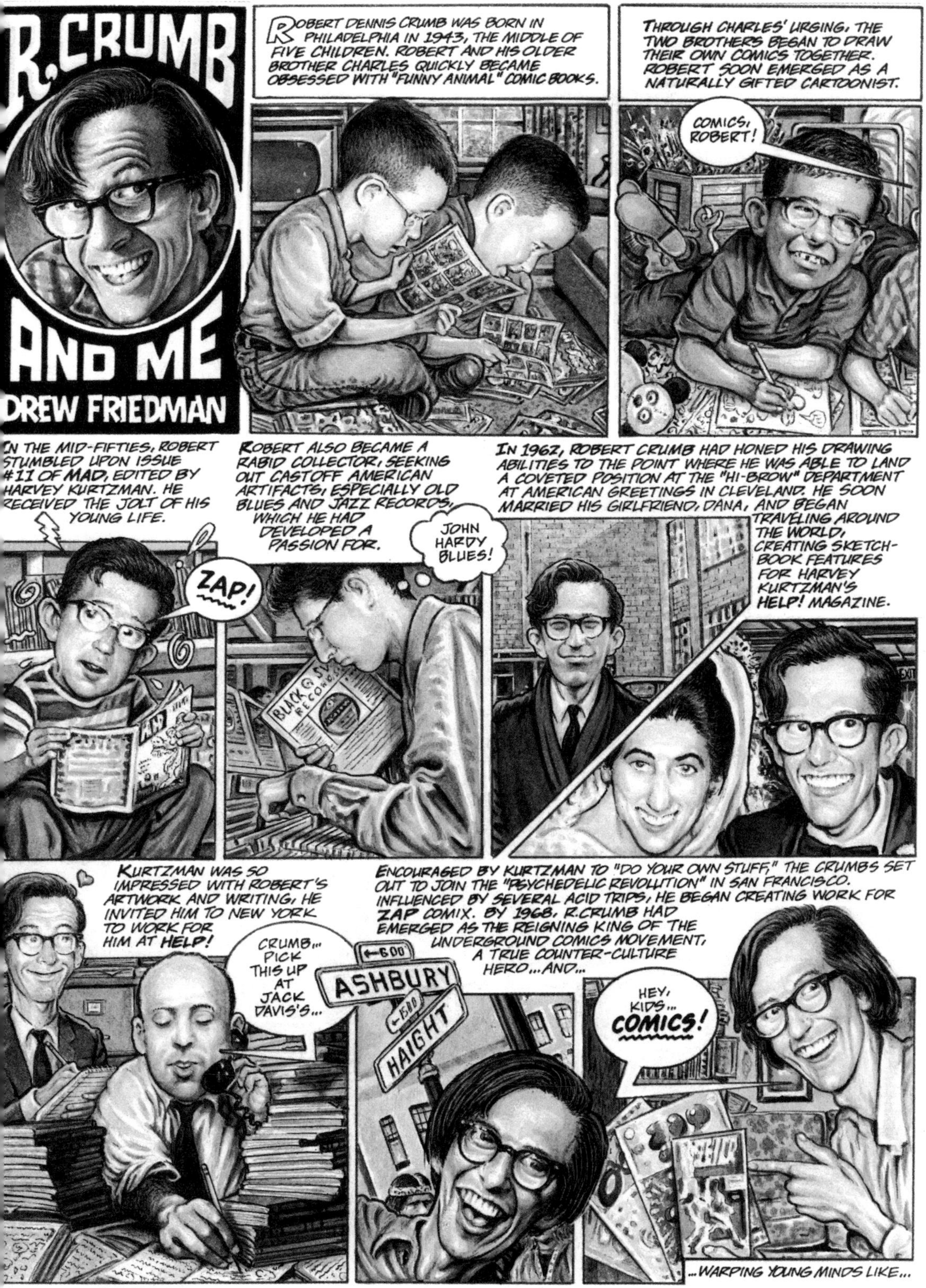

R. CRUMB AND ME
DREW FRIEDMAN
ROBERT DENNIS CRUMB WAS BORN IN PHILADELPHIA IN 1943, THE MIDDLE OF FIVE CHILDREN. ROBERT AND HIS OLDER BROTHER CHARLES QUICKLY BECAME OBSESSED WITH "FUNNY ANIMAL" COMIC BOOKS.
THROUGH CHARLES' URGING, THE TWO BROTHERS BEGAN TO DRAW THEIR OWN COMICS TOGETHER. ROBERT SOON EMERGED AS A NATURALLY GIFTED CARTOONIST.
COMICS, ROBERT!
IN THE MID-FIFTIES, ROBERT STUMBLED UPON ISSUE #11 OF MAD, EDITED BY HARVEY KURTZMAN. HE RECEIVED THE JOLT OF HIS YOUNG LIFE.
ZAP!
ROBERT ALSO BECAME A RABID COLLECTOR, SEEKING OUT CASTOFF AMERICAN ARTIFACTS, ESPECIALLY OLD BLUES AND JAZZ RECORDS, WHICH HE HAD DEVELOPED A PASSION FOR.
JOHN HARDY BLUES!
IN 1962, ROBERT CRUMB HAD HONED HIS DRAWING ABILITIES TO THE POINT WHERE HE WAS ABLE TO LAND A COVETED POSITION AT THE "HI-BROW" DEPARTMENT AT AMERICAN GREETINGS IN CLEVELAND. HE SOON MARRIED HIS GIRLFRIEND, DANA, AND BEGAN TRAVELING AROUND THE WORLD, CREATING SKETCH-BOOK FEATURES FOR HARVEY KURTZMAN'S HELP! MAGAZINE.
KURTZMAN WAS SO IMPRESSED WITH ROBERT'S ARTWORK AND WRITING, HE INVITED HIM TO NEW YORK TO WORK FOR HIM AT HELP!
CRUMB... PICK THIS UP AT JACK DAVIS'S...
ENCOURAGED BY KURTZMAN TO "DO YOUR OWN STUFF," THE CRUMBS SET OUT TO JOIN THE "PSYCHEDELIC REVOLUTION" IN SAN FRANCISCO. INFLUENCED BY SEVERAL ACID TRIPS, HE BEGAN CREATING WORK FOR ZAP COMIX. BY 1968, R. CRUMB HAD EMERGED AS THE REIGNING KING OF THE UNDERGROUND COMICS MOVEMENT, A TRUE COUNTER-CULTURE HERO... AND...
←600
ASHBURY
←1500
HAIGHT
HEY, KIDS... COMICS!
...WARPING YOUNG MINDS LIKE...


LETTERING BY PHIL FELIX

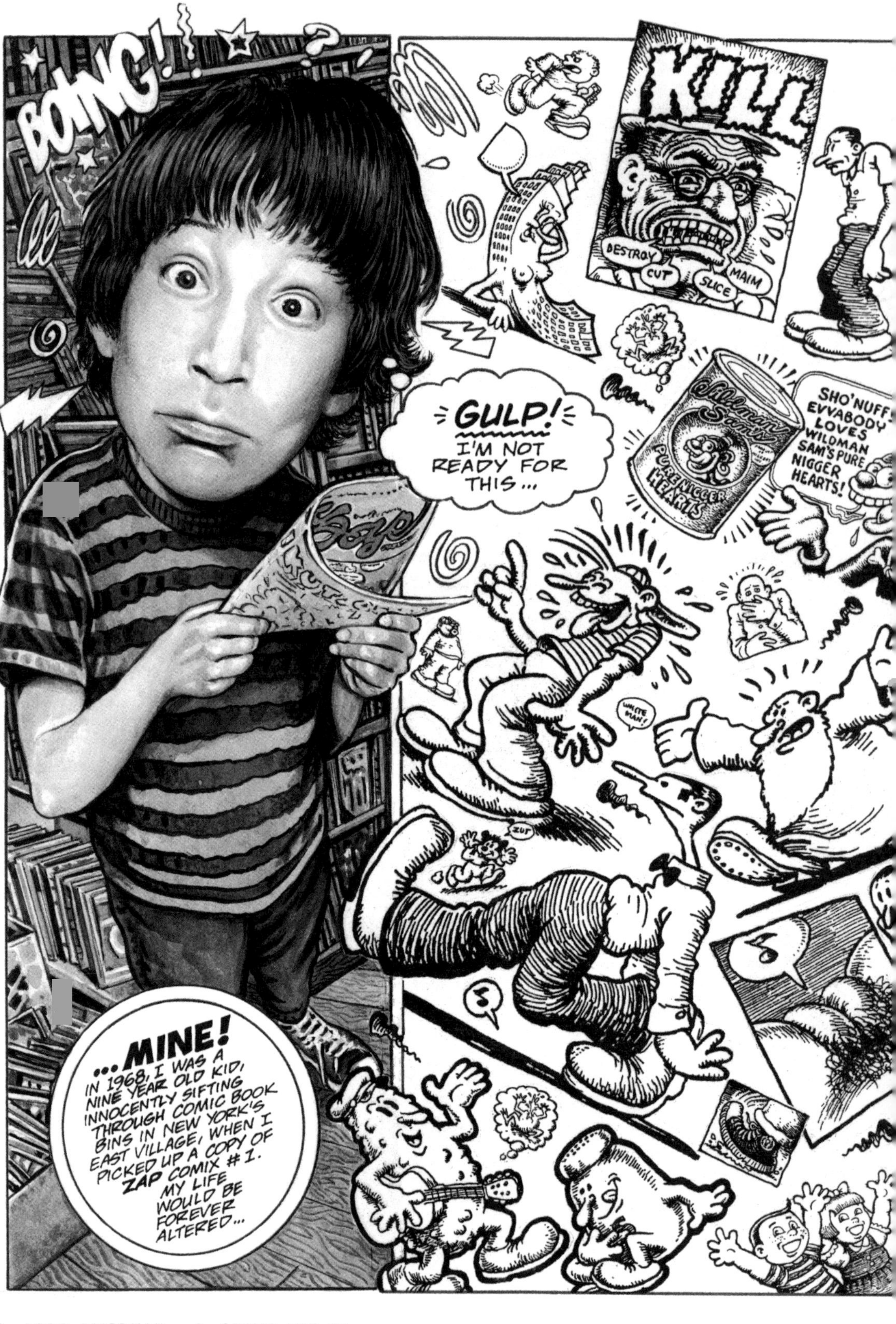
BOING!
KILL
DESTROY
CUT
SLICE
MAIM
GULP! I'M NOT READY FOR THIS...
Wildman Sam's PURE NIGGER HEARTS
SHO'NUFF! EVVABODY LOVES WILDMAN SAM'S PURE NIGGER HEARTS!
WHITE MAN!
ZUT
...MINE! IN 1968, I WAS A NINE YEAR OLD KID, INNOCENTLY SIFTING THROUGH COMIC BOOK BINS IN NEW YORK'S EAST VILLAGE, WHEN I PICKED UP A COPY OF ZAP COMIX #1. MY LIFE WOULD BE FOREVER ALTERED...

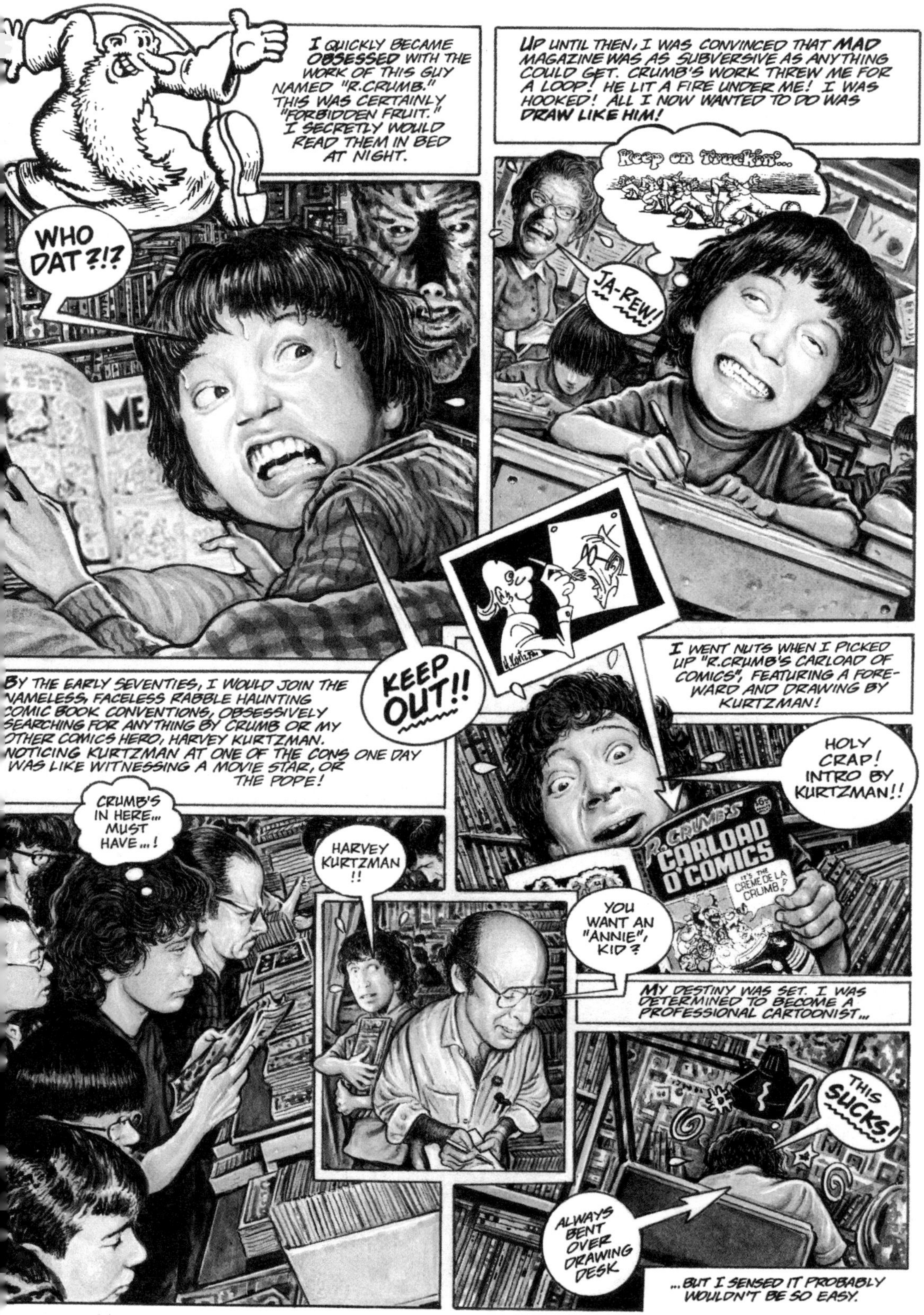

I QUICKLY BECAME OBSESSED WITH THE WORK OF THIS GUY NAMED "R.CRUMB." THIS WAS CERTAINLY "FORBIDDEN FRUIT." I SECRETLY WOULD READ THEM IN BED AT NIGHT.
WHO DAT ?!?
UP UNTIL THEN, I WAS CONVINCED THAT MAD MAGAZINE WAS AS SUBVERSIVE AS ANYTHING COULD GET. CRUMB'S WORK THREW ME FOR A LOOP! HE LIT A FIRE UNDER ME! I WAS HOOKED! ALL I NOW WANTED TO DO WAS DRAW LIKE HIM!
Keep on Truckin'...
JA-REW!
KEEP OUT!!
BY THE EARLY SEVENTIES, I WOULD JOIN THE NAMELESS, FACELESS RABBLE HAUNTING COMIC BOOK CONVENTIONS, OBSESSIVELY SEARCHING FOR ANYTHING BY CRUMB OR MY OTHER COMICS HERO, HARVEY KURTZMAN. NOTICING KURTZMAN AT ONE OF THE CONS ONE DAY WAS LIKE WITNESSING A MOVIE STAR, OR THE POPE!
I WENT NUTS WHEN I PICKED UP "R.CRUMB'S CARLOAD OF COMICS", FEATURING A FOREWARD AND DRAWING BY KURTZMAN!
HOLY CRAP! INTRO BY KURTZMAN!!
R. CRUMB'S CARLOAD O'COMICS
IT'S THE CREME DE LA CRUMB!
CRUMB'S IN HERE... MUST HAVE...!
HARVEY KURTZMAN !!
YOU WANT AN "ANNIE", KID?
MY DESTINY WAS SET. I WAS DETERMINED TO BECOME A PROFESSIONAL CARTOONIST...
THIS SUCKS!
ALWAYS BENT OVER DRAWING DESK
...BUT I SENSED IT PROBABLY WOULDN'T BE SO EASY.

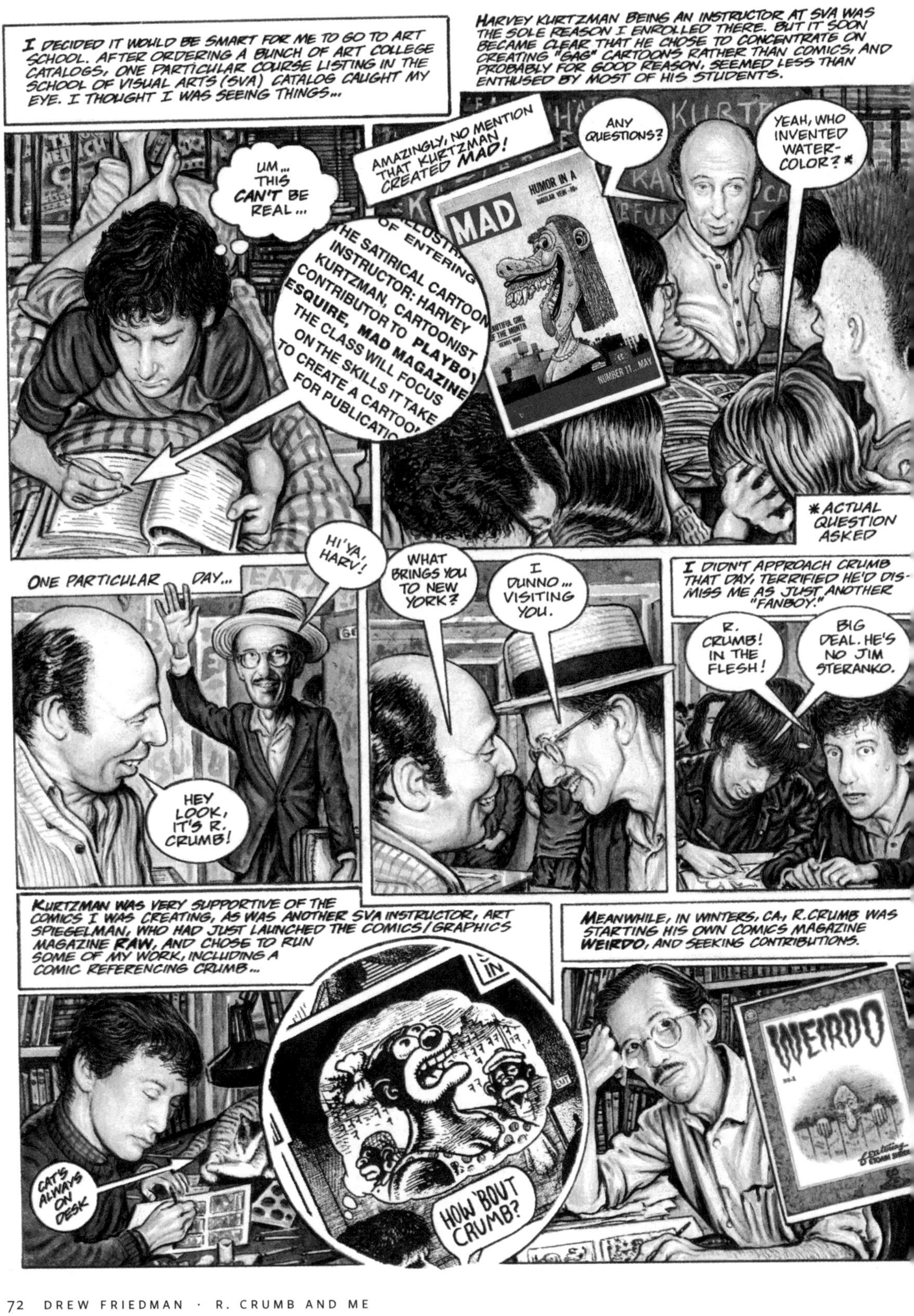
I DECIDED IT WOULD BE SMART FOR ME TO GO TO ART SCHOOL. AFTER ORDERING A BUNCH OF ART COLLEGE CATALOGS, ONE PARTICULAR COURSE LISTING IN THE SCHOOL OF VISUAL ARTS (SVA) CATALOG CAUGHT MY EYE. I THOUGHT I WAS SEEING THINGS...
UM... THIS CAN'T BE REAL...
THE SATIRICAL CARTOON INSTRUCTOR: HARVEY KURTZMAN, CARTOONIST CONTRIBUTOR TO PLAYBOY ESQUIRE, MAD MAGAZINE THE CLASS WILL FOCUS ON THE SKILLS IT TAKE TO CREATE A CARTOON FOR PUBLICATIO
HARVEY KURTZMAN BEING AN INSTRUCTOR AT SVA WAS THE SOLE REASON I ENROLLED THERE. BUT IT SOON BECAME CLEAR THAT HE CHOSE TO CONCENTRATE ON CREATING "GAG" CARTOONS RATHER THAN COMICS, AND PROBABLY FOR GOOD REASON, SEEMED LESS THAN ENTHUSED BY MOST OF HIS STUDENTS.
AMAZINGLY, NO MENTION THAT KURTZMAN CREATED MAD!
MAD
HUMOR IN A
NUMBER 11...MAY
ANY QUESTIONS?
YEAH, WHO INVENTED WATER-COLOR? *
* ACTUAL QUESTION ASKED
ONE PARTICULAR DAY...
HI'YA, HARV!
HEY LOOK, IT'S R. CRUMB!
WHAT BRINGS YOU TO NEW YORK?
I DUNNO... VISITING YOU.
I DIDN'T APPROACH CRUMB THAT DAY, TERRIFIED HE'D DISMISS ME AS JUST ANOTHER "FANBOY."
R. CRUMB! IN THE FLESH!
BIG DEAL. HE'S NO JIM STERANKO.
KURTZMAN WAS VERY SUPPORTIVE OF THE COMICS I WAS CREATING, AS WAS ANOTHER SVA INSTRUCTOR, ART SPIEGELMAN, WHO HAD JUST LAUNCHED THE COMICS/GRAPHICS MAGAZINE RAW, AND CHOSE TO RUN SOME OF MY WORK, INCLUDING A COMIC REFERENCING CRUMB...
CAT'S ALWAYS ON DESK
HOW 'BOUT CRUMB?
MEANWHILE, IN WINTERS, CA., R.CRUMB WAS STARTING HIS OWN COMICS MAGAZINE WEIRDO, AND SEEKING CONTRIBUTIONS.
WEIRDO

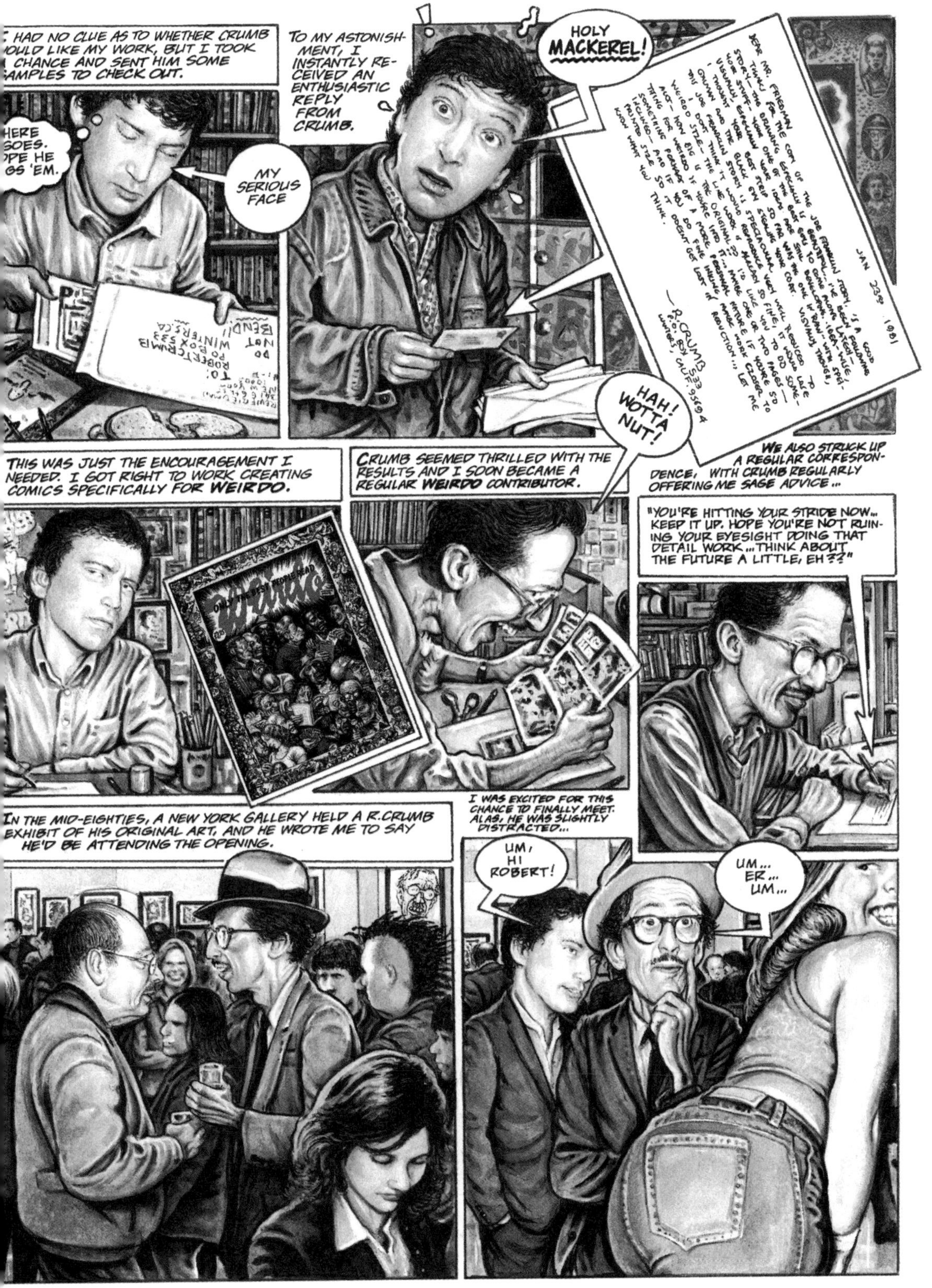

HAD NO CLUE AS TO WHETHER CRUMB OULD LIKE MY WORK, BUT I TOOK CHANCE AND SENT HIM SOME AMPLES TO CHECK OUT.
HERE GOES. OPE HE GS 'EM.
MY SERIOUS FACE
TO MY ASTONISHMENT, I INSTANTLY RECEIVED AN ENTHUSIASTIC REPLY FROM CRUMB.
HOLY MACKEREL!
JAN 23rd 1981
— R. CRUMB P.O. BOX 533 WINTERS, CALIF. 95694
HAH! WOTTA NUT!
THIS WAS JUST THE ENCOURAGEMENT I NEEDED. I GOT RIGHT TO WORK CREATING COMICS SPECIFICALLY FOR WEIRDO.
CRUMB SEEMED THRILLED WITH THE RESULTS AND I SOON BECAME A REGULAR WEIRDO CONTRIBUTOR.
WE ALSO STRUCK UP A REGULAR CORRESPONDENCE, WITH CRUMB REGULARLY OFFERING ME SAGE ADVICE...
"YOU'RE HITTING YOUR STRIDE NOW... KEEP IT UP. HOPE YOU'RE NOT RUINING YOUR EYESIGHT DOING THAT DETAIL WORK... THINK ABOUT THE FUTURE A LITTLE, EH??"
IN THE MID-EIGHTIES, A NEW YORK GALLERY HELD A R.CRUMB EXHIBIT OF HIS ORIGINAL ART, AND HE WROTE ME TO SAY HE'D BE ATTENDING THE OPENING.
I WAS EXCITED FOR THIS CHANCE TO FINALLY MEET. ALAS, HE WAS SLIGHTLY DISTRACTED...
UM, HI ROBERT!
UM... ER... UM...

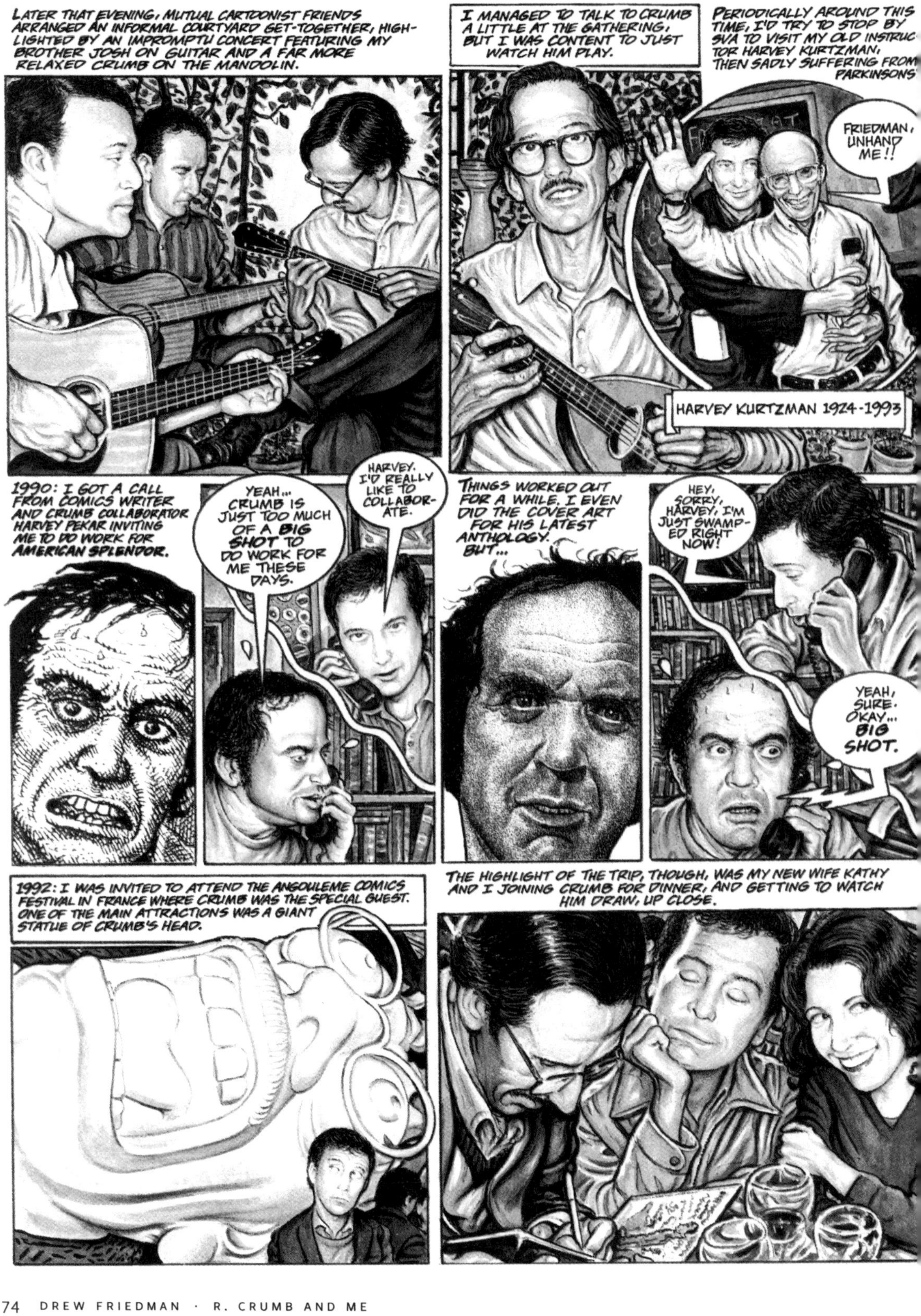
LATER THAT EVENING, MUTUAL CARTOONIST FRIENDS ARRANGED AN INFORMAL COURTYARD GET-TOGETHER, HIGHLIGHTED BY AN IMPROMPTU CONCERT FEATURING MY BROTHER JOSH ON GUITAR AND A FAR MORE RELAXED CRUMB ON THE MANDOLIN.
I MANAGED TO TALK TO CRUMB A LITTLE AT THE GATHERING, BUT I WAS CONTENT TO JUST WATCH HIM PLAY.
PERIODICALLY AROUND THIS TIME, I'D TRY TO STOP BY SVA TO VISIT MY OLD INSTRUCTOR HARVEY KURTZMAN, THEN SADLY SUFFERING FROM PARKINSONS
FRIEDMAN, UNHAND ME!!
HARVEY KURTZMAN 1924-1993
1990: I GOT A CALL FROM COMICS WRITER AND CRUMB COLLABORATOR HARVEY PEKAR INVITING ME TO DO WORK FOR AMERICAN SPLENDOR.
HARVEY. I'D REALLY LIKE TO COLLABORATE.
YEAH... CRUMB IS JUST TOO MUCH OF A BIG SHOT TO DO WORK FOR ME THESE DAYS.
THINGS WORKED OUT FOR A WHILE. I EVEN DID THE COVER ART FOR HIS LATEST ANTHOLOGY. BUT...
HEY, SORRY, HARVEY, I'M JUST SWAMPED RIGHT NOW!
YEAH, SURE. OKAY... BIG SHOT.
1992: I WAS INVITED TO ATTEND THE ANGOULEME COMICS FESTIVAL IN FRANCE WHERE CRUMB WAS THE SPECIAL GUEST. ONE OF THE MAIN ATTRACTIONS WAS A GIANT STATUE OF CRUMB'S HEAD.
THE HIGHLIGHT OF THE TRIP, THOUGH, WAS MY NEW WIFE KATHY AND I JOINING CRUMB FOR DINNER, AND GETTING TO WATCH HIM DRAW, UP CLOSE.

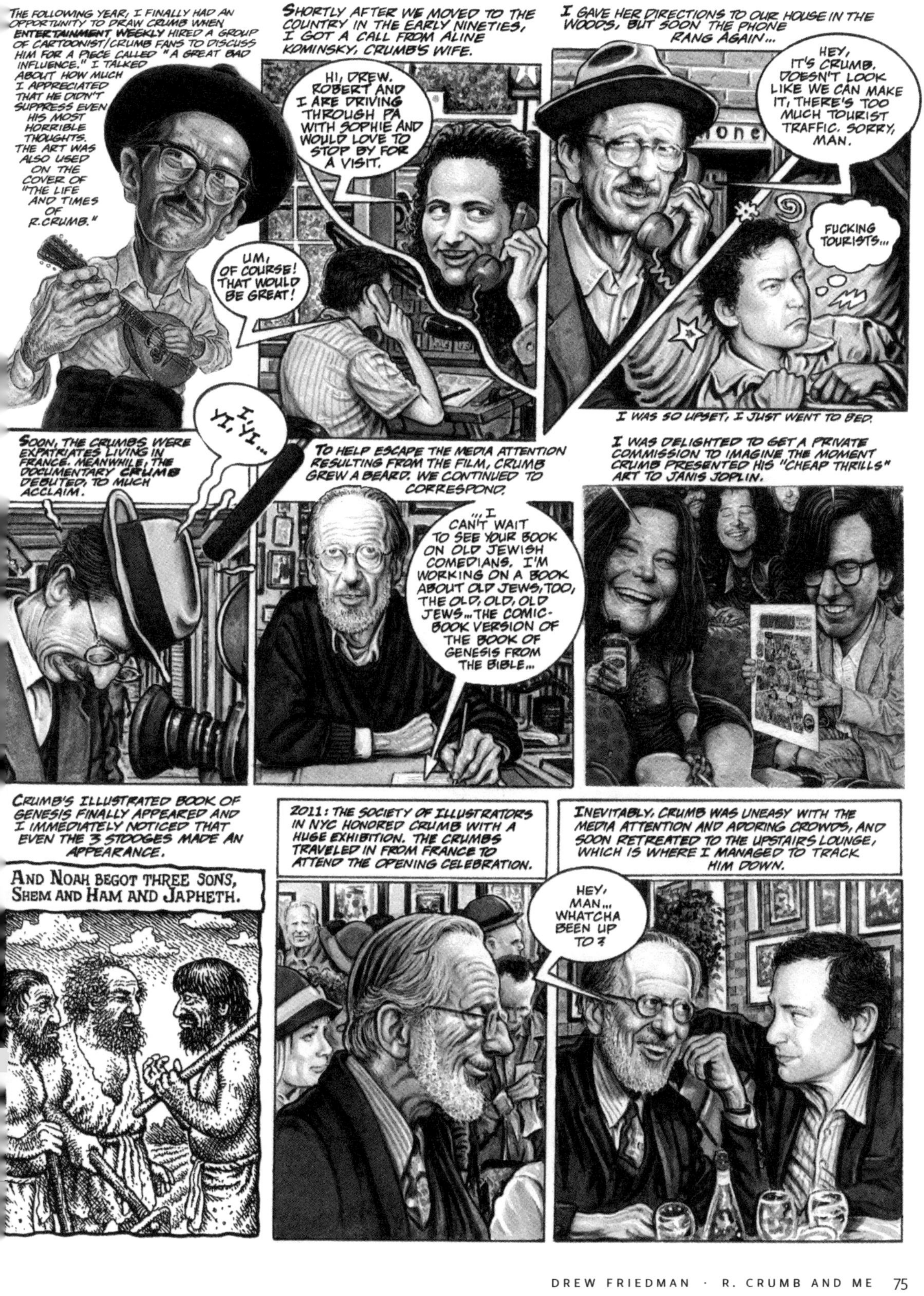

THE FOLLOWING YEAR, I FINALLY HAD AN OPPORTUNITY TO DRAW CRUMB WHEN ENTERTAINMENT WEEKLY HIRED A GROUP OF CARTOONIST/CRUMB FANS TO DISCUSS HIM FOR A PIECE CALLED "A GREAT BAD INFLUENCE." I TALKED ABOUT HOW MUCH I APPRECIATED THAT HE DIDN'T SUPPRESS EVEN HIS MOST HORRIBLE THOUGHTS. THE ART WAS ALSO USED ON THE COVER OF "THE LIFE AND TIMES OF R.CRUMB."
SHORTLY AFTER WE MOVED TO THE COUNTRY IN THE EARLY NINETIES, I GOT A CALL FROM ALINE KOMINSKY, CRUMB'S WIFE.
HI, DREW. ROBERT AND I ARE DRIVING THROUGH PA WITH SOPHIE AND WOULD LOVE TO STOP BY FOR A VISIT.
UM, OF COURSE! THAT WOULD BE GREAT!
I GAVE HER DIRECTIONS TO OUR HOUSE IN THE WOODS, BUT SOON THE PHONE RANG AGAIN...
HEY, IT'S CRUMB. DOESN'T LOOK LIKE WE CAN MAKE IT, THERE'S TOO MUCH TOURIST TRAFFIC. SORRY, MAN.
FUCKING TOURISTS...
I WAS SO UPSET, I JUST WENT TO BED.
SOON, THE CRUMBS WERE EXPATRIATES LIVING IN FRANCE. MEANWHILE, THE DOCUMENTARY CRUMB DEBUTED, TO MUCH ACCLAIM.
I, YI, YI...
TO HELP ESCAPE THE MEDIA ATTENTION RESULTING FROM THE FILM, CRUMB GREW A BEARD. WE CONTINUED TO CORRESPOND.
...I CAN'T WAIT TO SEE YOUR BOOK ON OLD JEWISH COMEDIANS. I'M WORKING ON A BOOK ABOUT OLD JEWS, TOO, THE OLD, OLD, OLD JEWS...THE COMIC-BOOK VERSION OF THE BOOK OF GENESIS FROM THE BIBLE...
I WAS DELIGHTED TO GET A PRIVATE COMMISSION TO IMAGINE THE MOMENT CRUMB PRESENTED HIS "CHEAP THRILLS" ART TO JANIS JOPLIN.
CRUMB'S ILLUSTRATED BOOK OF GENESIS FINALLY APPEARED AND I IMMEDIATELY NOTICED THAT EVEN THE 3 STOOGES MADE AN APPEARANCE.
AND NOAH BEGOT THREE SONS, SHEM AND HAM AND JAPHETH.
2011: THE SOCIETY OF ILLUSTRATORS IN NYC HONORED CRUMB WITH A HUGE EXHIBITION. THE CRUMBS TRAVELED IN FROM FRANCE TO ATTEND THE OPENING CELEBRATION.
INEVITABLY, CRUMB WAS UNEASY WITH THE MEDIA ATTENTION AND ADORING CROWDS, AND SOON RETREATED TO THE UPSTAIRS LOUNGE, WHICH IS WHERE I MANAGED TO TRACK HIM DOWN.
HEY, MAN... WHATCHA BEEN UP TO?

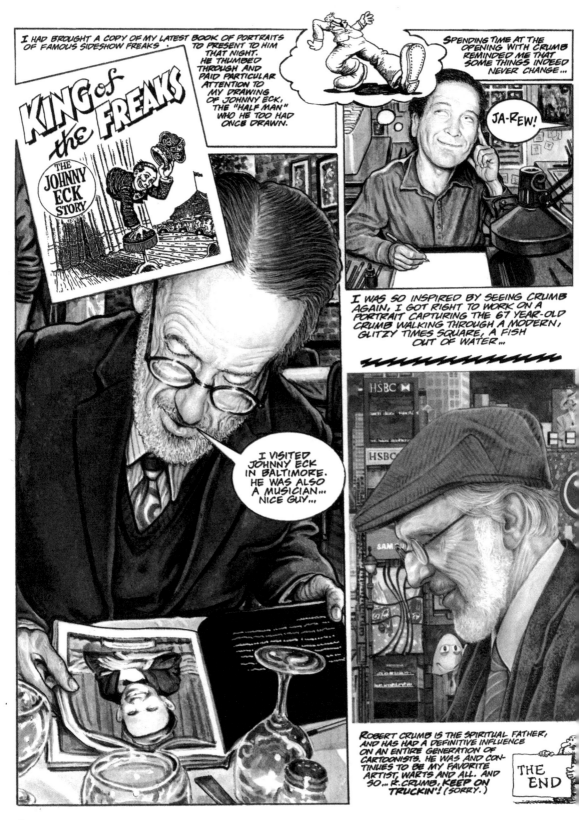

I HAD BROUGHT A COPY OF MY LATEST BOOK OF PORTRAITS OF FAMOUS SIDESHOW FREAKS TO PRESENT TO HIM THAT NIGHT. HE THUMBED THROUGH AND PAID PARTICULAR ATTENTION TO MY DRAWING OF JOHNNY ECK, THE "HALF MAN" WHO HE TOO HAD ONCE DRAWN.

KING of the FREAKS

THE JOHNNY ECK STORY

JA-REW!

SPENDING TIME AT THE OPENING WITH CRUMB REMINDED ME THAT SOME THINGS INDEED NEVER CHANGE...

I VISITED JOHNNY ECK IN BALTIMORE. HE WAS ALSO A MUSICIAN ... NICE GUY...

I WAS SO INSPIRED BY SEEING CRUMB AGAIN, I GOT RIGHT TO WORK ON A PORTRAIT CAPTURING THE 67 YEAR-OLD CRUMB WALKING THROUGH A MODERN, GLITZY TIMES SQUARE, A FISH OUT OF WATER...

HSBC
HSBC

ROBERT CRUMB IS THE SPIRITUAL FATHER, AND HAS HAD A DEFINITIVE INFLUENCE ON AN ENTIRE GENERATION OF CARTOONISTS. HE WAS AND CONTINUES TO BE MY FAVORITE ARTIST, WARTS AND ALL. AND SO ... R. CRUMB, KEEP ON TRUCKIN'! (SORRY.)

THE END

# Stroppy (*Excerpt*)

MARC BELL

MARC BELL'S
STROPPY
CASH PRIZES
D&Q

*excerpted from*

Stroppy

DRAWN AND QUARTERLY

8.4 × 10.6 inches • 64 pages

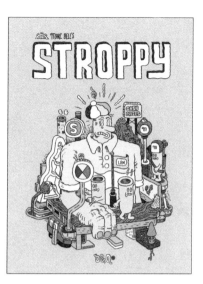

## Biography

Marc Bell was born in London, Ontario. His books include *Shrimpy and Paul and Friends* (Highwater Books, 2003), *The Stacks* (Drawn and Quarterly, 2004), *Hot Potatoe [sic]* (Drawn and Quarterly, 2009), *Pure Pajamas* (Drawn and Quarterly, 2011), and *Stroppy* (Drawn and Quarterly, 2015). His work was recently included in Afterimage at DePaul Art Museum (Chicago) and Drawn and Quarterly 25th Anniversary at Galerie Martel (Paris). marcbelldept.blogspot.ca

## Statement

This selection from *Stroppy* is the "set up" where we find our hero Stroppy being interfered with at work by a character named Sean. A series of other misfortunes fall upon Stroppy during the rest of the book. This is only the beginning, but it certainly sets the tone.

STROPPY IS AT WORK (AT MONSIEUR MOUSTACHE'S REMOTE VILLAGER PROCESSING PLANT*)

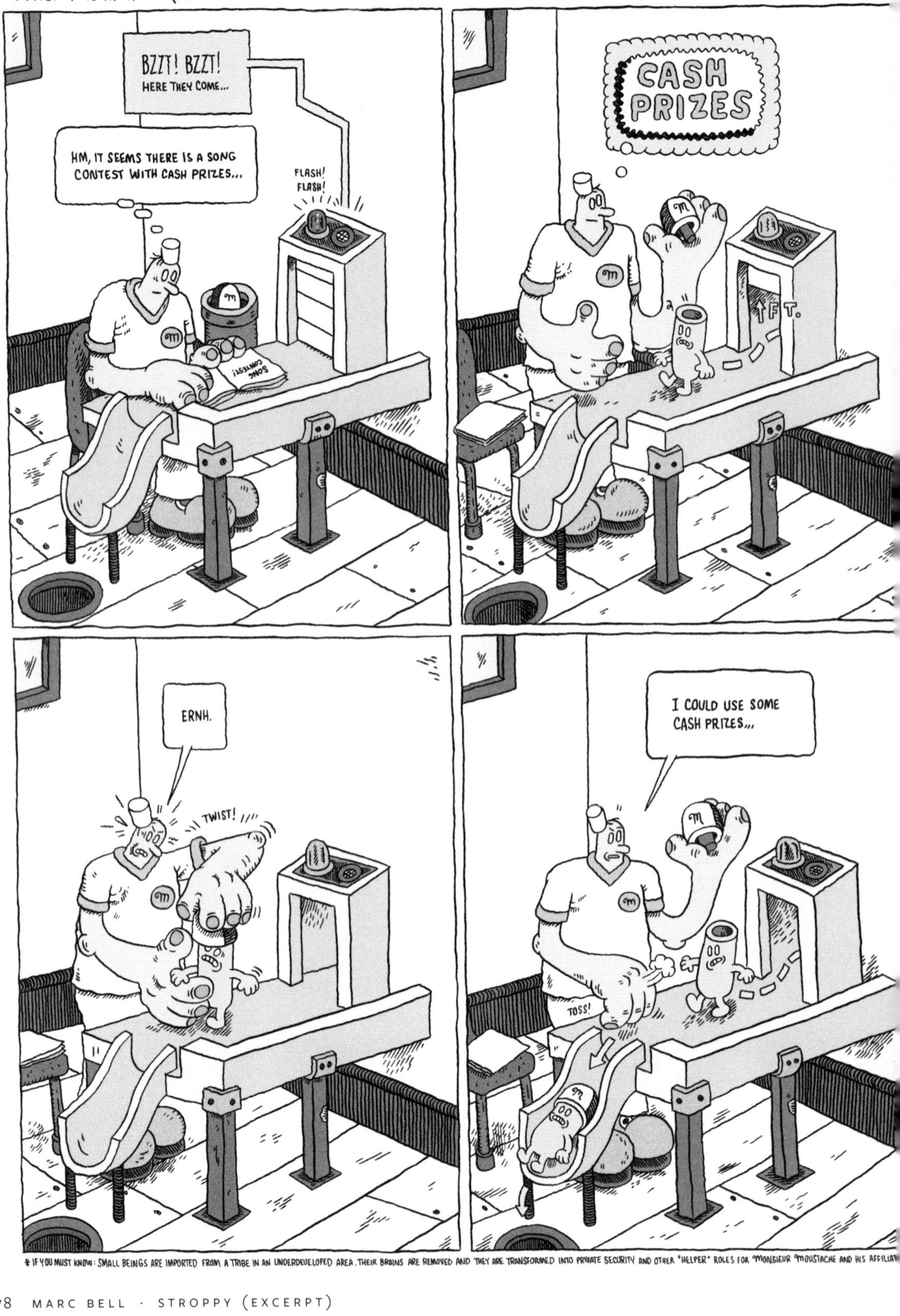
BZZT! BZZT!
HERE THEY COME...
HM, IT SEEMS THERE IS A SONG CONTEST WITH CASH PRIZES...
FLASH! FLASH!
SONG CONTEST!
CASH PRIZES
ERNH.
TWIST!
I COULD USE SOME CASH PRIZES...
TOSS!

* IF YOU MUST KNOW: SMALL BEINGS ARE IMPORTED FROM A TRIBE IN AN UNDERDEVELOPED AREA. THEIR BRAINS ARE REMOVED AND THEY ARE TRANSFORMED INTO PRIVATE SECURITY AND OTHER "HELPER" ROLES FOR MONSIEUR MOUSTACHE AND HIS AFFILIAT

THERE IS A VISITOR

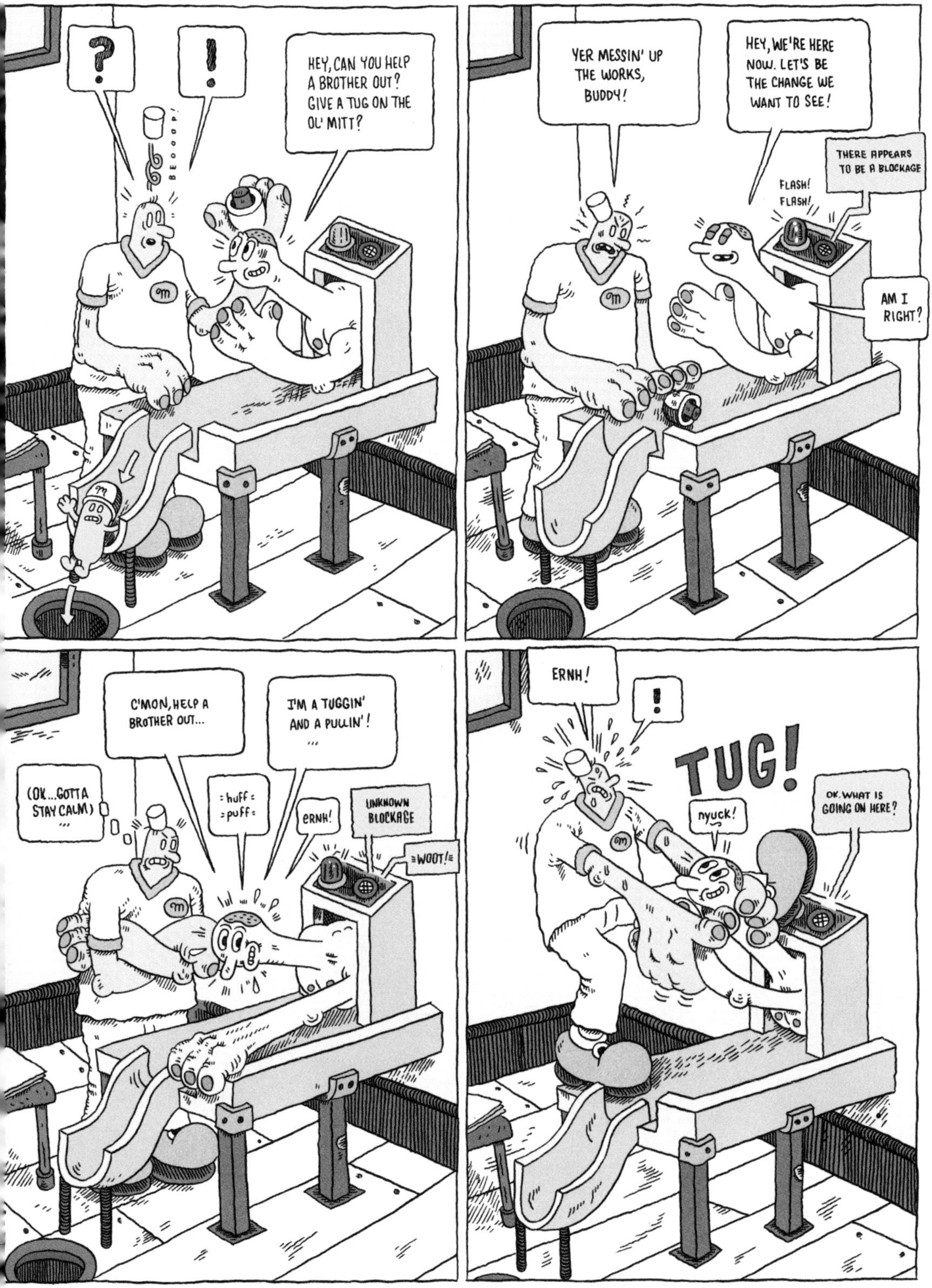
?
!
BEOOOP!
HEY, CAN YOU HELP A BROTHER OUT? GIVE A TUG ON THE OL' MITT?
YER MESSIN' UP THE WORKS, BUDDY!
HEY, WE'RE HERE NOW. LET'S BE THE CHANGE WE WANT TO SEE!
FLASH! FLASH!
THERE APPEARS TO BE A BLOCKAGE
AM I RIGHT?
C'MON, HELP A BROTHER OUT...
I'M A TUGGIN' AND A PULLIN'! ...
(OK...GOTTA STAY CALM) ...
=huff= =puff=
ERNH!
UNKNOWN BLOCKAGE
=WOOT!=
ERNH!
!
TUG!
nyuck!
OK. WHAT IS GOING ON HERE?

HIS NAME IS SEAN, HE WEARS NO SHIRT

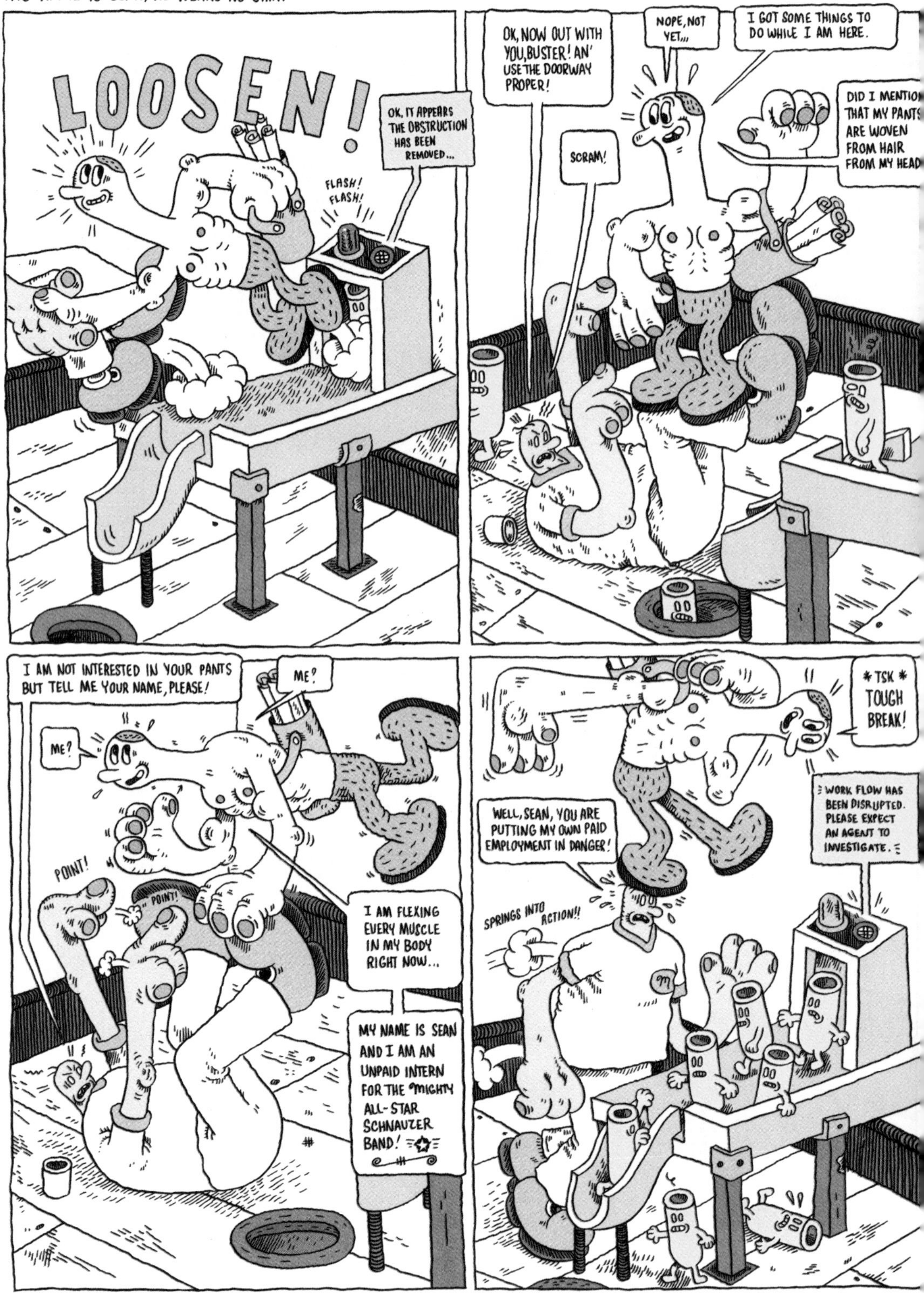

LOOSEN!
OK, IT APPEARS THE OBSTRUCTION HAS BEEN REMOVED...
FLASH! FLASH!
OK, NOW OUT WITH YOU, BUSTER! AN' USE THE DOORWAY PROPER!
NOPE, NOT YET...
I GOT SOME THINGS TO DO WHILE I AM HERE.
SCRAM!
DID I MENTIO THAT MY PANT ARE WOVEN FROM HAIR FROM MY HEAD
I AM NOT INTERESTED IN YOUR PANTS BUT TELL ME YOUR NAME, PLEASE!
ME?
ME?
POINT!
POINT!
I AM FLEXING EVERY MUSCLE IN MY BODY RIGHT NOW...
MY NAME IS SEAN AND I AM AN UNPAID INTERN FOR THE MIGHTY ALL-STAR SCHNAUZER BAND!
* TSK * TOUGH BREAK!
WELL, SEAN, YOU ARE PUTTING MY OWN PAID EMPLOYMENT IN DANGER!
WORK FLOW HAS BEEN DISRUPTED. PLEASE EXPECT AN AGENT TO INVESTIGATE.
SPRINGS INTO ACTION!!

MONSIEUR MOUSTACHE IS AT HOME

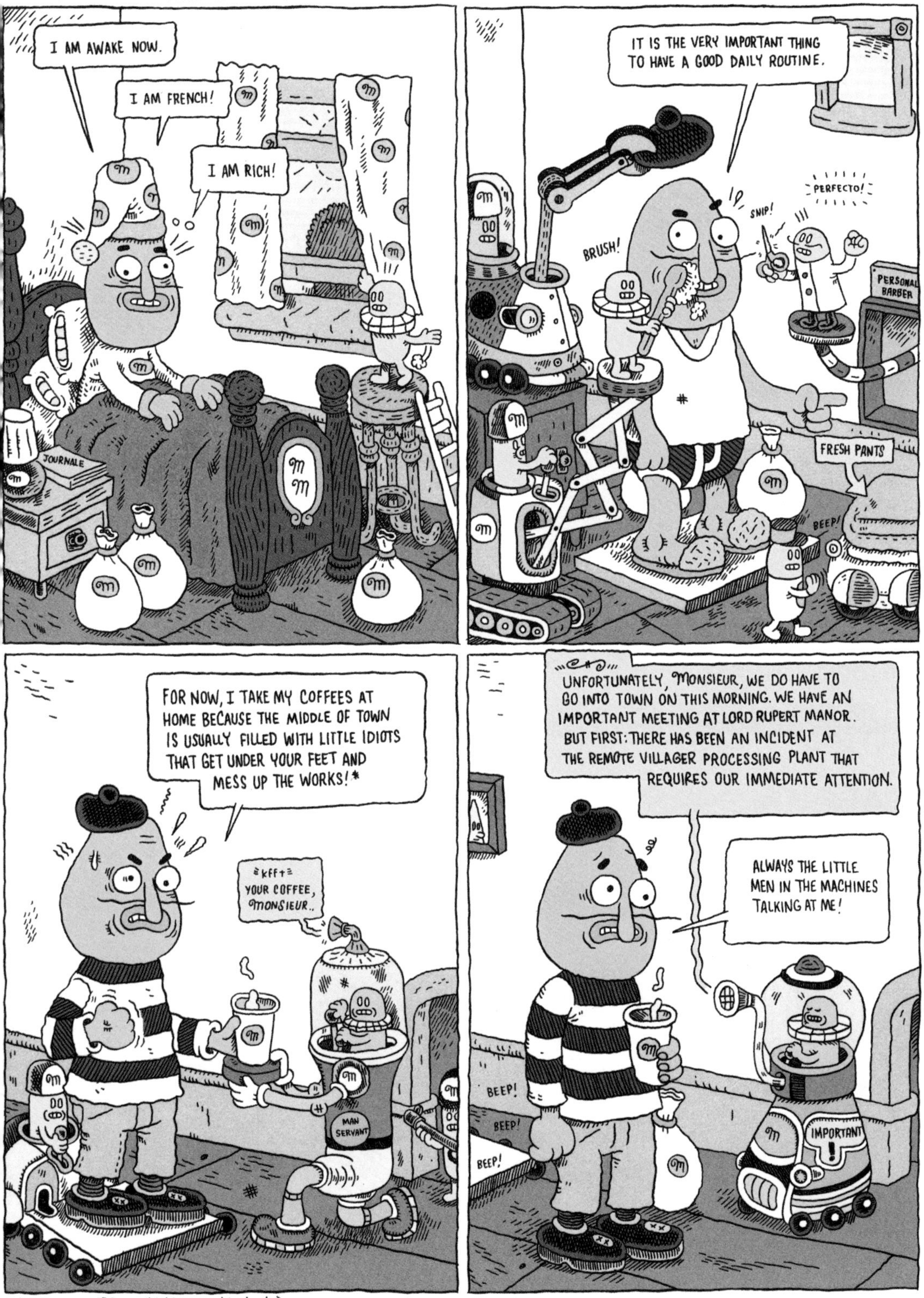
I AM AWAKE NOW.
I AM FRENCH!
I AM RICH!
JOURNALE
IT IS THE VERY IMPORTANT THING TO HAVE A GOOD DAILY ROUTINE.
BRUSH!
SNIP!
PERFECTO!
PERSONAL BARBER
FRESH PANTS
BEEP!
FOR NOW, I TAKE MY COFFEES AT HOME BECAUSE THE MIDDLE OF TOWN IS USUALLY FILLED WITH LITTLE IDIOTS THAT GET UNDER YOUR FEET AND MESS UP THE WORKS!*
kfft YOUR COFFEE, MONSIEUR..
MAN SERVANT
UNFORTUNATELY, MONSIEUR, WE DO HAVE TO GO INTO TOWN ON THIS MORNING. WE HAVE AN IMPORTANT MEETING AT LORD RUPERT MANOR. BUT FIRST: THERE HAS BEEN AN INCIDENT AT THE REMOTE VILLAGER PROCESSING PLANT THAT REQUIRES OUR IMMEDIATE ATTENTION.
ALWAYS THE LITTLE MEN IN THE MACHINES TALKING AT ME!
BEEP!
BEEP!
BEEP!
IMPORTANT

* SEE: WORN TUFF ELBOW #1 (fantagraphics books)

GOO IS EMPLOYED BY THE INTERNAL AUTHORITIES

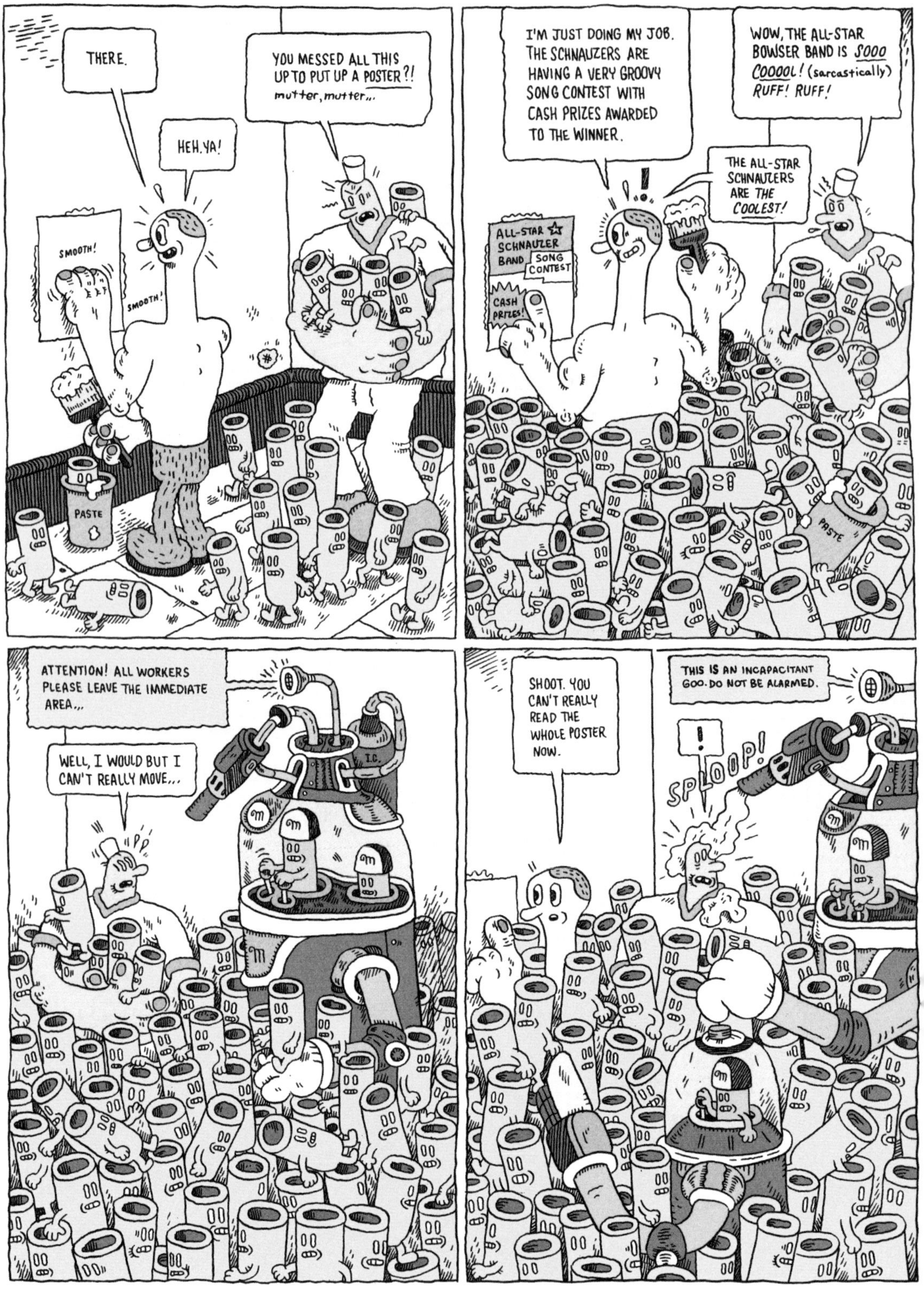

THERE.
HEH. YA!
SMOOTH!
SMOOTH!
YOU MESSED ALL THIS UP TO PUT UP A POSTER?!
mutter, mutter...
PASTE
I'M JUST DOING MY JOB. THE SCHNAUZERS ARE HAVING A VERY GROOVY SONG CONTEST WITH CASH PRIZES AWARDED TO THE WINNER.
ALL-STAR SCHNAUZER BAND
SONG CONTEST
CASH PRIZES!
THE ALL-STAR SCHNAUZERS ARE THE COOLEST!
WOW, THE ALL-STAR BOWSER BAND IS SOOO COOOOL! (sarcastically) RUFF! RUFF!
PASTE
ATTENTION! ALL WORKERS PLEASE LEAVE THE IMMEDIATE AREA...
WELL, I WOULD BUT I CAN'T REALLY MOVE...
SHOOT. YOU CAN'T REALLY READ THE WHOLE POSTER NOW.
THIS IS AN INCAPACITANT GOO. DO NOT BE ALARMED.
SPLOOP!

# MONSIEUR MOUSTACHE'S ROUTINE IS INTERRUPTED AGAIN

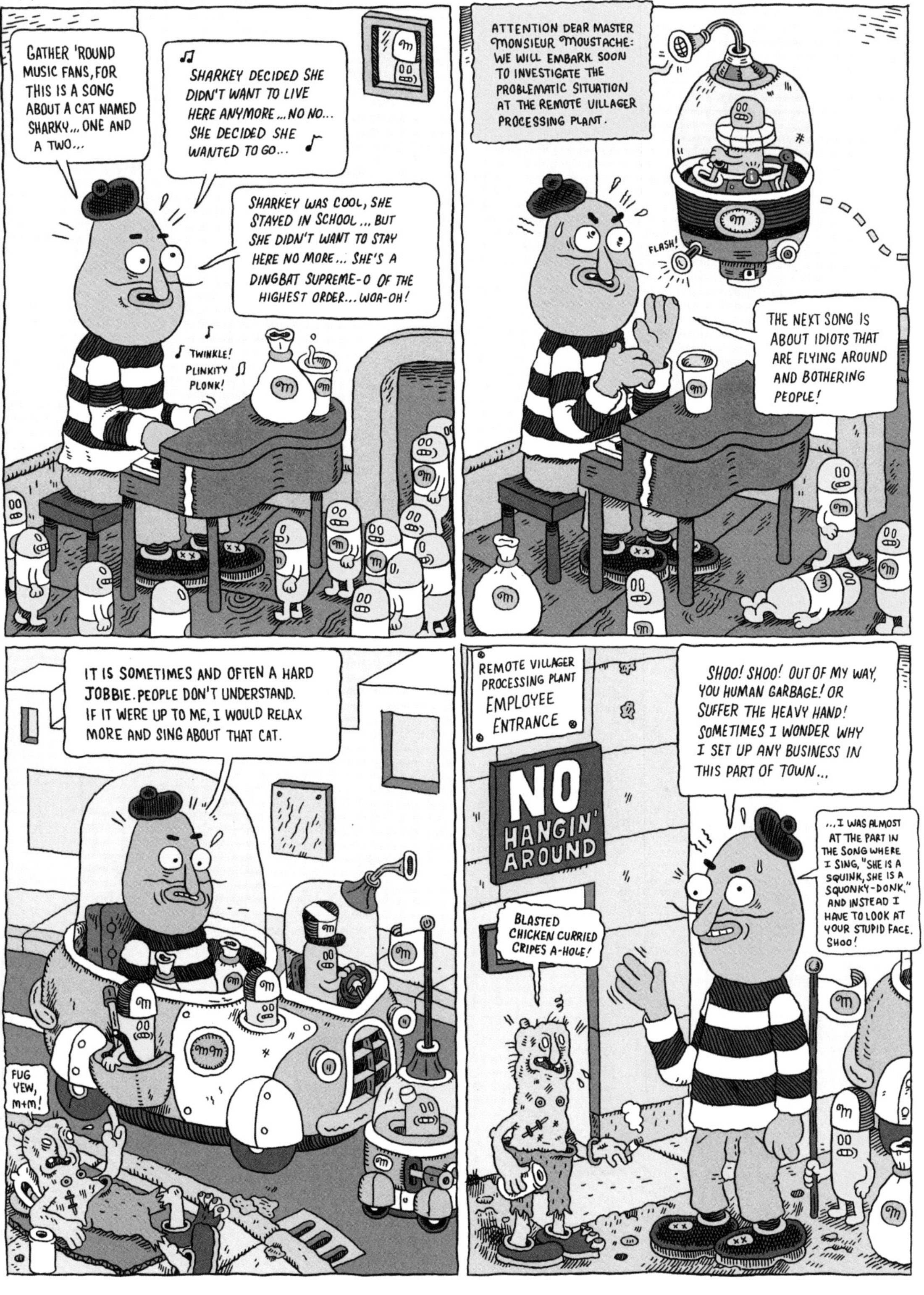
GATHER 'ROUND MUSIC FANS, FOR THIS IS A SONG ABOUT A CAT NAMED SHARKY... ONE AND A TWO...
SHARKEY DECIDED SHE DIDN'T WANT TO LIVE HERE ANYMORE... NO NO... SHE DECIDED SHE WANTED TO GO...
SHARKEY WAS COOL, SHE STAYED IN SCHOOL... BUT SHE DIDN'T WANT TO STAY HERE NO MORE... SHE'S A DINGBAT SUPREME-O OF THE HIGHEST ORDER... WOA-OH!
TWINKLE! PLINKITY PLONK!
ATTENTION DEAR MASTER MONSIEUR MOUSTACHE: WE WILL EMBARK SOON TO INVESTIGATE THE PROBLEMATIC SITUATION AT THE REMOTE VILLAGER PROCESSING PLANT.
FLASH!
THE NEXT SONG IS ABOUT IDIOTS THAT ARE FLYING AROUND AND BOTHERING PEOPLE!
IT IS SOMETIMES AND OFTEN A HARD JOBBIE. PEOPLE DON'T UNDERSTAND. IF IT WERE UP TO ME, I WOULD RELAX MORE AND SING ABOUT THAT CAT.
FUG YEW, M+M!
REMOTE VILLAGER PROCESSING PLANT EMPLOYEE ENTRANCE
NO HANGIN' AROUND
SHOO! SHOO! OUT OF MY WAY, YOU HUMAN GARBAGE! OR SUFFER THE HEAVY HAND! SOMETIMES I WONDER WHY I SET UP ANY BUSINESS IN THIS PART OF TOWN...
...I WAS ALMOST AT THE PART IN THE SONG WHERE I SING, "SHE IS A SQUINK, SHE IS A SQUONKY-DONK," AND INSTEAD I HAVE TO LOOK AT YOUR STUPID FACE. SHOO!
BLASTED CHICKEN CURRIED CRIPES A-HOLE!

DECISIONS ARE MADE

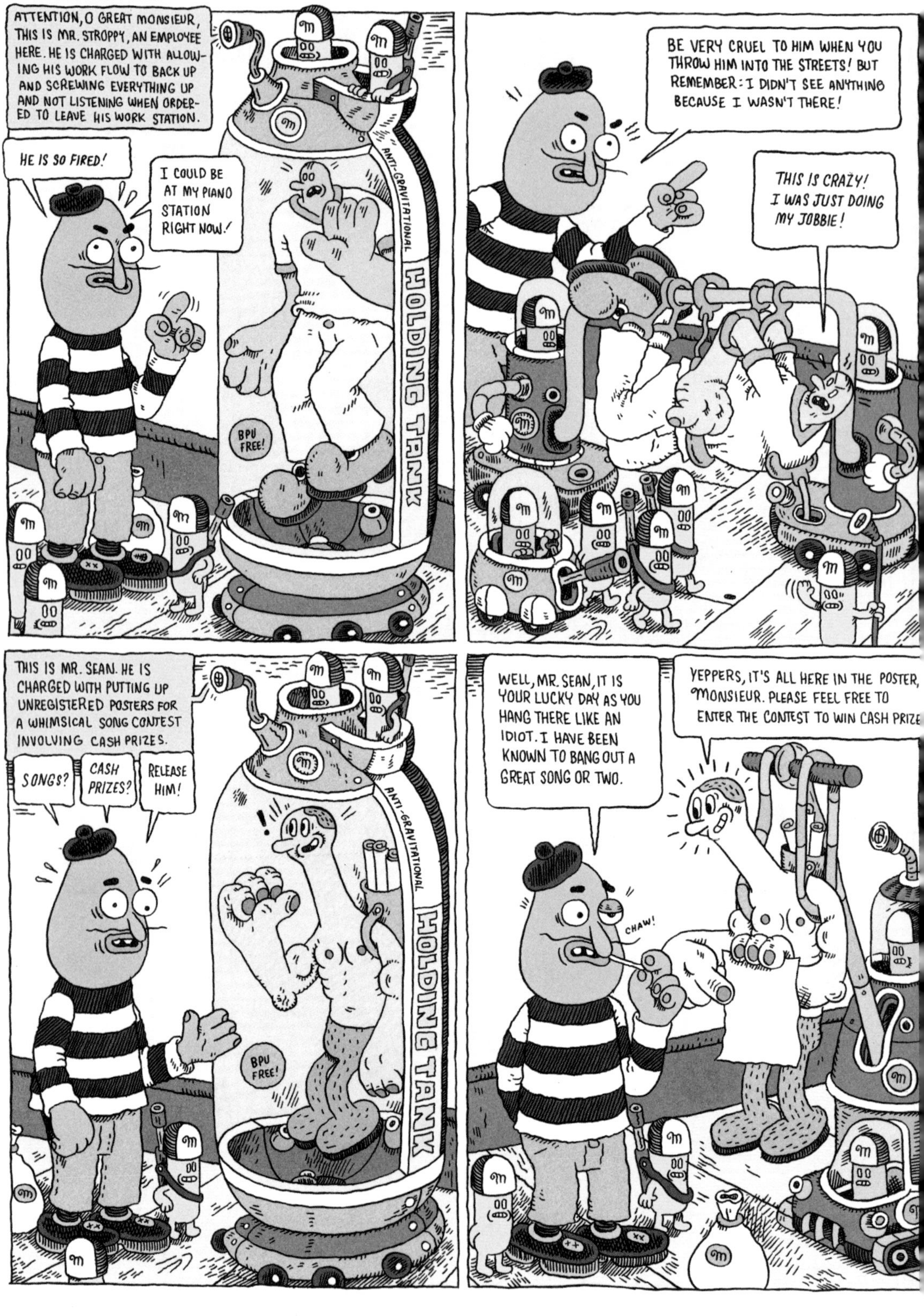

ATTENTION, O GREAT MONSIEUR, THIS IS MR. STROPPY, AN EMPLOYEE HERE. HE IS CHARGED WITH ALLOWING HIS WORK FLOW TO BACK UP AND SCREWING EVERYTHING UP AND NOT LISTENING WHEN ORDERED TO LEAVE HIS WORK STATION.
HE IS SO FIRED!
I COULD BE AT MY PIANO STATION RIGHT NOW!
ANTI-GRAVITATIONAL
HOLDING TANK
BPU FREE!
BE VERY CRUEL TO HIM WHEN YOU THROW HIM INTO THE STREETS! BUT REMEMBER: I DIDN'T SEE ANYTHING BECAUSE I WASN'T THERE!
THIS IS CRAZY! I WAS JUST DOING MY JOBBIE!
THIS IS MR. SEAN. HE IS CHARGED WITH PUTTING UP UNREGISTERED POSTERS FOR A WHIMSICAL SONG CONTEST INVOLVING CASH PRIZES.
SONGS?
CASH PRIZES?
RELEASE HIM!
ANTI-GRAVITATIONAL
HOLDING TANK
BPU FREE!
WELL, MR. SEAN, IT IS YOUR LUCKY DAY AS YOU HANG THERE LIKE AN IDIOT. I HAVE BEEN KNOWN TO BANG OUT A GREAT SONG OR TWO.
YEPPERS, IT'S ALL HERE IN THE POSTER, MONSIEUR. PLEASE FEEL FREE TO ENTER THE CONTEST TO WIN CASH PRIZE
CHAW!

STROPPY IS REMOVED FROM THE PREMISES

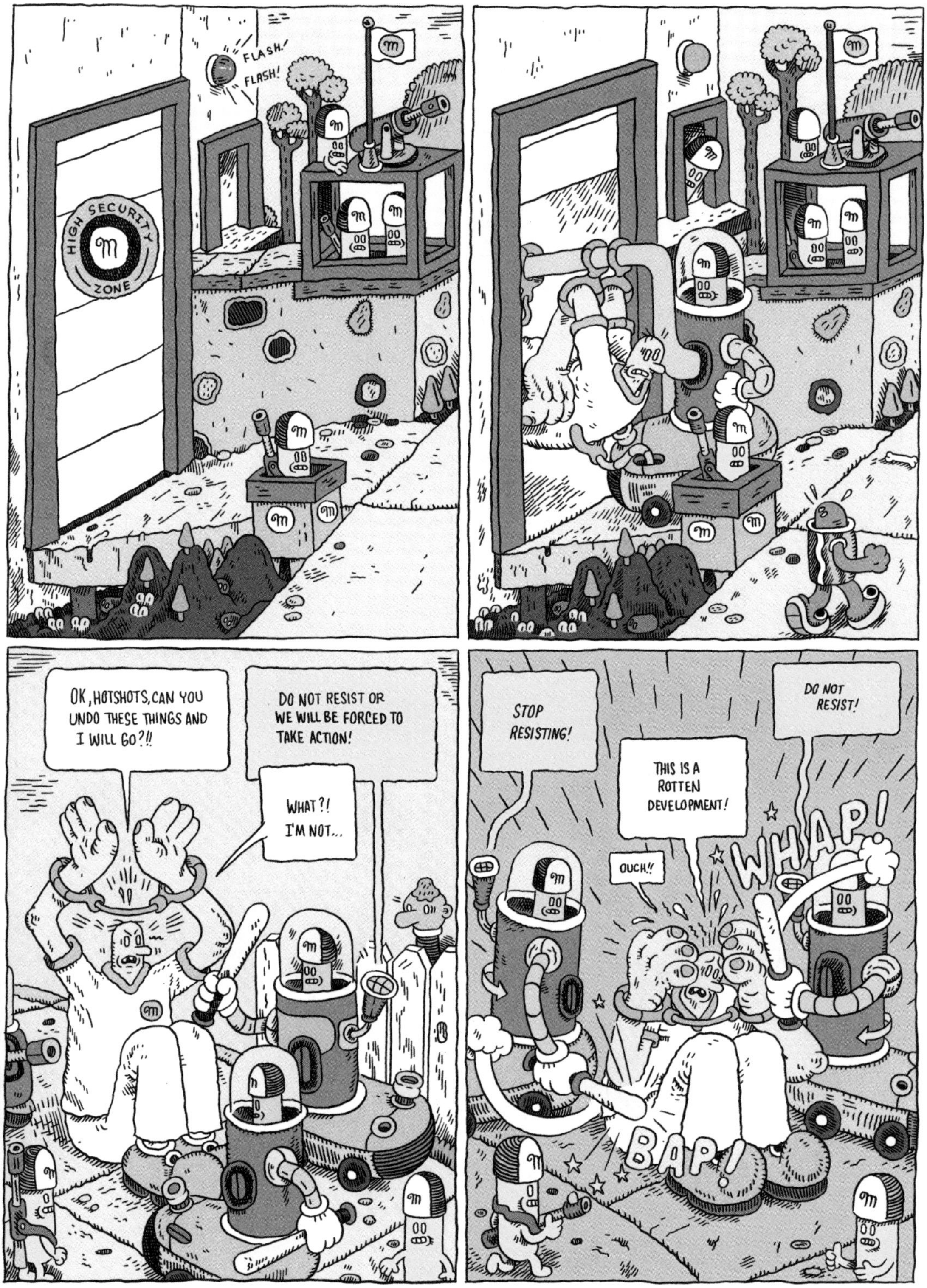

FLASH!
FLASH!
HIGH SECURITY ZONE
OK, HOTSHOTS, CAN YOU UNDO THESE THINGS AND I WILL GO?!!
DO NOT RESIST OR WE WILL BE FORCED TO TAKE ACTION!
WHAT?! I'M NOT...
STOP RESISTING!
DO NOT RESIST!
THIS IS A ROTTEN DEVELOPMENT!
OUCH!!
WHAP!
BAP!

STROPPY SUFFERS FURTHER HUMILIATIONS OUTSIDE HIS FORMER WORKPLACE

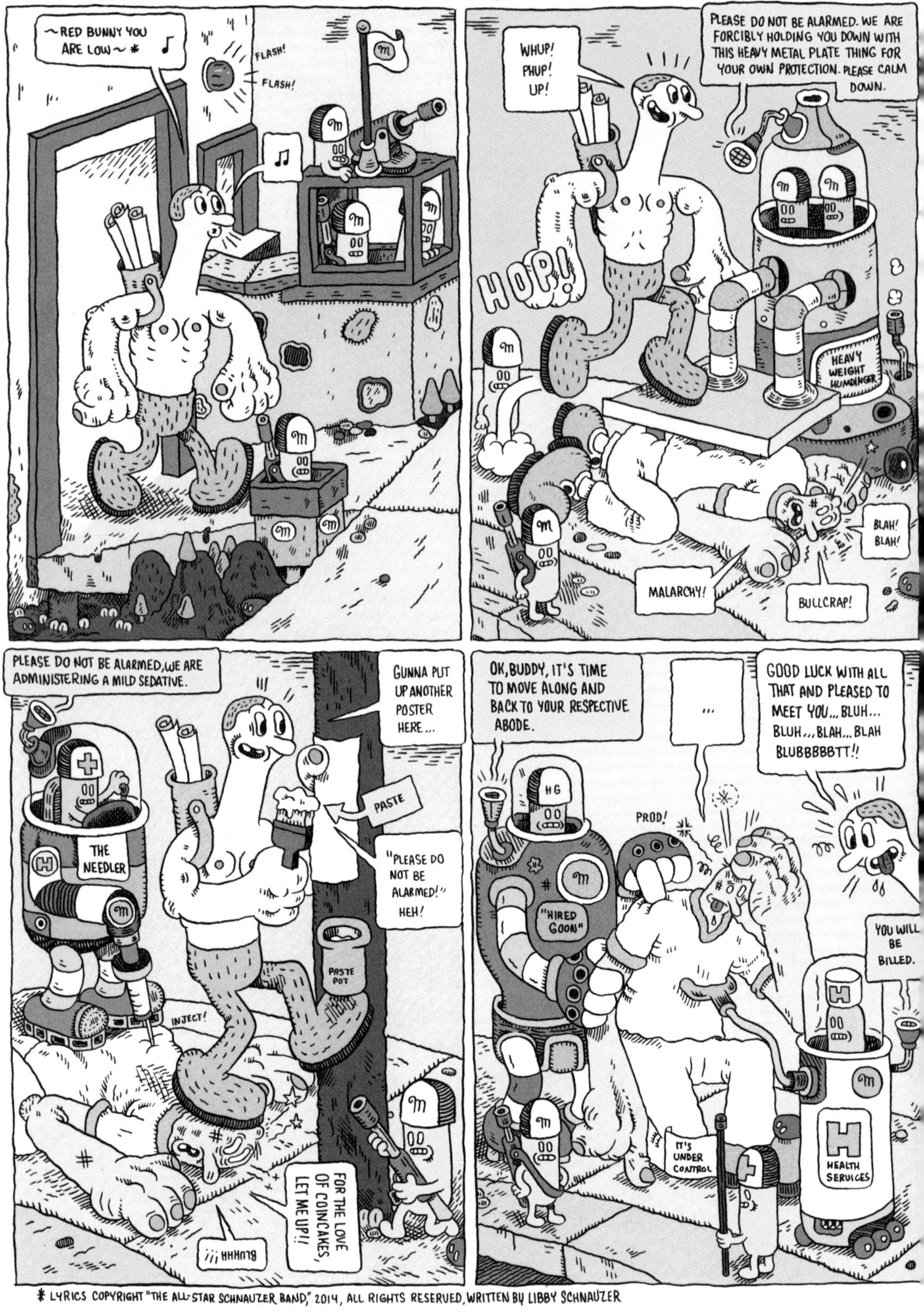

~RED BUNNY YOU ARE LOW~ *
FLASH!
FLASH!
WHUP! PHUP! UP!
PLEASE DO NOT BE ALARMED. WE ARE FORCIBLY HOLDING YOU DOWN WITH THIS HEAVY METAL PLATE THING FOR YOUR OWN PROTECTION. PLEASE CALM DOWN.
HOP!
HEAVY WEIGHT HUMDINGER
BLAH! BLAH!
MALARCHY!
BULLCRAP!
PLEASE DO NOT BE ALARMED, WE ARE ADMINISTERING A MILD SEDATIVE.
GUNNA PUT UP ANOTHER POSTER HERE...
PASTE
THE NEEDLER
"PLEASE DO NOT BE ALARMED!" HEH!
PASTE POT
INJECT!
FOR THE LOVE OF COINCAKES, LET ME UP!!
BLUHHH!!!
OK, BUDDY, IT'S TIME TO MOVE ALONG AND BACK TO YOUR RESPECTIVE ABODE.
...
GOOD LUCK WITH ALL THAT AND PLEASED TO MEET YOU... BLUH... BLUH... BLAH... BLAH BLUBBBBBTT!!
HG
PROD!
"HIRED GOON"
YOU WILL BE BILLED.
IT'S UNDER CONTROL
HEALTH SERVICES


* LYRICS COPYRIGHT "THE ALL-STAR SCHNAUZER BAND," 2014, ALL RIGHTS RESERVED, WRITTEN BY LIBBY SCHNAUZER

CLANCY THE POET HAPPENS BY

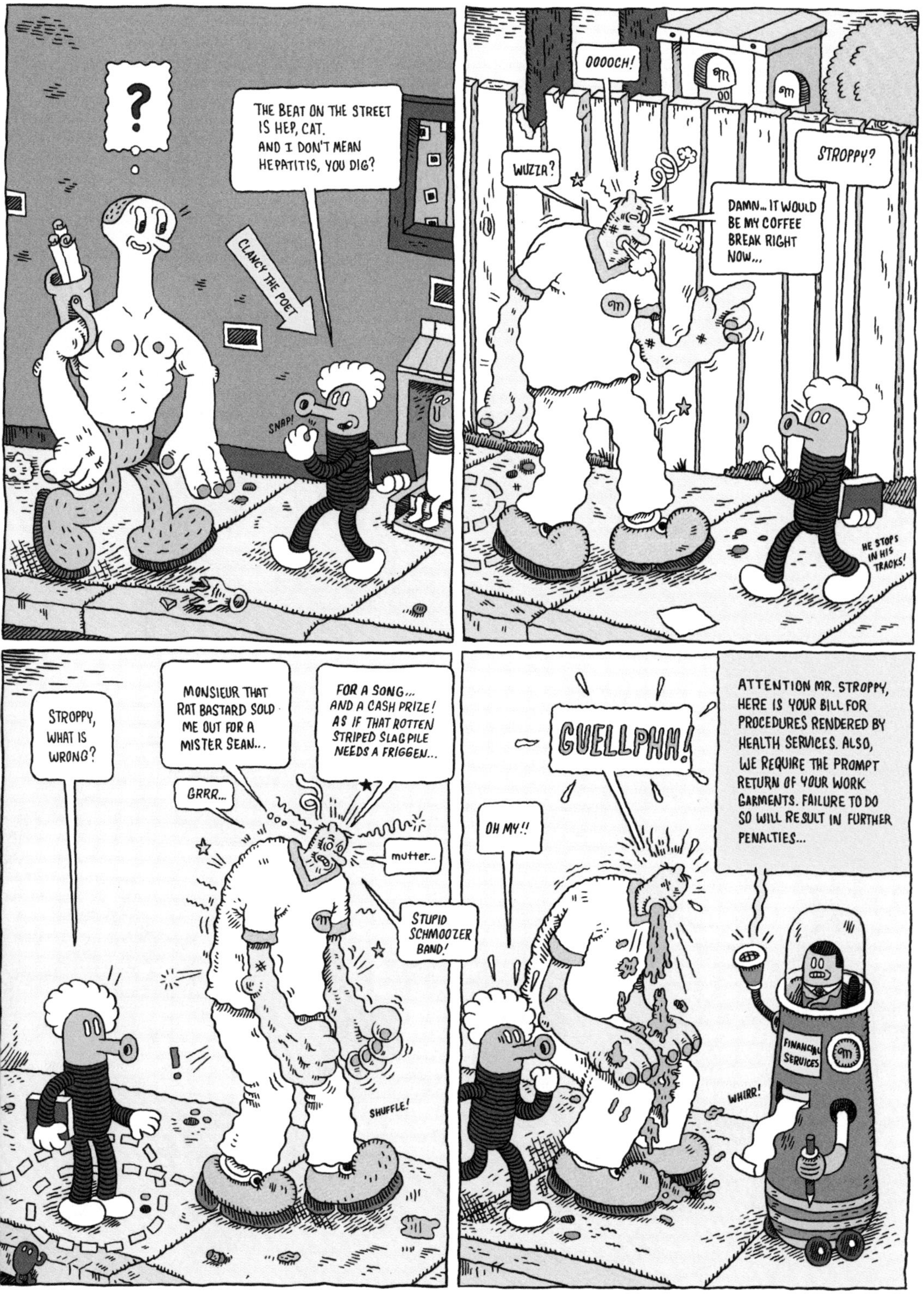
?
THE BEAT ON THE STREET IS HEP, CAT. AND I DON'T MEAN HEPATITIS, YOU DIG?
CLANCY THE POET
SNAP!
OOOOCH!
WUZZA?
STROPPY?
DAMN... IT WOULD BE MY COFFEE BREAK RIGHT NOW...
HE STOPS IN HIS TRACKS!
STROPPY, WHAT IS WRONG?
MONSIEUR THAT RAT BASTARD SOLD ME OUT FOR A MISTER SEAN...
FOR A SONG... AND A CASH PRIZE! AS IF THAT ROTTEN STRIPED SLAGPILE NEEDS A FRIGGEN...
GRRR...
mutter...
STUPID SCHMOOZER BAND!
SHUFFLE!
GUELLPHH!
OH MY!!
ATTENTION MR. STROPPY, HERE IS YOUR BILL FOR PROCEDURES RENDERED BY HEALTH SERVICES. ALSO, WE REQUIRE THE PROMPT RETURN OF YOUR WORK GARMENTS. FAILURE TO DO SO WILL RESULT IN FURTHER PENALTIES...
FINANCIAL SERVICES
WHIRR!

STROPPY TURNS IN HIS UNIFORM

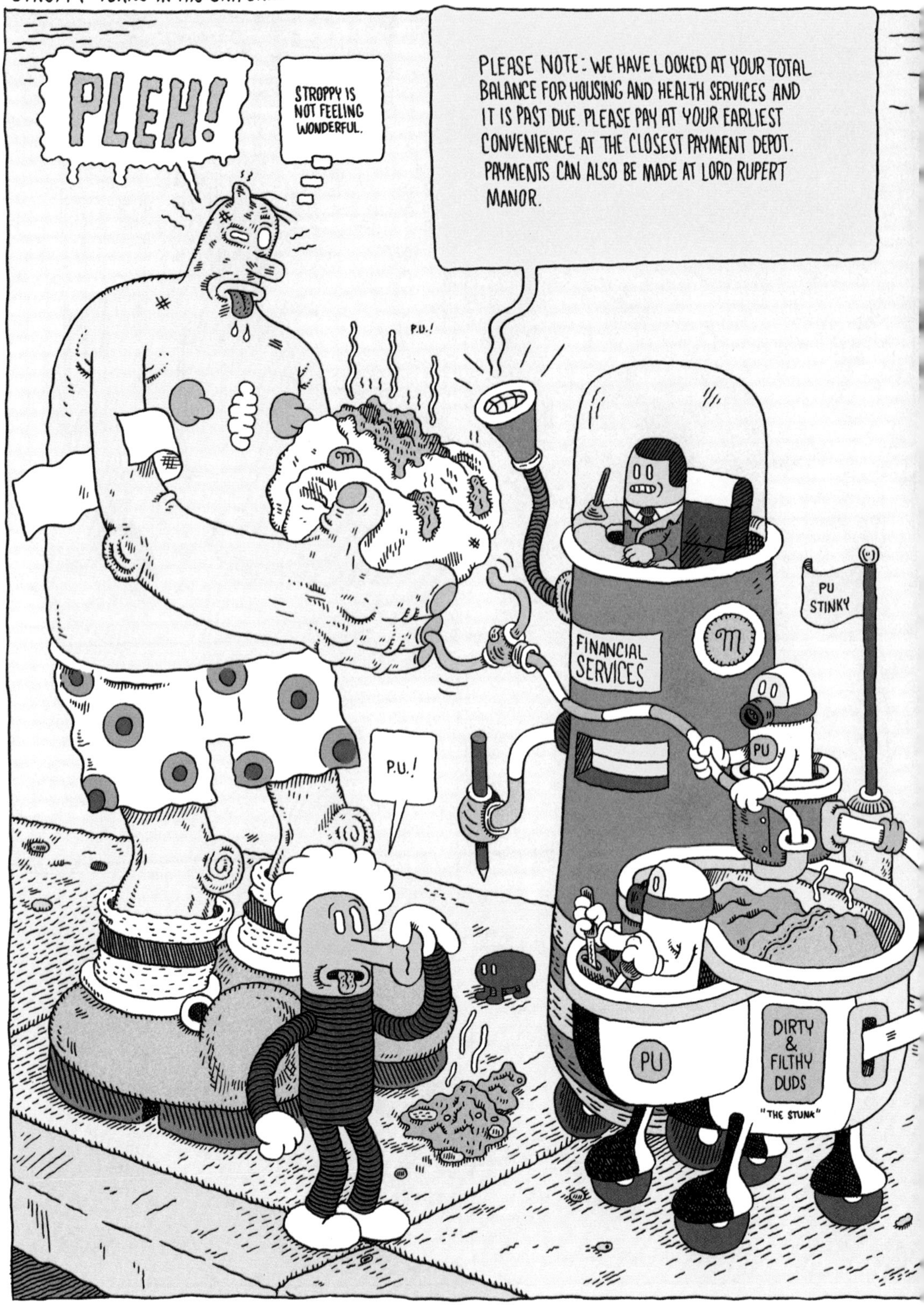
PLEH!
STROPPY IS NOT FEELING WONDERFUL.
PLEASE NOTE: WE HAVE LOOKED AT YOUR TOTAL BALANCE FOR HOUSING AND HEALTH SERVICES AND IT IS PAST DUE. PLEASE PAY AT YOUR EARLIEST CONVENIENCE AT THE CLOSEST PAYMENT DEPOT. PAYMENTS CAN ALSO BE MADE AT LORD RUPERT MANOR.
P.U.!
P.U.!
PU STINKY
FINANCIAL SERVICES
PU
PU
DIRTY & FILTHY DUDS
"THE STUNK"

# Powdered Milk, Vol. 14

## KEILER ROBERTS

*originally published in*

Powdered Milk, Vol. 14

SELF-PUBLISHED

5.5 × 8.5 inches • 16 pages

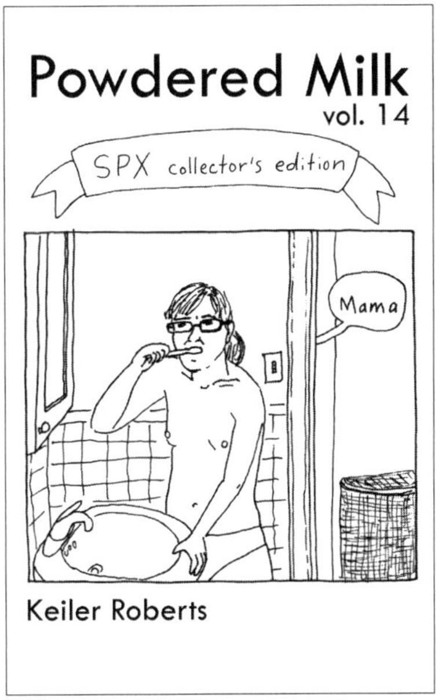
Powdered Milk
vol. 14
SPX collector's edition
Mama
Keiler Roberts

### Biography

Keiler Roberts's autobiographical comic series, *Powdered Milk*, has received three Ignatz Award nominations and has been published in the *Chicago Reader*, *Mutha Magazine*, *Nat. Brut*, *Darling Sleeper*, and *Newcity*. She was a special guest at CAKE (Chicago Alternative Comics Festival) in 2015 and Chicago Zine Fest in 2013. *Miseryland*, Roberts's third book, has been reviewed by *Publisher's Weekly*, *The Comics Journal*, *Broken Frontier*, *Sequential State*, and more. She was a panelist in the Chicago Architectural Biennial, and has performed readings of her comics at Brain Frame, Sector 2337 Gallery, Quimby's, and Two Cookie Minimum. Roberts teaches at the School of the Art Institute of Chicago and DePaul University. keilerroberts.com

### Statement

*Powdered Milk* is an ongoing autobiographical comic I started in 2009, a year before I had my daughter Xia. Parts of volume 14 were originally printed in *Mutha Magazine*. The entire minicomic was later included in my self-published book, *Miseryland*. The pages here show me redefining femininity, sexuality, and maternal instinct.

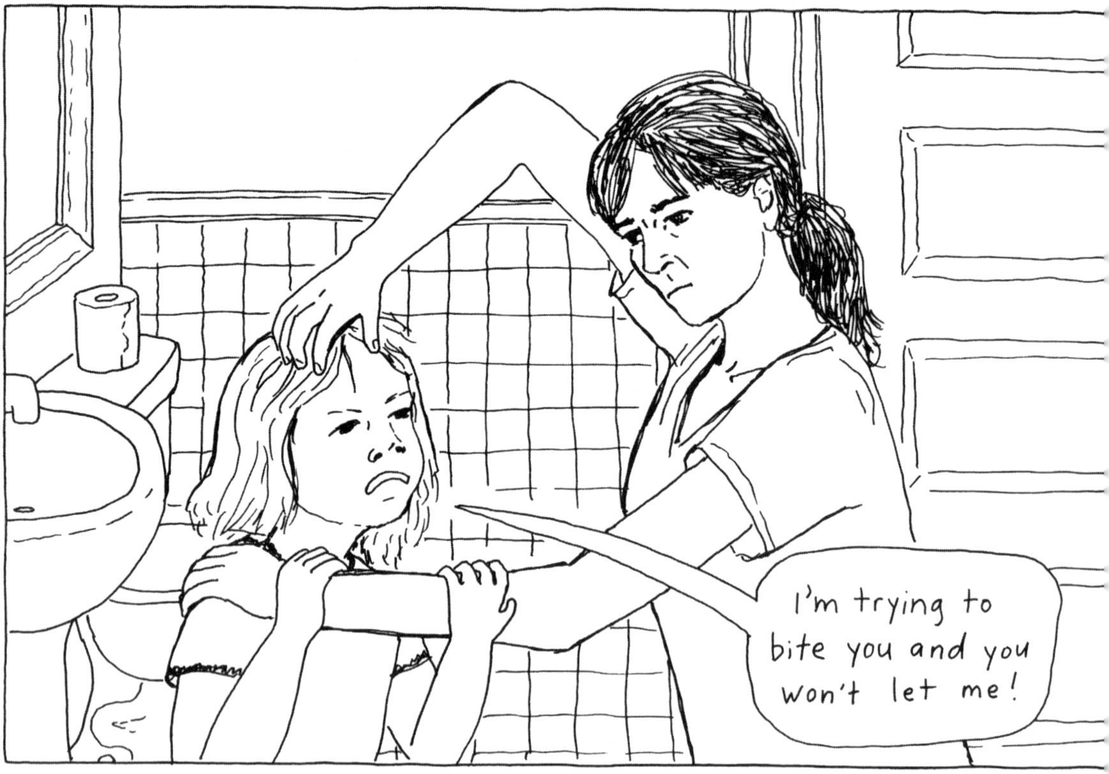
I'm trying to bite you and you won't let me!

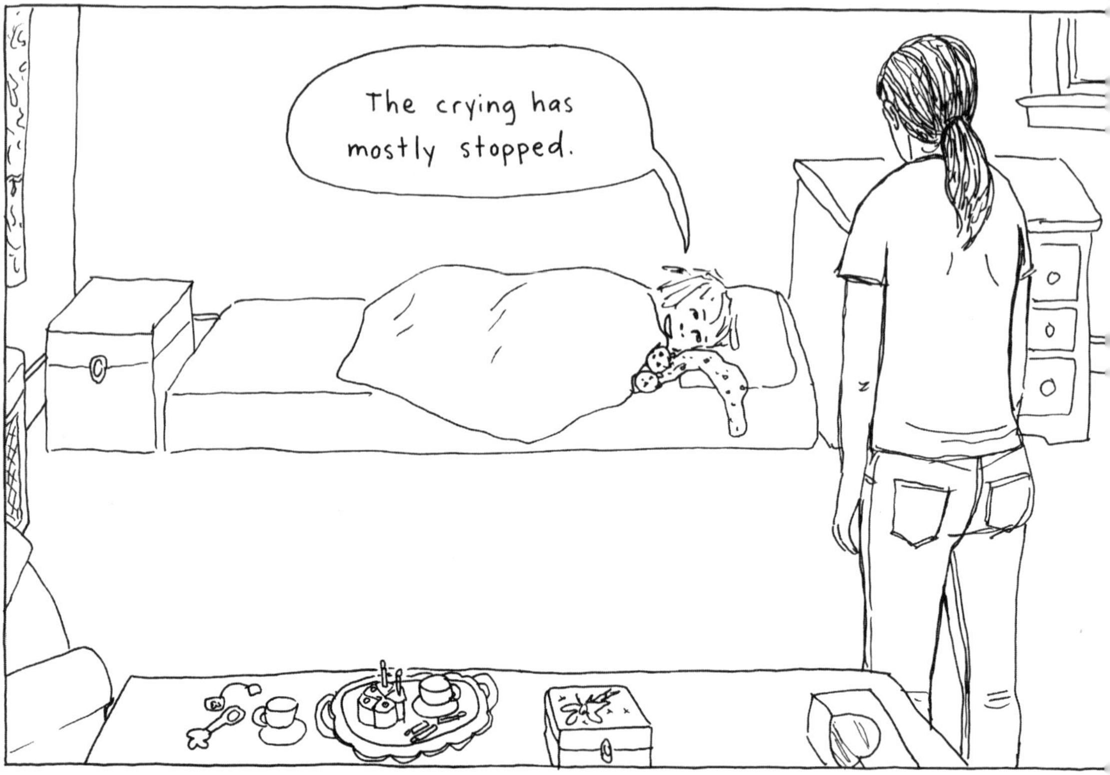
The crying has mostly stopped.

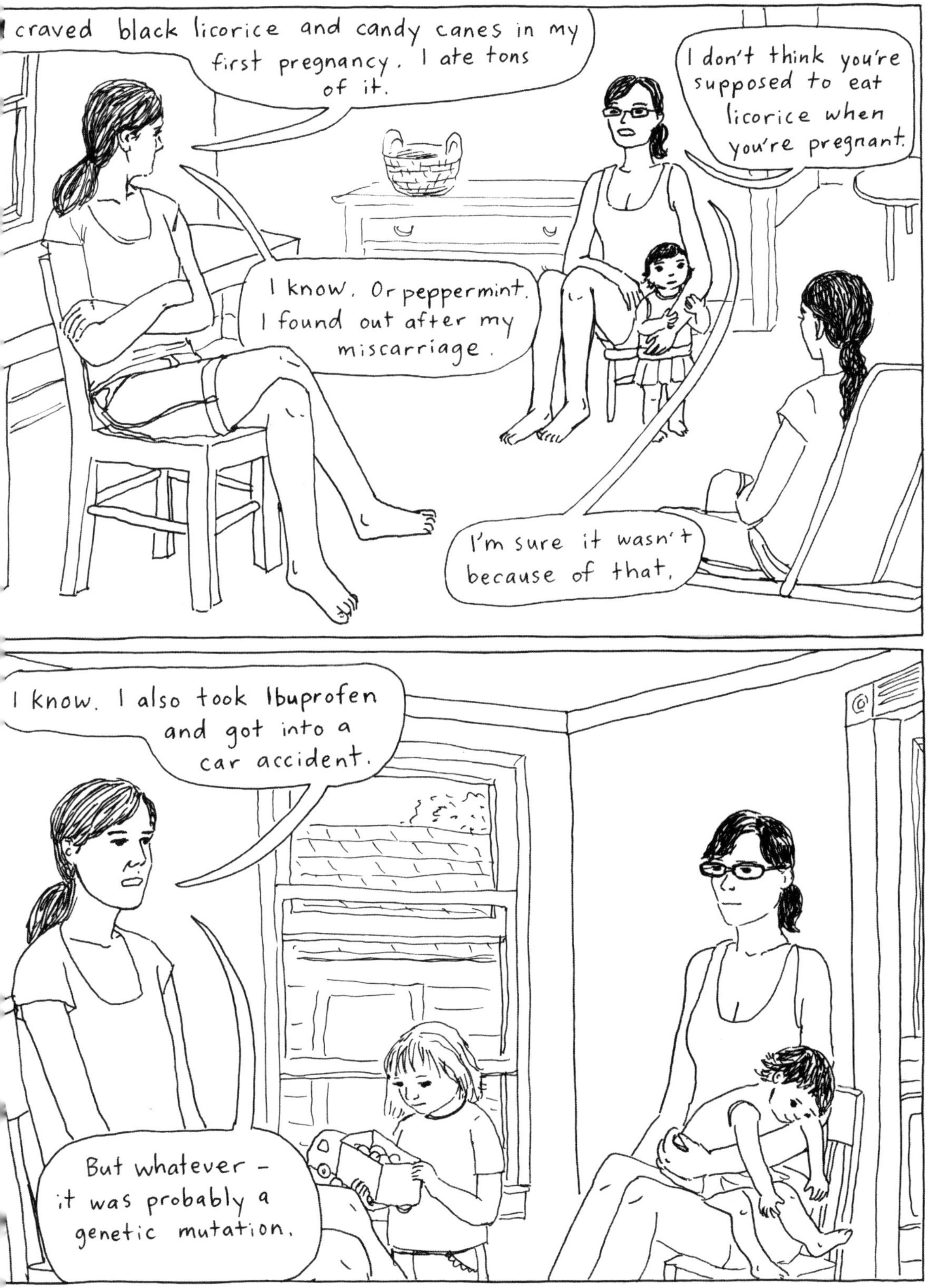
craved black licorice and candy canes in my first pregnancy. I ate tons of it.
I don't think you're supposed to eat licorice when you're pregnant.
I know. Or peppermint. I found out after my miscarriage.
I'm sure it wasn't because of that.
I know. I also took Ibuprofen and got into a car accident.
But whatever - it was probably a genetic mutation.

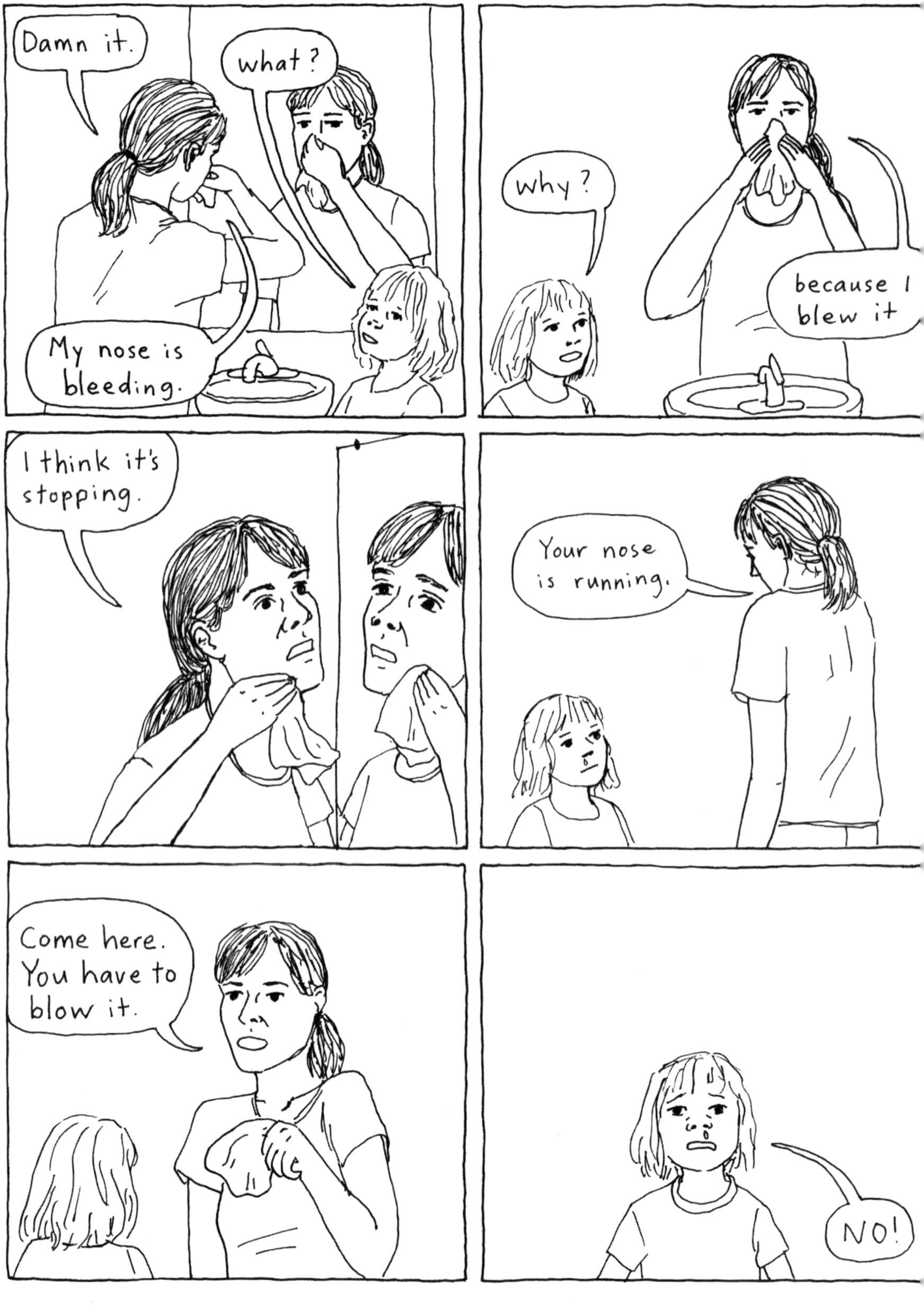
Damn it.
what?
My nose is bleeding.
why?
because I blew it
I think it's stopping.
Your nose is running.
Come here. You have to blow it.
NO!

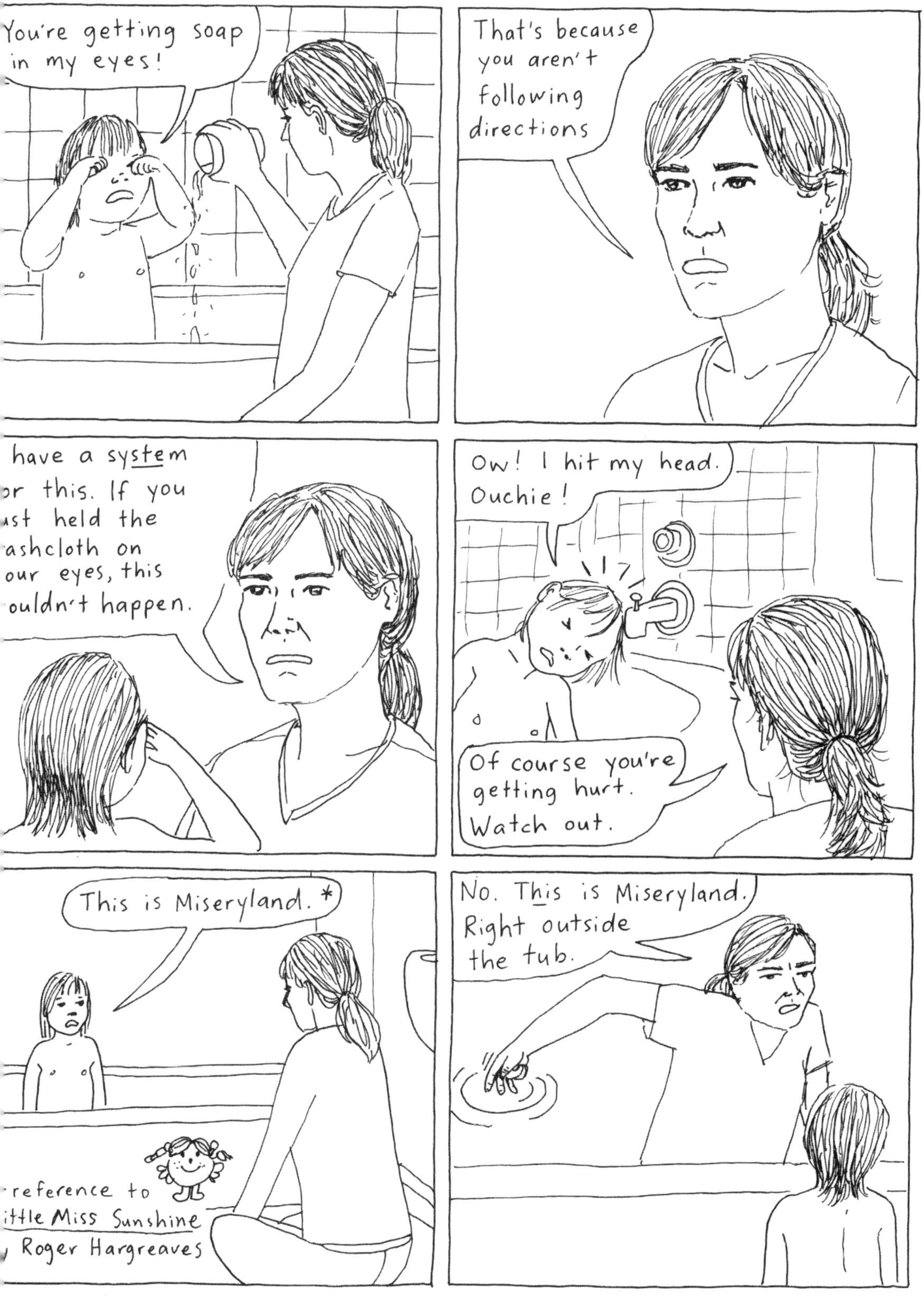
You're getting soap in my eyes!
That's because you aren't following directions
have a system r this. If you ust held the ashcloth on our eyes, this ouldn't happen.
Ow! I hit my head. Ouchie!
Of course you're getting hurt. Watch out.
This is Miseryland. *
No. This is Miseryland. Right outside the tub.
reference to ittle Miss Sunshine Roger Hargreaves

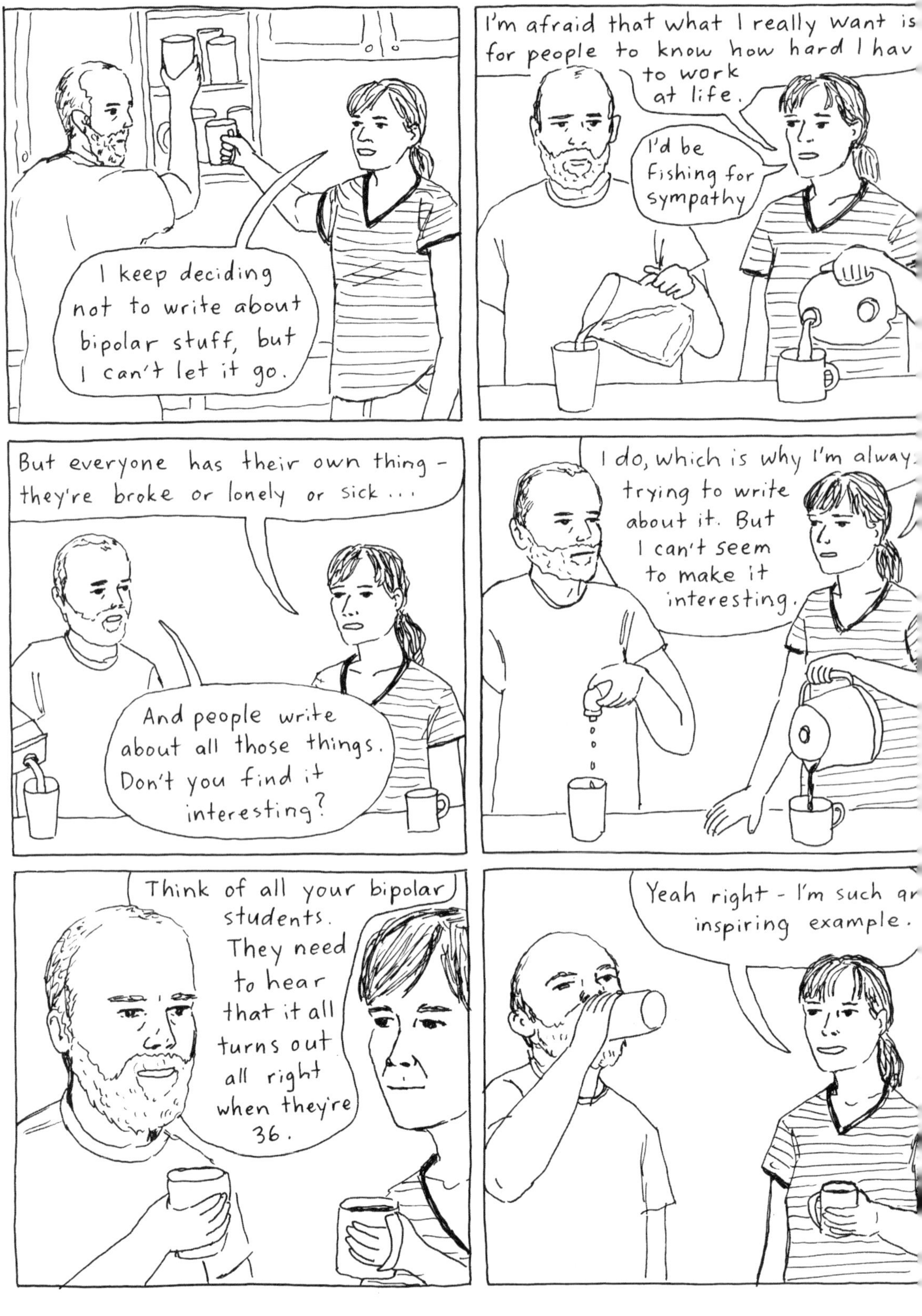
I keep deciding not to write about bipolar stuff, but I can't let it go.
I'm afraid that what I really want is for people to know how hard I hav to work at life.
I'd be fishing for sympathy
But everyone has their own thing - they're broke or lonely or sick . . .
And people write about all those things. Don't you find it interesting?
I do, which is why I'm alway trying to write about it. But I can't seem to make it interesting.
Think of all your bipolar students. They need to hear that it all turns out all right when they're 36.
Yeah right - I'm such ar inspiring example.

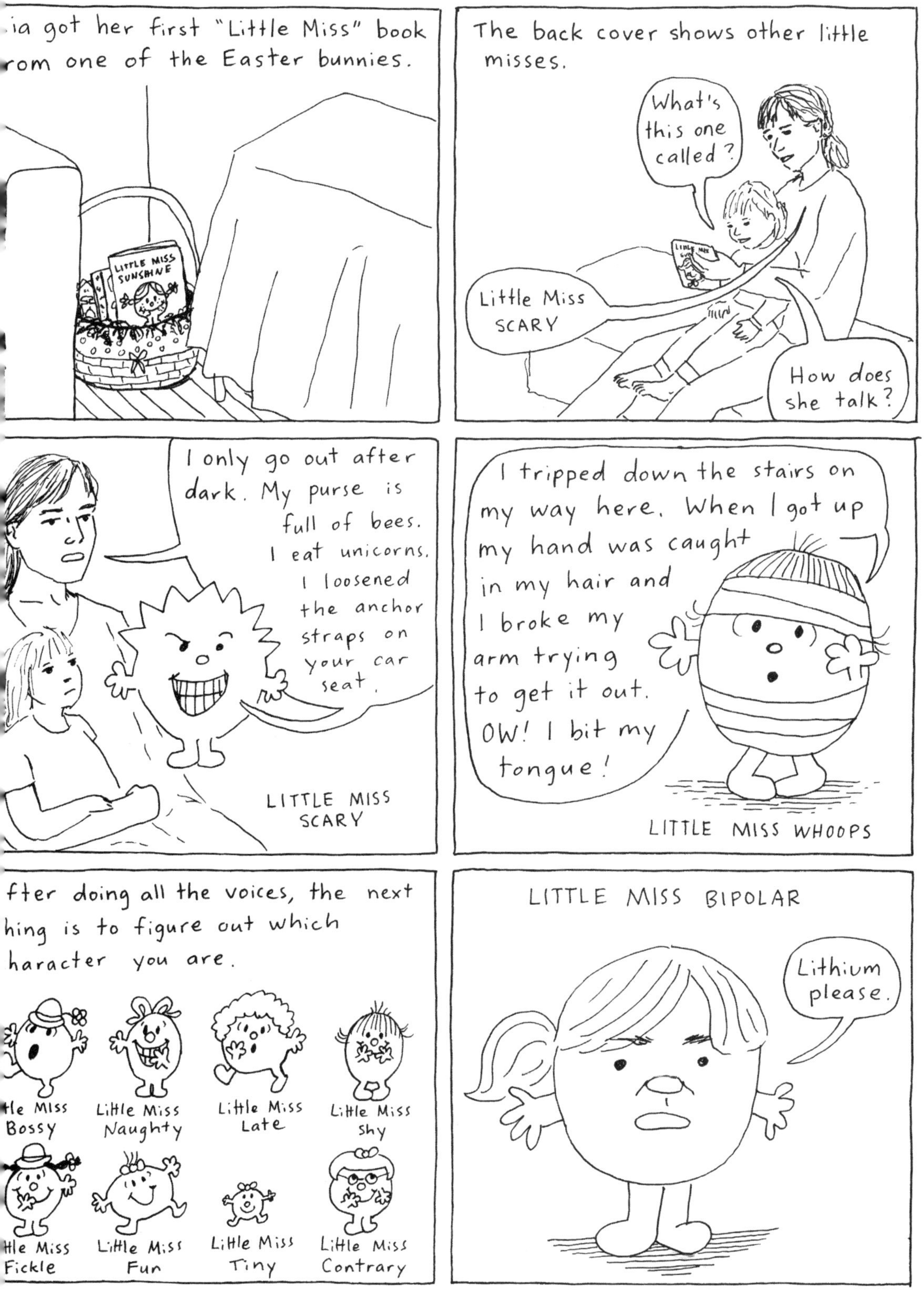
ia got her first "Little Miss" book rom one of the Easter bunnies.
LITTLE MISS SUNSHINE
The back cover shows other little misses.
What's this one called?
Little Miss SCARY
How does she talk?
I only go out after dark. My purse is full of bees. I eat unicorns. I loosened the anchor straps on your car seat.
LITTLE MISS SCARY
I tripped down the stairs on my way here. When I got up my hand was caught in my hair and I broke my arm trying to get it out. OW! I bit my tongue!
LITTLE MISS WHOOPS
fter doing all the voices, the next hing is to figure out which haracter you are.
tle Miss Bossy
Little Miss Naughty
Little Miss Late
Little Miss Shy
tle Miss Fickle
Little Miss Fun
Little Miss Tiny
Little Miss Contrary
LITTLE MISS BIPOLAR
Lithium please.

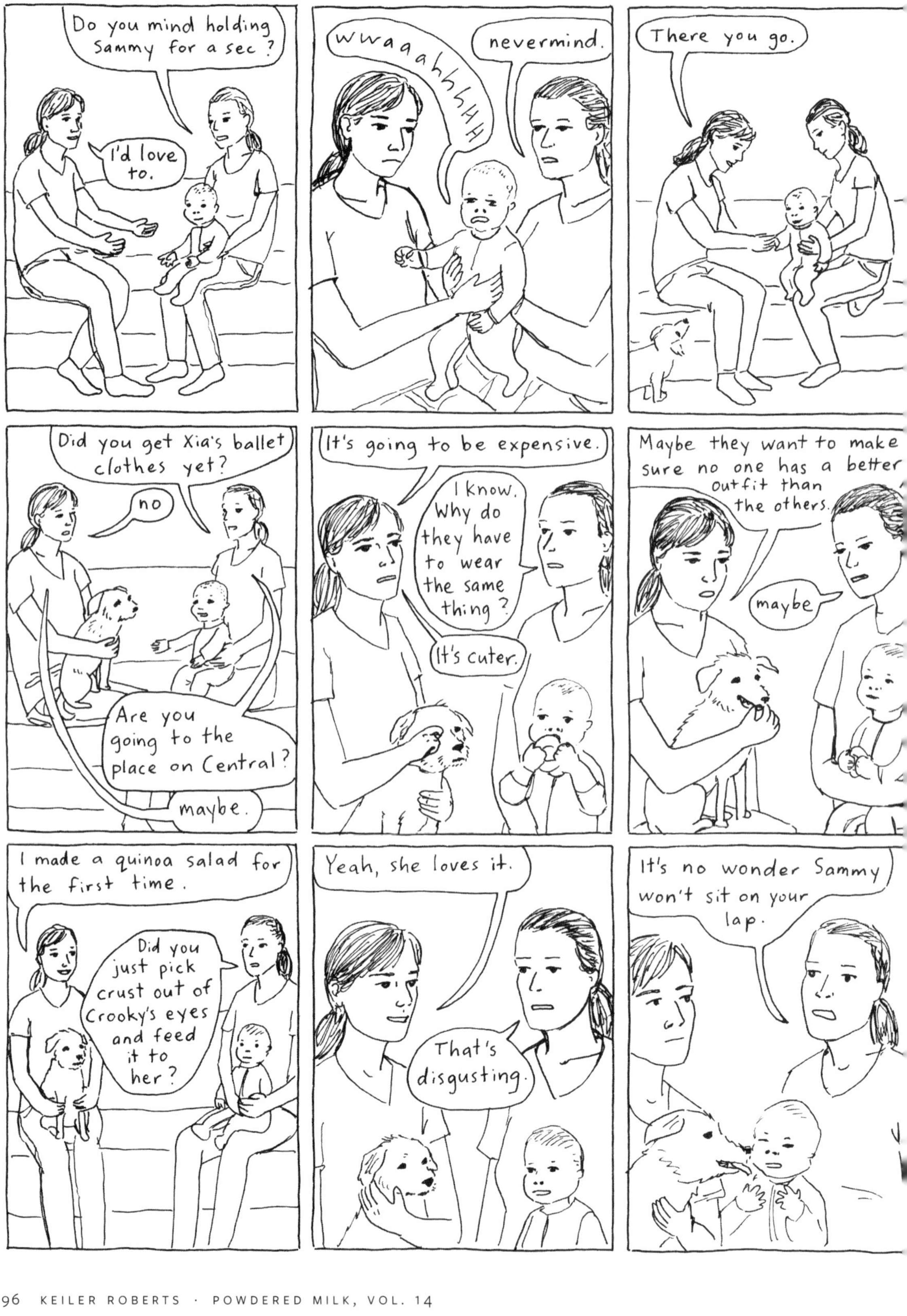
Do you mind holding Sammy for a sec?
I'd love to.
wwaaahhhHH
nevermind.
There you go.
Did you get Xia's ballet clothes yet?
no
Are you going to the place on Central?
maybe.
It's going to be expensive.
I know. Why do they have to wear the same thing?
It's cuter.
Maybe they want to make sure no one has a better outfit than the others.
maybe
I made a quinoa salad for the first time.
Did you just pick crust out of Crooky's eyes and feed it to her?
Yeah, she loves it.
That's disgusting.
It's no wonder Sammy won't sit on your lap.

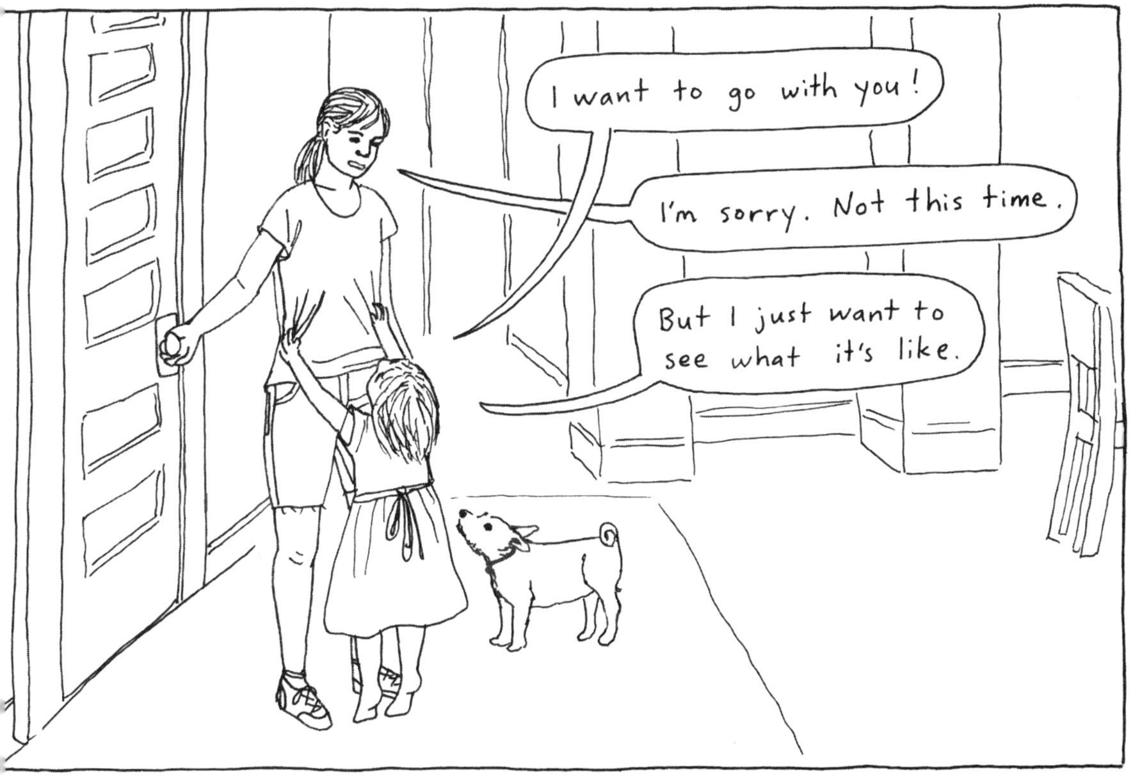
I want to go with you!
I'm sorry. Not this time.
But I just want to see what it's like.

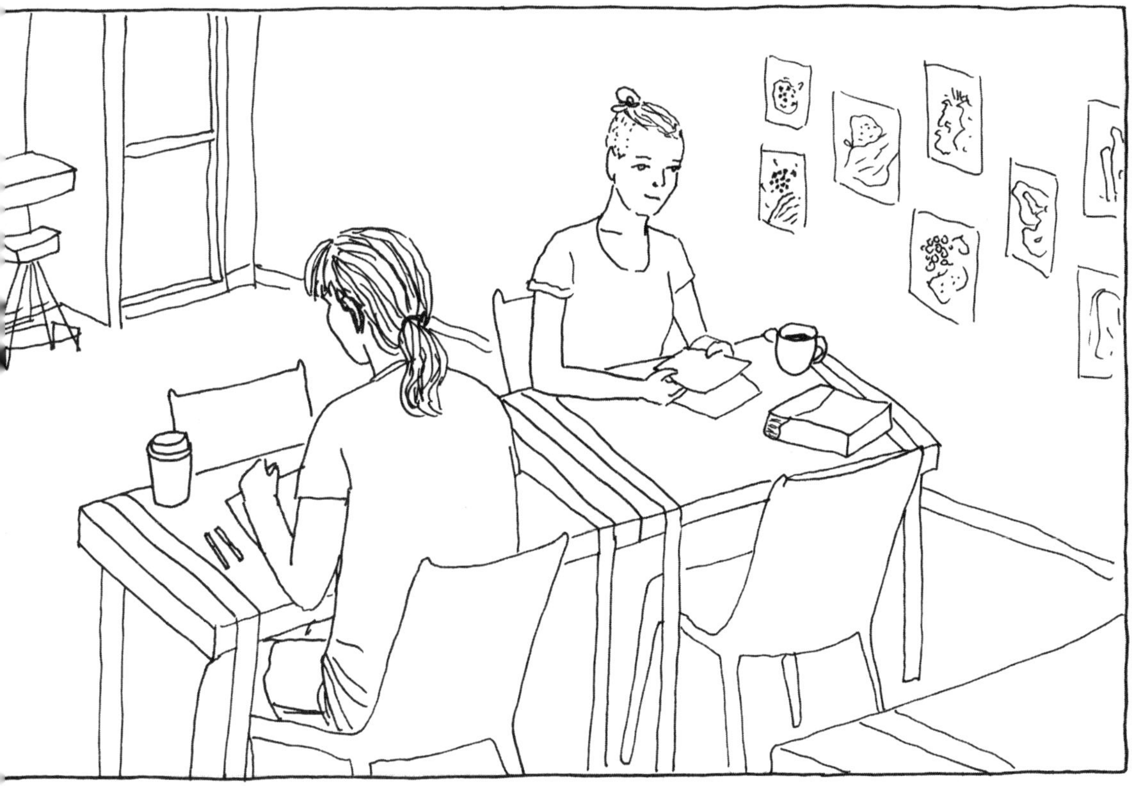

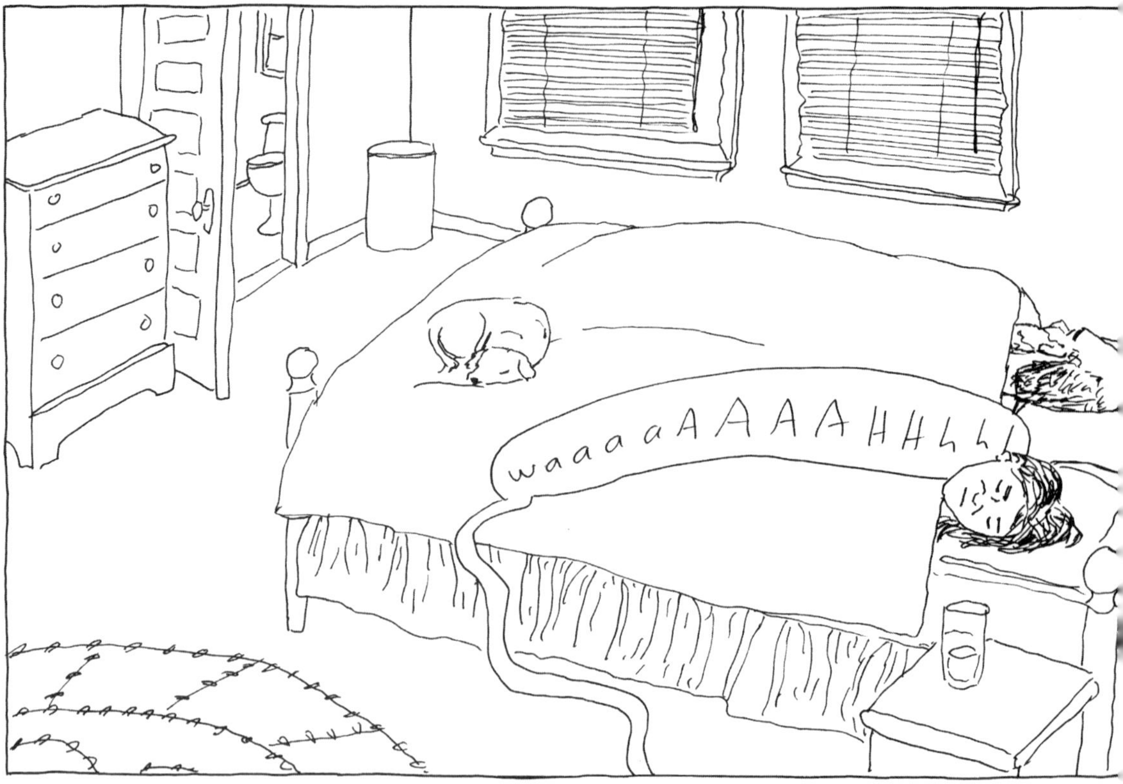
waaaaAAAAAHHhh

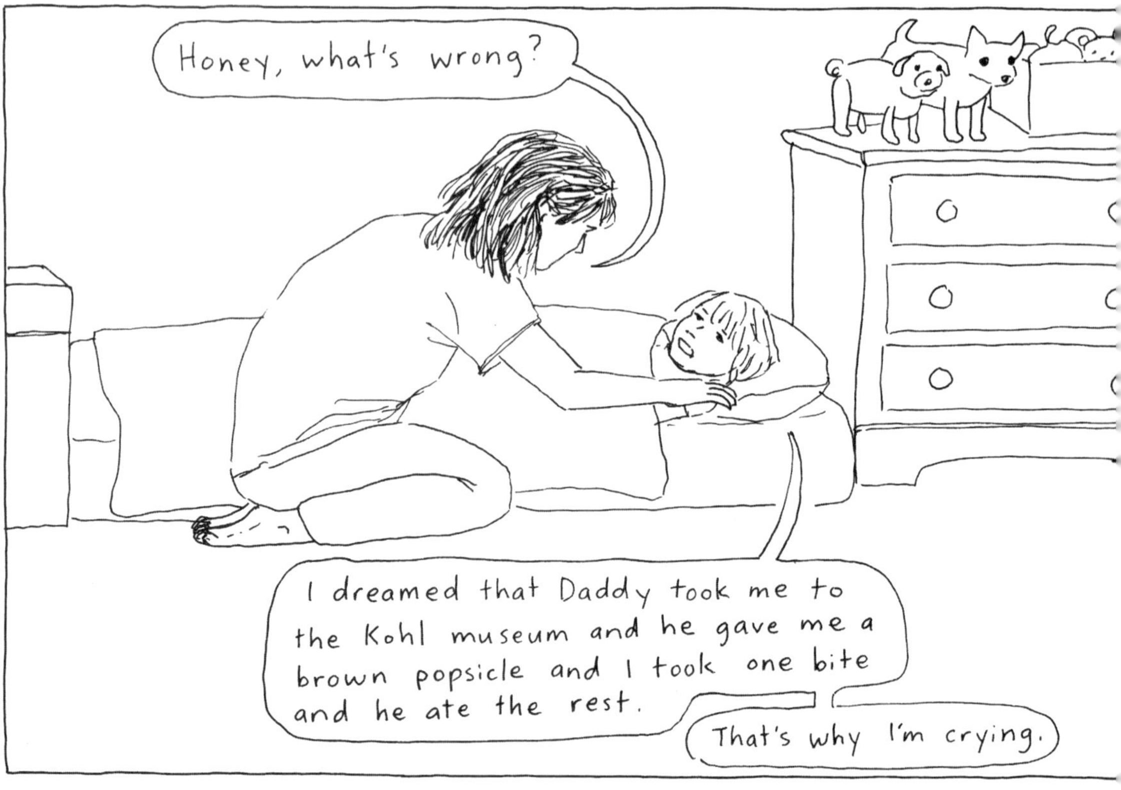
Honey, what's wrong?
I dreamed that Daddy took me to the Kohl museum and he gave me a brown popsicle and I took one bite and he ate the rest.
That's why I'm crying.

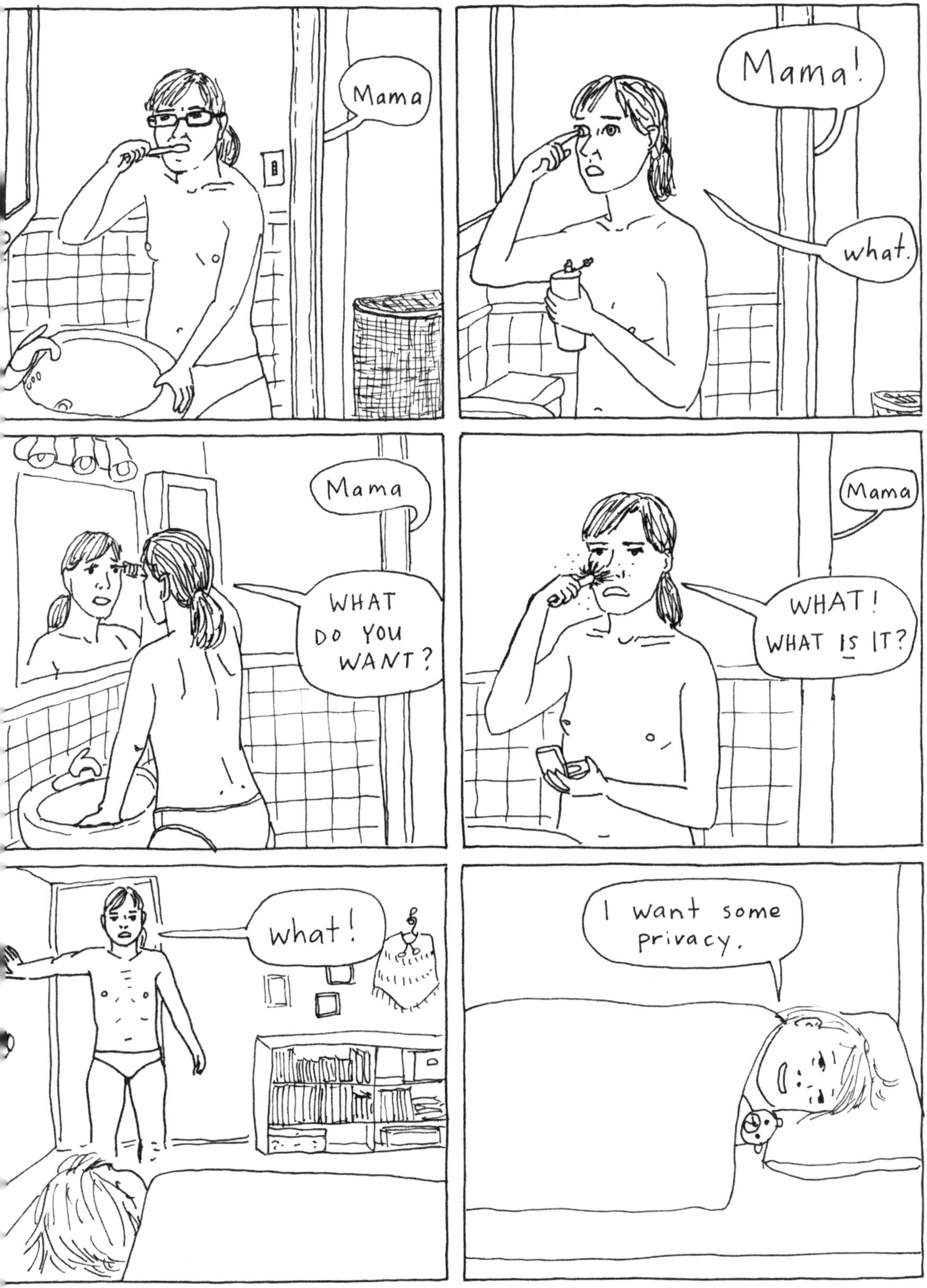
Mama
Mama!
what.
Mama
WHAT DO YOU WANT?
Mama
WHAT! WHAT IS IT?
what!
I want some privacy.

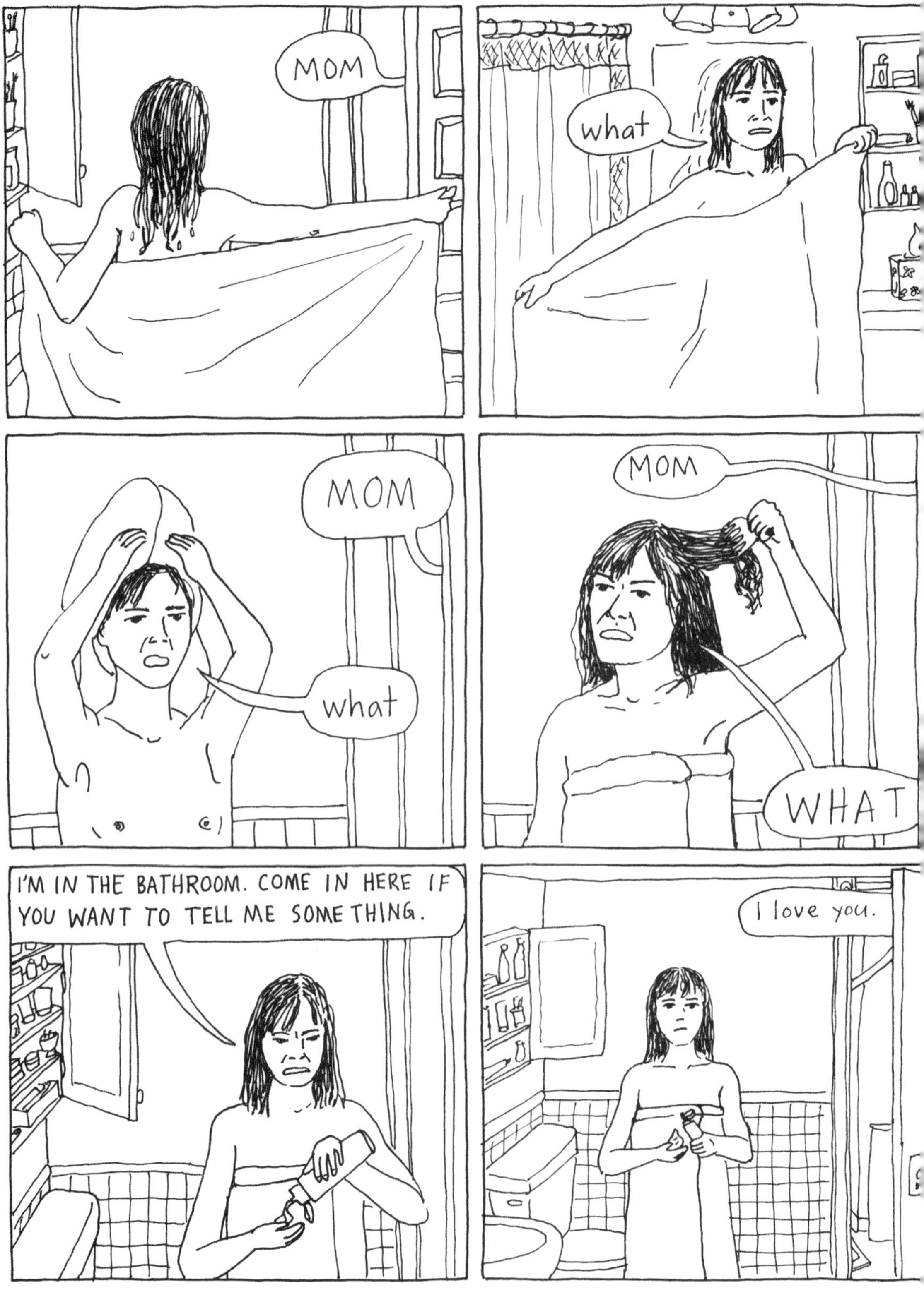
MOM
what
MOM
what
MOM
WHAT
I'M IN THE BATHROOM. COME IN HERE IF YOU WANT TO TELL ME SOMETHING.
I love you.

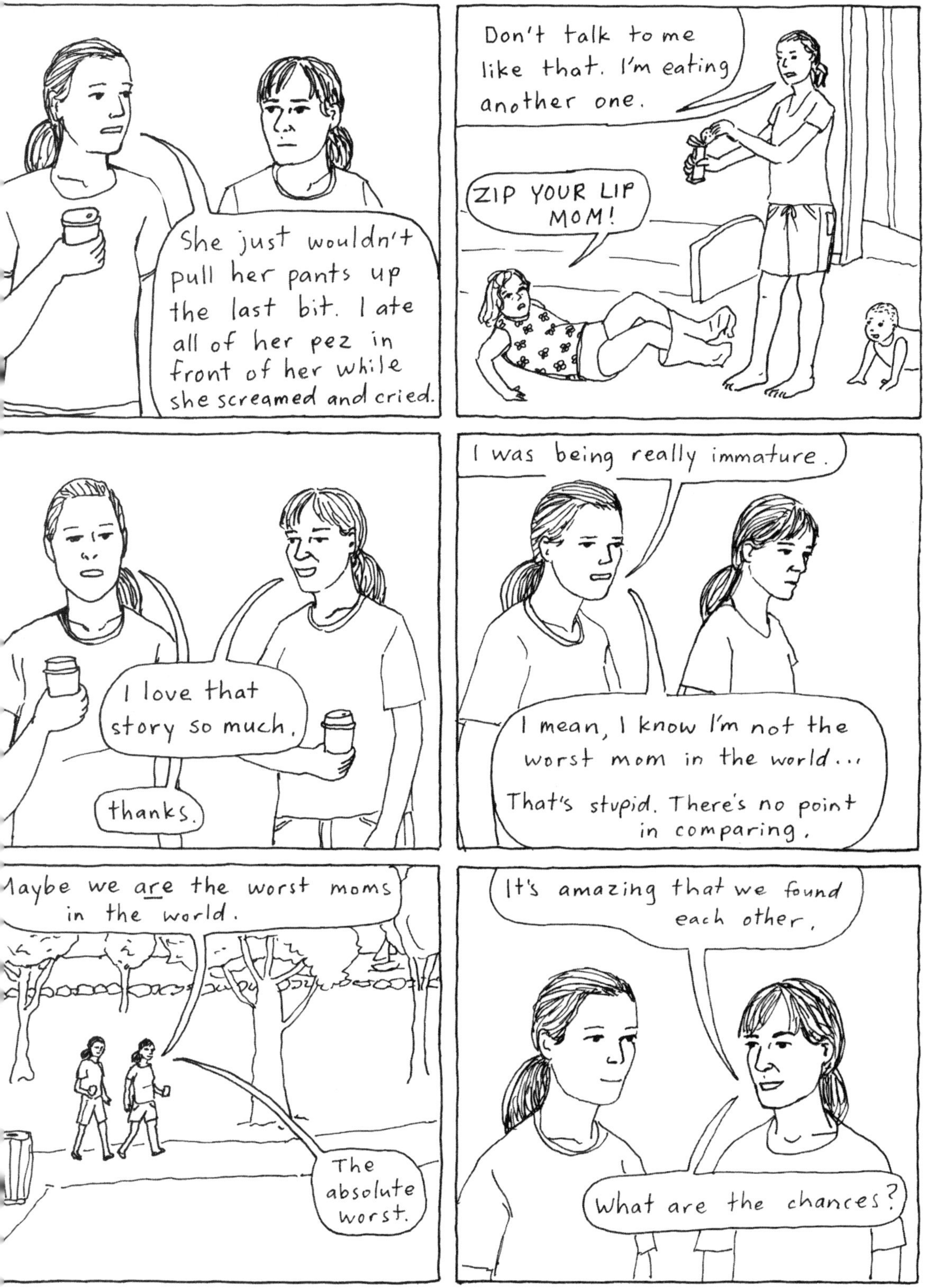
She just wouldn't pull her pants up the last bit. I ate all of her pez in front of her while she screamed and cried.
Don't talk to me like that. I'm eating another one.
ZIP YOUR LIP MOM!
I love that story so much.
thanks.
I was being really immature.
I mean, I know I'm not the worst mom in the world...
That's stupid. There's no point in comparing.
Maybe we are the worst moms in the world.
The absolute worst.
It's amazing that we found each other.
What are the chances?

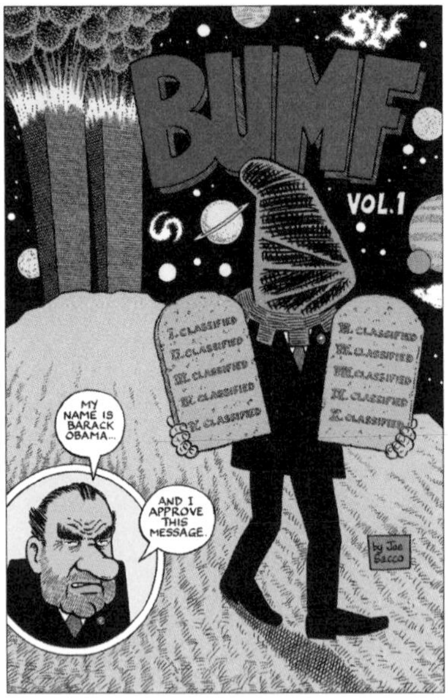
BUMF
VOL.1
I. CLASSIFIED
II. CLASSIFIED
III. CLASSIFIED
IV. CLASSIFIED
V. CLASSIFIED
VI. CLASSIFIED
VII. CLASSIFIED
VIII. CLASSIFIED
IX. CLASSIFIED
X. CLASSIFIED
MY NAME IS BARACK OBAMA...
AND I APPROVE THIS MESSAGE.
by Joe Sacco

# Milk

## JOE SACCO

*originally published in*

Bumf, Vol. 1
FANTAGRAPHICS
6.625 × 10.5 inches • 100 pages

## Biography

Joe Sacco is mostly known for doing comics journalism. *Bumf* is his return to satire.

## Statement

This excerpt is part of my book *Bumf*. *Bumf* is about our twenty-first-century world. I don't think we're going to make it.

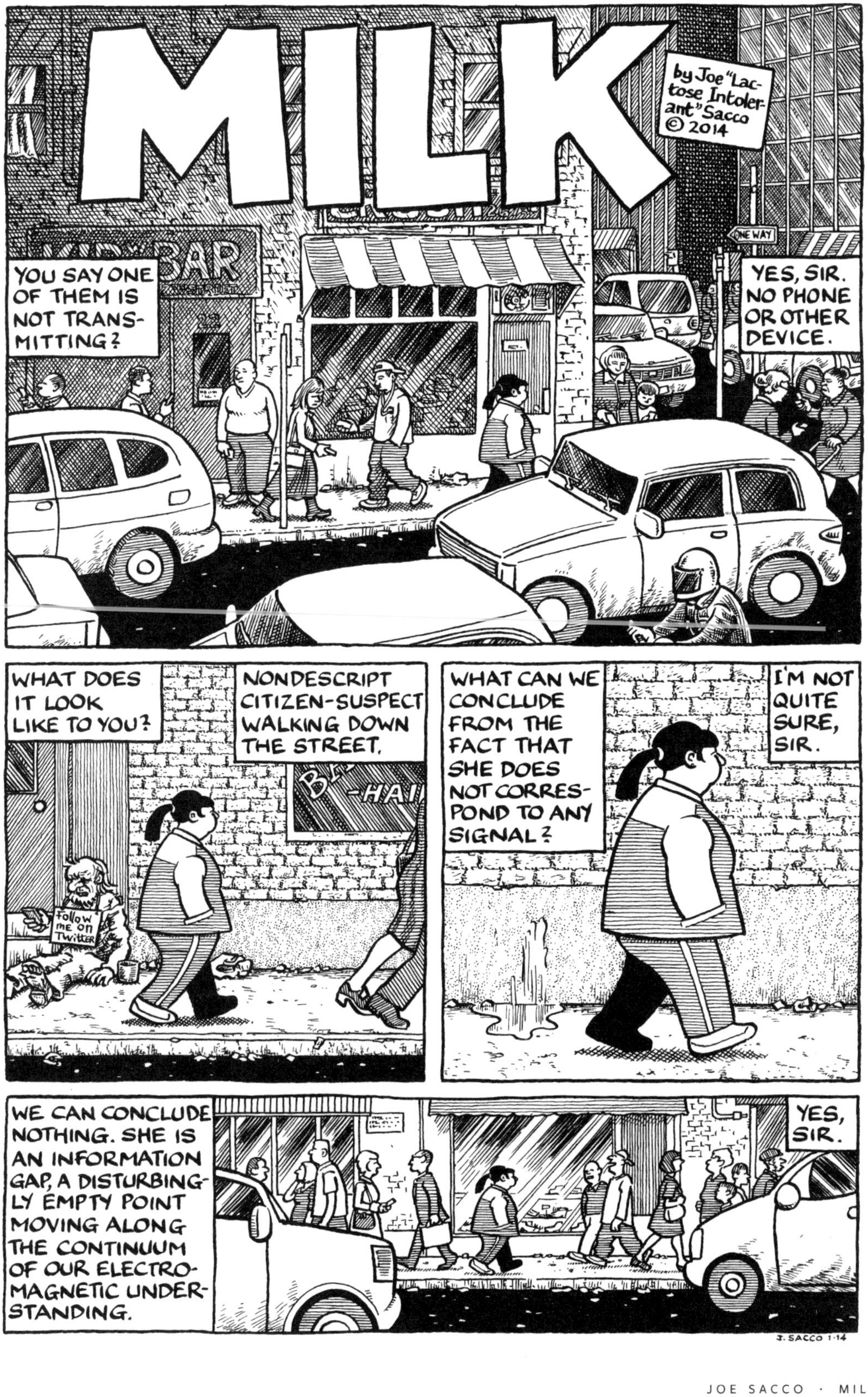
MILK
by Joe "Lactose Intolerant" Sacco © 2014
BAR
ONE WAY
YOU SAY ONE OF THEM IS NOT TRANSMITTING?
YES, SIR. NO PHONE OR OTHER DEVICE.
WHAT DOES IT LOOK LIKE TO YOU?
NONDESCRIPT CITIZEN-SUSPECT WALKING DOWN THE STREET.
Follow me on Twitter
WHAT CAN WE CONCLUDE FROM THE FACT THAT SHE DOES NOT CORRESPOND TO ANY SIGNAL?
I'M NOT QUITE SURE, SIR.
WE CAN CONCLUDE NOTHING. SHE IS AN INFORMATION GAP, A DISTURBINGLY EMPTY POINT MOVING ALONG THE CONTINUUM OF OUR ELECTROMAGNETIC UNDERSTANDING.
YES, SIR.
J. SACCO 1·14

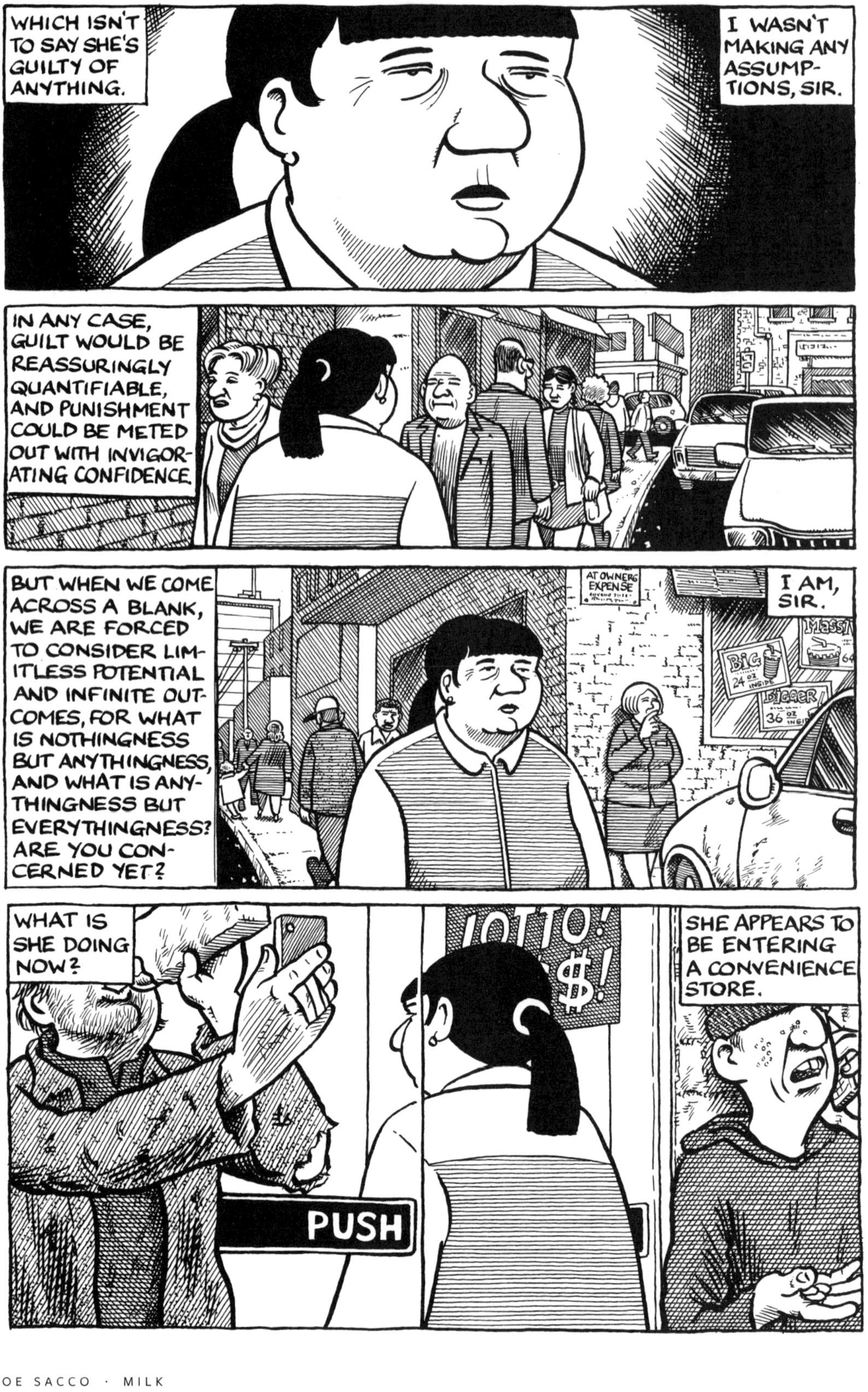
WHICH ISN'T TO SAY SHE'S GUILTY OF ANYTHING.
I WASN'T MAKING ANY ASSUMPTIONS, SIR.
IN ANY CASE, GUILT WOULD BE REASSURINGLY QUANTIFIABLE, AND PUNISHMENT COULD BE METED OUT WITH INVIGORATING CONFIDENCE.
BUT WHEN WE COME ACROSS A BLANK, WE ARE FORCED TO CONSIDER LIMITLESS POTENTIAL AND INFINITE OUTCOMES, FOR WHAT IS NOTHINGNESS BUT ANYTHINGNESS, AND WHAT IS ANYTHINGNESS BUT EVERYTHINGNESS? ARE YOU CONCERNED YET?
AT OWNERS EXPENSE
I AM, SIR.
WHAT IS SHE DOING NOW?
PUSH
SHE APPEARS TO BE ENTERING A CONVENIENCE STORE.

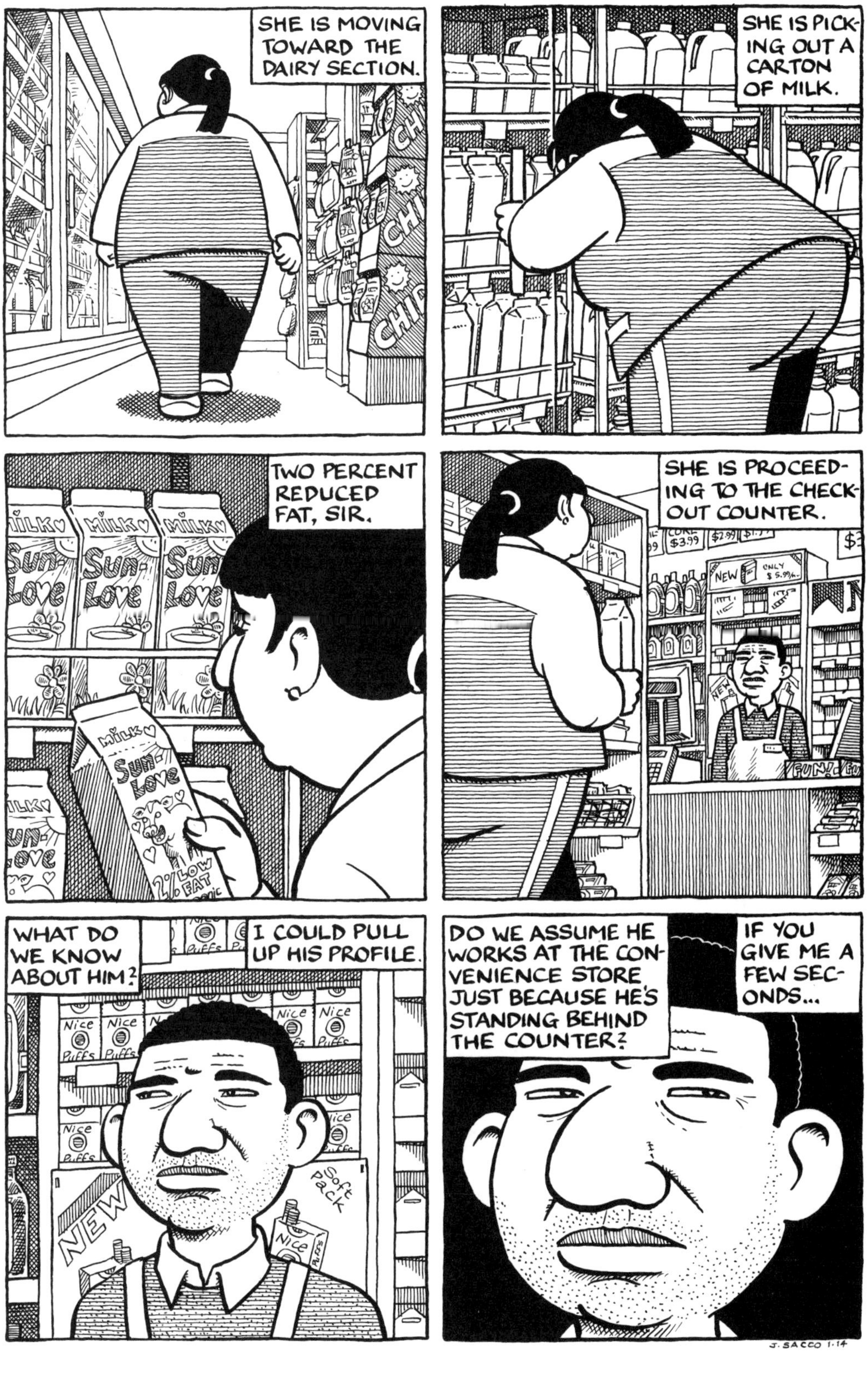
SHE IS MOVING TOWARD THE DAIRY SECTION.
SHE IS PICKING OUT A CARTON OF MILK.
TWO PERCENT REDUCED FAT, SIR.
MILK
Sun-Love
2% LOW FAT
SHE IS PROCEEDING TO THE CHECKOUT COUNTER.
NEW
WHAT DO WE KNOW ABOUT HIM?
I COULD PULL UP HIS PROFILE.
Nice Puffs
Soft Pack
NEW
DO WE ASSUME HE WORKS AT THE CONVENIENCE STORE JUST BECAUSE HE'S STANDING BEHIND THE COUNTER?
IF YOU GIVE ME A FEW SECONDS...
J. SACCO 1.14

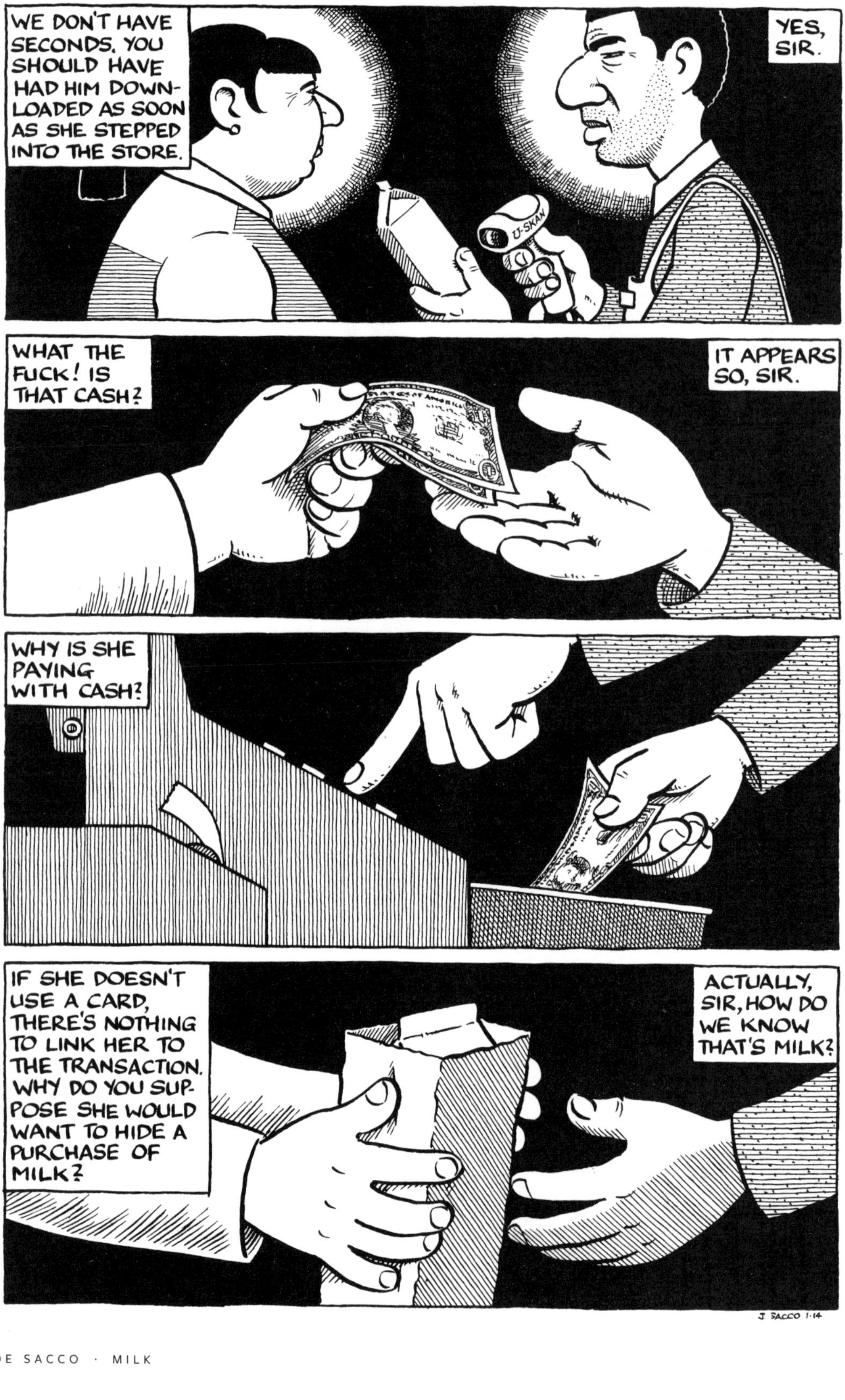
WE DON'T HAVE SECONDS. YOU SHOULD HAVE HAD HIM DOWN-LOADED AS SOON AS SHE STEPPED INTO THE STORE.
YES, SIR.
U-SKAN
WHAT THE FUCK! IS THAT CASH?
IT APPEARS SO, SIR.
WHY IS SHE PAYING WITH CASH?
IF SHE DOESN'T USE A CARD, THERE'S NOTHING TO LINK HER TO THE TRANSACTION. WHY DO YOU SUP-POSE SHE WOULD WANT TO HIDE A PURCHASE OF MILK?
ACTUALLY, SIR, HOW DO WE KNOW THAT'S MILK?
J. SACCO 1·14

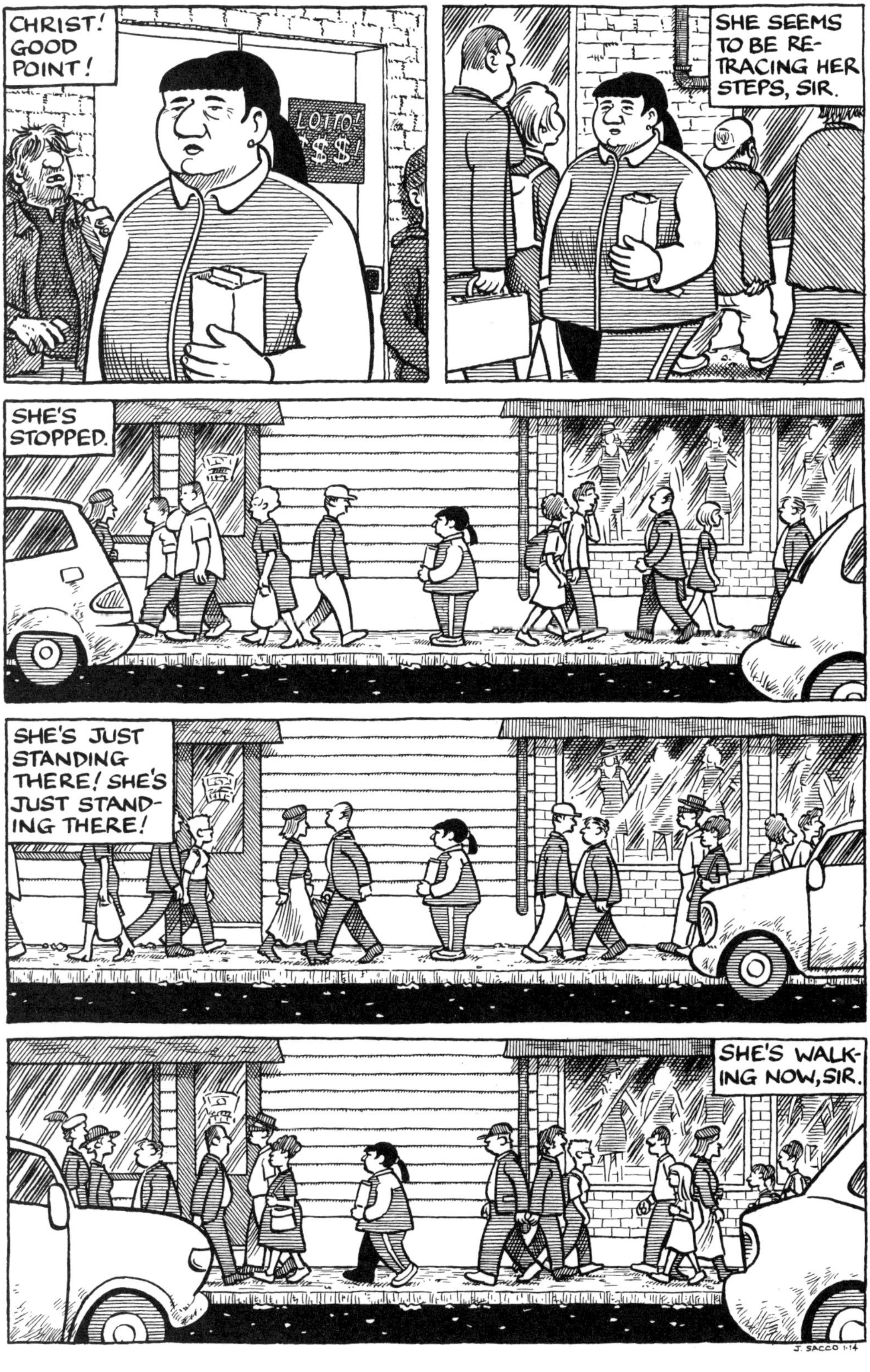
CHRIST! GOOD POINT!
LOTTO! $$$!
SHE SEEMS TO BE RE-TRACING HER STEPS, SIR.
SHE'S STOPPED.
SHE'S JUST STANDING THERE! SHE'S JUST STAND-ING THERE!
SHE'S WALK-ING NOW, SIR.
J. SACCO 1·14

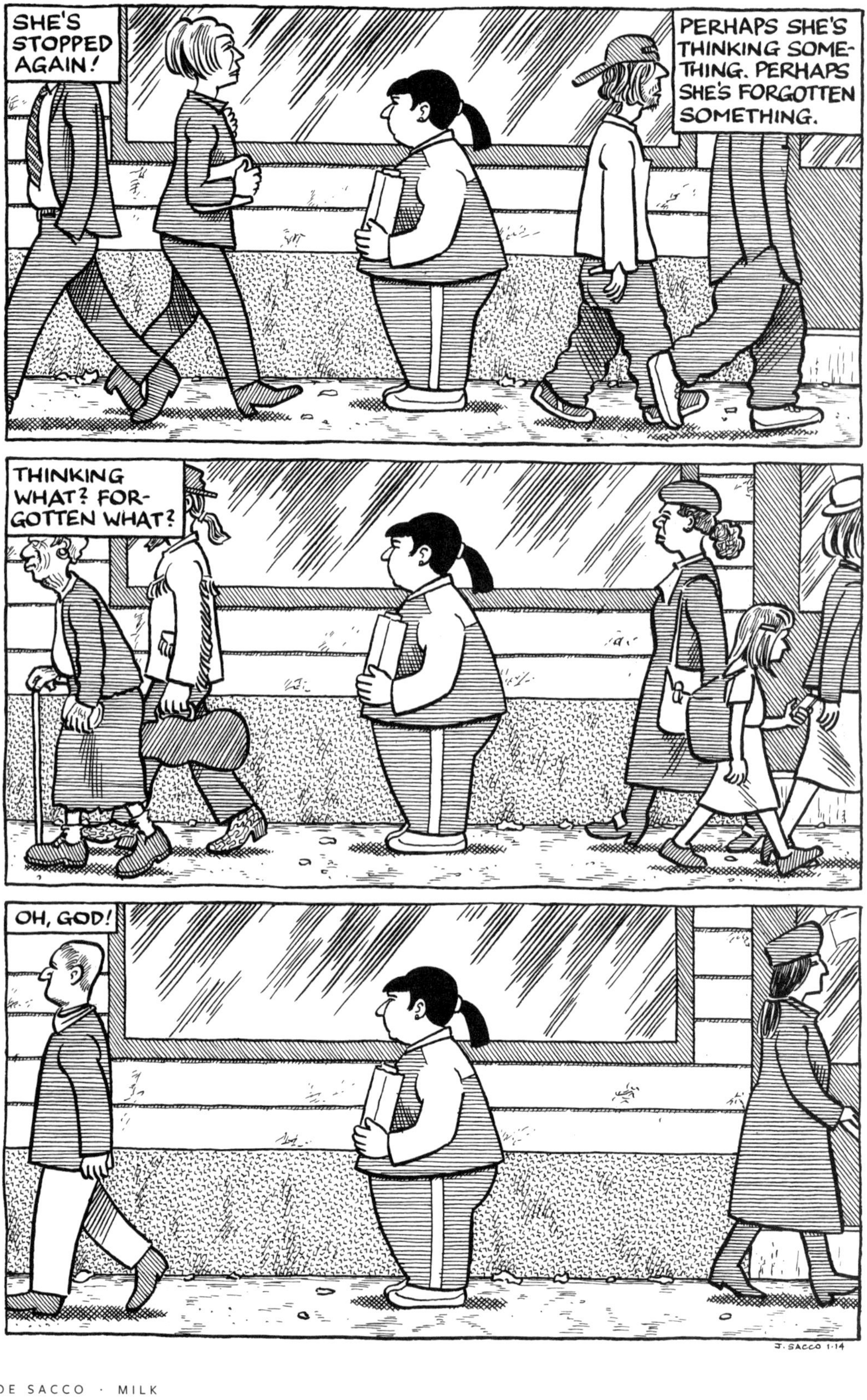
SHE'S STOPPED AGAIN!
PERHAPS SHE'S THINKING SOME-THING. PERHAPS SHE'S FORGOTTEN SOMETHING.
THINKING WHAT? FOR-GOTTEN WHAT?
OH, GOD!
J. SACCO 1·14

# The Dishrack

## GABRIELLE BELL

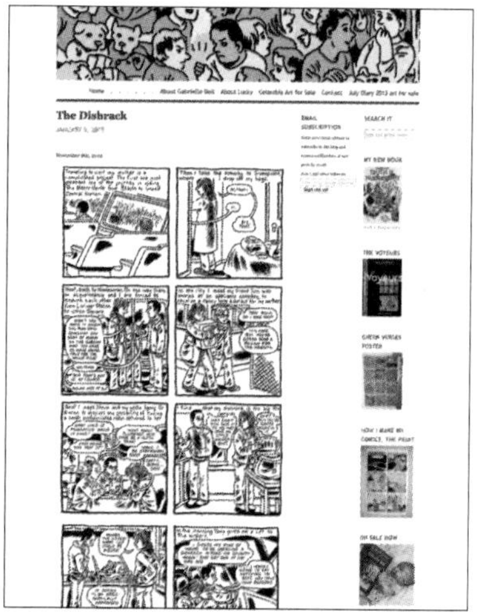
The Dishrack

*originally published at*

gabriellebell.com

SELF-PUBLISHED

digital

## Biography

Gabrielle Bell was born in London, England, and raised in California. She is the author of five books, including *The Voyeurs* and *Truth Is Fragmentary*. Her work has appeared in the *Guardian*, *VICE*, *McSweeney's*, *The Believer*, *Flare*, and *The Big Issue*. The title story of her 2009 collection, *Cecil and Jordan in New York*, was adapted for the screen by Bell and Michel Gondry for the triptych film *Tokyo!*. She lives in Beacon, New York.
gabriellebell.com

## Statement

This comic was written on an airplane. It was about the long journey (train, subway, car, plane, train, bus, truck) from my little town in northern New York to my old home in a remote area of northern California. Since I was only halfway there, I had to make up the future parts of the story, based on my past trips. Then when I arrived I adjusted the "future" part of the story according to how it actually went. Funnily enough, just as I was finishing the comic I was invited to participate in a comics show whose theme was time.

# Tuesday, November 11th

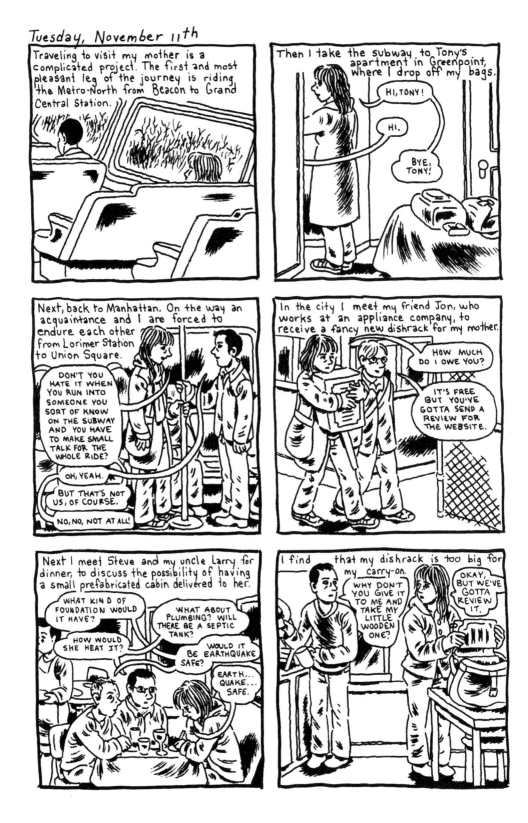

Traveling to visit my mother is a complicated project. The first and most pleasant leg of the journey is riding the Metro-North from Beacon to Grand Central Station.

Then I take the subway to Tony's apartment in Greenpoint, where I drop off my bags.

HI, TONY!

HI.

BYE, TONY!

Next, back to Manhattan. On the way an acquaintance and I are forced to endure each other from Lorimer Station to Union Square.

DON'T YOU HATE IT WHEN YOU RUN INTO SOMEONE YOU SORT OF KNOW ON THE SUBWAY AND YOU HAVE TO MAKE SMALL TALK FOR THE WHOLE RIDE?

OH, YEAH.

BUT THAT'S NOT US, OF COURSE.

NO, NO, NOT AT ALL!

In the city I meet my friend Jon, who works at an appliance company, to receive a fancy new dishrack for my mother.

HOW MUCH DO I OWE YOU?

IT'S FREE BUT YOU'VE GOTTA SEND A REVIEW FOR THE WEBSITE.

Next I meet Steve and my uncle Larry for dinner, to discuss the possibility of having a small prefabricated cabin delivered to her.

WHAT KIND OF FOUNDATION WOULD IT HAVE?

WHAT ABOUT PLUMBING? WILL THERE BE A SEPTIC TANK?

HOW WOULD SHE HEAT IT?

WOULD IT BE EARTHQUAKE SAFE?

EARTH... QUAKE... SAFE.

I find that my dishrack is too big for my carry-on.

WHY DON'T YOU GIVE IT TO ME AND TAKE MY LITTLE WOODEN ONE?

OKAY, BUT WE'VE GOTTA REVIEW IT.

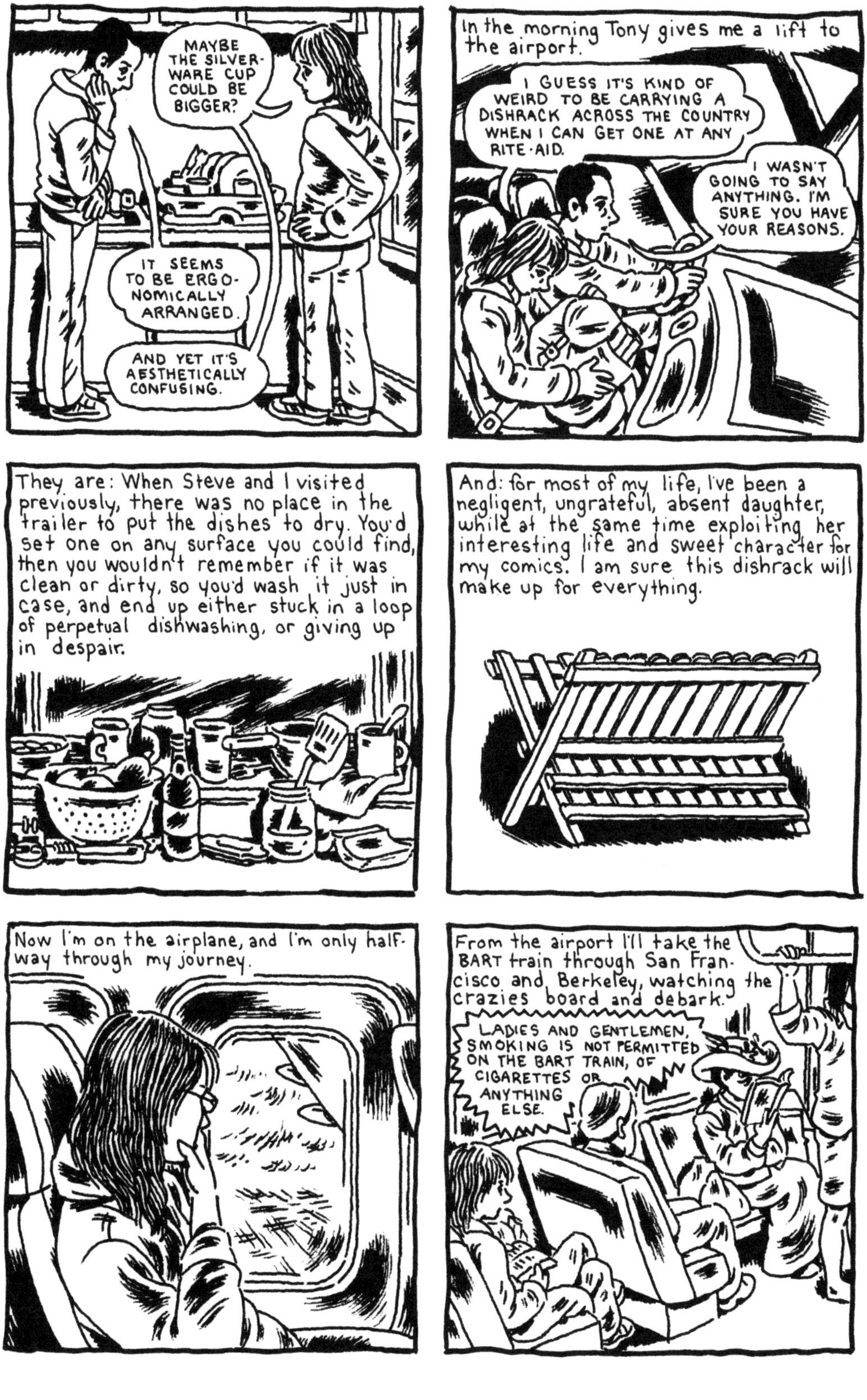
MAYBE THE SILVERWARE CUP COULD BE BIGGER?
IT SEEMS TO BE ERGONOMICALLY ARRANGED.
AND YET IT'S AESTHETICALLY CONFUSING.
In the morning Tony gives me a lift to the airport.
I GUESS IT'S KIND OF WEIRD TO BE CARRYING A DISHRACK ACROSS THE COUNTRY WHEN I CAN GET ONE AT ANY RITE-AID.
I WASN'T GOING TO SAY ANYTHING. I'M SURE YOU HAVE YOUR REASONS.
They are: When Steve and I visited previously, there was no place in the trailer to put the dishes to dry. You'd set one on any surface you could find, then you wouldn't remember if it was clean or dirty, so you'd wash it just in case, and end up either stuck in a loop of perpetual dishwashing, or giving up in despair.
And: for most of my life, I've been a negligent, ungrateful, absent daughter, while at the same time exploiting her interesting life and sweet character for my comics. I am sure this dishrack will make up for everything.
Now I'm on the airplane, and I'm only halfway through my journey.
From the airport I'll take the BART train through San Francisco and Berkeley, watching the crazies board and debark.
LADIES AND GENTLEMEN, SMOKING IS NOT PERMITTED ON THE BART TRAIN, OF CIGARETTES OR ANYTHING ELSE.

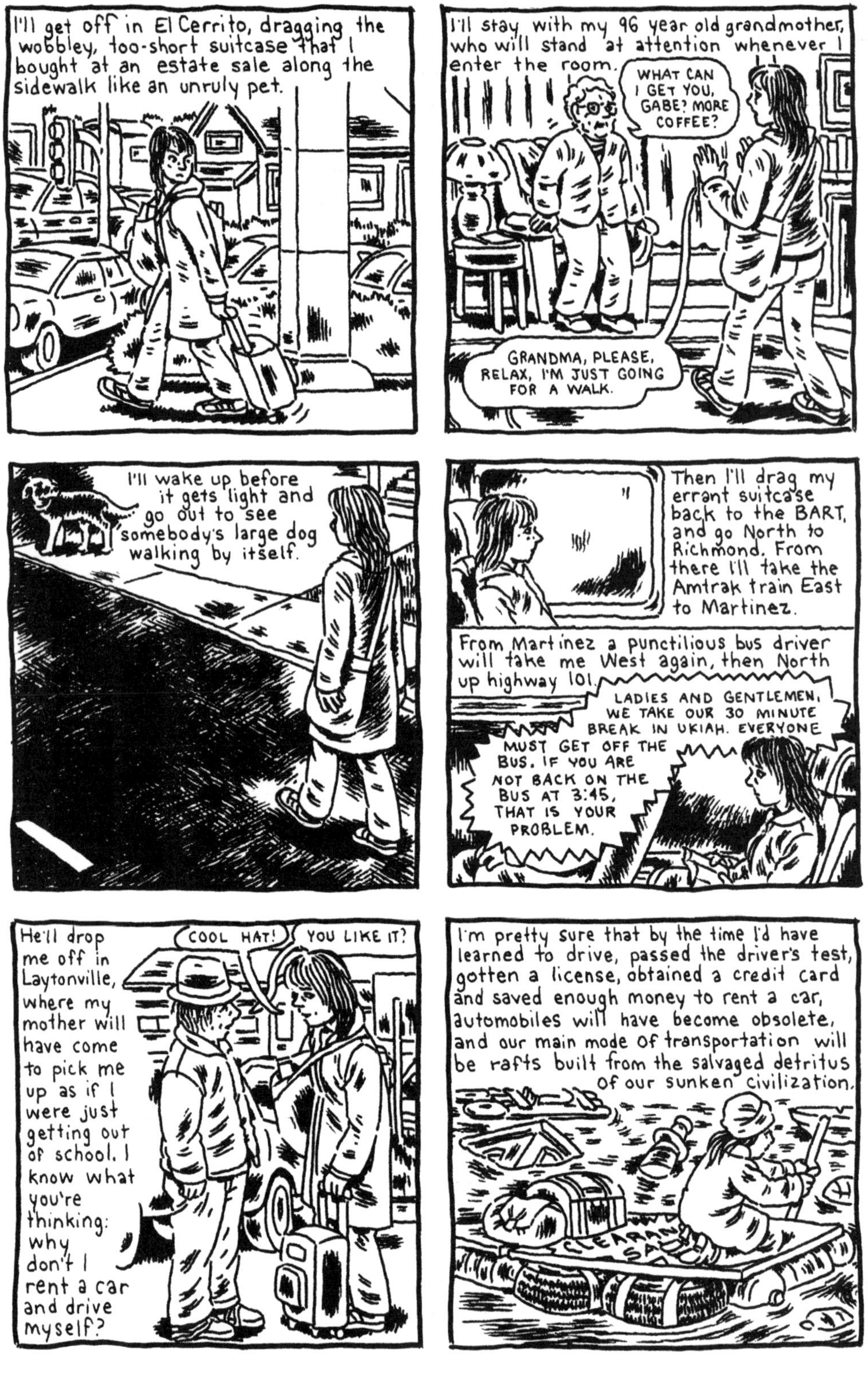
I'll get off in El Cerrito, dragging the wobbley, too-short suitcase that I bought at an estate sale along the sidewalk like an unruly pet.
I'll stay with my 96 year old grandmother, who will stand at attention whenever I enter the room.
WHAT CAN I GET YOU, GABE? MORE COFFEE?
GRANDMA, PLEASE, RELAX, I'M JUST GOING FOR A WALK.
I'll wake up before it gets light and go out to see somebody's large dog walking by itself.
Then I'll drag my errant suitcase back to the BART, and go North to Richmond. From there I'll take the Amtrak train East to Martinez.
From Martinez a punctilious bus driver will take me West again, then North up highway 101.
LADIES AND GENTLEMEN, WE TAKE OUR 30 MINUTE BREAK IN UKIAH. EVERYONE MUST GET OFF THE BUS. IF YOU ARE NOT BACK ON THE BUS AT 3:45, THAT IS YOUR PROBLEM.
He'll drop me off in Laytonville, where my mother will have come to pick me up as if I were just getting out of school. I know what you're thinking: why don't I rent a car and drive myself?
COOL HAT!
YOU LIKE IT?
I'm pretty sure that by the time I'd have learned to drive, passed the driver's test, gotten a license, obtained a credit card and saved enough money to rent a car, automobiles will have become obsolete, and our main mode of transportation will be rafts built from the salvaged detritus of our sunken civilization.

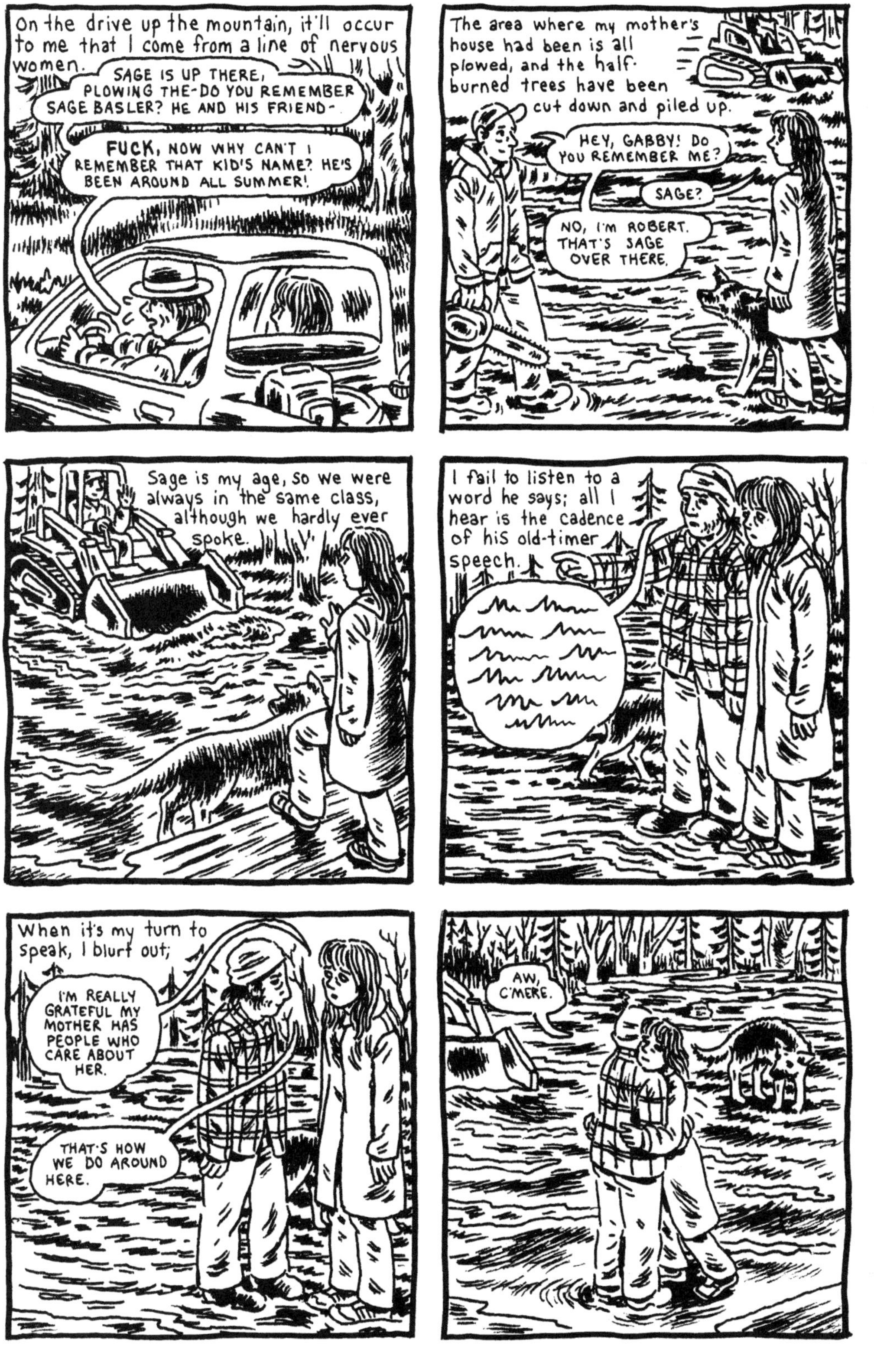
On the drive up the mountain, it'll occur to me that I come from a line of nervous women.
SAGE IS UP THERE, PLOWING THE- DO YOU REMEMBER SAGE BASLER? HE AND HIS FRIEND-
FUCK, NOW WHY CAN'T I REMEMBER THAT KID'S NAME? HE'S BEEN AROUND ALL SUMMER!
The area where my mother's house had been is all plowed, and the half-burned trees have been cut down and piled up.
HEY, GABBY! DO YOU REMEMBER ME?
SAGE?
NO, I'M ROBERT. THAT'S SAGE OVER THERE.
Sage is my age, so we were always in the same class, although we hardly ever spoke.
I fail to listen to a word he says; all I hear is the cadence of his old-timer speech.
When it's my turn to speak, I blurt out;
I'M REALLY GRATEFUL MY MOTHER HAS PEOPLE WHO CARE ABOUT HER.
THAT'S HOW WE DO AROUND HERE.
AW, C'MERE.

HELLO
SYLLABUS
LYNDA BARRY
FALL SEMESTER
SPRING SEMESTER
NOTES FROM AN ACCIDENTAL PROFESSOR
WHO IS THE TEACHER?

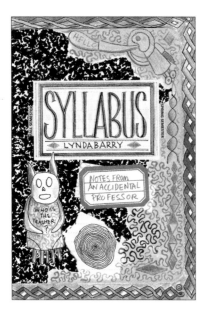

# Syllabus (*Excerpt*)

LYNDA BARRY

*excerpted from*

Syllabus

DRAWN AND QUARTERLY

7.5 × 9.8 • 200 pages

## Biography

Lynda Barry has worked as a painter, cartoonist, writer, illustrator, playwright, editor, commentator, and teacher and found that they are all very much alike. She is the author of the acclaimed graphic novel *One! Hundred! Demons!*, the cartoonist behind the long-running *Ernie Pook's Comeek*, and the author of the creative how-to memoir comic books *What It Is* and *Picture This*. She lives in Wisconsin, where she is an assistant professor of art and a Discovery Fellow at the University of Wisconsin-Madison. thenearsightedmonkey.tumblr.com

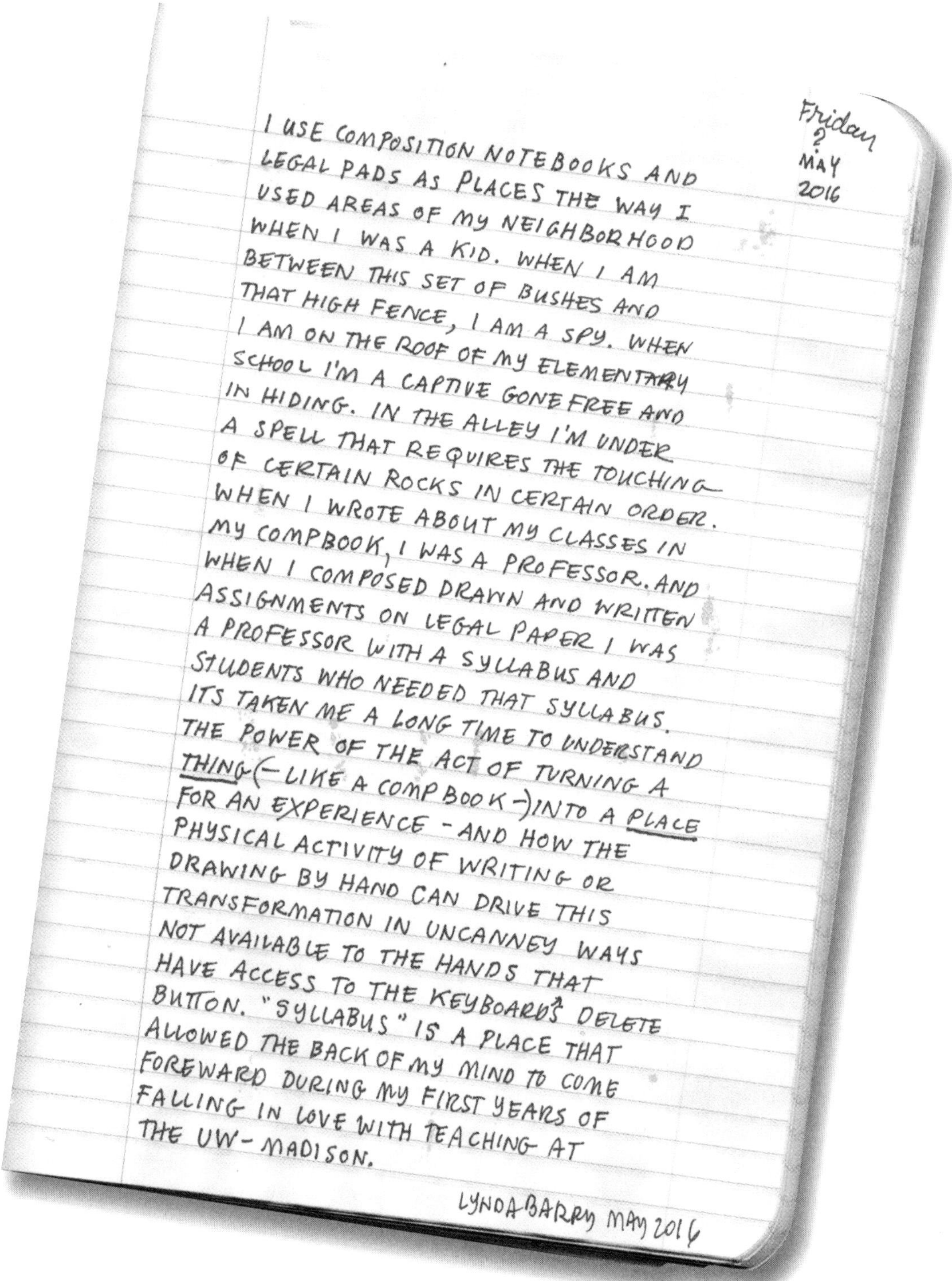

Friday ? MAY 2016

I USE COMPOSITION NOTEBOOKS AND LEGAL PADS AS PLACES THE WAY I USED AREAS OF MY NEIGHBORHOOD WHEN I WAS A KID. WHEN I AM BETWEEN THIS SET OF BUSHES AND THAT HIGH FENCE, I AM A SPY. WHEN I AM ON THE ROOF OF MY ELEMENTARY SCHOOL I'M A CAPTIVE GONE FREE AND IN HIDING. IN THE ALLEY I'M UNDER A SPELL THAT REQUIRES THE TOUCHING OF CERTAIN ROCKS IN CERTAIN ORDER. WHEN I WROTE ABOUT MY CLASSES IN MY COMPBOOK, I WAS A PROFESSOR. AND WHEN I COMPOSED DRAWN AND WRITTEN ASSIGNMENTS ON LEGAL PAPER I WAS A PROFESSOR WITH A SYLLABUS AND STUDENTS WHO NEEDED THAT SYLLABUS. ITS TAKEN ME A LONG TIME TO UNDERSTAND THE POWER OF THE ACT OF TURNING A <u>THING</u> (—LIKE A COMP BOOK—) INTO A <u>PLACE</u> FOR AN EXPERIENCE — AND HOW THE PHYSICAL ACTIVITY OF WRITING OR DRAWING BY HAND CAN DRIVE THIS TRANSFORMATION IN UNCANNEY WAYS NOT AVAILABLE TO THE HANDS THAT HAVE ACCESS TO THE KEYBOARD'S DELETE BUTTON. "SYLLABUS" IS A PLACE THAT ALLOWED THE BACK OF MY MIND TO COME FOREWARD DURING MY FIRST YEARS OF FALLING IN LOVE WITH TEACHING AT THE UW-MADISON.

LYNDA BARRY MAY 2016

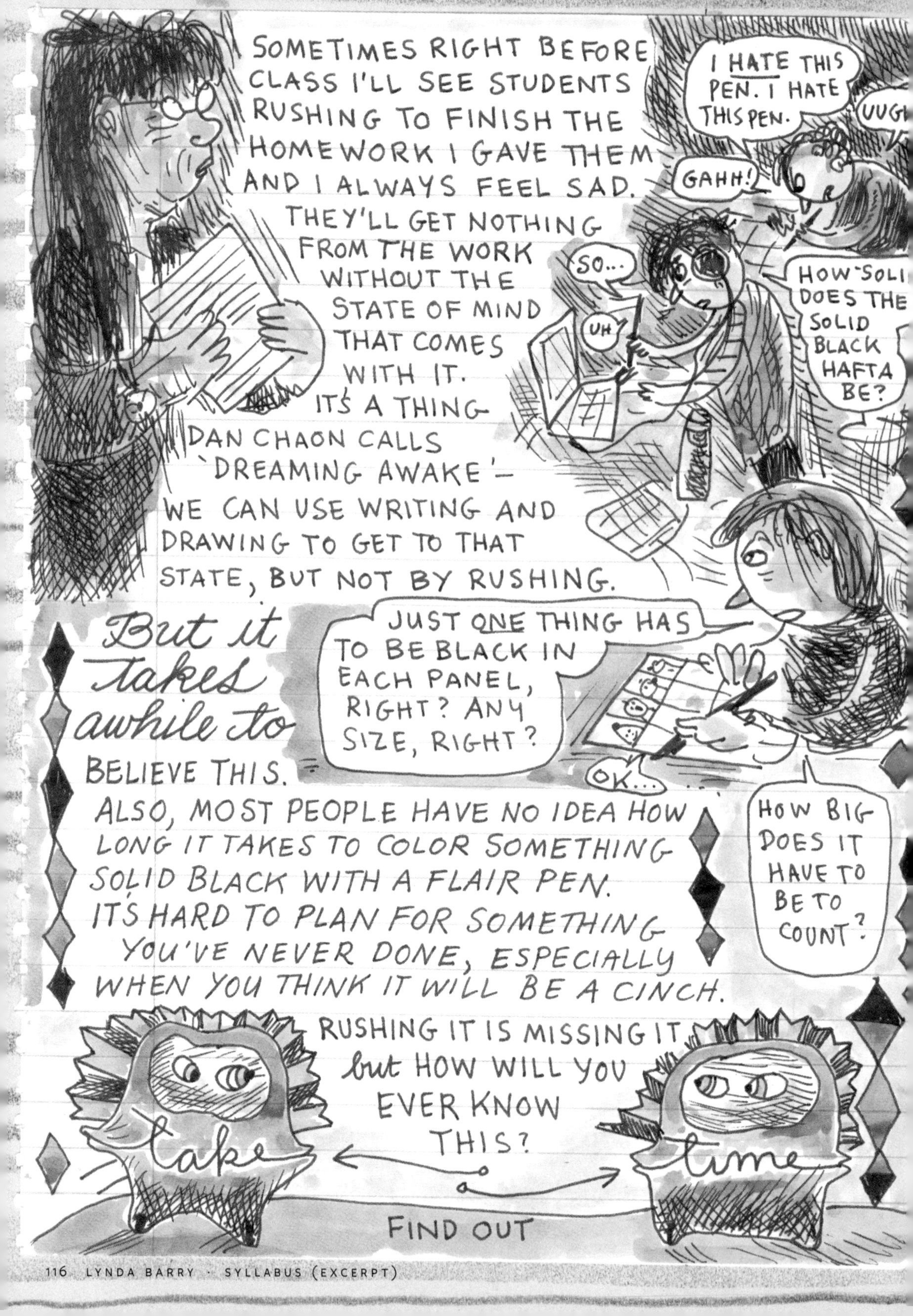
SOMETIMES RIGHT BEFORE CLASS I'LL SEE STUDENTS RUSHING TO FINISH THE HOMEWORK I GAVE THEM AND I ALWAYS FEEL SAD.
I HATE THIS PEN. I HATE THIS PEN.
UUG
GAHH!
THEY'LL GET NOTHING FROM THE WORK WITHOUT THE STATE OF MIND THAT COMES WITH IT.
SO...
UH
HOW-SOLI DOES THE SOLID BLACK HAFTA BE?
IT'S A THING DAN CHAON CALLS 'DREAMING AWAKE'— WE CAN USE WRITING AND DRAWING TO GET TO THAT STATE, BUT NOT BY RUSHING.
But it takes awhile to BELIEVE THIS.
JUST ONE THING HAS TO BE BLACK IN EACH PANEL, RIGHT? ANY SIZE, RIGHT?
OK...
ALSO, MOST PEOPLE HAVE NO IDEA HOW LONG IT TAKES TO COLOR SOMETHING SOLID BLACK WITH A FLAIR PEN. IT'S HARD TO PLAN FOR SOMETHING YOU'VE NEVER DONE, ESPECIALLY WHEN YOU THINK IT WILL BE A CINCH.
HOW BIG DOES IT HAVE TO BE TO COUNT?
RUSHING IT IS MISSING IT but HOW WILL YOU EVER KNOW THIS?
take
time
FIND OUT

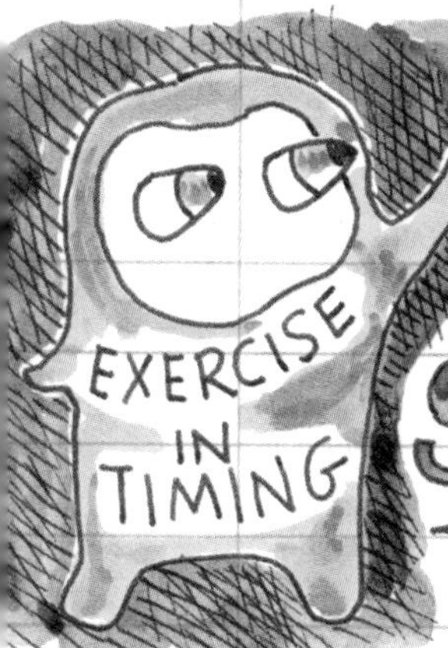
EXERCISE IN TIMING

# CAN DRAWING CHANGE OUR SENSE OF TIME?

YOU WILL NEED: A CLOCK,

YOUR COMP BOOK, NON-PHOTO BLUE PENCIL

YOUR UNIBALL PEN

A PHOTOGRAPH OF A GROUP OF PEOPLE POSING FOR A PHOTO - AT LEAST FIVE PEOPLE, NO MORE THAN TEN

SOME UNINTERRUPTED TIME

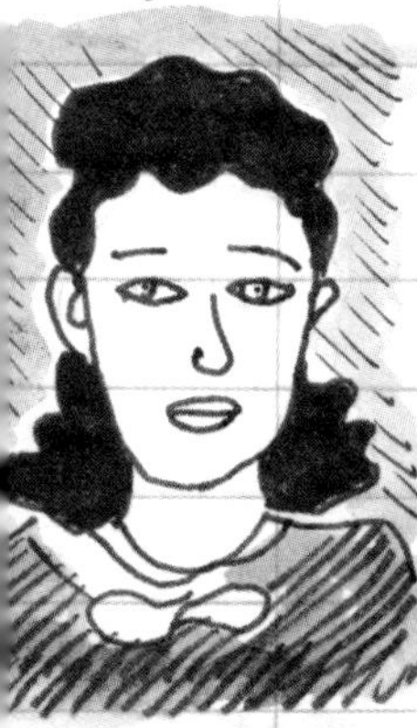

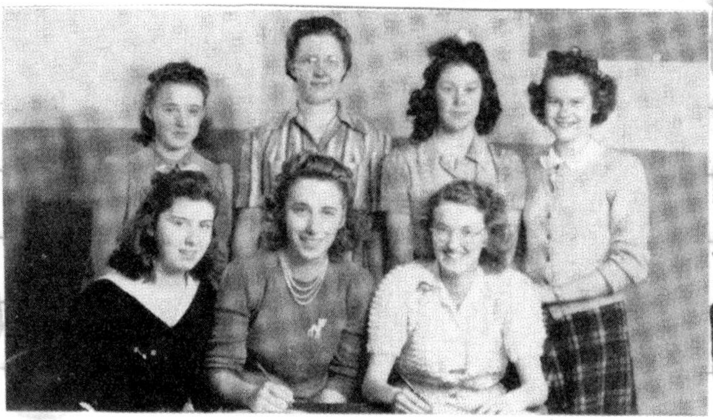

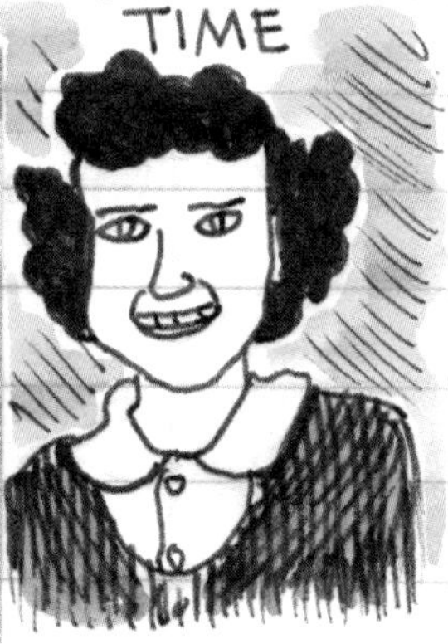

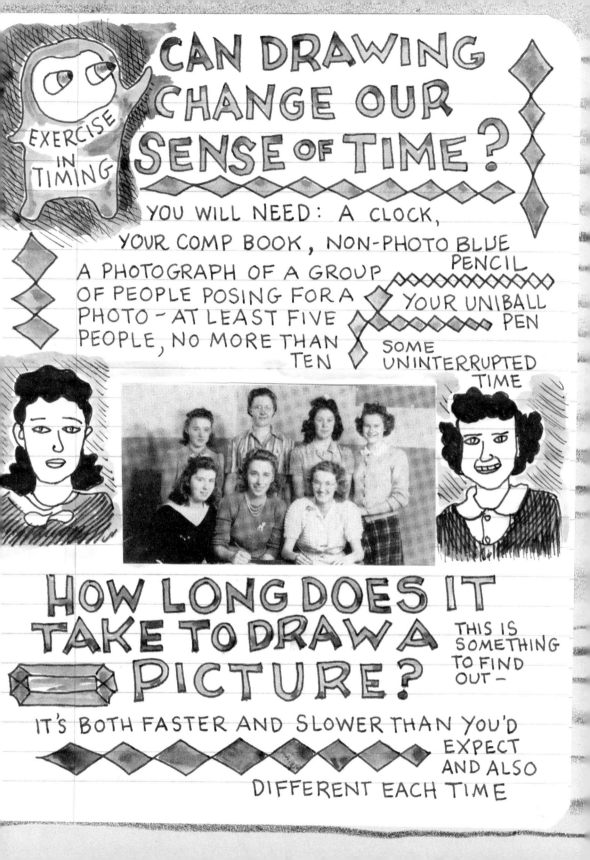

# HOW LONG DOES IT TAKE TO DRAW A PICTURE?

THIS IS SOMETHING TO FIND OUT -

IT'S BOTH FASTER AND SLOWER THAN YOU'D EXPECT AND ALSO DIFFERENT EACH TIME

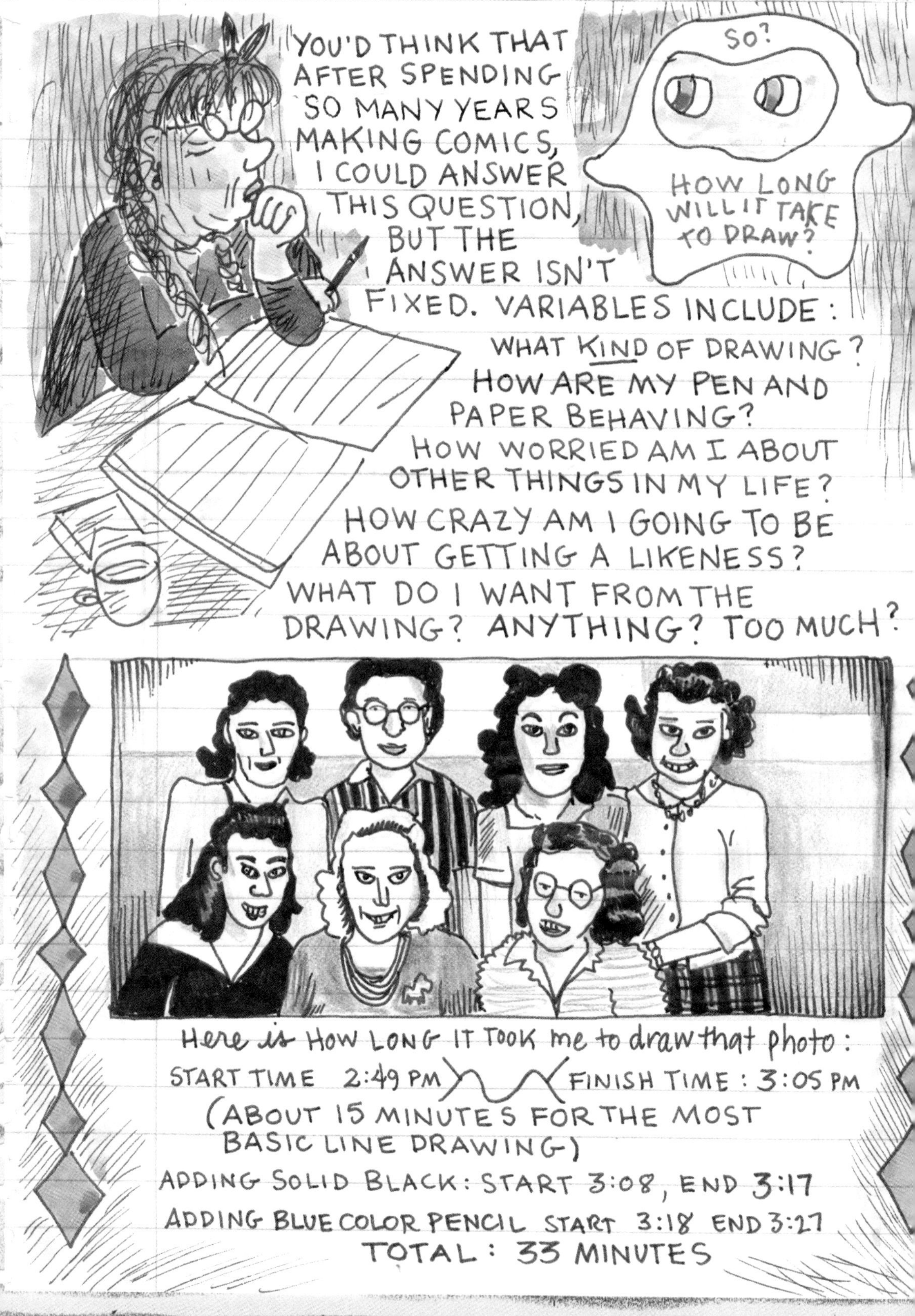
So?
HOW LONG WILL IT TAKE TO DRAW?
YOU'D THINK THAT AFTER SPENDING SO MANY YEARS MAKING COMICS, I COULD ANSWER THIS QUESTION, BUT THE ANSWER ISN'T FIXED. VARIABLES INCLUDE:
WHAT KIND OF DRAWING?
HOW ARE MY PEN AND PAPER BEHAVING?
HOW WORRIED AM I ABOUT OTHER THINGS IN MY LIFE?
HOW CRAZY AM I GOING TO BE ABOUT GETTING A LIKENESS?
WHAT DO I WANT FROM THE DRAWING? ANYTHING? TOO MUCH?
Here is HOW LONG IT TOOK me to draw that photo:
START TIME 2:49 PM
FINISH TIME: 3:05 PM
(ABOUT 15 MINUTES FOR THE MOST BASIC LINE DRAWING)
ADDING SOLID BLACK: START 3:08, END 3:17
ADDING BLUE COLOR PENCIL START 3:18 END 3:27
TOTAL: 33 MINUTES

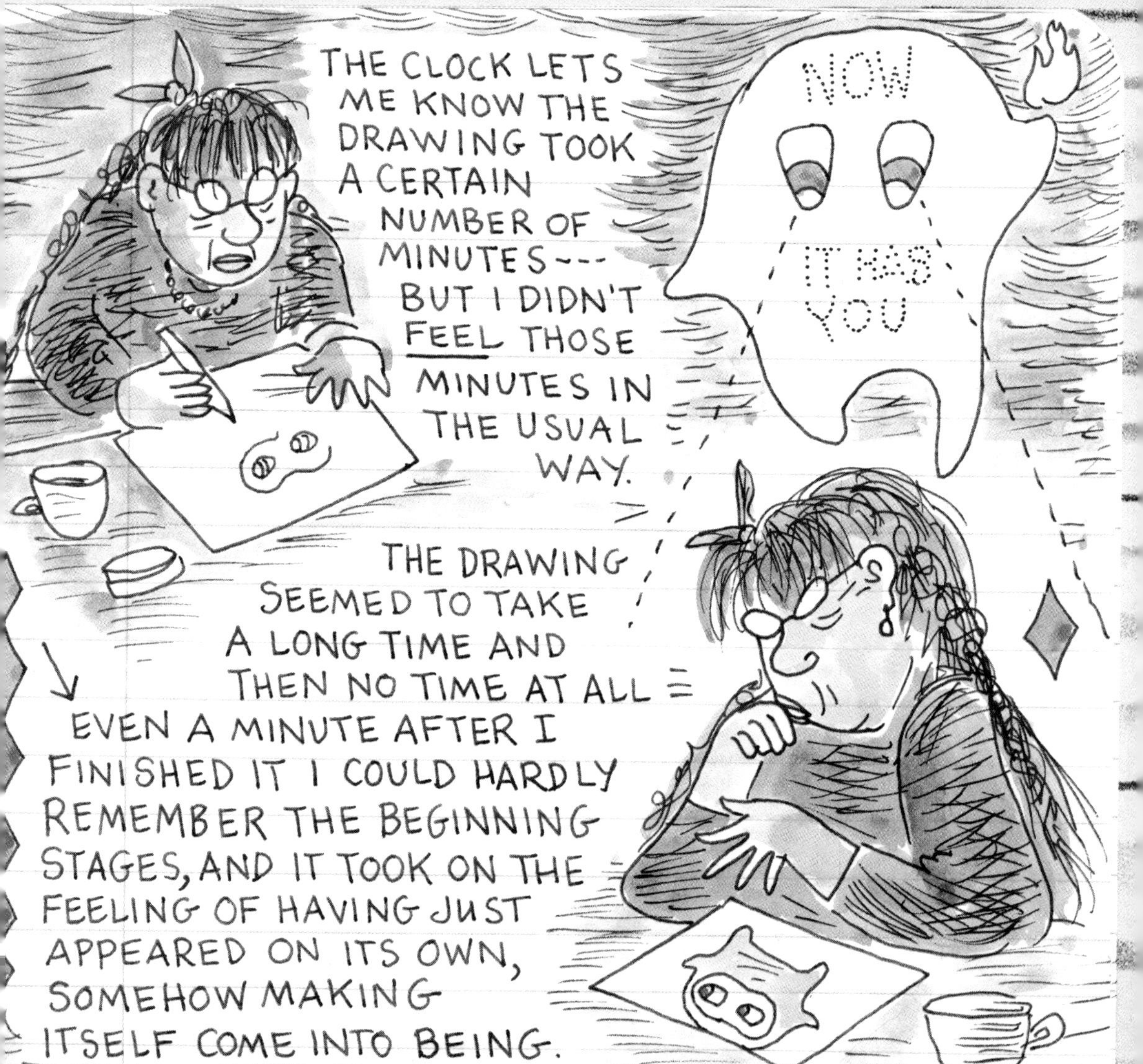
THE CLOCK LETS ME KNOW THE DRAWING TOOK A CERTAIN NUMBER OF MINUTES--- BUT I DIDN'T FEEL THOSE MINUTES IN THE USUAL WAY.
NOW
IT HAS YOU
THE DRAWING SEEMED TO TAKE A LONG TIME AND THEN NO TIME AT ALL
EVEN A MINUTE AFTER I FINISHED IT I COULD HARDLY REMEMBER THE BEGINNING STAGES, AND IT TOOK ON THE FEELING OF HAVING JUST APPEARED ON ITS OWN, SOMEHOW MAKING ITSELF COME INTO BEING.
I HAVE A NEPHEW WHO SAID HE WANTED A TIME MACHINE WITH A 'MEANWHILE' BUTTON. DRAWING IS SOMETHING LIKE THAT FOR ME. I FEEL LIKE I GO SOMEPLACE I CAN'T RECALL — AND WHEN I GET BACK, THERE IS A DRAWING, AND SOMEHOW I MADE IT, THOUGH IT'S LIKE IT HAS ALWAYS EXISTED.

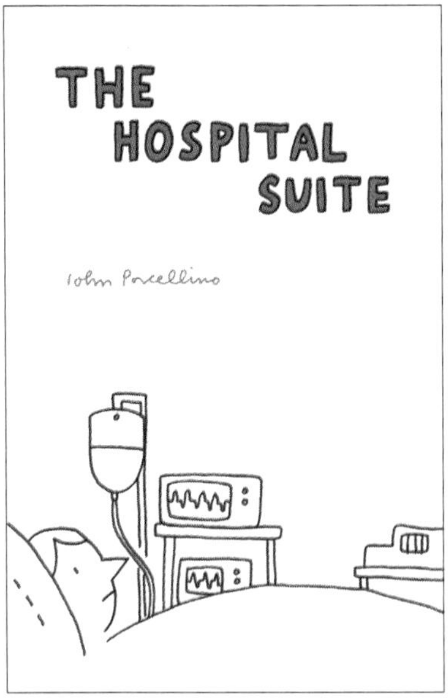
THE
HOSPITAL
SUITE
John Porcellino

# The Hospital Suite (*Excerpt*)

JOHN PORCELLINO

*excerpted from*

The Hospital Suite
DRAWN AND QUARTERLY
7.5 × 9.8 inches · 200 pages

## Biography

John Porcellino was born in Chicago in 1968, and has been writing, drawing, and publishing minicomics, comics, and graphic novels for over thirty years. His celebrated self-published series King-Cat Comics, begun in 1989, has inspired a generation of cartoonists. According to cartoonist Chris Ware, "John Porcellino's comics distill, in just a few lines and words, the feeling of simply being alive." king-cat.net

## Statement

*The Hospital Suite* is a collection of three stories concerning health issues I've experienced, both physical and mental. This excerpt is from the first story, also called "The Hospital Suite," in which, due to extreme abdominal pain, I undergo exploratory surgery. The rest of the book explores the physical and mental fallout from this experience, including a wide range of mysterious physical ailments and the development of Obsessive Compulsive Disorder.

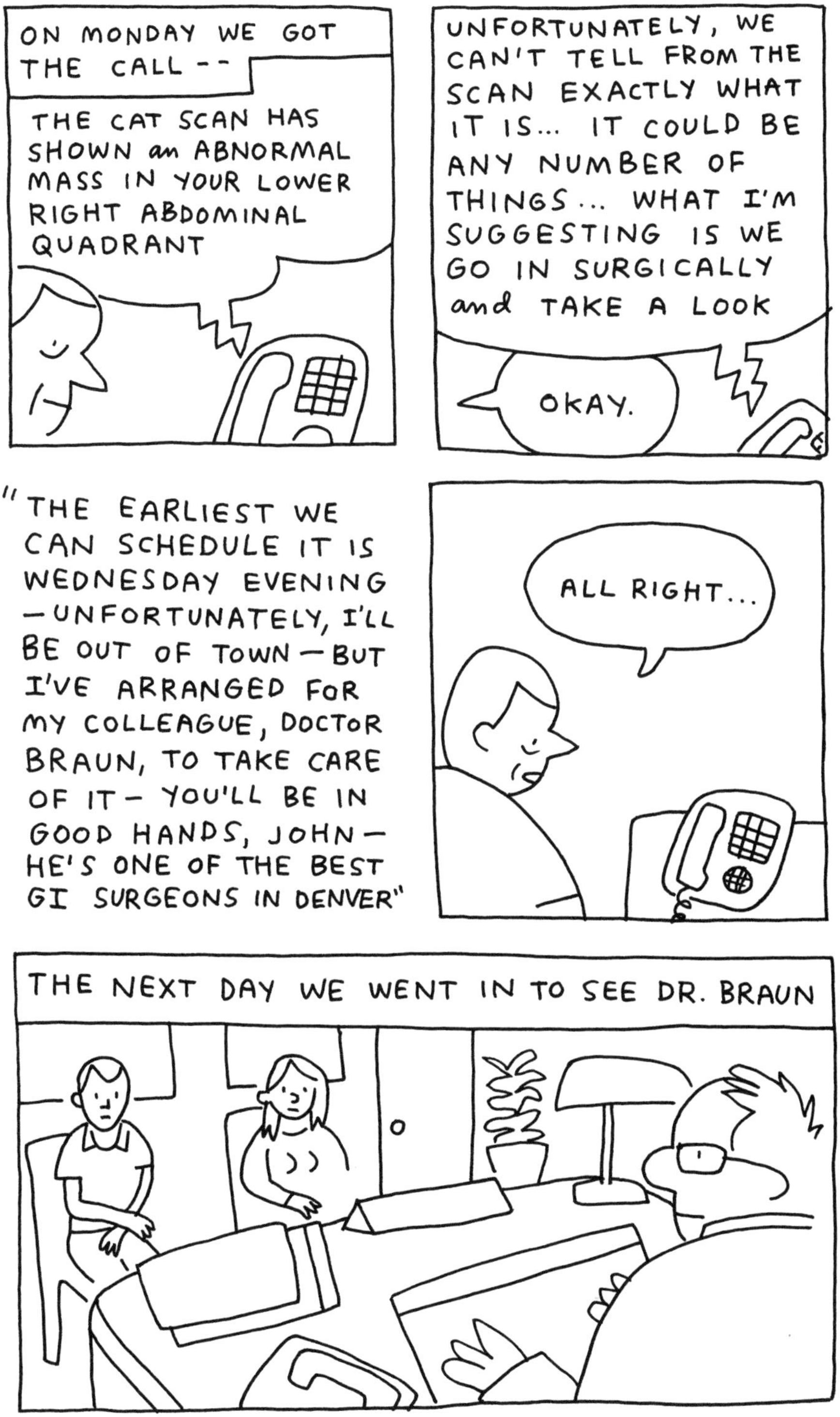
ON MONDAY WE GOT THE CALL --
THE CAT SCAN HAS SHOWN an ABNORMAL MASS IN YOUR LOWER RIGHT ABDOMINAL QUADRANT
UNFORTUNATELY, WE CAN'T TELL FROM THE SCAN EXACTLY WHAT IT IS... IT COULD BE ANY NUMBER OF THINGS... WHAT I'M SUGGESTING IS WE GO IN SURGICALLY and TAKE A LOOK
OKAY.
"THE EARLIEST WE CAN SCHEDULE IT IS WEDNESDAY EVENING — UNFORTUNATELY, I'LL BE OUT OF TOWN — BUT I'VE ARRANGED FOR MY COLLEAGUE, DOCTOR BRAUN, TO TAKE CARE OF IT — YOU'LL BE IN GOOD HANDS, JOHN — HE'S ONE OF THE BEST GI SURGEONS IN DENVER"
ALL RIGHT...
THE NEXT DAY WE WENT IN TO SEE DR. BRAUN

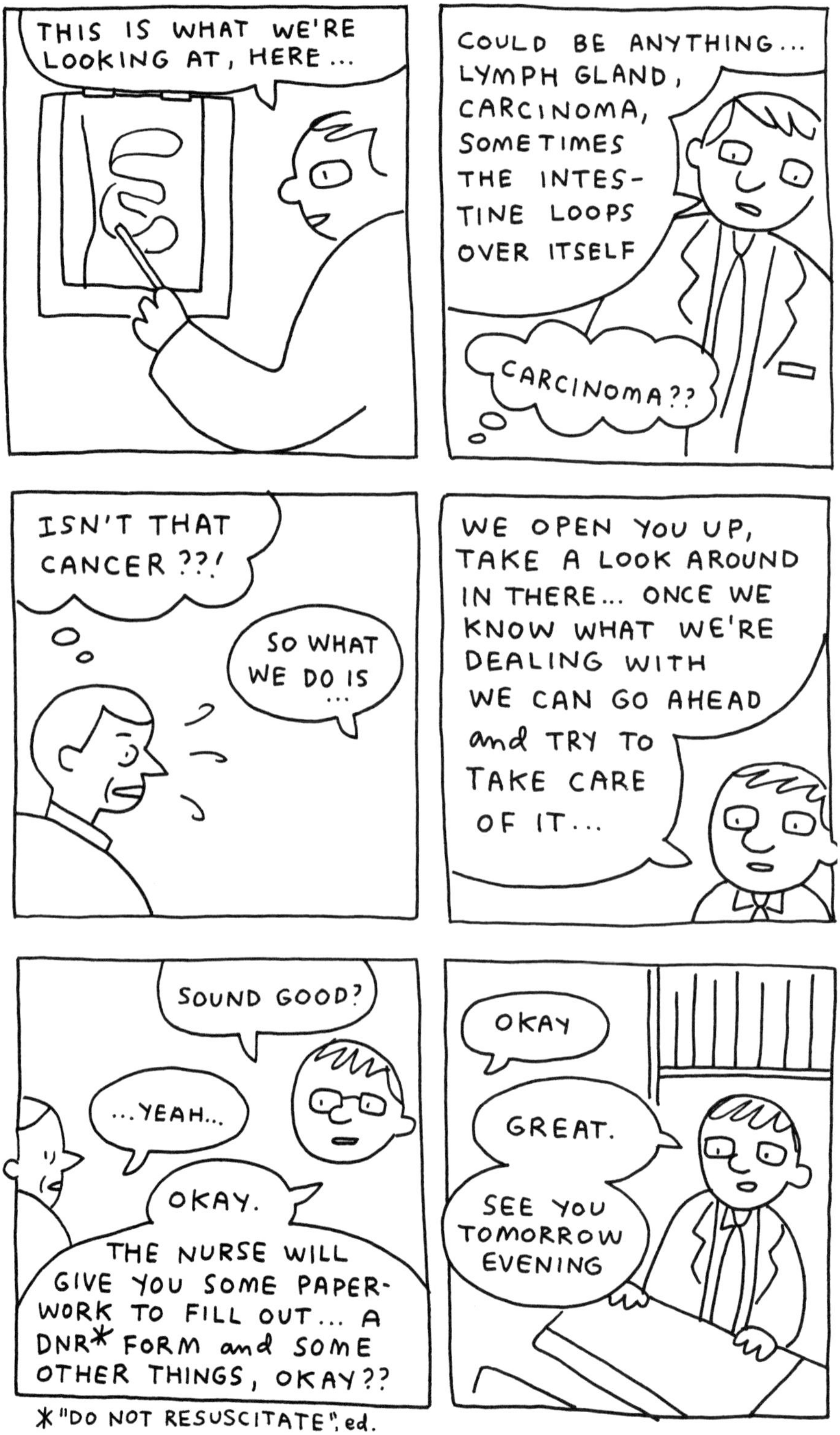
THIS IS WHAT WE'RE LOOKING AT, HERE...
COULD BE ANYTHING... LYMPH GLAND, CARCINOMA, SOMETIMES THE INTES-TINE LOOPS OVER ITSELF
CARCINOMA??
ISN'T THAT CANCER??!
SO WHAT WE DO IS ...
WE OPEN YOU UP, TAKE A LOOK AROUND IN THERE... ONCE WE KNOW WHAT WE'RE DEALING WITH WE CAN GO AHEAD and TRY TO TAKE CARE OF IT...
SOUND GOOD?
...YEAH...
OKAY.
THE NURSE WILL GIVE YOU SOME PAPER-WORK TO FILL OUT... A DNR* FORM and SOME OTHER THINGS, OKAY??
OKAY
GREAT.
SEE YOU TOMORROW EVENING

* "DO NOT RESUSCITATE", ed.

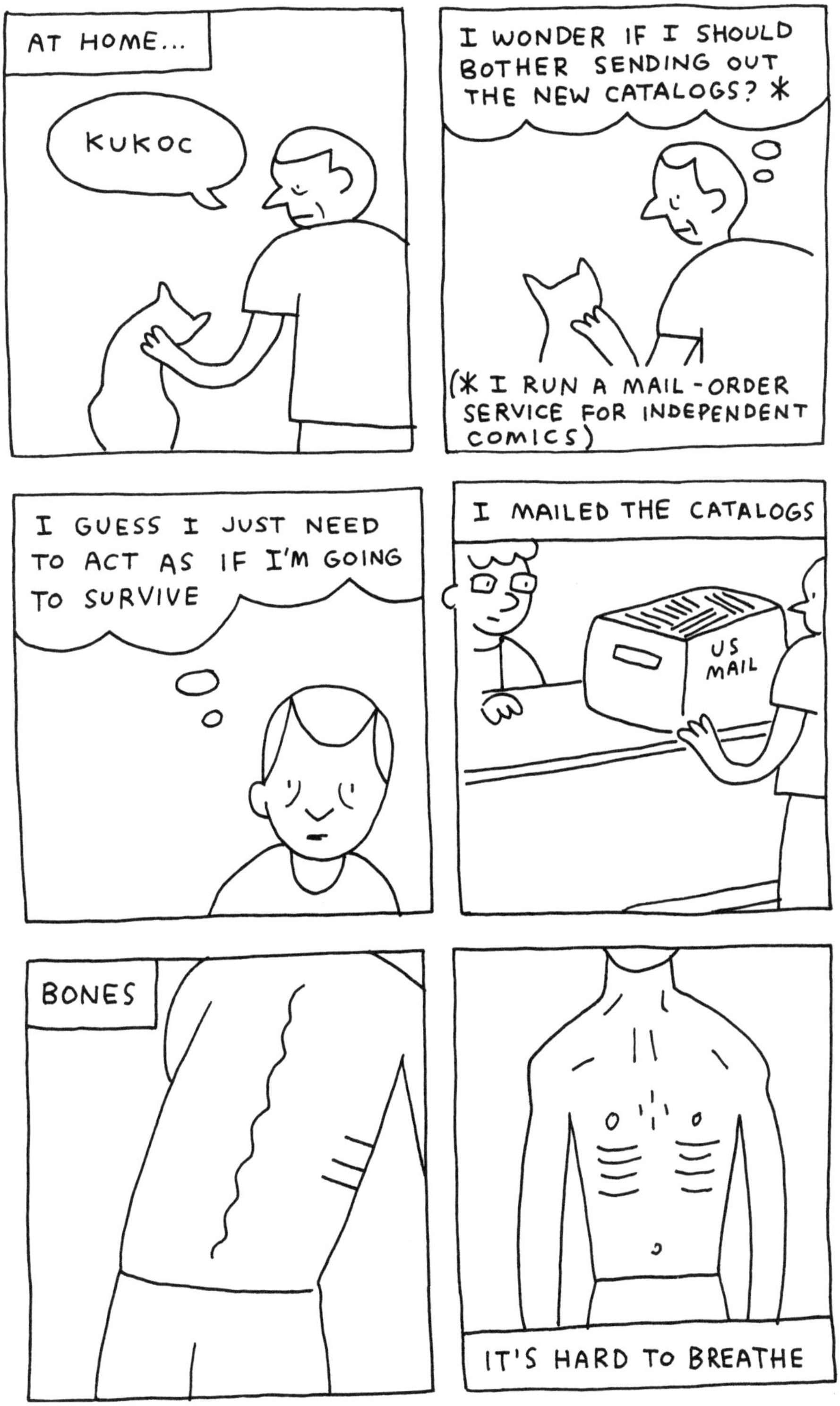
AT HOME...
KUKOC
I WONDER IF I SHOULD BOTHER SENDING OUT THE NEW CATALOGS? *
(* I RUN A MAIL-ORDER SERVICE FOR INDEPENDENT COMICS)
I GUESS I JUST NEED TO ACT AS IF I'M GOING TO SURVIVE
I MAILED THE CATALOGS
US MAIL
BONES
IT'S HARD TO BREATHE

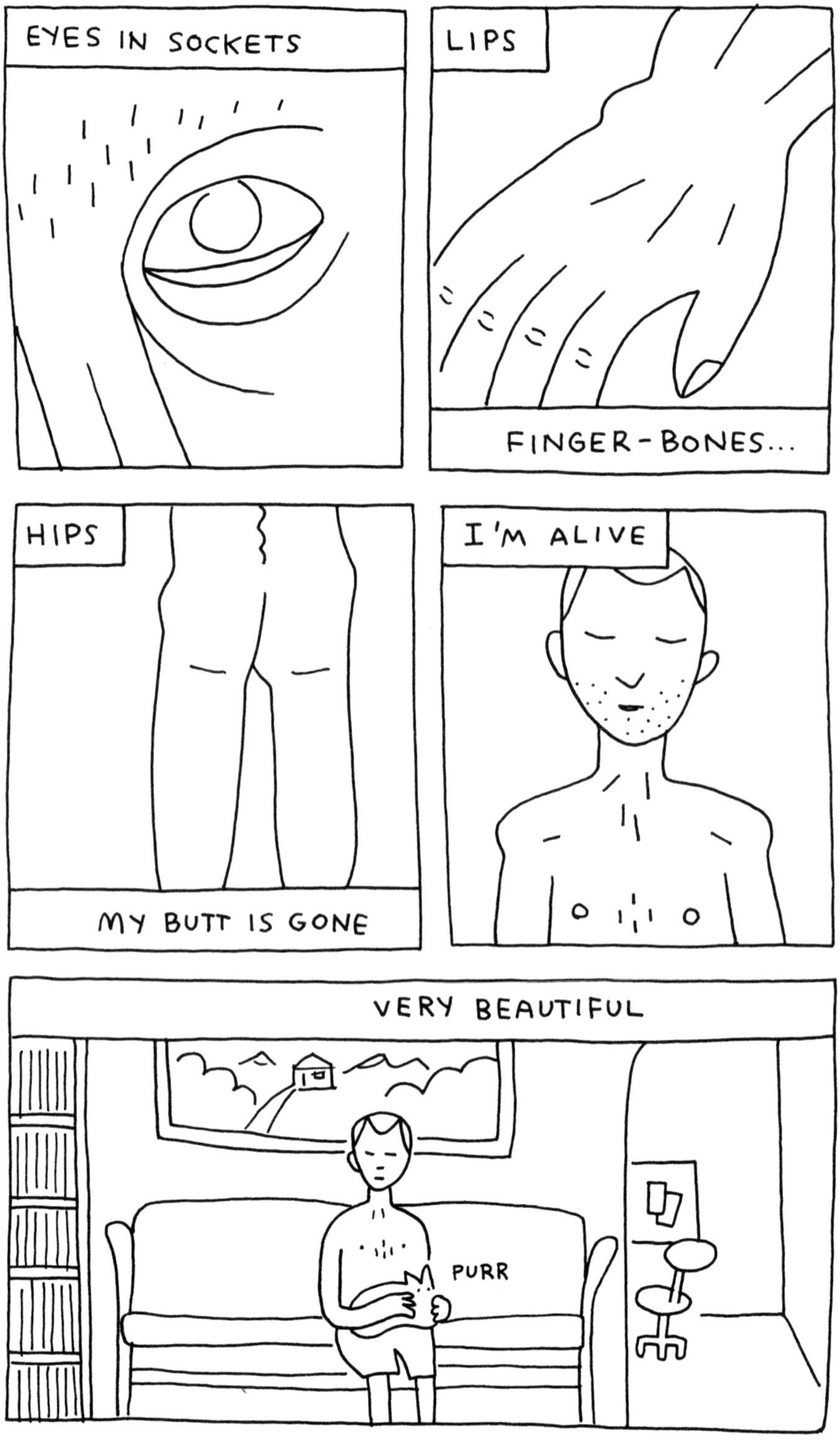
EYES IN SOCKETS
LIPS
FINGER-BONES...
HIPS
MY BUTT IS GONE
I'M ALIVE
VERY BEAUTIFUL
PURR

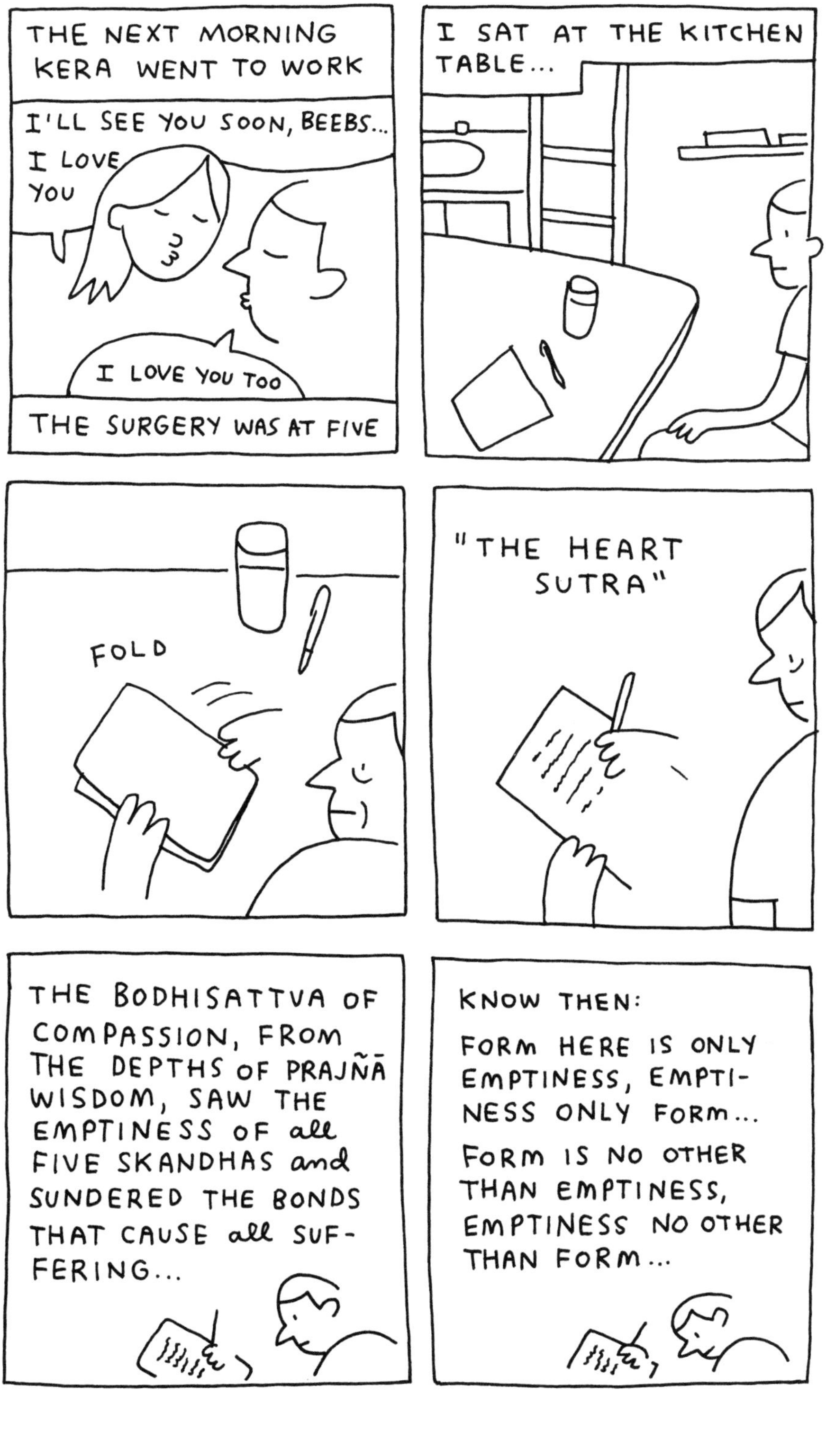
THE NEXT MORNING KERA WENT TO WORK
I'LL SEE YOU SOON, BEEBS... I LOVE YOU
I LOVE YOU TOO
THE SURGERY WAS AT FIVE
I SAT AT THE KITCHEN TABLE...
FOLD
"THE HEART SUTRA"
THE BODHISATTVA OF COMPASSION, FROM THE DEPTHS OF PRAJÑĀ WISDOM, SAW THE EMPTINESS OF all FIVE SKANDHAS and SUNDERED THE BONDS THAT CAUSE all SUF-FERING...
KNOW THEN:
FORM HERE IS ONLY EMPTINESS, EMPTI-NESS ONLY FORM...
FORM IS NO OTHER THAN EMPTINESS, EMPTINESS NO OTHER THAN FORM...

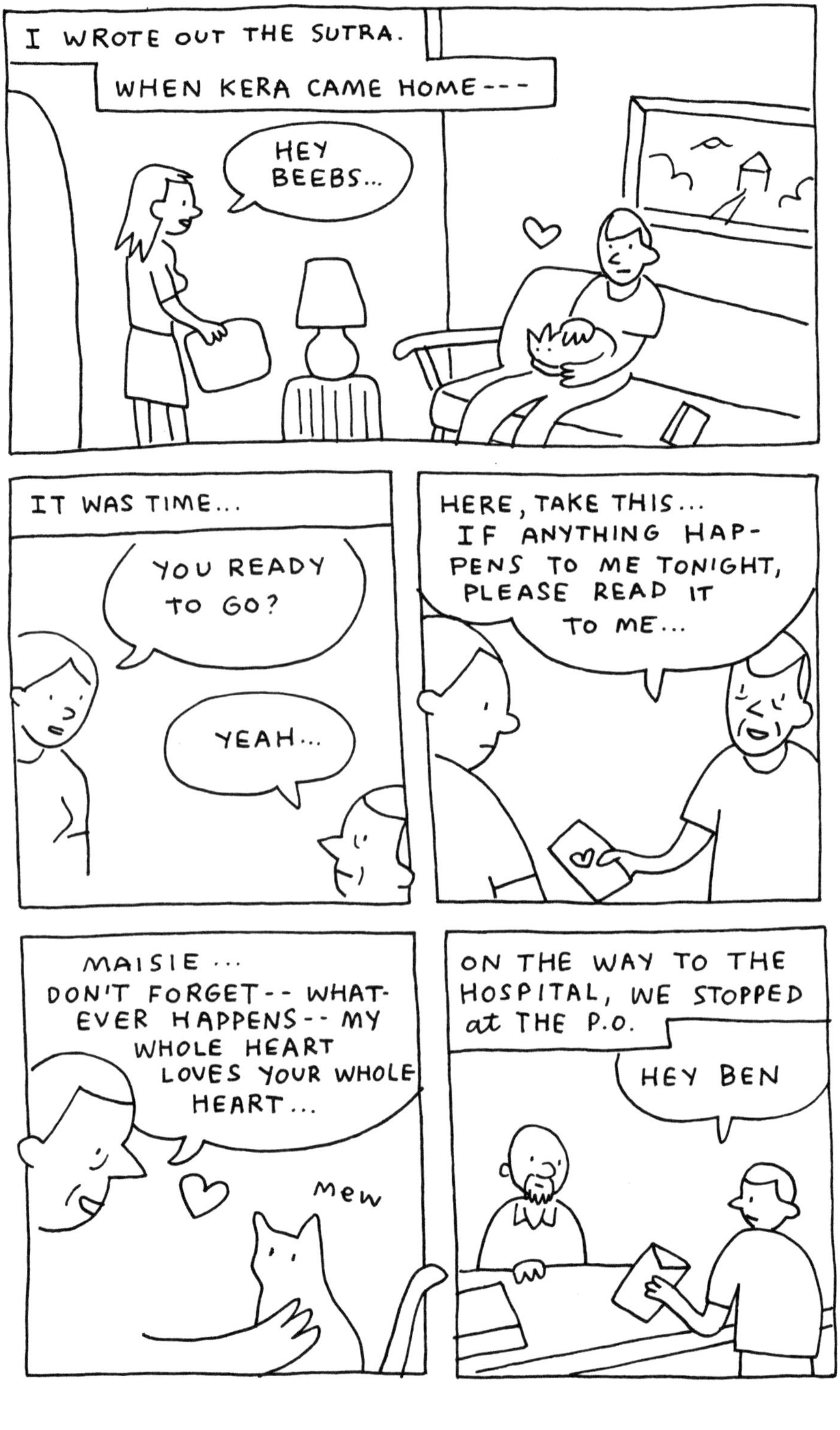
I WROTE OUT THE SUTRA.
WHEN KERA CAME HOME---
HEY BEEBS...
IT WAS TIME...
YOU READY TO GO?
YEAH...
HERE, TAKE THIS... IF ANYTHING HAPPENS TO ME TONIGHT, PLEASE READ IT TO ME...
MAISIE... DON'T FORGET-- WHATEVER HAPPENS-- MY WHOLE HEART LOVES YOUR WHOLE HEART...
mew
ON THE WAY TO THE HOSPITAL, WE STOPPED at THE P.O.
HEY BEN

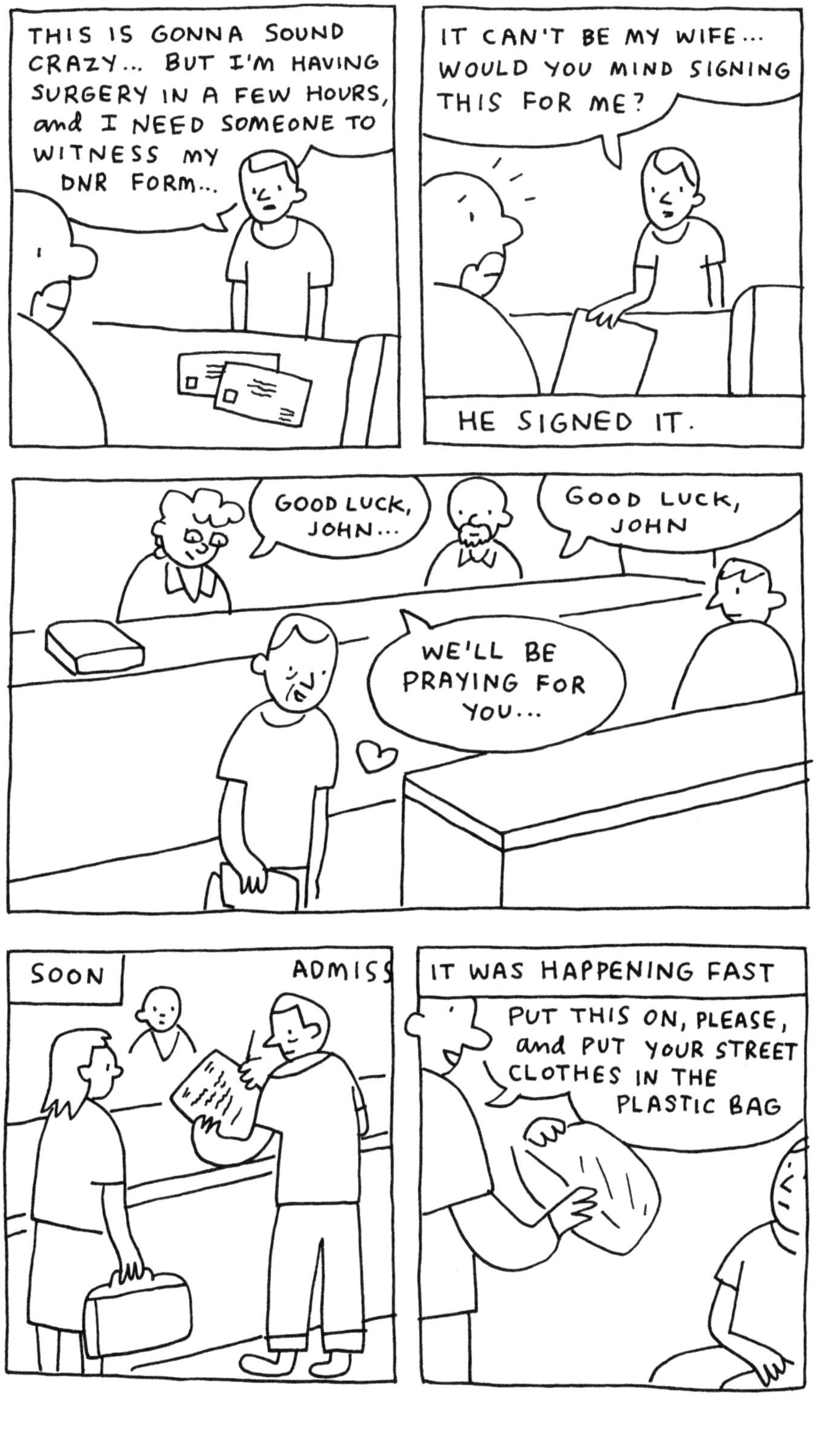
THIS IS GONNA SOUND CRAZY... BUT I'M HAVING SURGERY IN A FEW HOURS, and I NEED SOMEONE TO WITNESS MY DNR FORM...
IT CAN'T BE MY WIFE... WOULD YOU MIND SIGNING THIS FOR ME?
HE SIGNED IT.
GOOD LUCK, JOHN...
GOOD LUCK, JOHN
WE'LL BE PRAYING FOR YOU...
SOON
ADMISS
IT WAS HAPPENING FAST
PUT THIS ON, PLEASE, and PUT YOUR STREET CLOTHES IN THE PLASTIC BAG

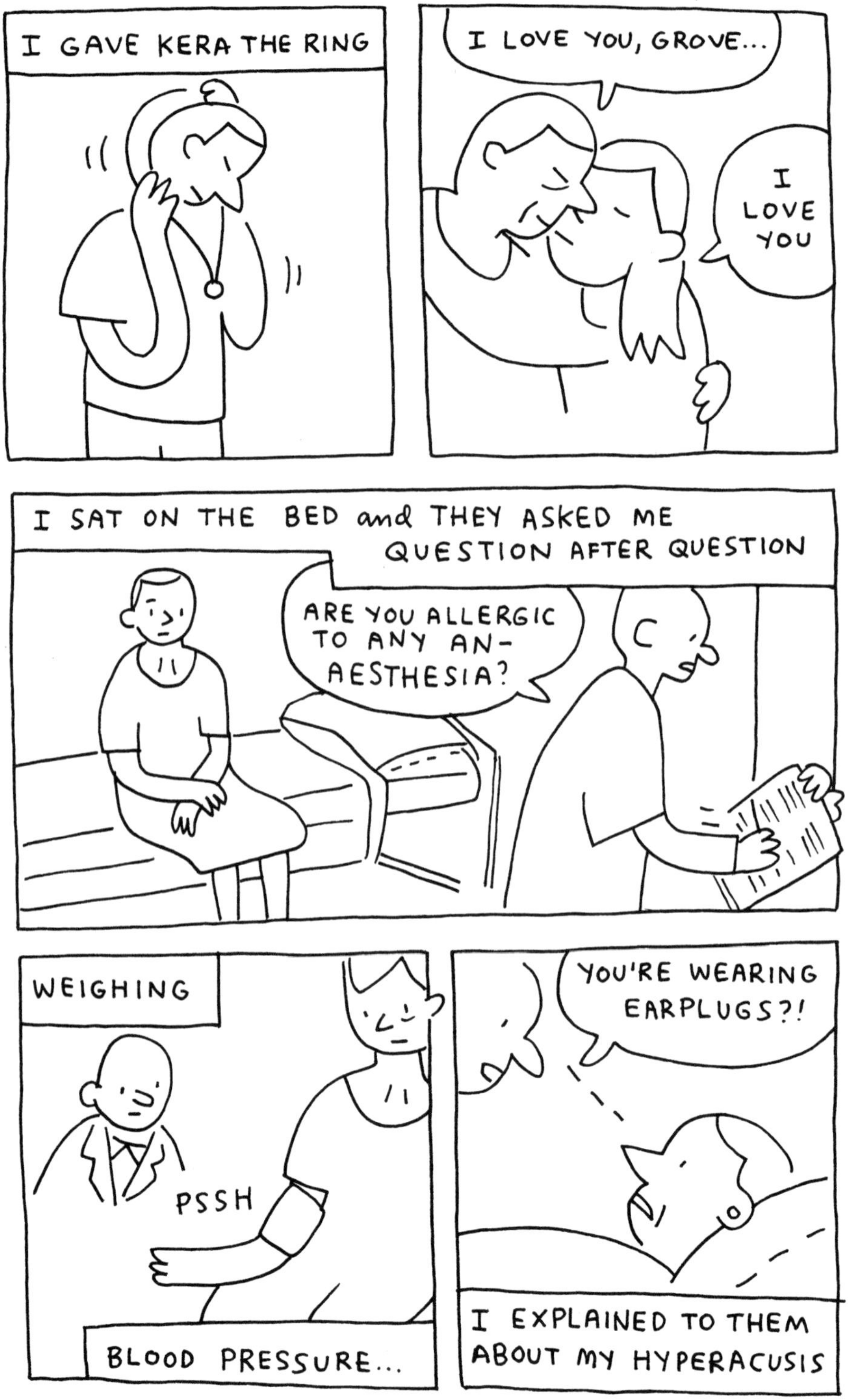
I GAVE KERA THE RING
I LOVE YOU, GROVE...
I LOVE YOU
I SAT ON THE BED and THEY ASKED ME QUESTION AFTER QUESTION
ARE YOU ALLERGIC TO ANY AN-AESTHESIA?
WEIGHING
PSSH
BLOOD PRESSURE...
YOU'RE WEARING EARPLUGS?!
I EXPLAINED TO THEM ABOUT MY HYPERACUSIS

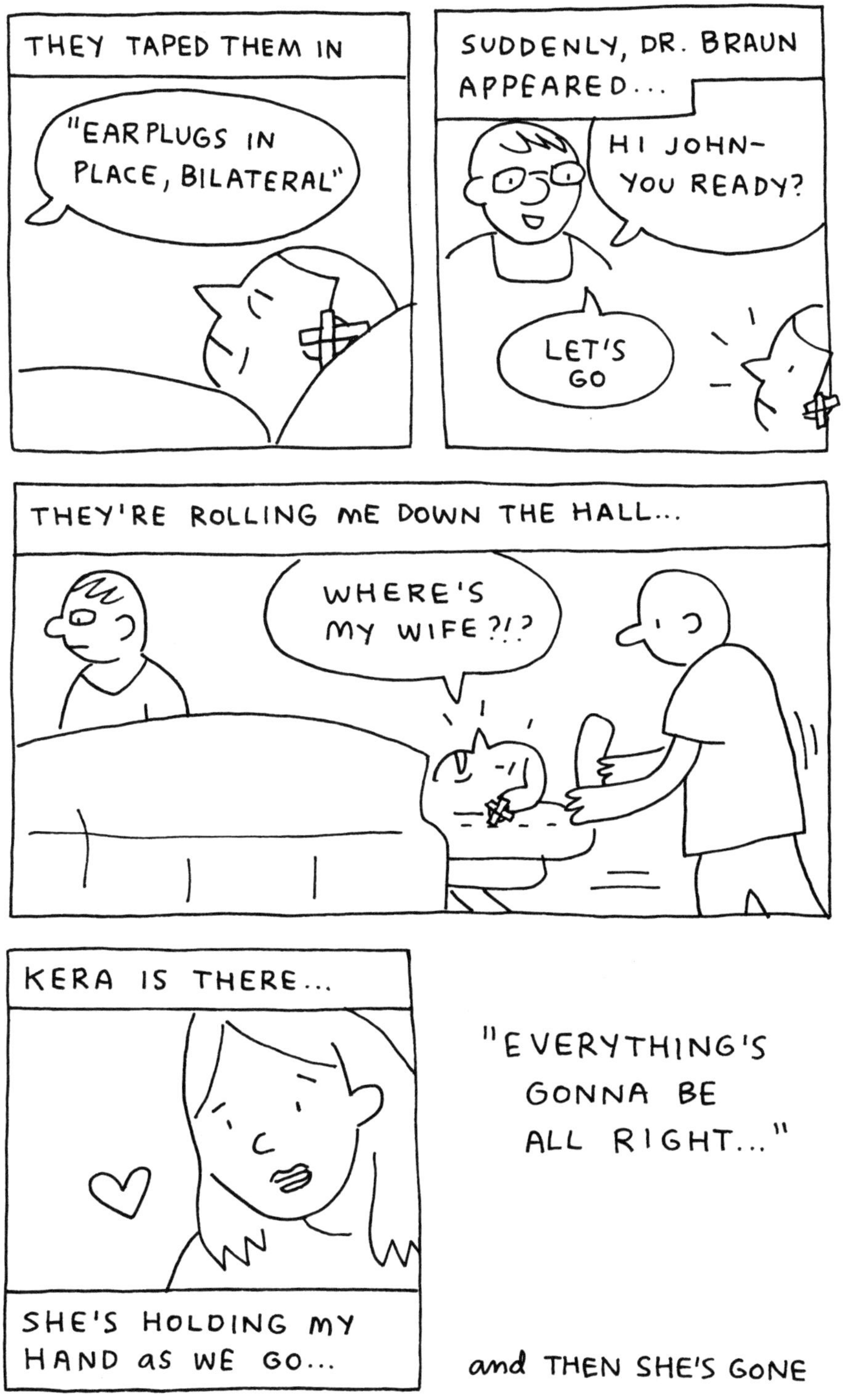
THEY TAPED THEM IN
"EARPLUGS IN PLACE, BILATERAL"
SUDDENLY, DR. BRAUN APPEARED...
HI JOHN- YOU READY?
LET'S GO
THEY'RE ROLLING ME DOWN THE HALL...
WHERE'S MY WIFE?!?
KERA IS THERE...
SHE'S HOLDING MY HAND as WE GO...
"EVERYTHING'S GONNA BE ALL RIGHT..."
and THEN SHE'S GONE

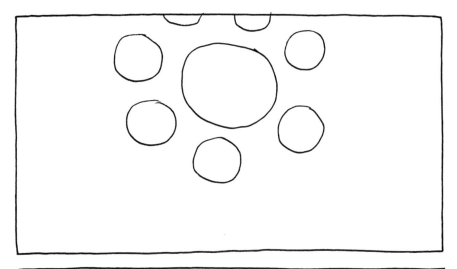

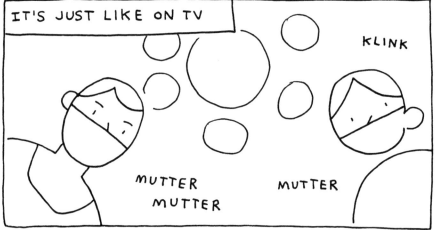

IT'S JUST LIKE ON TV

KLINK

MUTTER
MUTTER

MUTTER

DON'T
WORRY-
YOU'LL BE
FINE...

DR. BRAUN
IS THE BEST...

THEY'RE MAKING JOKES,
LAUGHING... TRYING
TO SET ME at EASE

HA

KLINK

EVERYONE HAS BEEN SO KIND...
JOHN?
IT'S DOCTOR BRAUN ...
WE'RE all SET TO GO...
WE'RE GOING TO BEGIN ADMINISTERING THE ANAESTHESIA... I'LL SEE YOU SOON...

I WASN'T AFRAID TO BE BORN...

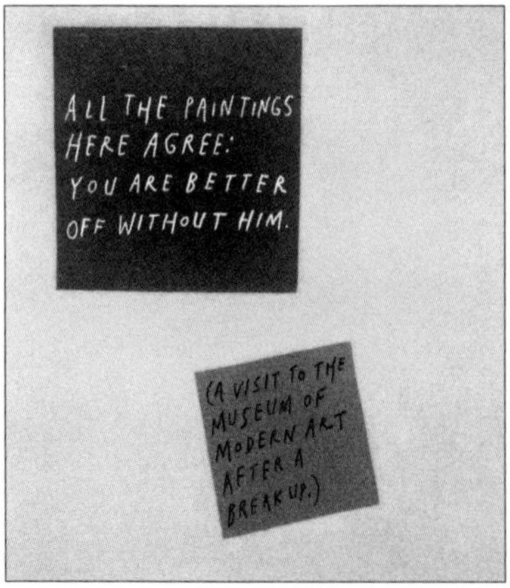
ALL THE PAINTINGS
HERE AGREE:
YOU ARE BETTER
OFF WITHOUT HIM.
(A VISIT TO THE
MUSEUM OF
MODERN ART
AFTER A
BREAKUP.)

# All the Paintings Here Agree

LIANA FINCK

*originally published at*

the-toast.net
digital

## Biography

Liana Finck's first book, *A Bintel Brief*, was published by Ecco Press in 2014. Her cartoons appear in *The New Yorker*. instagram.com/lianafinck/

## Statement

My heart was broken but I was free.

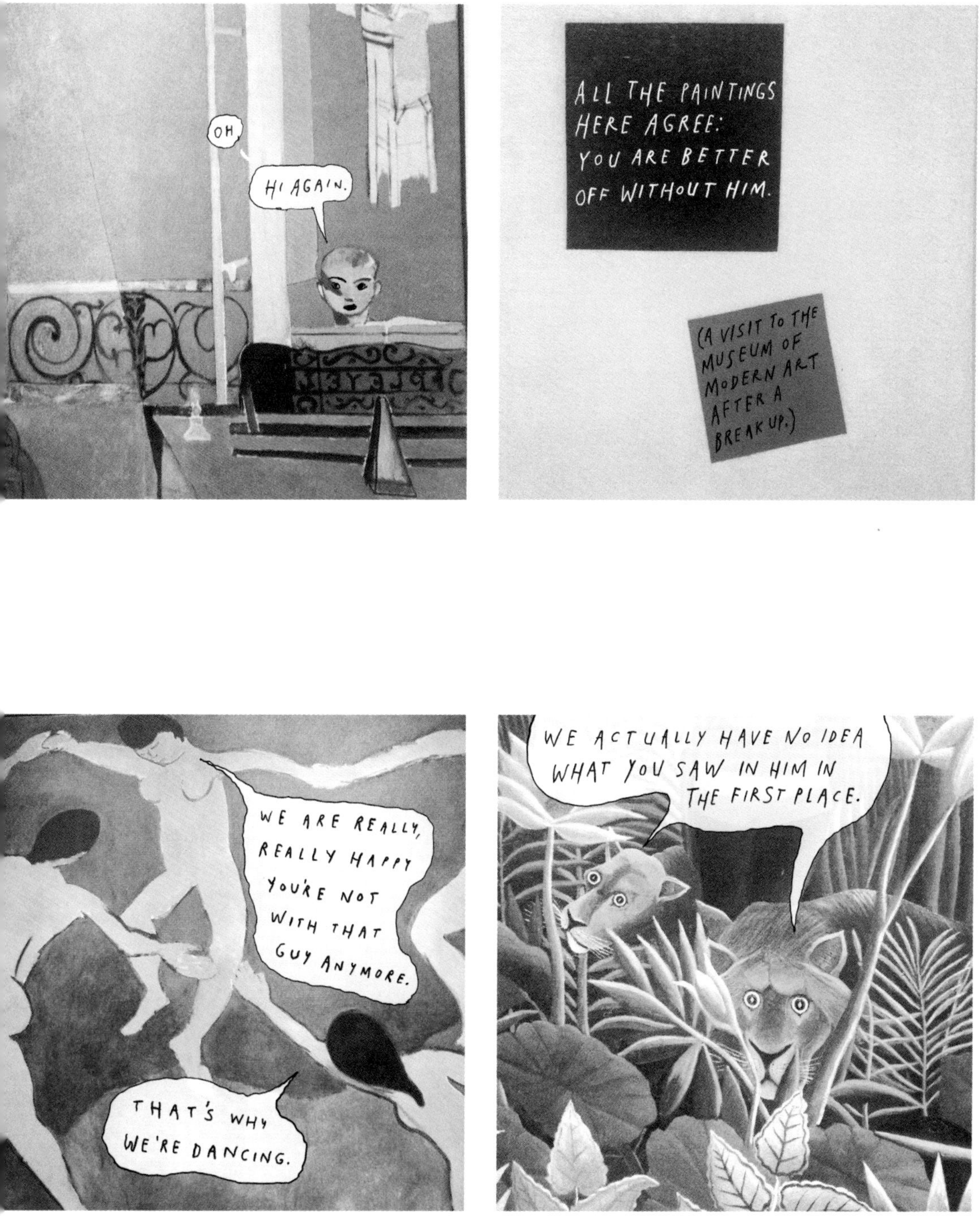

OH,
HI AGAIN.
ALL THE PAINTINGS HERE AGREE: YOU ARE BETTER OFF WITHOUT HIM.
(A VISIT TO THE MUSEUM OF MODERN ART AFTER A BREAK UP.)
WE ARE REALLY, REALLY HAPPY YOU'RE NOT WITH THAT GUY ANYMORE.
THAT'S WHY WE'RE DANCING.
WE ACTUALLY HAVE NO IDEA WHAT YOU SAW IN HIM IN THE FIRST PLACE.

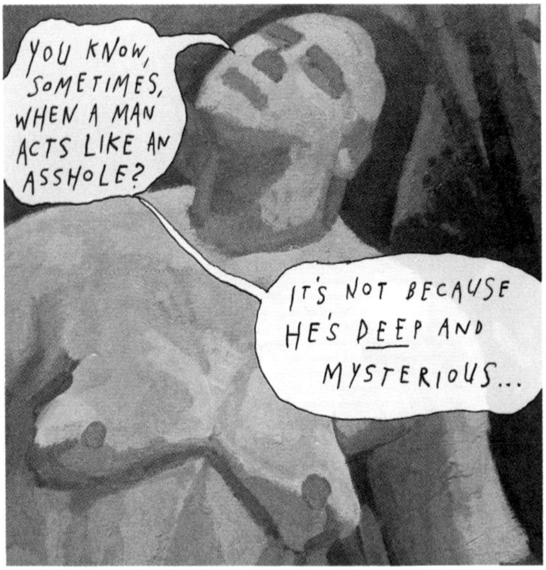
YOU KNOW, SOMETIMES, WHEN A MAN ACTS LIKE AN ASSHOLE?
IT'S NOT BECAUSE HE'S DEEP AND MYSTERIOUS...

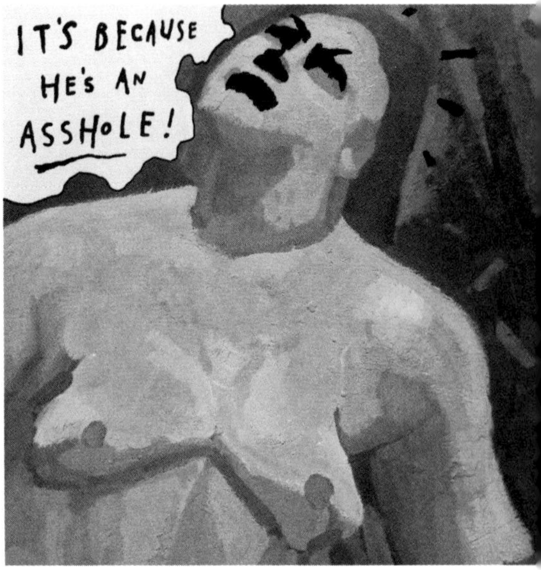
IT'S BECAUSE HE'S AN ASSHOLE!

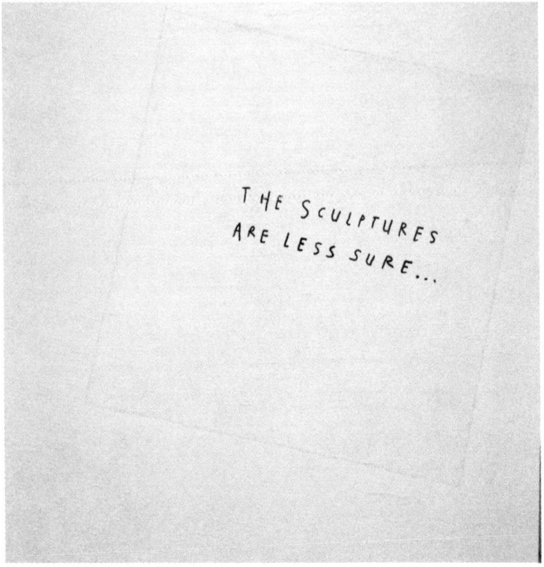
THE SCULPTURES ARE LESS SURE...

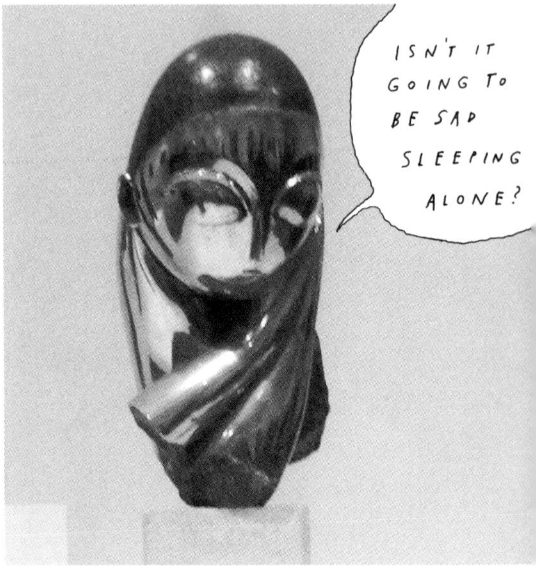
ISN'T IT GOING TO BE SAD SLEEPING ALONE?

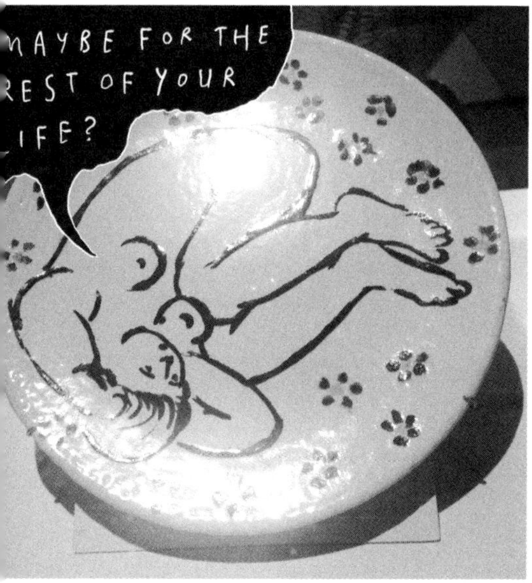
MAYBE FOR THE
REST OF YOUR
LIFE?

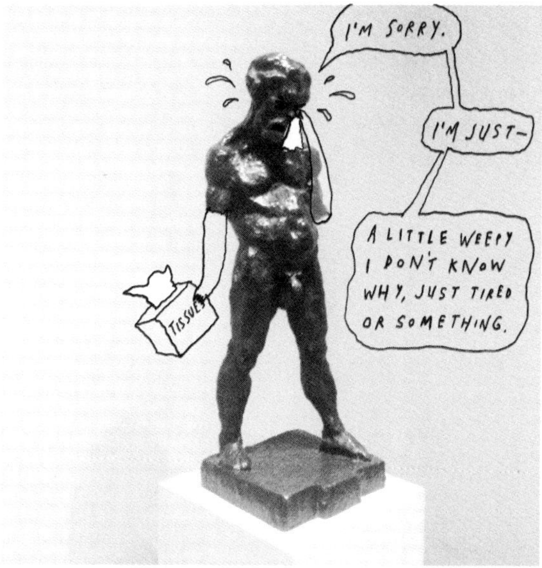
I'M SORRY.
I'M JUST-
A LITTLE WEEPY I DON'T KNOW WHY, JUST TIRED OR SOMETHING.
TISSUES

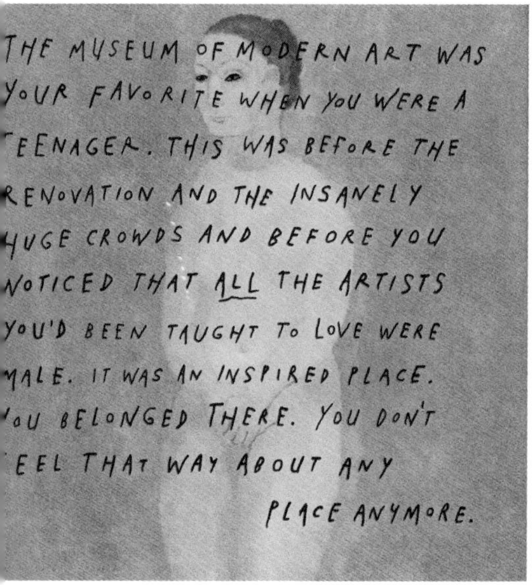
THE MUSEUM OF MODERN ART WAS YOUR FAVORITE WHEN YOU WERE A TEENAGER. THIS WAS BEFORE THE RENOVATION AND THE INSANELY HUGE CROWDS AND BEFORE YOU NOTICED THAT ALL THE ARTISTS YOU'D BEEN TAUGHT TO LOVE WERE MALE. IT WAS AN INSPIRED PLACE. YOU BELONGED THERE. YOU DON'T FEEL THAT WAY ABOUT ANY PLACE ANYMORE.

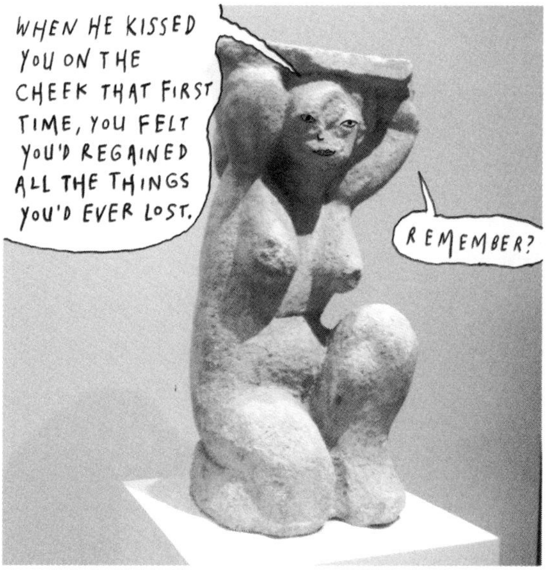
WHEN HE KISSED YOU ON THE CHEEK THAT FIRST TIME, YOU FELT YOU'D REGAINED ALL THE THINGS YOU'D EVER LOST.
REMEMBER?

YOU THOUGHT, "MY REAL LIFE IS ABOUT TO BEGIN NOW."
AND IT DID.

THE WORLD OPENED UP TO YOU.
YOU BECAME HAPPY
AND PERCEPTIVE
AND STRONG.

—WHICH WAS GOOD BECAUSE YOU NEEDED A LOT OF FAITH IN ORDER TO BE OK WHEN HE DISAPPEARED FOR AWHILE AND TO BE WARM WHEN HE WAS COLD AND TO LOVE HIM AND UNDERSTAND HIS SECRETIVENESS AND ALL HIS STRANGE NEUROSES.

YOU WOULD HAVE OUTGROWN HIM, YOU KNOW.
YOU'D ALREADY OUTGROWN HIM BY THE TIME HE LEFT YOU.

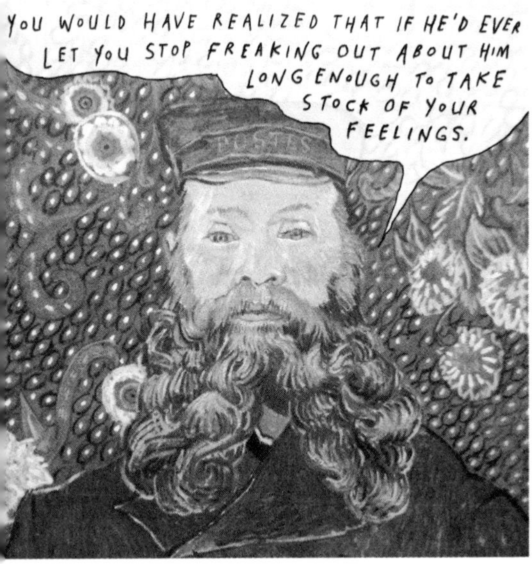
YOU WOULD HAVE REALIZED THAT IF HE'D EVER LET YOU STOP FREAKING OUT ABOUT HIM LONG ENOUGH TO TAKE STOCK OF YOUR FEELINGS.

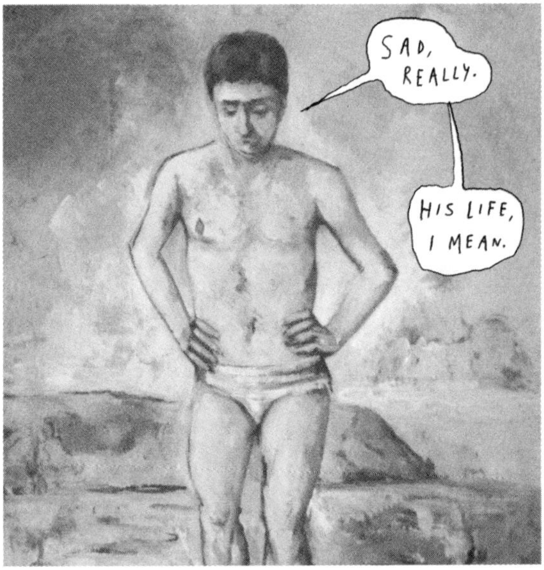
SAD, REALLY.
HIS LIFE, I MEAN.

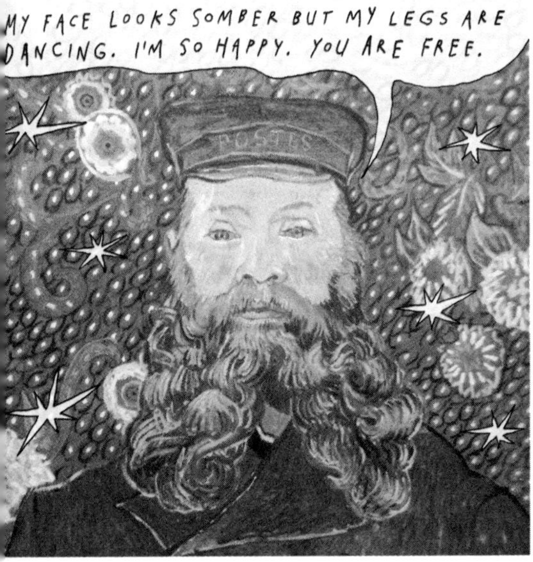
MY FACE LOOKS SOMBER BUT MY LEGS ARE DANCING. I'M SO HAPPY. YOU ARE FREE.

ARTISTS, IN ORDER OF APPEARANCE:

Henri Matisse, *The Piano Lesson*, 1916

Kazimir Malevich, *Painterly Realism of a Boy with a Knapsack—Color Masses in the Fourth Dimension*, 1915

Henri Matisse, *Dance (I)*, 1909

Henri Rousseau, *The Dream*, 1910

Andre Derain, *Bathers*, 1907

Kazimir Malevich, *Suprematist Composition: White on White*, 1918

Constantin Brancusi, *Mile Pogany*, 1913

Henri Matisse, *Female Nude*, 1907

Henri Matisse, *The Serf*, 1900-04

Pablo Picasso, *Standing Female Nude*, 1906

Amedeo Modigliani, *Caryatid*, 1914

Henri Matisse, *La Serpentine*, 1909

Alexander Calder, *Gibraltar*, 1936

Claude Monet, *Water Lilies*, 1914-26

Henri Matisse, *The Red Studio*, 1911

Vincent Van Gogh, *Portrait of The Postman*, 1889

Paul Cezanne, *The Bather*, 1898-1905

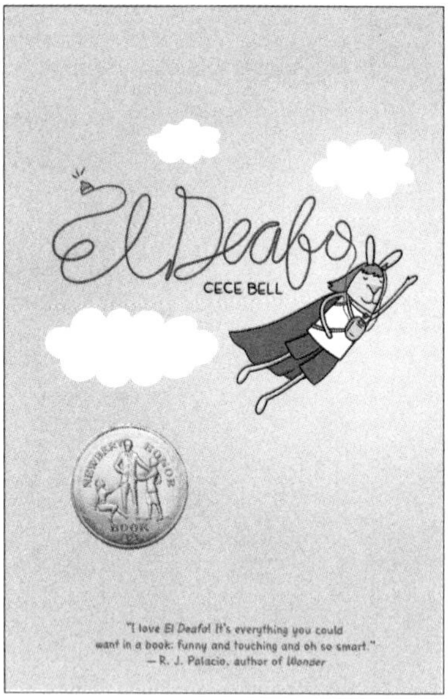
El Deafo
CECE BELL
NEWBERY HONOR BOOK
"I love El Deafo! It's everything you could want in a book: funny and touching and oh so smart."
— R. J. Palacio, author of Wonder

# El Deafo (*Excerpt*)

## CECE BELL

*excerpted from*

El Deafo
AMULET BOOKS / ABRAMS
6 × 9 inches · 248 pages

COLOR BY DAVID LASKY

### Biography

Cece Bell is an author and illustrator of books for children. She lives in an old church and works right next door in a new-ish barn. Her graphic memoir, *El Deafo*, which chronicles her childhood experiences with hearing loss, received a Newbery Honor and an Eisner Award in 2015. Cece's other books include the Geisel Honor book *Rabbit & Robot: The Sleepover*, *Bee-Wigged*, and the Sock Monkey series. She has also illustrated books written by her husband, Tom Angleberger, including the picture book *Crankee Doodle*, as well as the Inspector Flytrap chapter book series. cecebell.com

### Statement

The first thirty-three pages of *El Deafo* cover the nitty-gritty of my personal experience with hearing loss, as well as the nuts and bolts of hearing aid technology at the time. I describe the way I lost my hearing, the feelings (both physical and emotional) I experienced when I got my first hearing aid, and the frustrations I endured as I learned how to communicate by lip reading. These pages set the stage for *El Deafo*'s two main storylines: the one about the powerful (and gigantic) hearing aid that made me feel both isolated and a bit like a superhero, and the other (and ultimately more important) one about the quest to find a True Friend. The page describing my mother's realization that I could no longer hear were particularly painful to write and draw, especially now that I am a mother and could relive, somewhat at least, the experience through her eyes.

one

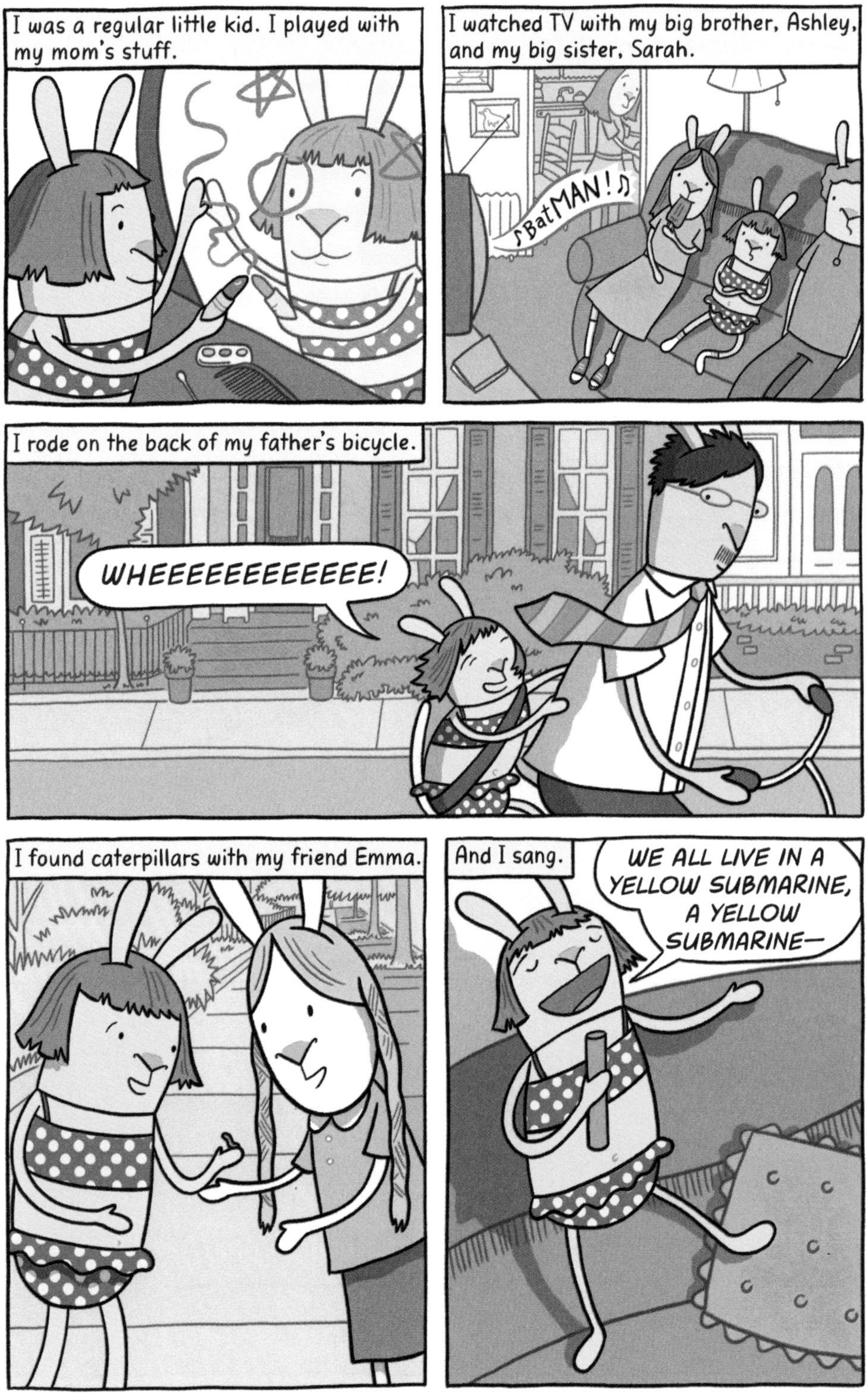
I was a regular little kid. I played with my mom's stuff.
I watched TV with my big brother, Ashley, and my big sister, Sarah.
♪BatMAN!♪
I rode on the back of my father's bicycle.
WHEEEEEEEEEEEE!
I found caterpillars with my friend Emma.
And I sang.
WE ALL LIVE IN A YELLOW SUBMARINE, A YELLOW SUBMARINE—

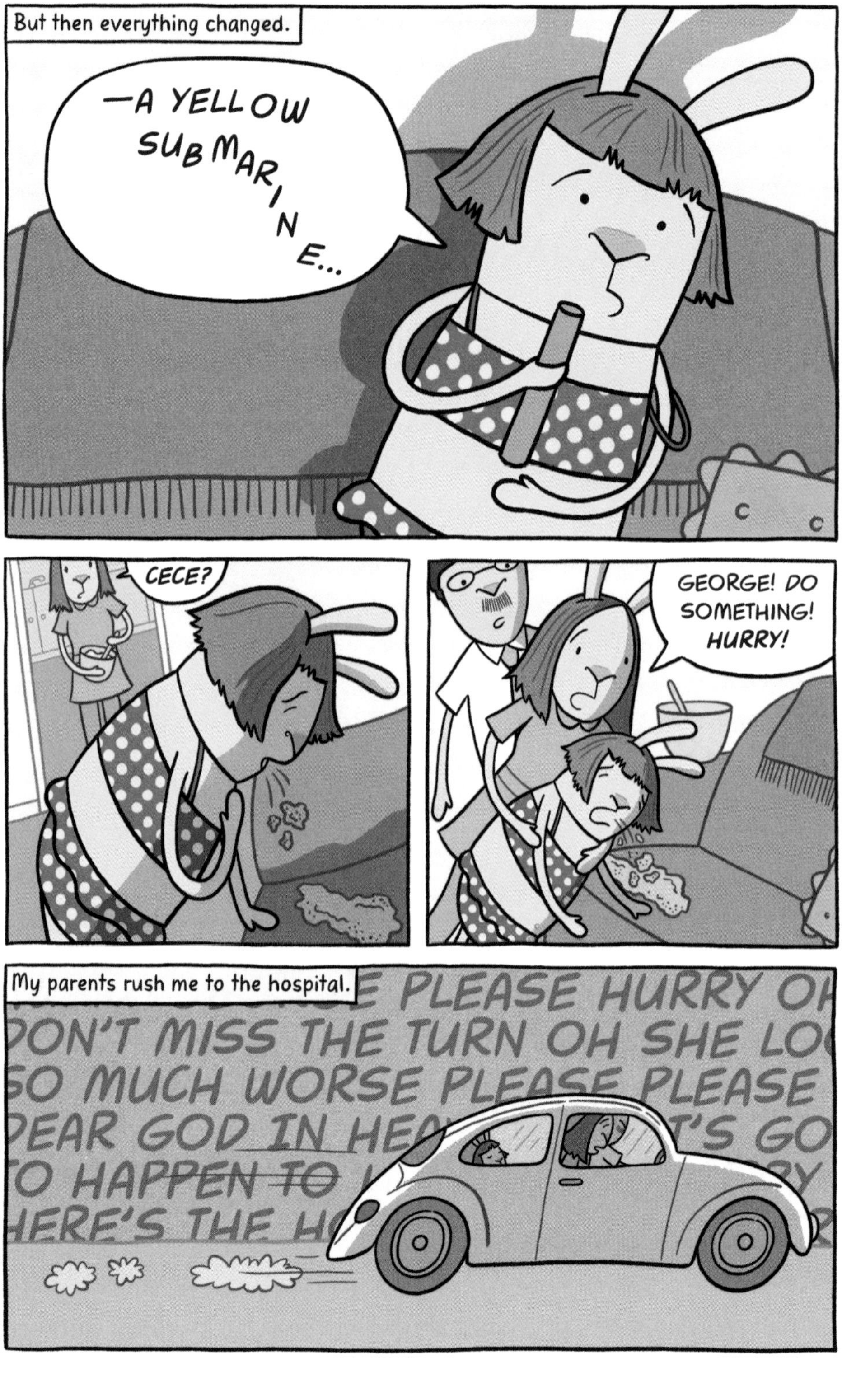
But then everything changed.
—A YELLOW SUBMARINE...
CECE?
GEORGE! DO SOMETHING! HURRY!
My parents rush me to the hospital.
PLEASE HURRY
DON'T MISS THE TURN OH SHE
SO MUCH WORSE PLEASE PLEASE
DEAR GOD IN
TO HAPPEN TO
HERE'S THE

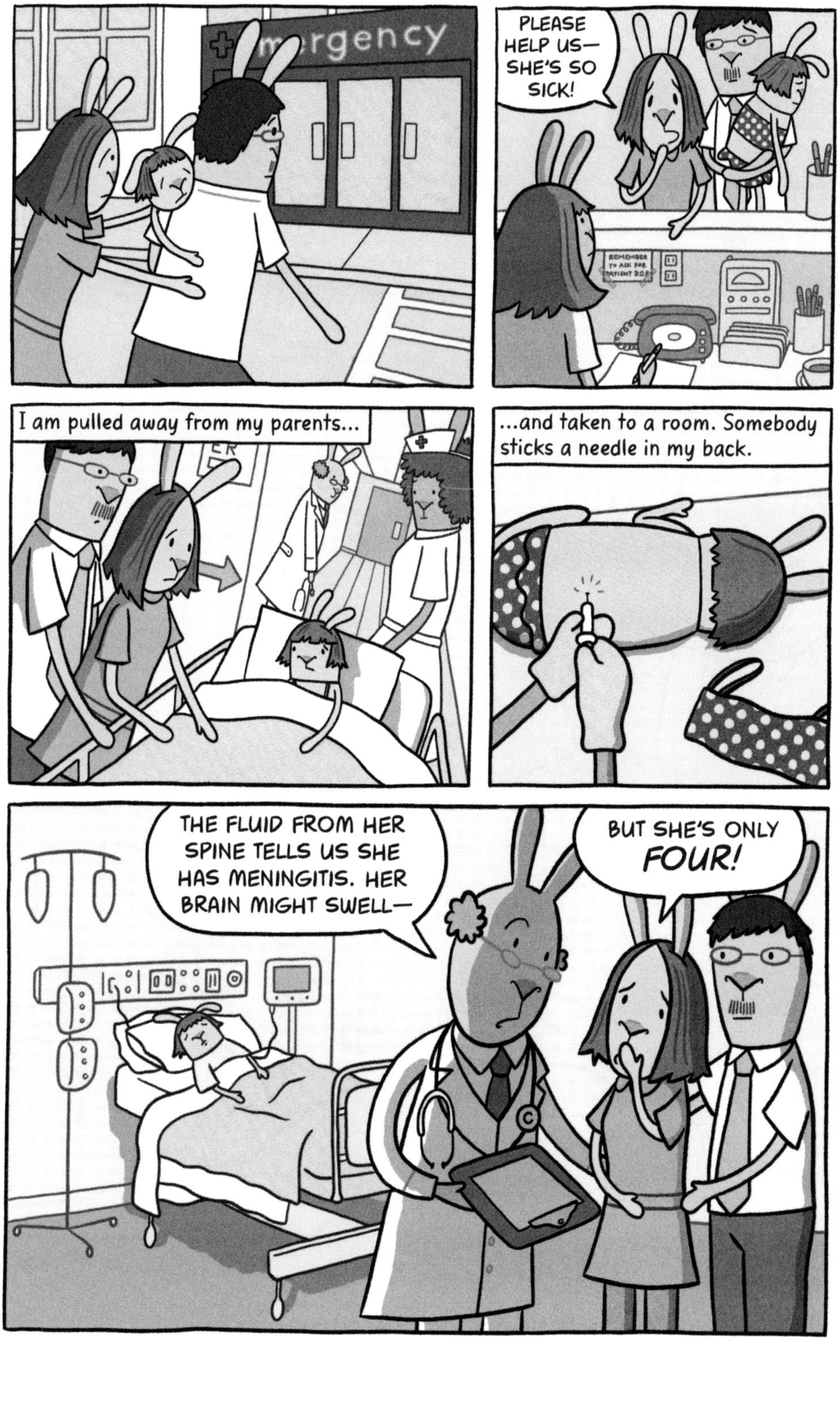
PLEASE HELP US— SHE'S SO SICK!
I am pulled away from my parents...
...and taken to a room. Somebody sticks a needle in my back.
THE FLUID FROM HER SPINE TELLS US SHE HAS MENINGITIS. HER BRAIN MIGHT SWELL—
BUT SHE'S ONLY *FOUR!*

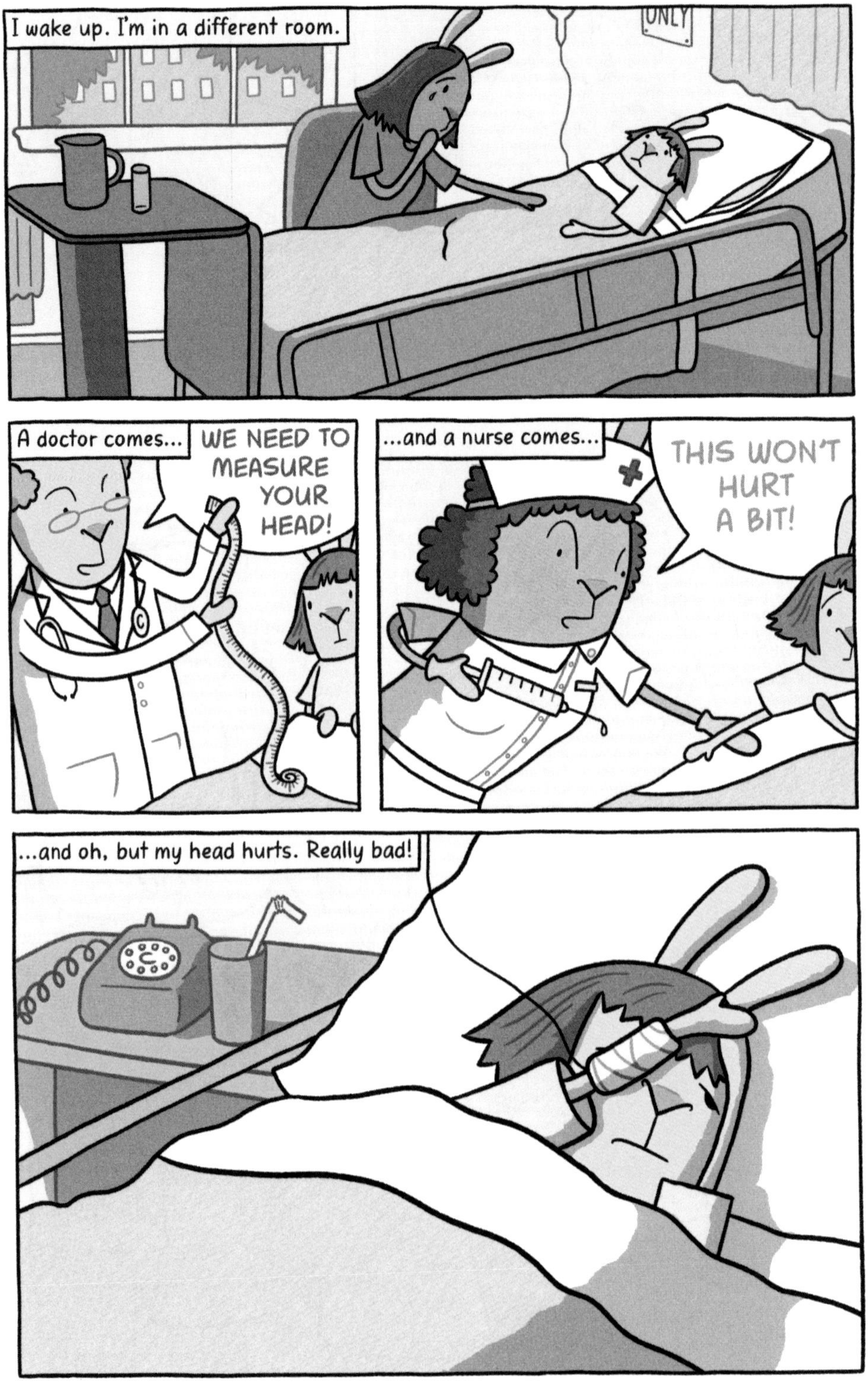
I wake up. I'm in a different room.
ONLY
A doctor comes...
WE NEED TO MEASURE YOUR HEAD!
...and a nurse comes...
THIS WON'T HURT A BIT!
...and oh, but my head hurts. Really bad!

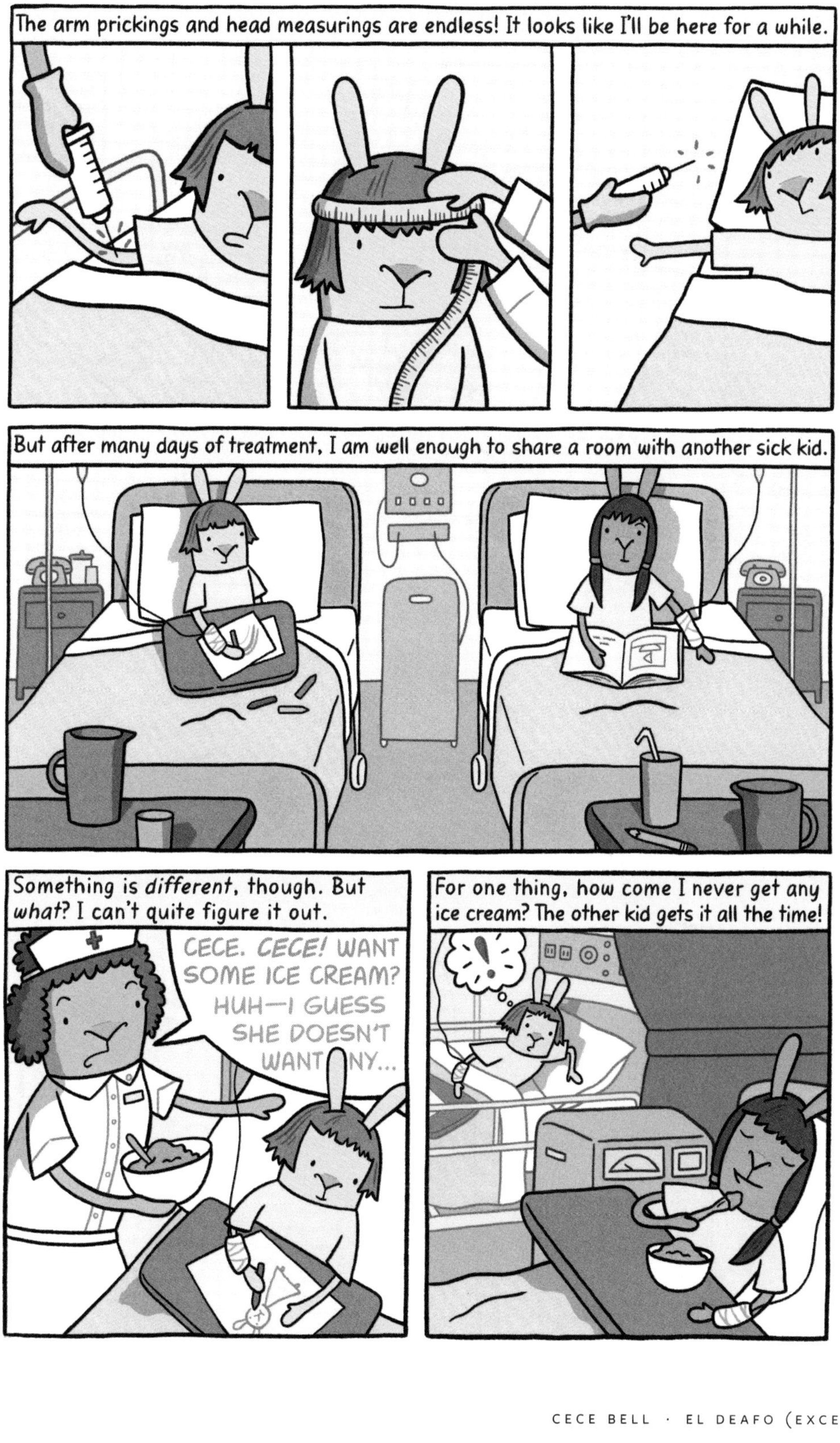

The arm prickings and head measurings are endless! It looks like I'll be here for a while.
But after many days of treatment, I am well enough to share a room with another sick kid.
Something is *different*, though. But *what*? I can't quite figure it out.
CECE. *CECE!* WANT SOME ICE CREAM? HUH—I GUESS SHE DOESN'T WANT ANY...
For one thing, how come I never get any ice cream? The other kid gets it all the time!

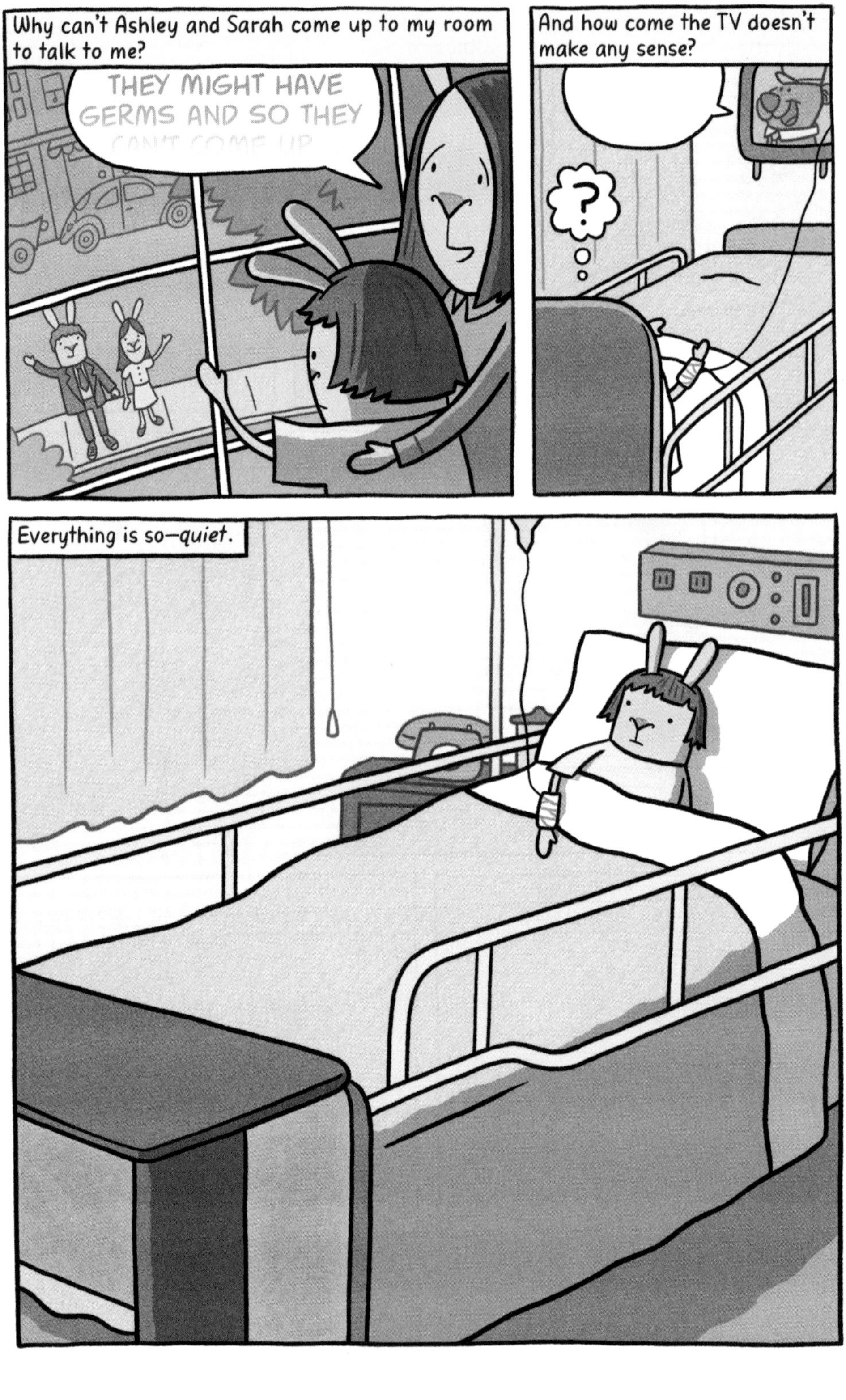
Why can't Ashley and Sarah come up to my room to talk to me?
THEY MIGHT HAVE GERMS AND SO THEY
And how come the TV doesn't make any sense?
?
Everything is so—*quiet*.

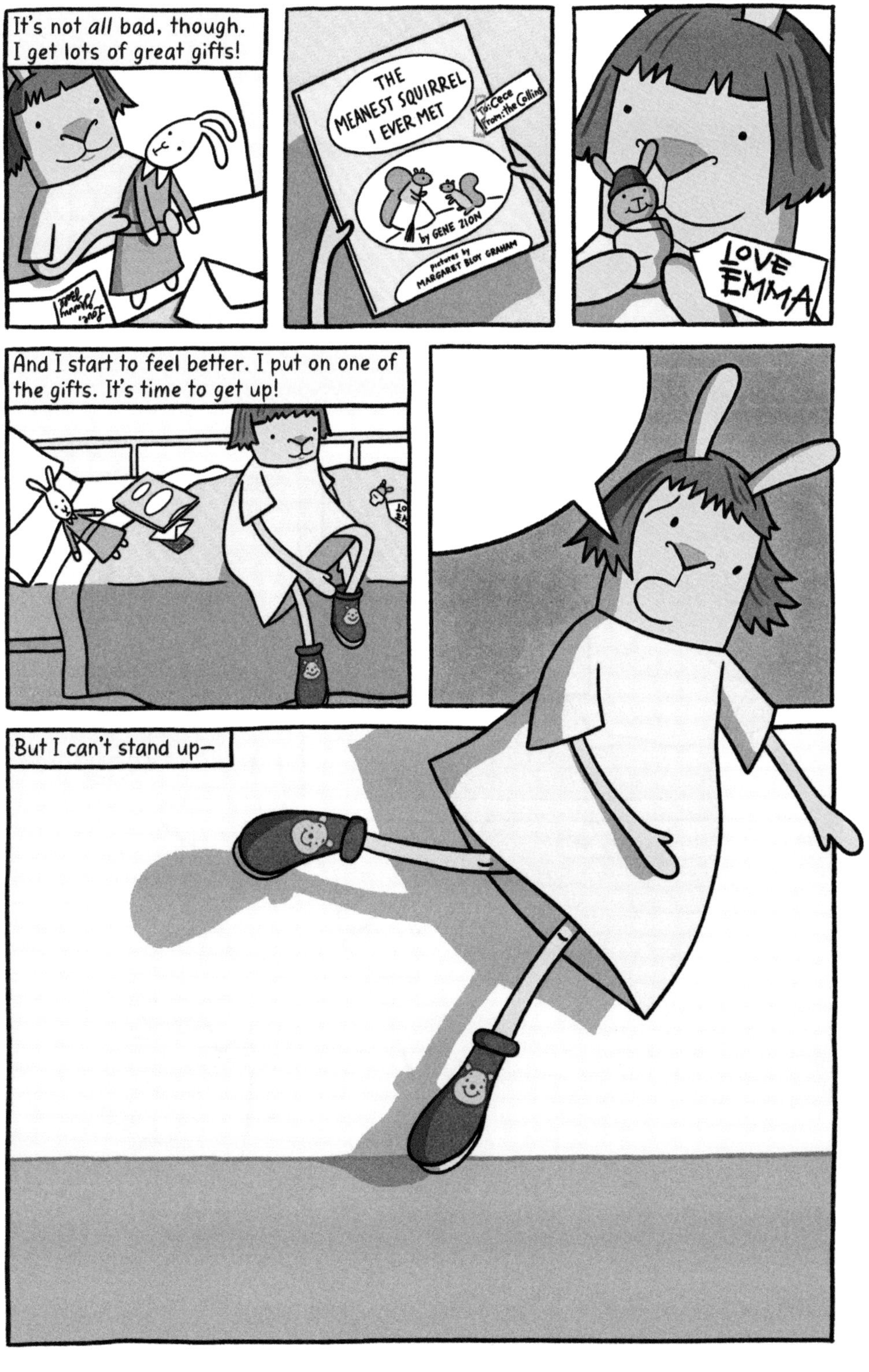
It's not *all* bad, though. I get lots of great gifts!
THE MEANEST SQUIRREL I EVER MET
To: Cece
From: the Collins
by GENE ZION
pictures by MARGARET BLOY GRAHAM
LOVE EMMA
And I start to feel better. I put on one of the gifts. It's time to get up!
But I can't stand up–

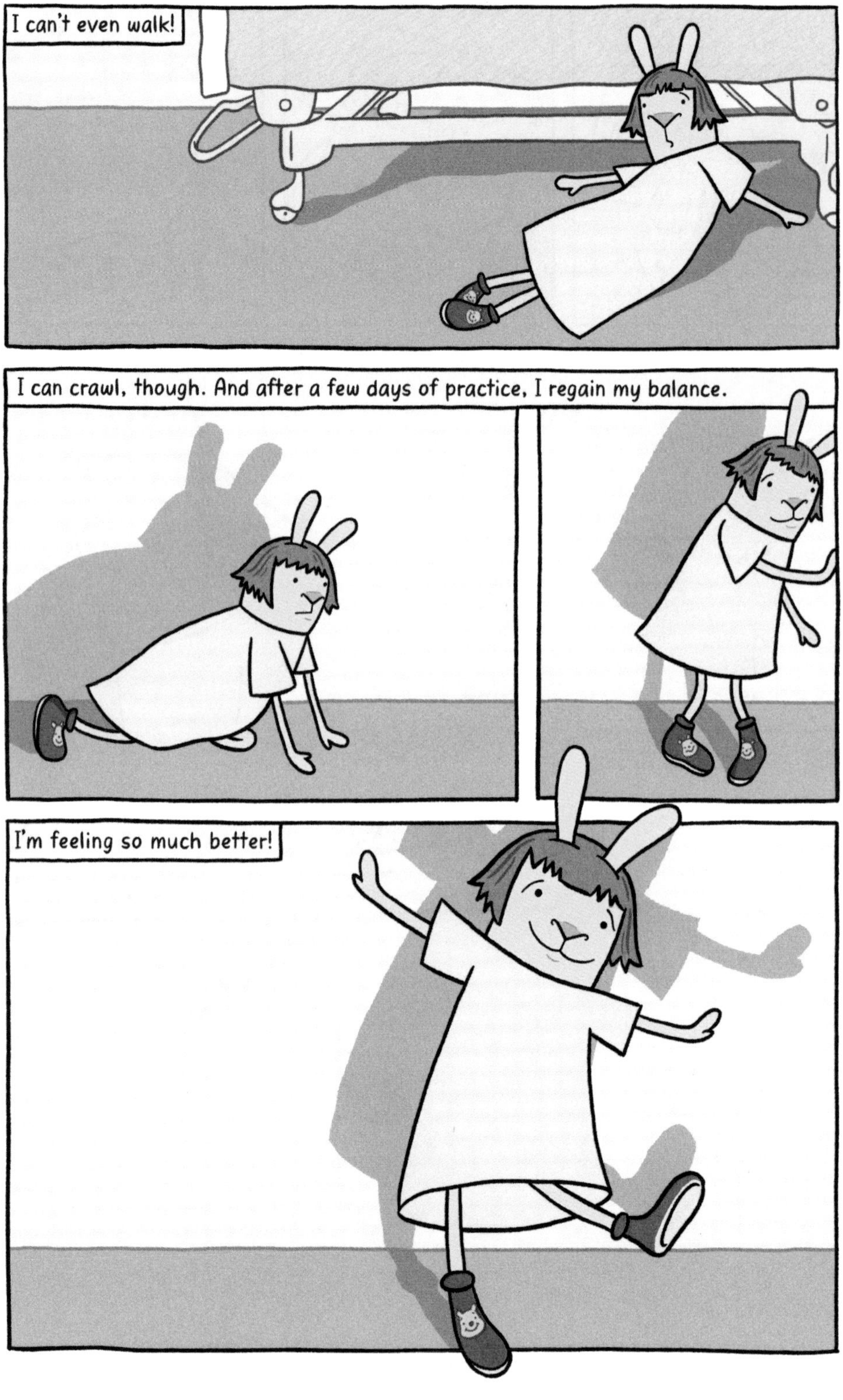

I can't even walk!
I can crawl, though. And after a few days of practice, I regain my balance.
I'm feeling so much better!

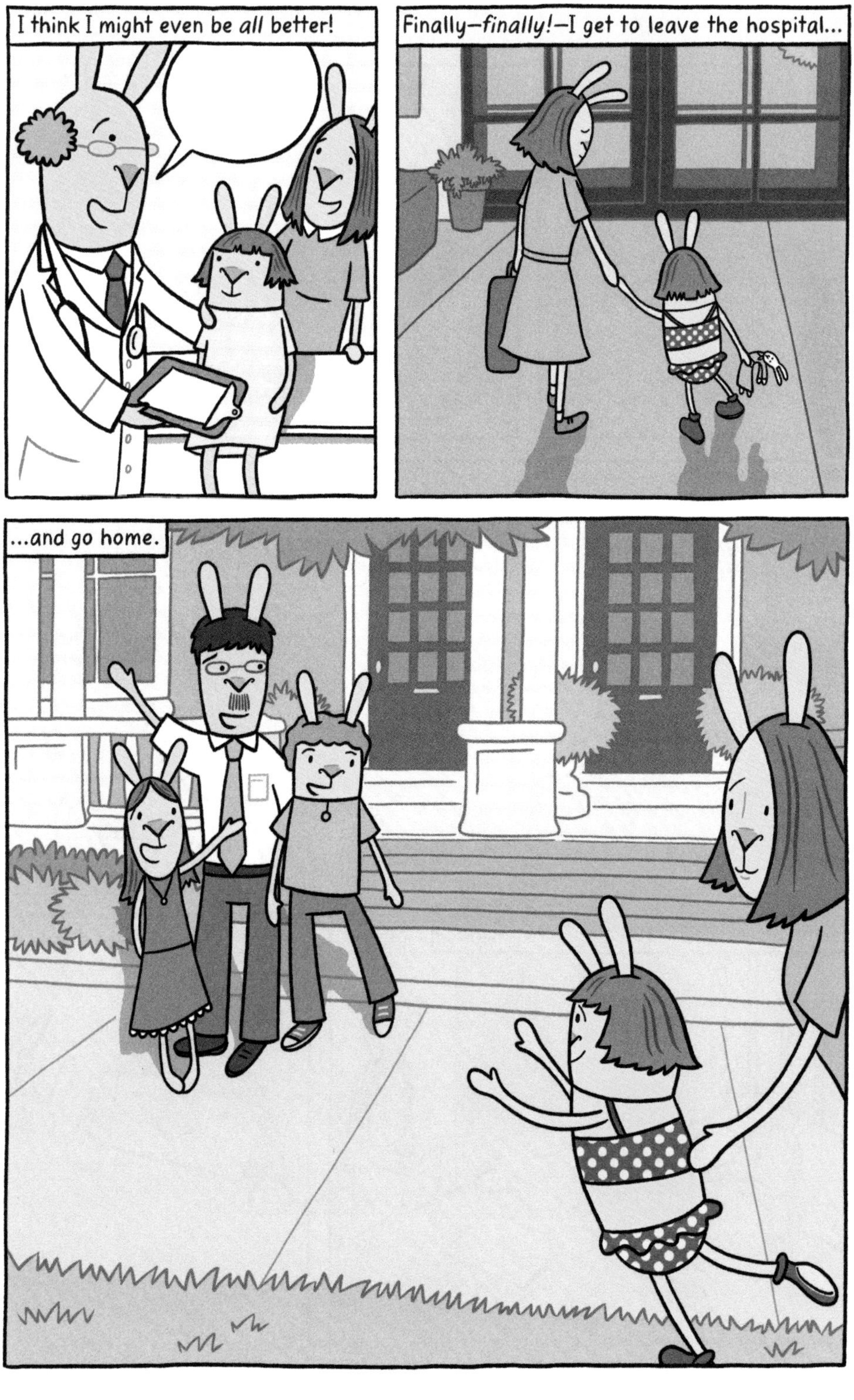
I think I might even be *all* better!
Finally—*finally!*—I get to leave the hospital...
...and go home.

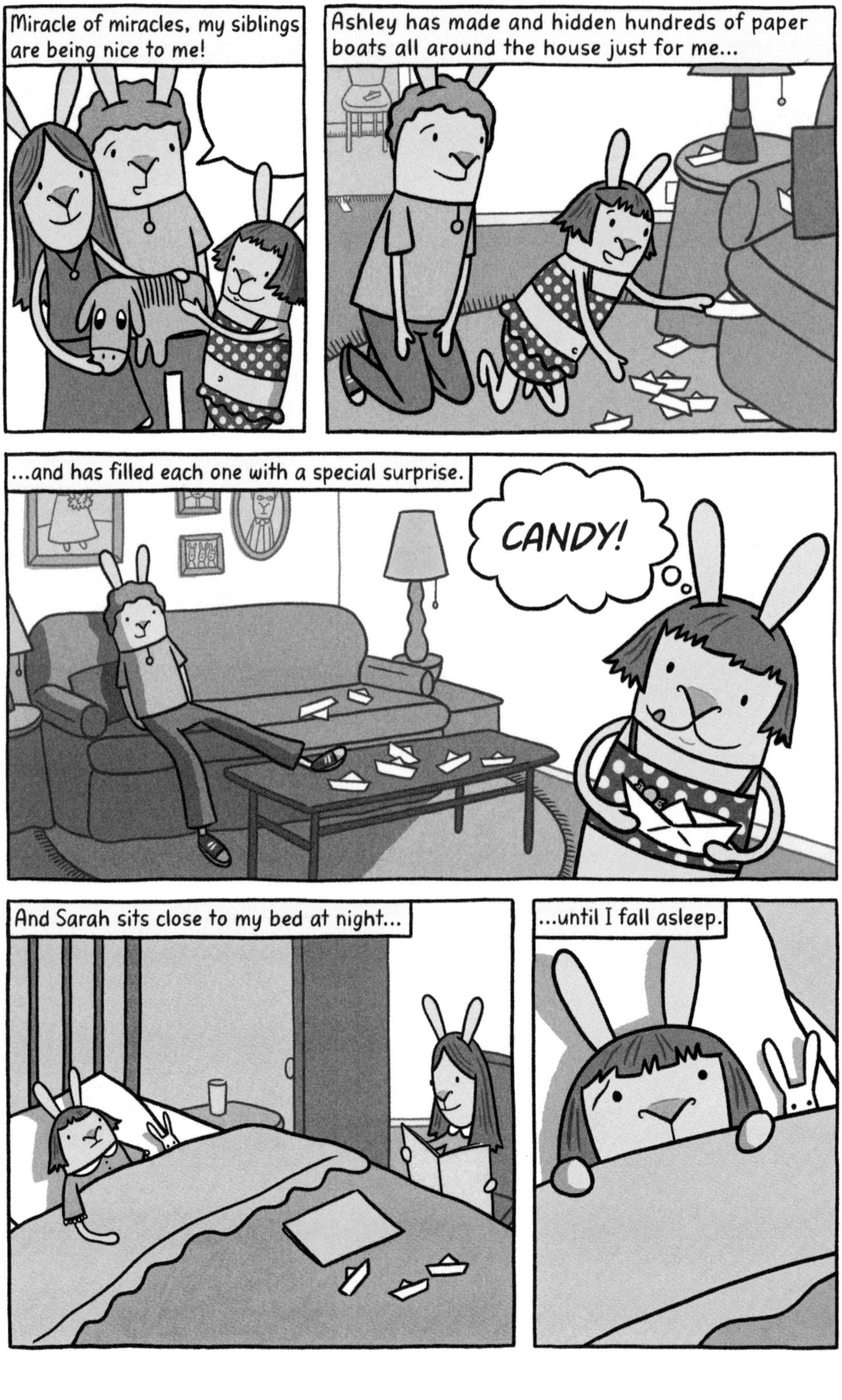
Miracle of miracles, my siblings are being nice to me!
Ashley has made and hidden hundreds of paper boats all around the house just for me...
...and has filled each one with a special surprise.
CANDY!
And Sarah sits close to my bed at night...
...until I fall asleep.

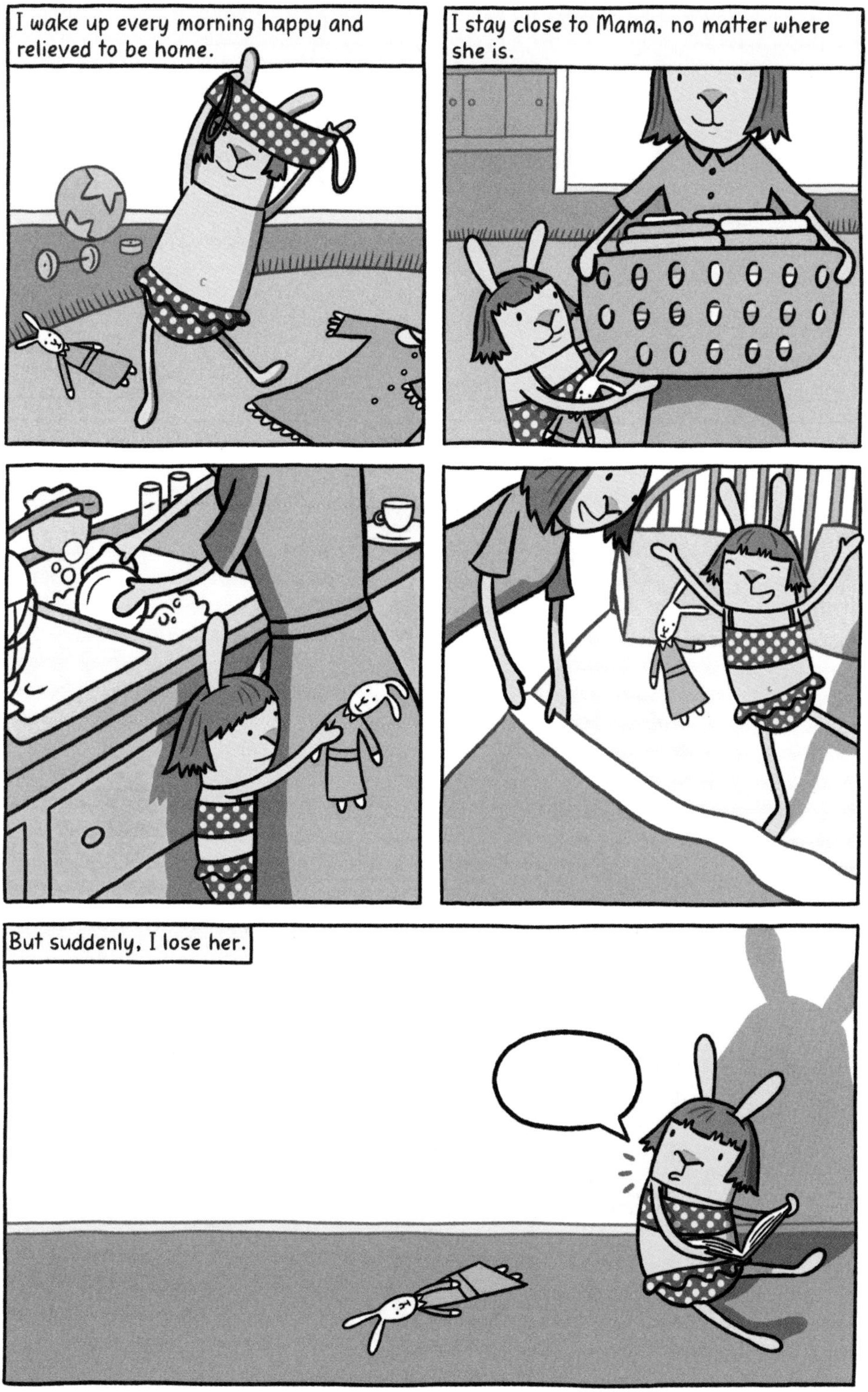
I wake up every morning happy and relieved to be home.
I stay close to Mama, no matter where she is.
But suddenly, I lose her.

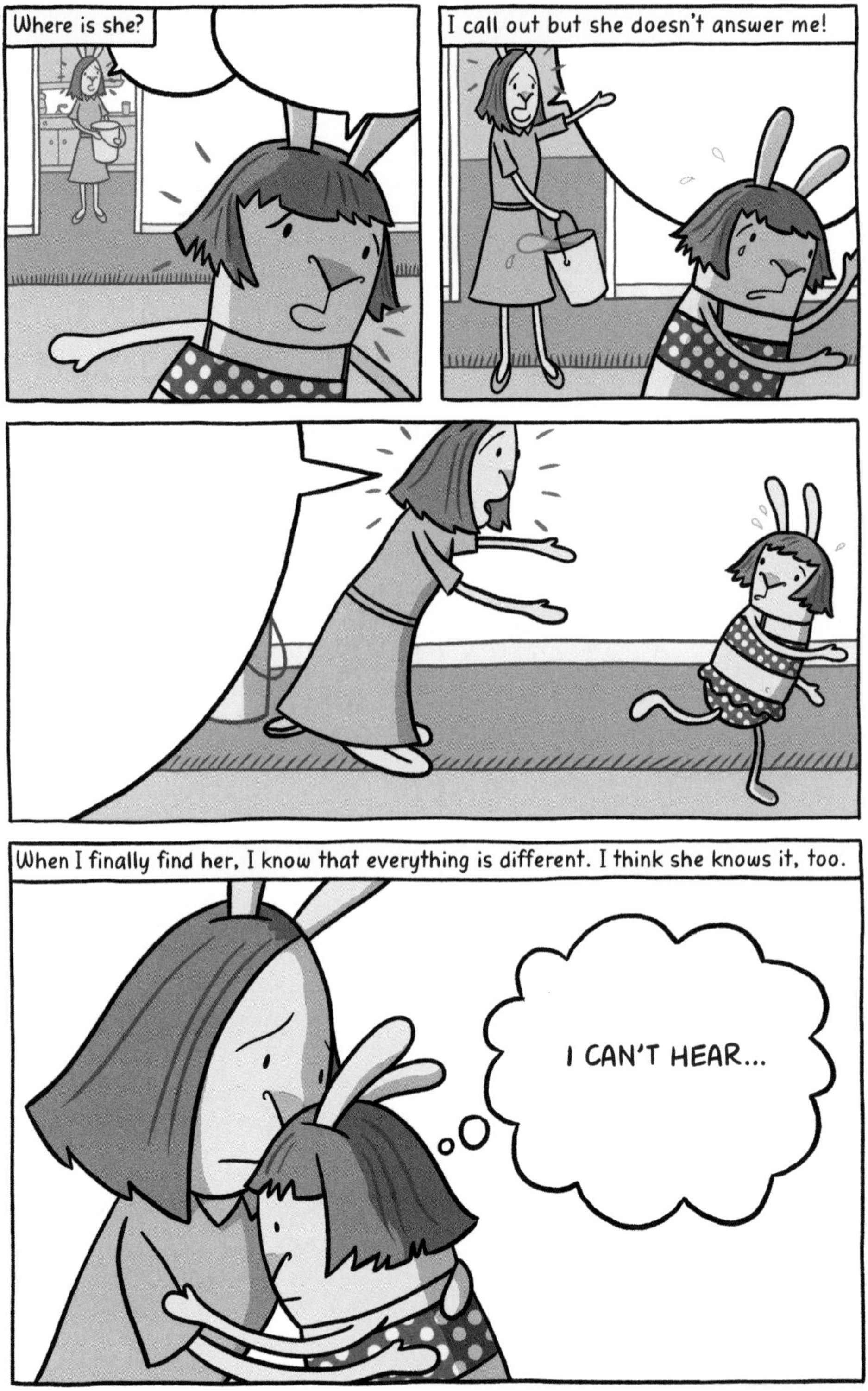
Where is she?
I call out but she doesn't answer me!
When I finally find her, I know that everything is different. I think she knows it, too.
I CAN'T HEAR...

# two

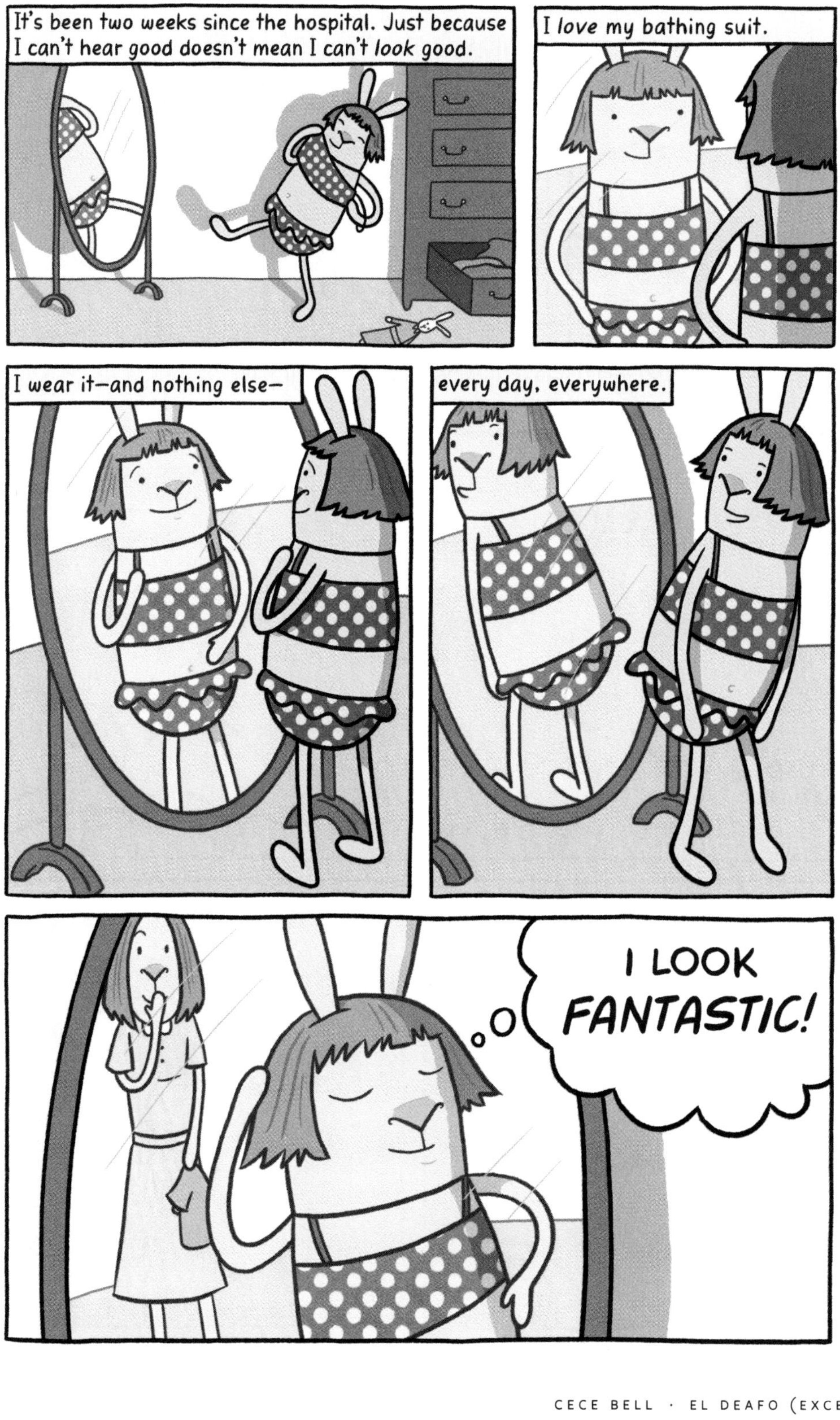

It's been two weeks since the hospital. Just because I can't hear good doesn't mean I can't *look* good.
I *love* my bathing suit.
I wear it—and nothing else—
every day, everywhere.
I LOOK FANTASTIC!

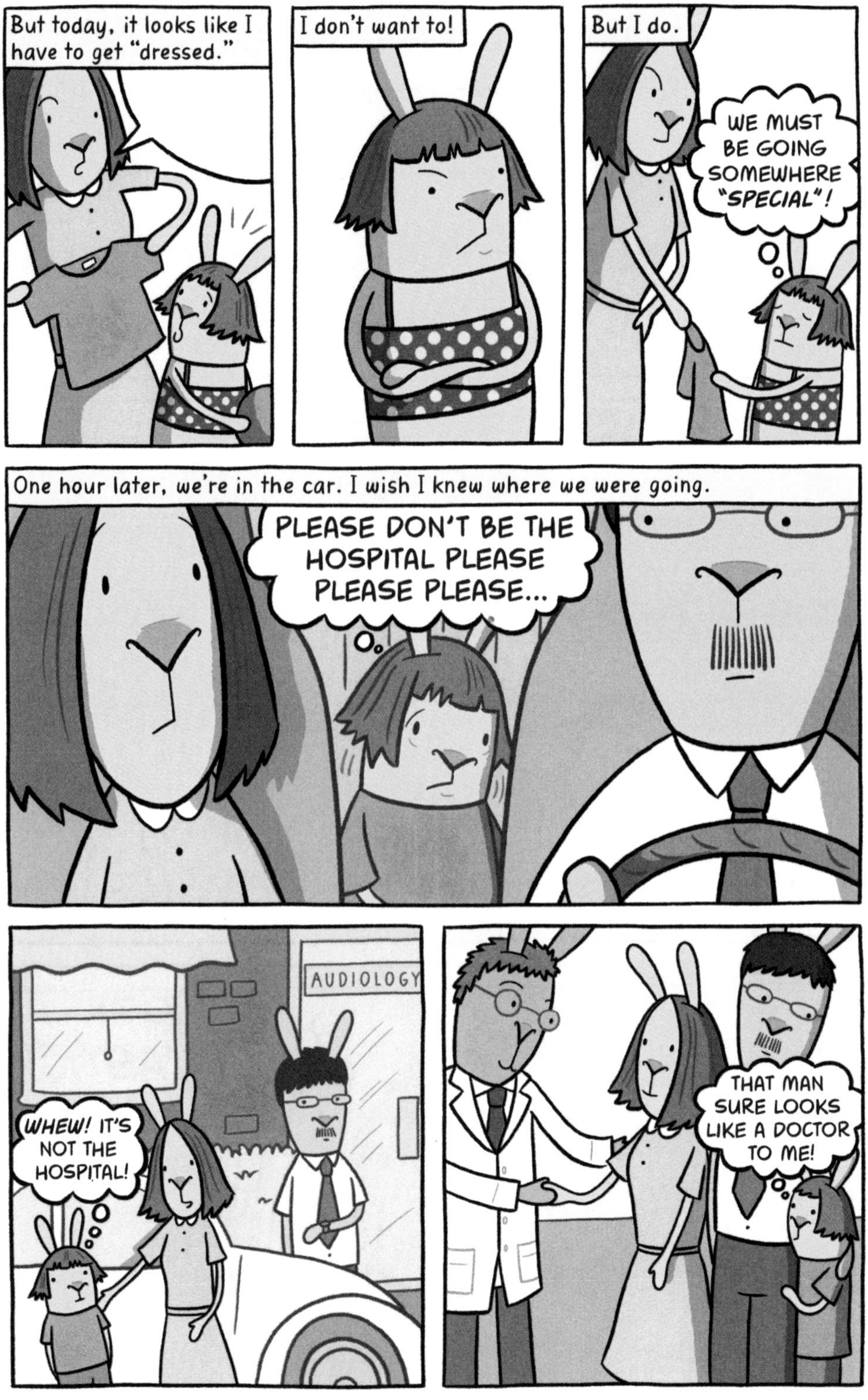

But today, it looks like I have to get "dressed."
I don't want to!
But I do.
WE MUST BE GOING SOMEWHERE "SPECIAL"!
One hour later, we're in the car. I wish I knew where we were going.
PLEASE DON'T BE THE HOSPITAL PLEASE PLEASE PLEASE...
AUDIOLOGY
WHEW! IT'S NOT THE HOSPITAL!
THAT MAN SURE LOOKS LIKE A DOCTOR TO ME!

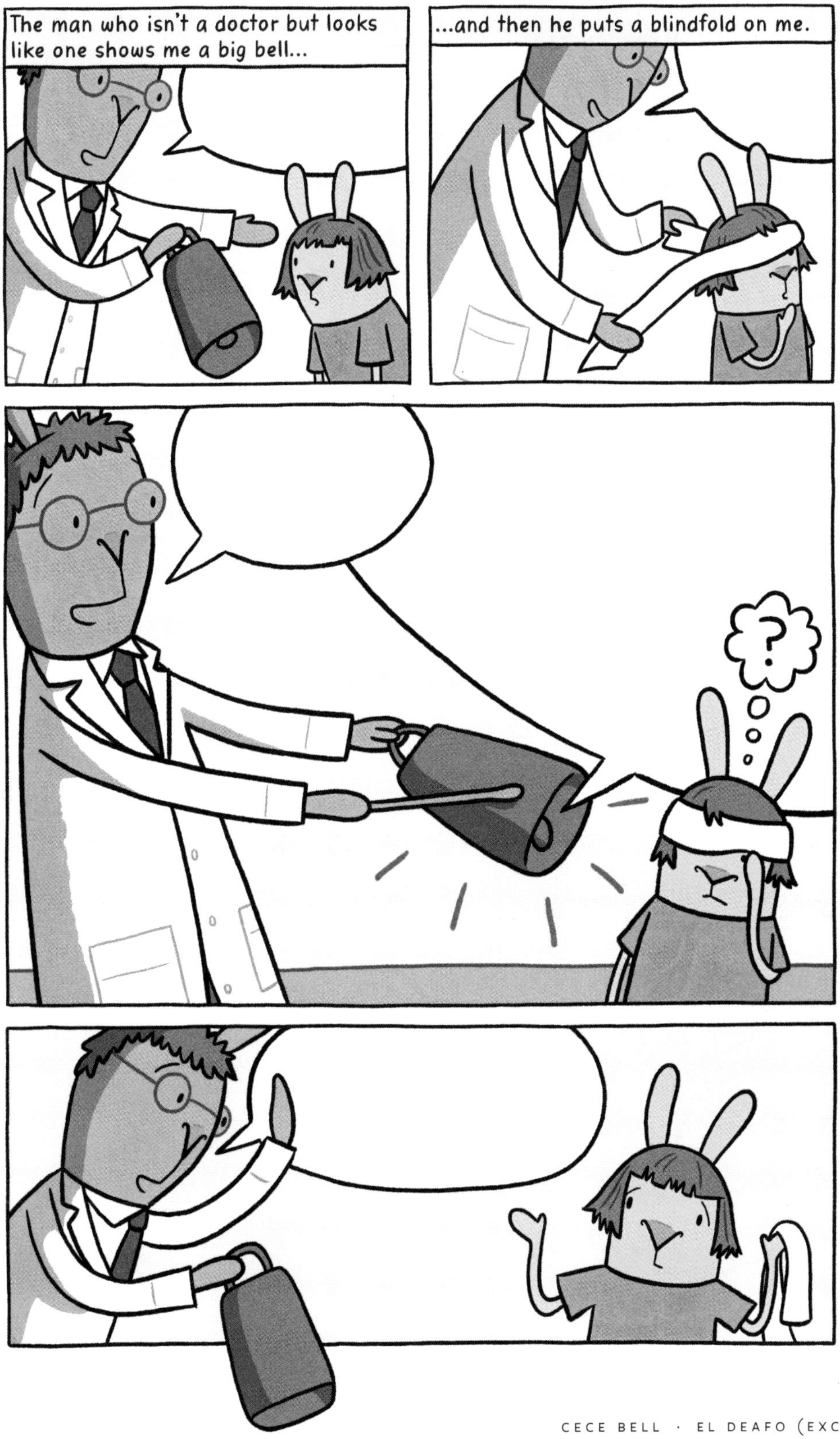
The man who isn't a doctor but looks like one shows me a big bell...
...and then he puts a blindfold on me.
?

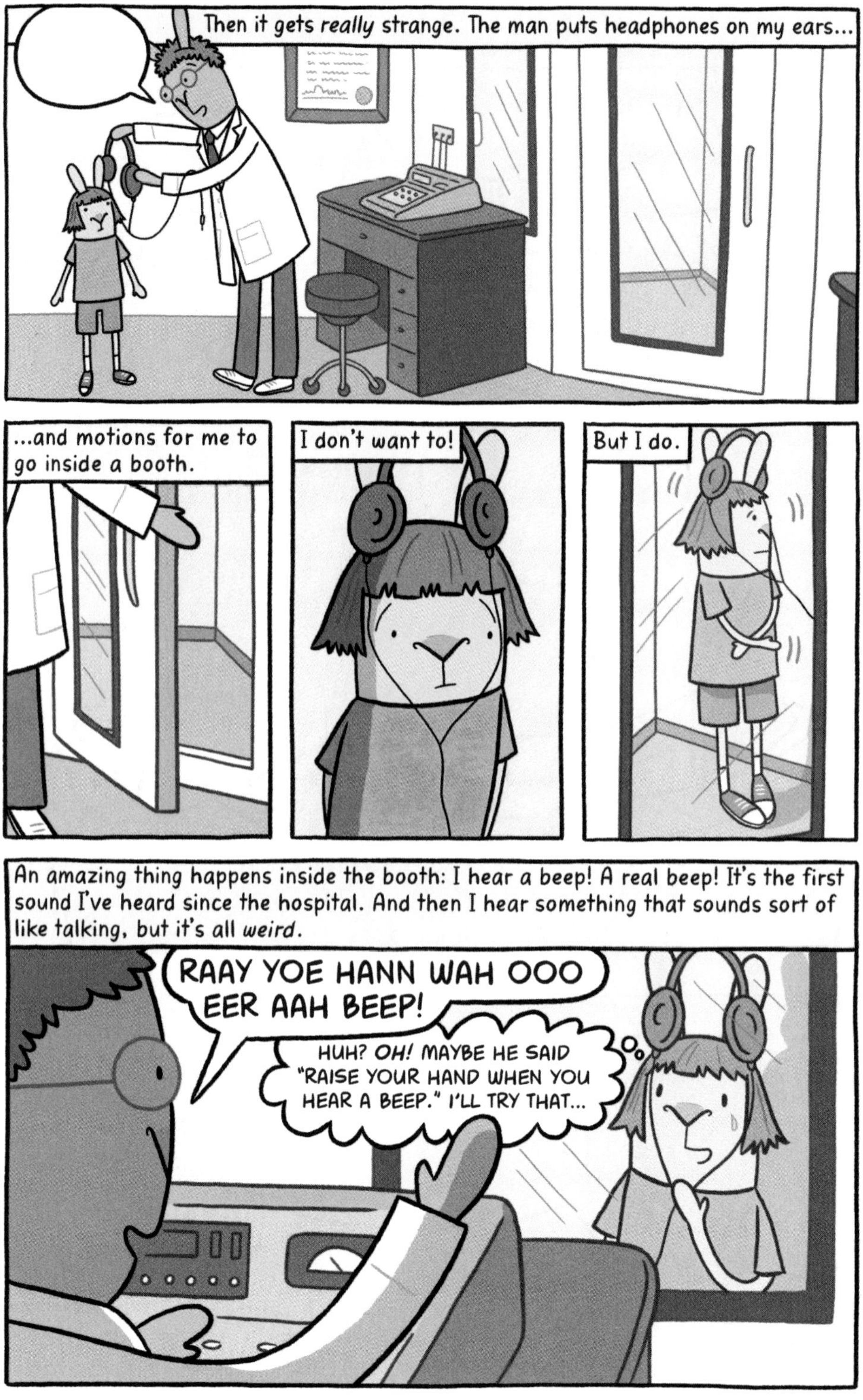
Then it gets *really* strange. The man puts headphones on my ears...
...and motions for me to go inside a booth.
I don't want to!
But I do.
An amazing thing happens inside the booth: I hear a beep! A real beep! It's the first sound I've heard since the hospital. And then I hear something that sounds sort of like talking, but it's all *weird*.
RAAY YOE HANN WAH OOO EER AAH BEEP!
HUH? *OH!* MAYBE HE SAID "RAISE YOUR HAND WHEN YOU HEAR A BEEP." I'LL TRY THAT...

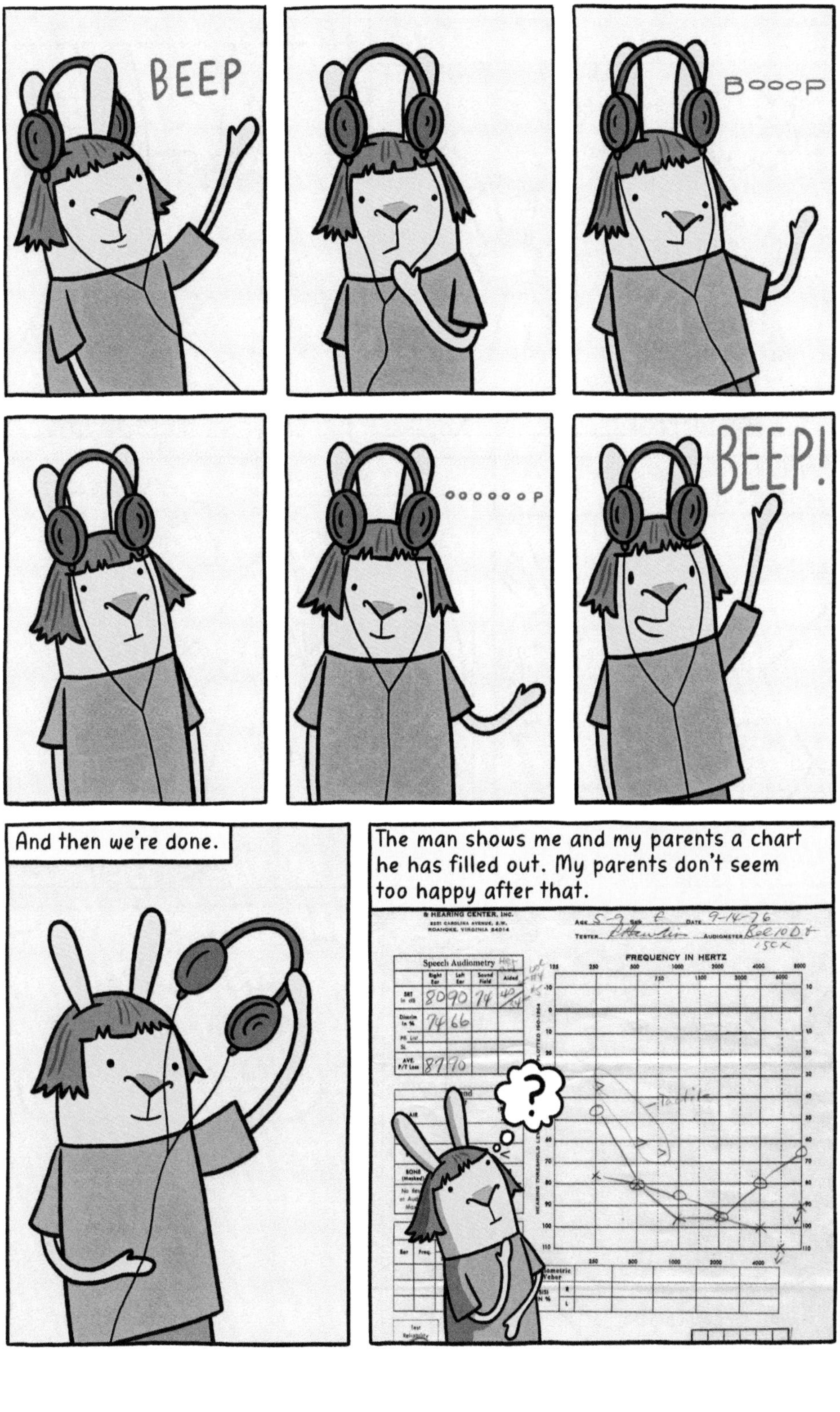
BEEP
Booop
oooooop
BEEP!
And then we're done.
The man shows me and my parents a chart he has filled out. My parents don't seem too happy after that.
FREQUENCY IN HERTZ
Speech Audiometry
?

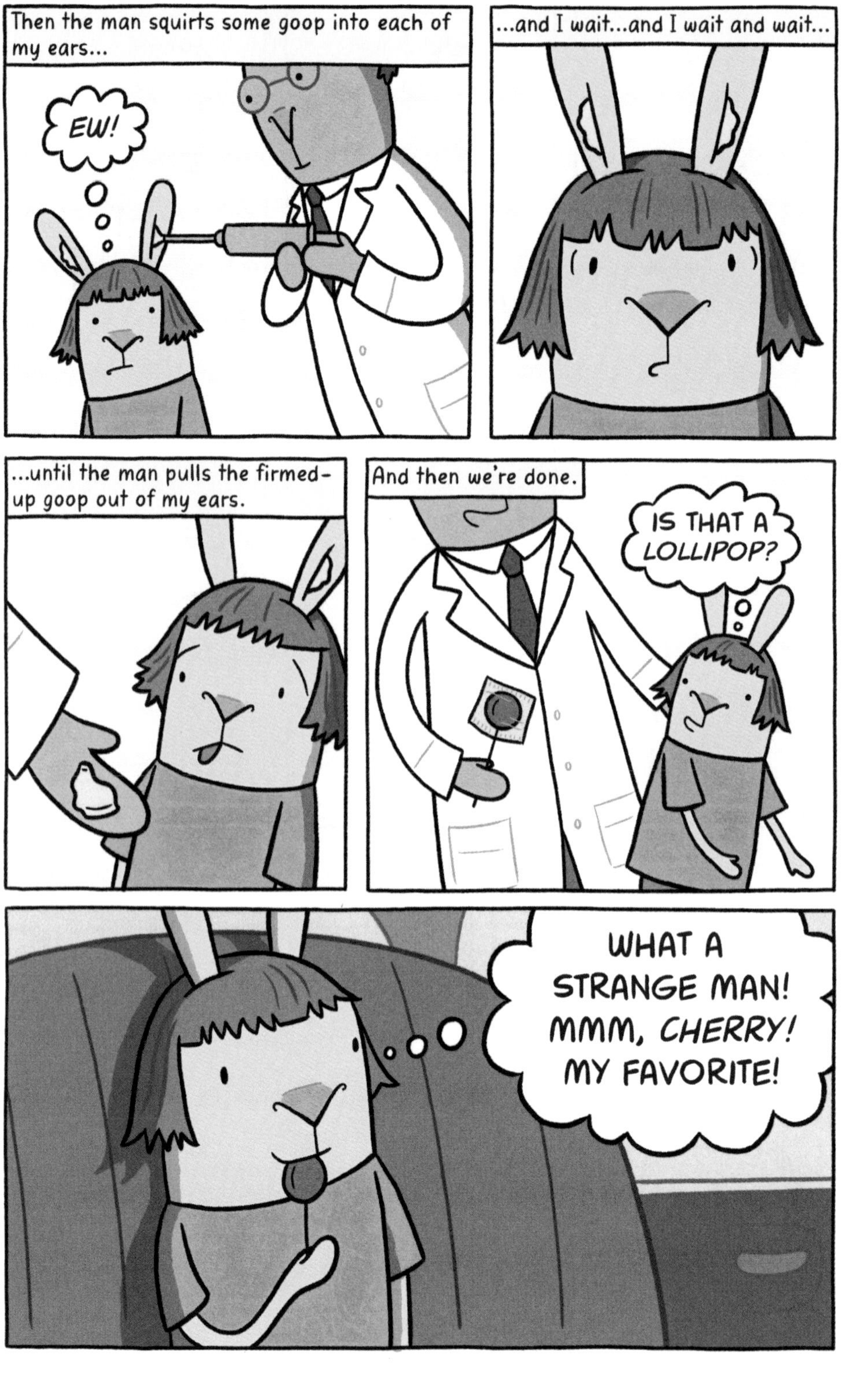

Then the man squirts some goop into each of my ears...
EW!
...and I wait...and I wait and wait...
...until the man pulls the firmed-up goop out of my ears.
And then we're done.
IS THAT A LOLLIPOP?
WHAT A STRANGE MAN! MMM, CHERRY! MY FAVORITE!

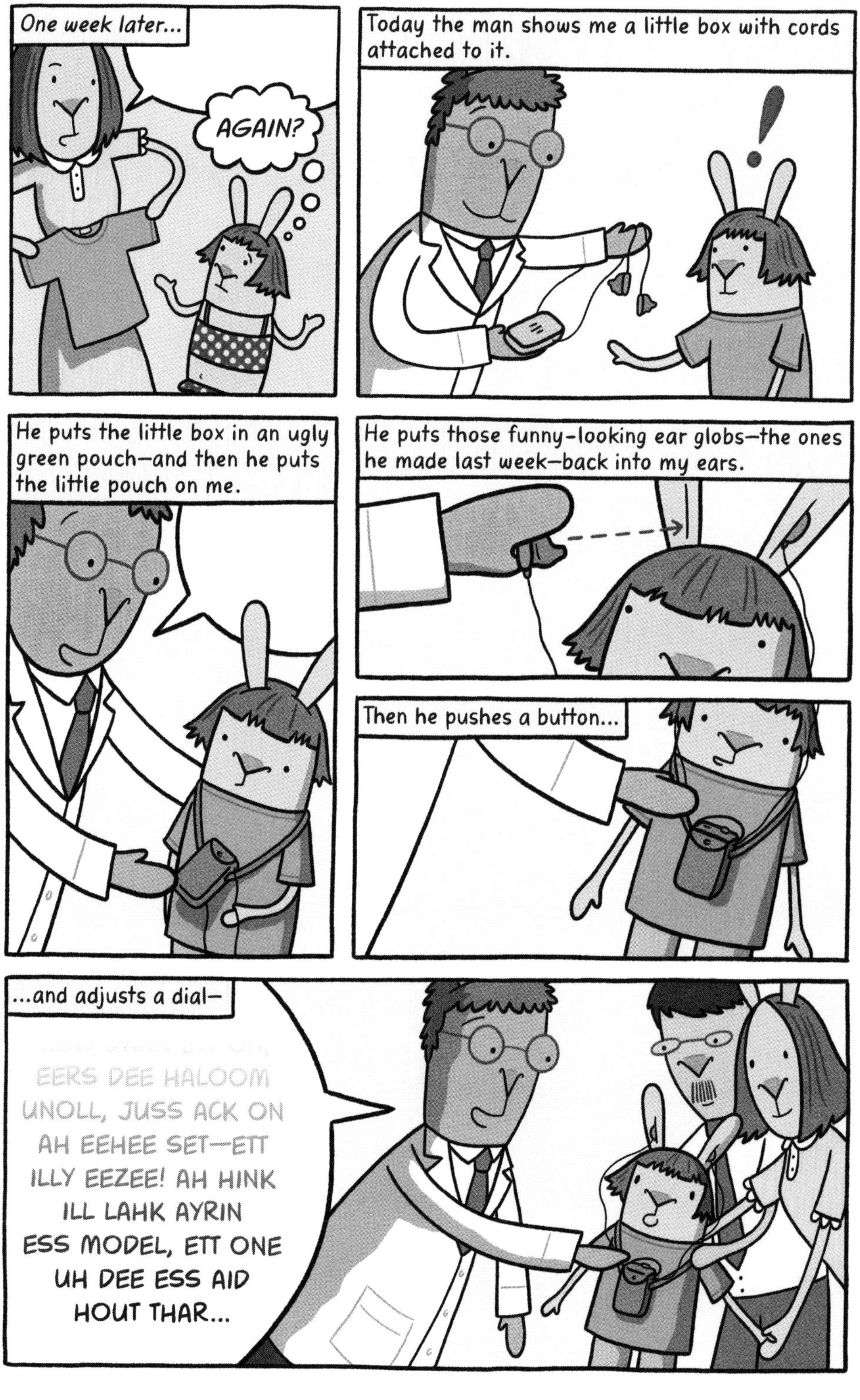
One week later...
AGAIN?
Today the man shows me a little box with cords attached to it.
!
He puts the little box in an ugly green pouch—and then he puts the little pouch on me.
He puts those funny-looking ear globs—the ones he made last week—back into my ears.
Then he pushes a button...
...and adjusts a dial—
EERS DEE HALOOM UNOLL, JUSS ACK ON AH EEHEE SET—ETT ILLY EEZEE! AH HINK ILL LAHK AYRIN ESS MODEL, ETT ONE UH DEE ESS AID HOUT THAR...

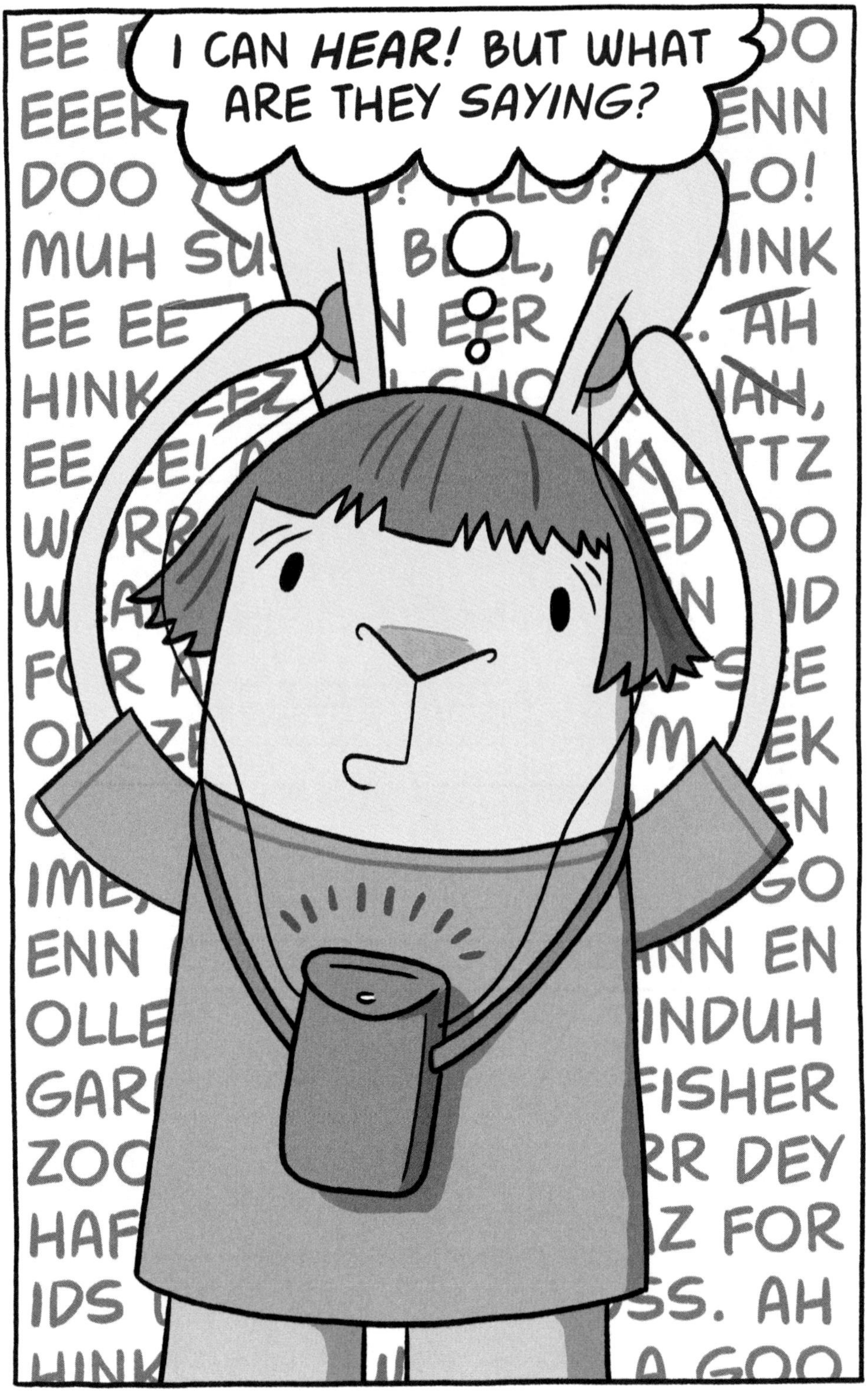
I CAN HEAR! BUT WHAT ARE THEY SAYING?

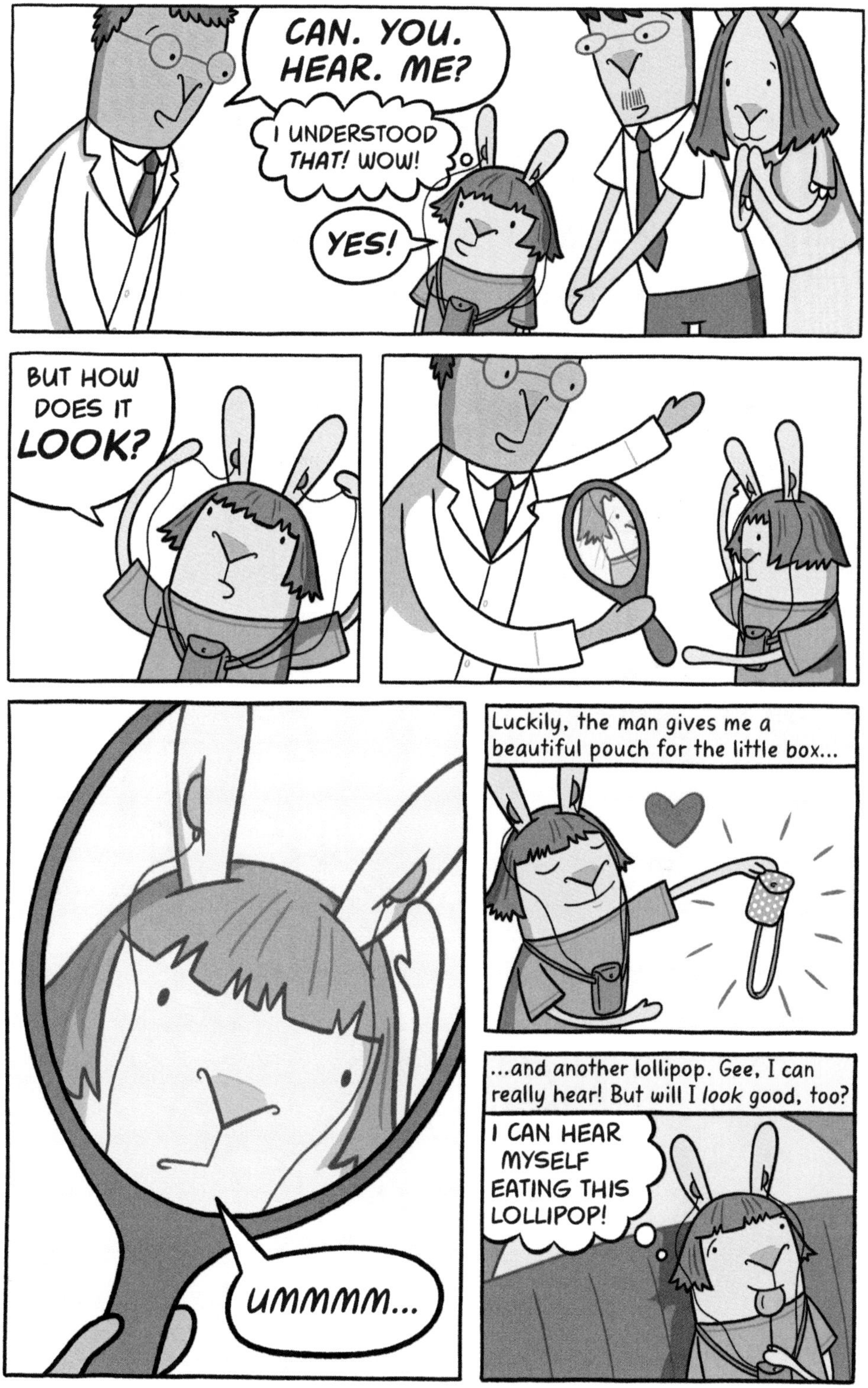

CAN. YOU. HEAR. ME?
I UNDERSTOOD THAT! WOW!
YES!
BUT HOW DOES IT LOOK?
UMMMM...
Luckily, the man gives me a beautiful pouch for the little box...
...and another lollipop. Gee, I can really hear! But will I look good, too?
I CAN HEAR MYSELF EATING THIS LOLLIPOP!

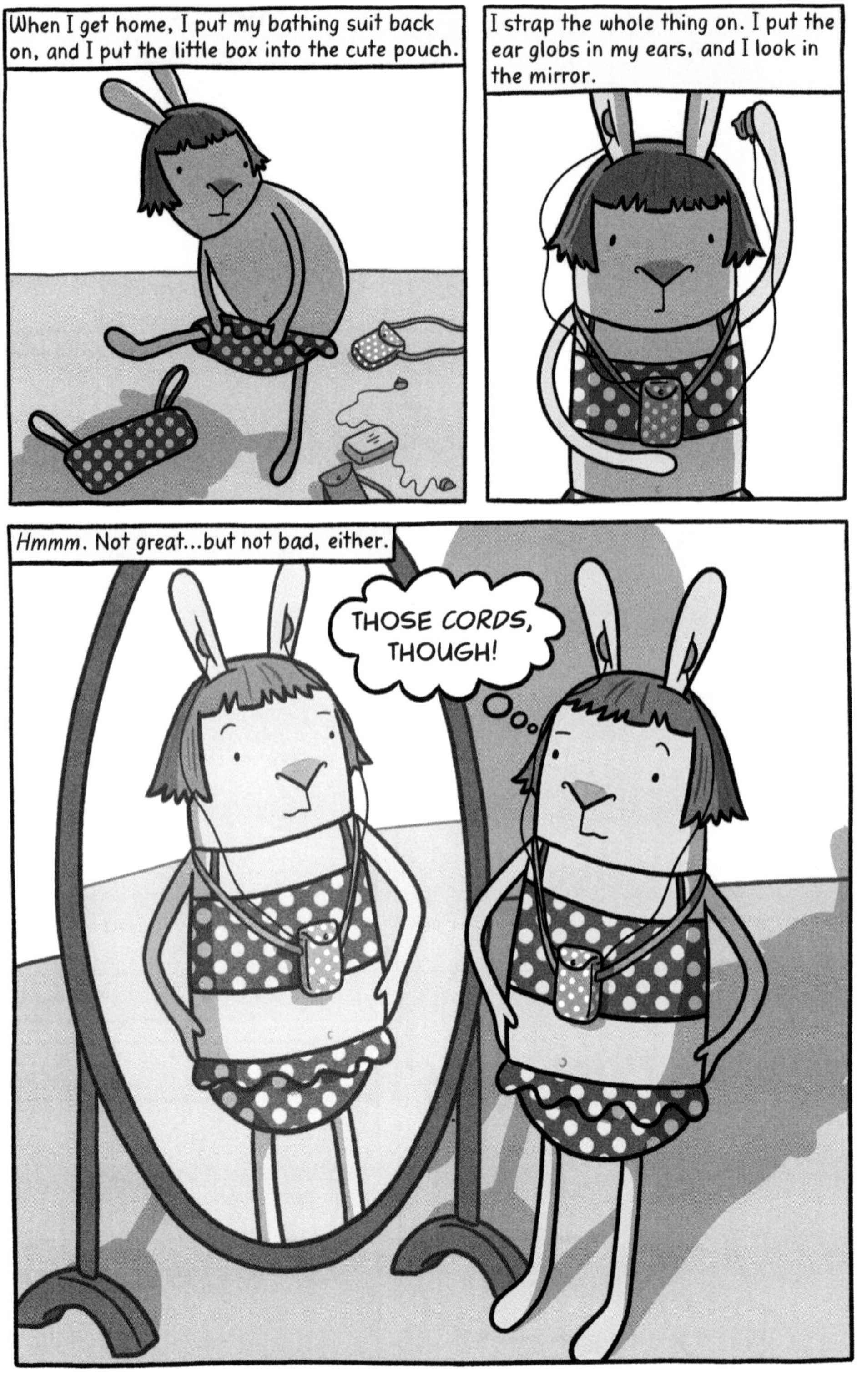
When I get home, I put my bathing suit back on, and I put the little box into the cute pouch.
I strap the whole thing on. I put the ear globs in my ears, and I look in the mirror.
*Hmmm*. Not great...but not bad, either.
THOSE CORDS, THOUGH!

# three

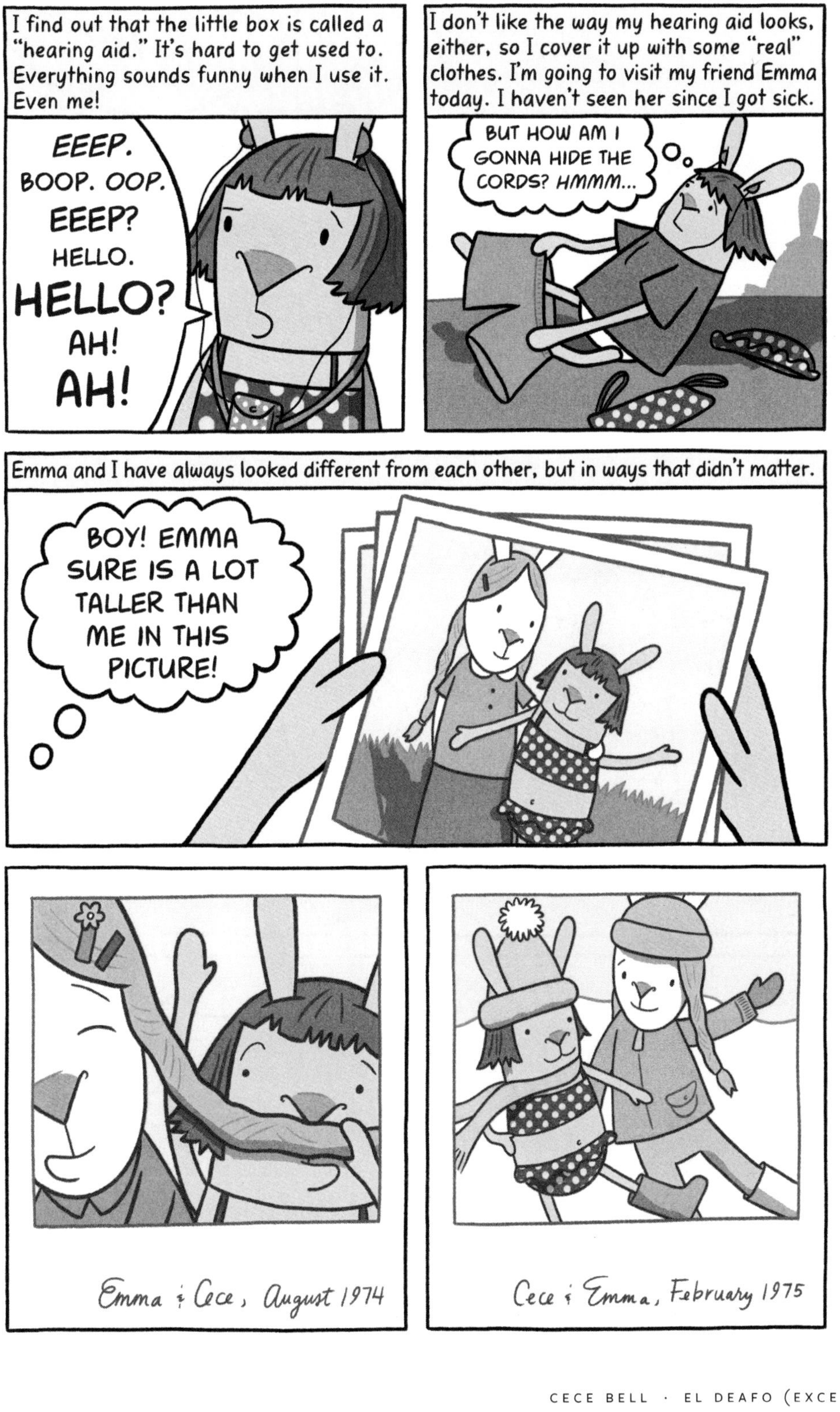
I find out that the little box is called a "hearing aid." It's hard to get used to. Everything sounds funny when I use it. Even me!
EEEP. BOOP. OOP. EEEP? HELLO. HELLO? AH! AH!
I don't like the way my hearing aid looks, either, so I cover it up with some "real" clothes. I'm going to visit my friend Emma today. I haven't seen her since I got sick.
BUT HOW AM I GONNA HIDE THE CORDS? HMMM...
Emma and I have always looked different from each other, but in ways that didn't matter.
BOY! EMMA SURE IS A LOT TALLER THAN ME IN THIS PICTURE!
Emma & Cece, August 1974
Cece & Emma, February 1975

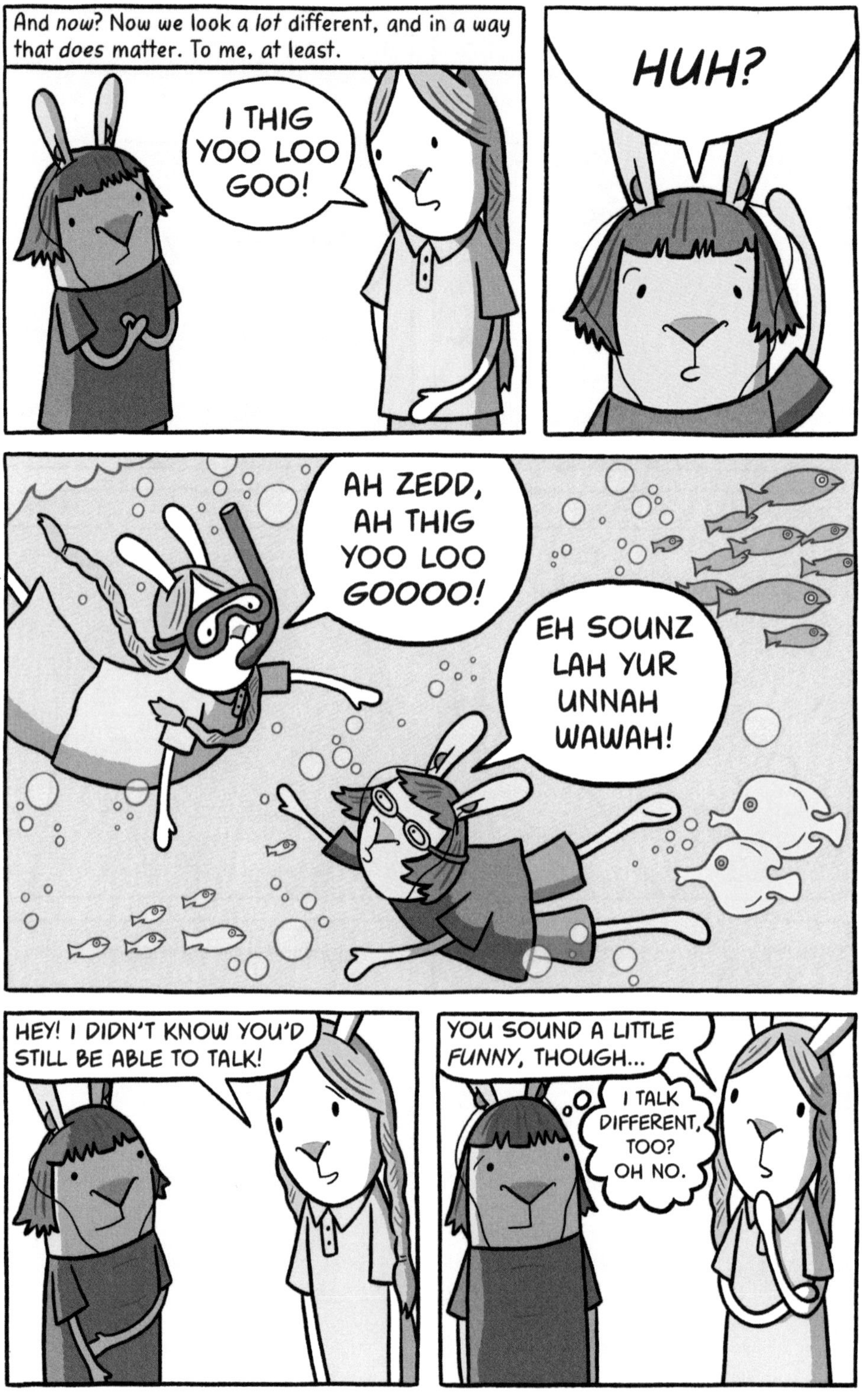

And *now*? Now we look a *lot* different, and in a way that *does* matter. To me, at least.
I THIG YOO LOO GOO!
HUH?
AH ZEDD, AH THIG YOO LOO GOOOO!
EH SOUNZ LAH YUR UNNAH WAWAH!
HEY! I DIDN'T KNOW YOU'D STILL BE ABLE TO TALK!
YOU SOUND A LITTLE *FUNNY*, THOUGH...
I TALK DIFFERENT, TOO? OH NO.

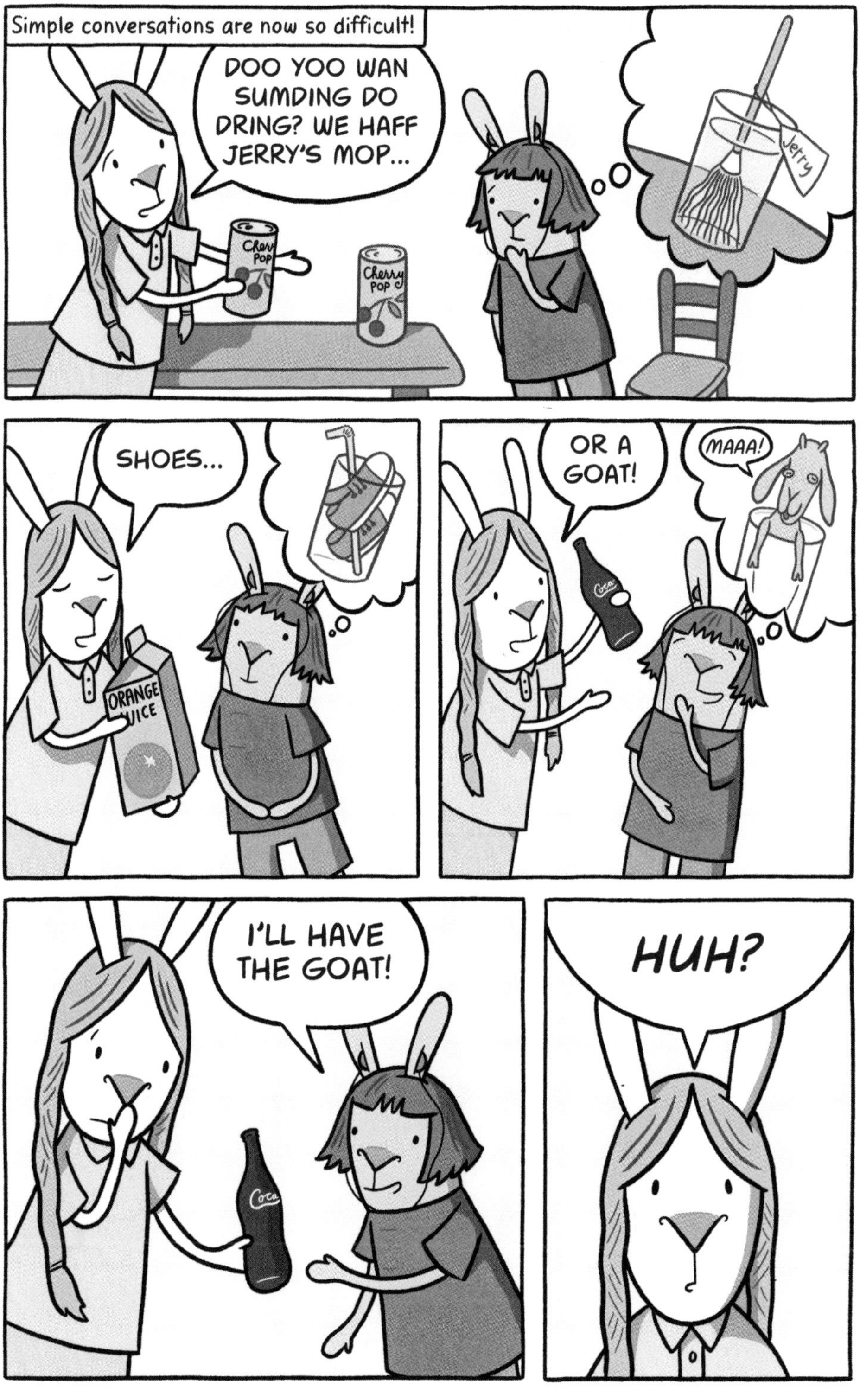
Simple conversations are now so difficult!
DOO YOO WAN SUMDING DO DRING? WE HAFF JERRY'S MOP...
Cherry POP
Cherry POP
Jerry
SHOES...
ORANGE JUICE
OR A GOAT!
MAAA!
Coca
I'LL HAVE THE GOAT!
Coca
HUH?

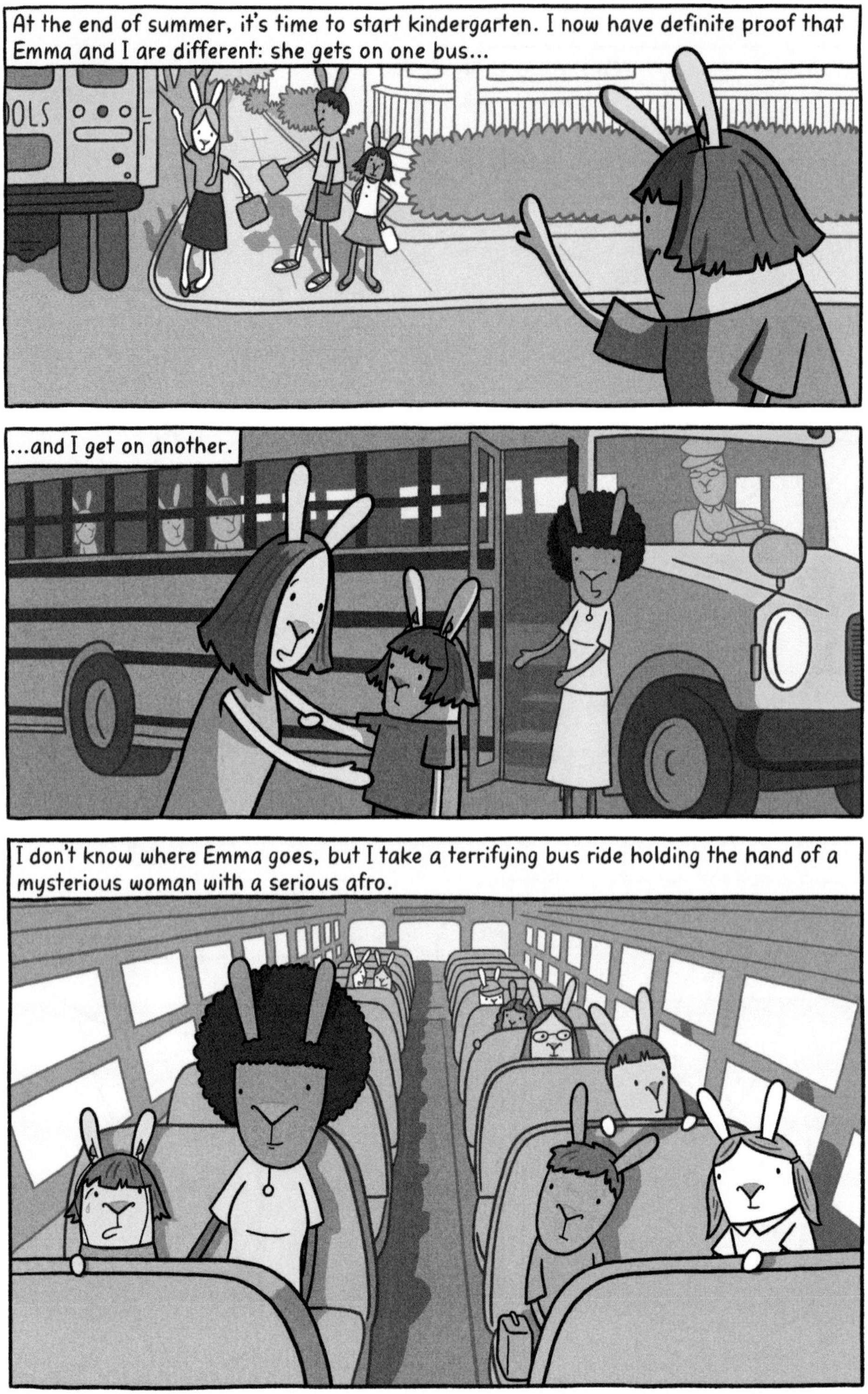
At the end of summer, it's time to start kindergarten. I now have definite proof that Emma and I are different: she gets on one bus...
...and I get on another.
I don't know where Emma goes, but I take a terrifying bus ride holding the hand of a mysterious woman with a serious afro.

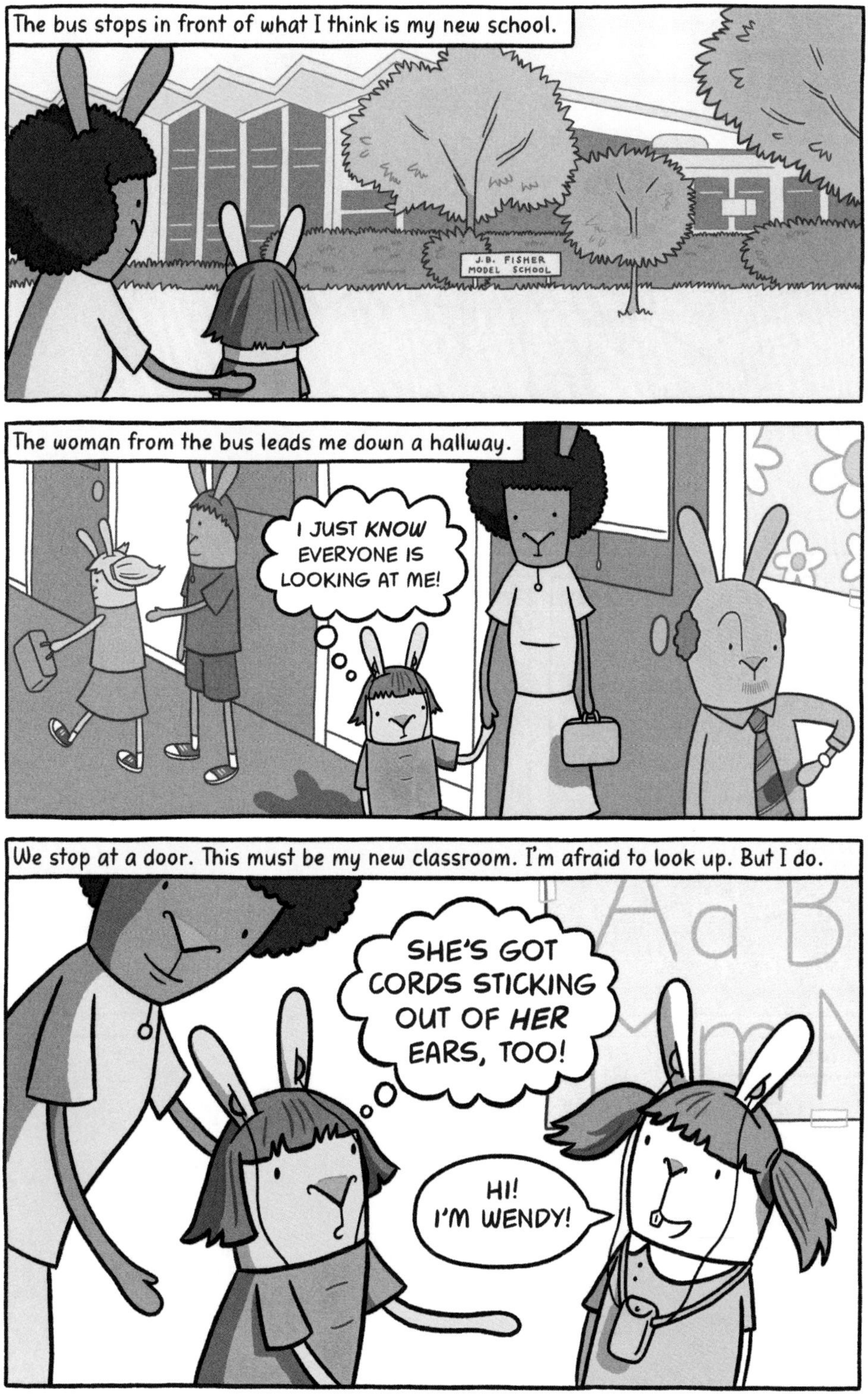
The bus stops in front of what I think is my new school.
J.B. FISHER MODEL SCHOOL
The woman from the bus leads me down a hallway.
I JUST KNOW EVERYONE IS LOOKING AT ME!
We stop at a door. This must be my new classroom. I'm afraid to look up. But I do.
SHE'S GOT CORDS STICKING OUT OF HER EARS, TOO!
HI! I'M WENDY!

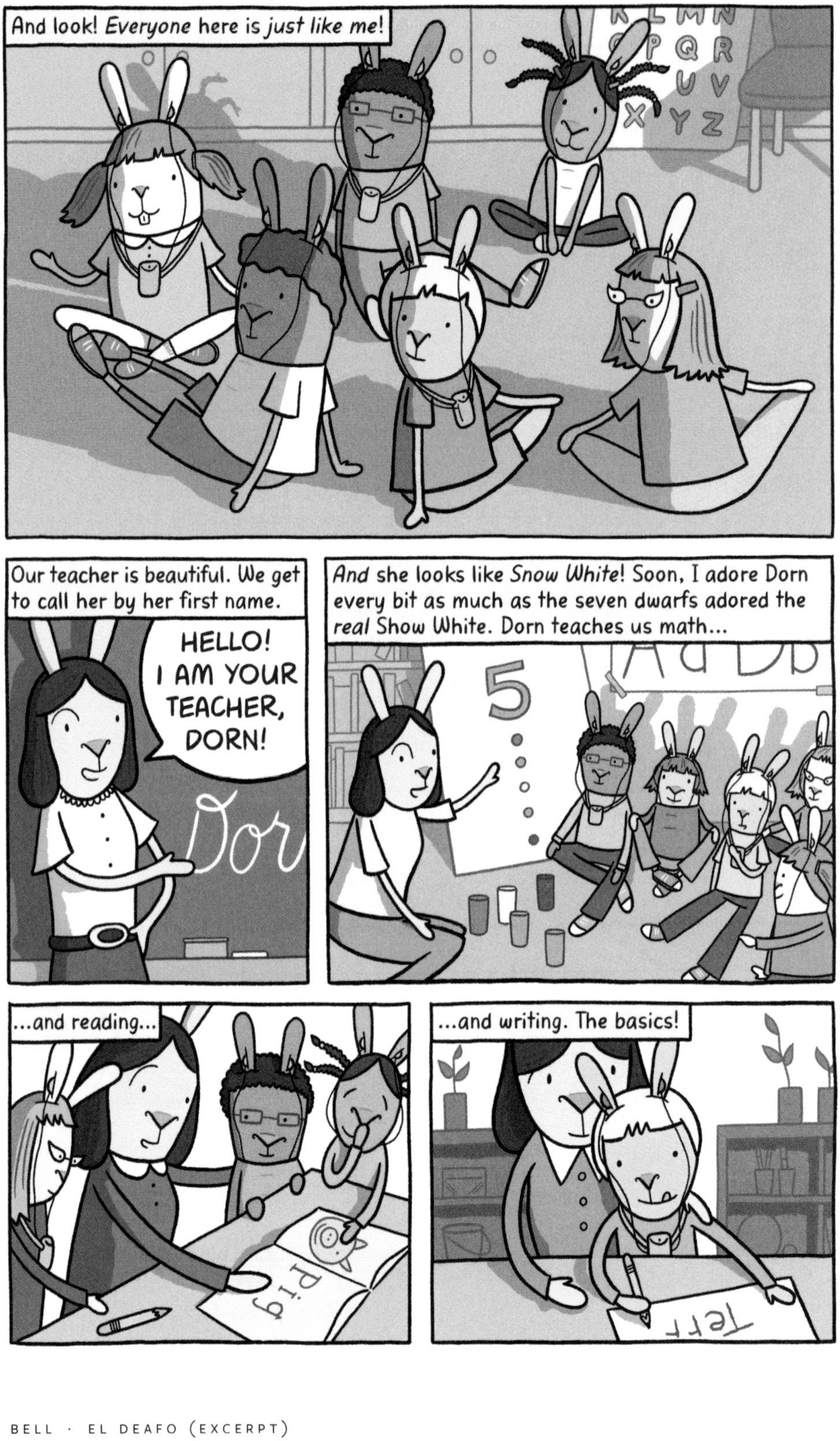
And look! *Everyone* here is *just like me*!
K L M N
O P Q R
U V
X Y Z
Our teacher is beautiful. We get to call her by her first name.
HELLO! I AM YOUR TEACHER, DORN!
Dor
*And* she looks like *Snow White*! Soon, I adore Dorn every bit as much as the seven dwarfs adored the *real* Show White. Dorn teaches us math...
5
...and reading...
Pig
...and writing. The basics!
Tett

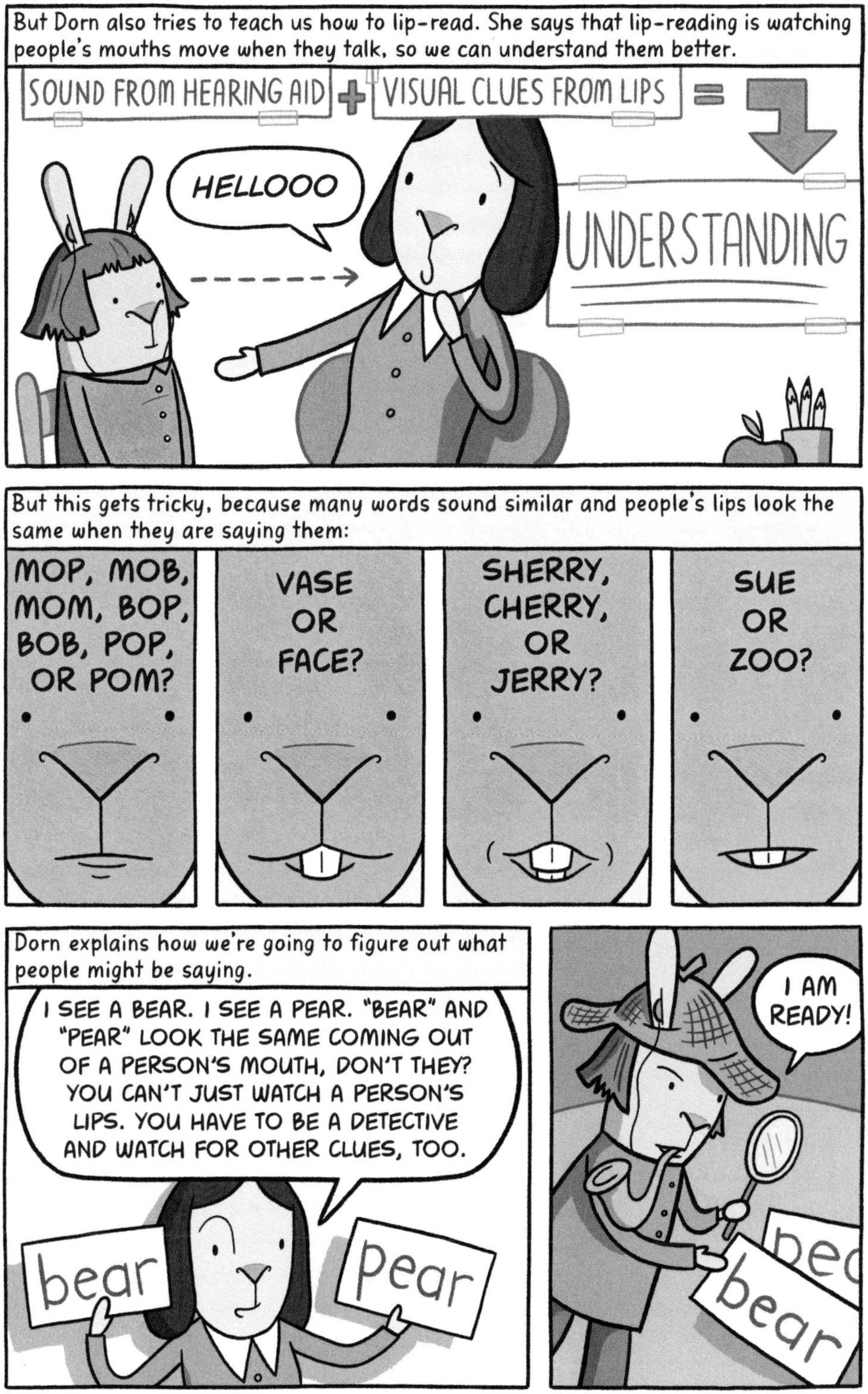
But Dorn also tries to teach us how to lip-read. She says that lip-reading is watching people's mouths move when they talk, so we can understand them better.
SOUND FROM HEARING AID
VISUAL CLUES FROM LIPS
UNDERSTANDING
HELLOOO
But this gets tricky, because many words sound similar and people's lips look the same when they are saying them:
MOP, MOB, MOM, BOP, BOB, POP, OR POM?
VASE OR FACE?
SHERRY, CHERRY, OR JERRY?
SUE OR ZOO?
Dorn explains how we're going to figure out what people might be saying.
I SEE A BEAR. I SEE A PEAR. "BEAR" AND "PEAR" LOOK THE SAME COMING OUT OF A PERSON'S MOUTH, DON'T THEY? YOU CAN'T JUST WATCH A PERSON'S LIPS. YOU HAVE TO BE A DETECTIVE AND WATCH FOR OTHER CLUES, TOO.
bear
pear
I AM READY!
bear

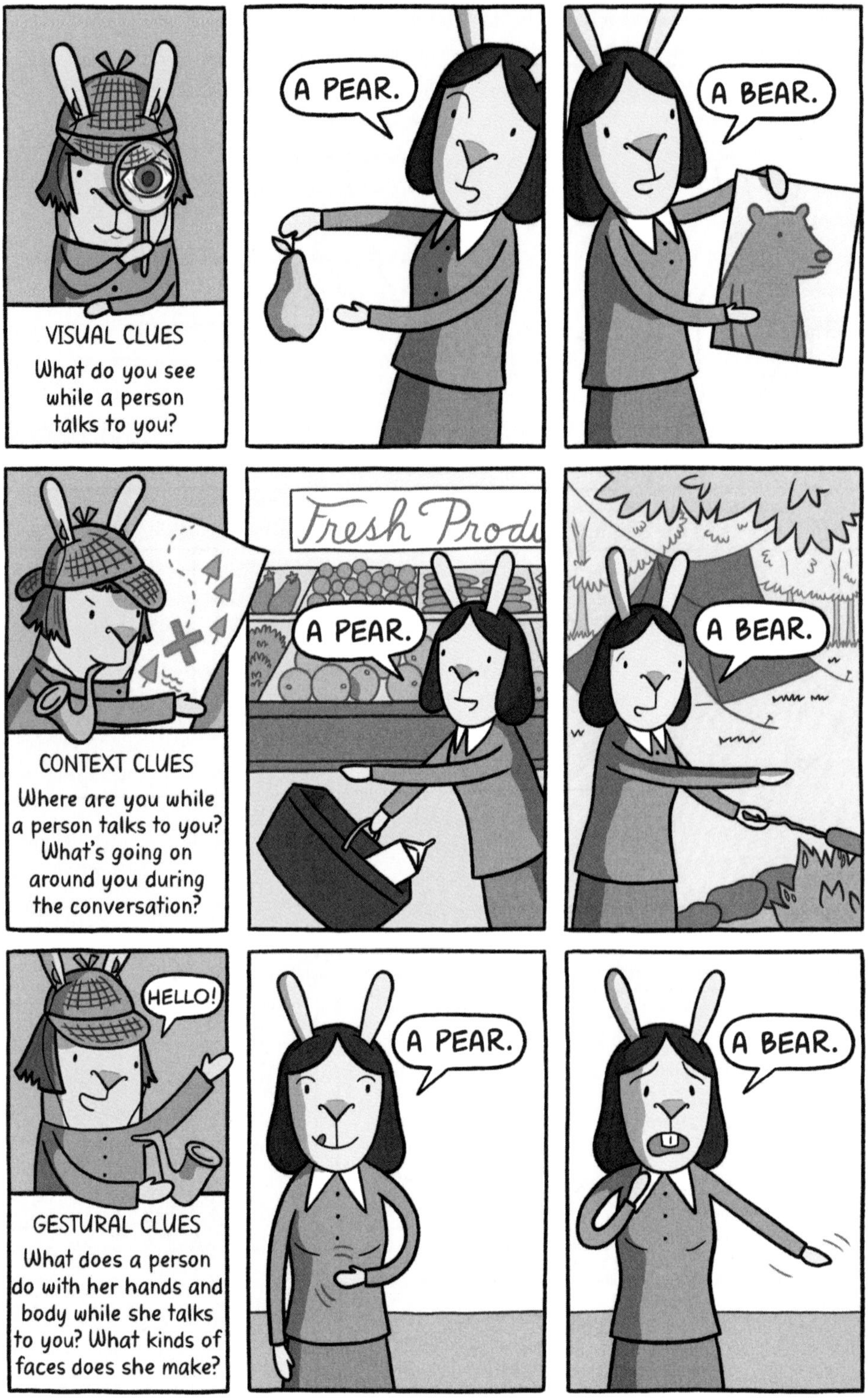
VISUAL CLUES
What do you see while a person talks to you?
A PEAR.
A BEAR.
CONTEXT CLUES
Where are you while a person talks to you? What's going on around you during the conversation?
Fresh Prod
A PEAR.
A BEAR.
HELLO!
GESTURAL CLUES
What does a person do with her hands and body while she talks to you? What kinds of faces does she make?
A PEAR.
A BEAR.

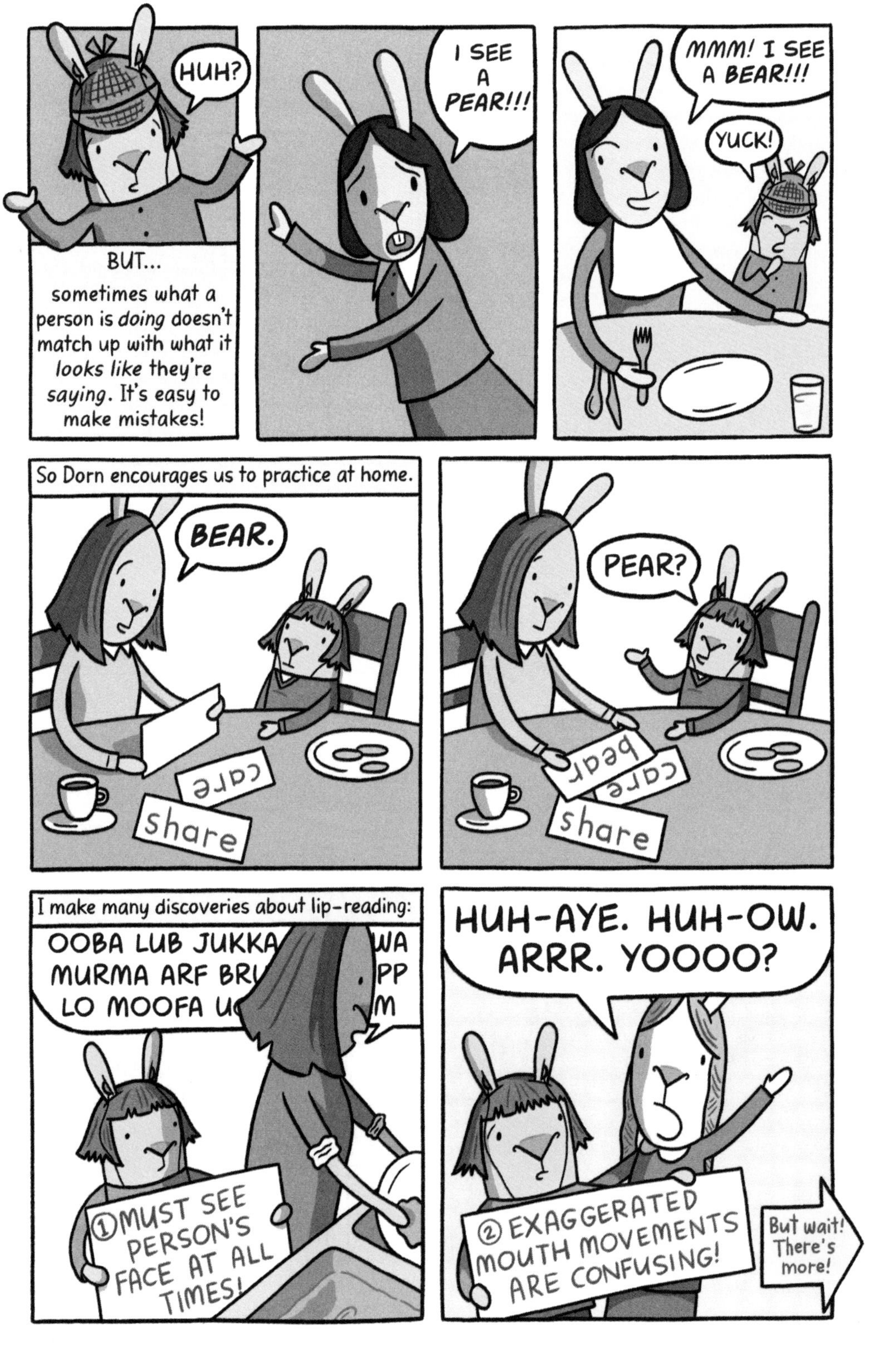
HUH?
BUT...
sometimes what a person is *doing* doesn't match up with what it *looks like* they're *saying*. It's easy to make mistakes!
I SEE A PEAR!!!
MMM! I SEE A BEAR!!!
YUCK!
So Dorn encourages us to practice at home.
BEAR.
care
share
PEAR?
bear
care
share
I make many discoveries about lip-reading:
OOBA LUB JUKKA WA MURMA ARF BR PP LO MOOFA U M
①MUST SEE PERSON'S FACE AT ALL TIMES!
HUH-AYE. HUH-OW. ARRR. YOOOO?
② EXAGGERATED MOUTH MOVEMENTS ARE CONFUSING!
But wait! There's more!

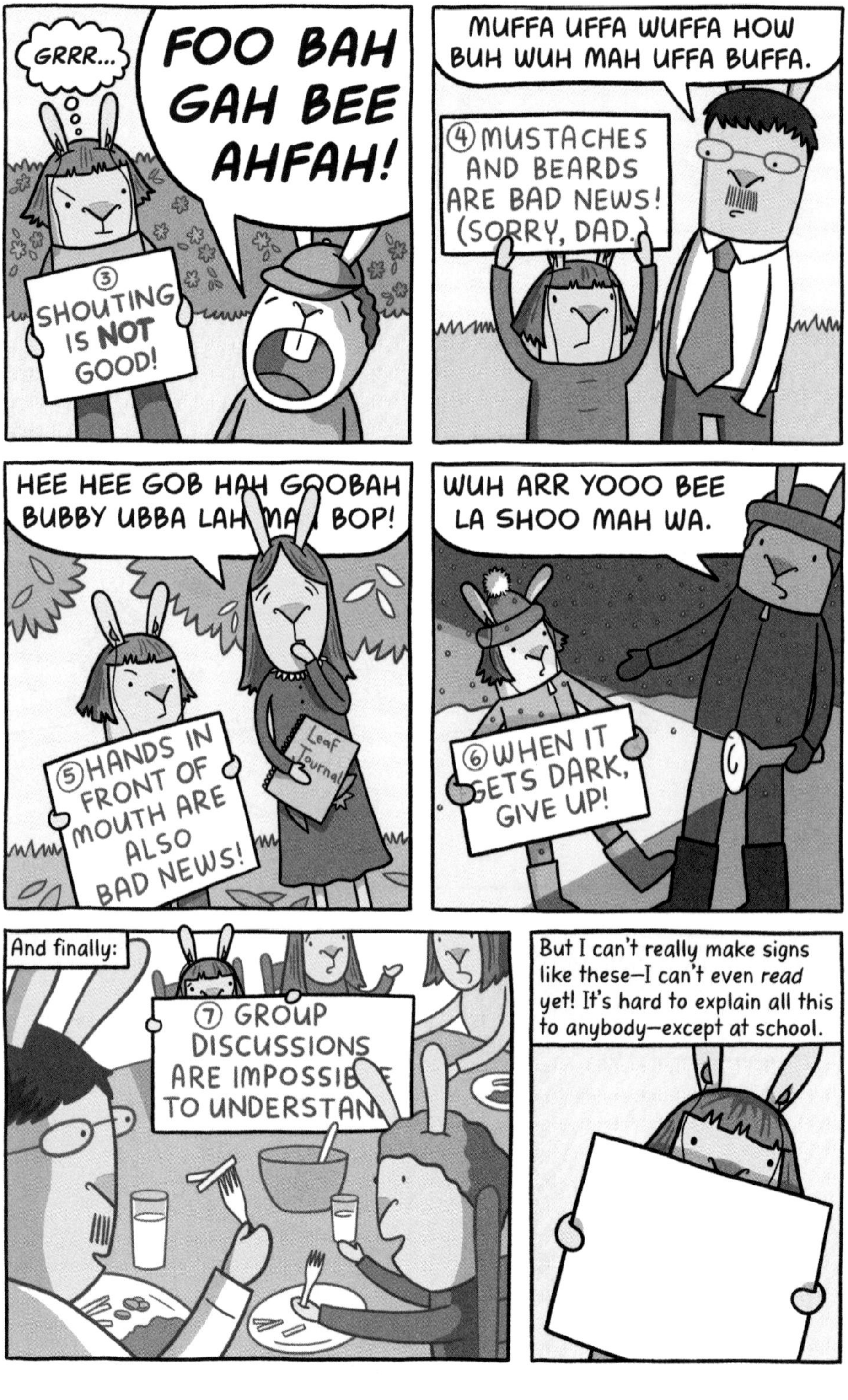
GRRR...
FOO BAH GAH BEE AHFAH!
③ SHOUTING IS NOT GOOD!
MUFFA UFFA WUFFA HOW BUH WUH MAH UFFA BUFFA.
④ MUSTACHES AND BEARDS ARE BAD NEWS! (SORRY, DAD.)
HEE HEE GOB HAH GOOBAH BUBBY UBBA LAH MAH BOP!
⑤ HANDS IN FRONT OF MOUTH ARE ALSO BAD NEWS!
Leaf Journal
WUH ARR YOOO BEE LA SHOO MAH WA.
⑥ WHEN IT GETS DARK, GIVE UP!
And finally:
⑦ GROUP DISCUSSIONS ARE IMPOSSIBLE TO UNDERSTAND
But I can't really make signs like these—I can't even *read* yet! It's hard to explain all this to anybody—except at school.

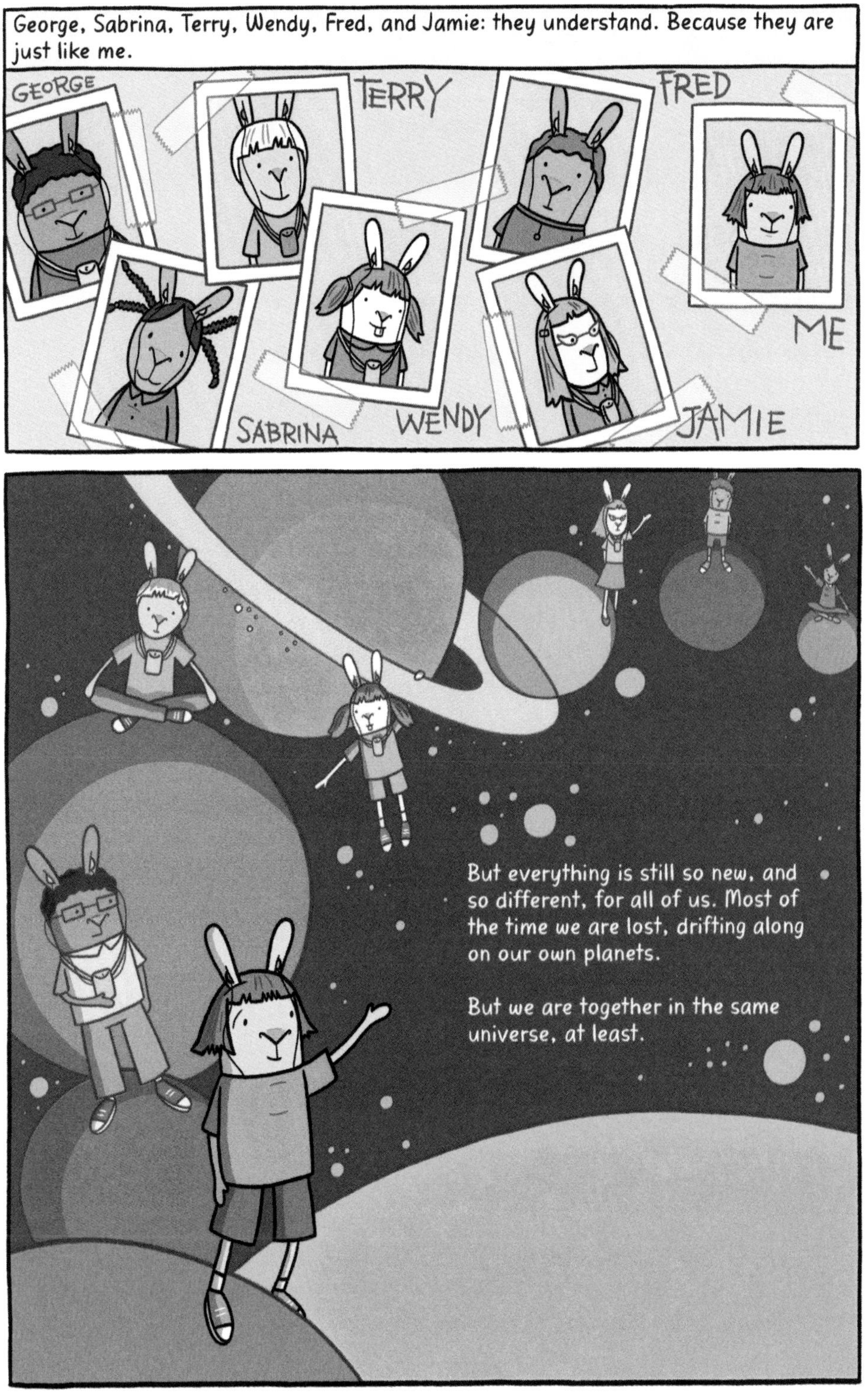
George, Sabrina, Terry, Wendy, Fred, and Jamie: they understand. Because they are just like me.
GEORGE
TERRY
FRED
ME
SABRINA
WENDY
JAMIE
But everything is still so new, and so different, for all of us. Most of the time we are lost, drifting along on our own planets.
But we are together in the same universe, at least.

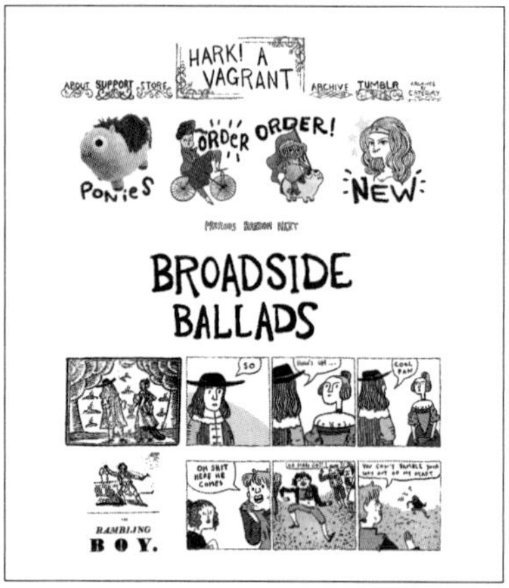
HARK! A VAGRANT
ABOUT
SUPPORT
STORE
ARCHIVE
TUMBLR
PONIES
ORDER ORDER!
NEW
BROADSIDE BALLADS
SO
COOL FAN
OH SHIT HERE HE COMES
YOU CAN'T RAMBLE YOUR WAY OUT OF MY HEART
RAMBLING
BOY.

# Broadside Ballads

KATE BEATON

*originally published at*

www.harkavagrant.com

SELF-PUBLISHED

digital

## Biography

Kate Beaton is a Canadian cartoonist from Nova Scotia. She is the author of the online work *Hark! A Vagrant*, the best-selling comic collection of the same name, and *Step Aside Pops*, both from Drawn and Quarterly. Her comics have appeared in *The New Yorker*, the *Guardian*, *Harper's Magazine*, the *National Post*, and the *American Bystander*. Her picture books *The Princess and the Pony* and *King Baby* are published by Scholastic. harkavagrant.com

## Statement

Broadside ballads were made for entertainment, and I've had great fun going through the Bodleian Library for them. The illustrations were often used over and over for different songs, and now they are being used again!

# BROADSIDE BALLADS

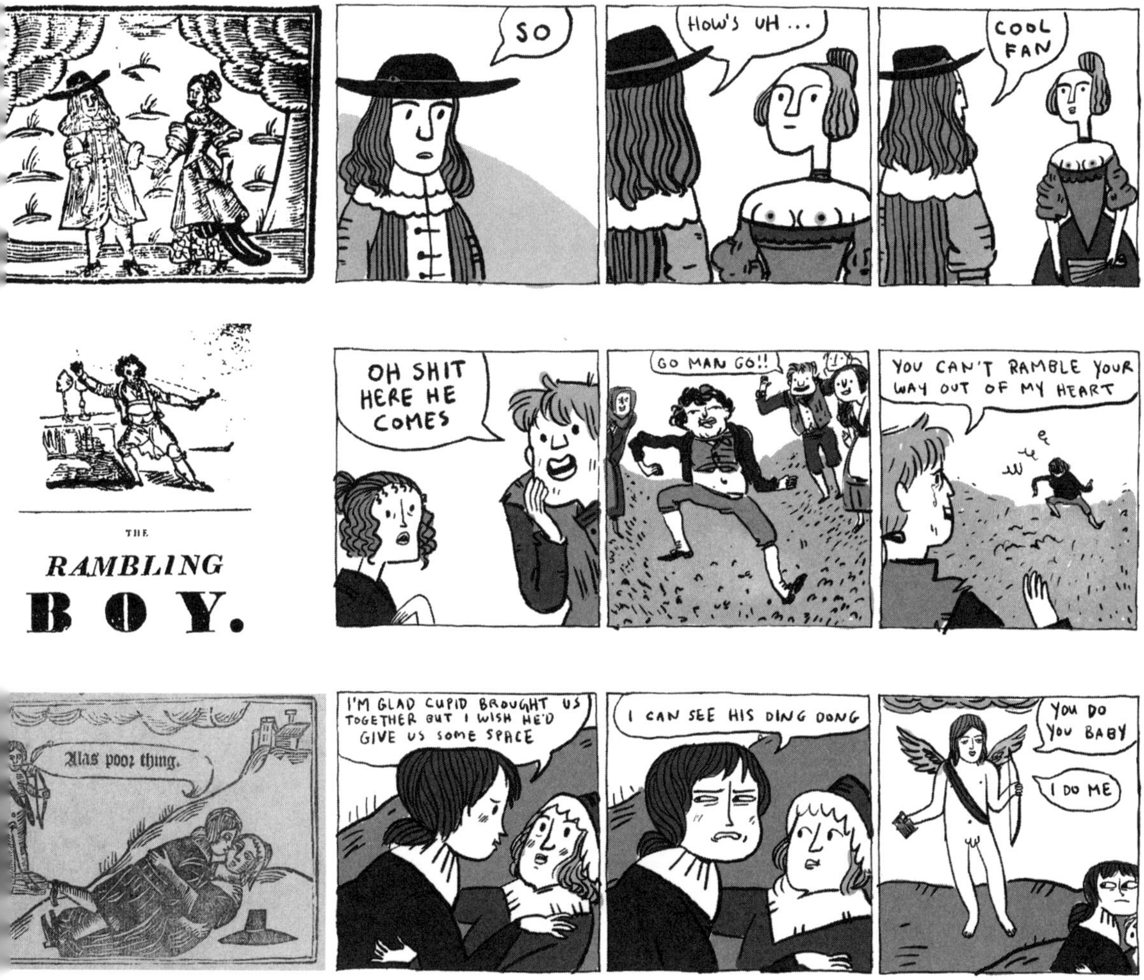
SO
HOW'S UH...
COOL FAN
THE RAMBLING BOY.
OH SHIT HERE HE COMES
GO MAN GO!!
YOU CAN'T RAMBLE YOUR WAY OUT OF MY HEART
Alas poor thing.
I'M GLAD CUPID BROUGHT US TOGETHER BUT I WISH HE'D GIVE US SOME SPACE
I CAN SEE HIS DING DONG
YOU DO YOU BABY
I DO ME

*All broadside images were taken from the Bodleian Library (ballads.bodleian.ox.ac.uk). The University of California also has a great collection (ebba.english.ucsb.edu). Please take a look! Broadside illustrations were often used over again for different songs, so it's not unusual to see them pop up in new places, though perhaps comic riffs is a new one.*

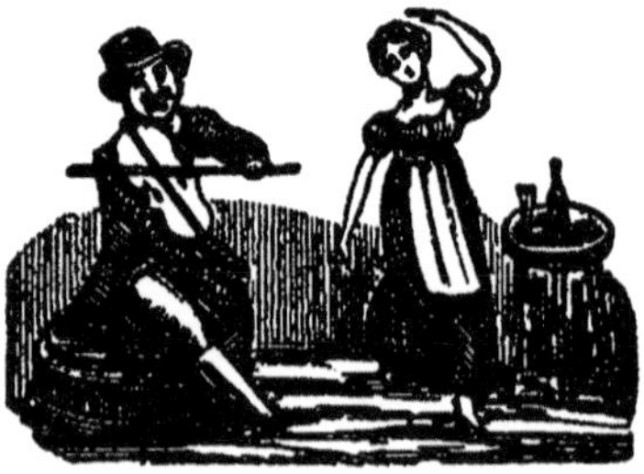

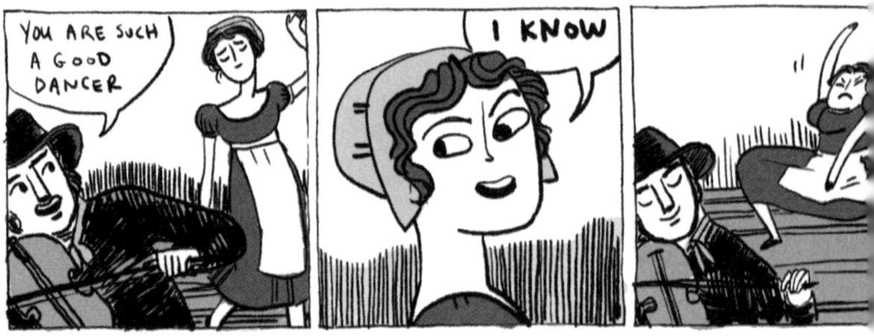
YOU ARE SUCH A GOOD DANCER
I KNOW

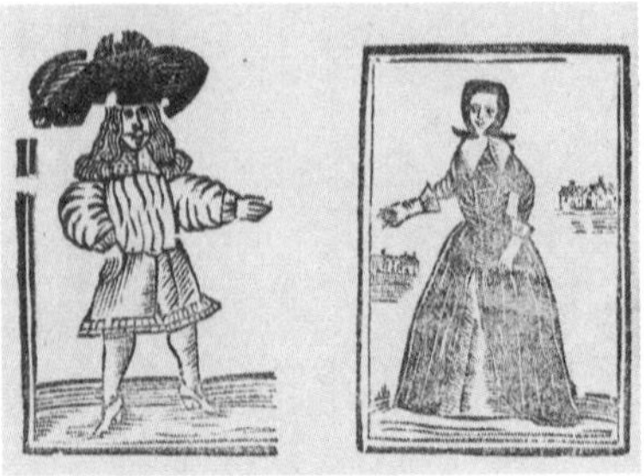

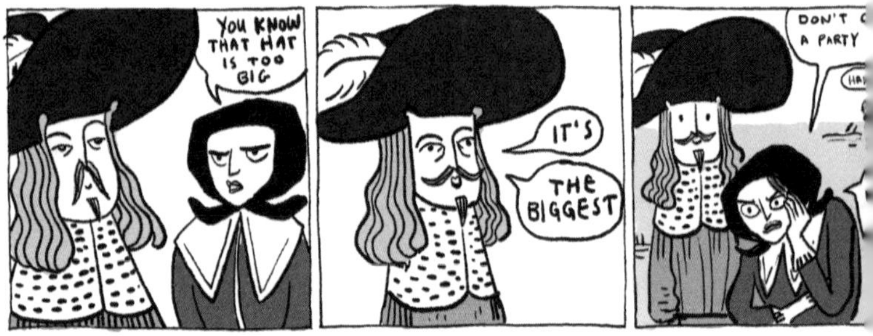
YOU KNOW THAT HAT IS TOO BIG
IT'S
THE BIGGEST

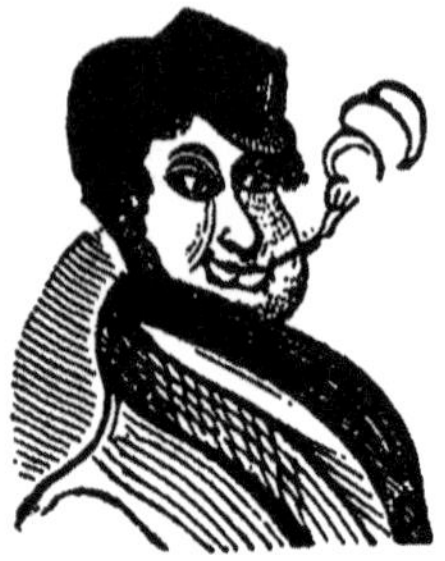

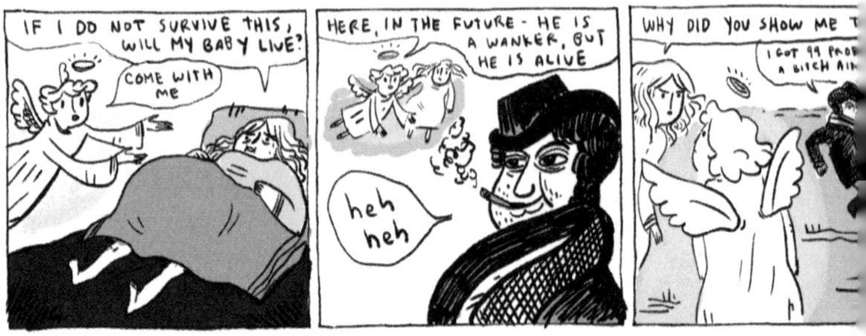
IF I DO NOT SURVIVE THIS, WILL MY BABY LIVE?
COME WITH ME
HERE, IN THE FUTURE - HE IS A WANKER, BUT HE IS ALIVE
heh heh

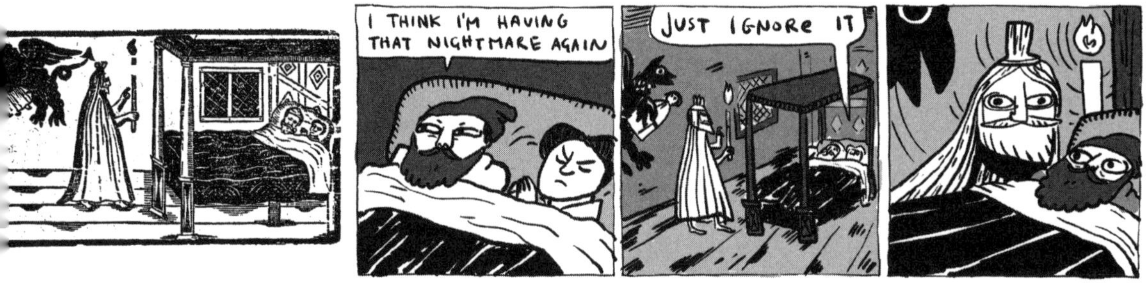
I THINK I'M HAVING THAT NIGHTMARE AGAIN
JUST IGNORE IT

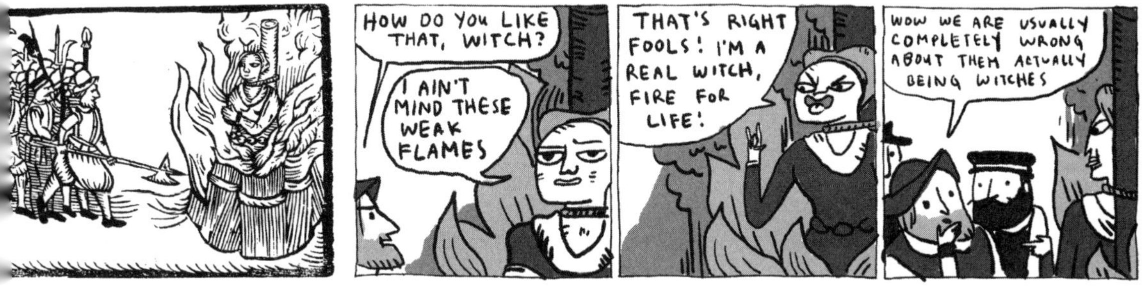
HOW DO YOU LIKE THAT, WITCH?
I AIN'T MIND THESE WEAK FLAMES
THAT'S RIGHT FOOLS! I'M A REAL WITCH, FIRE FOR LIFE!
WOW WE ARE USUALLY COMPLETELY WRONG ABOUT THEM ACTUALLY BEING WITCHES

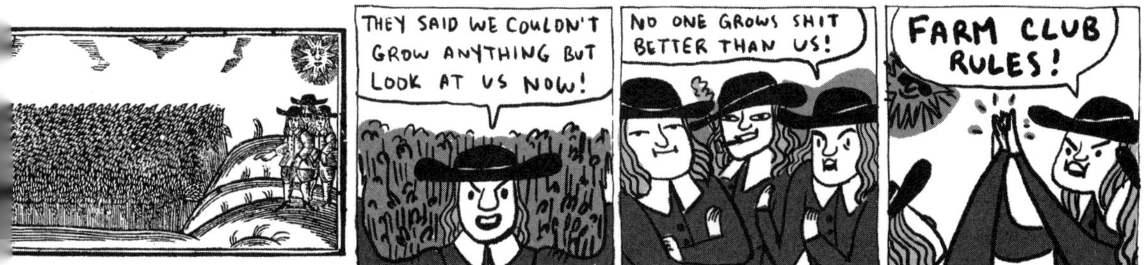
THEY SAID WE COULDN'T GROW ANYTHING BUT LOOK AT US NOW!
NO ONE GROWS SHIT BETTER THAN US!
FARM CLUB RULES!

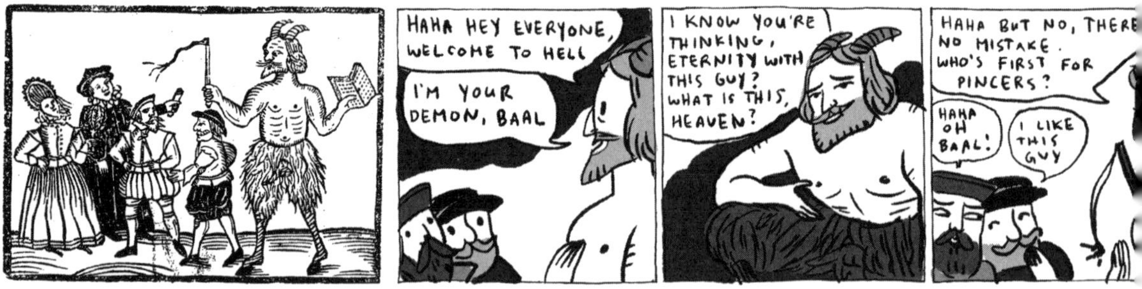
HAHA HEY EVERYONE, WELCOME TO HELL
I'M YOUR DEMON, BAAL
I KNOW YOU'RE THINKING, ETERNITY WITH THIS GUY? WHAT IS THIS, HEAVEN?
HAHA BUT NO, THERE
NO MISTAKE. WHO'S FIRST FOR PINCERS?
HAHA OH BAAL!
I LIKE THIS GUY

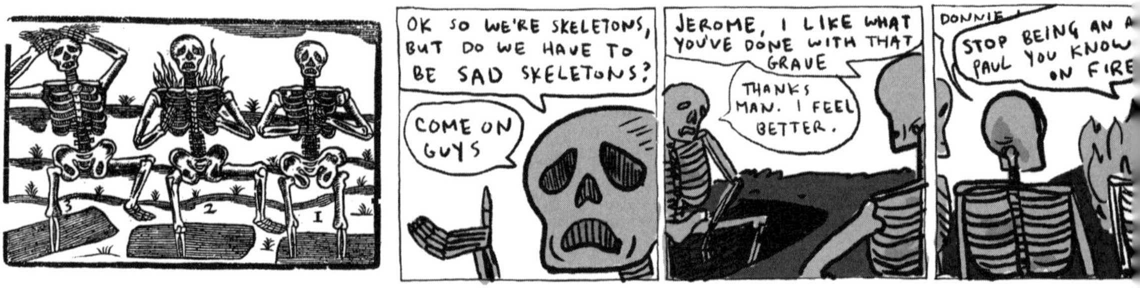
3
2
I
OK SO WE'RE SKELETONS, BUT DO WE HAVE TO BE SAD SKELETONS?
COME ON GUYS
JEROME, I LIKE WHAT YOU'VE DONE WITH THAT GRAVE
THANKS MAN. I FEEL BETTER.
DONNIE
STOP BEING AN A
PAUL YOU KNOW
ON FIRE

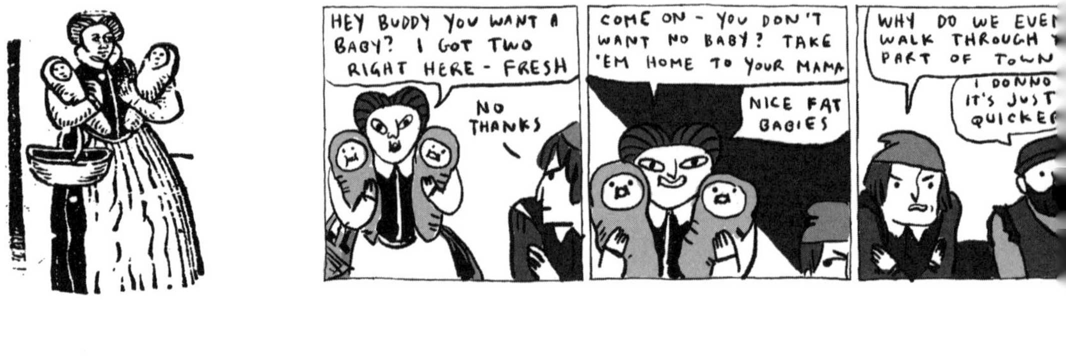
HEY BUDDY YOU WANT A BABY? I GOT TWO RIGHT HERE - FRESH
NO THANKS
COME ON - YOU DON'T WANT NO BABY? TAKE 'EM HOME TO YOUR MAMA
NICE FAT BABIES
WHY DO WE EVE
WALK THROUGH
PART OF TOWN
I DONNO IT'S JUST QUICKE

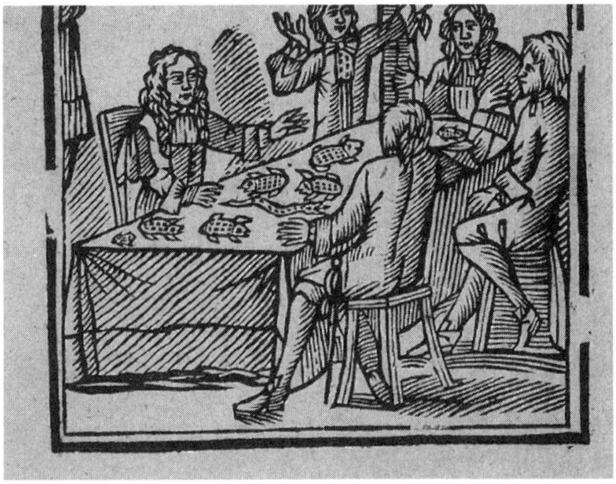

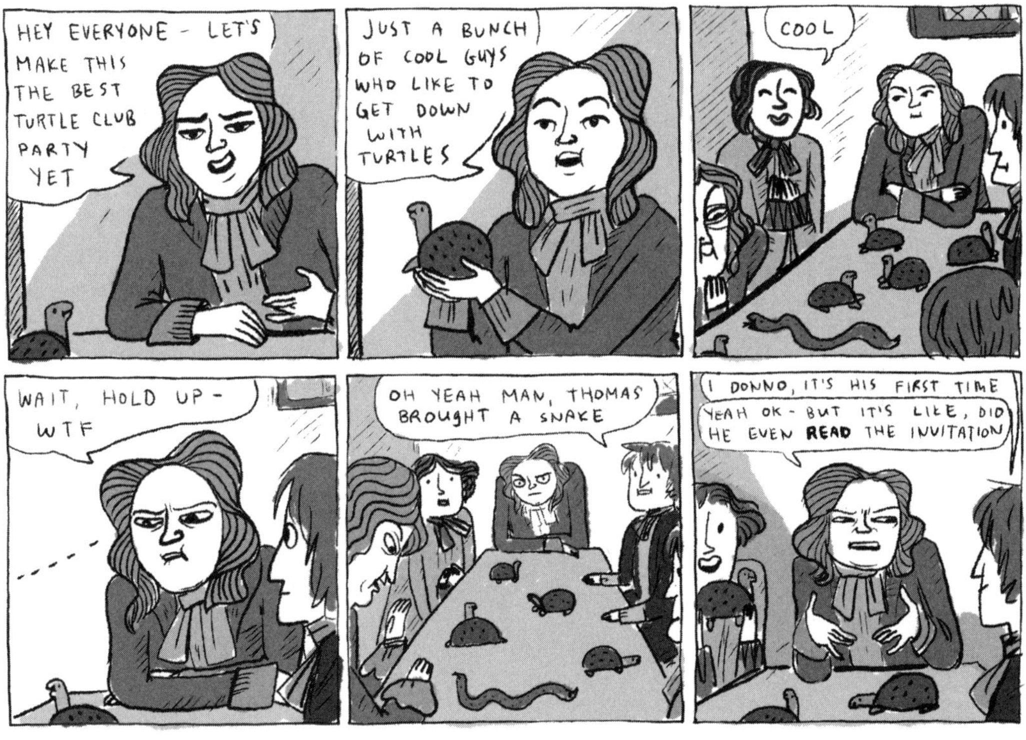
HEY EVERYONE - LET'S MAKE THIS THE BEST TURTLE CLUB PARTY YET
JUST A BUNCH OF COOL GUYS WHO LIKE TO GET DOWN WITH TURTLES
COOL
WAIT, HOLD UP - WTF
OH YEAH MAN, THOMAS BROUGHT A SNAKE
I DONNO, IT'S HIS FIRST TIME
YEAH OK - BUT IT'S LIKE, DID HE EVEN **READ** THE INVITATION

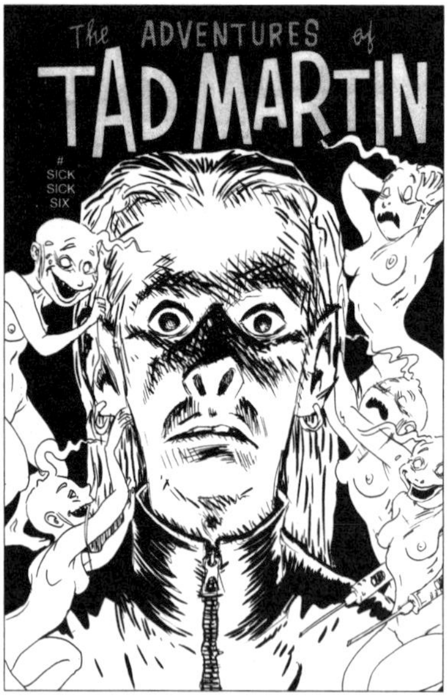
The ADVENTURES of
TAD MARTIN
#
SICK
SICK
SIX

# The Corpse, the Ghost and the Hollow-Weenie (*Excerpt*)

CASANOVA FRANKENSTEIN

*excerpted from*

The Adventures of TAD MARTIN #6

PROFANITY HILL / TEENAGE DINOSAUR

6.6 × 10.1 inches • 40 pages

## Biography

Casanova Frankenstein was born into a family of crazy people in the summer of 1967. He was raised in a segregated black neighborhood built on reclaimed landfill, near the Chicago city incinerator. He escaped in 1985 to pursue an art degree at Texas Tech University. Casanova has been creating art since he was three years old, but never had a show. His main concern is pursuing his craft, despite any obstacles.
cnfrankenstein.daportfolio.com

## Statement

The piece included is a recording of actual events in the life of the artist. Names have been changed to avoid ostracism. The purpose of the piece is to serve as an example of an individual's ability to overcome hardship and evolve as a human being.

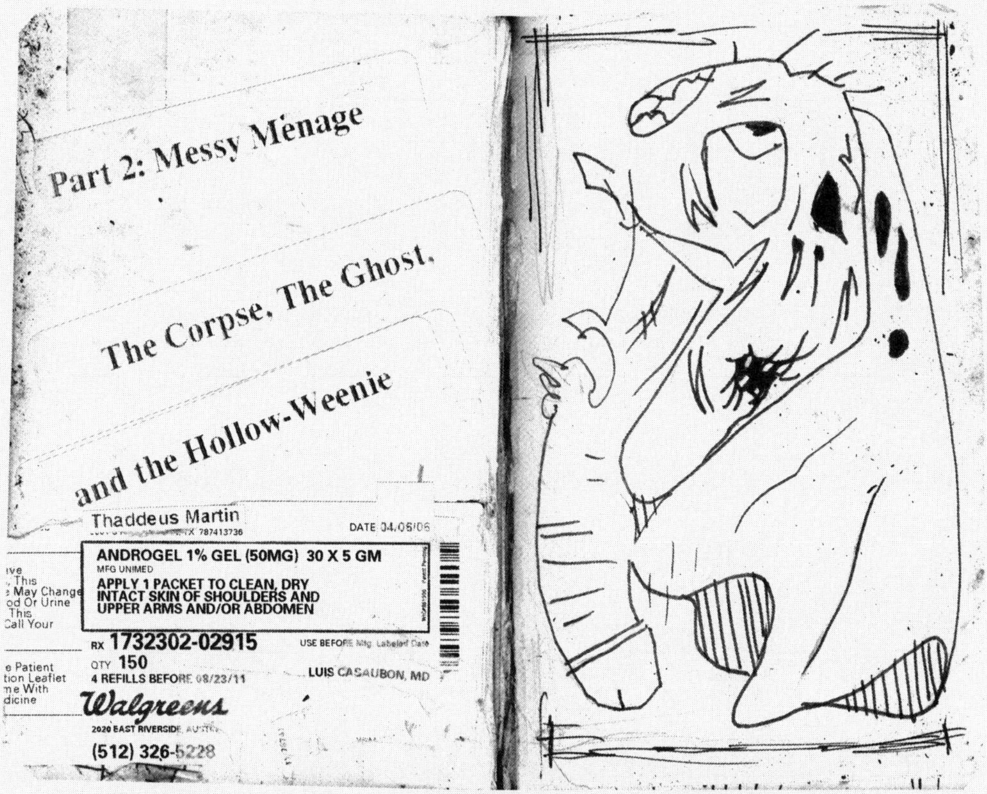

Part 2: Messy Ménage
The Corpse, The Ghost,
and the Hollow-Weenie
Thaddeus Martin
DATE 04/06/06
ANDROGEL 1% GEL (50MG) 30 X 5 GM
MFG UNIMED
APPLY 1 PACKET TO CLEAN, DRY INTACT SKIN OF SHOULDERS AND UPPER ARMS AND/OR ABDOMEN
RX 1732302-02915
USE BEFORE Mfg. Labeled Date
QTY 150
4 REFILLS BEFORE 08/23/11
LUIS CASAUBON, MD
Walgreens
2020 EAST RIVERSIDE, AUSTIN
(512) 326-5228


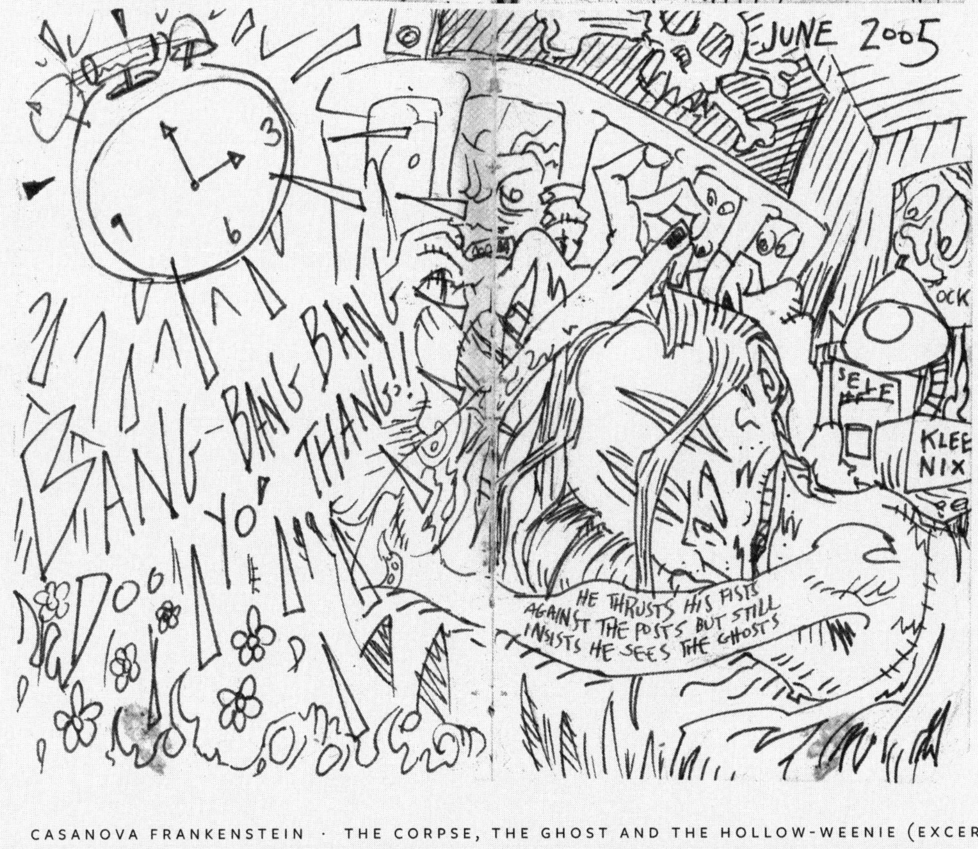

JUNE 2005
BANG-BANG-BANG
THANG!!
YO'
KLEENIX
HE THRUSTS HIS FISTS AGAINST THE POSTS BUT STILL INSISTS HE SEES THE GHOSTS

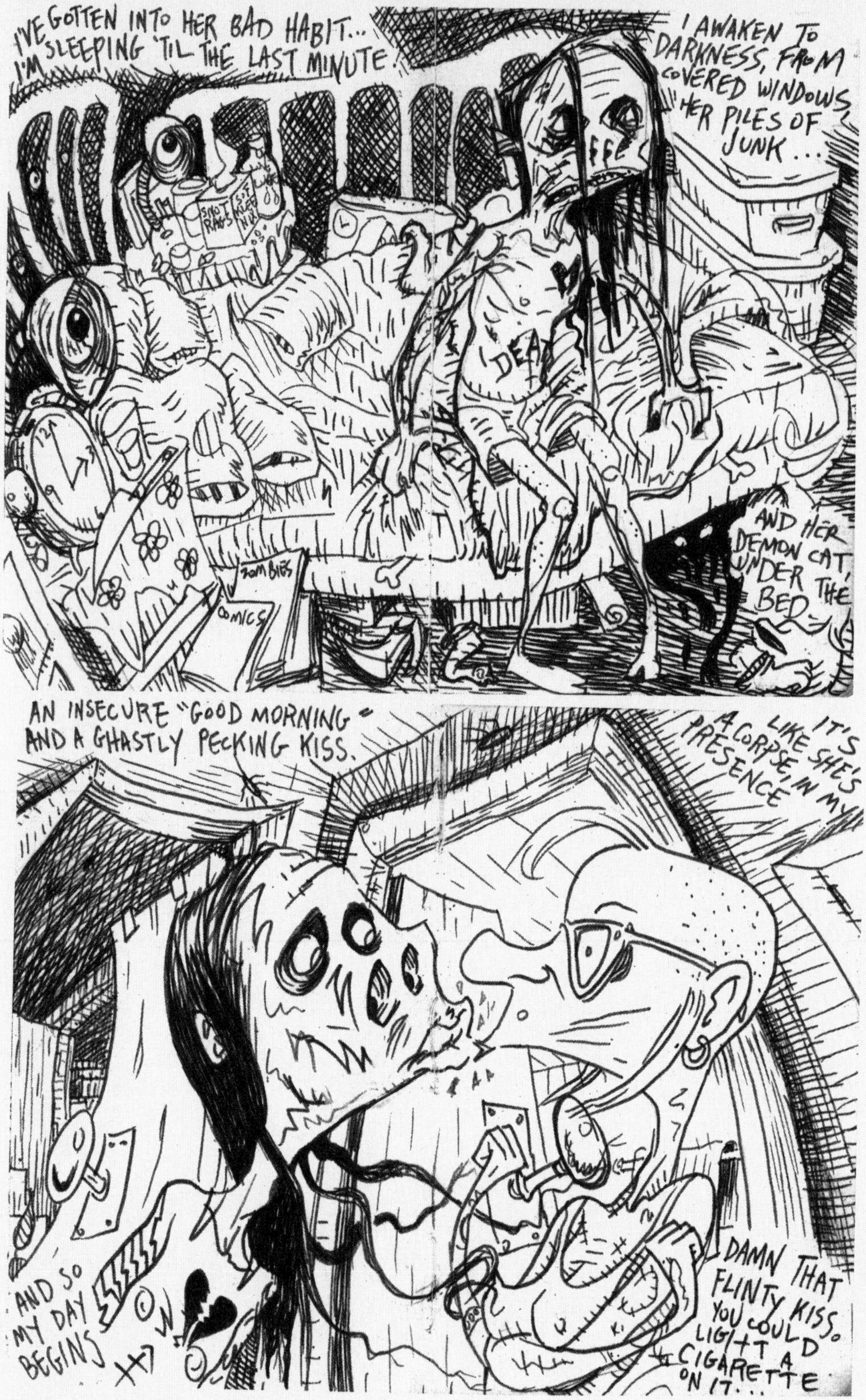
I'VE GOTTEN INTO HER BAD HABIT... I'M SLEEPING 'TIL THE LAST MINUTE!
I AWAKEN TO DARKNESS, FROM COVERED WINDOWS, HER PILES OF JUNK...
AND HER DEMON CAT, UNDER THE BED
ZOMBIES
COMICS
DEAD
AN INSECURE "GOOD MORNING" AND A GHASTLY PECKING KISS.
IT'S LIKE SHE'S A CORPSE, IN MY PRESENCE
AND SO MY DAY BEGINS
DAMN THAT FLINTY KISS. YOU COULD LIGHT A CIGARETTE ON IT...

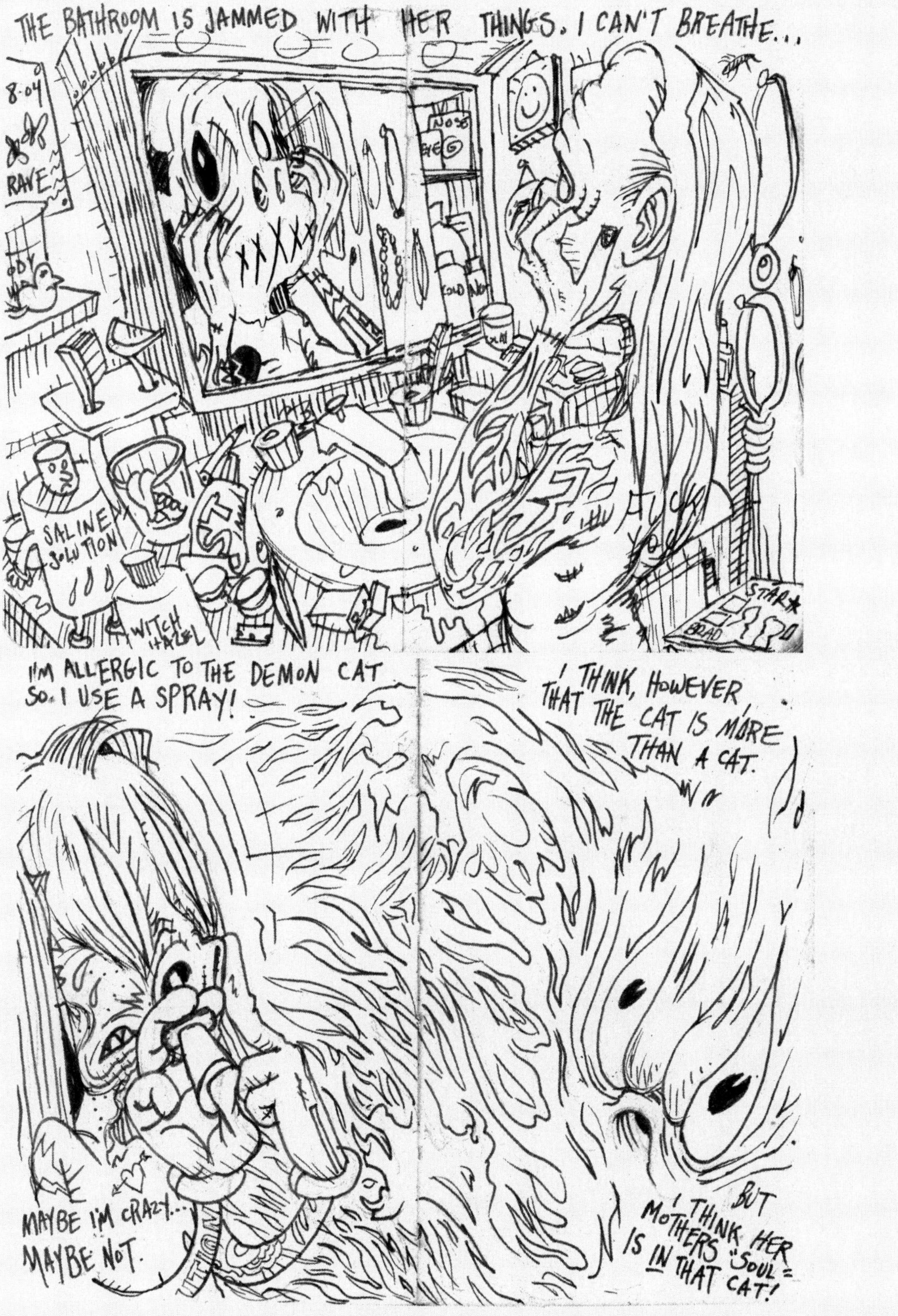
THE BATHROOM IS JAMMED WITH HER THINGS. I CAN'T BREATHE...
8.04
RAVE
SALINE SOLUTION
WITCH HAZEL
STAR★
BRAD
I'M ALLERGIC TO THE DEMON CAT SO. I USE A SPRAY!
I THINK, HOWEVER, THAT THE CAT IS MORE THAN A CAT.
MAYBE I'M CRAZY... MAYBE NOT.
BUT I THINK HER MOTHERS "SOUL" IS IN THAT CAT!

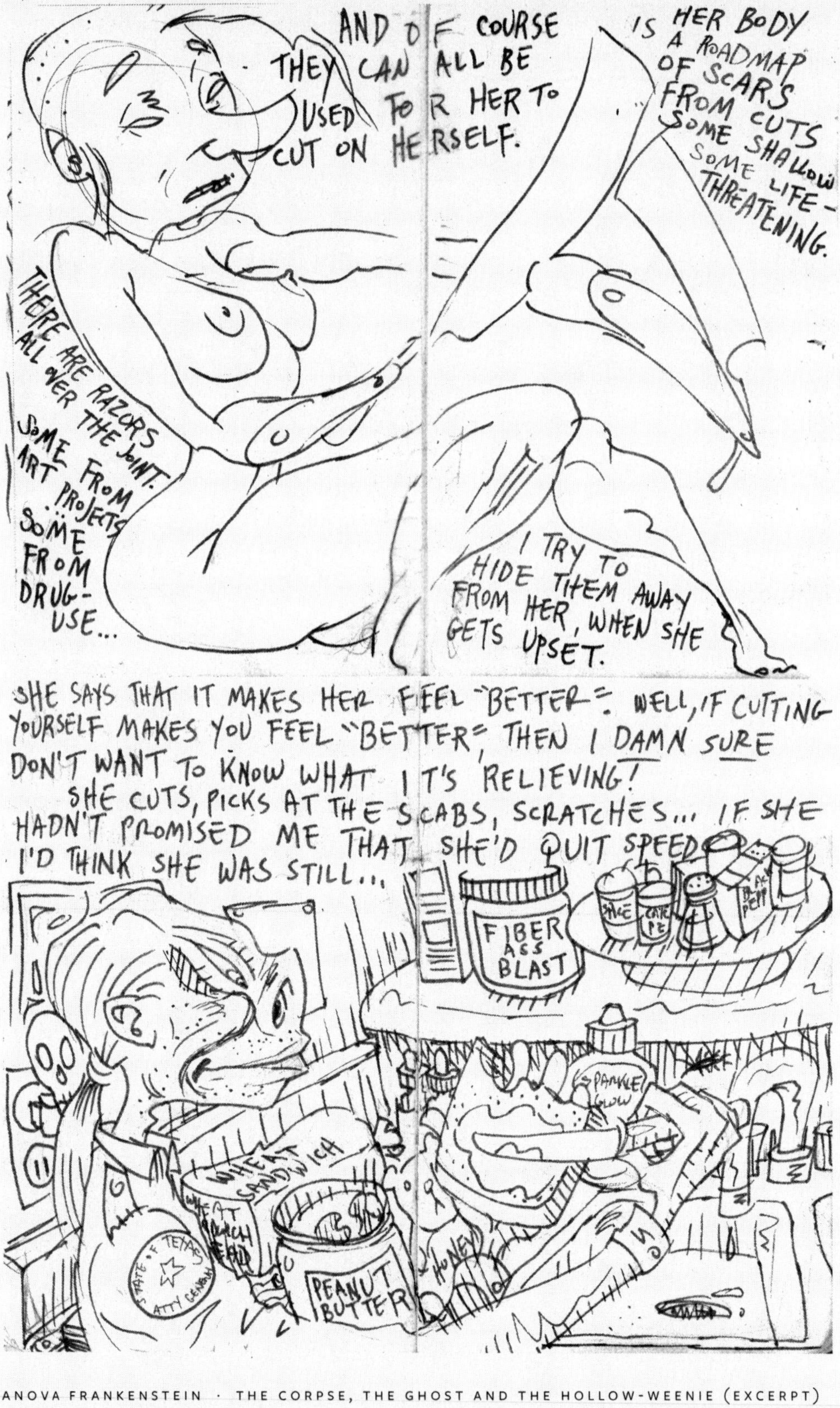

AND OF COURSE THEY CAN ALL BE USED FOR HER TO CUT ON HERSELF.
IS HER BODY A ROADMAP OF SCARS FROM CUTS SOME SHALLOW SOME LIFE-THREATENING.
THERE ARE RAZORS ALL OVER THE JOINT. SOME FROM ART PROJECTS... SOME FROM DRUG-USE...
I TRY TO HIDE THEM AWAY FROM HER, WHEN SHE GETS UPSET.
SHE SAYS THAT IT MAKES HER FEEL "BETTER". WELL, IF CUTTING YOURSELF MAKES YOU FEEL "BETTER", THEN I DAMN SURE DON'T WANT TO KNOW WHAT IT'S RELIEVING!
SHE CUTS, PICKS AT THE SCABS, SCRATCHES... IF SHE HADN'T PROMISED ME THAT SHE'D QUIT SPEED I'D THINK SHE WAS STILL...
FIBER ASS BLAST
WHEAT SANDWICH
PEANUT BUTTER
HONEY
SPARKLE GLOW

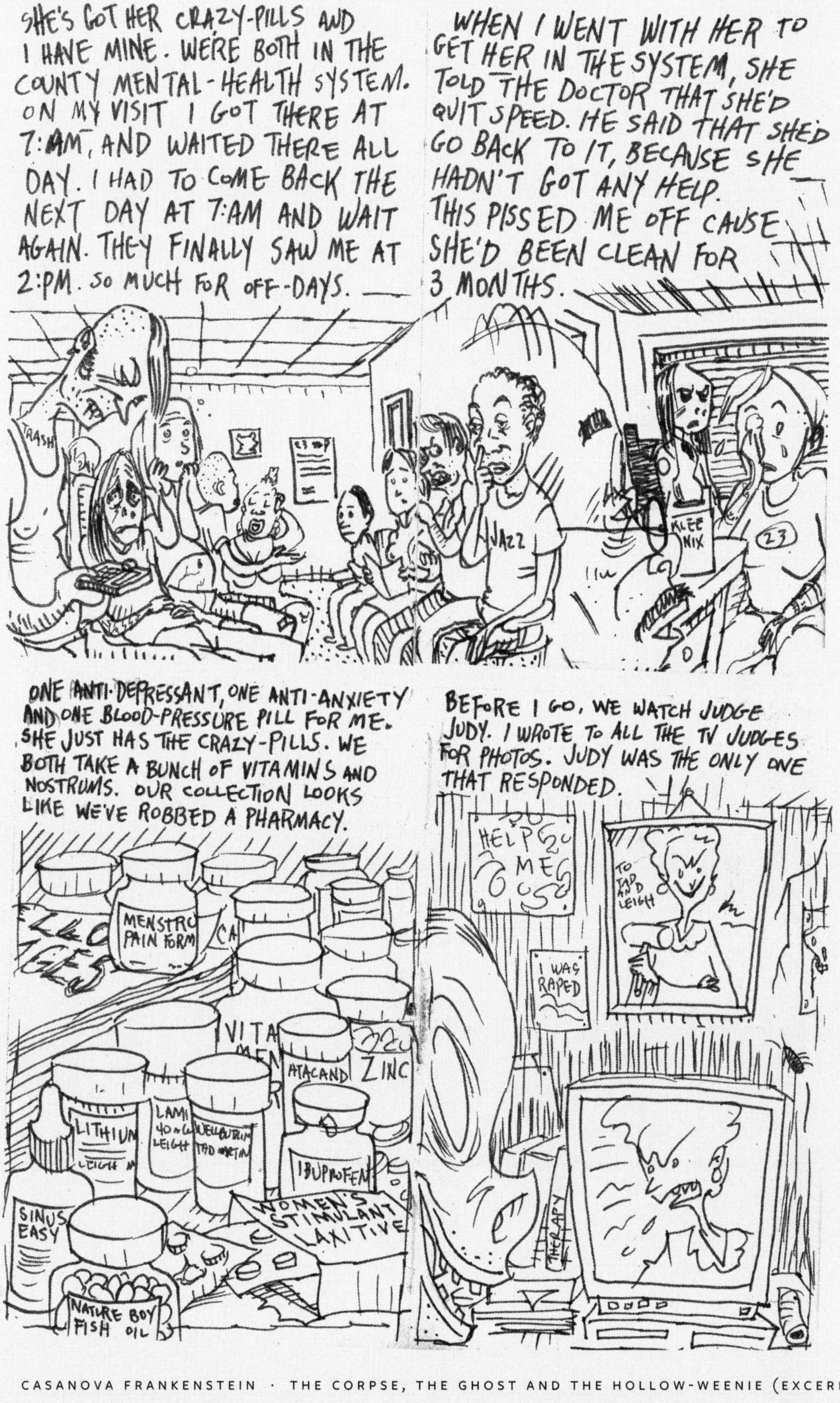
SHE'S GOT HER CRAZY-PILLS AND I HAVE MINE. WE'RE BOTH IN THE COUNTY MENTAL-HEALTH SYSTEM. ON MY VISIT I GOT THERE AT 7:AM, AND WAITED THERE ALL DAY. I HAD TO COME BACK THE NEXT DAY AT 7:AM AND WAIT AGAIN. THEY FINALLY SAW ME AT 2:PM. SO MUCH FOR OFF-DAYS.
WHEN I WENT WITH HER TO GET HER IN THE SYSTEM, SHE TOLD THE DOCTOR THAT SHE'D QUIT SPEED. HE SAID THAT SHE'D GO BACK TO IT, BECAUSE SHE HADN'T GOT ANY HELP. THIS PISSED ME OFF CAUSE SHE'D BEEN CLEAN FOR 3 MONTHS.
TRASH
JAZZ
KLEENIX
23
ONE ANTI-DEPRESSANT, ONE ANTI-ANXIETY AND ONE BLOOD-PRESSURE PILL FOR ME. SHE JUST HAS THE CRAZY-PILLS. WE BOTH TAKE A BUNCH OF VITAMINS AND NOSTRUMS. OUR COLLECTION LOOKS LIKE WE'VE ROBBED A PHARMACY.
MENSTRU PAIN FORM
VITA MEN
ATACAND
ZINC
LITHIUM LEIGH
LAMI 40mg LEIGH
WELLBUTRIN TAD MARTIN
IBUPROFEN
WOMEN'S STIMULANT LAXITIVE
SINUS EASY
NATURE BOY FISH OIL
BEFORE I GO, WE WATCH JUDGE JUDY. I WROTE TO ALL THE TV JUDGES FOR PHOTOS. JUDY WAS THE ONLY ONE THAT RESPONDED.
HELP ME
TO TAD AND LEIGH
I WAS RAPED
THERAPY

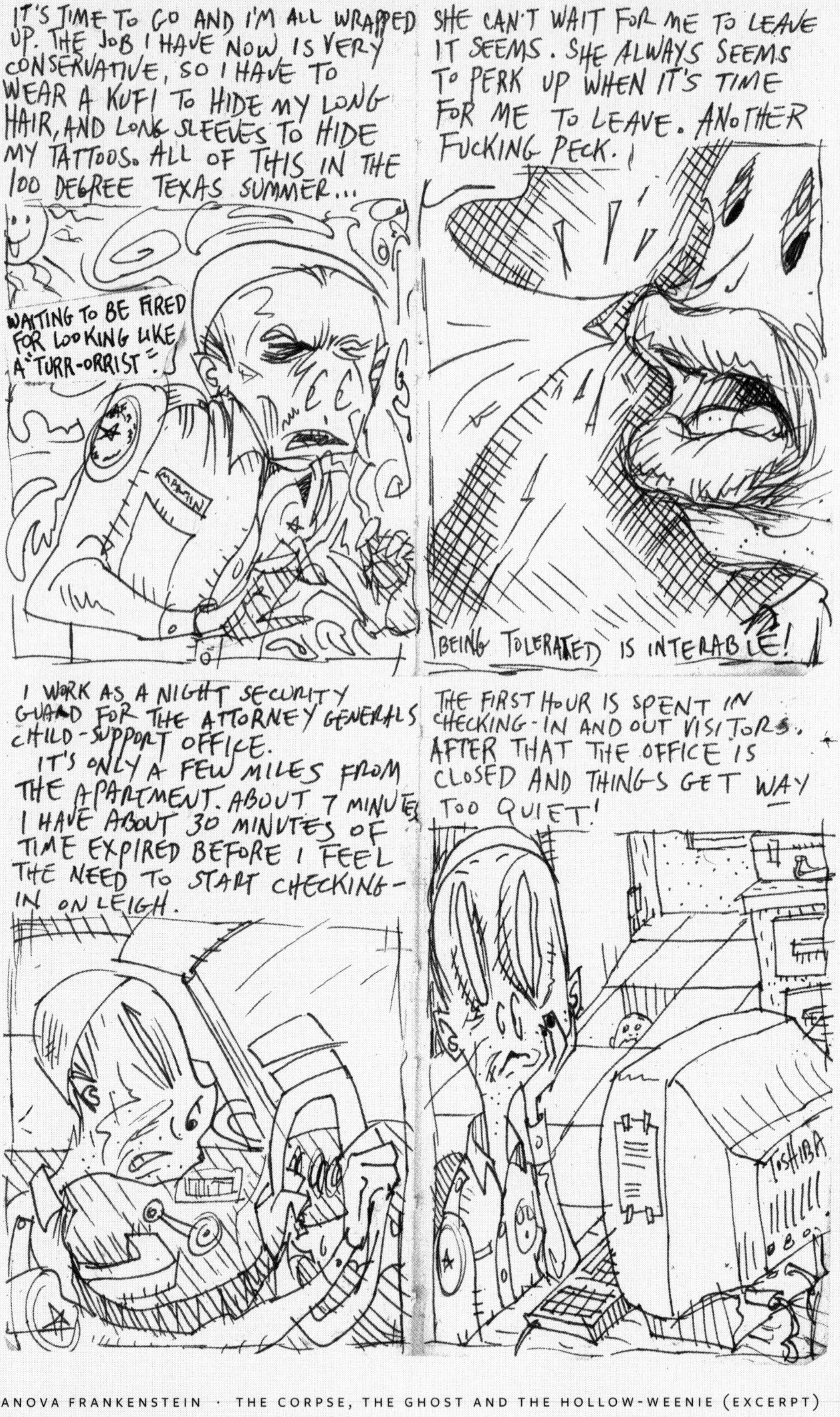
IT'S TIME TO GO AND I'M ALL WRAPPED UP. THE JOB I HAVE NOW IS VERY CONSERVATIVE, SO I HAVE TO WEAR A KUFI TO HIDE MY LONG HAIR, AND LONG SLEEVES TO HIDE MY TATTOOS. ALL OF THIS IN THE 100 DEGREE TEXAS SUMMER...
WAITING TO BE FIRED FOR LOOKING LIKE A "TURR-ORRIST"!
SHE CAN'T WAIT FOR ME TO LEAVE IT SEEMS. SHE ALWAYS SEEMS TO PERK UP WHEN IT'S TIME FOR ME TO LEAVE. ANOTHER FUCKING PECK.
BEING TOLERATED IS INTERABLE!
I WORK AS A NIGHT SECURITY GUARD FOR THE ATTORNEY GENERALS CHILD-SUPPORT OFFICE.
IT'S ONLY A FEW MILES FROM THE APARTMENT. ABOUT 7 MINUTES I HAVE ABOUT 30 MINUTES OF TIME EXPIRED BEFORE I FEEL THE NEED TO START CHECKING-IN ON LEIGH.
THE FIRST HOUR IS SPENT IN CHECKING-IN AND OUT VISITORS. AFTER THAT THE OFFICE IS CLOSED AND THINGS GET WAY TOO QUIET!
TOSHIBA

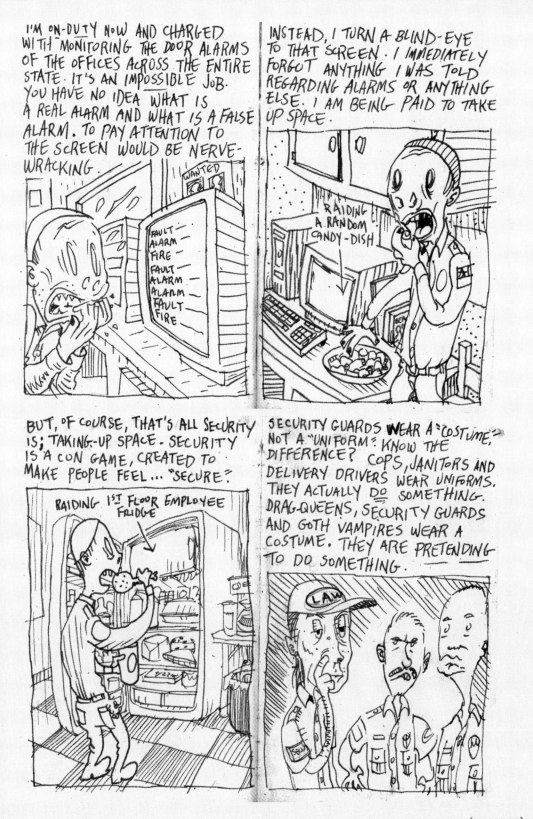

I'M ON-DUTY NOW AND CHARGED WITH MONITORING THE DOOR ALARMS OF THE OFFICES ACROSS THE ENTIRE STATE. IT'S AN IMPOSSIBLE JOB. YOU HAVE NO IDEA WHAT IS A REAL ALARM AND WHAT IS A FALSE ALARM. TO PAY ATTENTION TO THE SCREEN WOULD BE NERVE-WRACKING.

WANTED

FAULT
ALARM
FIRE
FAULT
ALARM
ALARM
FAULT
FIRE

INSTEAD, I TURN A BLIND-EYE TO THAT SCREEN. I IMMEDIATELY FORGOT ANYTHING I WAS TOLD REGARDING ALARMS OR ANYTHING ELSE. I AM BEING PAID TO TAKE UP SPACE.

RAIDING A RANDOM CANDY-DISH

BUT, OF COURSE, THAT'S ALL SECURITY IS; TAKING-UP SPACE. SECURITY IS A CON GAME, CREATED TO MAKE PEOPLE FEEL... "SECURE."

RAIDING 1ST FLOOR EMPLOYEE FRIDGE

HELLO?

PIZZA

SECURITY GUARDS WEAR A "COSTUME," NOT A "UNIFORM." KNOW THE DIFFERENCE? COPS, JANITORS AND DELIVERY DRIVERS WEAR UNIFORMS. THEY ACTUALLY DO SOMETHING. DRAG-QUEENS, SECURITY GUARDS AND GOTH VAMPIRES WEAR A COSTUME. THEY ARE PRETENDING TO DO SOMETHING.

LAW

SECURITY GUARDS ARE NOT COPS. BUT THE CON IS TO CONVINCE PEOPLE THAT THEY ARE COPS. THAT'S WHY MY LONG HAIR AND TATTOOS ARE UNWELCOME. THOSE THINGS WORK AGAINST THE COP ILLUSION.

LOOKING LIKE A COP WITHOUT BEING A COP IS DANGEROUS. IF SOME DISGRUNTLED FATHER COMES IN, AND ATTACKS ONE OF THE CASEWORKERS, I WOULD BE EXPECTED TO STEP IN. NO WEAPON, NO TRAINING, AND NO CONFIDENCE.

JOHNATHAN LAW

DOOR SHAKER

UMMM, SIR...

$10/HR

THE ABSURDITY OF MY SITUATION SOMETIMES HITS ME, IN A WAVE... OF ABSURDITY.

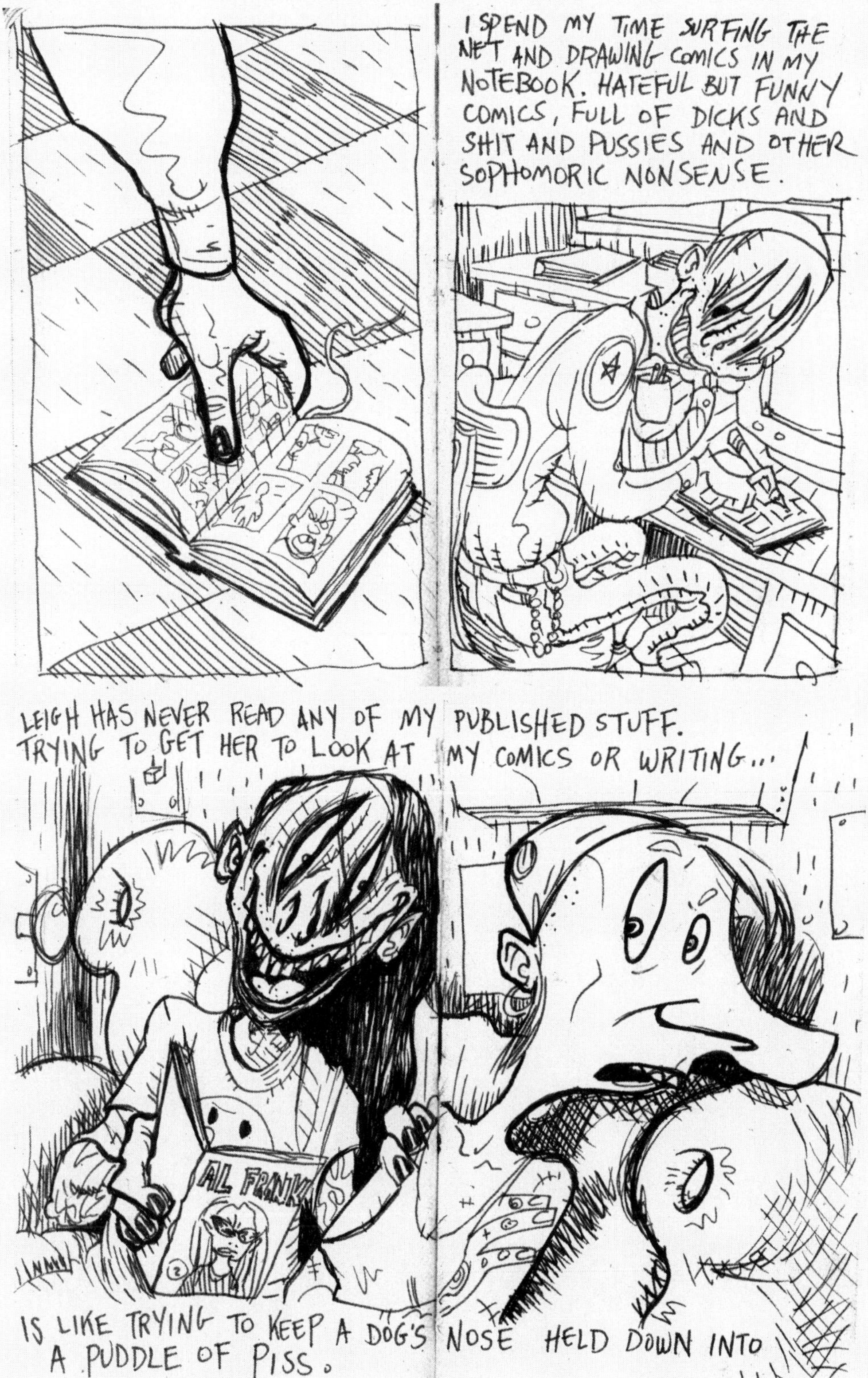
I SPEND MY TIME SURFING THE NET AND DRAWING COMICS IN MY NOTEBOOK. HATEFUL BUT FUNNY COMICS, FULL OF DICKS AND SHIT AND PUSSIES AND OTHER SOPHOMORIC NONSENSE.
LEIGH HAS NEVER READ ANY OF MY PUBLISHED STUFF. TRYING TO GET HER TO LOOK AT MY COMICS OR WRITING...
AL FRANK
IS LIKE TRYING TO KEEP A DOG'S NOSE HELD DOWN INTO A PUDDLE OF PISS.

AROUND 9:30 I USUALLY START TO SWEAT, CAUSE LEIGH IS GETTING READY TO GO OUT. I'M ALREADY PICTURING THE WORST.

I'M PICTURING THE TALL "FUCK ME" HEELS SHE DANCES IN UNTIL THE NAILS ON HER BIG TOES TURN BLACK AND FALL OFF.

 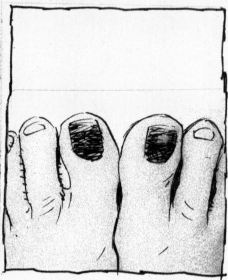

AND THE CROTCHLESS TIGHTS SHE FAVORS... SHE SAYS THEY'RE EASY CAUSE SHE DOESN'T HAVE TO TAKE THEM OFF TO PEE. I SAY THEY'RE EASY CAUSE YOU DON'T HAVE TO TAKE THEM OFF TO FUCK SOME GUY IN A STALL.

I ALSO PICTURE THE FAR-EASTSIDE JOOK-JOINT, IN A NEIGHBORHOOD WITH TWO STREETLIGHTS AND OF HER GETTING TO HER CAR AFTER BOOTY-SHAKING ALL NIGHT.

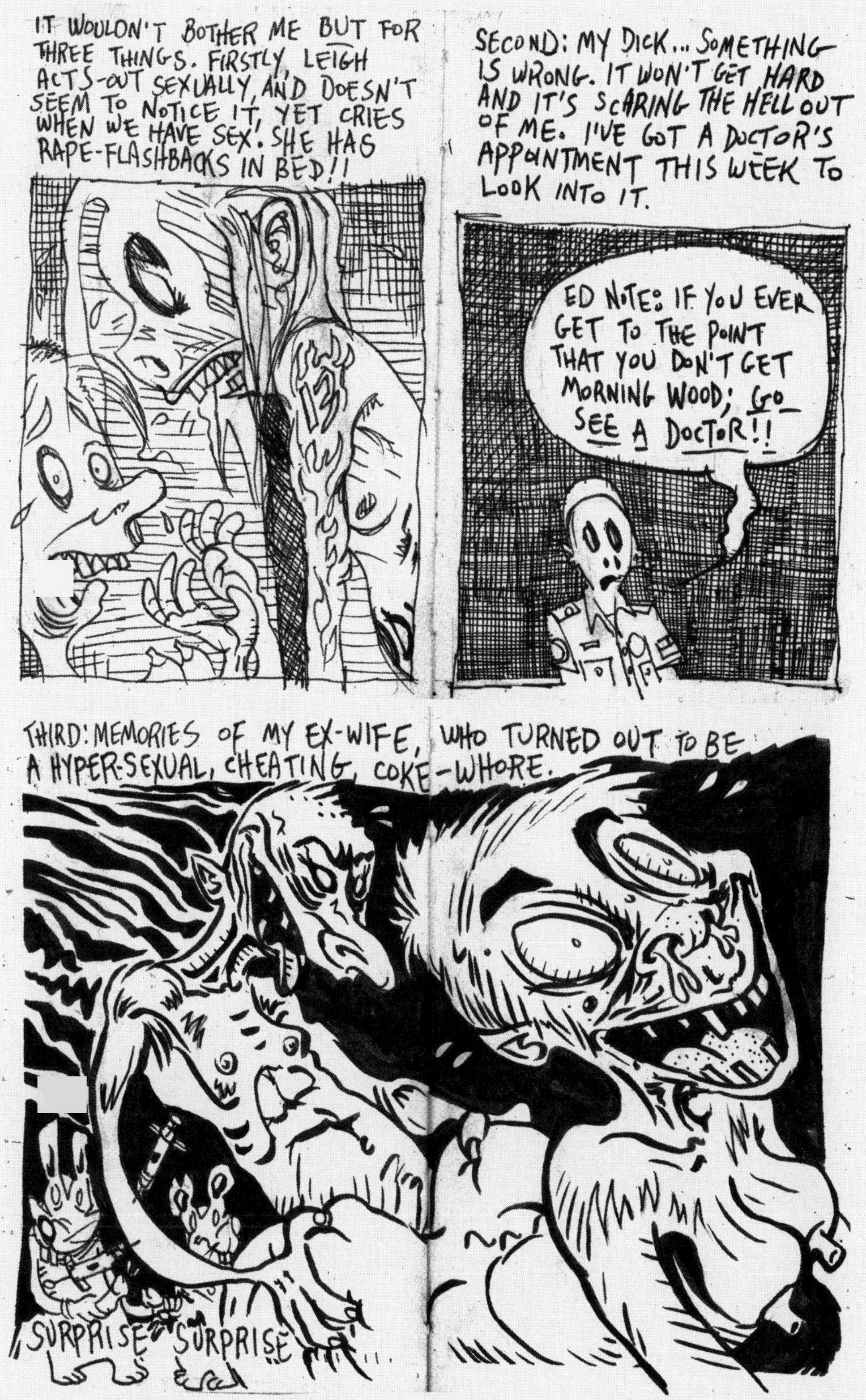
IT WOULDN'T BOTHER ME BUT FOR THREE THINGS. FIRSTLY, LEIGH ACTS-OUT SEXUALLY, AND DOESN'T SEEM TO NOTICE IT, YET CRIES WHEN WE HAVE SEX! SHE HAS RAPE-FLASHBACKS IN BED!!
SECOND: MY DICK... SOMETHING IS WRONG. IT WON'T GET HARD AND IT'S SCARING THE HELL OUT OF ME. I'VE GOT A DOCTOR'S APPOINTMENT THIS WEEK TO LOOK INTO IT.
ED NOTE: IF YOU EVER GET TO THE POINT THAT YOU DON'T GET MORNING WOOD; GO SEE A DOCTOR!!
THIRD: MEMORIES OF MY EX-WIFE, WHO TURNED OUT TO BE A HYPER-SEXUAL, CHEATING, COKE-WHORE.
SURPRISE SURPRISE

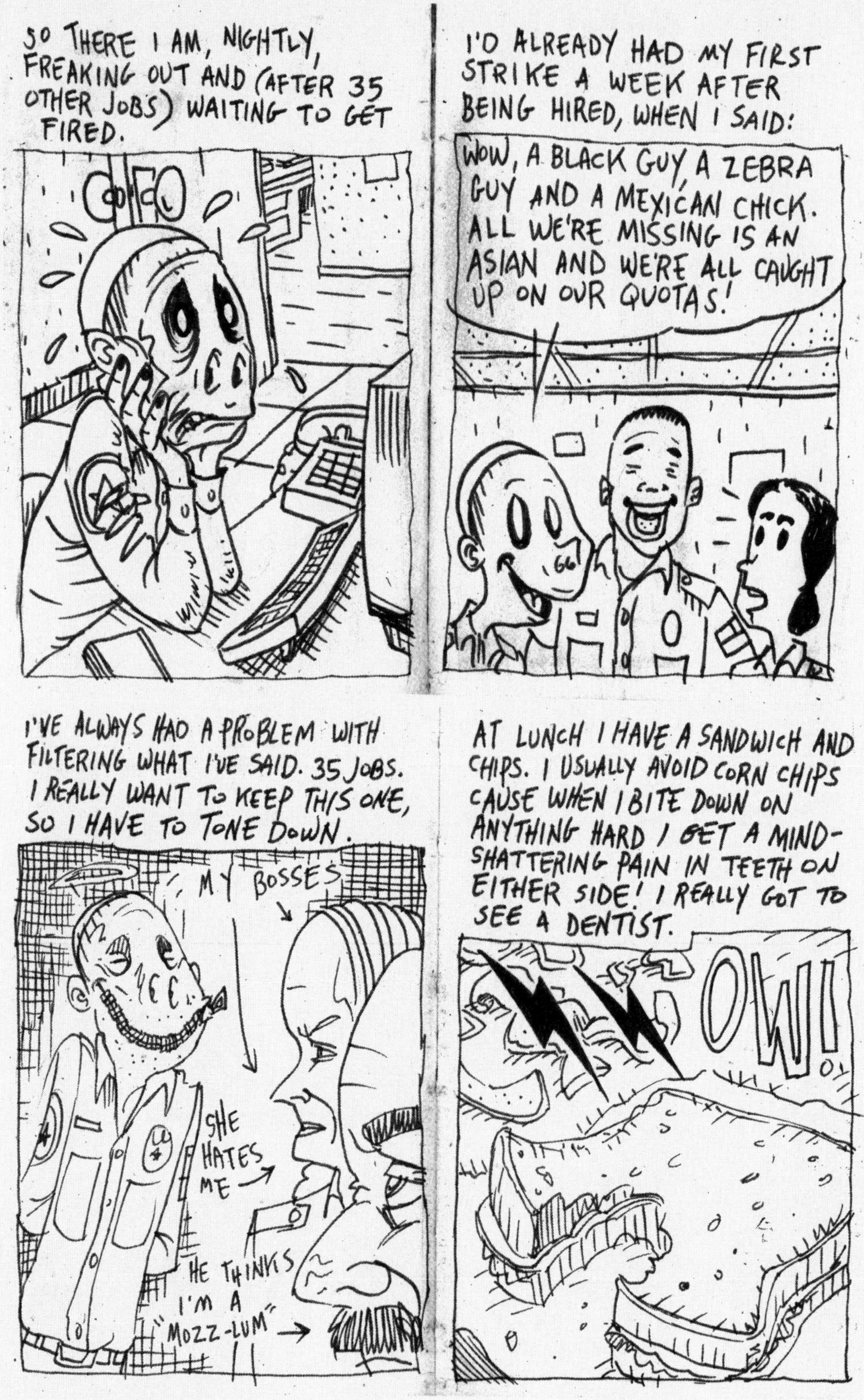
SO THERE I AM, NIGHTLY, FREAKING OUT AND (AFTER 35 OTHER JOBS) WAITING TO GET FIRED.
I'D ALREADY HAD MY FIRST STRIKE A WEEK AFTER BEING HIRED, WHEN I SAID:
WOW, A BLACK GUY, A ZEBRA GUY AND A MEXICAN CHICK. ALL WE'RE MISSING IS AN ASIAN AND WE'RE ALL CAUGHT UP ON OUR QUOTAS!
I'VE ALWAYS HAD A PROBLEM WITH FILTERING WHAT I'VE SAID. 35 JOBS. I REALLY WANT TO KEEP THIS ONE, SO I HAVE TO TONE DOWN.
MY BOSSES
SHE HATES ME
HE THINKS I'M A "MOZZ-LUM"
AT LUNCH I HAVE A SANDWICH AND CHIPS. I USUALLY AVOID CORN CHIPS CAUSE WHEN I BITE DOWN ON ANYTHING HARD I GET A MIND-SHATTERING PAIN IN TEETH ON EITHER SIDE! I REALLY GOT TO SEE A DENTIST.
OW!

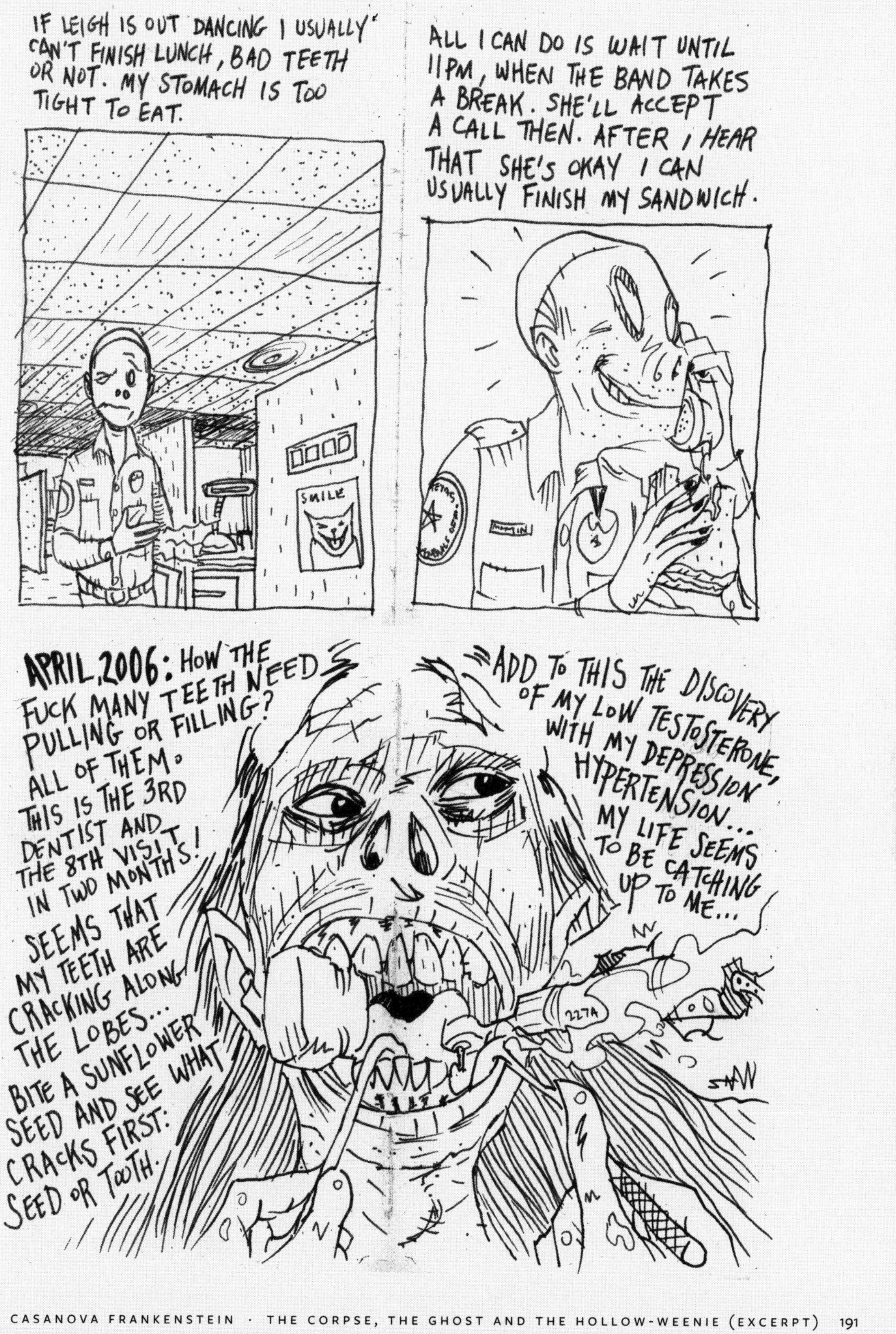
IF LEIGH IS OUT DANCING I USUALLY CAN'T FINISH LUNCH, BAD TEETH OR NOT. MY STOMACH IS TOO TIGHT TO EAT.
SMILE
ALL I CAN DO IS WAIT UNTIL 11PM, WHEN THE BAND TAKES A BREAK. SHE'LL ACCEPT A CALL THEN. AFTER I HEAR THAT SHE'S OKAY I CAN USUALLY FINISH MY SANDWICH.
APRIL, 2006: HOW THE FUCK MANY TEETH NEED PULLING OR FILLING? ALL OF THEM. THIS IS THE 3RD DENTIST AND THE 8TH VISIT IN TWO MONTH'S!
SEEMS THAT MY TEETH ARE CRACKING ALONG THE LOBES... BITE A SUNFLOWER SEED AND SEE WHAT CRACKS FIRST: SEED OR TOOTH.
ADD TO THIS THE DISCOVERY OF MY LOW TESTOSTERONE, WITH MY DEPRESSION, HYPERTENSION... MY LIFE SEEMS TO BE CATCHING UP TO ME...
227A
SNW

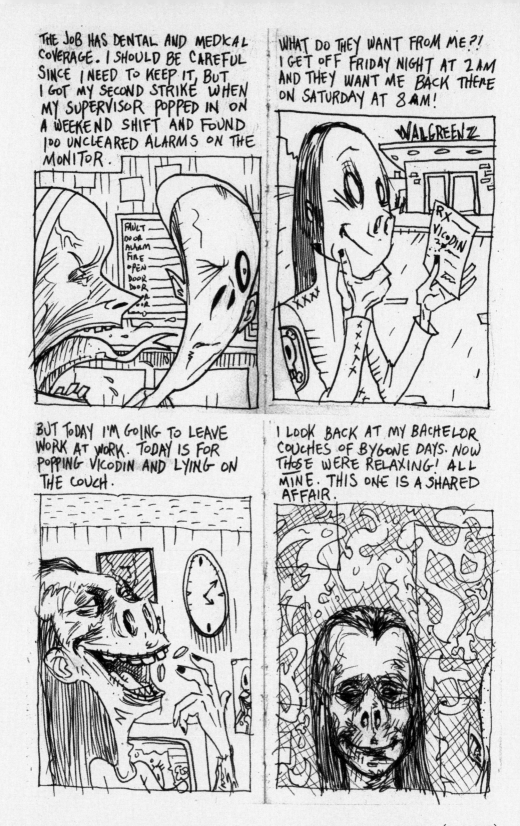

THE JOB HAS DENTAL AND MEDICAL COVERAGE. I SHOULD BE CAREFUL SINCE I NEED TO KEEP IT, BUT I GOT MY SECOND STRIKE WHEN MY SUPERVISOR POPPED IN ON A WEEKEND SHIFT AND FOUND 100 UNCLEARED ALARMS ON THE MONITOR.
FAULT
DOOR
ALARM
FIRE
OPEN
DOOR
DOOR
WHAT DO THEY WANT FROM ME?! I GET OFF FRIDAY NIGHT AT 2AM AND THEY WANT ME BACK THERE ON SATURDAY AT 8AM!
WALGREENZ
RX
VICODIN
BUT TODAY I'M GOING TO LEAVE WORK AT WORK. TODAY IS FOR POPPING VICODIN AND LYING ON THE COUCH.
I LOOK BACK AT MY BACHELOR COUCHES OF BYGONE DAYS. NOW THOSE WERE RELAXING! ALL MINE. THIS ONE IS A SHARED AFFAIR.

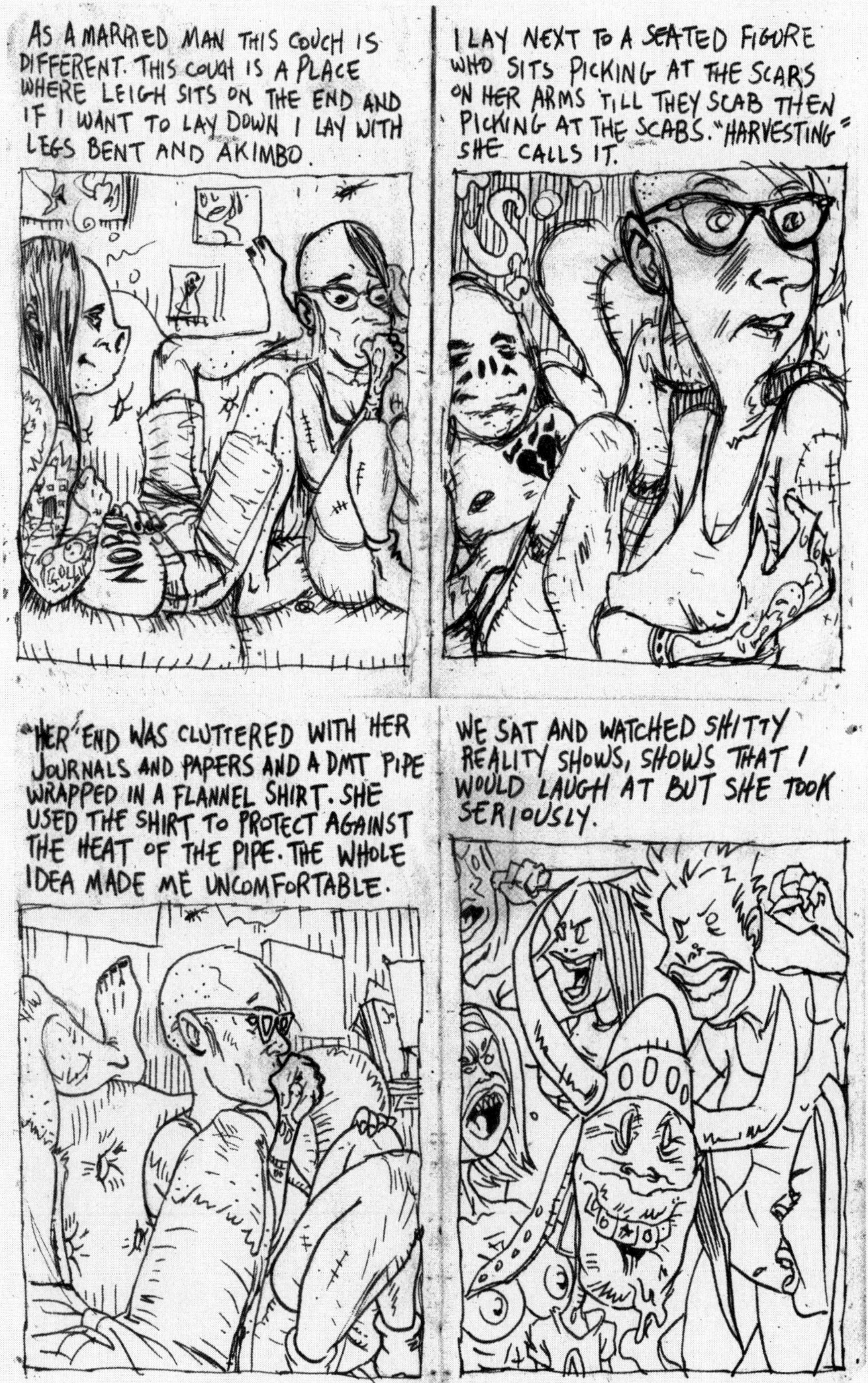
AS A MARRIED MAN THIS COUCH IS DIFFERENT. THIS COUCH IS A PLACE WHERE LEIGH SITS ON THE END AND IF I WANT TO LAY DOWN I LAY WITH LEGS BENT AND AKIMBO.
I LAY NEXT TO A SEATED FIGURE WHO SITS PICKING AT THE SCARS ON HER ARMS 'TILL THEY SCAB THEN PICKING AT THE SCABS. "HARVESTING" SHE CALLS IT.
"HER" END WAS CLUTTERED WITH HER JOURNALS AND PAPERS AND A DMT PIPE WRAPPED IN A FLANNEL SHIRT. SHE USED THE SHIRT TO PROTECT AGAINST THE HEAT OF THE PIPE. THE WHOLE IDEA MADE ME UNCOMFORTABLE.
WE SAT AND WATCHED SHITTY REALITY SHOWS, SHOWS THAT I WOULD LAUGH AT BUT SHE TOOK SERIOUSLY.

SHE HAD A SPECIAL RELATIONSHIP WITH THE STARS. A RELATIONSHIP LIKE HER FAILED ACTRESS MOTHER HAD. LIKE HER MOTHER SHE READ THE ENQUIRER AND STAR.

SHE TALKED ABOUT TRYING TO GET INTO COMEDY WITH HER STORIES. I'D TRIED TO EXPLAIN TO HER THAT TRAGIC STORIES OF RAPE AS A TODDLER AND TEEN AND BEING CHOKED UNCONSCIOUS BY YOUR DRUGGED-OUT MOTHER WEREN'T FUNNY.

BUT WHAT DID I KNOW? SHE NEVER LAUGHED AT ANYTHING I SAID. SHE JUST ASKED HER INVISIBLE CRAZY DEAD MOTHER FOR LIFE ADVICE.

AND SO, WE WERE NEVER JUST A MARRIED COUPLE. WE WERE A THREESOME. A GHOST, A SEXUAL CORPSE AND A LIMP-NOODLE. WHAT A CLUSTER FUCK...

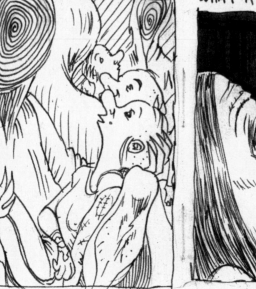

HA...

I ALWAYS LAY ON THIS COUCH ON MY OFF-DAYS BUT WITH VICODIN IT IS MUCH BETTER. VICODIN HELPS BLOCK OUT THE DISTURBING MONOLOGUE.

HER MONOLOGUE OF HER MOTHER'S ALCOHOLISM. OF HER MOTHER LOSING HER TO THE STATE AT AGE TWO. OF HER MOTHER THEN CONNING SOME DOPE INTO A RELATIONSHIP WHERE THEY KIDNAP THE 3 YEAR OLD LEIGH FROM FOSTER-CARE AND FLEE TO A TEXAS COMMUNE FROM OHIO.

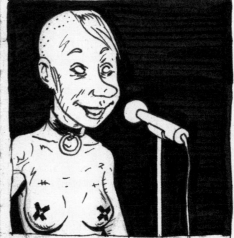

STORIES OF LIVING IN POVERTY IN AUSTIN FROM MOTEL TO MOTEL. OF WINDING UP WORKING WITH HER MOTHER ON COSTUMES AND PROPS FOR THE LIVE-COMEDY THEATER WHERE HER MOTHER WAS ALSO A PERFORMER.

HER MOTHER HER MOTHER HER MOTHER... HER MOTHER THE STRIPPER, HER MOTHER THE ACTRESS, HER MOTHER THE SPEED-FREAK, HER MOTHER THE PROSTITUTE, HER MOTHER THE CON-WOMAN. HER MOTHER WHO SUICIDED WHEN LEIGH WAS 25, FURTHER CRACKING HER REALITY. HER MOTHER THE SPIRITUALIST, HER MOTHER THE RACIST, HER MOTHER THE WITCH...

THE VICODIN HELPS SO MUCH THAT I LOOK FORWARD TO ROOT-CANALS AND EXTRACTIONS, SO THAT I CAN LISTEN TO THIS NEUROTIC MESS WITHOUT CARING.
I CAN LISTEN TO LEIGH TALK ABOUT HAVING TO FEED HER SUPPOSEDLY HELPLESS MOTHER AND CLEAN-UP AFTER HER AND HOW THE WOMAN WAS NICER DRUNK THAN SOBER, SO SHE LIKED THE DRUNK SIDE MORE.
FUCK YOU
OR THE HOT-TUB HER MOTHER HAD AND SITTING THERE IN THE WATER WITH HER MOTHER.
A WITCHES' CAULDRON OF INSANITY.
DOIN' THE ROBOT ON THE MOON WITH MIDGET SANTA IN A BACKPACK WHILE DRESSED LIKE TELEKON GARY NUMAN
AND WHEN LEIGH MAKES STATEMENTS LIKE, "MY MOTHER WAS SEXUALLY FRUSTRATED. I SOMETIMES THINK I WOULD HAVE BEEN THE ONLY ONE WHO COULD HAVE MADE HER CUM!". I CAN LET THOSE TYPE STATEMENTS FLOAT AWAY ON A CLOUD OF OPIOID PLEASURE AND BLOODY SPIT.
BEEP-BOOP

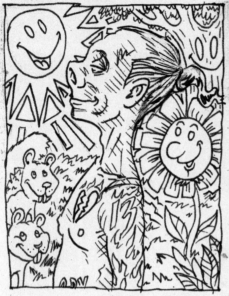

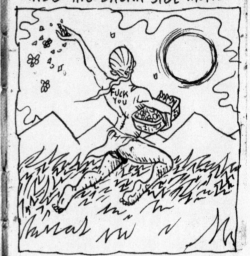

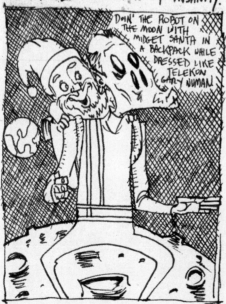

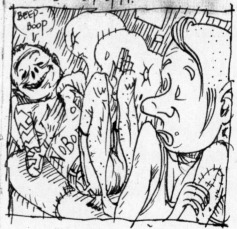

JULY 2006: IT STARTED WITH ME GOING IN TO WORK. JUST ANOTHER DAY, I THOUGHT. I PARKED AND STARTED FOR THE DOOR WITH MY BAG OF ART STUFF.

ALL OF A SUDDEN, THE MANAGER OF SECURITY COMES AROUND THE BUILDING AND STOPS ME. HE'S GOT AN EVIL GRIN ON HIS FACE AS HE ASKS ME FOR MY BADGE AND ID CARD.

HE EXPLAINS THAT A NUDE PICTURE WAS FOUND ON THE COPY MACHINE. I'D LEFT IT THERE THE NIGHT BEFORE WHEN I WAS TRYING TO ENLARGE IT.

I EXPLAINED TO HIM THAT I WAS WORKING ON A DRAWING. I WENT IN MY BAG AND PULLED OUT THE DRAWING TO SHOW HIM.

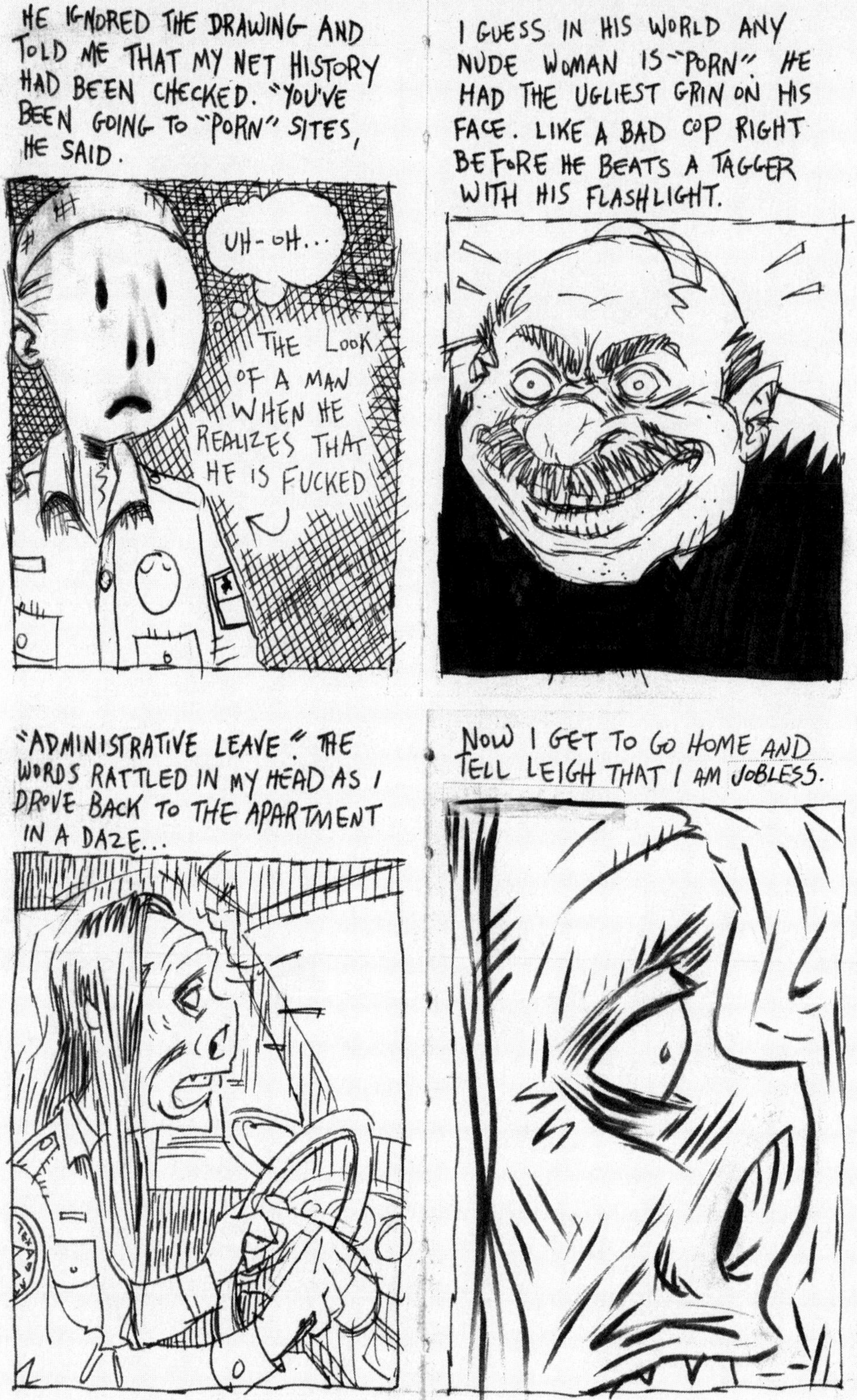
HE IGNORED THE DRAWING AND TOLD ME THAT MY NET HISTORY HAD BEEN CHECKED. "YOU'VE BEEN GOING TO "PORN" SITES, HE SAID.
UH-OH...
THE LOOK OF A MAN WHEN HE REALIZES THAT HE IS FUCKED
I GUESS IN HIS WORLD ANY NUDE WOMAN IS "PORN". HE HAD THE UGLIEST GRIN ON HIS FACE. LIKE A BAD COP RIGHT BEFORE HE BEATS A TAGGER WITH HIS FLASHLIGHT.
"ADMINISTRATIVE LEAVE." THE WORDS RATTLED IN MY HEAD AS I DROVE BACK TO THE APARTMENT IN A DAZE...
NOW I GET TO GO HOME AND TELL LEIGH THAT I AM JOBLESS.

# Fashion Cat

ALEX SCHUBERT

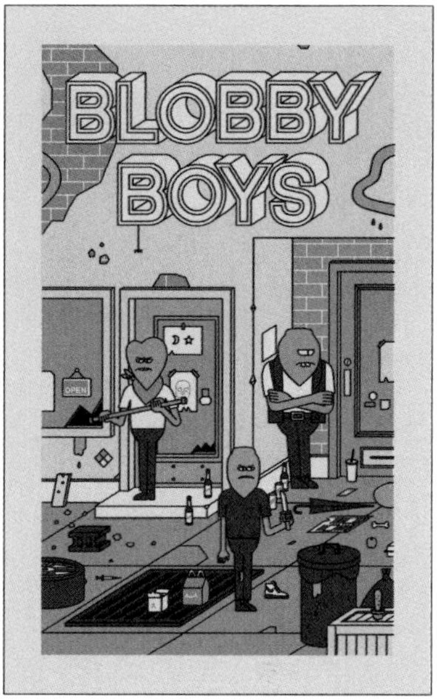
BLOBBY
BOYS
OPEN

*originally published in*

Blobby Boys 2

KOYAMA PRESS

5.5 × 8.5 inches • 52 pages

## Biography

Alex Schubert is from Mascoutah, Illinois, and now lives in Los Angeles. He is a frequent contributor to *VICE*. His book series, *Blobby Boys*, is published by Koyama Press. As an animation designer, his clients include Target, FOX ADHD, and Disney XD. zinepolice.com

## Statement

I was watching a documentary about Basquiat, and my girlfriend mumbled something that sounded like "All Night Fashion Cat." I have no clue what she was really saying.

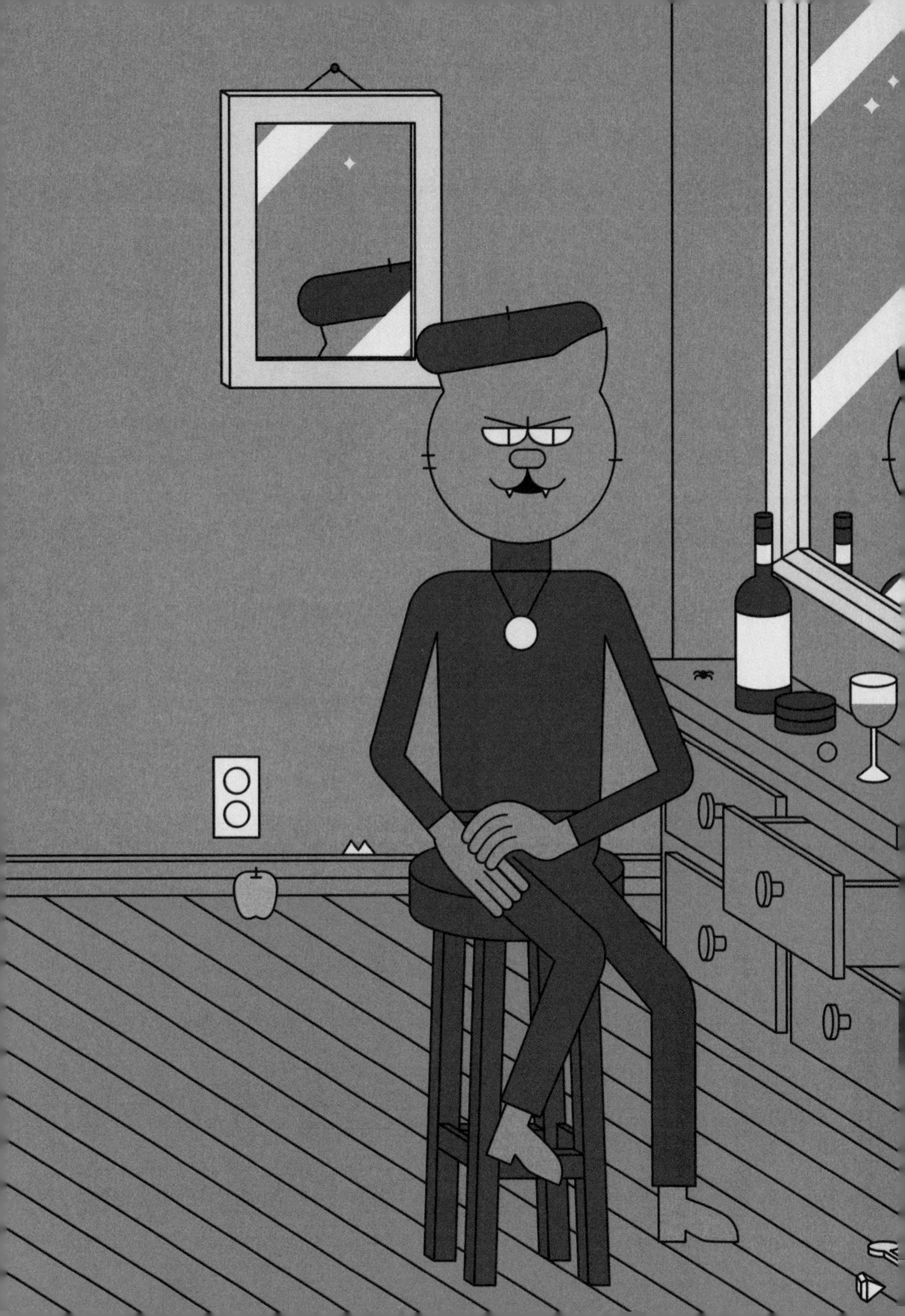

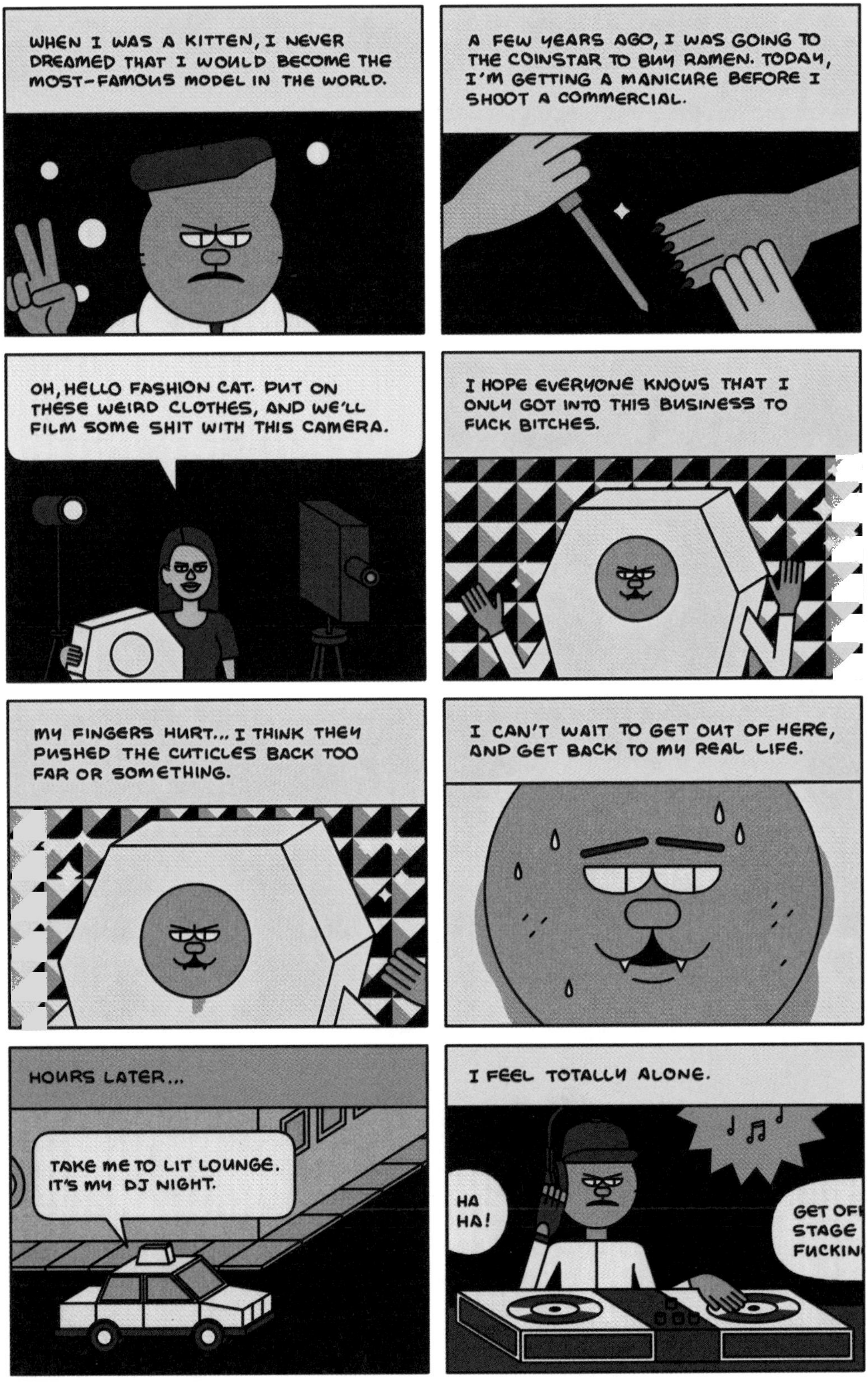
WHEN I WAS A KITTEN, I NEVER DREAMED THAT I WOULD BECOME THE MOST-FAMOUS MODEL IN THE WORLD.
A FEW YEARS AGO, I WAS GOING TO THE COINSTAR TO BUY RAMEN. TODAY, I'M GETTING A MANICURE BEFORE I SHOOT A COMMERCIAL.
OH, HELLO FASHION CAT. PUT ON THESE WEIRD CLOTHES, AND WE'LL FILM SOME SHIT WITH THIS CAMERA.
I HOPE EVERYONE KNOWS THAT I ONLY GOT INTO THIS BUSINESS TO FUCK BITCHES.
MY FINGERS HURT... I THINK THEY PUSHED THE CUTICLES BACK TOO FAR OR SOMETHING.
I CAN'T WAIT TO GET OUT OF HERE, AND GET BACK TO MY REAL LIFE.
HOURS LATER...
TAKE ME TO LIT LOUNGE. IT'S MY DJ NIGHT.
I FEEL TOTALLY ALONE.
HA HA!
GET OF STAGE FUCKIN

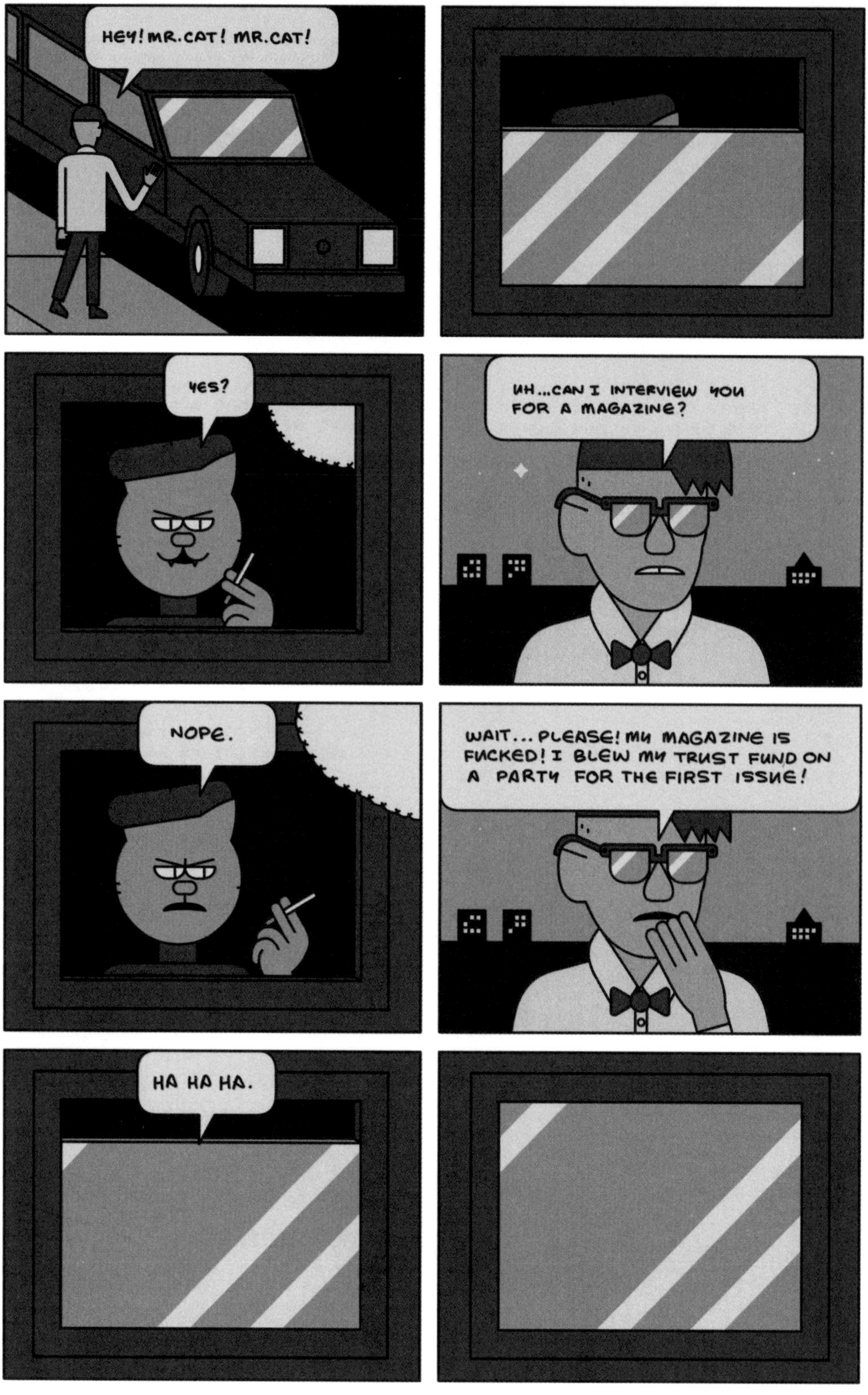
HEY! MR. CAT! MR. CAT!
YES?
UH...CAN I INTERVIEW YOU FOR A MAGAZINE?
NOPE.
WAIT... PLEASE! MY MAGAZINE IS FUCKED! I BLEW MY TRUST FUND ON A PARTY FOR THE FIRST ISSUE!
HA HA HA.

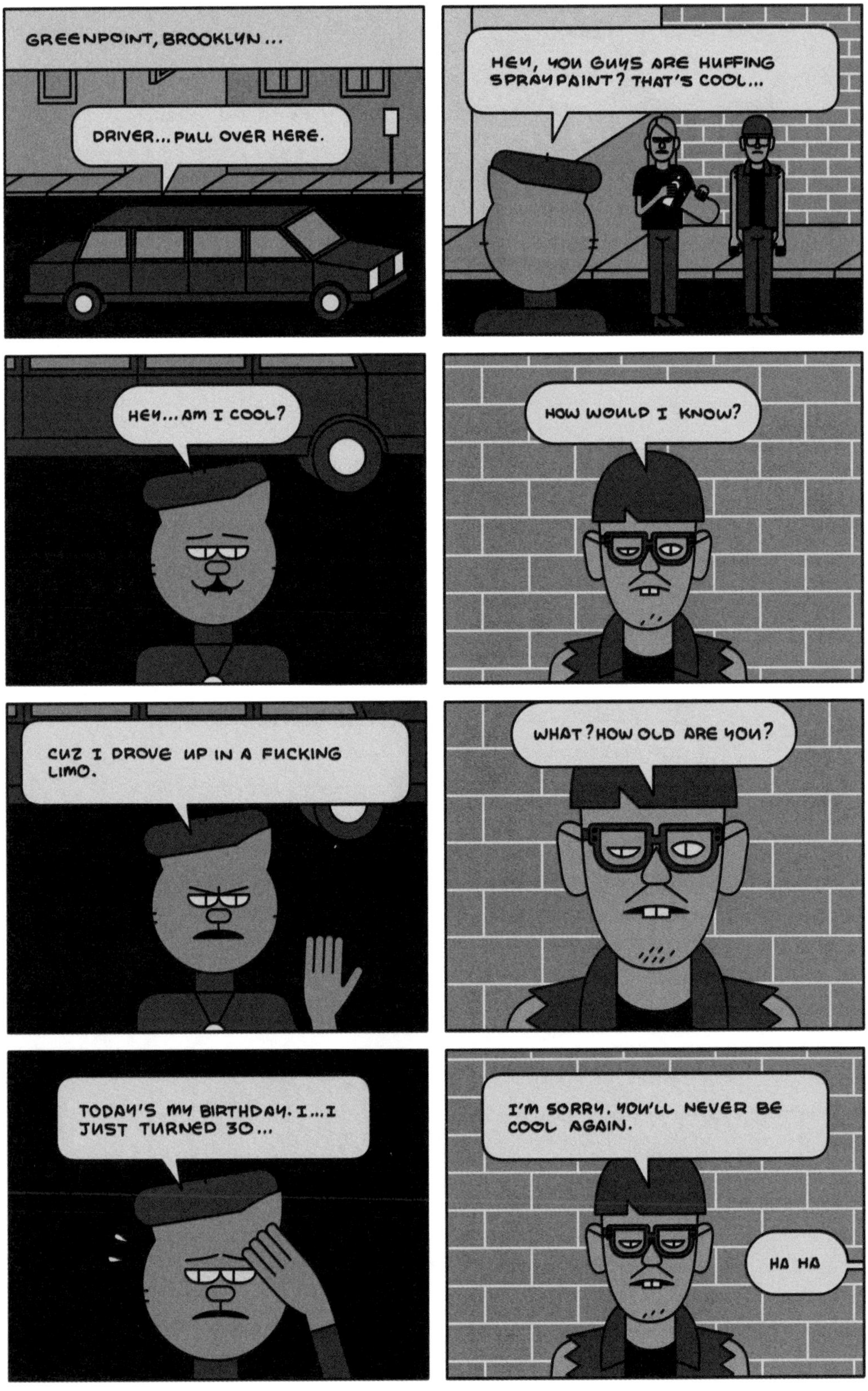
GREENPOINT, BROOKLYN...
DRIVER... PULL OVER HERE.
HEY, YOU GUYS ARE HUFFING SPRAYPAINT? THAT'S COOL...
HEY... AM I COOL?
HOW WOULD I KNOW?
CUZ I DROVE UP IN A FUCKING LIMO.
WHAT? HOW OLD ARE YOU?
TODAY'S MY BIRTHDAY. I...I JUST TURNED 30...
I'M SORRY. YOU'LL NEVER BE COOL AGAIN.
HA HA

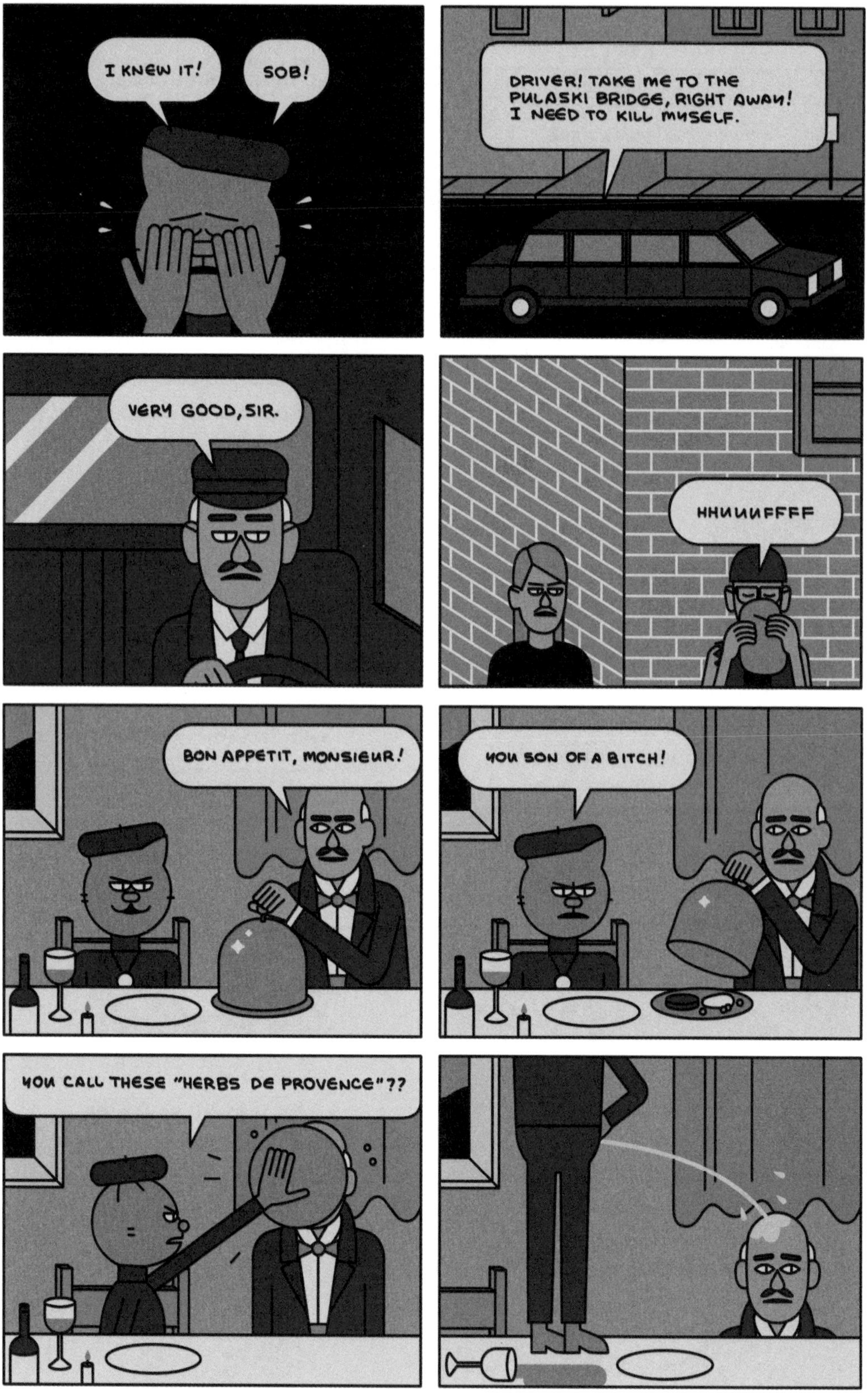
I KNEW IT!
SOB!
DRIVER! TAKE ME TO THE PULASKI BRIDGE, RIGHT AWAY! I NEED TO KILL MYSELF.
VERY GOOD, SIR.
HHUUUFFFF
BON APPETIT, MONSIEUR!
YOU SON OF A BITCH!
YOU CALL THESE "HERBS DE PROVENCE"??

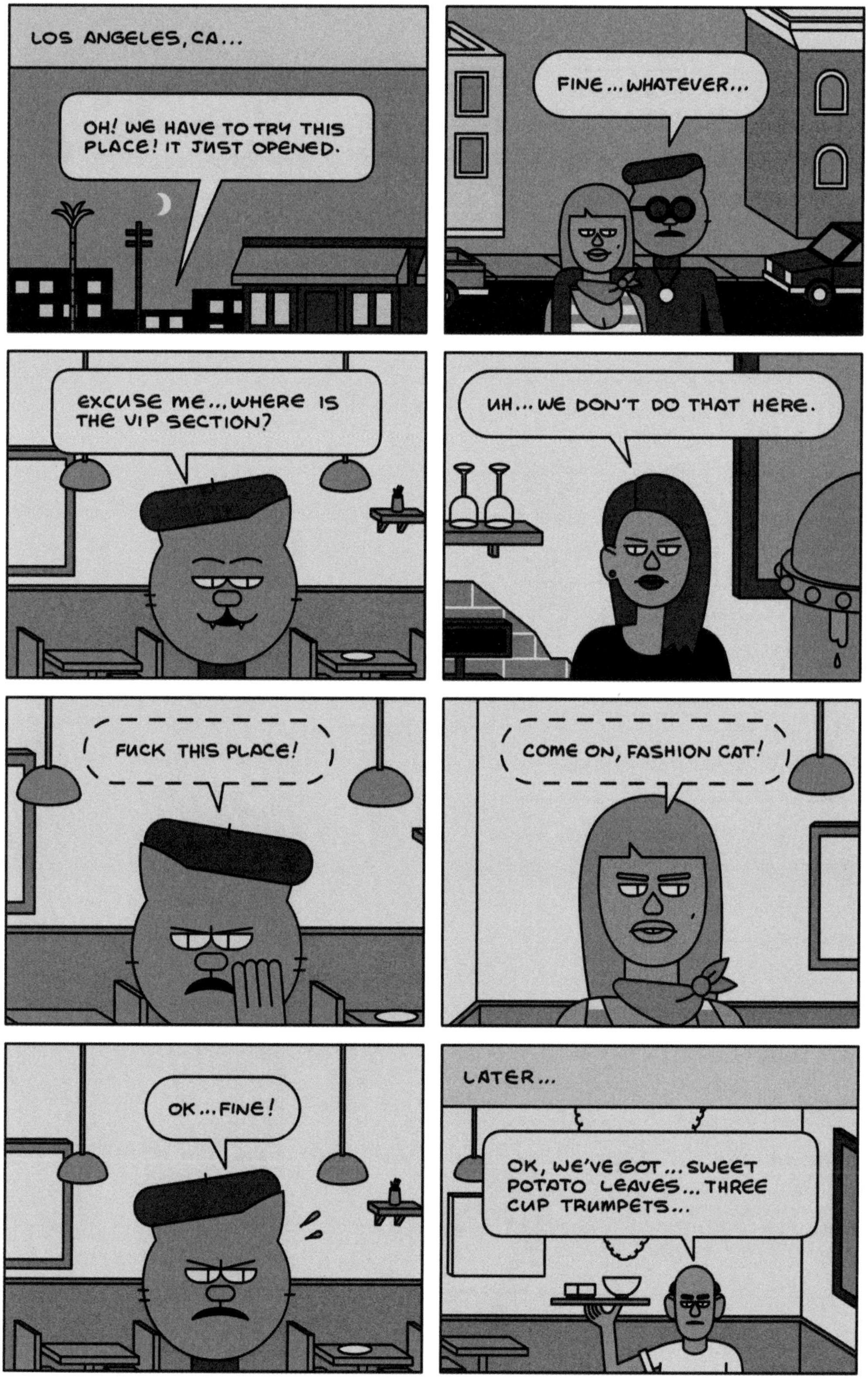
LOS ANGELES, CA...
OH! WE HAVE TO TRY THIS PLACE! IT JUST OPENED.
FINE... WHATEVER...
EXCUSE ME... WHERE IS THE VIP SECTION?
UH... WE DON'T DO THAT HERE.
FUCK THIS PLACE!
COME ON, FASHION CAT!
OK... FINE!
LATER...
OK, WE'VE GOT... SWEET POTATO LEAVES... THREE CUP TRUMPETS...

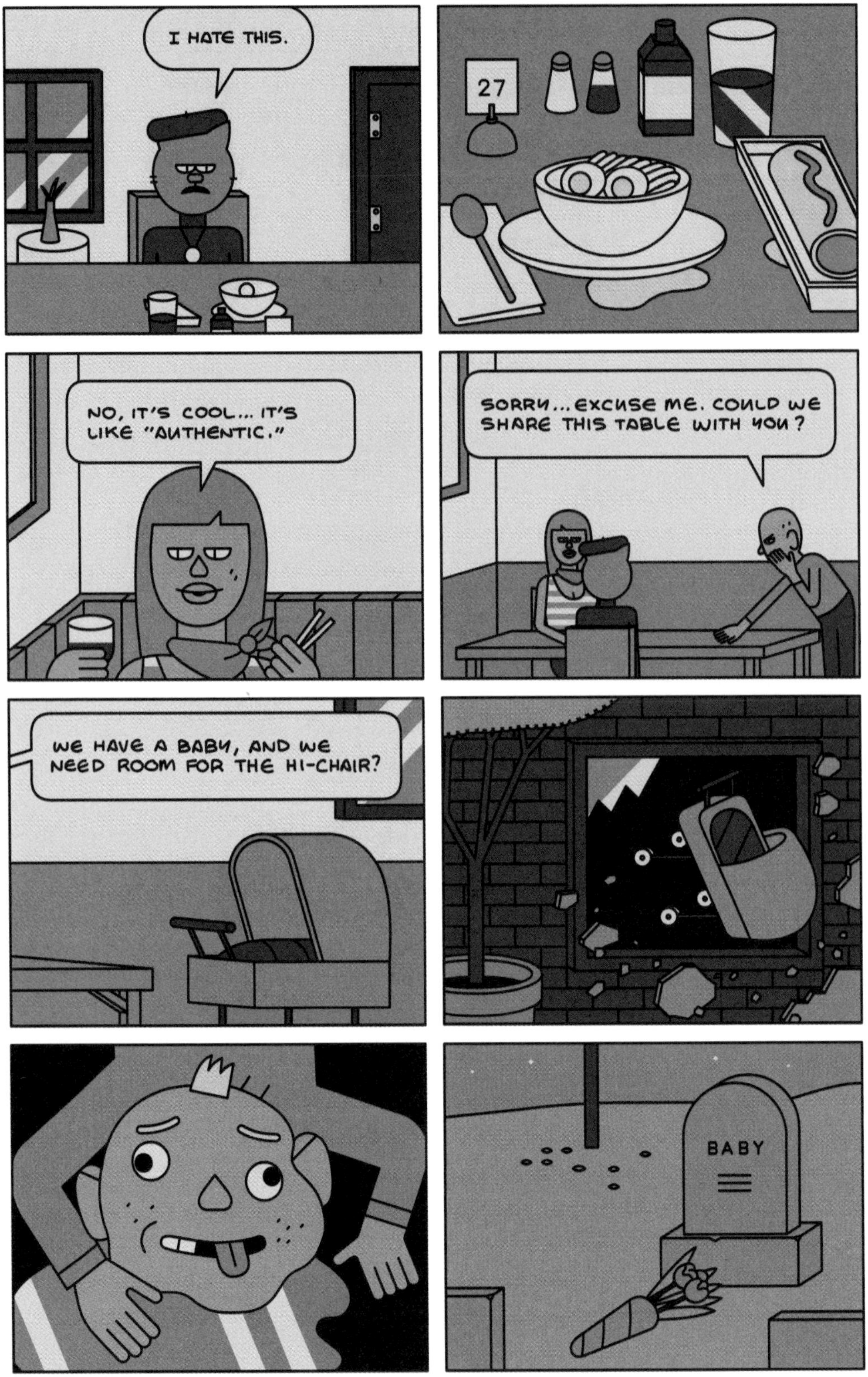
I HATE THIS.
27
NO, IT'S COOL... IT'S LIKE "AUTHENTIC."
SORRY... EXCUSE ME. COULD WE SHARE THIS TABLE WITH YOU?
WE HAVE A BABY, AND WE NEED ROOM FOR THE HI-CHAIR?
BABY

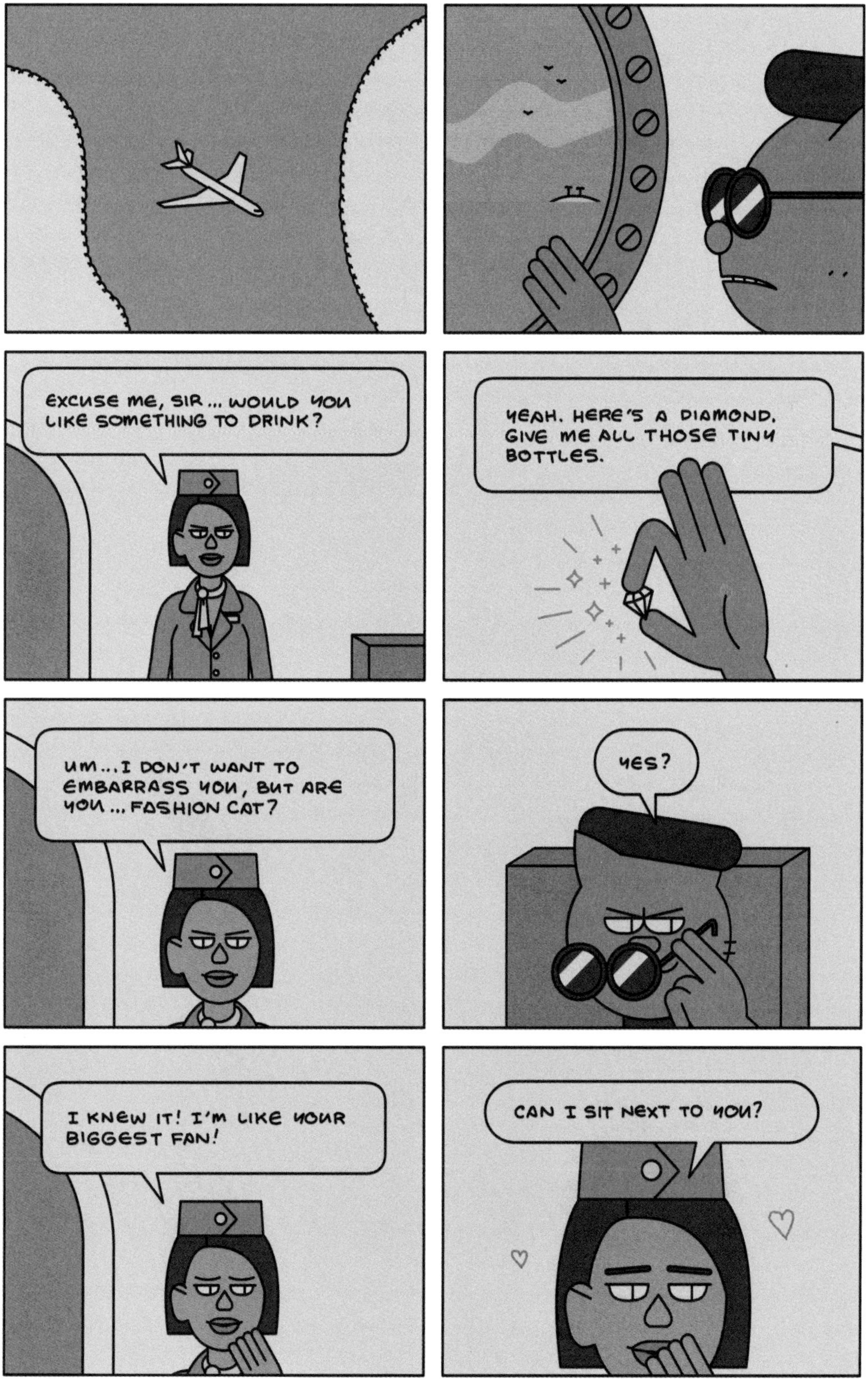
EXCUSE ME, SIR... WOULD YOU LIKE SOMETHING TO DRINK?
YEAH. HERE'S A DIAMOND. GIVE ME ALL THOSE TINY BOTTLES.
UM...I DON'T WANT TO EMBARRASS YOU, BUT ARE YOU... FASHION CAT?
YES?
I KNEW IT! I'M LIKE YOUR BIGGEST FAN!
CAN I SIT NEXT TO YOU?

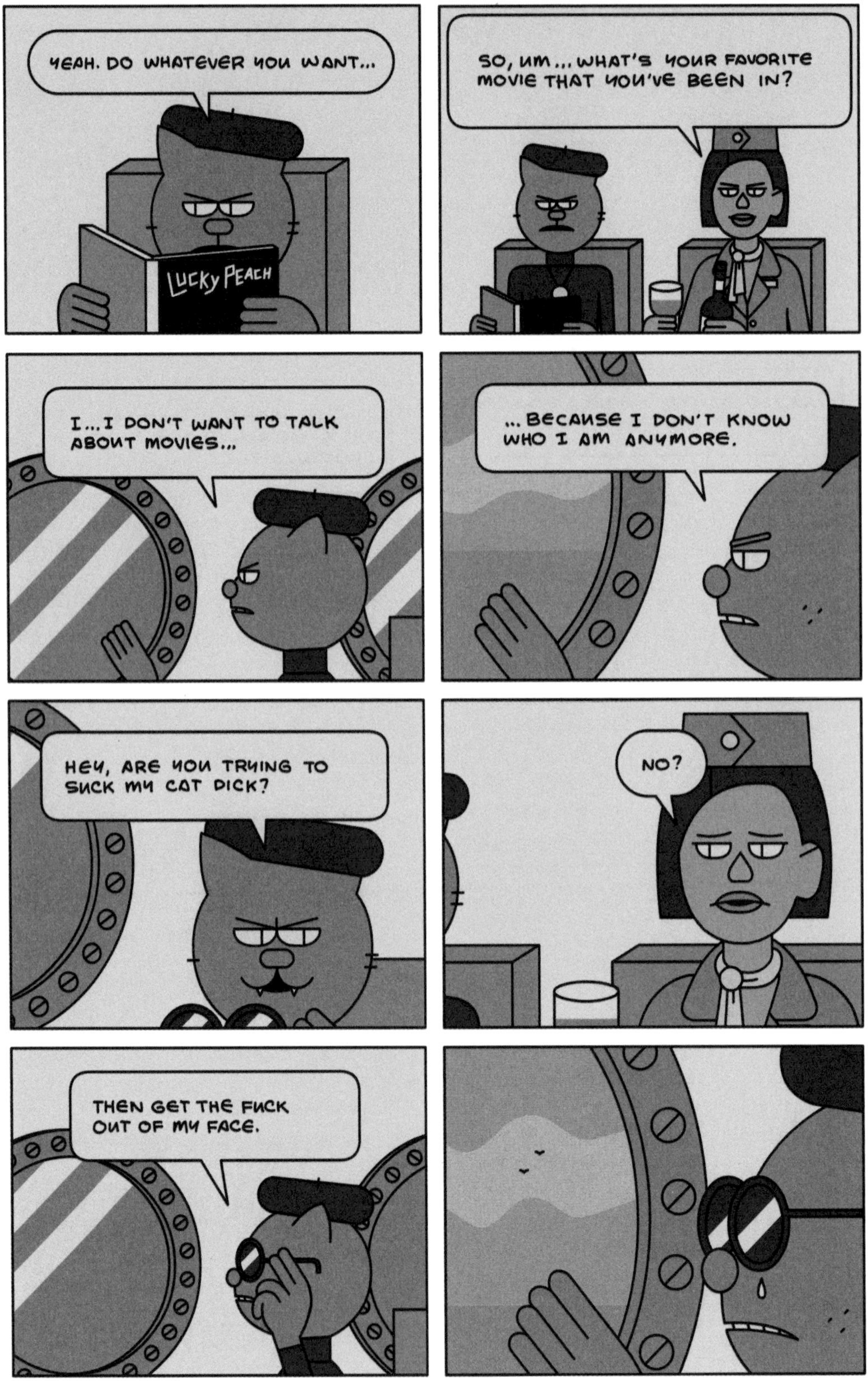
YEAH. DO WHATEVER YOU WANT...
LUCKY PEACH
SO, UM... WHAT'S YOUR FAVORITE MOVIE THAT YOU'VE BEEN IN?
I... I DON'T WANT TO TALK ABOUT MOVIES...
...BECAUSE I DON'T KNOW WHO I AM ANYMORE.
HEY, ARE YOU TRYING TO SUCK MY CAT DICK?
NO?
THEN GET THE FUCK OUT OF MY FACE.

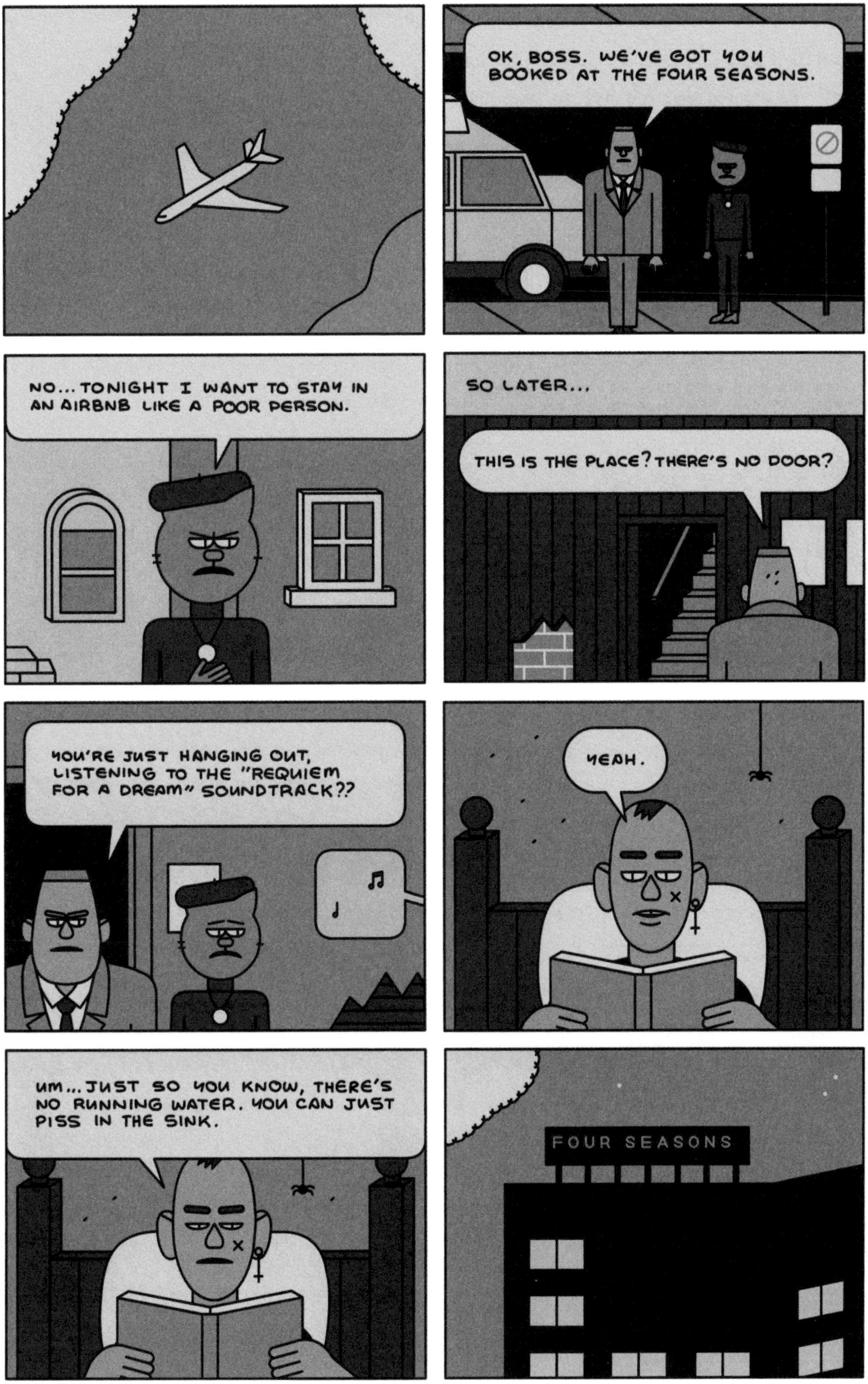
OK, BOSS. WE'VE GOT YOU BOOKED AT THE FOUR SEASONS.
NO... TONIGHT I WANT TO STAY IN AN AIRBNB LIKE A POOR PERSON.
SO LATER...
THIS IS THE PLACE? THERE'S NO DOOR?
YOU'RE JUST HANGING OUT, LISTENING TO THE "REQUIEM FOR A DREAM" SOUNDTRACK??
YEAH.
UM... JUST SO YOU KNOW, THERE'S NO RUNNING WATER. YOU CAN JUST PISS IN THE SINK.
FOUR SEASONS

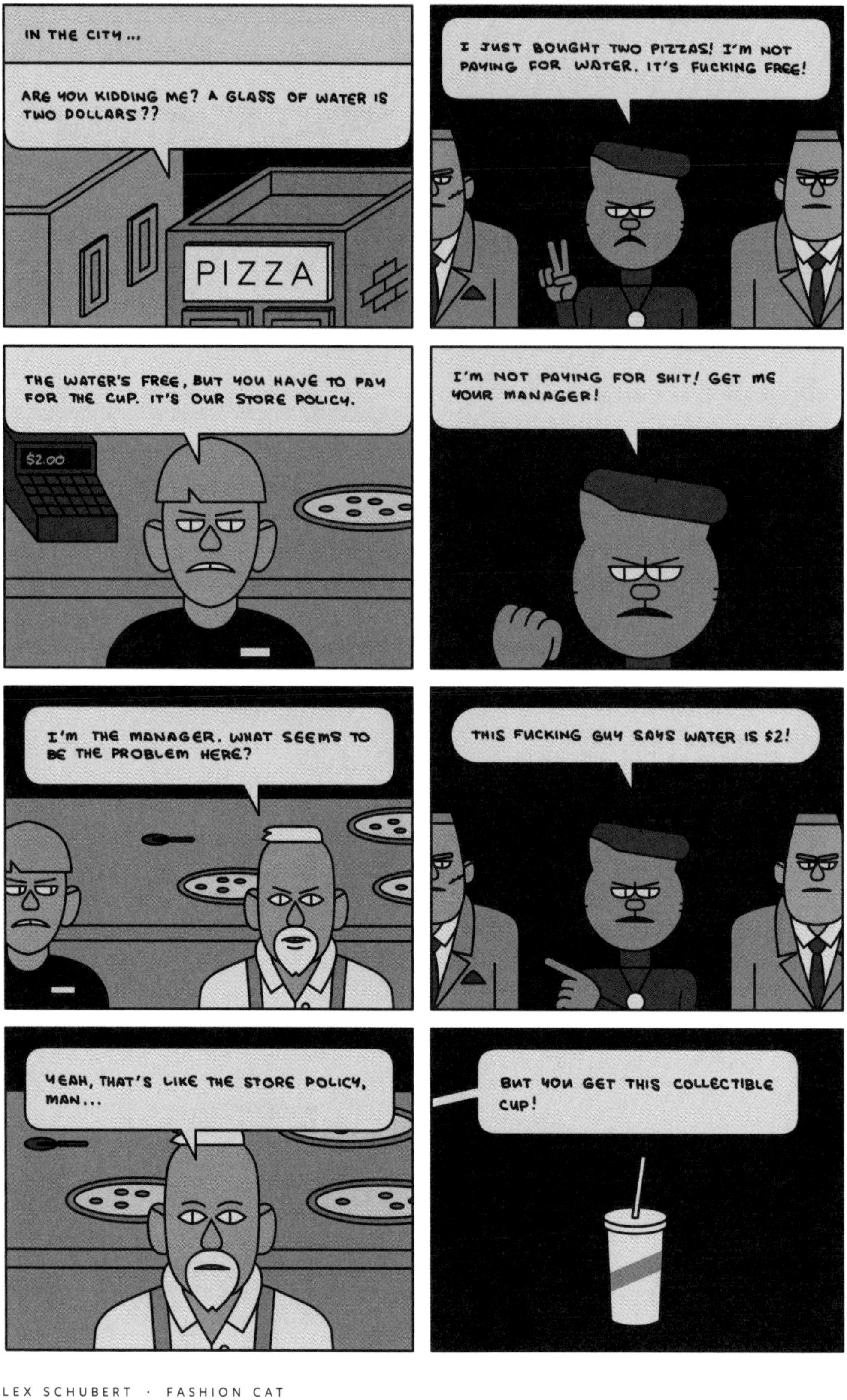
IN THE CITY...
ARE YOU KIDDING ME? A GLASS OF WATER IS TWO DOLLARS??
PIZZA
I JUST BOUGHT TWO PIZZAS! I'M NOT PAYING FOR WATER. IT'S FUCKING FREE!
THE WATER'S FREE, BUT YOU HAVE TO PAY FOR THE CUP. IT'S OUR STORE POLICY.
$2.00
I'M NOT PAYING FOR SHIT! GET ME YOUR MANAGER!
I'M THE MANAGER. WHAT SEEMS TO BE THE PROBLEM HERE?
THIS FUCKING GUY SAYS WATER IS $2!
YEAH, THAT'S LIKE THE STORE POLICY, MAN...
BUT YOU GET THIS COLLECTIBLE CUP!

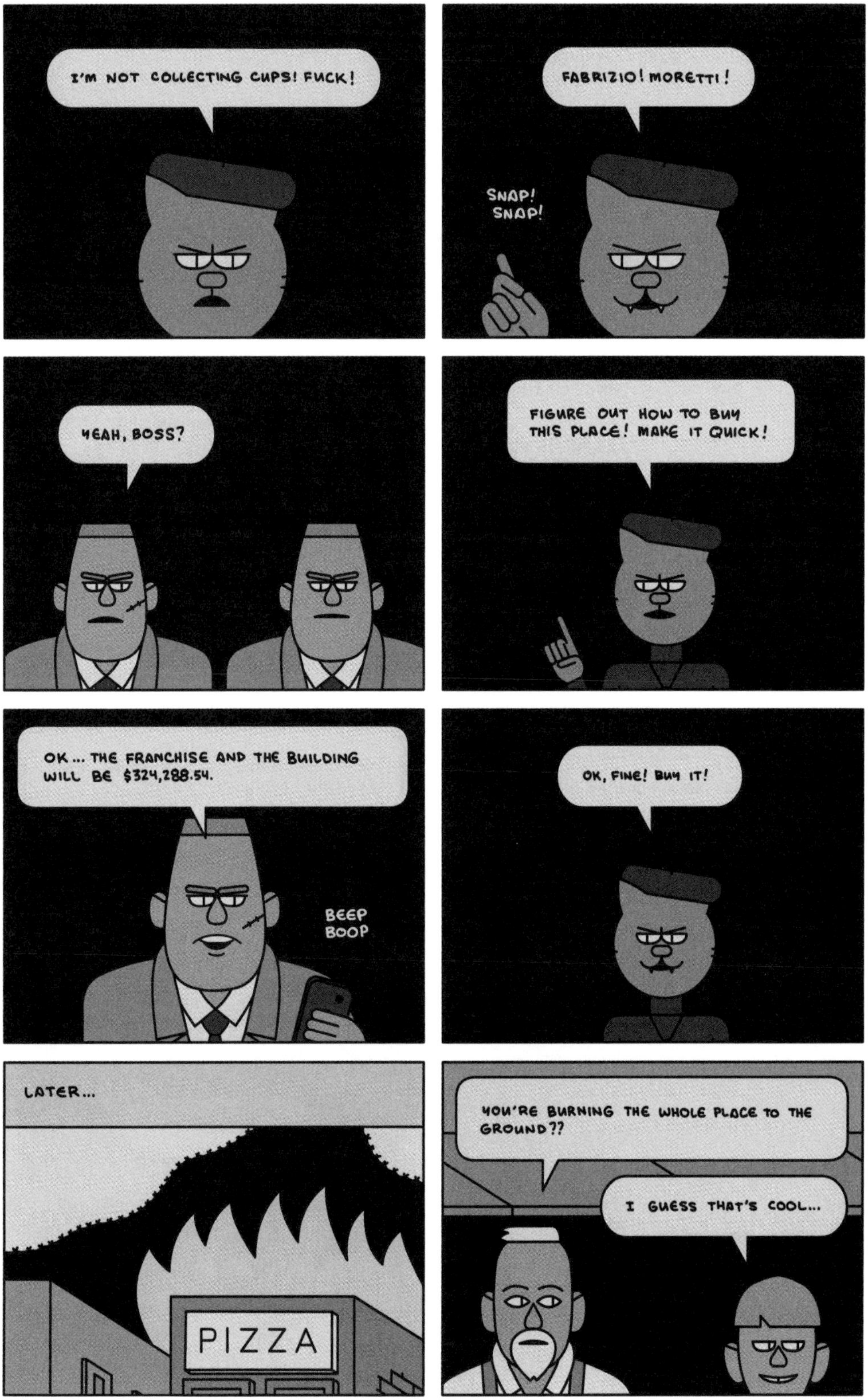

I'M NOT COLLECTING CUPS! FUCK!
FABRIZIO! MORETTI!
SNAP! SNAP!
YEAH, BOSS?
FIGURE OUT HOW TO BUY THIS PLACE! MAKE IT QUICK!
OK... THE FRANCHISE AND THE BUILDING WILL BE $324,288.54.
BEEP BOOP
OK, FINE! BUY IT!
LATER...
PIZZA
YOU'RE BURNING THE WHOLE PLACE TO THE GROUND??
I GUESS THAT'S COOL...

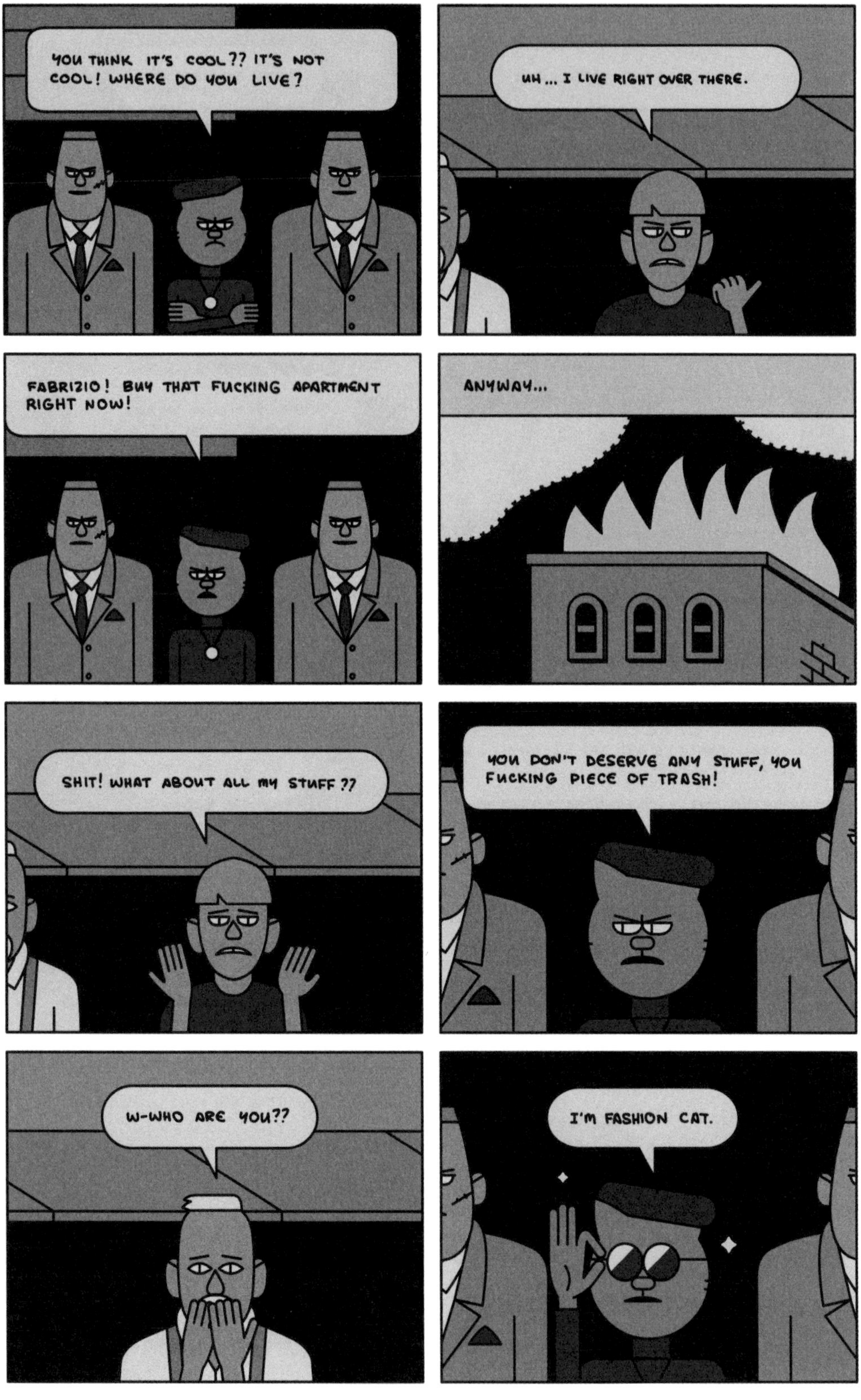
YOU THINK IT'S COOL?? IT'S NOT COOL! WHERE DO YOU LIVE?
UH... I LIVE RIGHT OVER THERE.
FABRIZIO! BUY THAT FUCKING APARTMENT RIGHT NOW!
ANYWAY...
SHIT! WHAT ABOUT ALL MY STUFF??
YOU DON'T DESERVE ANY STUFF, YOU FUCKING PIECE OF TRASH!
W-WHO ARE YOU??
I'M FASHION CAT.

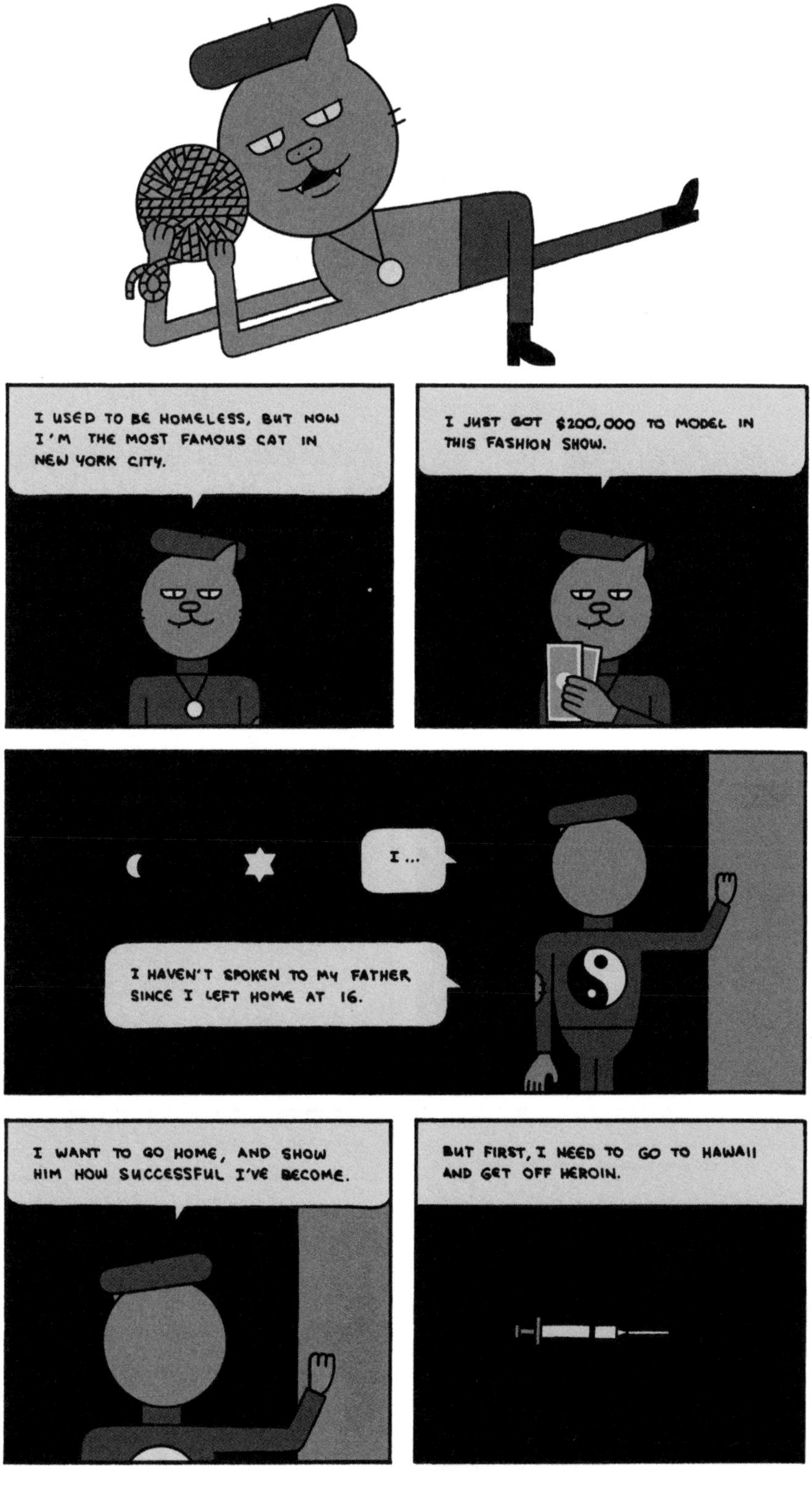
I USED TO BE HOMELESS, BUT NOW I'M THE MOST FAMOUS CAT IN NEW YORK CITY.
I JUST GOT $200,000 TO MODEL IN THIS FASHION SHOW.
I...
I HAVEN'T SPOKEN TO MY FATHER SINCE I LEFT HOME AT 16.
I WANT TO GO HOME, AND SHOW HIM HOW SUCCESSFUL I'VE BECOME.
BUT FIRST, I NEED TO GO TO HAWAII AND GET OFF HEROIN.

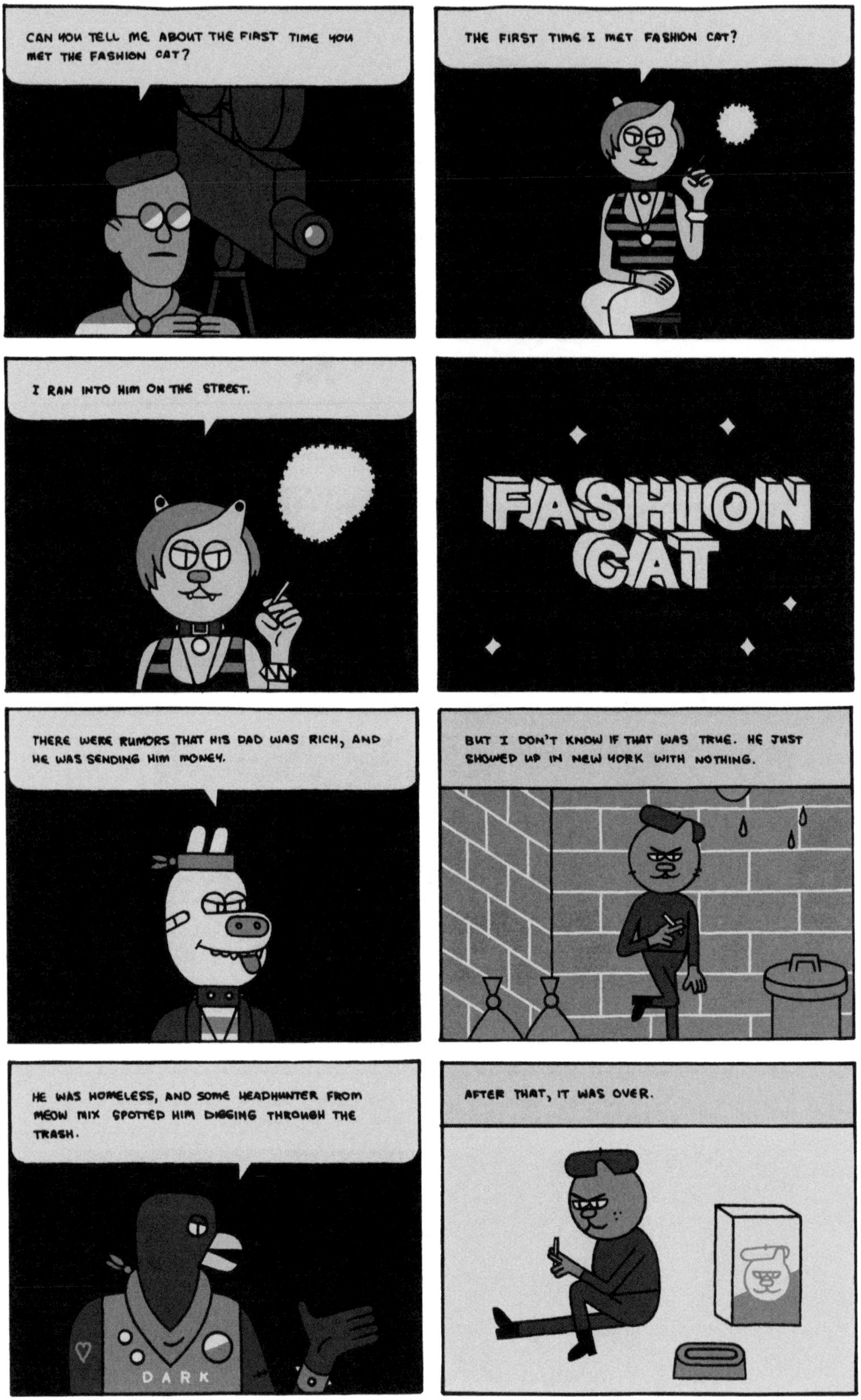
CAN YOU TELL ME ABOUT THE FIRST TIME YOU MET THE FASHION CAT?
THE FIRST TIME I MET FASHION CAT?
I RAN INTO HIM ON THE STREET.
FASHION CAT
THERE WERE RUMORS THAT HIS DAD WAS RICH, AND HE WAS SENDING HIM MONEY.
BUT I DON'T KNOW IF THAT WAS TRUE. HE JUST SHOWED UP IN NEW YORK WITH NOTHING.
HE WAS HOMELESS, AND SOME HEADHUNTER FROM MEOW MIX SPOTTED HIM DIGGING THROUGH THE TRASH.
DARK
AFTER THAT, IT WAS OVER.

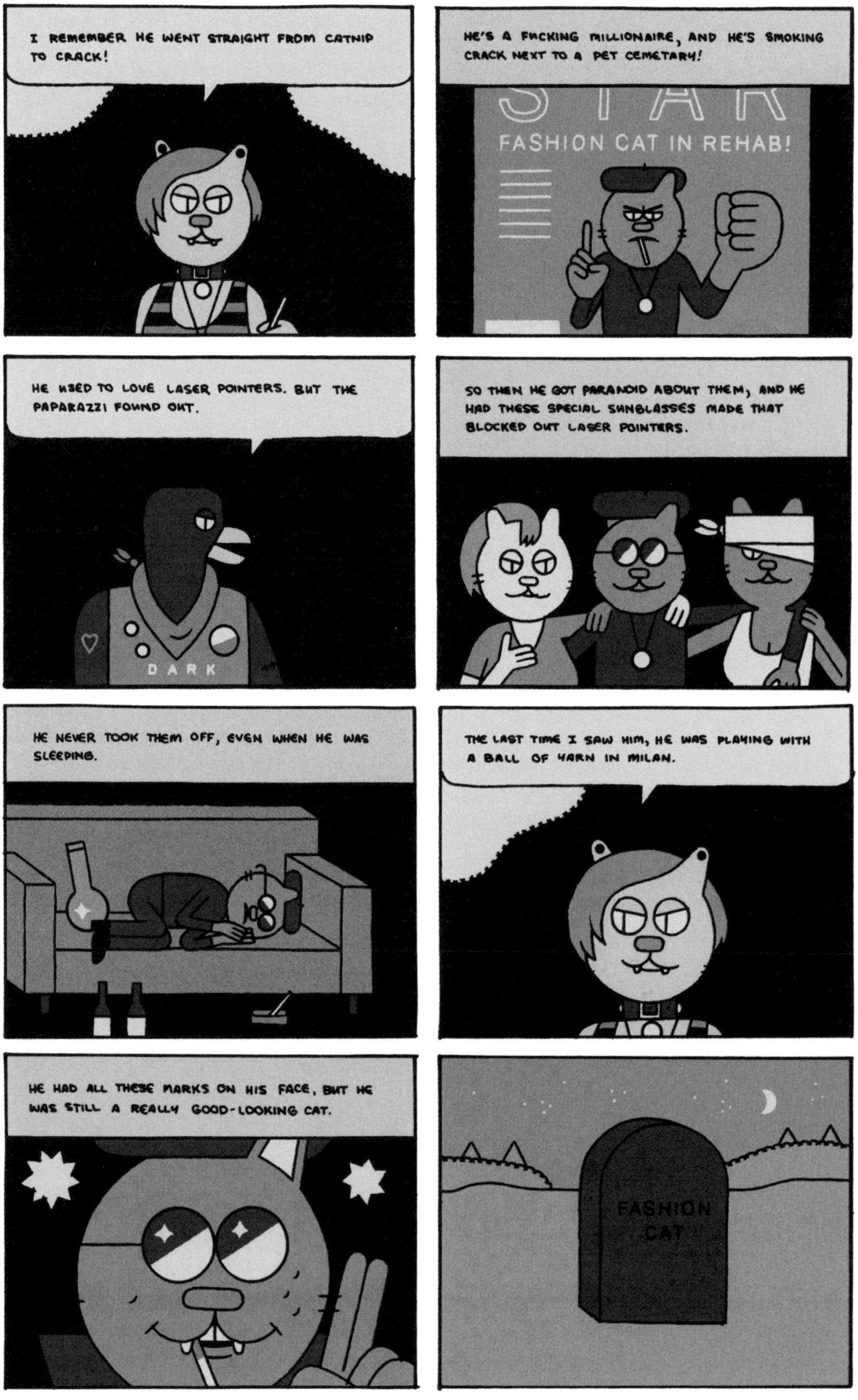
I REMEMBER HE WENT STRAIGHT FROM CATNIP TO CRACK!
HE'S A FUCKING MILLIONAIRE, AND HE'S SMOKING CRACK NEXT TO A PET CEMETARY!
FASHION CAT IN REHAB!
HE USED TO LOVE LASER POINTERS. BUT THE PAPARAZZI FOUND OUT.
DARK
SO THEN HE GOT PARANOID ABOUT THEM, AND HE HAD THESE SPECIAL SUNGLASSES MADE THAT BLOCKED OUT LASER POINTERS.
HE NEVER TOOK THEM OFF, EVEN WHEN HE WAS SLEEPING.
THE LAST TIME I SAW HIM, HE WAS PLAYING WITH A BALL OF YARN IN MILAN.
HE HAD ALL THESE MARKS ON HIS FACE, BUT HE WAS STILL A REALLY GOOD-LOOKING CAT.
FASHION CAT

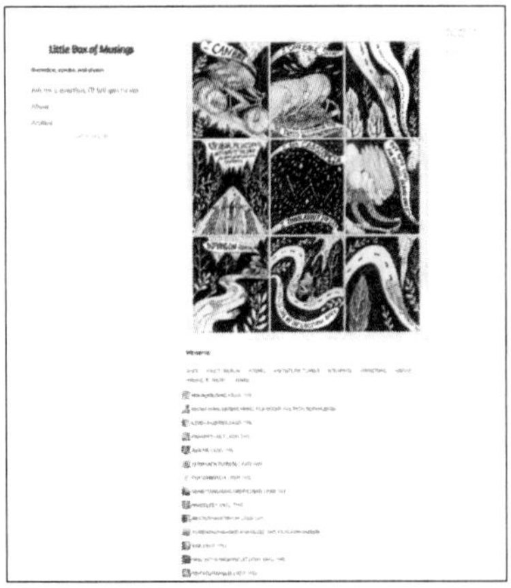
Little Box of Musings

# Bike Fast, Coney Island, AND Home

SOPHIA ZDON

*originally published on*

sophiazdon.tumblr.com

SELF-PUBLISHED

digital

## Biography

Sophia Zdon was a feral child raised by wolves found north of civilization deep in the wild wilds of Minnesota. She graduated from the School of Visual Arts in 2015.
sophiazdon.com

## Statement

These three comics were a part of my senior thesis at SVA. Ever since I was little, I've wanted to tell stories. I was always excited to have created something new that hadn't existed in the world before I'd thought of it. Creating these comics was a cathartic process. I lost my father three years ago and making art and writing helped me process his loss.

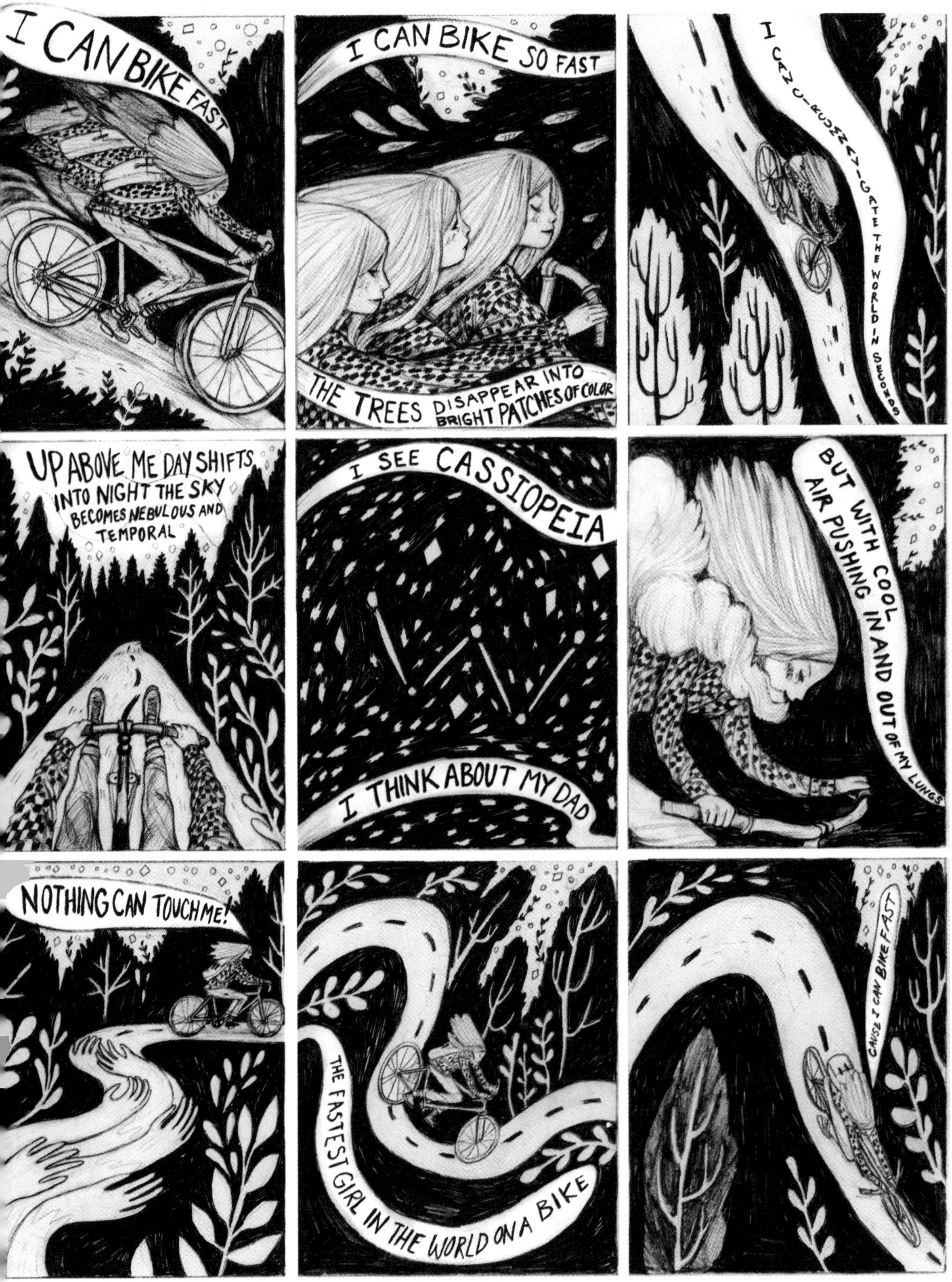
I CAN BIKE FAST
I CAN BIKE SO FAST
THE TREES DISAPPEAR INTO BRIGHT PATCHES OF COLOR
I CAN CIRCUMNAVIGATE THE WORLD IN SECONDS
UP ABOVE ME DAY SHIFTS INTO NIGHT THE SKY BECOMES NEBULOUS AND TEMPORAL
I SEE CASSIOPEIA
I THINK ABOUT MY DAD
BUT WITH COOL AIR PUSHING IN AND OUT OF MY LUNGS
NOTHING CAN TOUCH ME!
THE FASTEST GIRL IN THE WORLD ON A BIKE
CAUSE I CAN BIKE FAST

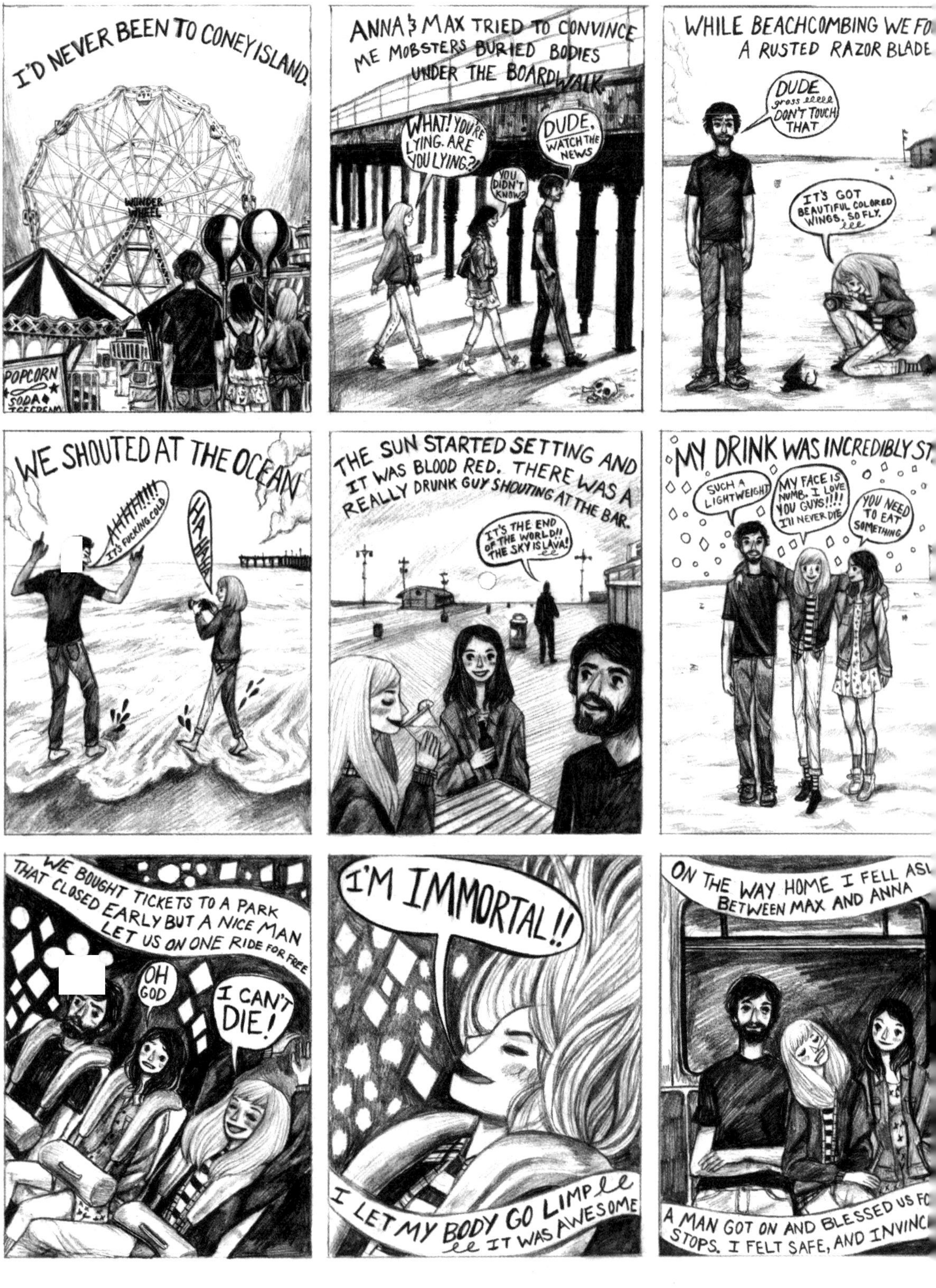

I'D NEVER BEEN TO CONEY ISLAND.
WONDER WHEEL
POPCORN
SODA
ANNA & MAX TRIED TO CONVINCE ME MOBSTERS BURIED BODIES UNDER THE BOARDWALK.
WHAT! YOU'RE LYING. ARE YOU LYING?!
YOU DIDN'T KNOW?
DUDE, WATCH THE NEWS
WHILE BEACHCOMBING WE FO
A RUSTED RAZOR BLADE
DUDE gross DON'T TOUCH THAT
IT'S GOT BEAUTIFUL COLORED WINGS, SO FLY.
WE SHOUTED AT THE OCEAN
AHHH!!!! IT'S FUCKING COLD
HA HA HA
THE SUN STARTED SETTING AND IT WAS BLOOD RED. THERE WAS A REALLY DRUNK GUY SHOUTING AT THE BAR.
IT'S THE END OF THE WORLD!! THE SKY IS LAVA!
MY DRINK WAS INCREDIBLY ST
SUCH A LIGHTWEIGHT
MY FACE IS NUMB. I LOVE YOU GUYS!!!! I'll NEVER DIE
YOU NEED TO EAT SOMETHING
WE BOUGHT TICKETS TO A PARK THAT CLOSED EARLY BUT A NICE MAN LET US ON ONE RIDE FOR FREE
OH GOD
I CAN'T DIE!
I'M IMMORTAL!!
I LET MY BODY GO LIMP IT WAS AWESOME
ON THE WAY HOME I FELL AS
BETWEEN MAX AND ANNA
A MAN GOT ON AND BLESSED US FO
STOPS. I FELT SAFE, AND INVINC

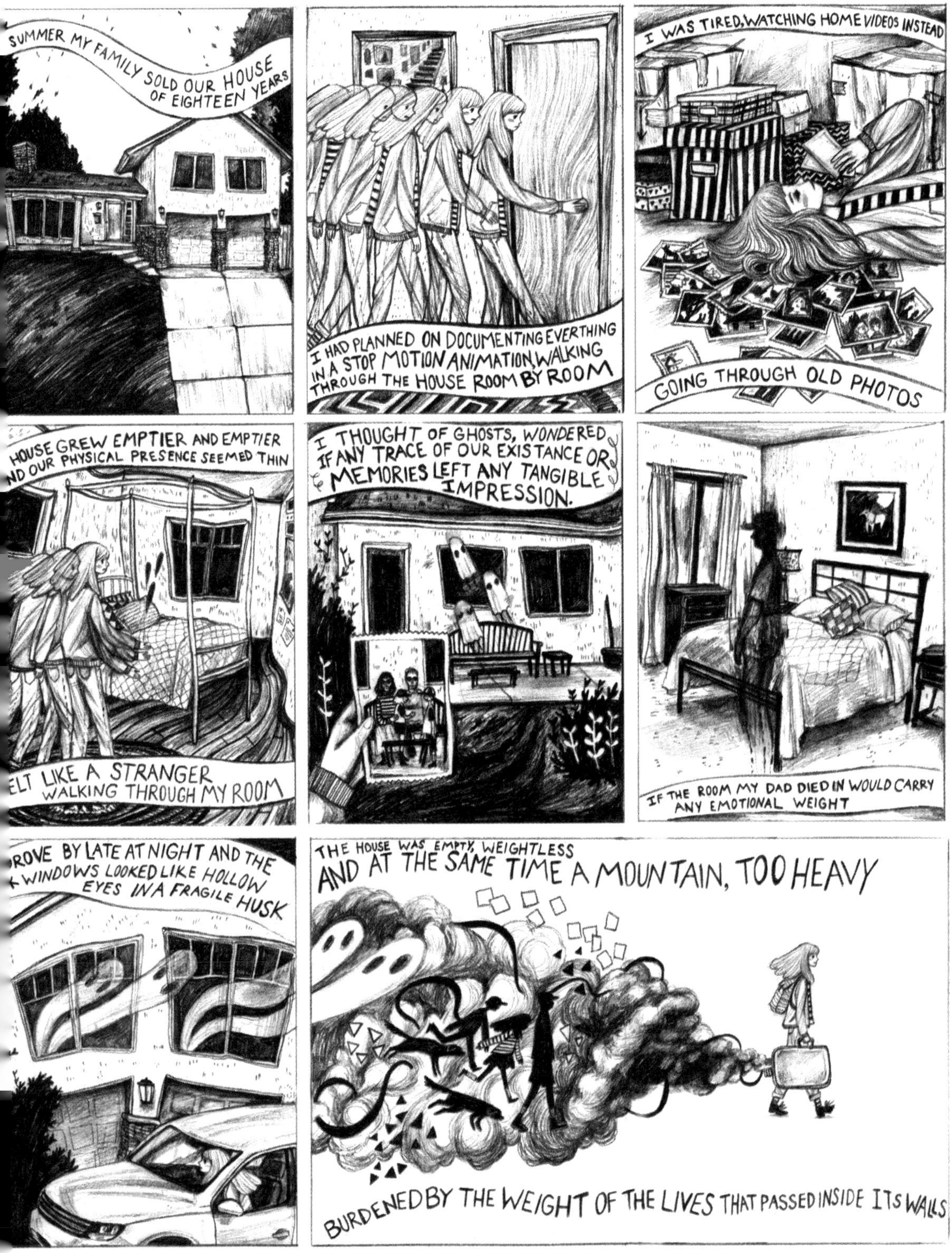

SUMMER MY FAMILY SOLD OUR HOUSE OF EIGHTEEN YEARS
I HAD PLANNED ON DOCUMENTING EVERTHING IN A STOP MOTION ANIMATION, WALKING THROUGH THE HOUSE ROOM BY ROOM
I WAS TIRED, WATCHING HOME VIDEOS INSTEAD
GOING THROUGH OLD PHOTOS
HOUSE GREW EMPTIER AND EMPTIER
ND OUR PHYSICAL PRESENCE SEEMED THIN
ELT LIKE A STRANGER WALKING THROUGH MY ROOM
I THOUGHT OF GHOSTS, WONDERED IF ANY TRACE OF OUR EXISTANCE OR MEMORIES LEFT ANY TANGIBLE IMPRESSION.
IF THE ROOM MY DAD DIED IN WOULD CARRY ANY EMOTIONAL WEIGHT
ROVE BY LATE AT NIGHT AND THE
WINDOWS LOOKED LIKE HOLLOW EYES IN A FRAGILE HUSK
THE HOUSE WAS EMPTY, WEIGHTLESS
AND AT THE SAME TIME A MOUNTAIN, TOO HEAVY
BURDENED BY THE WEIGHT OF THE LIVES THAT PASSED INSIDE ITS WALLS

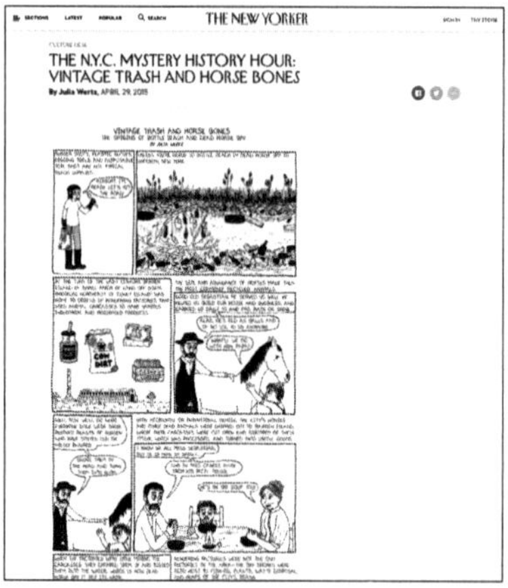
THE NEW YORKER
THE N.Y.C. MYSTERY HISTORY HOUR:
VINTAGE TRASH AND HORSE BONES
By Julia Wertz, APRIL 29, 2015
VINTAGE TRASH AND HORSE BONES

# Vintage Trash and Horse Bones

## JULIA WERTZ

*originally published on*

www.newyorker.com

CONDÉ NAST

digital

## Biography

Julia Wertz is a professional cartoonist and amateur historian. She has published five graphic novels and does monthly history comics for *The New Yorker* and *Harper's Magazine*. juliawertz.com

## Statement

This piece is part of a monthly series about New York history.

# VINTAGE TRASH AND HORSE BONES
## THE ORIGINS OF BOTTLE BEACH AND DEAD HORSE BAY
BY JULIA WERTZ

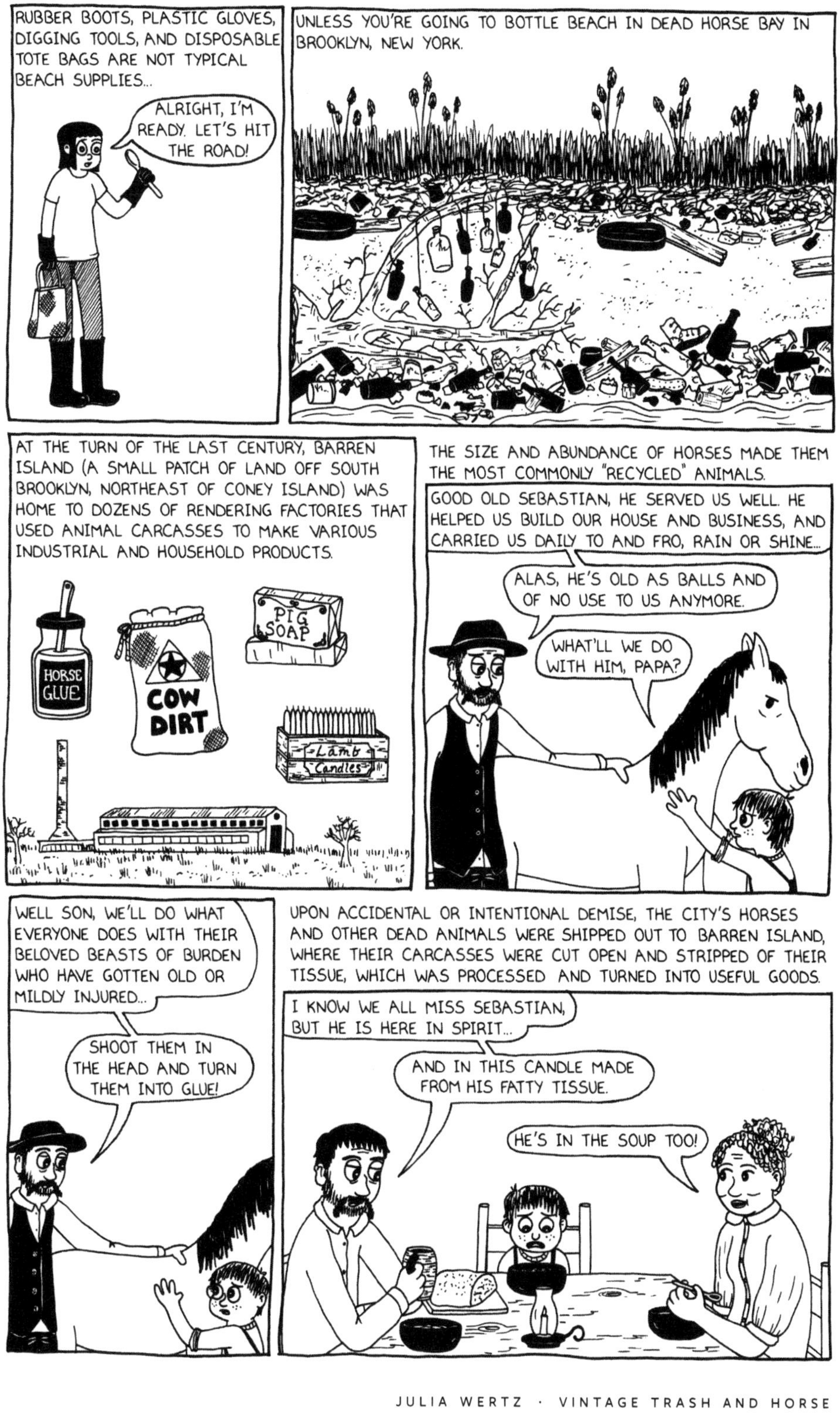
RUBBER BOOTS, PLASTIC GLOVES, DIGGING TOOLS, AND DISPOSABLE TOTE BAGS ARE NOT TYPICAL BEACH SUPPLIES...
ALRIGHT, I'M READY. LET'S HIT THE ROAD!
UNLESS YOU'RE GOING TO BOTTLE BEACH IN DEAD HORSE BAY IN BROOKLYN, NEW YORK.
AT THE TURN OF THE LAST CENTURY, BARREN ISLAND (A SMALL PATCH OF LAND OFF SOUTH BROOKLYN, NORTHEAST OF CONEY ISLAND) WAS HOME TO DOZENS OF RENDERING FACTORIES THAT USED ANIMAL CARCASSES TO MAKE VARIOUS INDUSTRIAL AND HOUSEHOLD PRODUCTS.
HORSE GLUE
COW DIRT
PIG SOAP
Lamb Candles
THE SIZE AND ABUNDANCE OF HORSES MADE THEM THE MOST COMMONLY "RECYCLED" ANIMALS.
GOOD OLD SEBASTIAN, HE SERVED US WELL. HE HELPED US BUILD OUR HOUSE AND BUSINESS, AND CARRIED US DAILY TO AND FRO, RAIN OR SHINE...
ALAS, HE'S OLD AS BALLS AND OF NO USE TO US ANYMORE.
WHAT'LL WE DO WITH HIM, PAPA?
WELL SON, WE'LL DO WHAT EVERYONE DOES WITH THEIR BELOVED BEASTS OF BURDEN WHO HAVE GOTTEN OLD OR MILDLY INJURED...
SHOOT THEM IN THE HEAD AND TURN THEM INTO GLUE!
UPON ACCIDENTAL OR INTENTIONAL DEMISE, THE CITY'S HORSES AND OTHER DEAD ANIMALS WERE SHIPPED OUT TO BARREN ISLAND, WHERE THEIR CARCASSES WERE CUT OPEN AND STRIPPED OF THEIR TISSUE, WHICH WAS PROCESSED AND TURNED INTO USEFUL GOODS.
I KNOW WE ALL MISS SEBASTIAN, BUT HE IS HERE IN SPIRIT...
AND IN THIS CANDLE MADE FROM HIS FATTY TISSUE.
HE'S IN THE SOUP TOO!

WHEN THE FACTORIES WERE DONE MINING THE CARCASSES, THEY CHOPPED THEM UP AND TOSSED THEM INTO THE WATER, WHICH IS HOW DEAD HORSE BAY IT GOT ITS NAME.

♪ hi-ho hi-ho ♪♪ into the bay you go!

RENDERING FACTORIES WERE NOT THE ONLY FACTORIES IN THE AREA—THE BAY SHORES WERE ALSO HOST TO FISH-OIL PLANTS, WASTE DISPOSAL, AND HEAPS OF THE CITY'S TRASH.

OOF, SMELLS LIKE SOMEONE MURDERED A FART OUT THERE. THE ROTTEN FISH IS BARELY MASKING THE SMELL OF THE ROTTING ANIMAL CARCASSES. WHAT'S FOR DINNER? UGH, SEBASTIAN STEW AGAIN? WE NEED TO START RAISING PIGS, GET SOME BACON UP IN THIS MOTHER.

BY THE NINETEEN-TWENTIES, THE FACTORIES WERE MOSTLY GONE, SINCE THE AUTOMOBILE REPLACED HORSES AS MEANS OF TRANSPORTATION, RENDERING THE RENDERING FACTORIES OBSOLETE. IN THEIR PLACE GREW A MASSIVE AND RAPIDLY EXPANDING LANDFILL. SOME OF THAT TRASH, ALONG WITH COAL AND SAND, WAS USED TO CONNECT BARREN ISLAND TO BROOKLYN, CREATING WHAT WAS LATER NAMED FLOYD BENNETT FIELD. IN THE NINETEEN-THIRTIES THE LANDFILL AT DEAD HORSE BAY WAS CAPPED AND FILLED IN WITH MARSHLANDS AND WATER. BUT IN NINETEEN-FIFTIES, THE CAP BURST, FILLING THE BAY WITH GARBAGE AND BONES.

SINCE THEN, THE GARBAGE HAS BEEN CONTINUALLY WASHING UP, FILLING THE SHORELINE MOSTLY WITH BOTTLES, BUT ALSO WITH SHOES, TOYS, APPLIANCES AND OTHER REMNANTS OF A BYGONE ERA.

ON QUIET DAYS AT BOTTLE BEACH, IF YOU STAND CLOSE TO THE WATER, YOU CAN HEAR THE MELODIC TINKLING OF THE SEA WASHING OVER THE BROKEN GLASS.

IT'S ALL JUST SO BEAUTIFUL...

THIS DISGUSTING HEAP OF GARBAGE IS MAKING ME HAVE FEELINGS!

DISCLAIMER: BOTTLE BEACH IS PART OF THE GATEWAY NATIONAL RECREATION AREA, AND WHILE IT IS TECHNICALLY CONSIDERED ILLEGAL TO REMOVE ANYTHING FROM NATIONAL PARKS, NO ONE WILL STOP YOU FROM TAKING A FEW BOTTLES AND TRINKETS, SINCE YOU ARE LITERALLY CLEANING UP GARBAGE.

# Here (*Excerpt*)

RICHARD McGUIRE

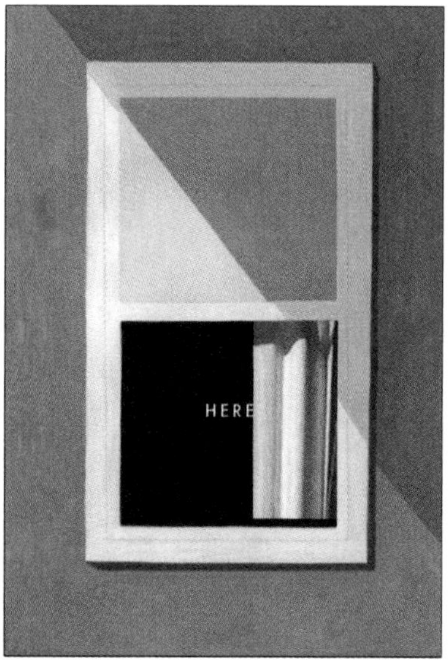
HERE

*excerpted from*

Here

PANTHEON

6.8 × 9.5 inches • 304 pages

## Biography

Richard McGuire is a multidisciplinary artist who has produced an enormously diverse body of work, including children's books, animated films, toys, comics, and sound sculpture installations. McGuire is also cofounder and bassist for the seminal early '80s post-punk band Liquid Liquid. His work has been featured in *McSweeney's*, the *New York Times*, *Le Monde*, *Libération*, and on numerous covers of *The New Yorker*. His deeply influential short story "Here," published in 1989 by Françoise Mouly and Art Spiegelman in the magazine *RAW*, was reinvented and released as a graphic novel in 2014 to international acclaim and awards. richard-mcguire.com

## Statement

*Here* started as a six-page comic that first appeared in *RAW* in 1989. The story centers on the corner of a living room in a suburban home. The perspective of this view never changes throughout the story; by introducing multiple panels we get glimpses into the distant past and far into the future. Twenty-five years after its publication I reimagined and expanded the original idea into a three-hundred-page book.

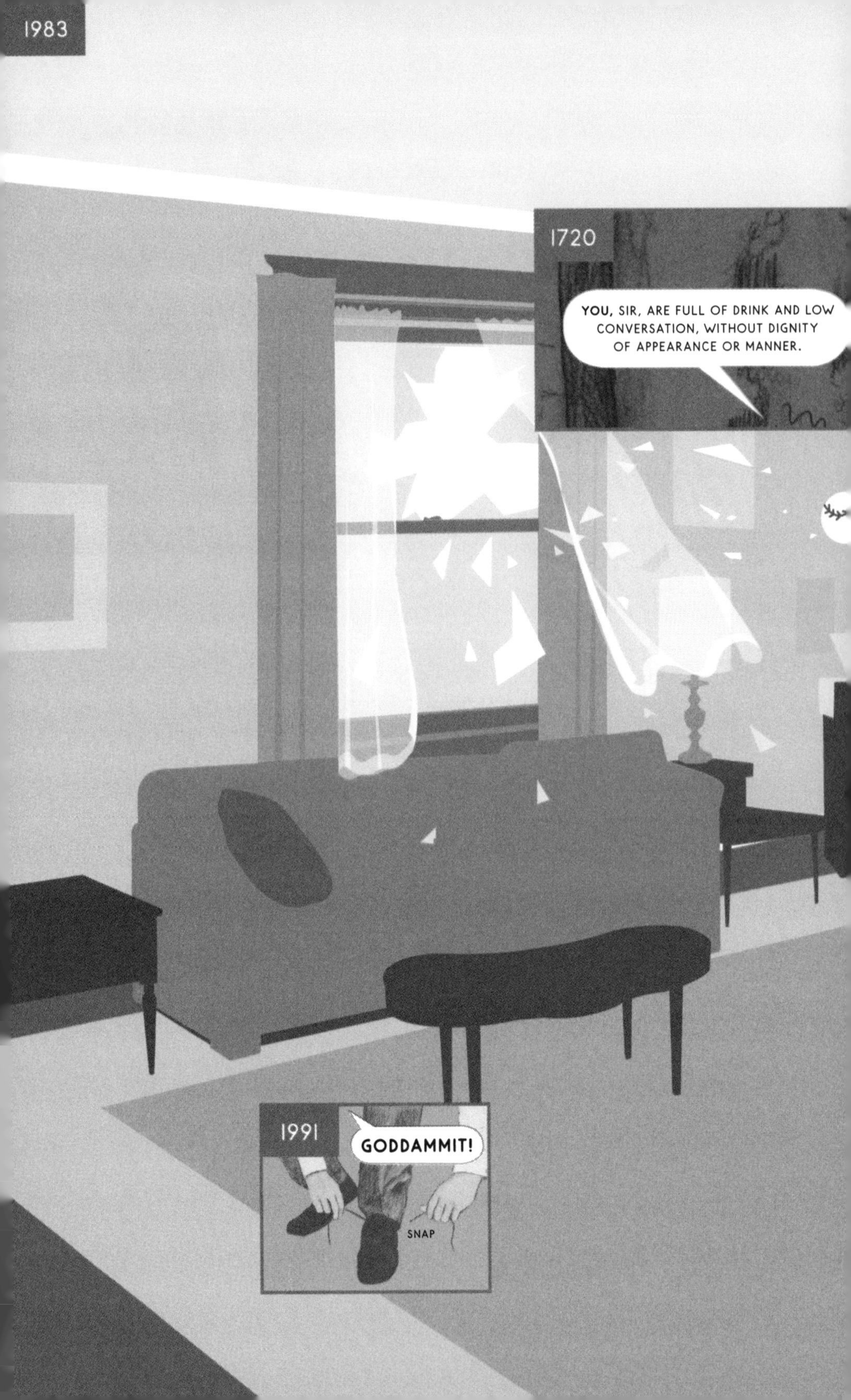
1983
1720
YOU, SIR, ARE FULL OF DRINK AND LOW CONVERSATION, WITHOUT DIGNITY OF APPEARANCE OR MANNER.
1991
GODDAMMIT!
SNAP

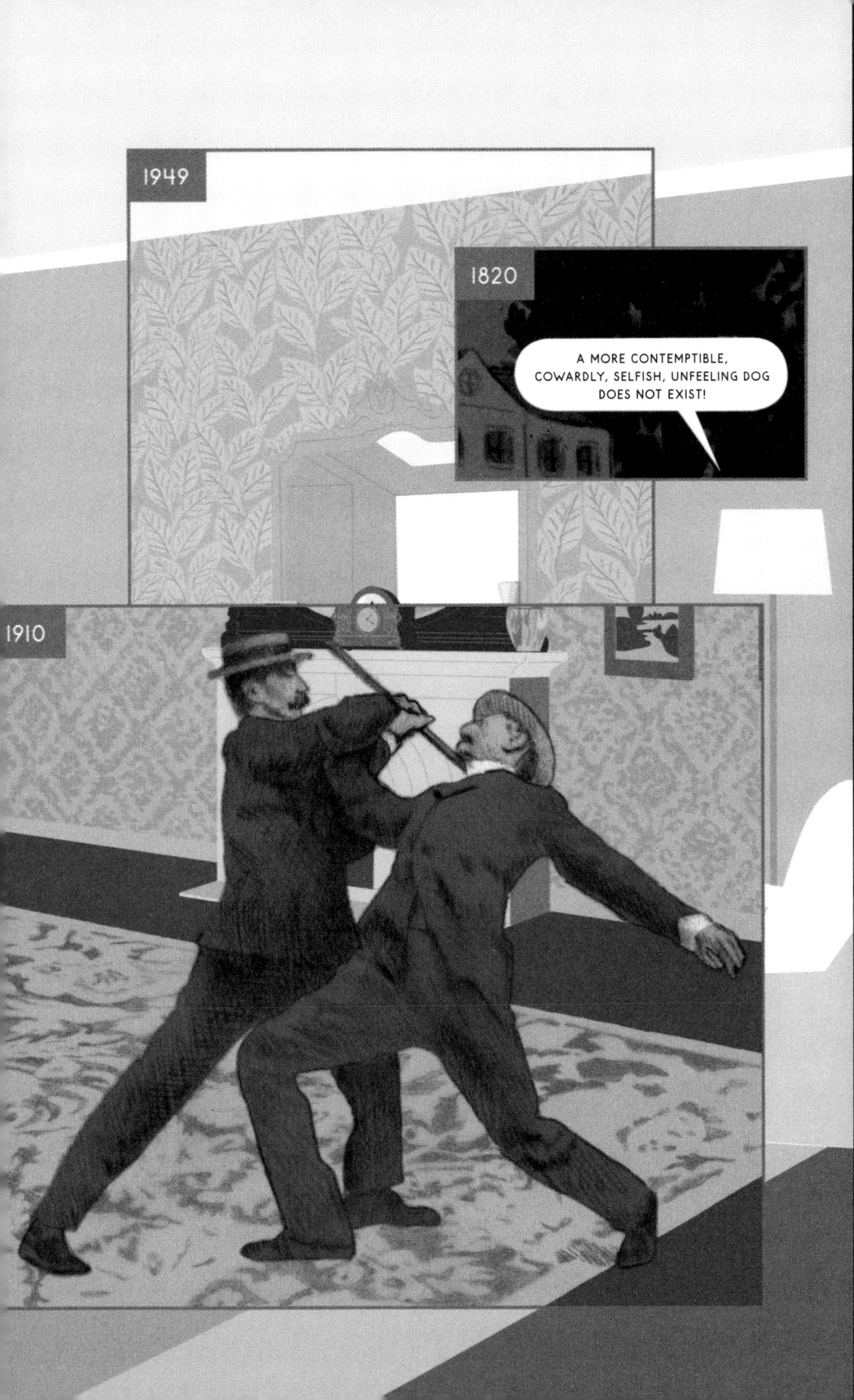
1949
1820
A MORE CONTEMPTIBLE, COWARDLY, SELFISH, UNFEELING DOG DOES NOT EXIST!
1910

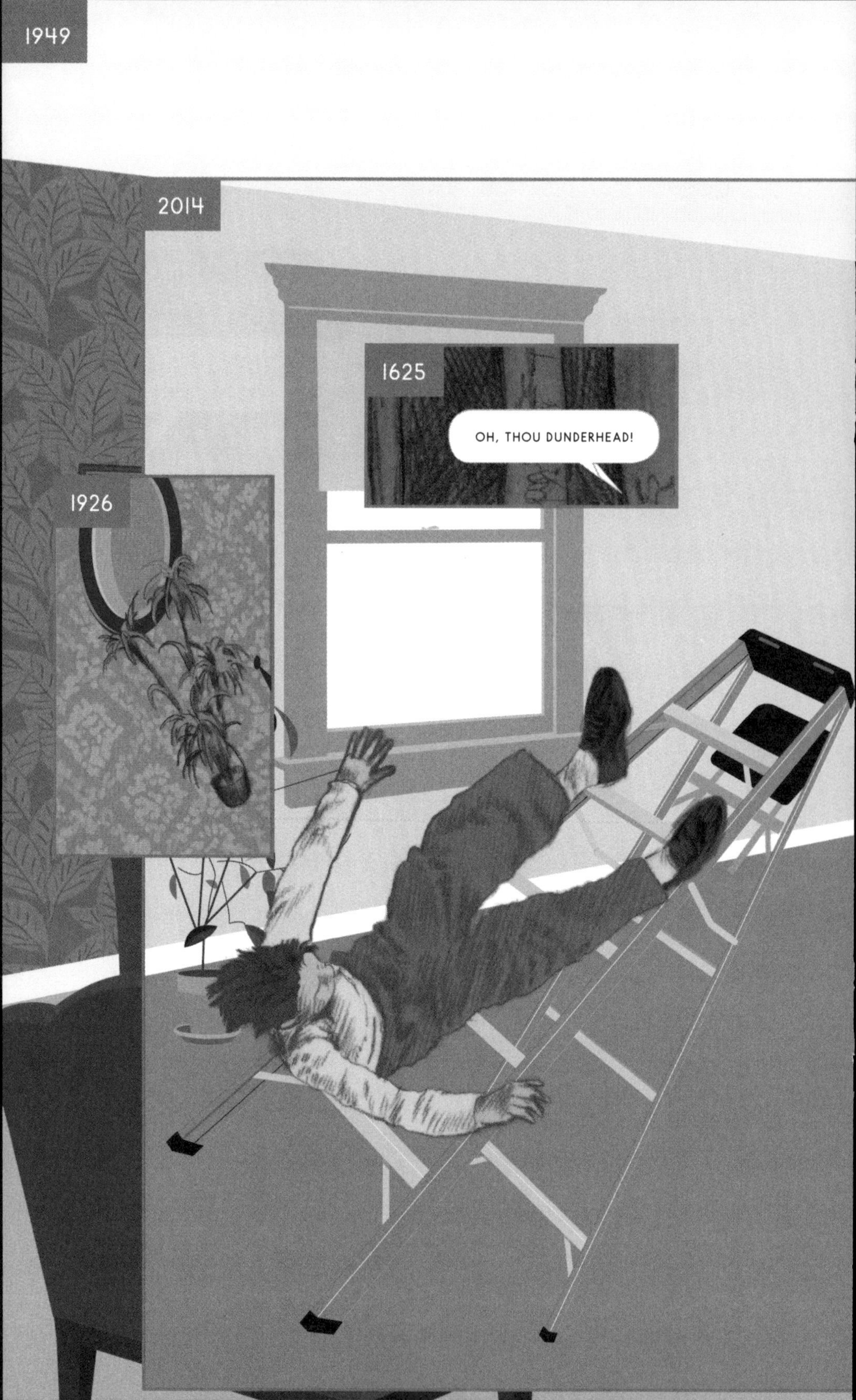
1949
2014
1625
OH, THOU DUNDERHEAD!
1926

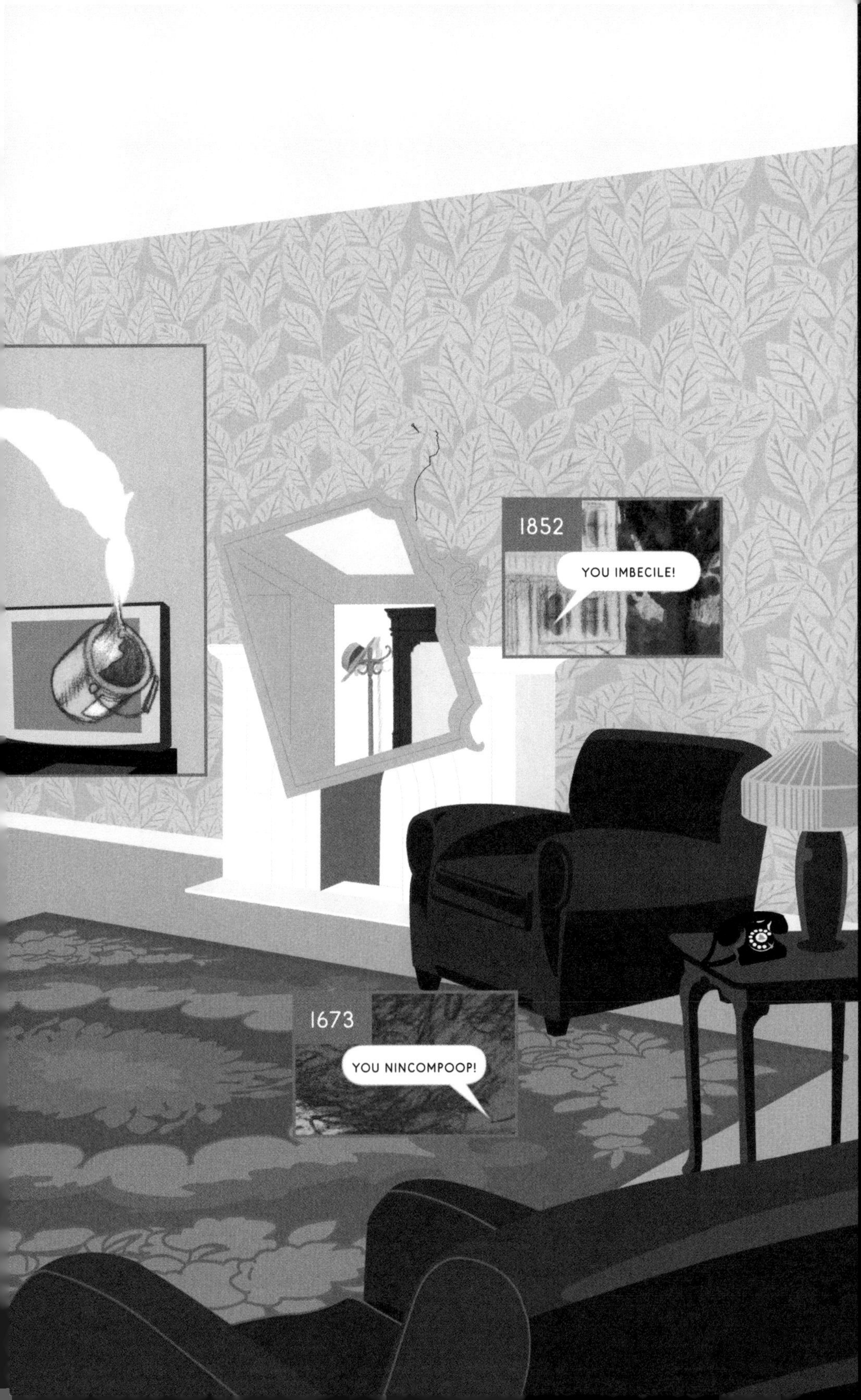
1852
YOU IMBECILE!
1673
YOU NINCOMPOOP!

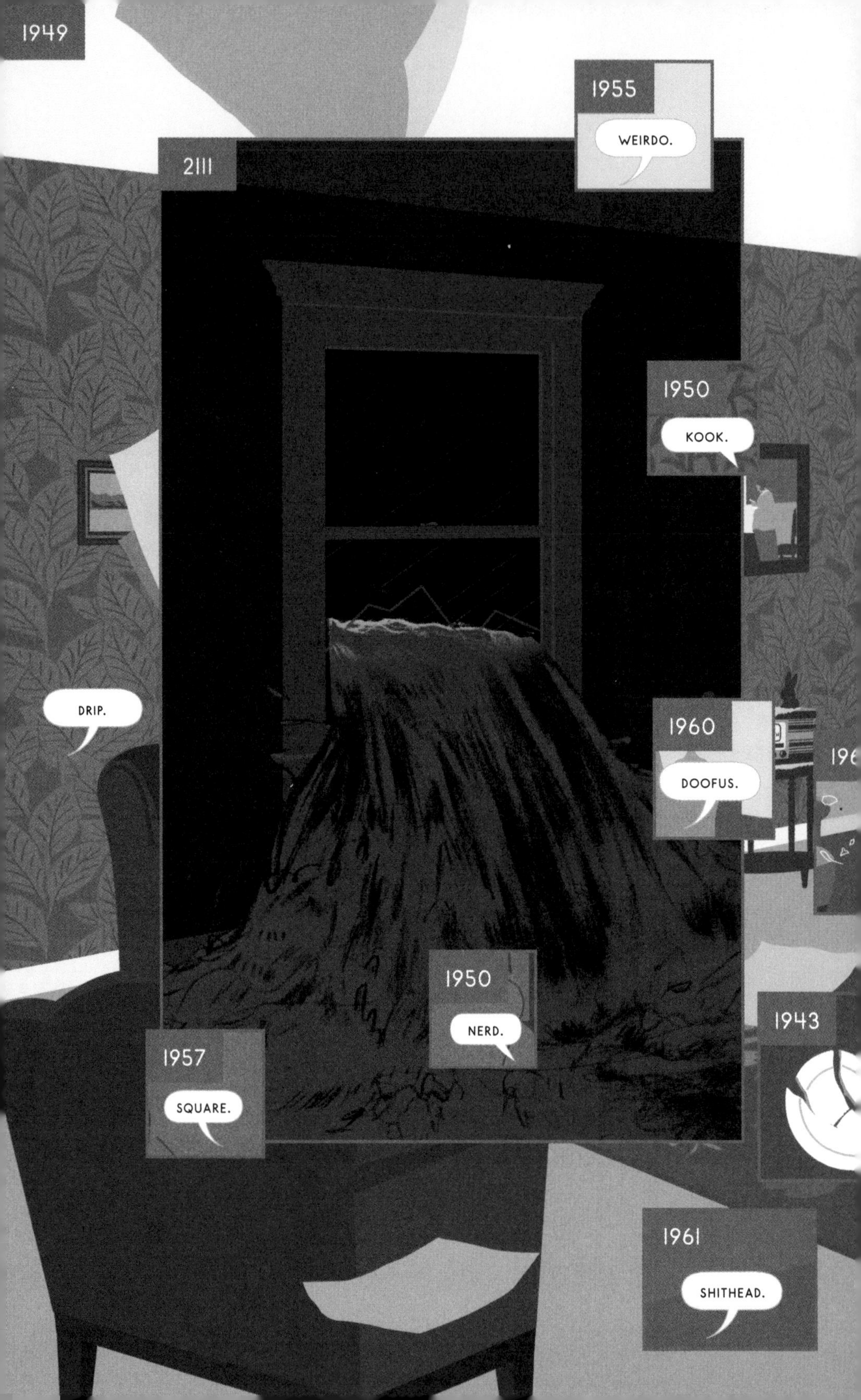

1949
2111
1955
WEIRDO.
1950
KOOK.
DRIP.
1960
DOOFUS.
1950
NERD.
1957
SQUARE.
1943
1961
SHITHEAD.

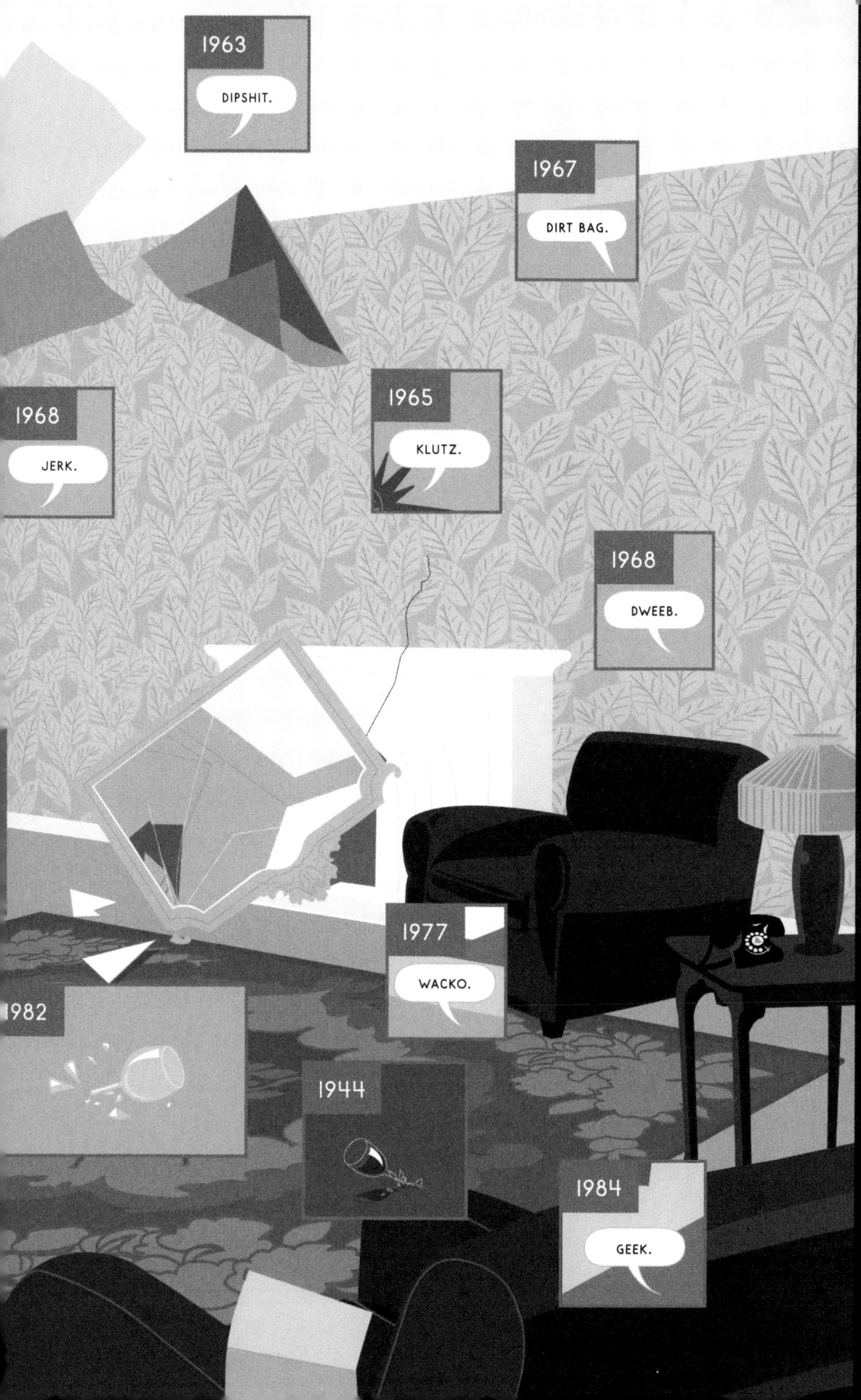
1963
DIPSHIT.
1967
DIRT BAG.
1968
JERK.
1965
KLUTZ.
1968
DWEEB.
1977
WACKO.
1982
1944
1984
GEEK.

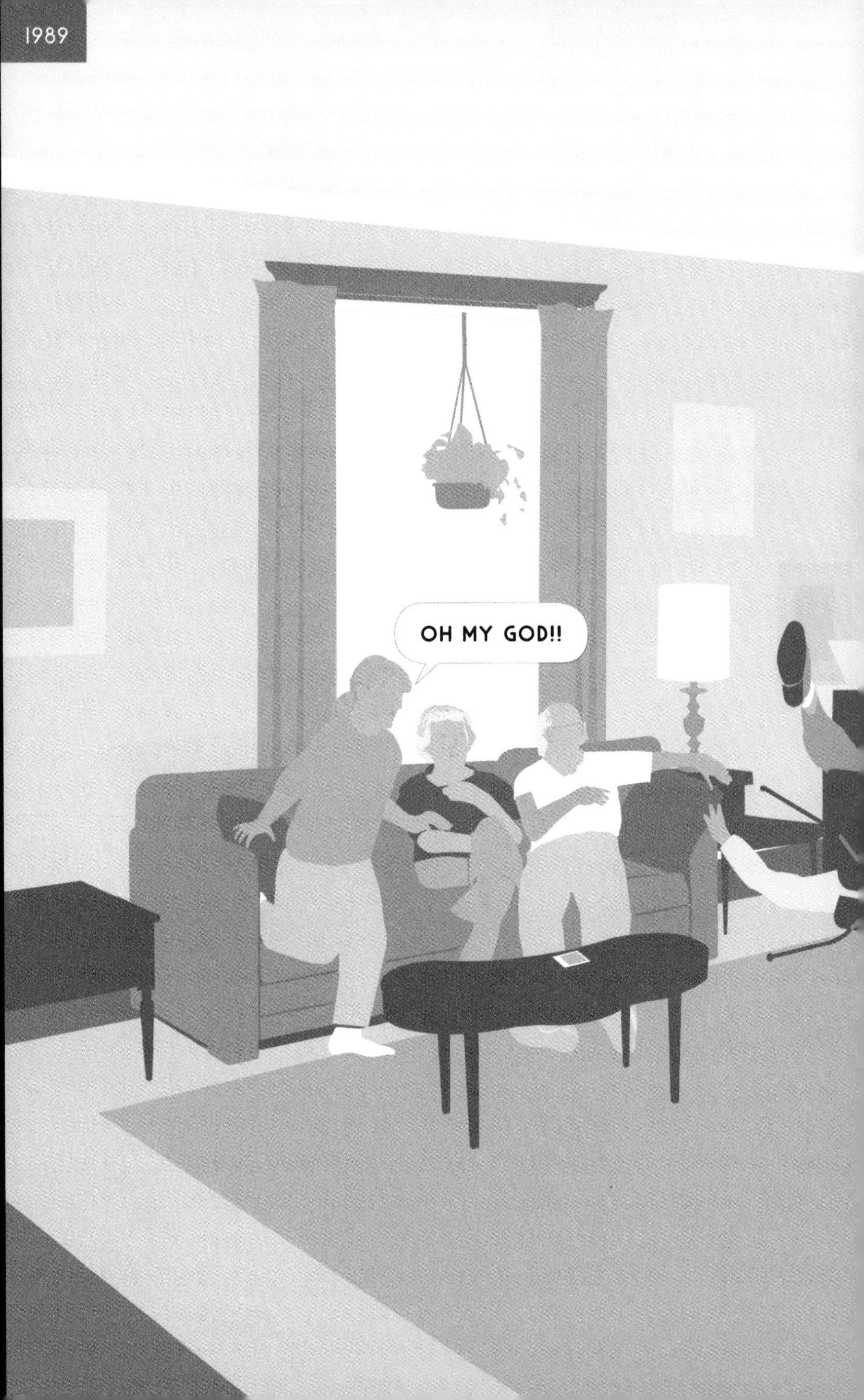
1989
OH MY GOD!!

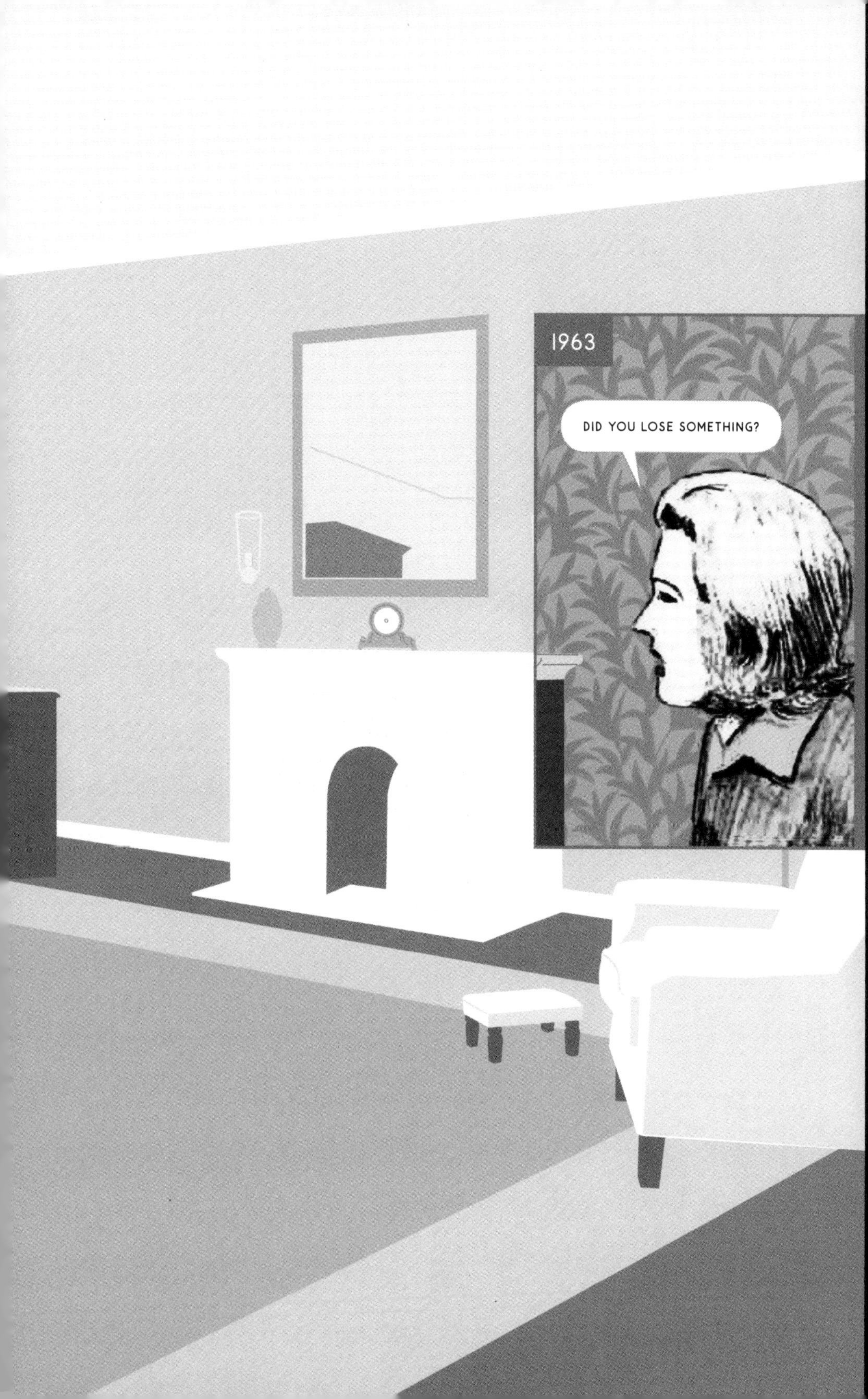
1963
DID YOU LOSE SOMETHING?

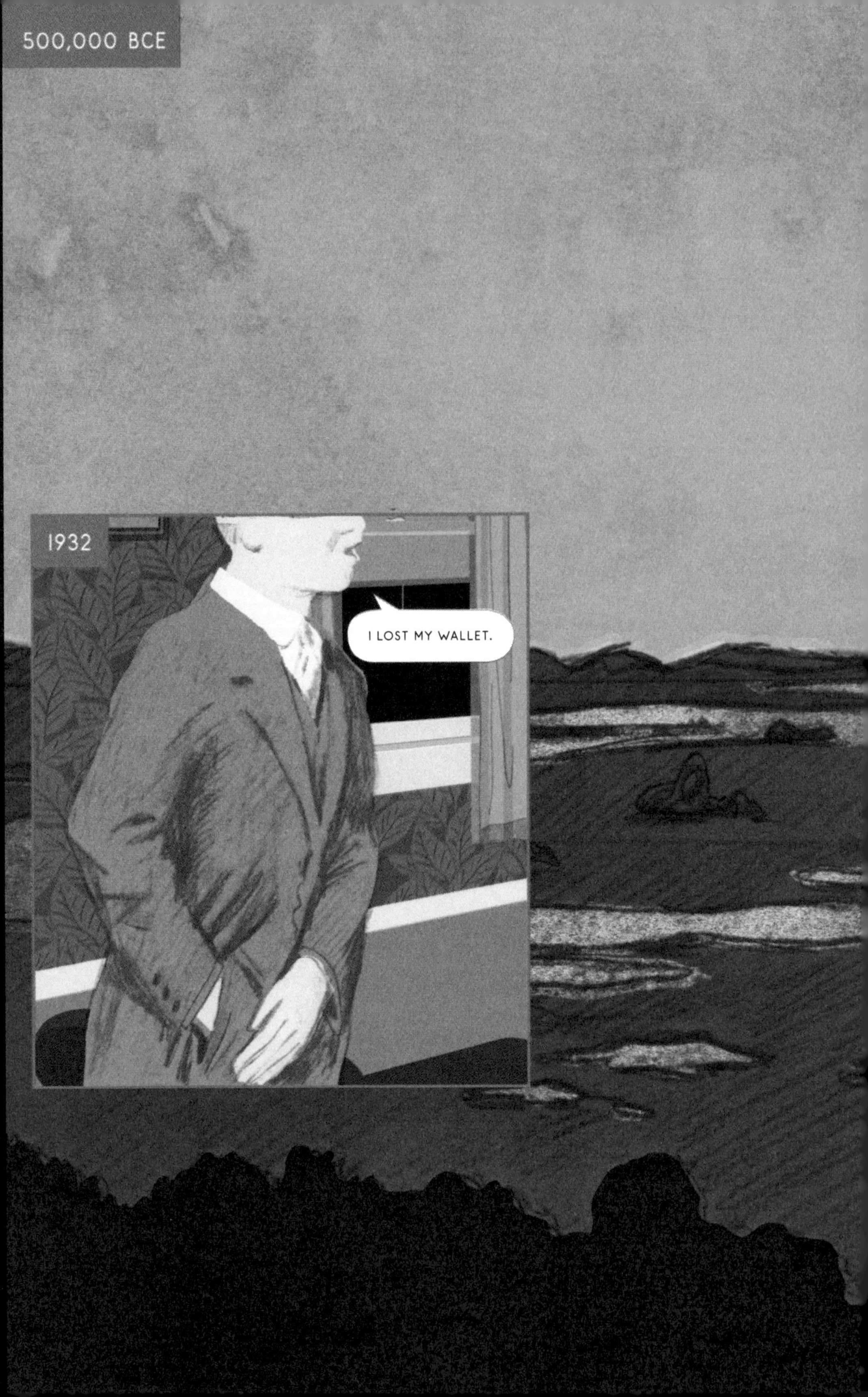
500,000 BCE
1932
I LOST MY WALLET.

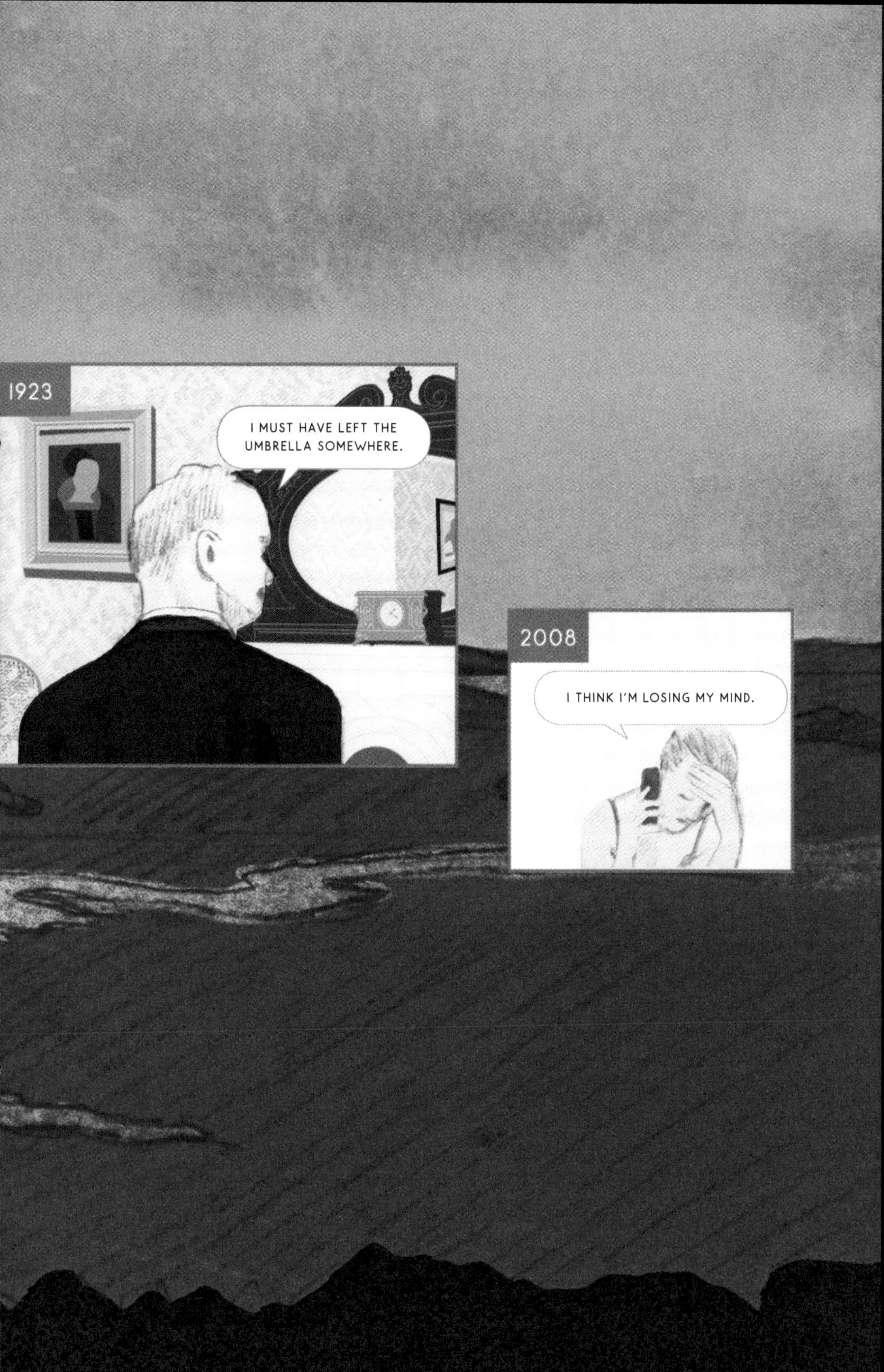
1923
I MUST HAVE LEFT THE UMBRELLA SOMEWHERE.
2008
I THINK I'M LOSING MY MIND.

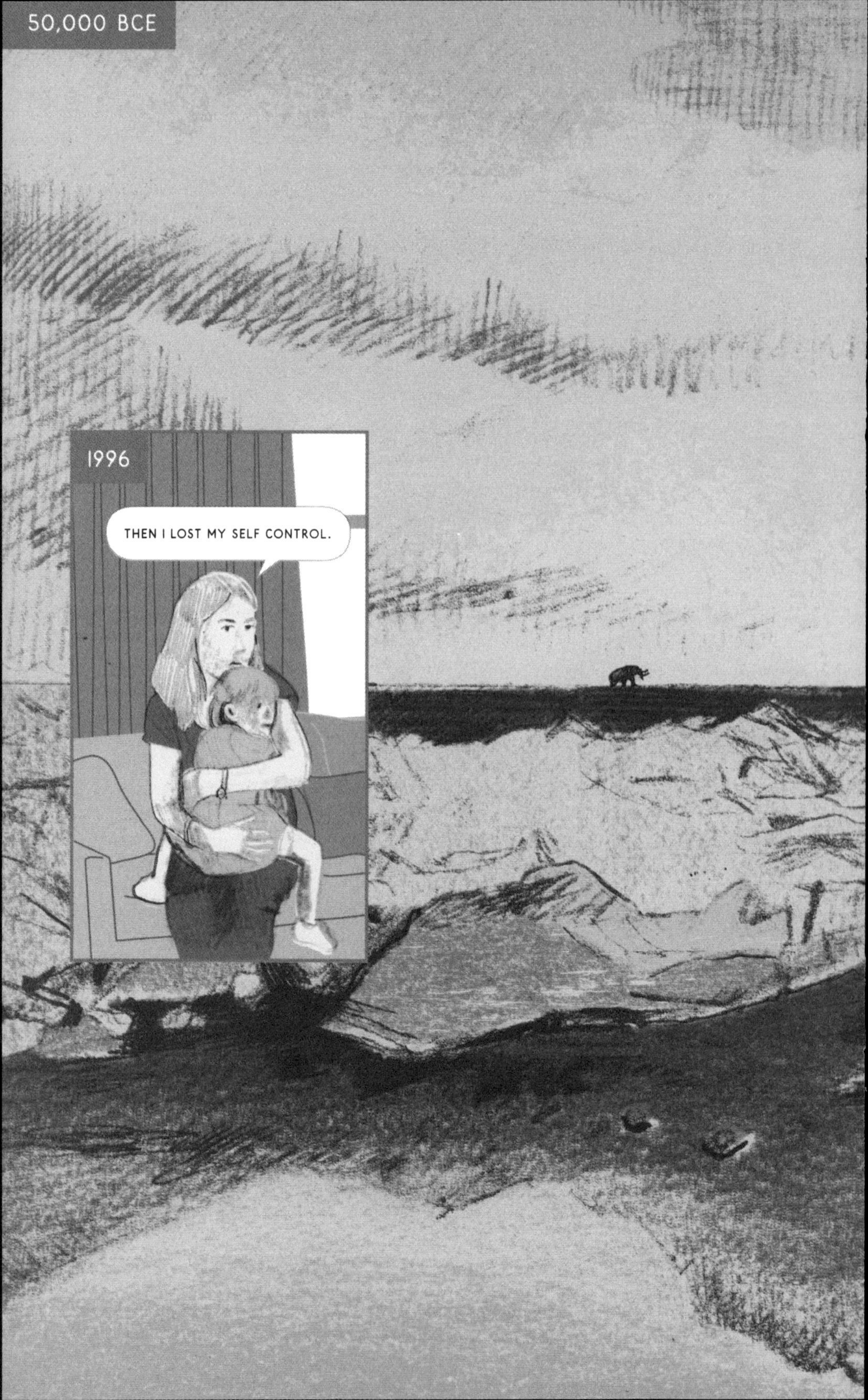
50,000 BCE
1996
THEN I LOST MY SELF CONTROL.

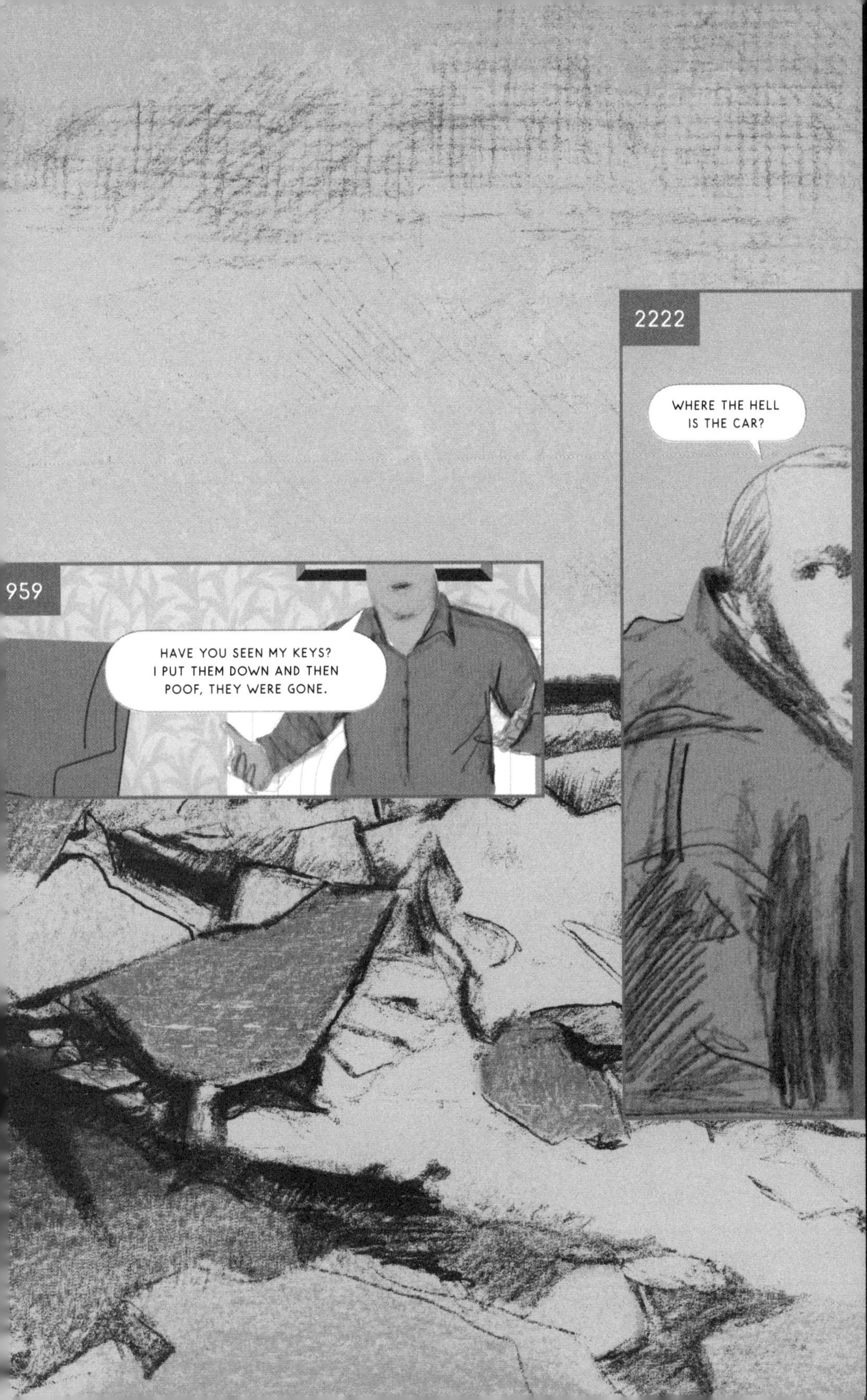
959
HAVE YOU SEEN MY KEYS? I PUT THEM DOWN AND THEN POOF, THEY WERE GONE.
2222
WHERE THE HELL IS THE CAR?

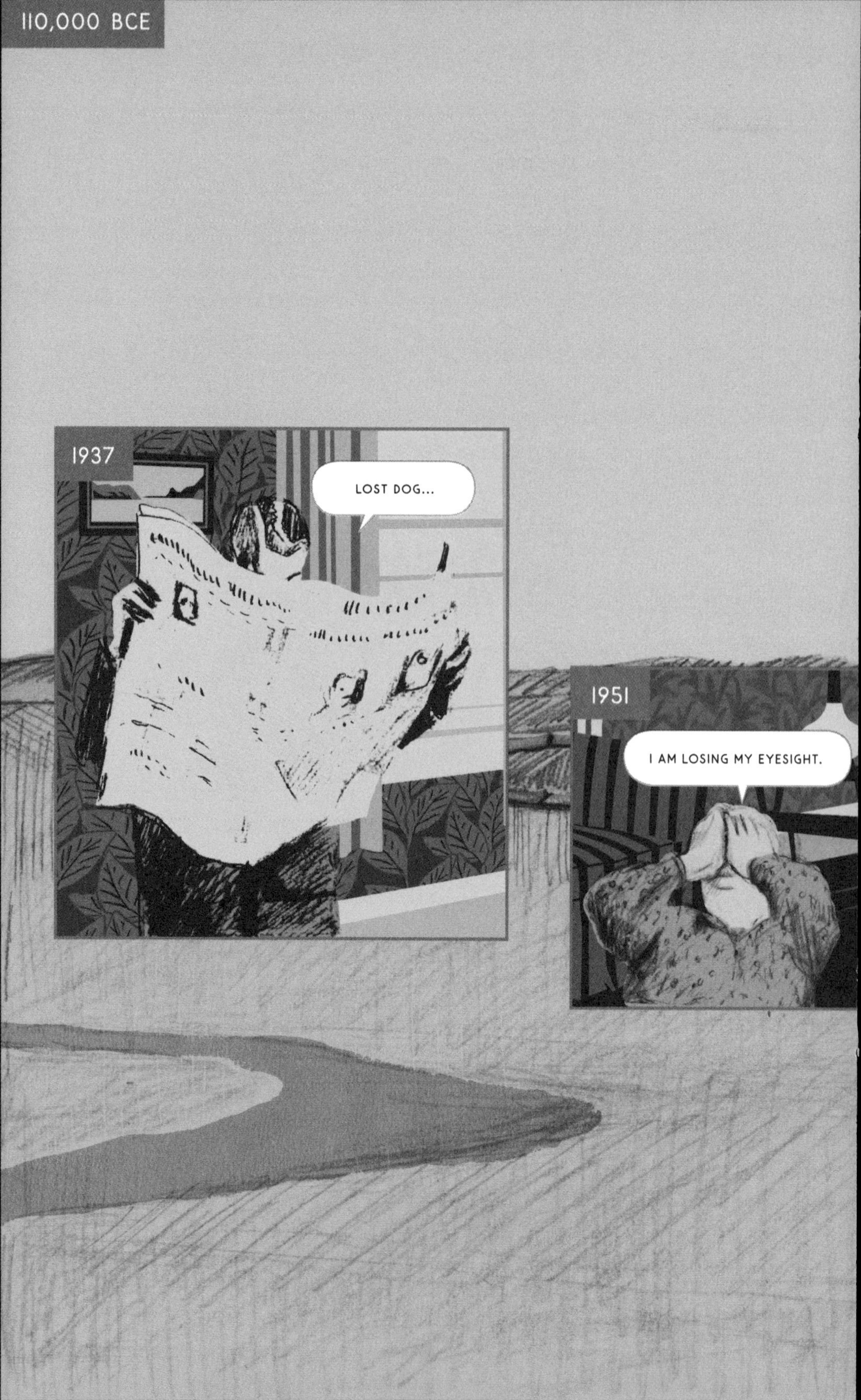
110,000 BCE
1937
LOST DOG...
1951
I AM LOSING MY EYESIGHT.

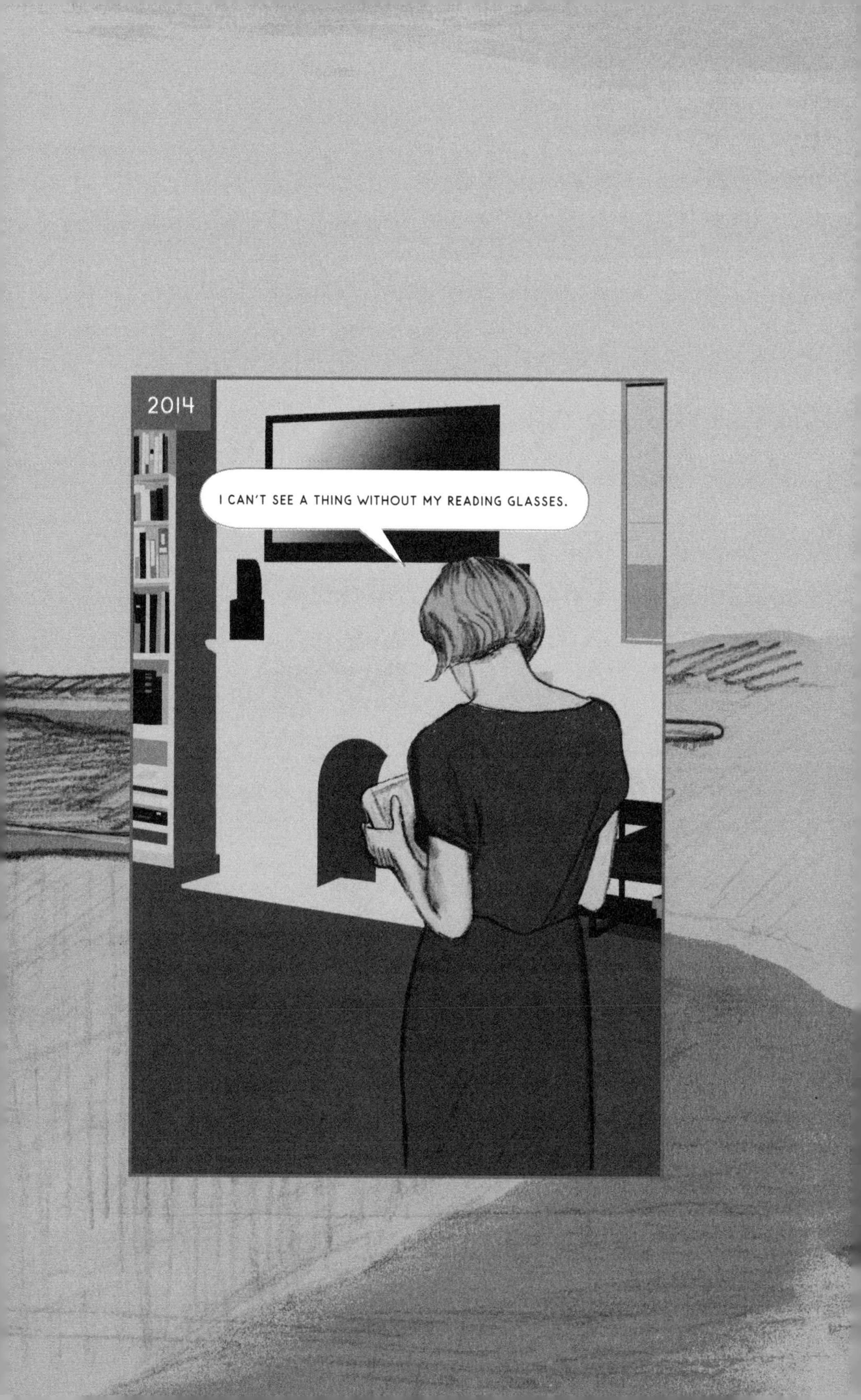
2014
I CAN'T SEE A THING WITHOUT MY READING GLASSES.

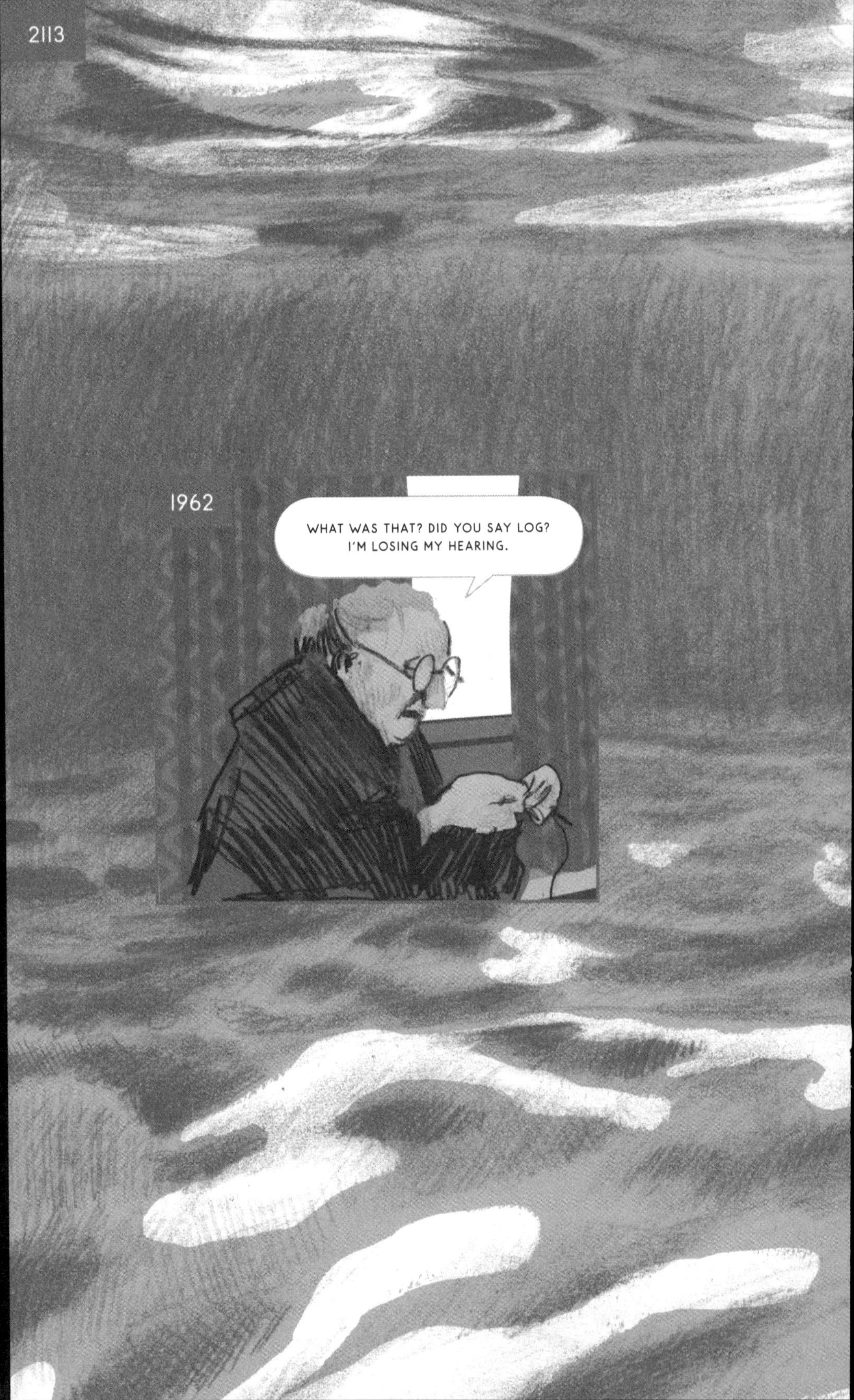
2113
1962
WHAT WAS THAT? DID YOU SAY LOG?
I'M LOSING MY HEARING.

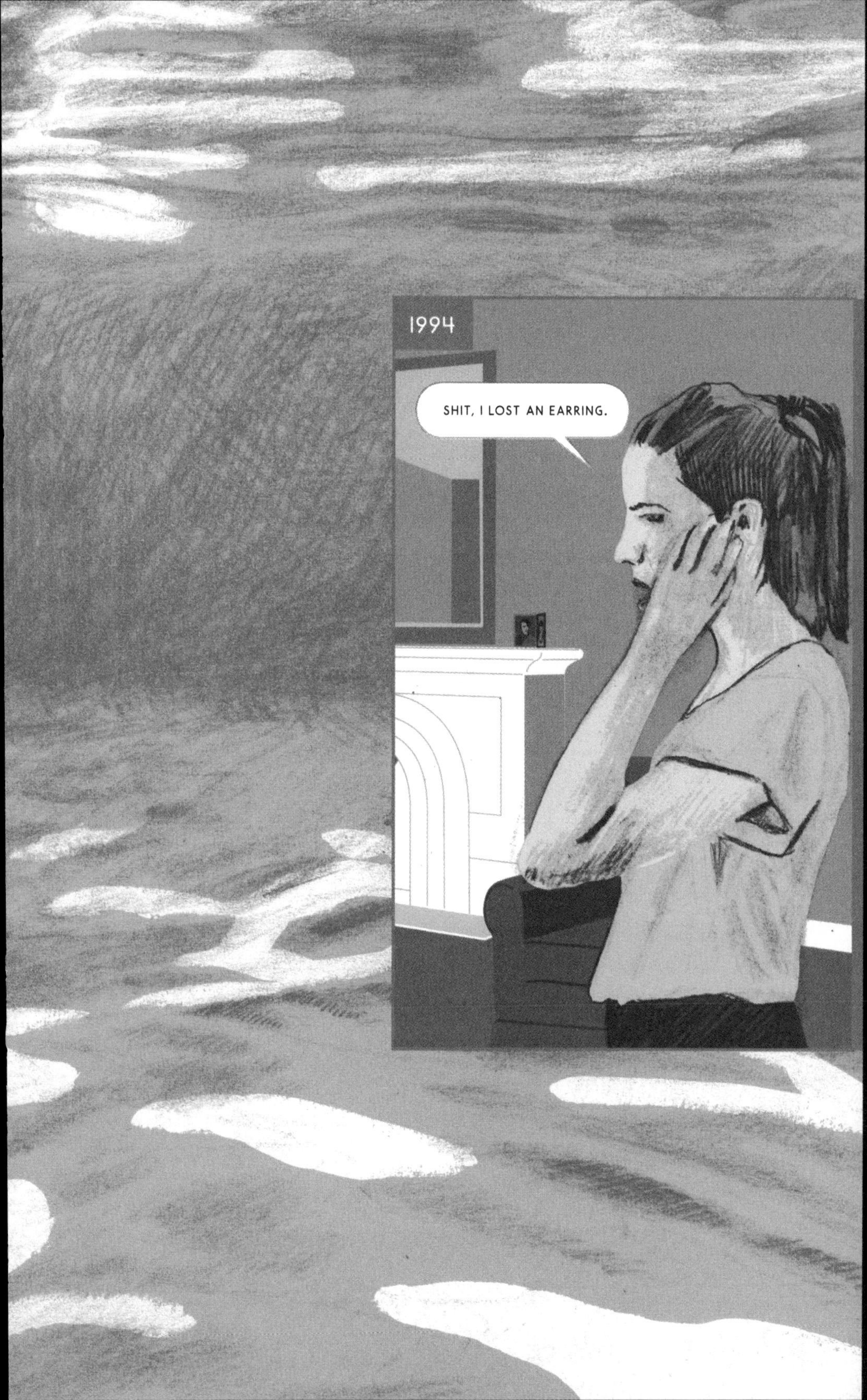
1994
SHIT, I LOST AN EARRING.

1,000,000 BCE

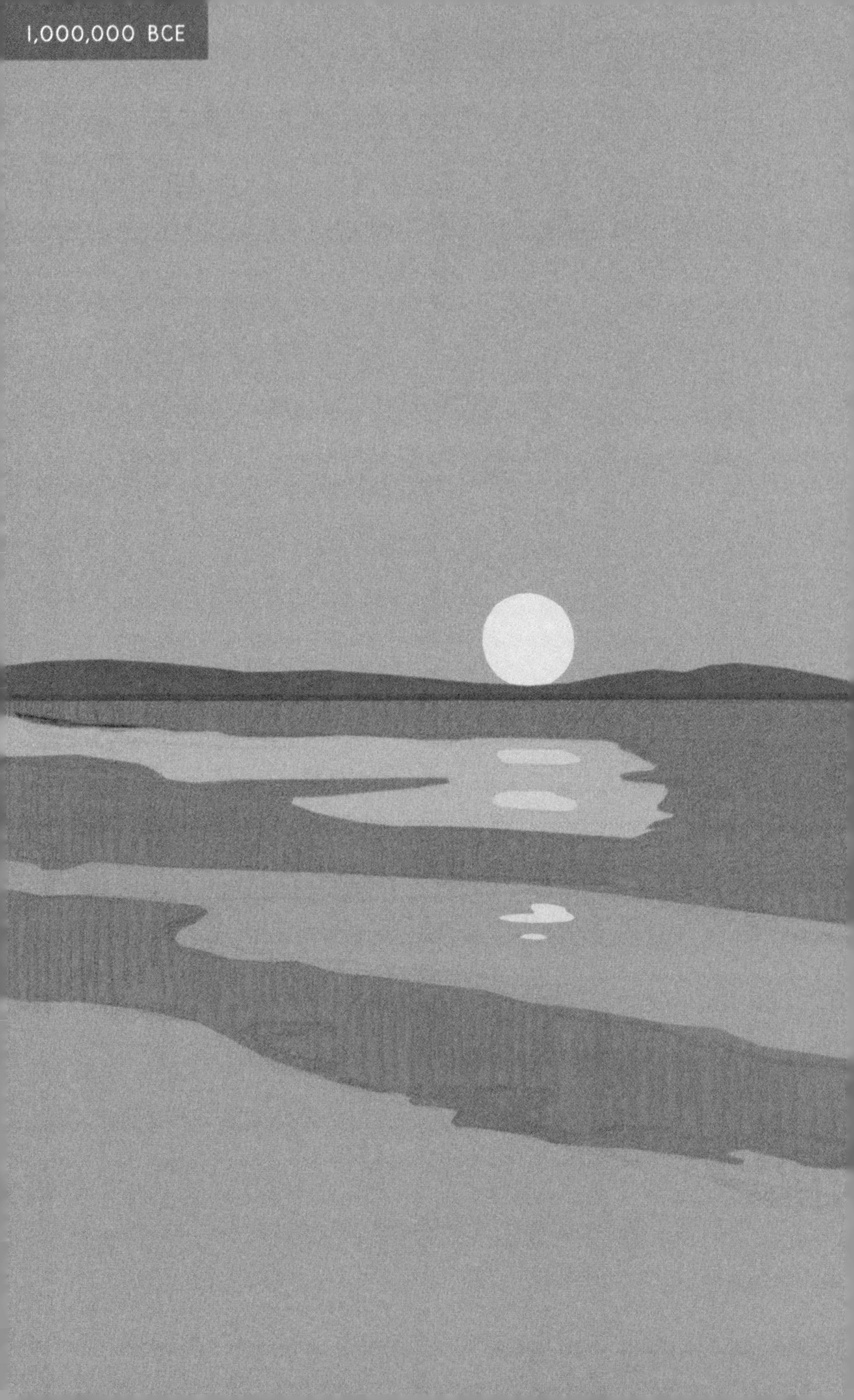

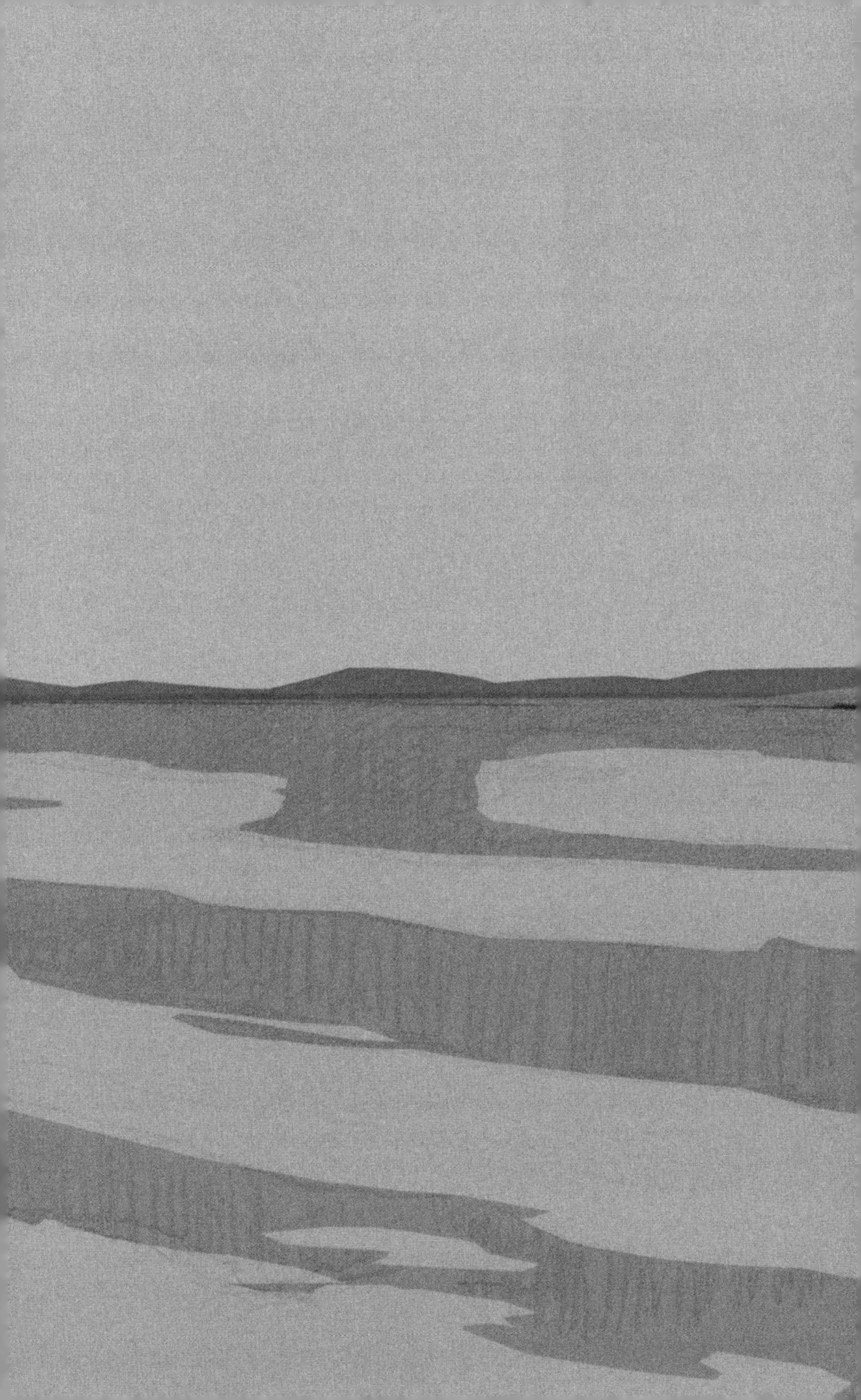

A FAMILY HISTORY
FATHERLAND
NINA BUNJEVAC

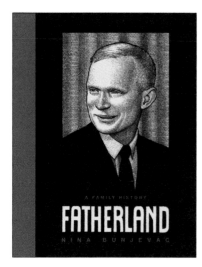

# Dissident Years (*Excerpt*)

## NINA BUNJEVAC

*excerpted from*

Fatherland

LIVERIGHT / NORTON

8.8 × 11.1 inches • 160 pages

## Biography

Nina Bunjevac is a Toronto-based cartoonist and illustrator. She is the author of *Heartless* (Conundrum Press, 2012) and *Fatherland* (Jonathan Cape, 2014). ninabunjevac.com

## Statement

*Fatherland* follows my father's life from his birthplace in pre- and World War II–era Croatia to his exile in Canada, his involvement in a radical Serbian nationalist terrorist group in Canada, and his subsequent death in 1977. The book is divided into two parts; the first being told from the maternal perspective, and the second one told from the paternal perspective of my family. These parts are further divided into chapters, and go back and forward in time.

"Dissident Years" is the second chapter in part two, entitled "Exile." There were quite a few gaps and long pauses in my father's biography—such as during WWII, and his three-year imprisonment in the early 1950's—which conveniently coincided with the most crucial points of Yugoslavian history. This provided an opportunity to fill the gaps with historical facts, in order to familiarize readers with the historical background of the story, which has had such a strong influence on its players. This story in particular gave me an opportunity to talk about the "normalcy" of my childhood in socialist Yugoslavia, which revisionists these days seem to negate and paint with the same brush as that of Stalin's Russia.

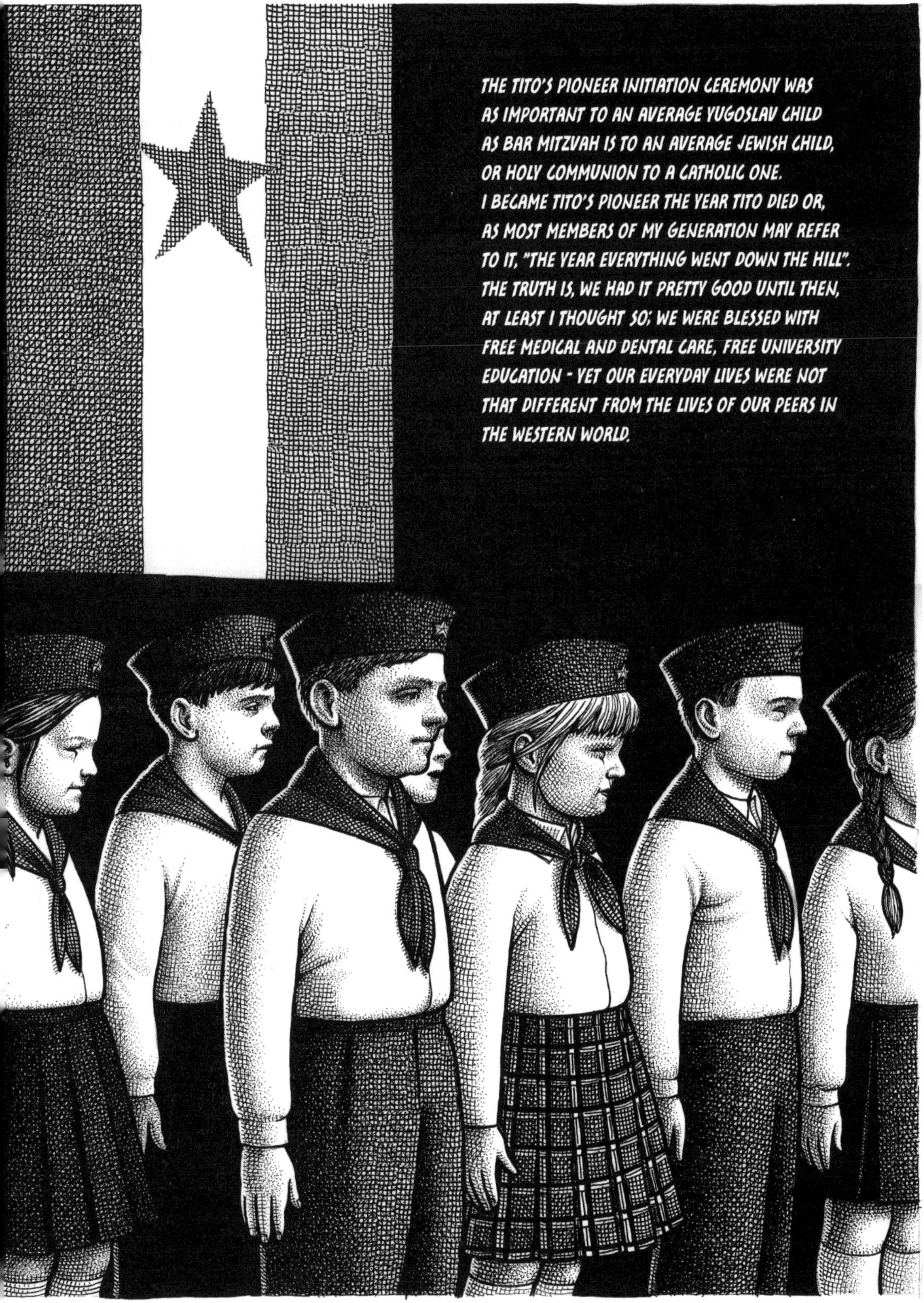
THE TITO'S PIONEER INITIATION CEREMONY WAS AS IMPORTANT TO AN AVERAGE YUGOSLAV CHILD AS BAR MITZVAH IS TO AN AVERAGE JEWISH CHILD, OR HOLY COMMUNION TO A CATHOLIC ONE. I BECAME TITO'S PIONEER THE YEAR TITO DIED OR, AS MOST MEMBERS OF MY GENERATION MAY REFER TO IT, "THE YEAR EVERYTHING WENT DOWN THE HILL". THE TRUTH IS, WE HAD IT PRETTY GOOD UNTIL THEN, AT LEAST I THOUGHT SO; WE WERE BLESSED WITH FREE MEDICAL AND DENTAL CARE, FREE UNIVERSITY EDUCATION - YET OUR EVERYDAY LIVES WERE NOT THAT DIFFERENT FROM THE LIVES OF OUR PEERS IN THE WESTERN WORLD.

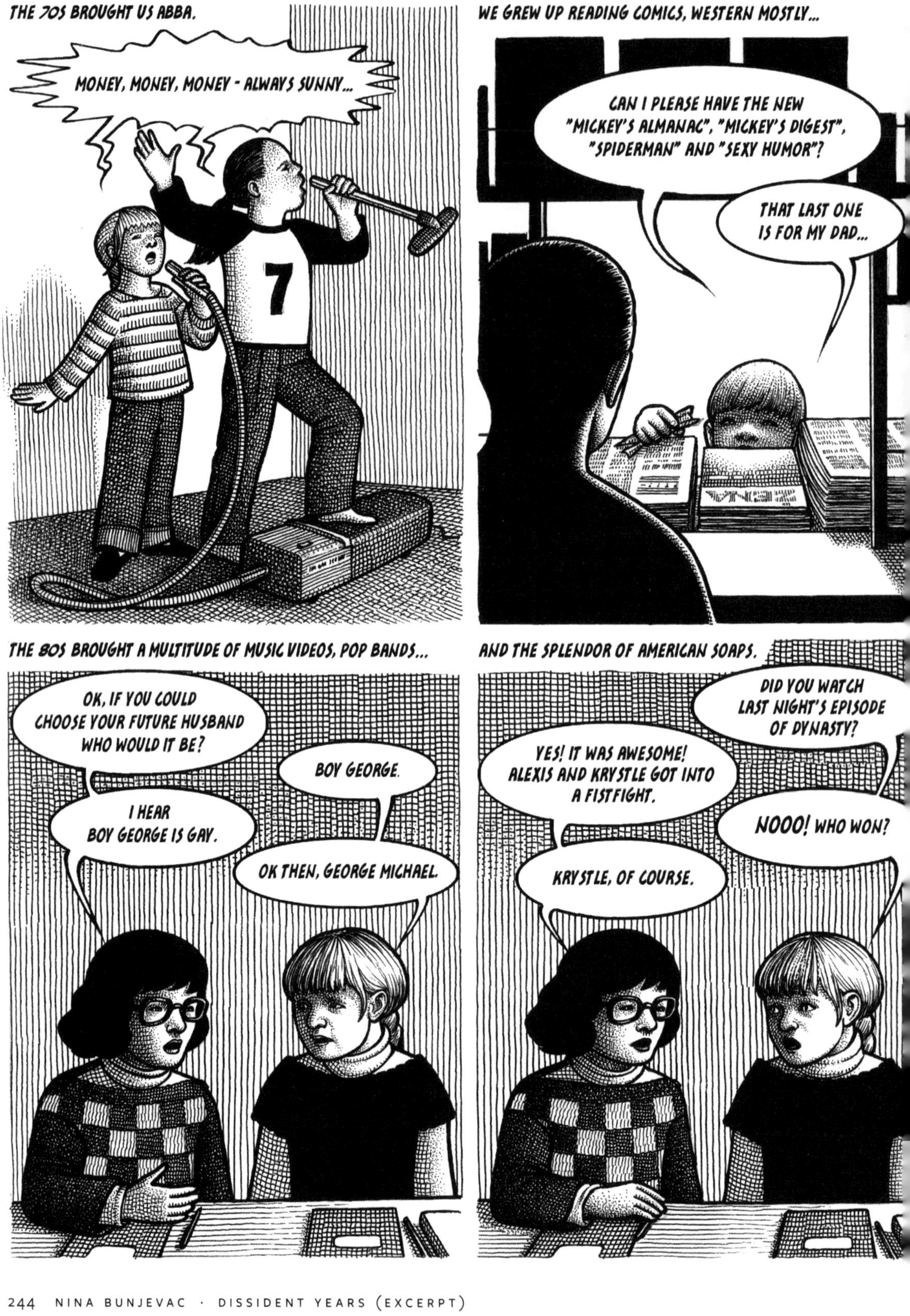
THE 70S BROUGHT US ABBA.
MONEY, MONEY, MONEY - ALWAYS SUNNY...
WE GREW UP READING COMICS, WESTERN MOSTLY...
CAN I PLEASE HAVE THE NEW "MICKEY'S ALMANAC", "MICKEY'S DIGEST", "SPIDERMAN" AND "SEXY HUMOR"?
THAT LAST ONE IS FOR MY DAD...
THE 80S BROUGHT A MULTITUDE OF MUSIC VIDEOS, POP BANDS...
OK, IF YOU COULD CHOOSE YOUR FUTURE HUSBAND WHO WOULD IT BE?
BOY GEORGE.
I HEAR BOY GEORGE IS GAY.
OK THEN, GEORGE MICHAEL.
AND THE SPLENDOR OF AMERICAN SOAPS.
DID YOU WATCH LAST NIGHT'S EPISODE OF DYNASTY?
YES! IT WAS AWESOME! ALEXIS AND KRYSTLE GOT INTO A FISTFIGHT.
NOOO! WHO WON?
KRYSTLE, OF COURSE.

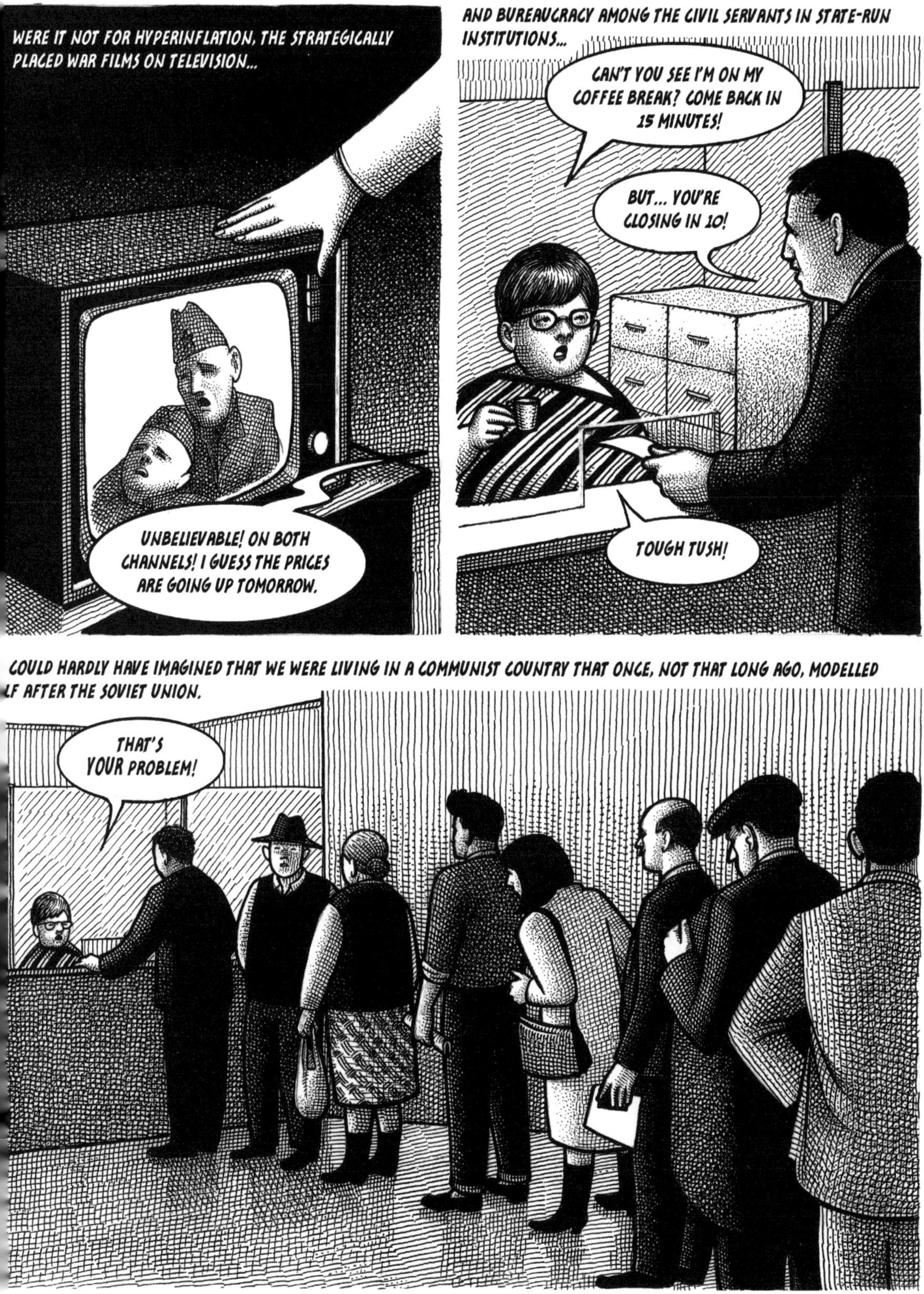

WERE IT NOT FOR HYPERINFLATION, THE STRATEGICALLY PLACED WAR FILMS ON TELEVISION...
UNBELIEVABLE! ON BOTH CHANNELS! I GUESS THE PRICES ARE GOING UP TOMORROW.
AND BUREAUCRACY AMONG THE CIVIL SERVANTS IN STATE-RUN INSTITUTIONS...
CAN'T YOU SEE I'M ON MY COFFEE BREAK? COME BACK IN 15 MINUTES!
BUT... YOU'RE CLOSING IN 10!
TOUGH TUSH!
COULD HARDLY HAVE IMAGINED THAT WE WERE LIVING IN A COMMUNIST COUNTRY THAT ONCE, NOT THAT LONG AGO, MODELLED
LF AFTER THE SOVIET UNION.
THAT'S YOUR PROBLEM!

FOR SOME REASON OR OTHER THOSE OLD PRO-SOVIET DAYS WERE ONLY WHISPERED ABOUT IN MY FAMILY.

AS A CHILD, ONE THING I LOVED MORE THAN LISTENING TO GROWNUPS ENGAGED IN CONVERSATION WAS OVERHEARING THINGS I WASN'T SUPPOSED TO HEAR IN THE FIRST PLACE.

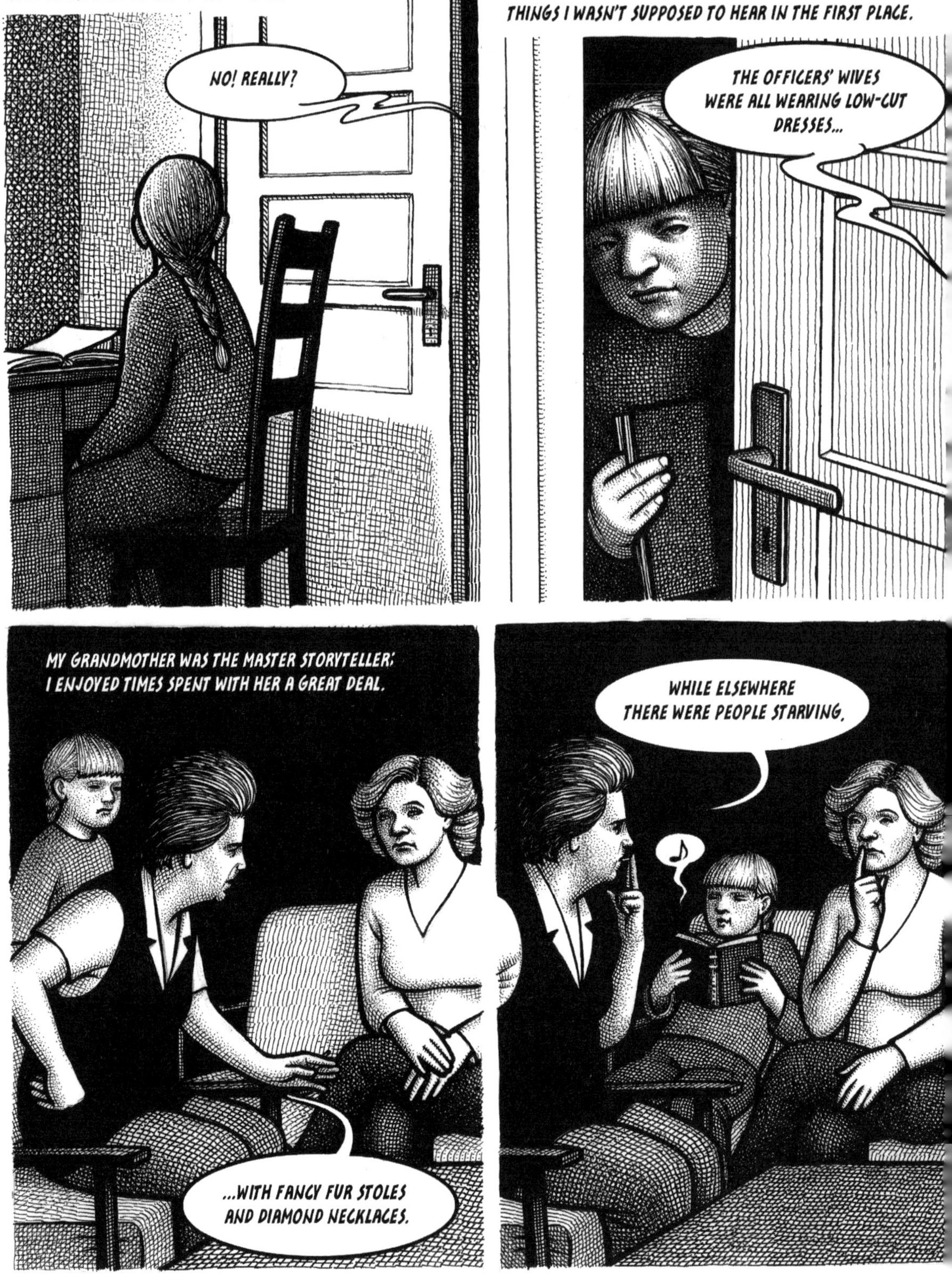
NO! REALLY?
THE OFFICERS' WIVES WERE ALL WEARING LOW-CUT DRESSES...
MY GRANDMOTHER WAS THE MASTER STORYTELLER; I ENJOYED TIMES SPENT WITH HER A GREAT DEAL.
...WITH FANCY FUR STOLES AND DIAMOND NECKLACES.
WHILE ELSEWHERE THERE WERE PEOPLE STARVING.

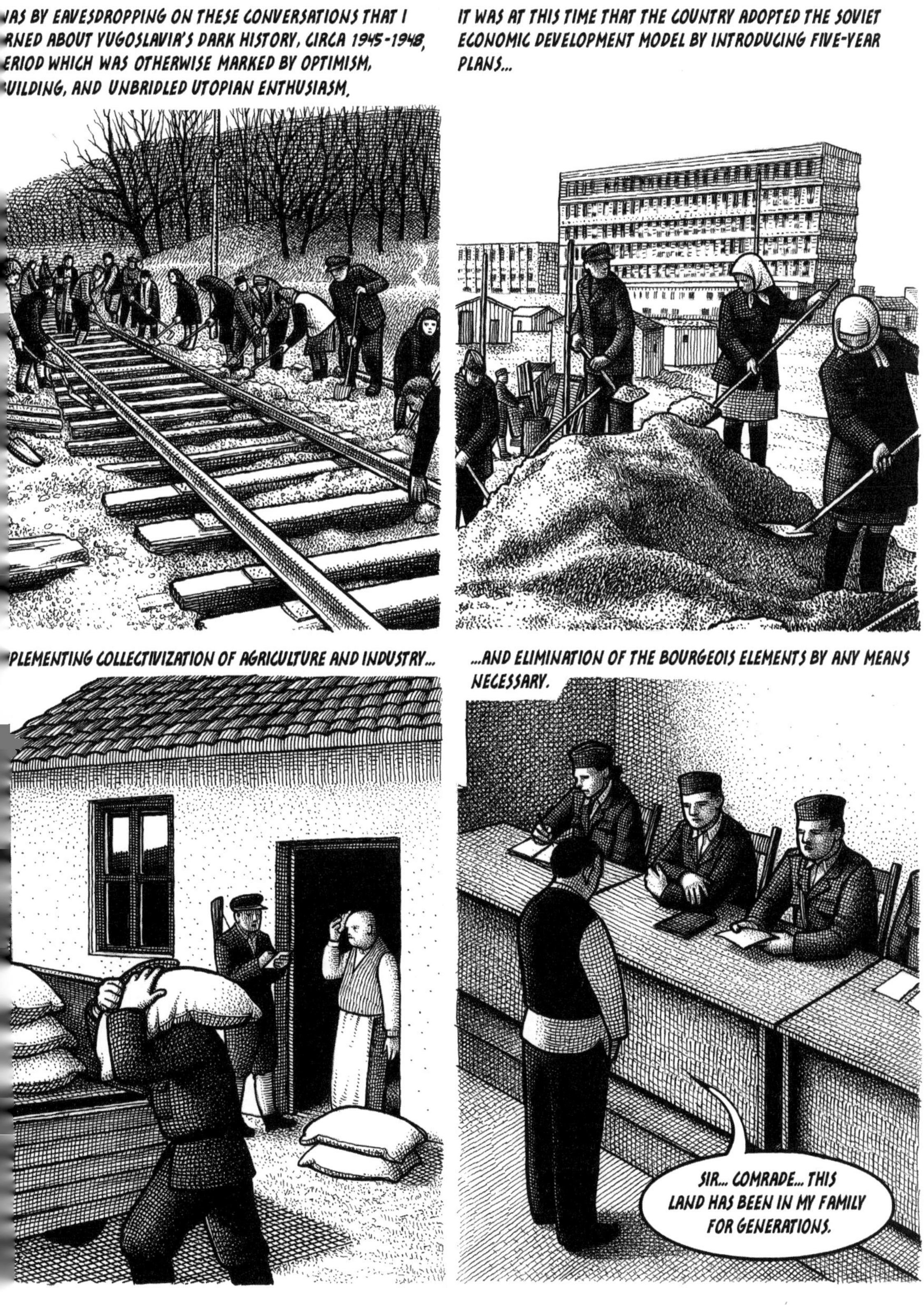
IAS BY EAVESDROPPING ON THESE CONVERSATIONS THAT I
RNED ABOUT YUGOSLAVIA'S DARK HISTORY, CIRCA 1945-1948,
ERIOD WHICH WAS OTHERWISE MARKED BY OPTIMISM,
UILDING, AND UNBRIDLED UTOPIAN ENTHUSIASM.
IT WAS AT THIS TIME THAT THE COUNTRY ADOPTED THE SOVIET ECONOMIC DEVELOPMENT MODEL BY INTRODUCING FIVE-YEAR PLANS...
PLEMENTING COLLECTIVIZATION OF AGRICULTURE AND INDUSTRY...
...AND ELIMINATION OF THE BOURGEOIS ELEMENTS BY ANY MEANS NECESSARY.
SIR... COMRADE... THIS LAND HAS BEEN IN MY FAMILY FOR GENERATIONS.

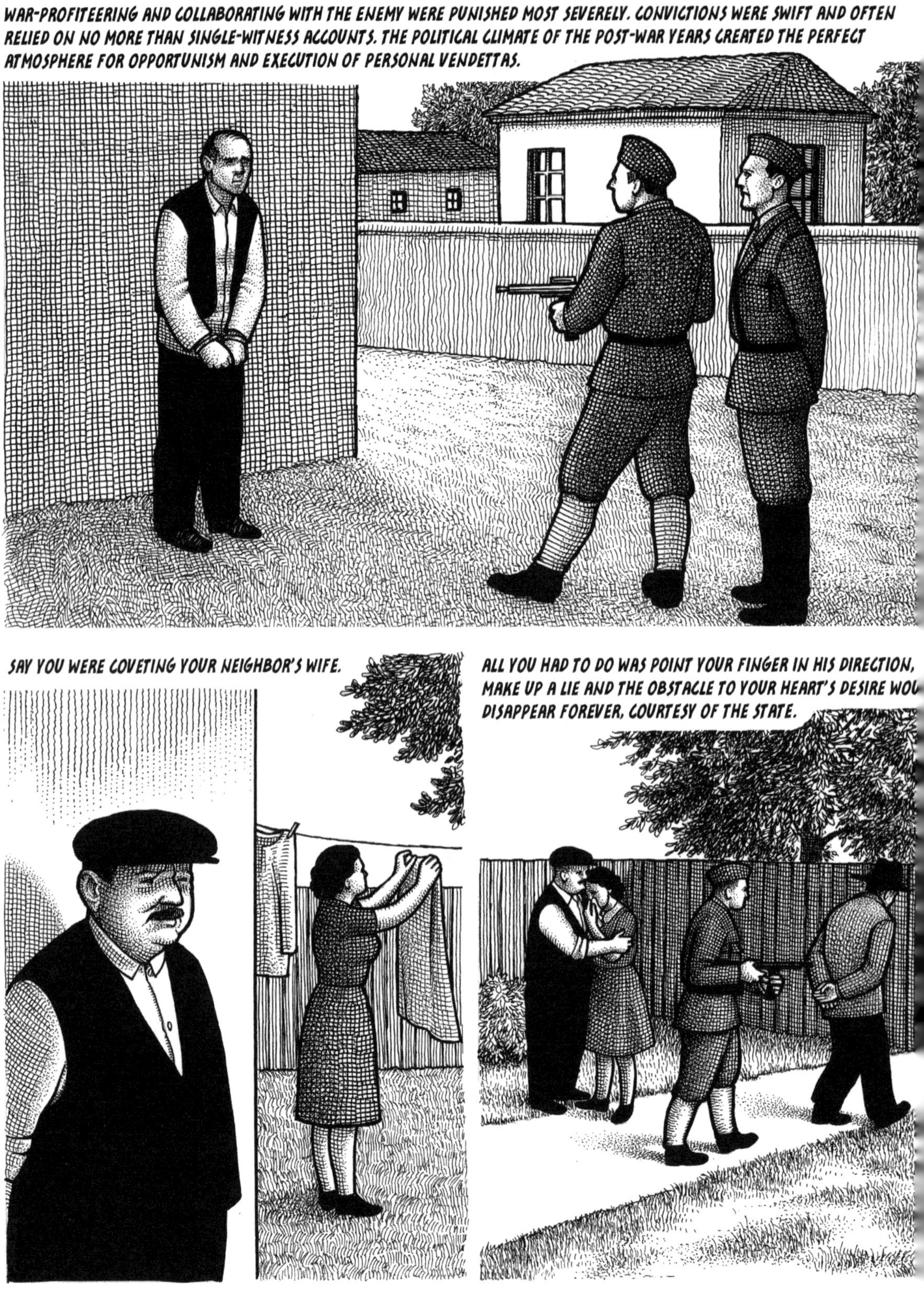
WAR-PROFITEERING AND COLLABORATING WITH THE ENEMY WERE PUNISHED MOST SEVERELY. CONVICTIONS WERE SWIFT AND OFTEN RELIED ON NO MORE THAN SINGLE-WITNESS ACCOUNTS. THE POLITICAL CLIMATE OF THE POST-WAR YEARS CREATED THE PERFECT ATMOSPHERE FOR OPPORTUNISM AND EXECUTION OF PERSONAL VENDETTAS.
SAY YOU WERE COVETING YOUR NEIGHBOR'S WIFE.
ALL YOU HAD TO DO WAS POINT YOUR FINGER IN HIS DIRECTION, MAKE UP A LIE AND THE OBSTACLE TO YOUR HEART'S DESIRE WOU
DISAPPEAR FOREVER, COURTESY OF THE STATE.

HE SITUATION ESCALATED IN 1948 WHEN YUGOSLAVIA GOT XPELLED FROM THE COMINFORM FOLLOWING THE TITO-STALIN ISPUTE ABOUT AIDING THE COMMUNIST UPRISING IN GREECE ND THE POTENTIAL UNIFICATION OF YUGOSLAVIA AND BULGARIA.

HAT FOLLOWED WAS AN ECONOMIC MBARGO IMPOSED BY OTHER MEMBER OUNTRIES OF THE COMINFORM.

BLESSING IN DISGUISE, THE EMBARGO OULD NUDGE THE COUNTRY TO EDEFINE ITS FOREIGN POLICY ND DEVELOP ECONOMIC TIES WITH ON-COMMUNIST COUNTRIES.

UGOSLAVIA WOULD EVENTUALLY MBARK ON THE SOCIALIST PATH, UT NOT BEFORE HAVING O DEAL WITH THE "SOVIET LEMENT" WITHIN ITS OWN ORDERS FIRST.

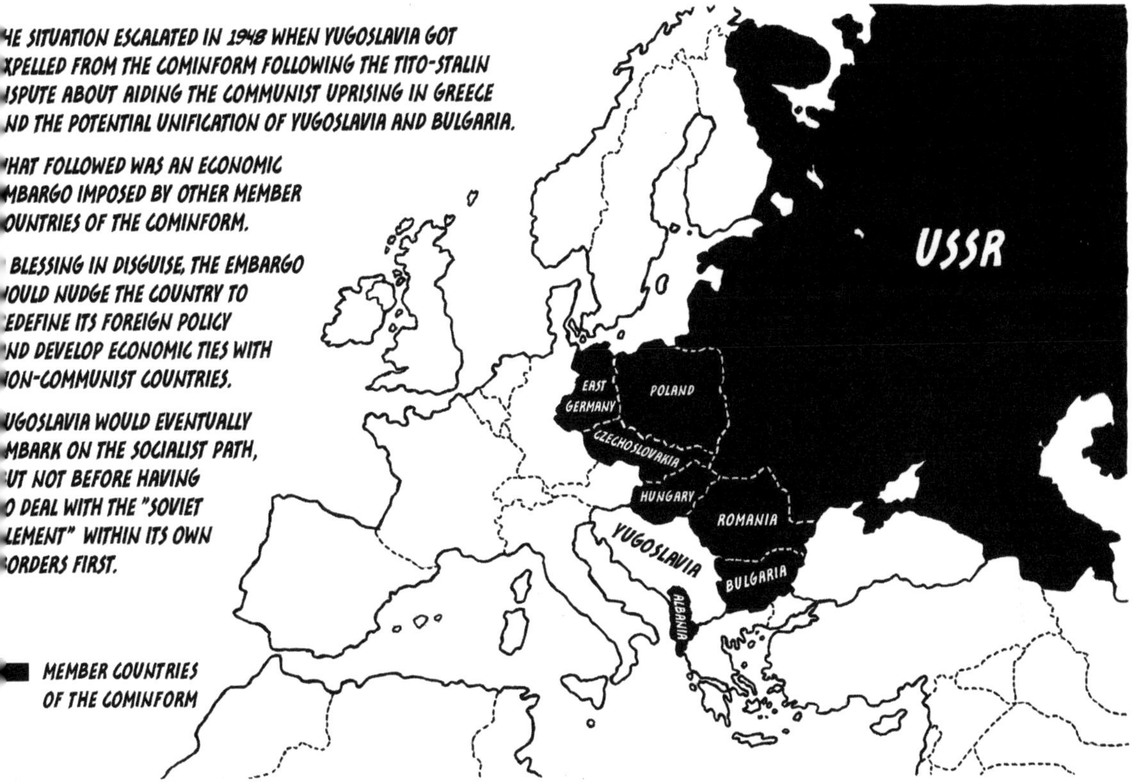
USSR
EAST GERMANY
POLAND
CZECHOSLOVAKIA
HUNGARY
ROMANIA
YUGOSLAVIA
BULGARIA
ALBANIA
MEMBER COUNTRIES OF THE COMINFORM

E HOLY "LENIN-STALIN-TITO" TRINITY WAS BROKEN, SYMPATHIZING H STALIN WOULD HAVE ONE PEGGED A "STALINIST", AN ADDITION AN ALREADY LENGTHY LIST OF THINGS "ONE DARE NOT EVEN TALK OUT".

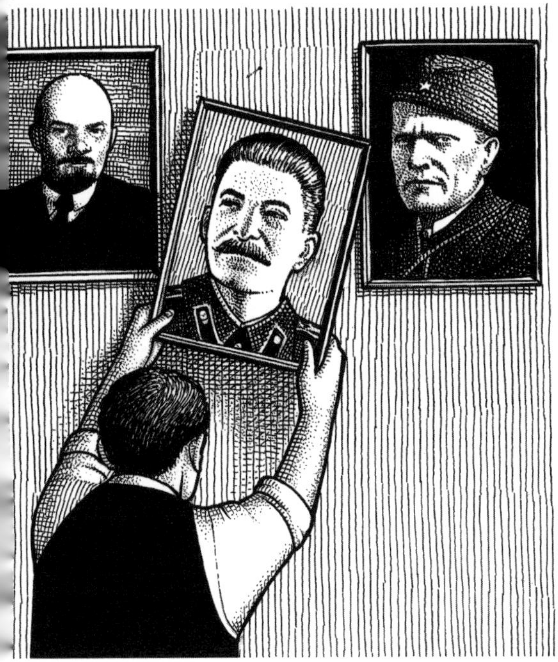

STORIES WERE TOLD ABOUT "GOLI OTOK" - THE PRISON WHICH WAS BUILT FOR THE SPECIFIC PURPOSE OF DEALING WITH THE ENEMIES OF THE STATE - AND THE SEVERE AND INHUMANE TREATMENT OF ITS INMATES.

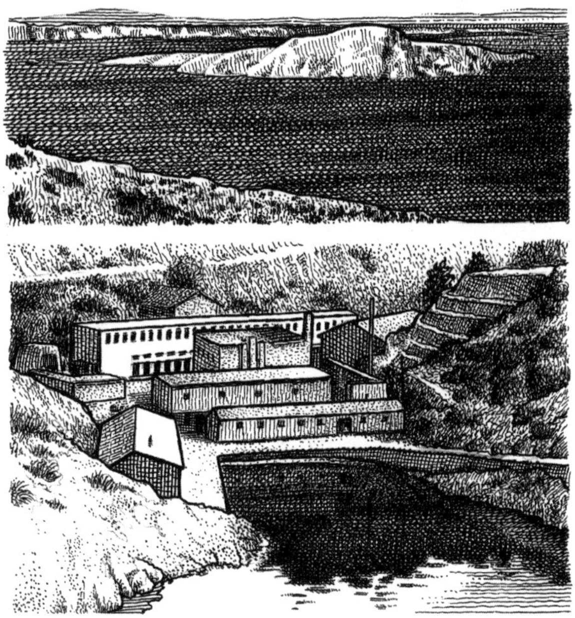

WHAT WAS WHISPERED ABOUT THE MOST, AND WHAT SEEMED TO BOTHER MY GRANDMOTHER IMMENSELY WAS THE INTERNMENT AND EXPULSION OF ETHNIC GERMANS FROM THE NORTHERN PROVINCE OF VOJVODINA. ALTHOUGH A LARGE PERCENTAGE OF THE GERMAN POPULATION DID SUPPORT AND JOIN THE WEHRMACHT DURING WWII, MANY INNOCENT PEOPLE PERISHED ALONG THE WAY BETWEEN 1945 AND 1948, SOLELY BY VIRTUE OF THEIR ETHNICITY.

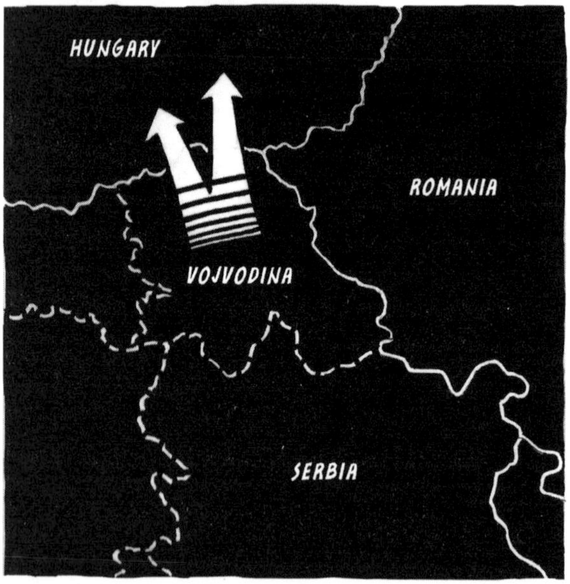
HUNGARY
ROMANIA
VOJVODINA
SERBIA

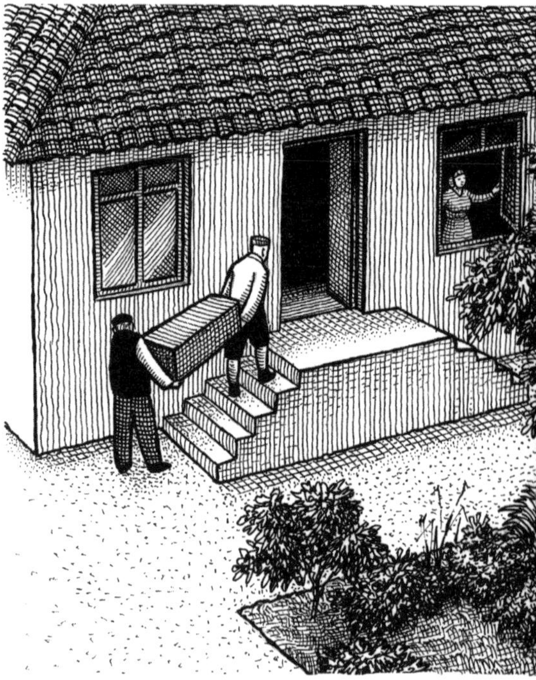

CONFISCATED PROPERTIES THAT ONCE BELONGED TO GERMAN FAMILIES WERE THEN GIVEN TO DESERVING MEMBERS OF THE COMMUNIST PARTY; IN MOST CASES FORMER PARTISANS.

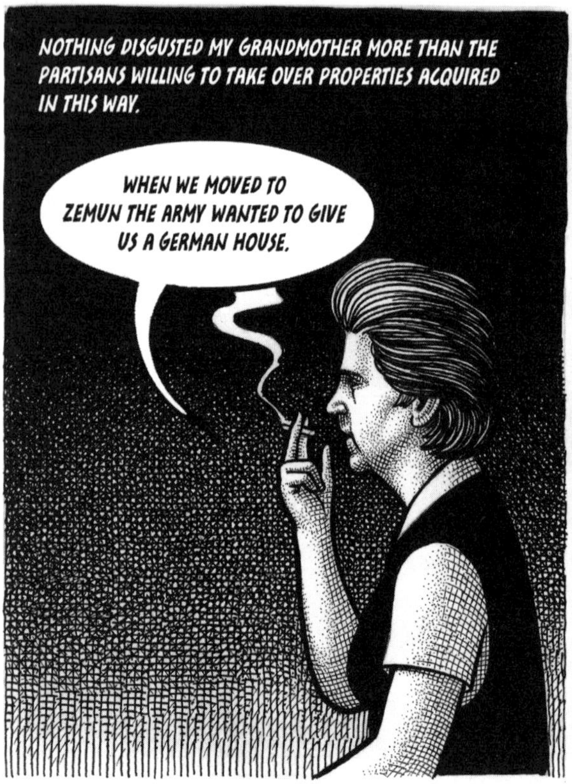
NOTHING DISGUSTED MY GRANDMOTHER MORE THAN THE PARTISANS WILLING TO TAKE OVER PROPERTIES ACQUIRED IN THIS WAY.
WHEN WE MOVED TO ZEMUN THE ARMY WANTED TO GIVE US A GERMAN HOUSE.

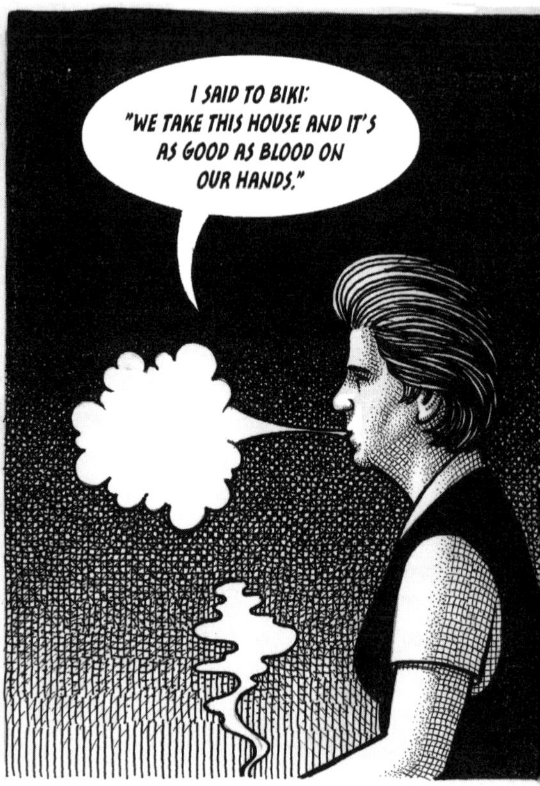
I SAID TO BIKI: "WE TAKE THIS HOUSE AND IT'S AS GOOD AS BLOOD ON OUR HANDS."

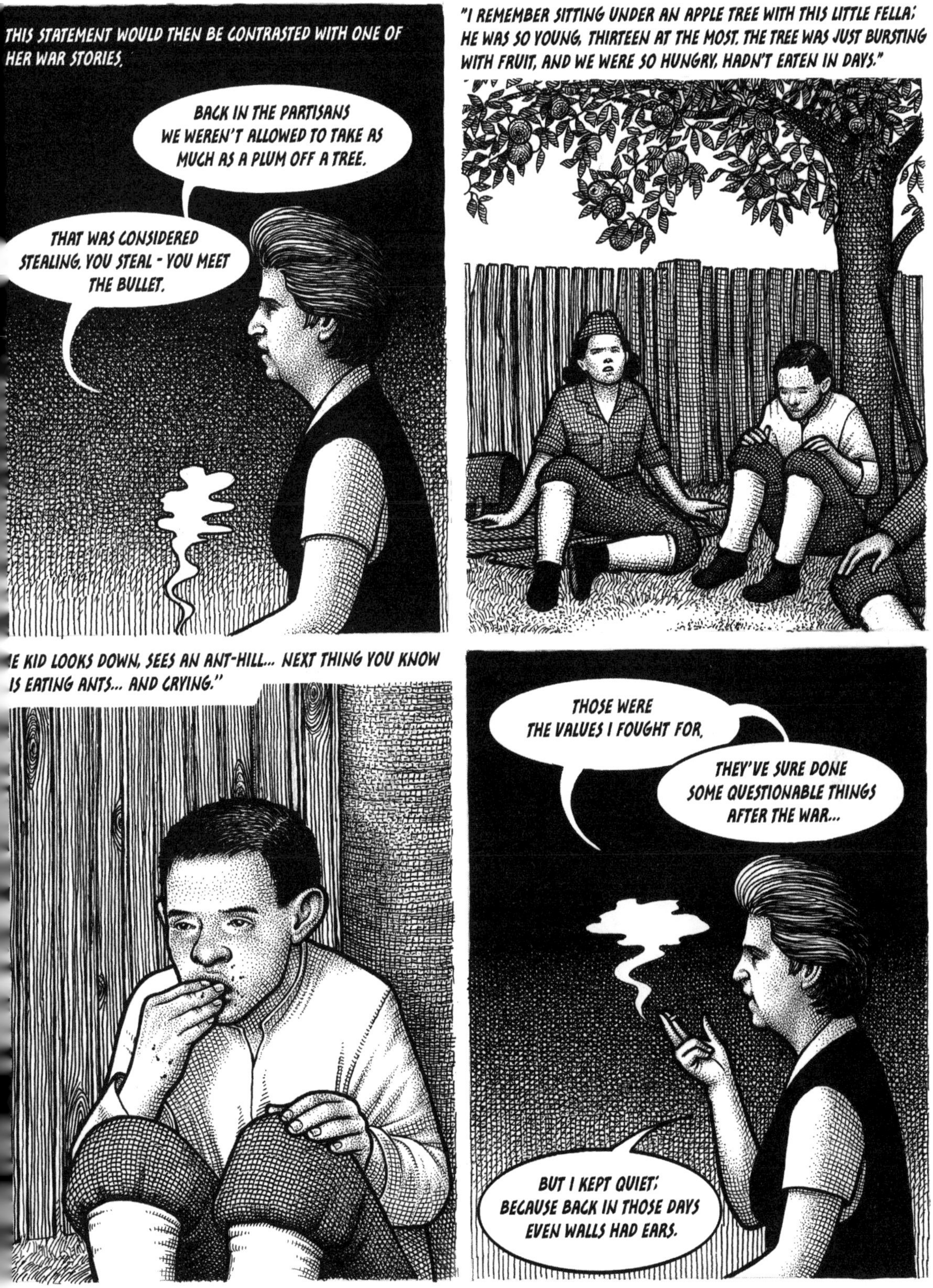
THIS STATEMENT WOULD THEN BE CONTRASTED WITH ONE OF HER WAR STORIES.
BACK IN THE PARTISANS WE WEREN'T ALLOWED TO TAKE AS MUCH AS A PLUM OFF A TREE.
THAT WAS CONSIDERED STEALING. YOU STEAL - YOU MEET THE BULLET.
"I REMEMBER SITTING UNDER AN APPLE TREE WITH THIS LITTLE FELLA; HE WAS SO YOUNG, THIRTEEN AT THE MOST. THE TREE WAS JUST BURSTING WITH FRUIT, AND WE WERE SO HUNGRY, HADN'T EATEN IN DAYS."
E KID LOOKS DOWN, SEES AN ANT-HILL... NEXT THING YOU KNOW IS EATING ANTS... AND CRYING."
THOSE WERE THE VALUES I FOUGHT FOR.
THEY'VE SURE DONE SOME QUESTIONABLE THINGS AFTER THE WAR...
BUT I KEPT QUIET; BECAUSE BACK IN THOSE DAYS EVEN WALLS HAD EARS.

SHE WAS WISE TO KEEP QUIET, FOR CRITICIZING THE GOVERNMENT WAS NOT TOLERATED ALL THAT WELL, EVEN IF THE CRITICISM CAME FRO TOP PARTY OFFICIALS. SUCH WAS THE CASE OF MILOVAN DJILAS, ONE OF THE KEY FIGURES IN THE COMMUNIST RESISTANCE, A MAN SECON ONLY TO TITO. DJILAS WAS SEVERELY CRITICAL OF THE EMERGENCE OF A NEW CLASS IN WHAT WAS ESSENTIALLY A NO-CLASS SYSTEM.

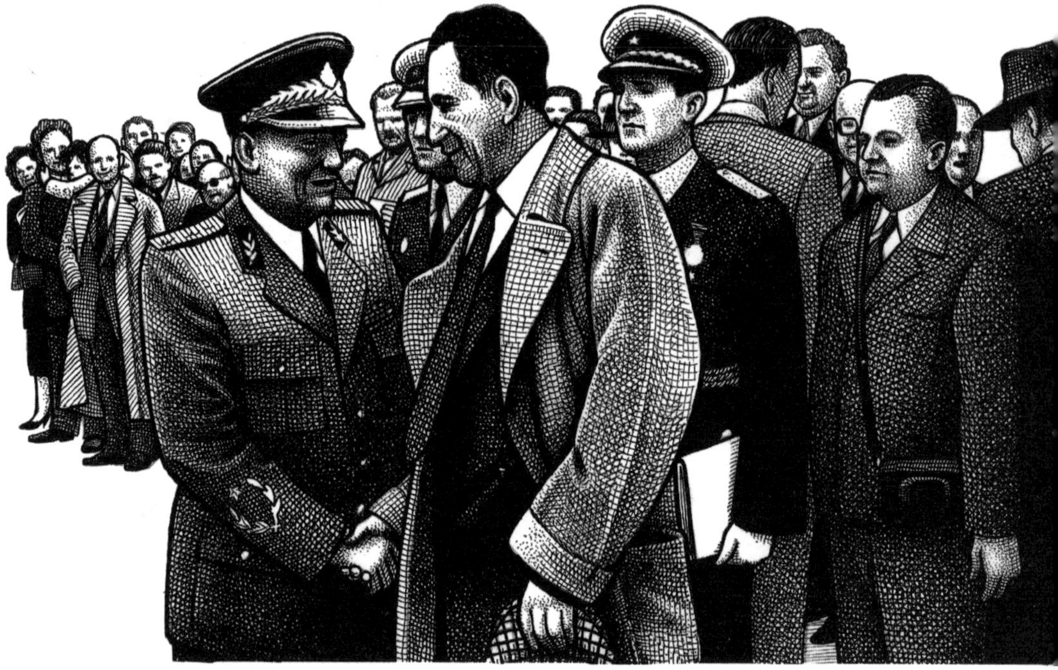

WHAT HE WAS REFERRING TO WAS THE LAVISH LIFE-STYLE ENJOYED BY THE ELITE PARTY MEMBERS, WHILE MOST PEOPLE LIVED WELL BELOW THE POVERTY LINE.

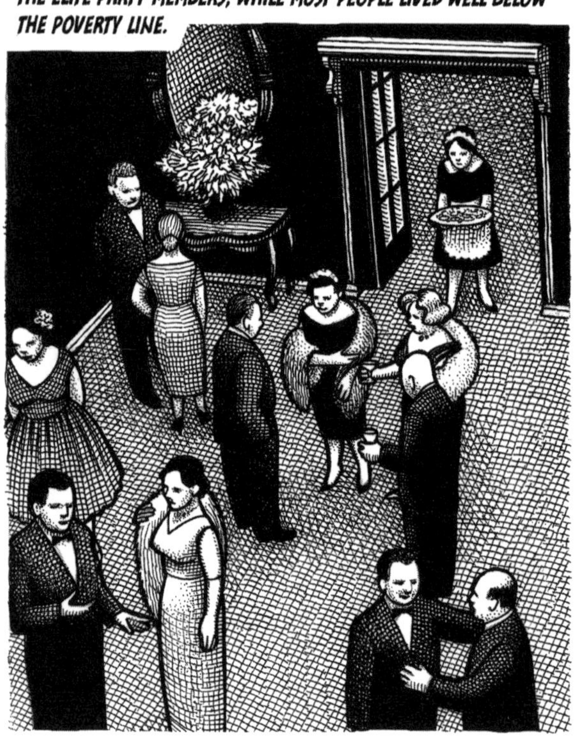

IN 1954 DJILAS PUBLISHED OVER A DOZEN ESSAYS ON THAT VERY SUBJECT IN *BORBA*, THE OFFICIAL PAPER OF THE COMMUNIST PAR ALTHOUGH WIDELY READ AND POPULAR, DJILAS'S WRITING WAS SE AS A GESTURE OF DISLOYALTY TO THE PARTY, AND WOULD EVENTUA CAUSE HIS EXPULSION FROM THE CENTRAL COMMITTEE.

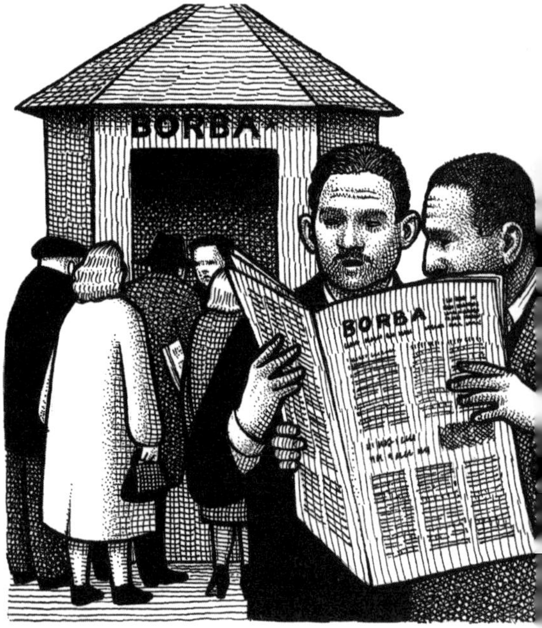
BORBA
BORBA

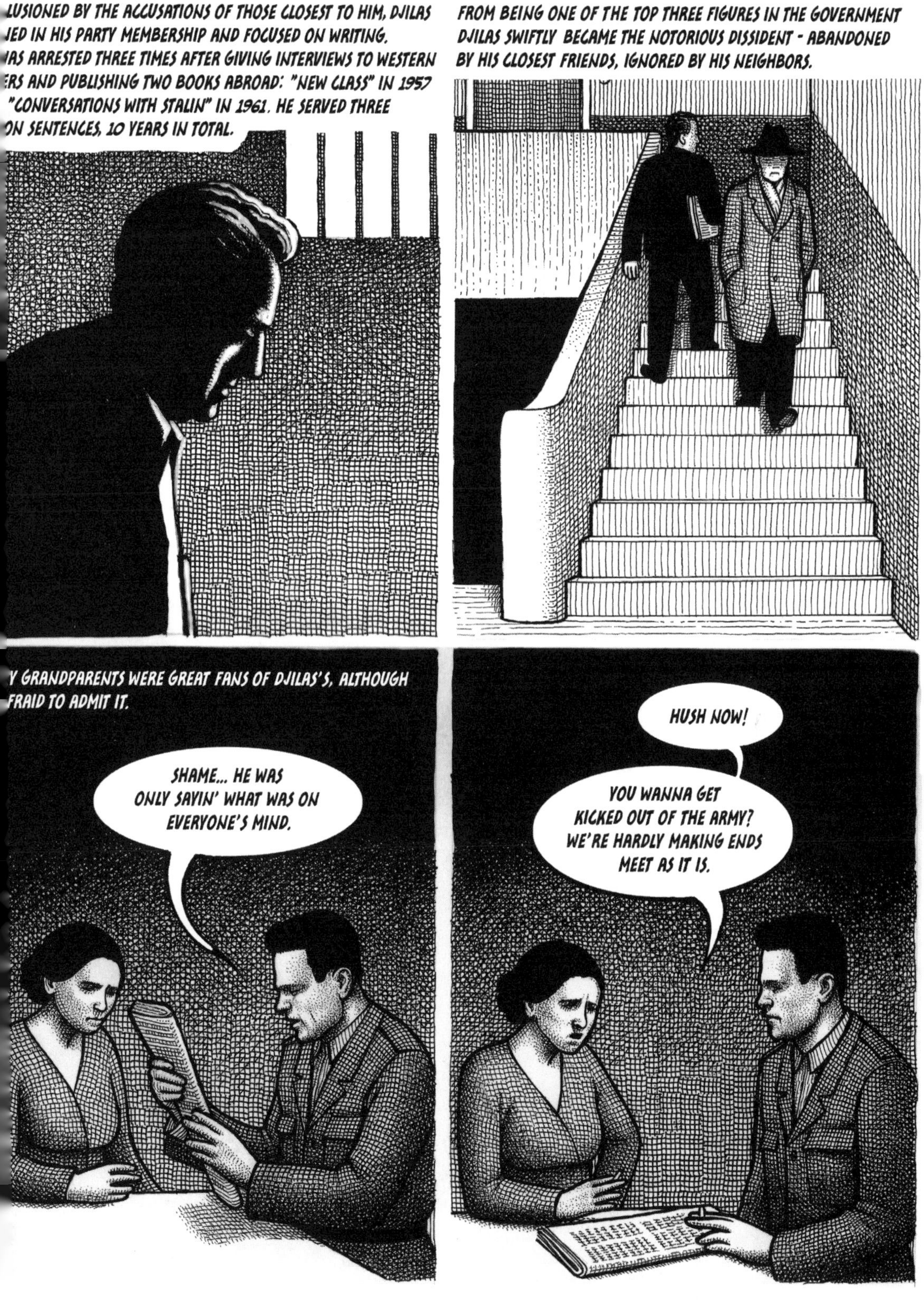
LUSIONED BY THE ACCUSATIONS OF THOSE CLOSEST TO HIM, DJILAS
IED IN HIS PARTY MEMBERSHIP AND FOCUSED ON WRITING.
IAS ARRESTED THREE TIMES AFTER GIVING INTERVIEWS TO WESTERN
ERS AND PUBLISHING TWO BOOKS ABROAD: "NEW CLASS" IN 1957
"CONVERSATIONS WITH STALIN" IN 1961. HE SERVED THREE
ON SENTENCES, 10 YEARS IN TOTAL.
FROM BEING ONE OF THE TOP THREE FIGURES IN THE GOVERNMENT DJILAS SWIFTLY BECAME THE NOTORIOUS DISSIDENT - ABANDONED BY HIS CLOSEST FRIENDS, IGNORED BY HIS NEIGHBORS.
Y GRANDPARENTS WERE GREAT FANS OF DJILAS'S, ALTHOUGH
FRAID TO ADMIT IT.
SHAME... HE WAS ONLY SAYIN' WHAT WAS ON EVERYONE'S MIND.
HUSH NOW!
YOU WANNA GET KICKED OUT OF THE ARMY? WE'RE HARDLY MAKING ENDS MEET AS IT IS.

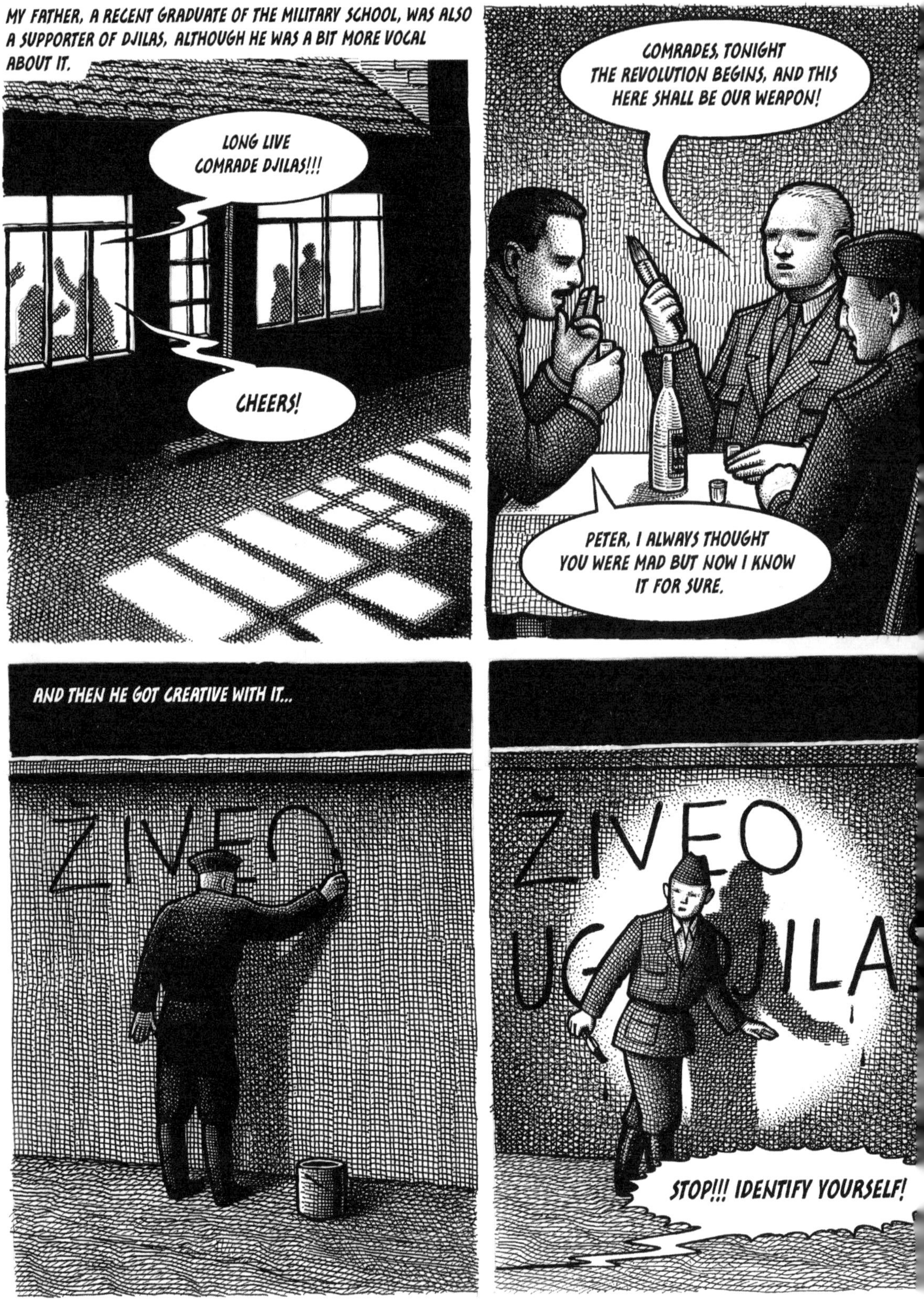
MY FATHER, A RECENT GRADUATE OF THE MILITARY SCHOOL, WAS ALSO A SUPPORTER OF DJILAS, ALTHOUGH HE WAS A BIT MORE VOCAL ABOUT IT.
LONG LIVE COMRADE DJILAS!!!
CHEERS!
COMRADES, TONIGHT THE REVOLUTION BEGINS, AND THIS HERE SHALL BE OUR WEAPON!
PETER, I ALWAYS THOUGHT YOU WERE MAD BUT NOW I KNOW IT FOR SURE.
AND THEN HE GOT CREATIVE WITH IT...
ŽIVEO
ŽIVEO
STOP!!! IDENTIFY YOURSELF!

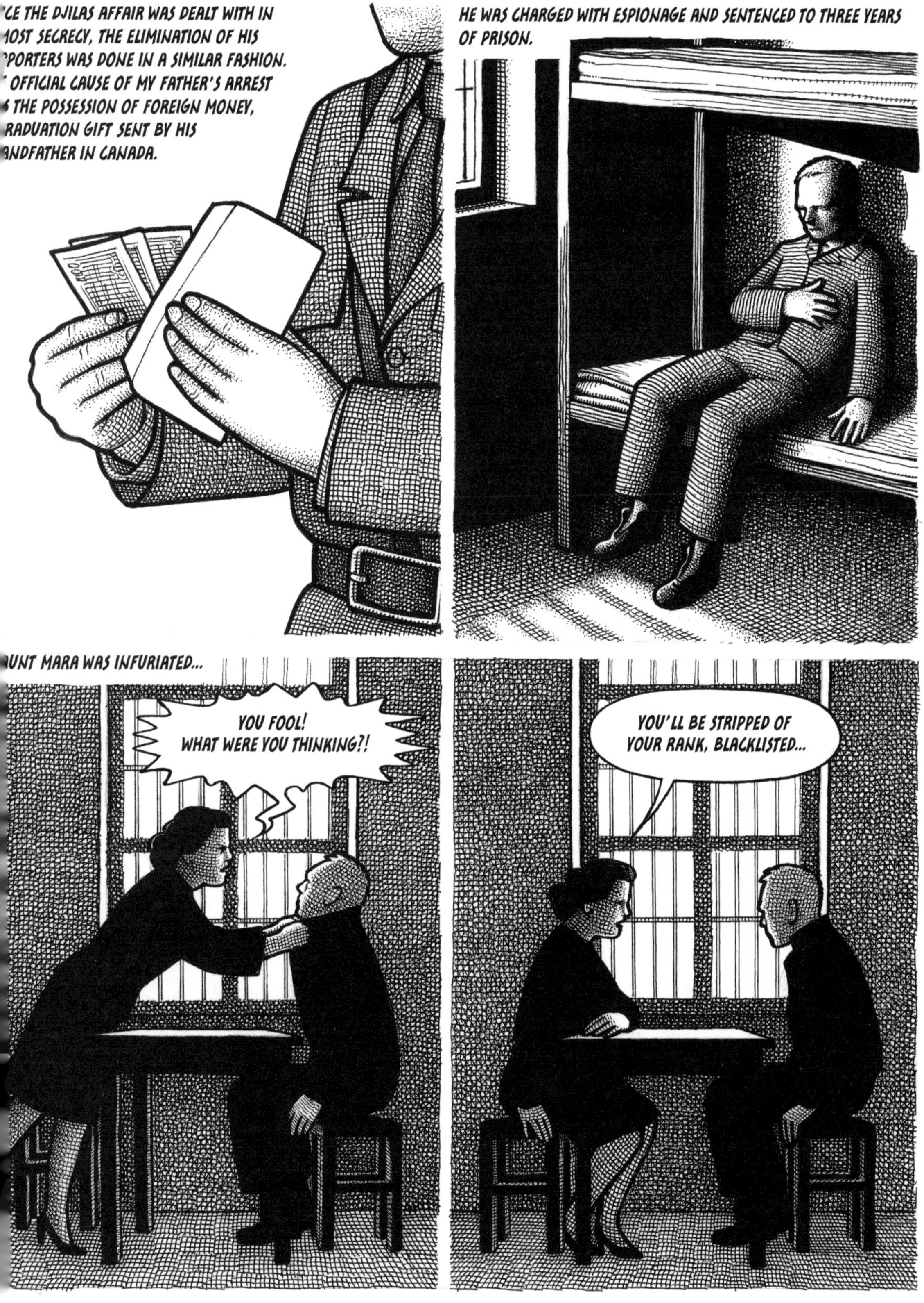

CE THE DJILAS AFFAIR WAS DEALT WITH IN
MOST SECRECY, THE ELIMINATION OF HIS
PORTERS WAS DONE IN A SIMILAR FASHION.
OFFICIAL CAUSE OF MY FATHER'S ARREST
S THE POSSESSION OF FOREIGN MONEY,
RADUATION GIFT SENT BY HIS
NDFATHER IN CANADA.
HE WAS CHARGED WITH ESPIONAGE AND SENTENCED TO THREE YEARS OF PRISON.
UNT MARA WAS INFURIATED...
YOU FOOL! WHAT WERE YOU THINKING?!
YOU'LL BE STRIPPED OF YOUR RANK, BLACKLISTED...

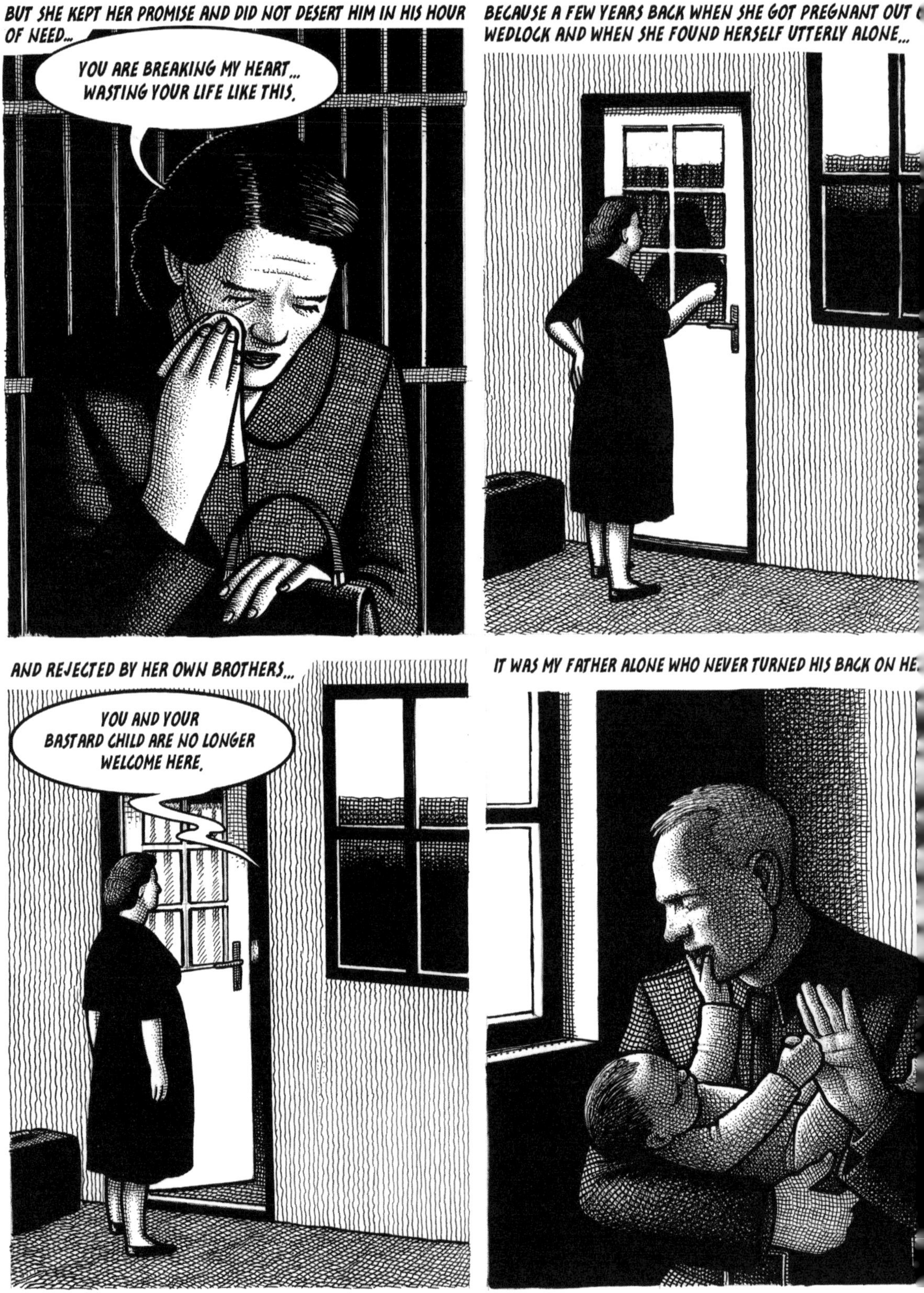
BUT SHE KEPT HER PROMISE AND DID NOT DESERT HIM IN HIS HOUR OF NEED...
YOU ARE BREAKING MY HEART... WASTING YOUR LIFE LIKE THIS.
BECAUSE A FEW YEARS BACK WHEN SHE GOT PREGNANT OUT
WEDLOCK AND WHEN SHE FOUND HERSELF UTTERLY ALONE...
AND REJECTED BY HER OWN BROTHERS...
YOU AND YOUR BASTARD CHILD ARE NO LONGER WELCOME HERE.
IT WAS MY FATHER ALONE WHO NEVER TURNED HIS BACK ON HE

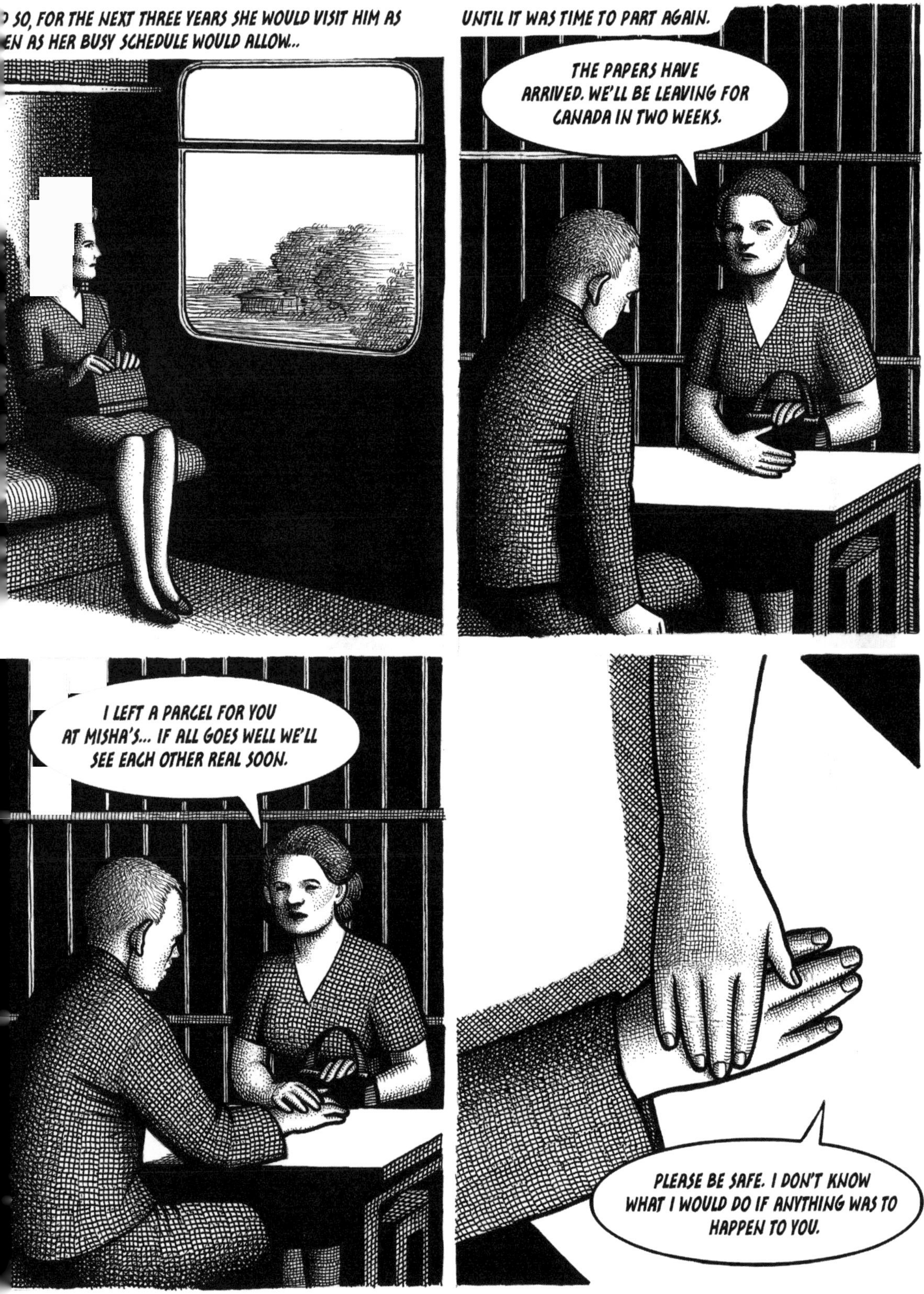
D SO, FOR THE NEXT THREE YEARS SHE WOULD VISIT HIM AS
EN AS HER BUSY SCHEDULE WOULD ALLOW...
UNTIL IT WAS TIME TO PART AGAIN.
THE PAPERS HAVE ARRIVED. WE'LL BE LEAVING FOR CANADA IN TWO WEEKS.
I LEFT A PARCEL FOR YOU AT MISHA'S... IF ALL GOES WELL WE'LL SEE EACH OTHER REAL SOON.
PLEASE BE SAFE. I DON'T KNOW WHAT I WOULD DO IF ANYTHING WAS TO HAPPEN TO YOU.

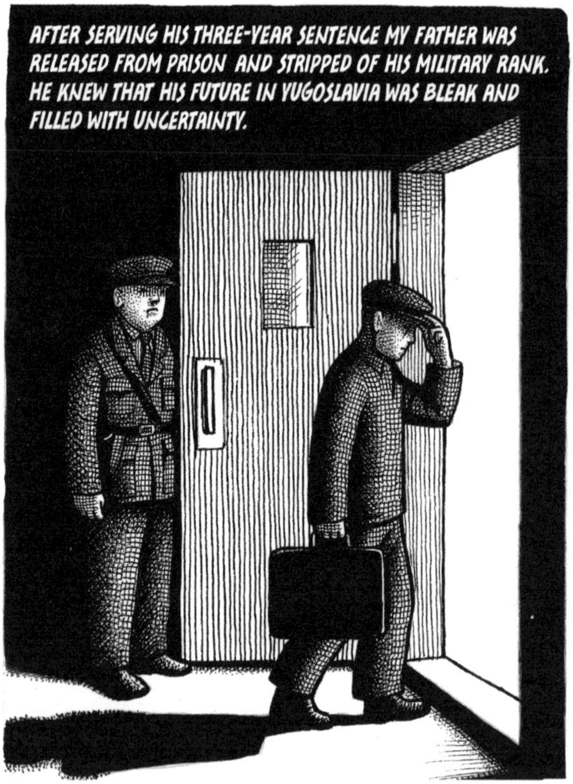
AFTER SERVING HIS THREE-YEAR SENTENCE MY FATHER WAS RELEASED FROM PRISON AND STRIPPED OF HIS MILITARY RANK. HE KNEW THAT HIS FUTURE IN YUGOSLAVIA WAS BLEAK AND FILLED WITH UNCERTAINTY.

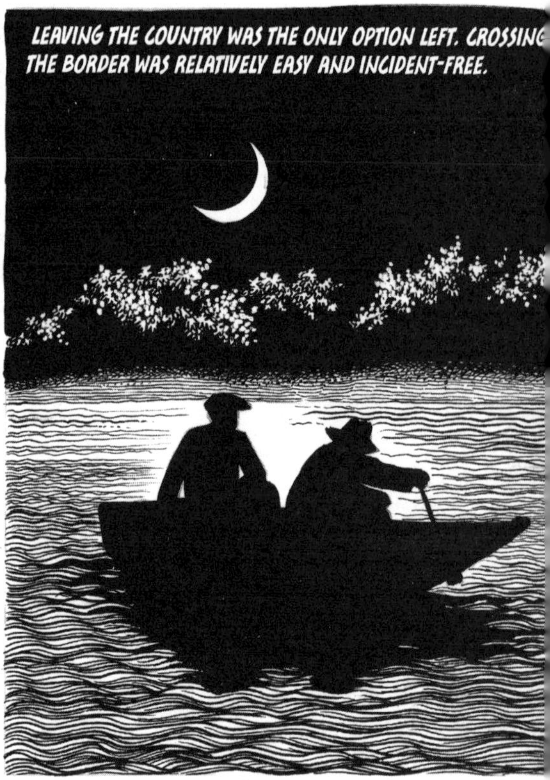
LEAVING THE COUNTRY WAS THE ONLY OPTION LEFT. CROSSING THE BORDER WAS RELATIVELY EASY AND INCIDENT-FREE.

WAITING FOR PERMISSION TO ENTER CANADA WAS A THREE-MONTH ORDEAL, DURING WHICH HE REMAINED AT THE INTERNMENT CAMP IN UPPER AUSTRIA...

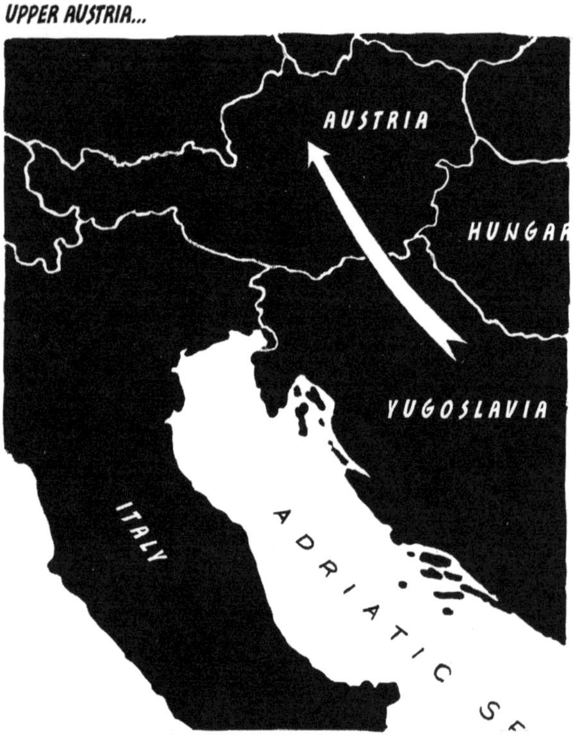
AUSTRIA
HUNGAR
YUGOSLAVIA
ITALY
ADRIATIC SE

CONCURRENTLY WITH NIKOLA KAVAJA, AN EXILED MILITARY OFFI
MUCH LIKE HIMSELF, WITH A SIMILAR BONE TO PICK. THIS MEETIN
WAS TO INFLUENCE MY FATHER POLITICALLY AND IDEOLOGICALLY MORE THAN ANY OTHER BEFORE.

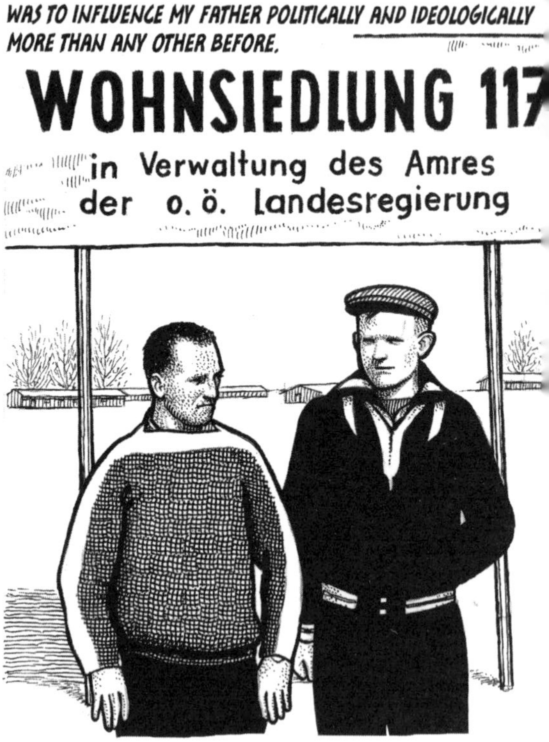
WOHNSIEDLUNG 117
in Verwaltung des Amres
der o. ö. Landesregierung

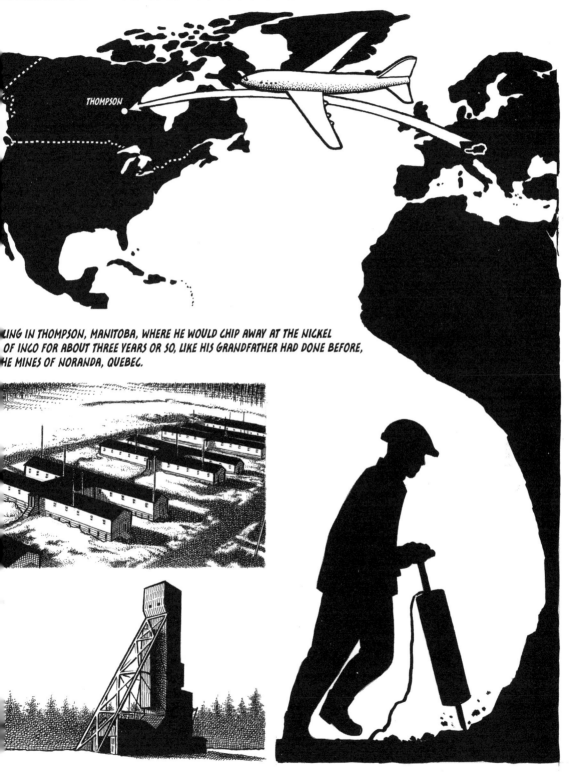

...HE EARLY SPRING OF 1959 HE MADE THE TRANSATLANTIC JOURNEY TO CANADA...

THOMPSON

...LING IN THOMPSON, MANITOBA, WHERE HE WOULD CHIP AWAY AT THE NICKEL
...OF INCO FOR ABOUT THREE YEARS OR SO, LIKE HIS GRANDFATHER HAD DONE BEFORE,
...HE MINES OF NORANDA, QUEBEC.

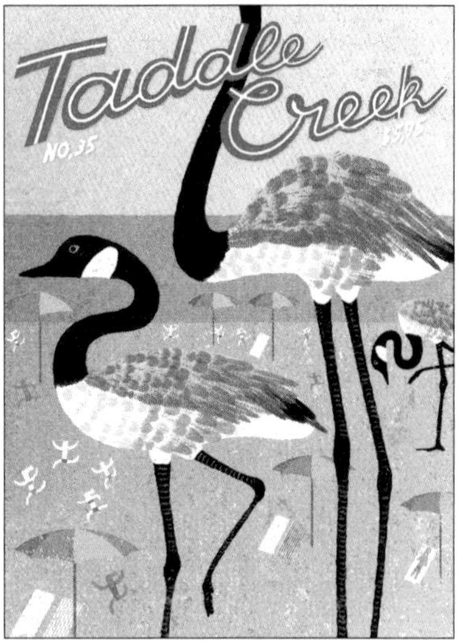
Taddle Creek
NO. 35

# mom

## DAVE LAPP

*originally published in*

Taddle Creek, vol. XVII, no. 2

VITALIS PUBLISHING

8 × 10.75 inches • 22 pages

### Biography

Dave Lapp is a teacher and cartoonist living in Toronto, Canada. He has been doing some form of alternative comics for over two decades. Dave's first graphic novel, *Drop-In* (Conundrum Press), is a collection of stories about his work as an art teacher in one of Canada's poorest neighborhoods. *Drop-In* received "best book" nominations from the Ignatz and Doug Wright awards. Dave's second book is *Children of the Atom* (Conundrum), a collection of 240 strange, sweet, sorrowful, philosophical strips featuring Franklin-Boy and Jim-Jam Girl. His most recent book, *People Around Here* (Conundrum), was released in 2012. *People Around Here* collects a decade's worth of cartoons developed from observations of people and places in Toronto. Dave is currently working on a five-hundred-page graphic novel collecting stories from when he was a child. davelappcomics.blogspot.ca

### Statement

Mom was dying and for the first time in my life I was going to miss a deadline. But mom died sooner than we thought. God, I was sad, but I didn't want to break the streak. With sheer ferocity against that damned thing that wanted me to give up, I forced this page out. I wanted all the agonizing memories out. So now they're out, now time's passed, now there's peace. My gosh, once you share your story with others and they share theirs, well, that's what it's all about. Thanks to Conan Tobias for allowing me such freedom.

# mom

dave lapp

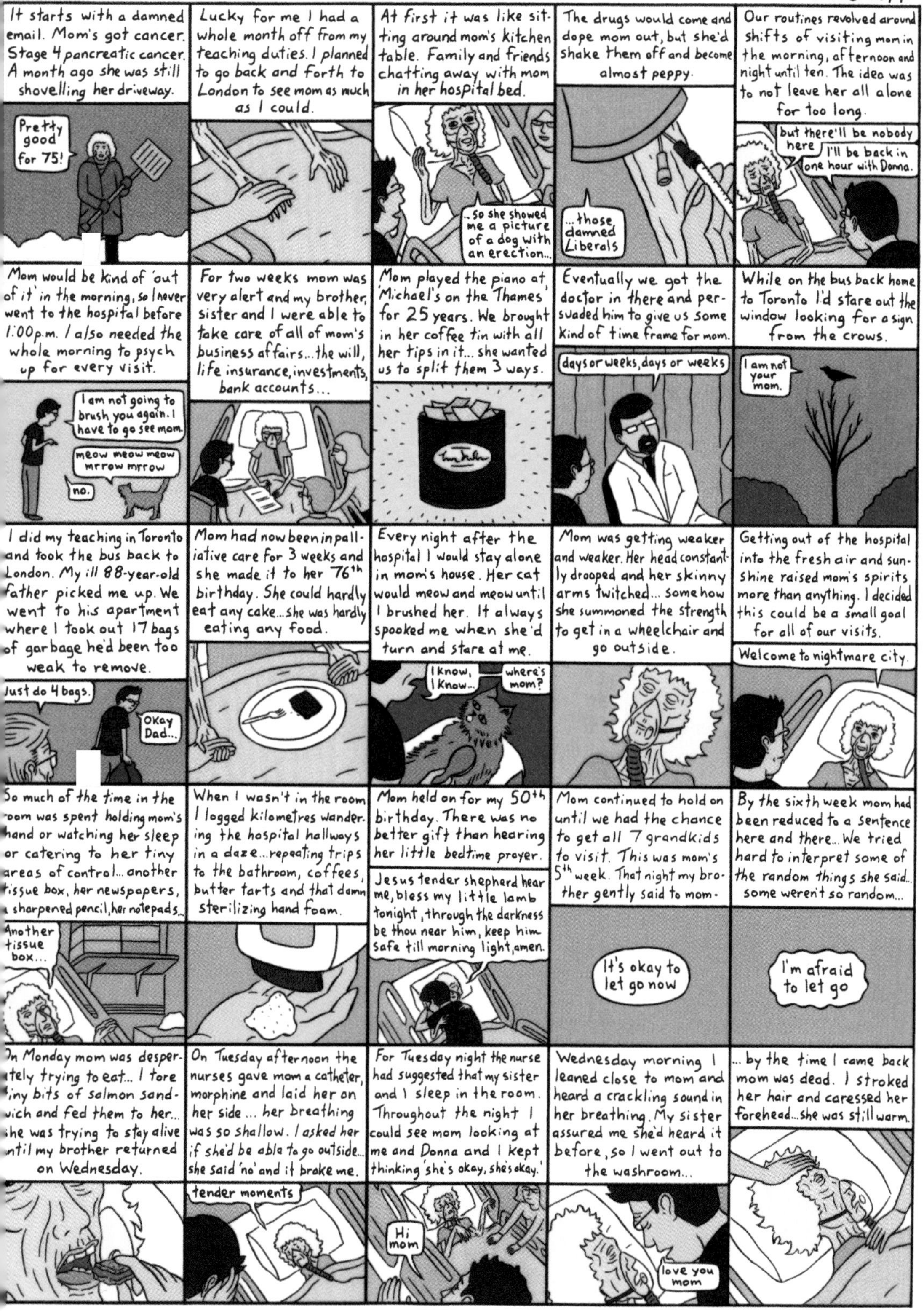

It starts with a damned email. Mom's got cancer. Stage 4 pancreatic cancer. A month ago she was still shovelling her driveway.
Pretty good for 75!
Lucky for me I had a whole month off from my teaching duties. I planned to go back and forth to London to see mom as much as I could.
At first it was like sitting around mom's kitchen table. Family and friends chatting away with mom in her hospital bed.
...so she showed me a picture of a dog with an erection...
The drugs would come and dope mom out, but she'd shake them off and become almost peppy.
...those damned Liberals
Our routines revolved around shifts of visiting mom in the morning, afternoon and night until ten. The idea was to not leave her all alone for too long.
but there'll be nobody here
I'll be back in one hour with Donna.
Mom would be kind of 'out of it' in the morning, so I never went to the hospital before 1:00 p.m. I also needed the whole morning to psych up for every visit.
I am not going to brush you again. I have to go see mom.
meow meow meow mrrow mrrow
no.
For two weeks mom was very alert and my brother, sister and I were able to take care of all of mom's business affairs... the will, life insurance, investments, bank accounts...
Mom played the piano at 'Michael's on the Thames' for 25 years. We brought in her coffee tin with all her tips in it... she wanted us to split them 3 ways.
Eventually we got the doctor in there and persuaded him to give us some kind of time frame for mom.
days or weeks, days or weeks
While on the bus back home to Toronto I'd stare out the window looking for a sign from the crows.
I am not your mom.
I did my teaching in Toronto and took the bus back to London. My ill 88-year-old father picked me up. We went to his apartment where I took out 17 bags of garbage he'd been too weak to remove.
Just do 4 bags.
Okay Dad...
Mom had now been in palliative care for 3 weeks and she made it to her 76th birthday. She could hardly eat any cake... she was hardly eating any food.
Every night after the hospital I would stay alone in mom's house. Her cat would meow and meow until I brushed her. It always spooked me when she'd turn and stare at me.
I know, I know...
where's mom?
Mom was getting weaker and weaker. Her head constantly drooped and her skinny arms twitched... somehow she summoned the strength to get in a wheelchair and go outside.
Getting out of the hospital into the fresh air and sunshine raised mom's spirits more than anything. I decided this could be a small goal for all of our visits.
Welcome to nightmare city.
So much of the time in the room was spent holding mom's hand or watching her sleep or catering to her tiny areas of control... another tissue box, her newspapers, a sharpened pencil, her notepads...
Another tissue box...
When I wasn't in the room I logged kilometres wandering the hospital hallways in a daze... repeating trips to the bathroom, coffees, butter tarts and that damn sterilizing hand foam.
Mom held on for my 50th birthday. There was no better gift than hearing her little bedtime prayer.
Jesus tender shepherd hear me, bless my little lamb tonight, through the darkness be thou near him, keep him safe till morning light, amen.
Mom continued to hold on until we had the chance to get all 7 grandkids to visit. This was mom's 5th week. That night my brother gently said to mom-
It's okay to let go now
By the sixth week mom had been reduced to a sentence here and there... We tried hard to interpret some of the random things she said... some weren't so random...
I'm afraid to let go
On Monday mom was desperately trying to eat... I tore tiny bits of salmon sandwich and fed them to her... she was trying to stay alive until my brother returned on Wednesday.
On Tuesday afternoon the nurses gave mom a catheter, morphine and laid her on her side... her breathing was so shallow. I asked her if she'd be able to go outside... she said 'no' and it broke me.
tender moments
For Tuesday night the nurse had suggested that my sister and I sleep in the room. Throughout the night I could see mom looking at me and Donna and I kept thinking 'she's okay, she's okay.'
Hi mom
Wednesday morning I leaned close to mom and heard a crackling sound in her breathing. My sister assured me she'd heard it before, so I went out to the washroom...
love you mom
... by the time I came back mom was dead. I stroked her hair and caressed her forehead... she was still warm.

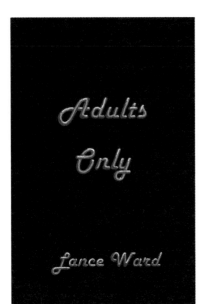

# Adults Only (*Excerpt*)

## LANCE WARD

*excerpted from*

## Adults Only
SELF-PUBLISHED
6 × 9 inches  •  86 pages

## Biography

Lance Ward refuses to let his mental illness define him. He is a Minnesota cartoonist and the creator of such books as *Stovetop* and the *A-Hole!* comics series. His graphic novel *Kmart Shoes* was nominated for a 2013 Minnesota Book Award. He is also an accomplished painter and a member of the International Cartoonist Conspiracy. tatertotdiaperman.wordpress.com

## Statement

I don't pre-draw any of the panels. I can't with this subject matter. I grab a blank sheet of custom frames and dive right in with the ink pen. I have to get it out. I time-travel back to the events, reliving the emotions and mistakes. It's a mind purge, so I don't have to think about it anymore. These particular pages, this comic, this confession, were the hardest to create.

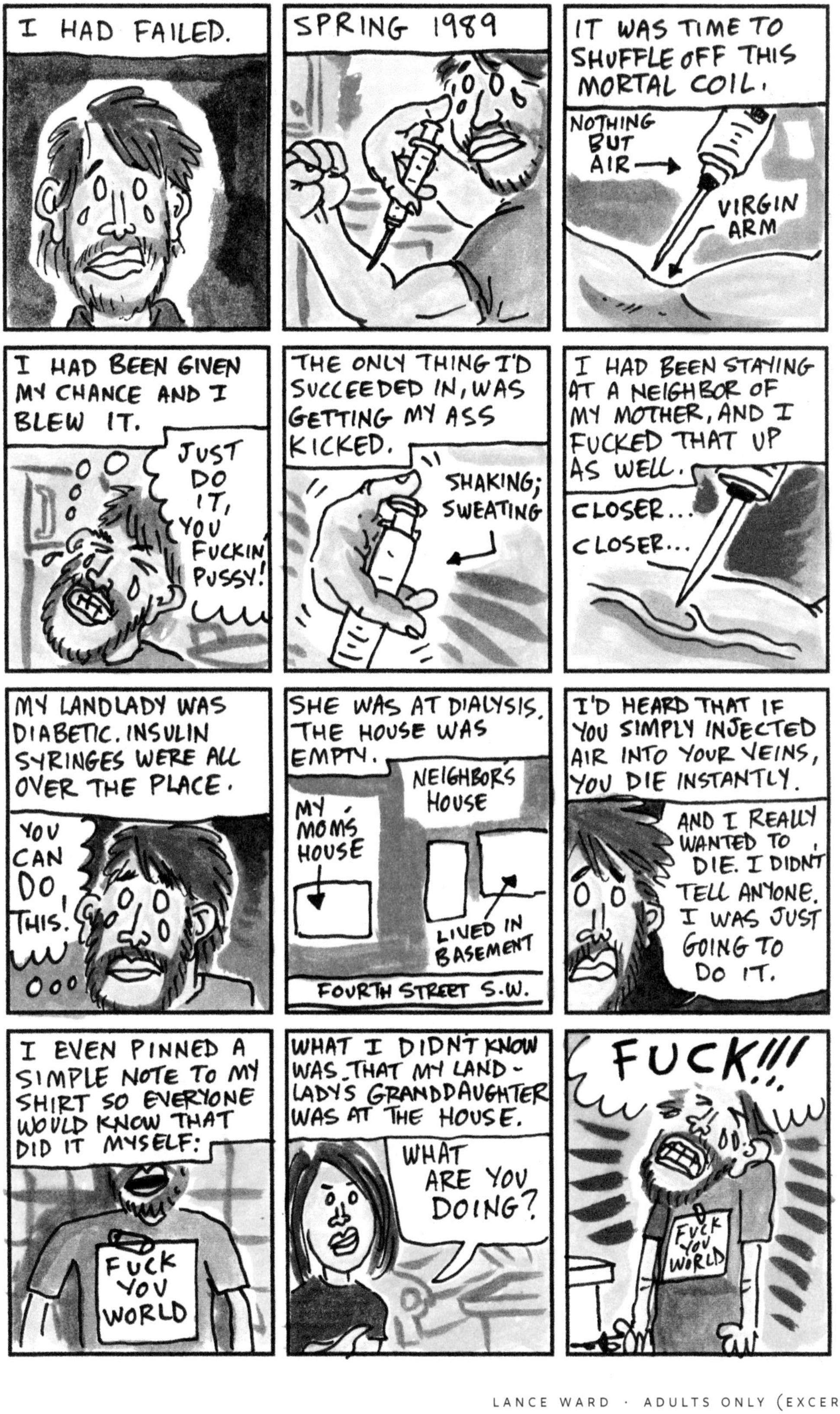
I HAD FAILED.
SPRING 1989
IT WAS TIME TO SHUFFLE OFF THIS MORTAL COIL.
NOTHING BUT AIR
VIRGIN ARM
I HAD BEEN GIVEN MY CHANCE AND I BLEW IT.
JUST DO IT, YOU FUCKIN' PUSSY!
THE ONLY THING I'D SUCCEEDED IN, WAS GETTING MY ASS KICKED.
SHAKING; SWEATING
I HAD BEEN STAYING AT A NEIGHBOR OF MY MOTHER, AND I FUCKED THAT UP AS WELL.
CLOSER...
CLOSER...
MY LANDLADY WAS DIABETIC. INSULIN SYRINGES WERE ALL OVER THE PLACE.
YOU CAN DO THIS!
SHE WAS AT DIALYSIS. THE HOUSE WAS EMPTY.
NEIGHBOR'S HOUSE
MY MOM'S HOUSE
LIVED IN BASEMENT
FOURTH STREET S.W.
I'D HEARD THAT IF YOU SIMPLY INJECTED AIR INTO YOUR VEINS, YOU DIE INSTANTLY.
AND I REALLY WANTED TO DIE. I DIDN'T TELL ANYONE. I WAS JUST GOING TO DO IT.
I EVEN PINNED A SIMPLE NOTE TO MY SHIRT SO EVERYONE WOULD KNOW THAT DID IT MYSELF:
FUCK YOU WORLD
WHAT I DIDN'T KNOW WAS THAT MY LANDLADY'S GRANDDAUGHTER WAS AT THE HOUSE.
WHAT ARE YOU DOING?
FUCK!!!
FUCK YOU WORLD

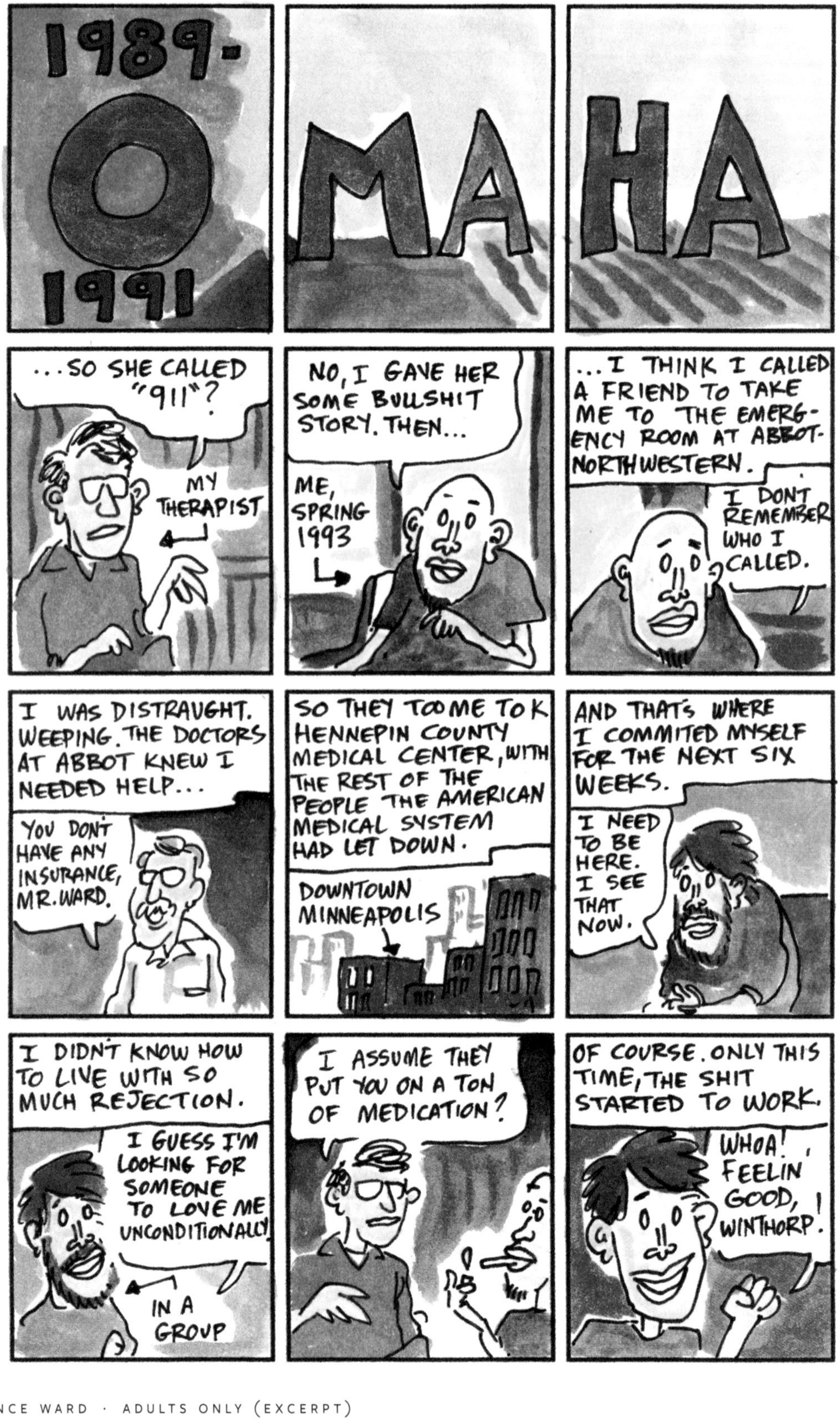
1989-
OMAHA
1991
...SO SHE CALLED "911"?
MY THERAPIST
NO, I GAVE HER SOME BULLSHIT STORY. THEN...
ME, SPRING 1993
...I THINK I CALLED A FRIEND TO TAKE ME TO THE EMERGENCY ROOM AT ABBOT-NORTHWESTERN.
I DONT REMEMBER WHO I CALLED.
I WAS DISTRAUGHT. WEEPING. THE DOCTORS AT ABBOT KNEW I NEEDED HELP...
YOU DON'T HAVE ANY INSURANCE, MR. WARD.
SO THEY TOOK ME TO HENNEPIN COUNTY MEDICAL CENTER, WITH THE REST OF THE PEOPLE THE AMERICAN MEDICAL SYSTEM HAD LET DOWN.
DOWNTOWN MINNEAPOLIS
AND THAT'S WHERE I COMMITED MYSELF FOR THE NEXT SIX WEEKS.
I NEED TO BE HERE. I SEE THAT NOW.
I DIDN'T KNOW HOW TO LIVE WITH SO MUCH REJECTION.
I GUESS I'M LOOKING FOR SOMEONE TO LOVE ME UNCONDITIONALLY!
IN A GROUP
I ASSUME THEY PUT YOU ON A TON OF MEDICATION?
OF COURSE. ONLY THIS TIME, THE SHIT STARTED TO WORK.
WHOA! FEELIN' GOOD, WINTHORP!

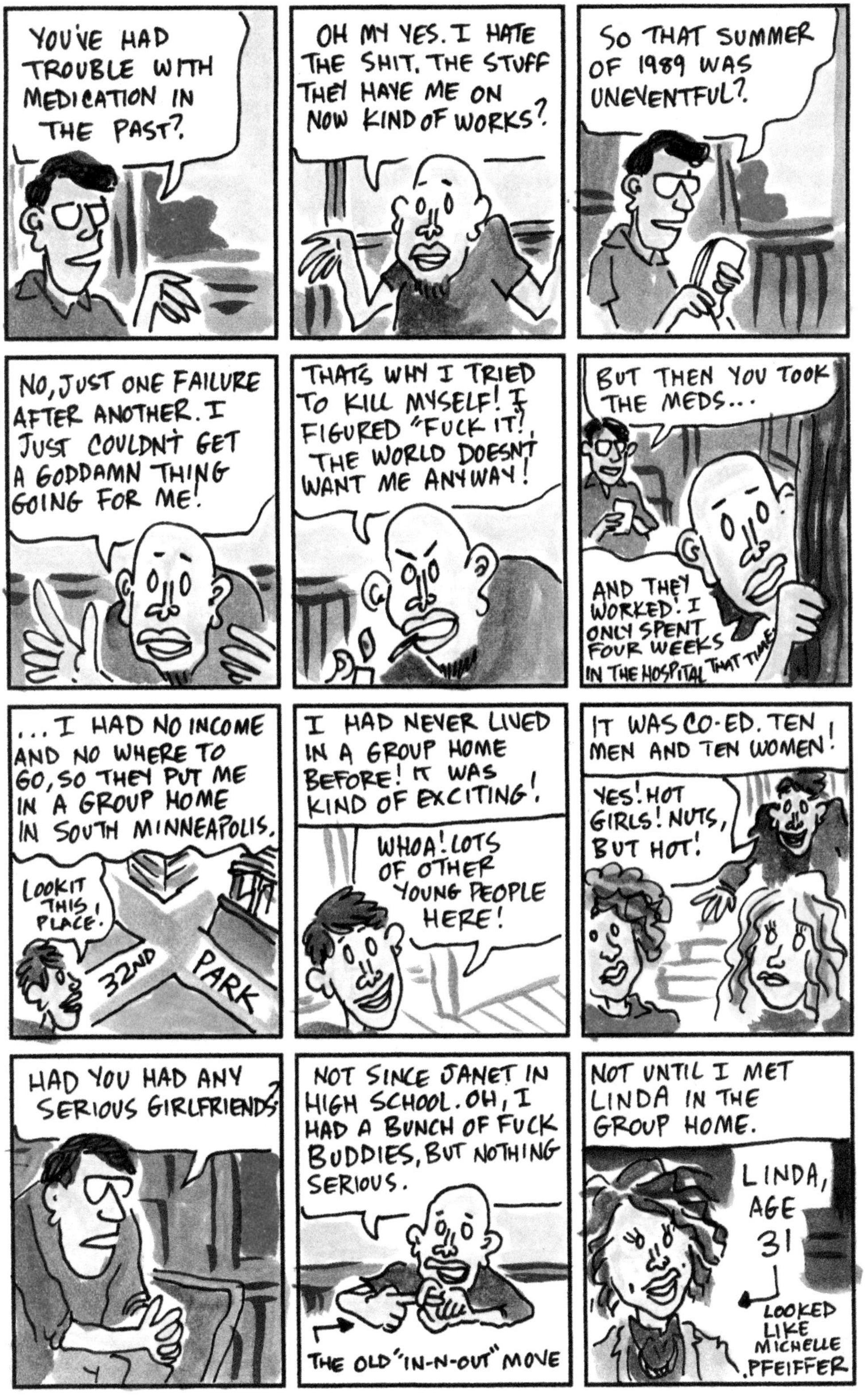
YOU'VE HAD TROUBLE WITH MEDICATION IN THE PAST?
OH MY YES. I HATE THE SHIT. THE STUFF THEY HAVE ME ON NOW KIND OF WORKS?
SO THAT SUMMER OF 1989 WAS UNEVENTFUL?
NO, JUST ONE FAILURE AFTER ANOTHER. I JUST COULDN'T GET A GODDAMN THING GOING FOR ME!
THATS WHY I TRIED TO KILL MYSELF! I FIGURED "FUCK IT!, THE WORLD DOESN'T WANT ME ANYWAY!
BUT THEN YOU TOOK THE MEDS...
AND THEY WORKED! I ONLY SPENT FOUR WEEKS IN THE HOSPITAL THAT TIME.
...I HAD NO INCOME AND NO WHERE TO GO, SO THEY PUT ME IN A GROUP HOME IN SOUTH MINNEAPOLIS.
LOOKIT THIS PLACE!
32ND
PARK
I HAD NEVER LIVED IN A GROUP HOME BEFORE! IT WAS KIND OF EXCITING!
WHOA! LOTS OF OTHER YOUNG PEOPLE HERE!
IT WAS CO-ED. TEN MEN AND TEN WOMEN!
YES! HOT GIRLS! NUTS, BUT HOT!
HAD YOU HAD ANY SERIOUS GIRLFRIENDS?
NOT SINCE JANET IN HIGH SCHOOL. OH, I HAD A BUNCH OF FUCK BUDDIES, BUT NOTHING SERIOUS.
THE OLD "IN-N-OUT" MOVE
NOT UNTIL I MET LINDA IN THE GROUP HOME.
LINDA, AGE 31
LOOKED LIKE MICHELLE PFEIFFER

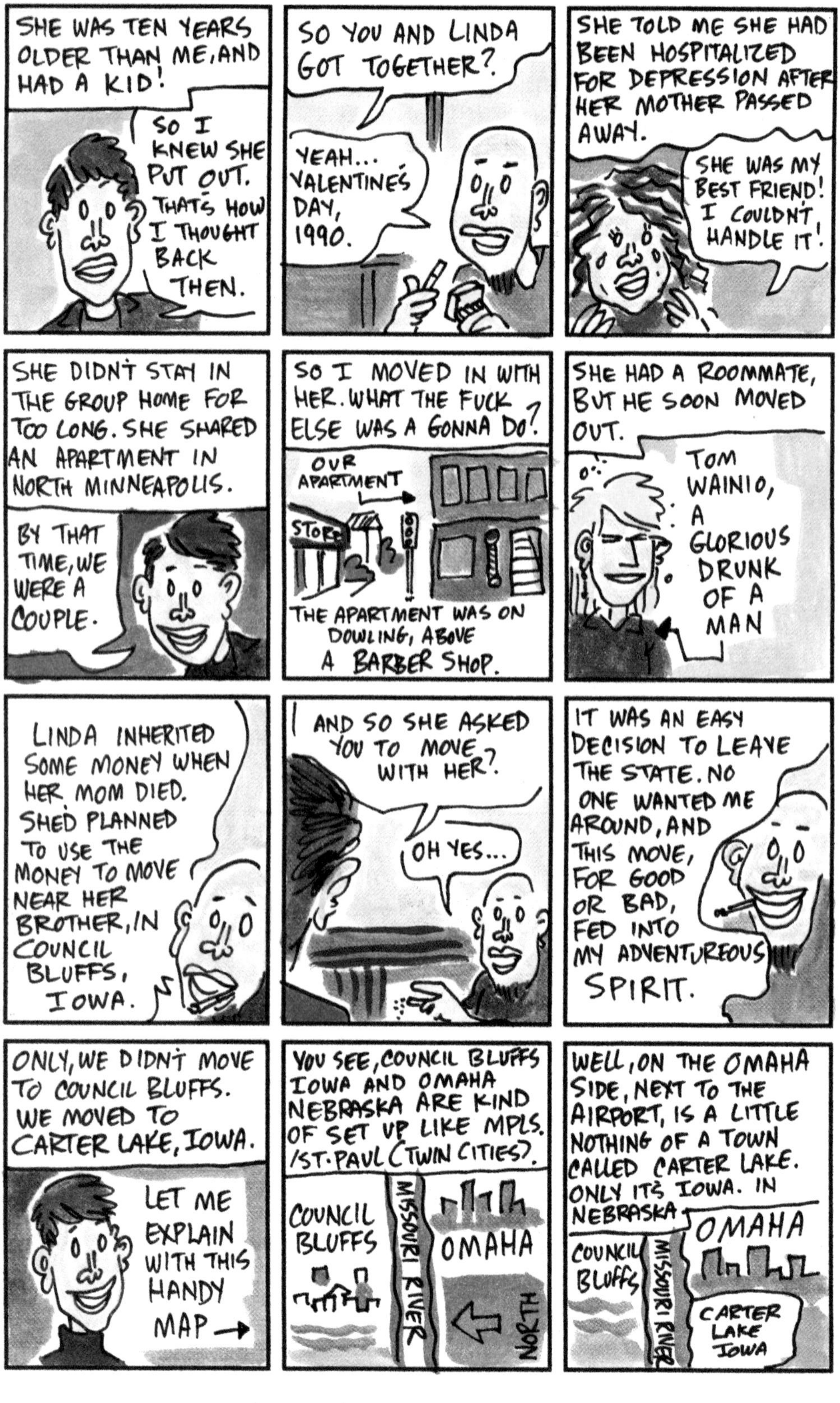
SHE WAS TEN YEARS OLDER THAN ME, AND HAD A KID!
SO I KNEW SHE PUT OUT. THAT'S HOW I THOUGHT BACK THEN.
SO YOU AND LINDA GOT TOGETHER?
YEAH... VALENTINE'S DAY, 1990.
SHE TOLD ME SHE HAD BEEN HOSPITALIZED FOR DEPRESSION AFTER HER MOTHER PASSED AWAY.
SHE WAS MY BEST FRIEND! I COULDN'T HANDLE IT!
SHE DIDN'T STAY IN THE GROUP HOME FOR TOO LONG. SHE SHARED AN APARTMENT IN NORTH MINNEAPOLIS.
BY THAT TIME, WE WERE A COUPLE.
SO I MOVED IN WITH HER. WHAT THE FUCK ELSE WAS A GONNA DO?
OUR APARTMENT
STORE
THE APARTMENT WAS ON DOWLING, ABOVE A BARBER SHOP.
SHE HAD A ROOMMATE, BUT HE SOON MOVED OUT.
TOM WAINIO, A GLORIOUS DRUNK OF A MAN
LINDA INHERITED SOME MONEY WHEN HER MOM DIED. SHE'D PLANNED TO USE THE MONEY TO MOVE NEAR HER BROTHER, IN COUNCIL BLUFFS, IOWA.
AND SO SHE ASKED YOU TO MOVE WITH HER?
OH YES...
IT WAS AN EASY DECISION TO LEAVE THE STATE. NO ONE WANTED ME AROUND, AND THIS MOVE, FOR GOOD OR BAD, FED INTO MY ADVENTUREOUS SPIRIT.
ONLY, WE DIDN'T MOVE TO COUNCIL BLUFFS. WE MOVED TO CARTER LAKE, IOWA.
LET ME EXPLAIN WITH THIS HANDY MAP
YOU SEE, COUNCIL BLUFFS IOWA AND OMAHA NEBRASKA ARE KIND OF SET UP LIKE MPLS./ST. PAUL (TWIN CITIES).
COUNCIL BLUFFS
MISSOURI RIVER
OMAHA
NORTH
WELL, ON THE OMAHA SIDE, NEXT TO THE AIRPORT, IS A LITTLE NOTHING OF A TOWN CALLED CARTER LAKE. ONLY IT'S IOWA. IN NEBRASKA.
OMAHA
COUNCIL BLUFFS
MISSOURI RIVER
CARTER LAKE IOWA

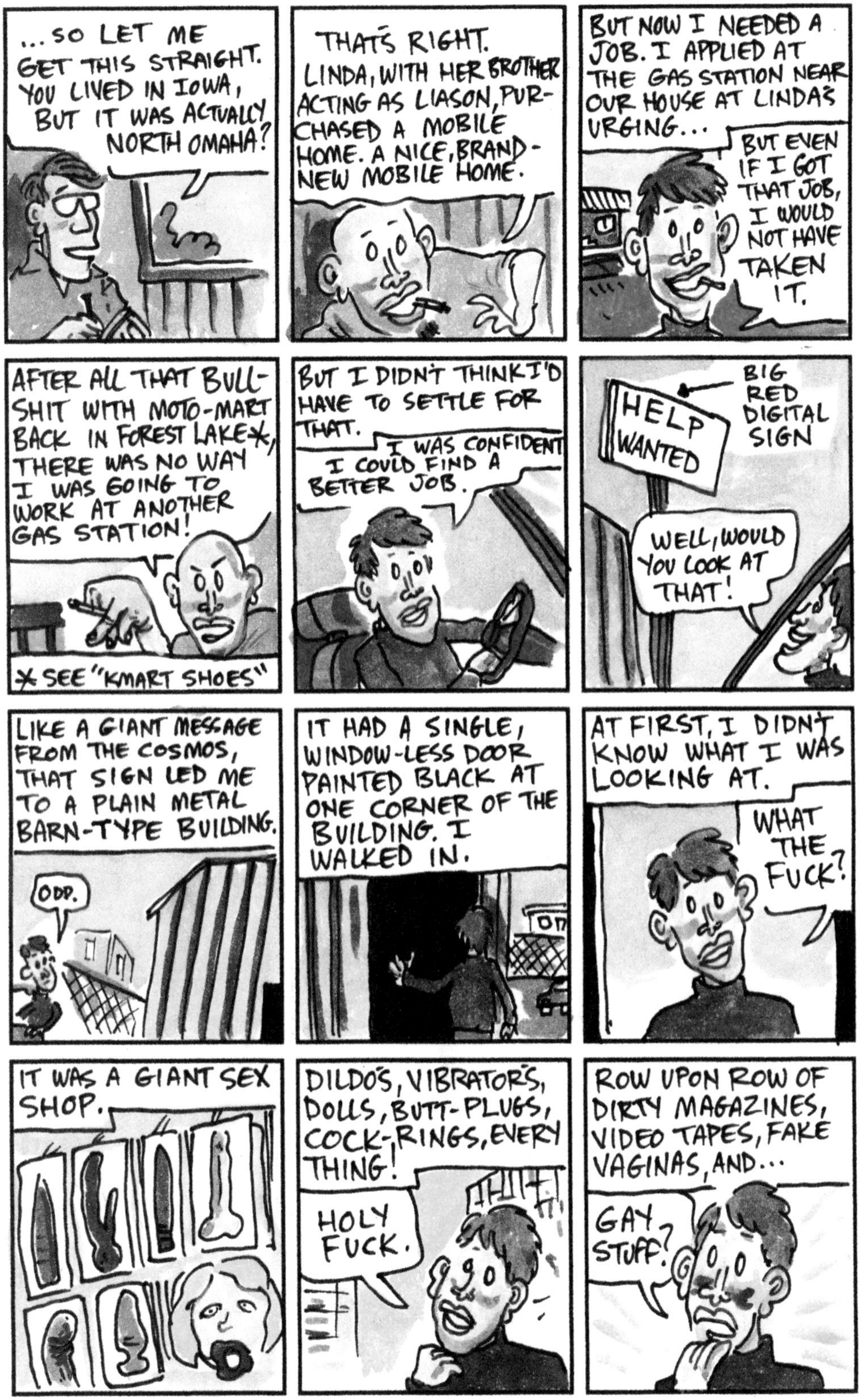
...SO LET ME GET THIS STRAIGHT. YOU LIVED IN IOWA, BUT IT WAS ACTUALLY NORTH OMAHA?
THAT'S RIGHT. LINDA, WITH HER BROTHER ACTING AS LIASON, PURCHASED A MOBILE HOME. A NICE, BRAND-NEW MOBILE HOME.
BUT NOW I NEEDED A JOB. I APPLIED AT THE GAS STATION NEAR OUR HOUSE AT LINDA'S URGING...
BUT EVEN IF I GOT THAT JOB, I WOULD NOT HAVE TAKEN IT.
AFTER ALL THAT BULLSHIT WITH MOTO-MART BACK IN FOREST LAKE*, THERE WAS NO WAY I WAS GOING TO WORK AT ANOTHER GAS STATION!
* SEE "KMART SHOES"
BUT I DIDN'T THINK I'D HAVE TO SETTLE FOR THAT.
I WAS CONFIDENT I COULD FIND A BETTER JOB.
HELP WANTED
BIG RED DIGITAL SIGN
WELL, WOULD YOU LOOK AT THAT!
LIKE A GIANT MESSAGE FROM THE COSMOS, THAT SIGN LED ME TO A PLAIN METAL BARN-TYPE BUILDING.
ODD.
IT HAD A SINGLE, WINDOW-LESS DOOR PAINTED BLACK AT ONE CORNER OF THE BUILDING. I WALKED IN.
AT FIRST, I DIDN'T KNOW WHAT I WAS LOOKING AT.
WHAT THE FUCK?
IT WAS A GIANT SEX SHOP.
DILDO'S, VIBRATOR'S, DOLLS, BUTT-PLUGS, COCK-RINGS, EVERY THING!
HOLY FUCK.
ROW UPON ROW OF DIRTY MAGAZINES, VIDEO TAPES, FAKE VAGINAS, AND...
GAY STUFF?

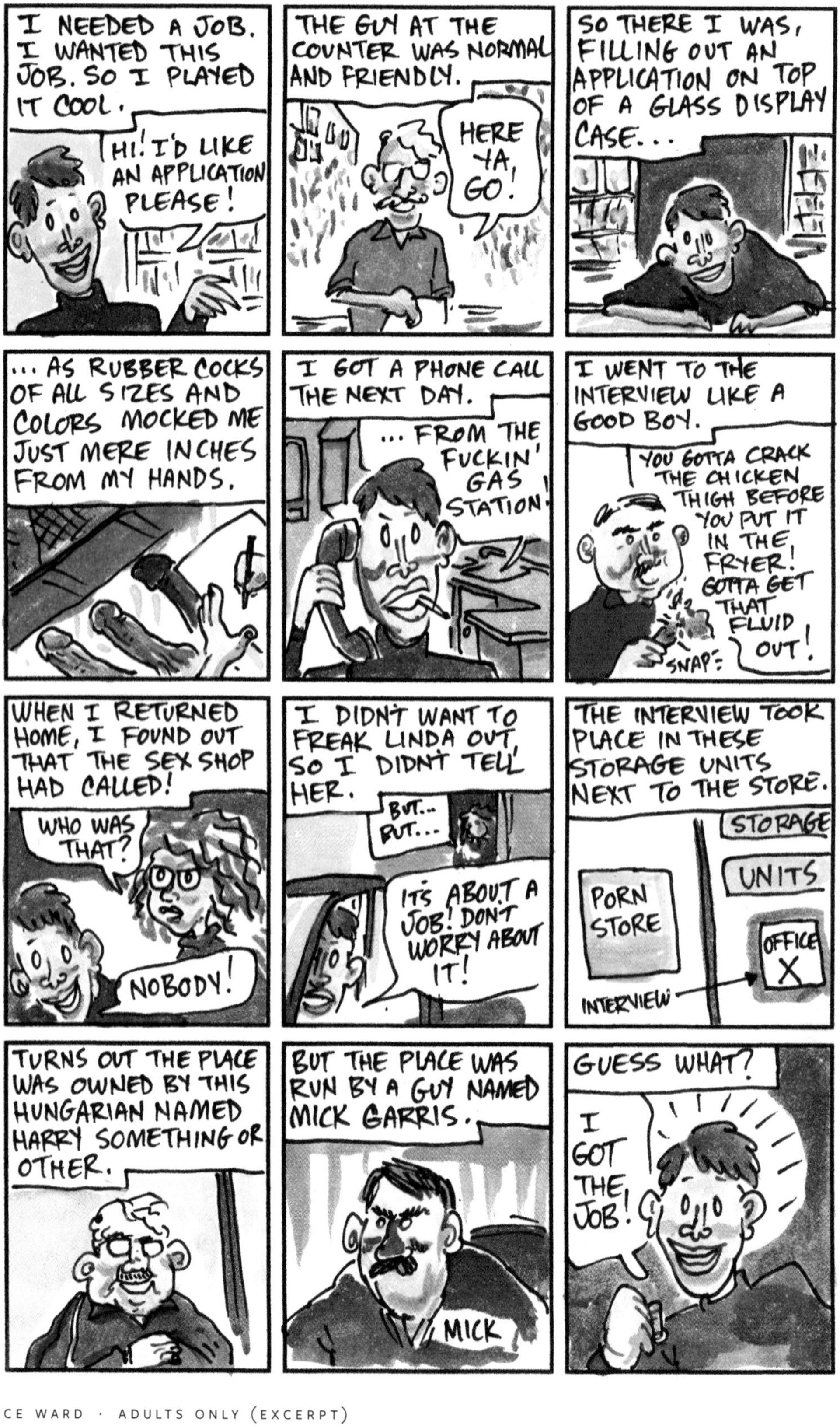
I NEEDED A JOB. I WANTED THIS JOB. SO I PLAYED IT COOL.
HI! I'D LIKE AN APPLICATION PLEASE!
THE GUY AT THE COUNTER WAS NORMAL AND FRIENDLY.
HERE YA, GO!
SO THERE I WAS, FILLING OUT AN APPLICATION ON TOP OF A GLASS DISPLAY CASE...
...AS RUBBER COCKS OF ALL SIZES AND COLORS MOCKED ME JUST MERE INCHES FROM MY HANDS.
I GOT A PHONE CALL THE NEXT DAY.
...FROM THE FUCKIN' GAS STATION!
I WENT TO THE INTERVIEW LIKE A GOOD BOY.
YOU GOTTA CRACK THE CHICKEN THIGH BEFORE YOU PUT IT IN THE FRYER! GOTTA GET THAT FLUID OUT!
SNAP
WHEN I RETURNED HOME, I FOUND OUT THAT THE SEX SHOP HAD CALLED!
WHO WAS THAT?
NOBODY!
I DIDN'T WANT TO FREAK LINDA OUT, SO I DIDN'T TELL HER.
BUT... BUT...
IT'S ABOUT A JOB! DON'T WORRY ABOUT IT!
THE INTERVIEW TOOK PLACE IN THESE STORAGE UNITS NEXT TO THE STORE.
STORAGE
UNITS
PORN STORE
OFFICE X
INTERVIEW
TURNS OUT THE PLACE WAS OWNED BY THIS HUNGARIAN NAMED HARRY SOMETHING OR OTHER.
BUT THE PLACE WAS RUN BY A GUY NAMED MICK GARRIS.
MICK
GUESS WHAT?
I GOT THE JOB!

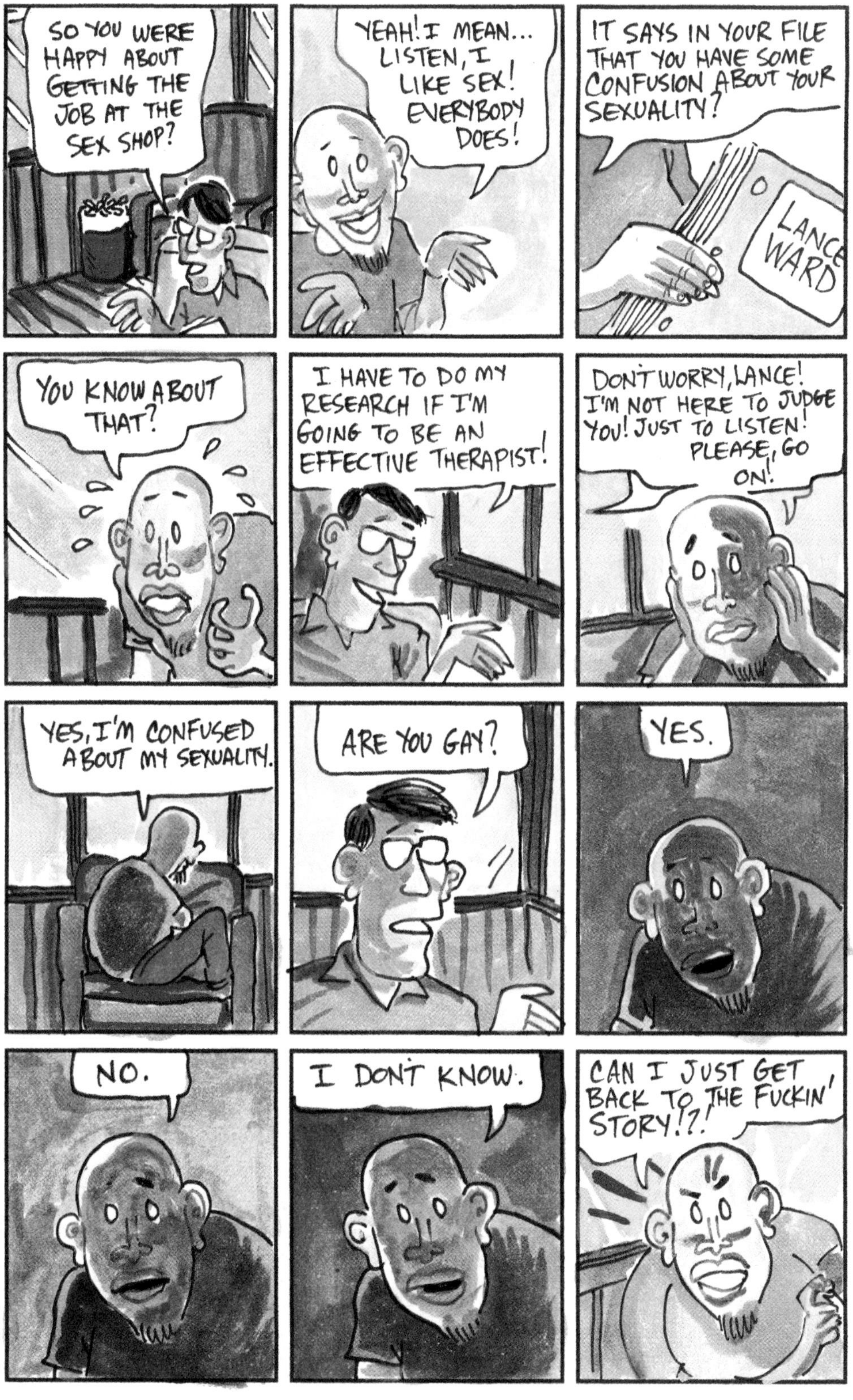
SO YOU WERE HAPPY ABOUT GETTING THE JOB AT THE SEX SHOP?
YEAH! I MEAN... LISTEN, I LIKE SEX! EVERYBODY DOES!
IT SAYS IN YOUR FILE THAT YOU HAVE SOME CONFUSION ABOUT YOUR SEXUALITY?
LANCE WARD
YOU KNOW ABOUT THAT?
I HAVE TO DO MY RESEARCH IF I'M GOING TO BE AN EFFECTIVE THERAPIST!
DON'T WORRY, LANCE! I'M NOT HERE TO JUDGE YOU! JUST TO LISTEN! PLEASE, GO ON!
YES, I'M CONFUSED ABOUT MY SEXUALITY.
ARE YOU GAY?
YES.
NO.
I DON'T KNOW.
CAN I JUST GET BACK TO THE FUCKIN' STORY!?!

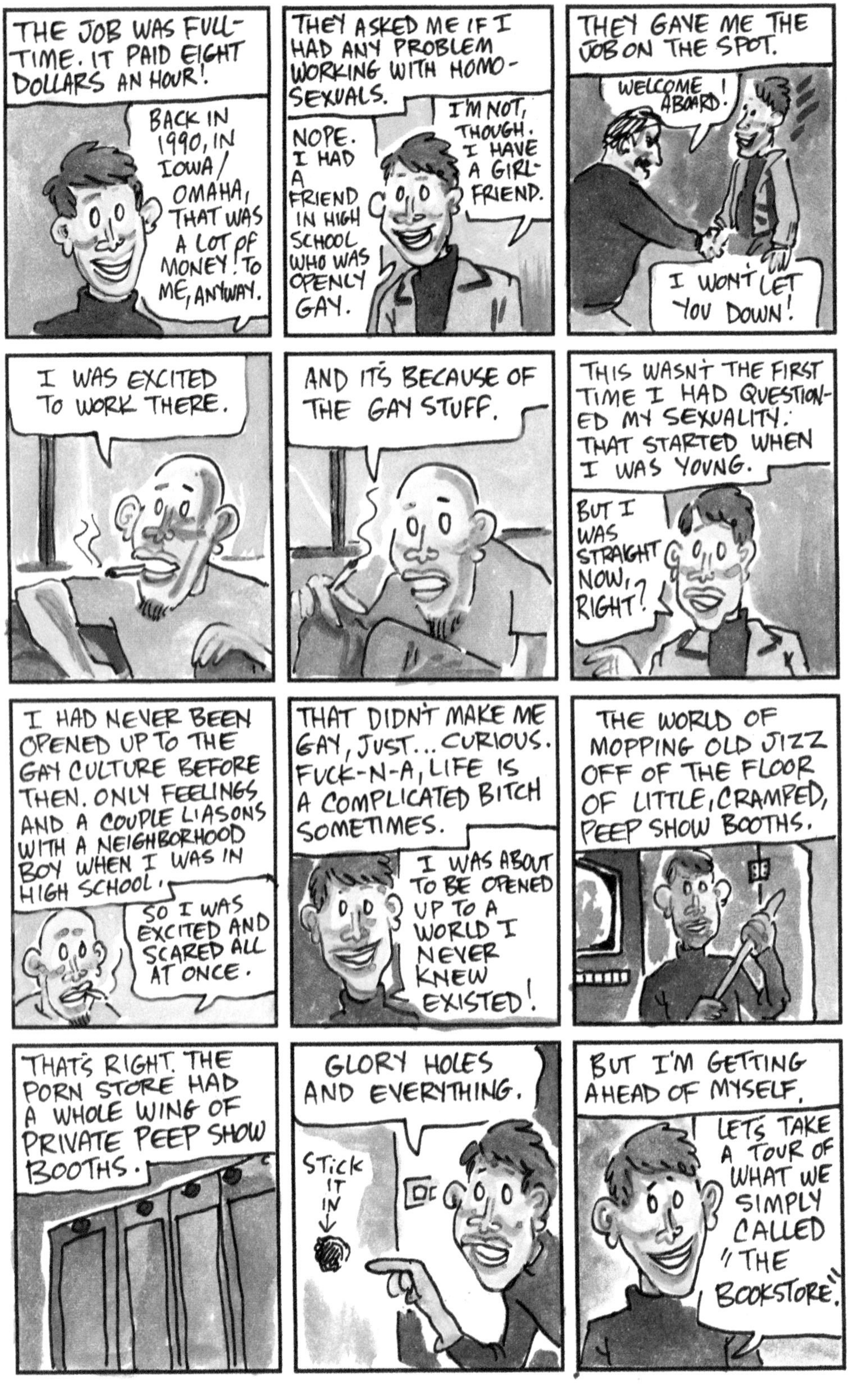

THE JOB WAS FULL-TIME. IT PAID EIGHT DOLLARS AN HOUR!
BACK IN 1990, IN IOWA/OMAHA, THAT WAS A LOT OF MONEY! TO ME, ANYWAY.
THEY ASKED ME IF I HAD ANY PROBLEM WORKING WITH HOMO-SEXUALS.
NOPE. I HAD A FRIEND IN HIGH SCHOOL WHO WAS OPENLY GAY.
I'M NOT, THOUGH. I HAVE A GIRL-FRIEND.
THEY GAVE ME THE JOB ON THE SPOT.
WELCOME ABOARD!
I WON'T LET YOU DOWN!
I WAS EXCITED TO WORK THERE.
AND IT'S BECAUSE OF THE GAY STUFF.
THIS WASN'T THE FIRST TIME I HAD QUESTION-ED MY SEXUALITY. THAT STARTED WHEN I WAS YOUNG.
BUT I WAS STRAIGHT NOW, RIGHT?
I HAD NEVER BEEN OPENED UP TO THE GAY CULTURE BEFORE THEN. ONLY FEELINGS AND A COUPLE LIASONS WITH A NEIGHBORHOOD BOY WHEN I WAS IN HIGH SCHOOL.
SO I WAS EXCITED AND SCARED ALL AT ONCE.
THAT DIDN'T MAKE ME GAY, JUST... CURIOUS. FUCK-N-A, LIFE IS A COMPLICATED BITCH SOMETIMES.
I WAS ABOUT TO BE OPENED UP TO A WORLD I NEVER KNEW EXISTED!
THE WORLD OF MOPPING OLD JIZZ OFF OF THE FLOOR OF LITTLE, CRAMPED, PEEP SHOW BOOTHS.
THAT'S RIGHT. THE PORN STORE HAD A WHOLE WING OF PRIVATE PEEP SHOW BOOTHS.
GLORY HOLES AND EVERYTHING.
STICK IT IN
BUT I'M GETTING AHEAD OF MYSELF.
LET'S TAKE A TOUR OF WHAT WE SIMPLY CALLED "THE BOOKSTORE".

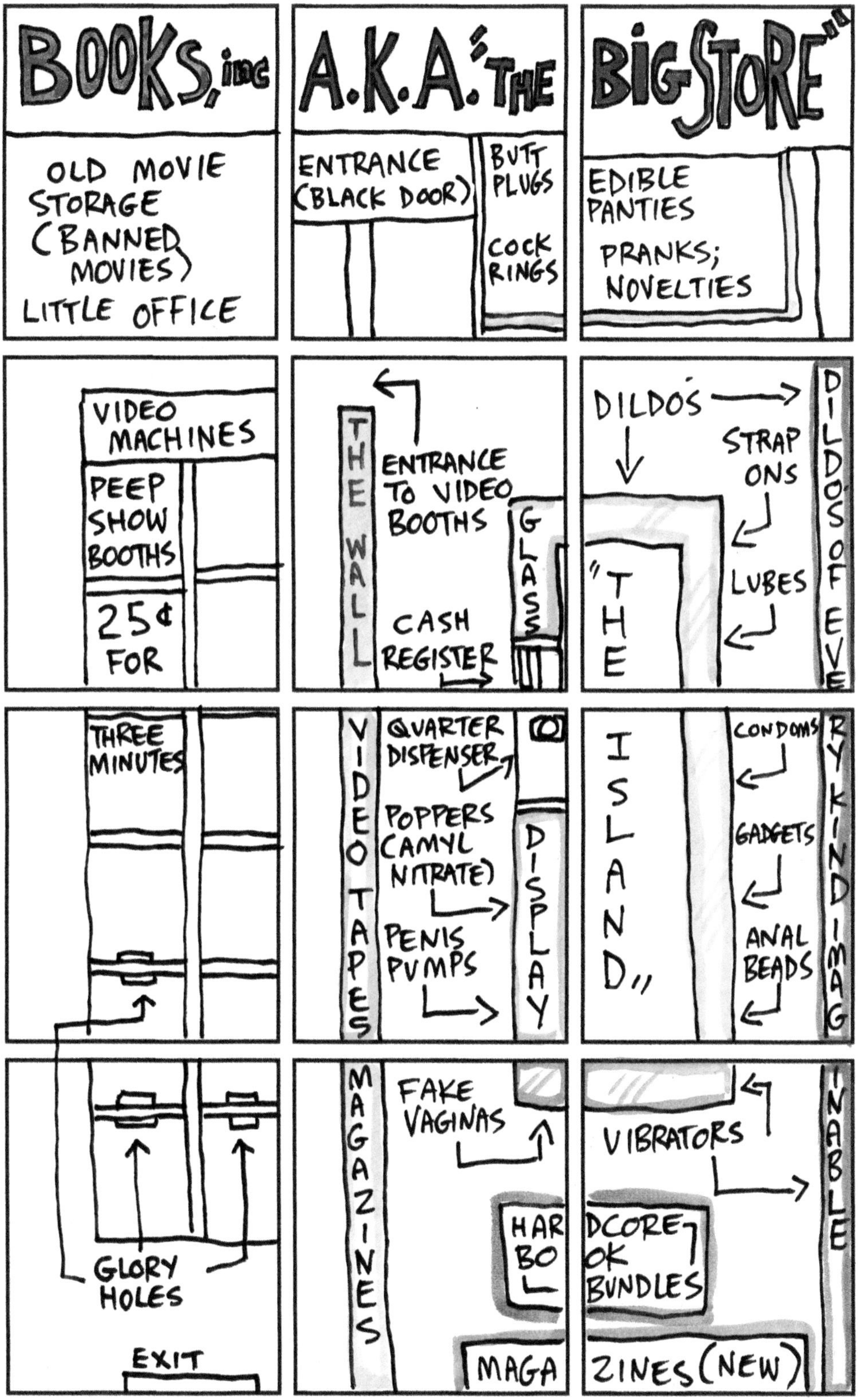
BOOKS, inc
A.K.A. "THE
BIG STORE"
OLD MOVIE STORAGE (BANNED MOVIES)
LITTLE OFFICE
ENTRANCE (BLACK DOOR)
BUTT PLUGS
COCK RINGS
EDIBLE PANTIES
PRANKS; NOVELTIES
VIDEO MACHINES
PEEP SHOW BOOTHS
25¢
FOR
THE WALL
ENTRANCE TO VIDEO BOOTHS
GLASS
CASH REGISTER
DILDOS
STRAP ONS
LUBES
DILDOS OF EVE
"THE
THREE MINUTES
VIDEO TAPES
QUARTER DISPENSER
POPPERS (AMYL NITRATE)
PENIS PUMPS
DISPLAY
ISLAND"
CONDOMS
GADGETS
ANAL BEADS
RY KIND IMAG
GLORY HOLES
EXIT
MAGAZINES
FAKE VAGINAS
HAR
BO
DCORE
OK BUNDLES
MAGA
ZINES (NEW)
VIBRATORS
INABLE

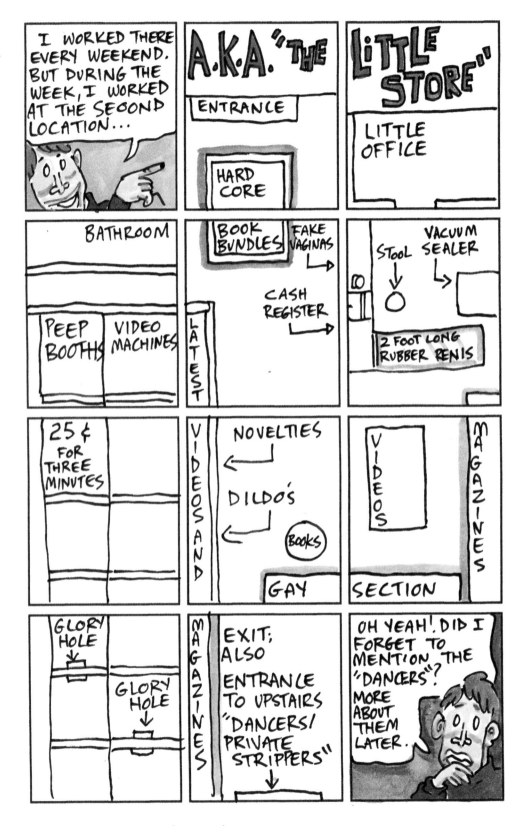

I WORKED THERE EVERY WEEKEND. BUT DURING THE WEEK, I WORKED AT THE SECOND LOCATION...

A.K.A. "THE

ENTRANCE

HARD CORE

LITTLE STORE"

LITTLE OFFICE

BATHROOM

PEEP BOOTHS | VIDEO MACHINES

BOOK BUNDLES | FAKE VAGINAS

LATEST

CASH REGISTER

VACUUM SEALER

STOOL

2 FOOT LONG RUBBER PENIS

25¢ FOR THREE MINUTES

VIDEOS AND

NOVELTIES

DILDO'S

BOOKS

GAY

VIDEOS

MAGAZINES

SECTION

GLORY HOLE

GLORY HOLE

MAGAZINES

EXIT; ALSO

ENTRANCE TO UPSTAIRS "DANCERS/ PRIVATE STRIPPERS"

OH YEAH! DID I FORGET TO MENTION THE "DANCERS"? MORE ABOUT THEM LATER.

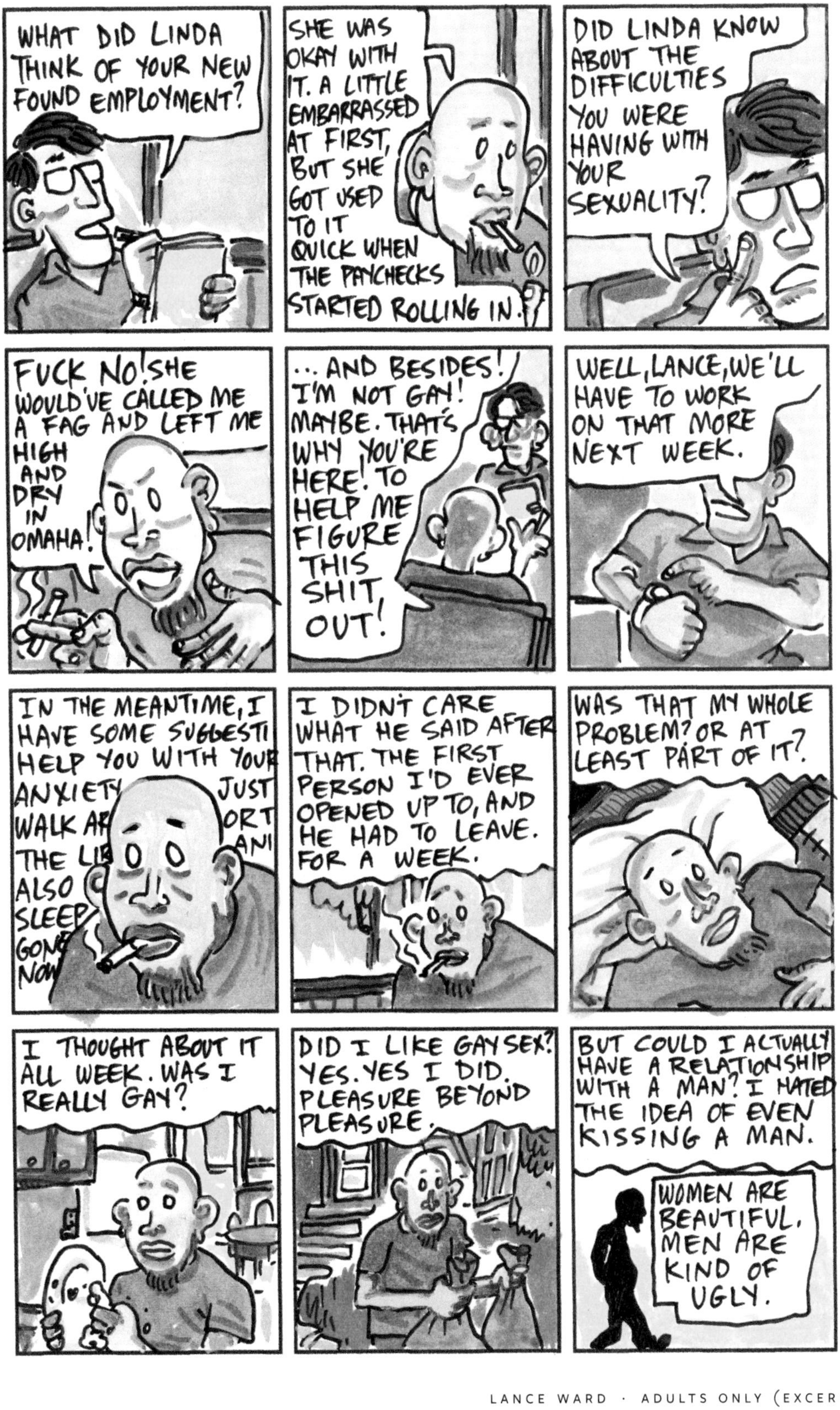
WHAT DID LINDA THINK OF YOUR NEW FOUND EMPLOYMENT?
SHE WAS OKAY WITH IT. A LITTLE EMBARRASSED AT FIRST, BUT SHE GOT USED TO IT QUICK WHEN THE PAYCHECKS STARTED ROLLING IN.
DID LINDA KNOW ABOUT THE DIFFICULTIES YOU WERE HAVING WITH YOUR SEXUALITY?
FUCK NO! SHE WOULD'VE CALLED ME A FAG AND LEFT ME HIGH AND DRY IN OMAHA!
...AND BESIDES! I'M NOT GAY! MAYBE. THAT'S WHY YOU'RE HERE! TO HELP ME FIGURE THIS SHIT OUT!
WELL, LANCE, WE'LL HAVE TO WORK ON THAT MORE NEXT WEEK.
IN THE MEANTIME, I HAVE SOME SUGGESTI HELP YOU WITH YOUR ANXIETY JUST WALK AR ORT THE LI ANI ALSO SLEEP GONE NOW
I DIDN'T CARE WHAT HE SAID AFTER THAT. THE FIRST PERSON I'D EVER OPENED UP TO, AND HE HAD TO LEAVE. FOR A WEEK.
WAS THAT MY WHOLE PROBLEM? OR AT LEAST PART OF IT?
I THOUGHT ABOUT IT ALL WEEK. WAS I REALLY GAY?
DID I LIKE GAY SEX? YES. YES I DID. PLEASURE BEYOND PLEASURE.
BUT COULD I ACTUALLY HAVE A RELATIONSHIP WITH A MAN? I HATED THE IDEA OF EVEN KISSING A MAN.
WOMEN ARE BEAUTIFUL, MEN ARE KIND OF UGLY.

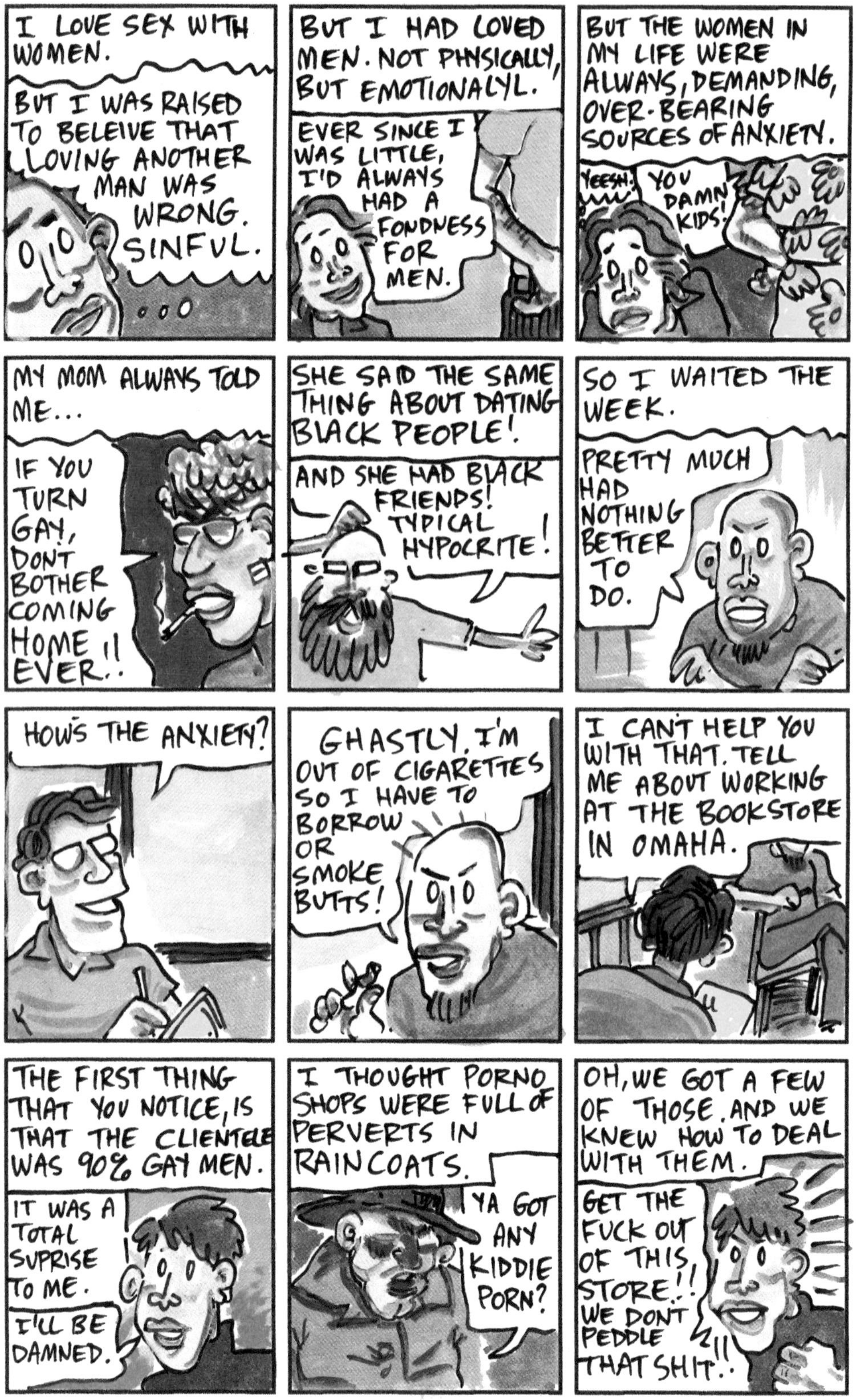
I LOVE SEX WITH WOMEN.
BUT I WAS RAISED TO BELEIVE THAT LOVING ANOTHER MAN WAS WRONG. SINFUL.
...
BUT I HAD LOVED MEN. NOT PHYSICALLY, BUT EMOTIONALYL.
EVER SINCE I WAS LITTLE, I'D ALWAYS HAD A FONDNESS FOR MEN.
BUT THE WOMEN IN MY LIFE WERE ALWAYS, DEMANDING, OVER-BEARING SOURCES OF ANXIETY.
YEESH!
YOU DAMN KIDS!
MY MOM ALWAYS TOLD ME...
IF YOU TURN GAY, DON'T BOTHER COMING HOME EVER!!
SHE SAID THE SAME THING ABOUT DATING BLACK PEOPLE!
AND SHE HAD BLACK FRIENDS! TYPICAL HYPOCRITE!
SO I WAITED THE WEEK.
PRETTY MUCH HAD NOTHING BETTER TO DO.
HOW'S THE ANXIETY?
GHASTLY. I'M OUT OF CIGARETTES SO I HAVE TO BORROW OR SMOKE BUTTS!
I CAN'T HELP YOU WITH THAT. TELL ME ABOUT WORKING AT THE BOOKSTORE IN OMAHA.
THE FIRST THING THAT YOU NOTICE, IS THAT THE CLIENTELE WAS 90% GAY MEN.
IT WAS A TOTAL SUPRISE TO ME.
I'LL BE DAMNED.
I THOUGHT PORNO SHOPS WERE FULL OF PERVERTS IN RAINCOATS.
YA GOT ANY KIDDIE PORN?
OH, WE GOT A FEW OF THOSE. AND WE KNEW HOW TO DEAL WITH THEM.
GET THE FUCK OUT OF THIS STORE!! WE DON'T PEDDLE THAT SHIT!!

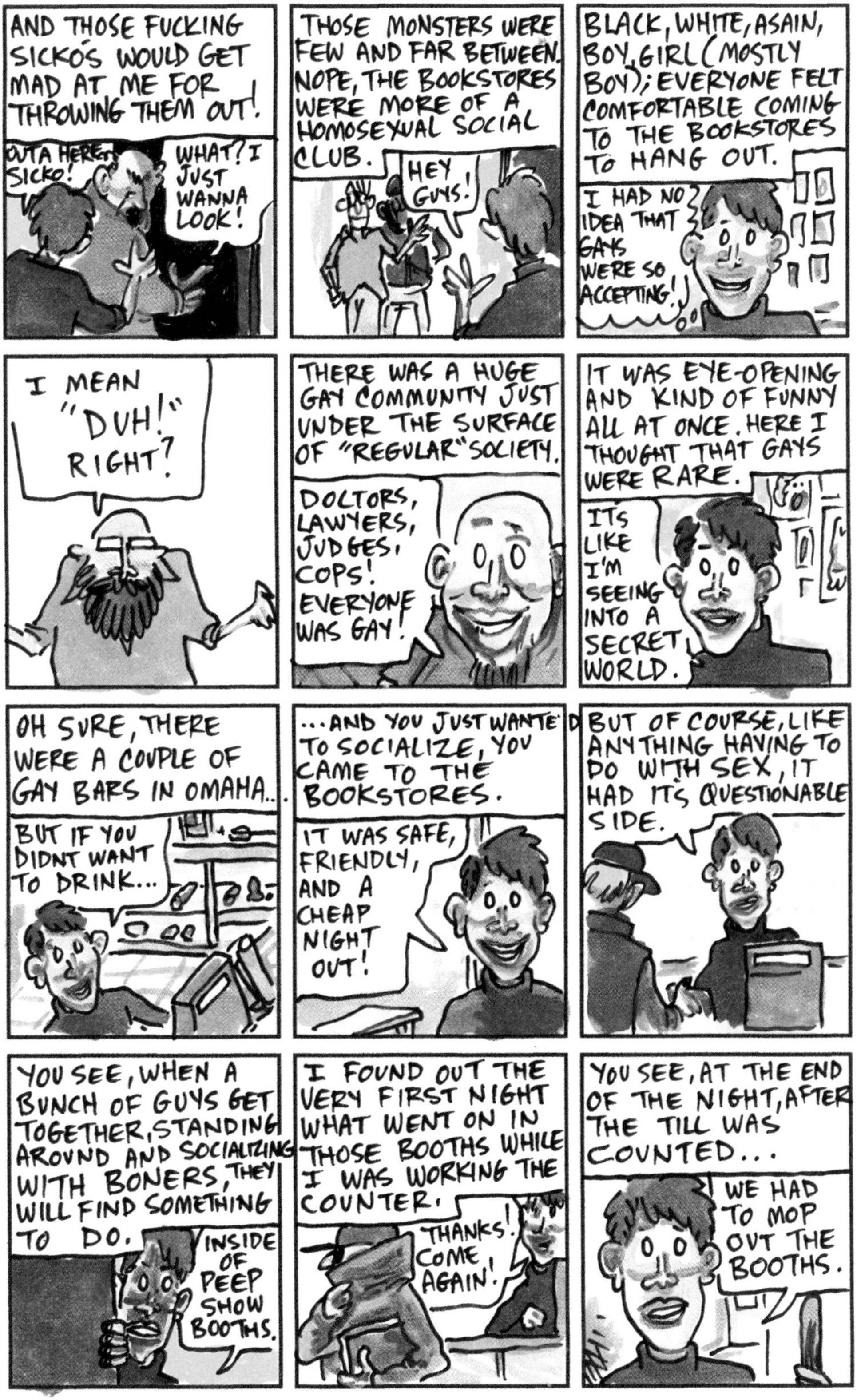
AND THOSE FUCKING SICKO'S WOULD GET MAD AT ME FOR THROWING THEM OUT!
OUTA HERE, SICKO!
WHAT? I JUST WANNA LOOK!
THOSE MONSTERS WERE FEW AND FAR BETWEEN. NOPE, THE BOOKSTORES WERE MORE OF A HOMOSEXUAL SOCIAL CLUB.
HEY GUYS!
BLACK, WHITE, ASAIN, BOY, GIRL (MOSTLY BOY); EVERYONE FELT COMFORTABLE COMING TO THE BOOKSTORES TO HANG OUT.
I HAD NO IDEA THAT GAYS WERE SO ACCEPTING!
I MEAN "DUH!" RIGHT?
THERE WAS A HUGE GAY COMMUNITY JUST UNDER THE SURFACE OF "REGULAR" SOCIETY.
DOCTORS, LAWYERS, JUDGES, COPS! EVERYONE WAS GAY!
IT WAS EYE-OPENING AND KIND OF FUNNY ALL AT ONCE. HERE I THOUGHT THAT GAYS WERE RARE.
ITS LIKE I'M SEEING INTO A SECRET WORLD.
OH SURE, THERE WERE A COUPLE OF GAY BARS IN OMAHA...
BUT IF YOU DIDNT WANT TO DRINK...
...AND YOU JUST WANTED TO SOCIALIZE, YOU CAME TO THE BOOKSTORES.
IT WAS SAFE, FRIENDLY, AND A CHEAP NIGHT OUT!
BUT OF COURSE, LIKE ANYTHING HAVING TO DO WITH SEX, IT HAD ITS QUESTIONABLE SIDE.
YOU SEE, WHEN A BUNCH OF GUYS GET TOGETHER, STANDING AROUND AND SOCIALIZING WITH BONERS, THEY WILL FIND SOMETHING TO DO.
INSIDE OF PEEP SHOW BOOTHS.
I FOUND OUT THE VERY FIRST NIGHT WHAT WENT ON IN THOSE BOOTHS WHILE I WAS WORKING THE COUNTER.
THANKS! COME AGAIN!
YOU SEE, AT THE END OF THE NIGHT, AFTER THE TILL WAS COUNTED...
WE HAD TO MOP OUT THE BOOTHS.

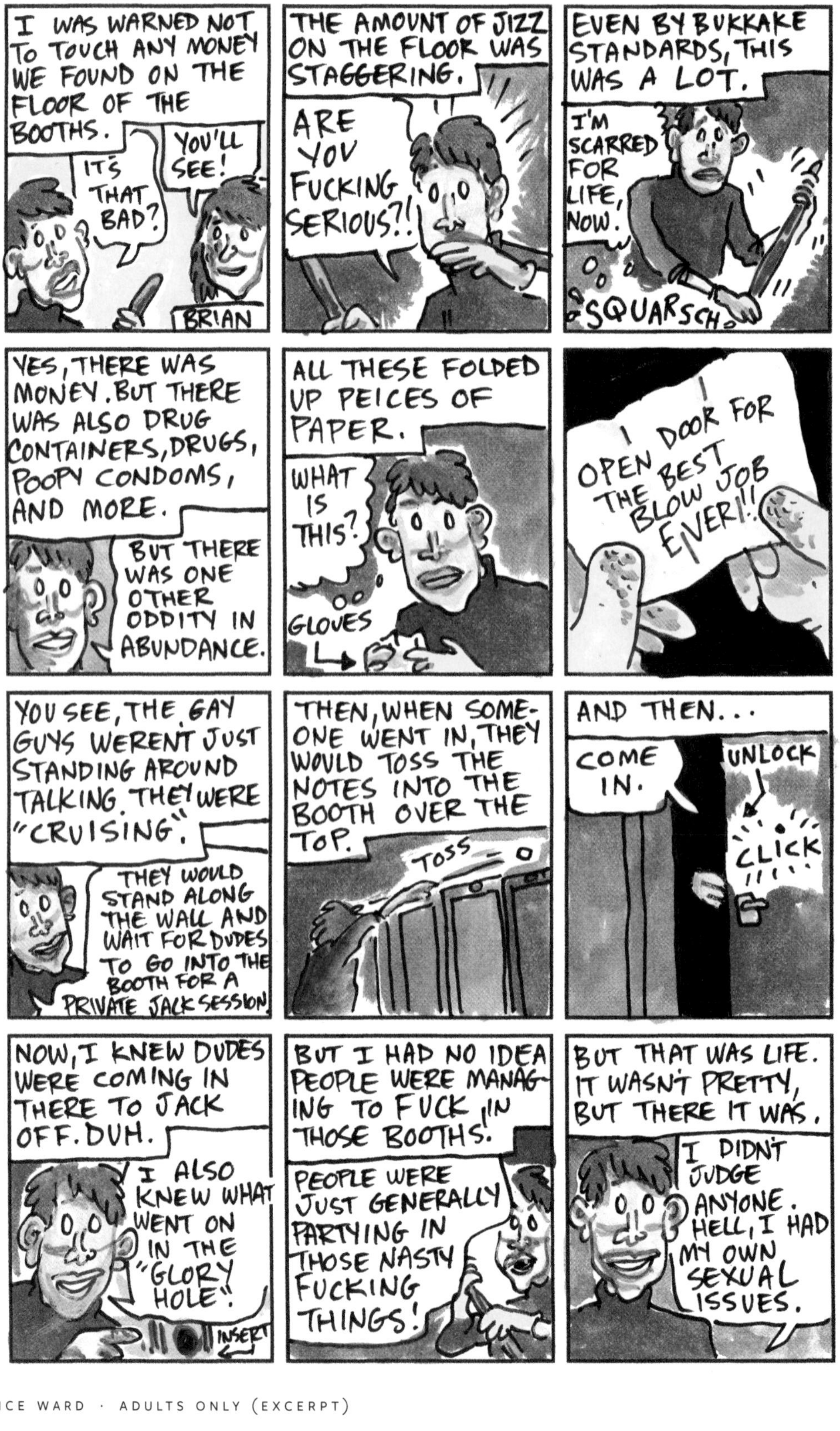
I WAS WARNED NOT TO TOUCH ANY MONEY WE FOUND ON THE FLOOR OF THE BOOTHS.
IT'S THAT BAD?
YOU'LL SEE!
BRIAN
THE AMOUNT OF JIZZ ON THE FLOOR WAS STAGGERING.
ARE YOU FUCKING SERIOUS?!
EVEN BY BUKKAKE STANDARDS, THIS WAS A LOT.
I'M SCARRED FOR LIFE, NOW.
SQUARSCH
YES, THERE WAS MONEY. BUT THERE WAS ALSO DRUG CONTAINERS, DRUGS, POOPY CONDOMS, AND MORE.
BUT THERE WAS ONE OTHER ODDITY IN ABUNDANCE.
ALL THESE FOLDED UP PEICES OF PAPER.
WHAT IS THIS?
GLOVES
I OPEN DOOR FOR THE BEST BLOW JOB EVER!!
YOU SEE, THE GAY GUYS WERENT JUST STANDING AROUND TALKING. THEY WERE "CRUISING".
THEY WOULD STAND ALONG THE WALL AND WAIT FOR DUDES TO GO INTO THE BOOTH FOR A PRIVATE JACK SESSION.
THEN, WHEN SOME-ONE WENT IN, THEY WOULD TOSS THE NOTES INTO THE BOOTH OVER THE TOP.
TOSS
AND THEN...
COME IN.
UNLOCK
CLICK
NOW, I KNEW DUDES WERE COMING IN THERE TO JACK OFF. DUH.
I ALSO KNEW WHAT WENT ON IN THE "GLORY HOLE".
INSERT
BUT I HAD NO IDEA PEOPLE WERE MANAG-ING TO FUCK IN THOSE BOOTHS!
PEOPLE WERE JUST GENERALLY PARTYING IN THOSE NASTY FUCKING THINGS!
BUT THAT WAS LIFE. IT WASN'T PRETTY, BUT THERE IT WAS.
I DIDN'T JUDGE ANYONE. HELL, I HAD MY OWN SEXUAL ISSUES.

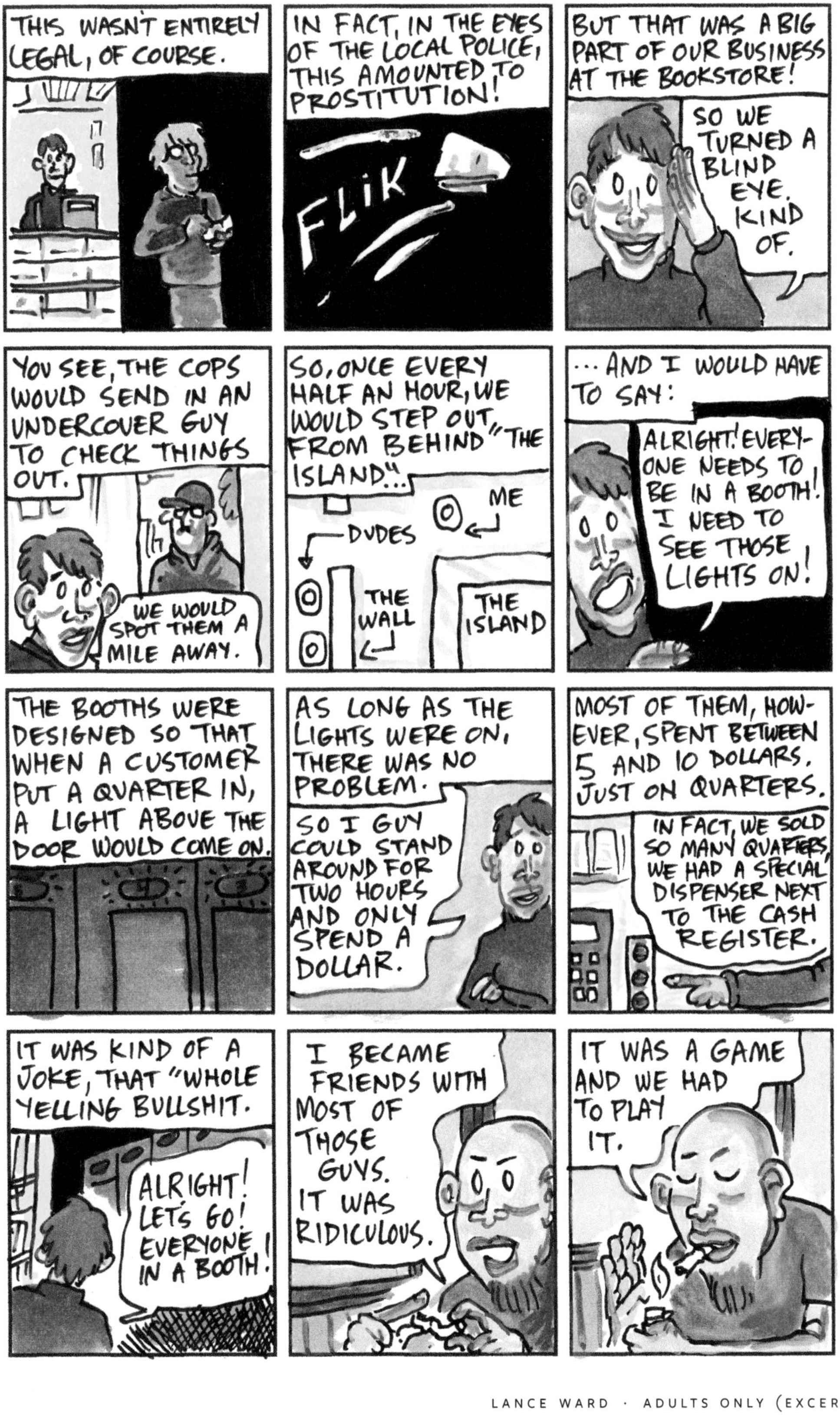
THIS WASN'T ENTIRELY LEGAL, OF COURSE.
IN FACT, IN THE EYES OF THE LOCAL POLICE, THIS AMOUNTED TO PROSTITUTION!
FLIK
BUT THAT WAS A BIG PART OF OUR BUSINESS AT THE BOOKSTORE!
SO WE TURNED A BLIND EYE. KIND OF.
YOU SEE, THE COPS WOULD SEND IN AN UNDERCOVER GUY TO CHECK THINGS OUT.
WE WOULD SPOT THEM A MILE AWAY.
SO, ONCE EVERY HALF AN HOUR, WE WOULD STEP OUT FROM BEHIND "THE ISLAND"...
ME
DUDES
THE WALL
THE ISLAND
... AND I WOULD HAVE TO SAY:
ALRIGHT! EVERYONE NEEDS TO BE IN A BOOTH! I NEED TO SEE THOSE LIGHTS ON!
THE BOOTHS WERE DESIGNED SO THAT WHEN A CUSTOMER PUT A QUARTER IN, A LIGHT ABOVE THE DOOR WOULD COME ON.
AS LONG AS THE LIGHTS WERE ON, THERE WAS NO PROBLEM.
SO I GUY COULD STAND AROUND FOR TWO HOURS AND ONLY SPEND A DOLLAR.
MOST OF THEM, HOWEVER, SPENT BETWEEN 5 AND 10 DOLLARS, JUST ON QUARTERS.
IN FACT, WE SOLD SO MANY QUARTERS, WE HAD A SPECIAL DISPENSER NEXT TO THE CASH REGISTER.
IT WAS KIND OF A JOKE, THAT "WHOLE YELLING BULLSHIT.
ALRIGHT! LET'S GO! EVERYONE IN A BOOTH!
I BECAME FRIENDS WITH MOST OF THOSE GUYS. IT WAS RIDICULOUS.
IT WAS A GAME AND WE HAD TO PLAY IT.

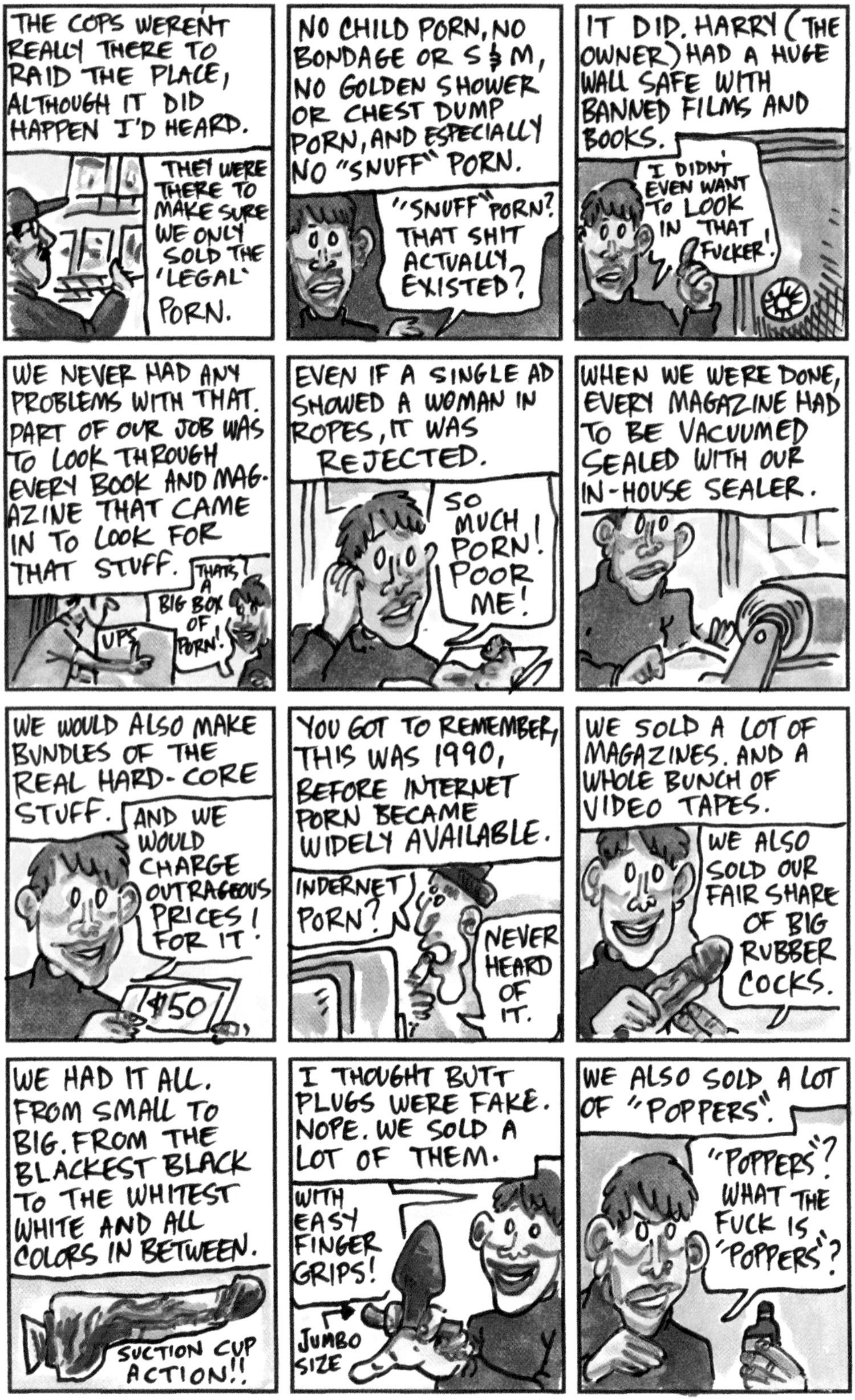
THE COPS WEREN'T REALLY THERE TO RAID THE PLACE, ALTHOUGH IT DID HAPPEN I'D HEARD.
THEY WERE THERE TO MAKE SURE WE ONLY SOLD THE 'LEGAL' PORN.
NO CHILD PORN, NO BONDAGE OR S&M, NO GOLDEN SHOWER OR CHEST DUMP PORN, AND ESPECIALLY NO "SNUFF" PORN.
"SNUFF" PORN? THAT SHIT ACTUALLY EXISTED?
IT DID. HARRY (THE OWNER) HAD A HUGE WALL SAFE WITH BANNED FILMS AND BOOKS.
I DIDN'T EVEN WANT TO LOOK IN THAT FUCKER!
WE NEVER HAD ANY PROBLEMS WITH THAT. PART OF OUR JOB WAS TO LOOK THROUGH EVERY BOOK AND MAGAZINE THAT CAME IN TO LOOK FOR THAT STUFF.
UPS
THAT'S A BIG BOX OF PORN!
EVEN IF A SINGLE AD SHOWED A WOMAN IN ROPES, IT WAS REJECTED.
SO MUCH PORN! POOR ME!
WHEN WE WERE DONE, EVERY MAGAZINE HAD TO BE VACUUMED SEALED WITH OUR IN-HOUSE SEALER.
WE WOULD ALSO MAKE BUNDLES OF THE REAL HARD-CORE STUFF.
AND WE WOULD CHARGE OUTRAGEOUS PRICES FOR IT.
$150
YOU GOT TO REMEMBER, THIS WAS 1990, BEFORE INTERNET PORN BECAME WIDELY AVAILABLE.
INDERNET PORN?
NEVER HEARD OF IT.
WE SOLD A LOT OF MAGAZINES. AND A WHOLE BUNCH OF VIDEO TAPES.
WE ALSO SOLD OUR FAIR SHARE OF BIG RUBBER COCKS.
WE HAD IT ALL. FROM SMALL TO BIG. FROM THE BLACKEST BLACK TO THE WHITEST WHITE AND ALL COLORS IN BETWEEN.
SUCTION CUP ACTION!!
I THOUGHT BUTT PLUGS WERE FAKE. NOPE. WE SOLD A LOT OF THEM.
WITH EASY FINGER GRIPS!
JUMBO SIZE
WE ALSO SOLD A LOT OF "POPPERS".
"POPPERS"? WHAT THE FUCK IS "POPPERS"?

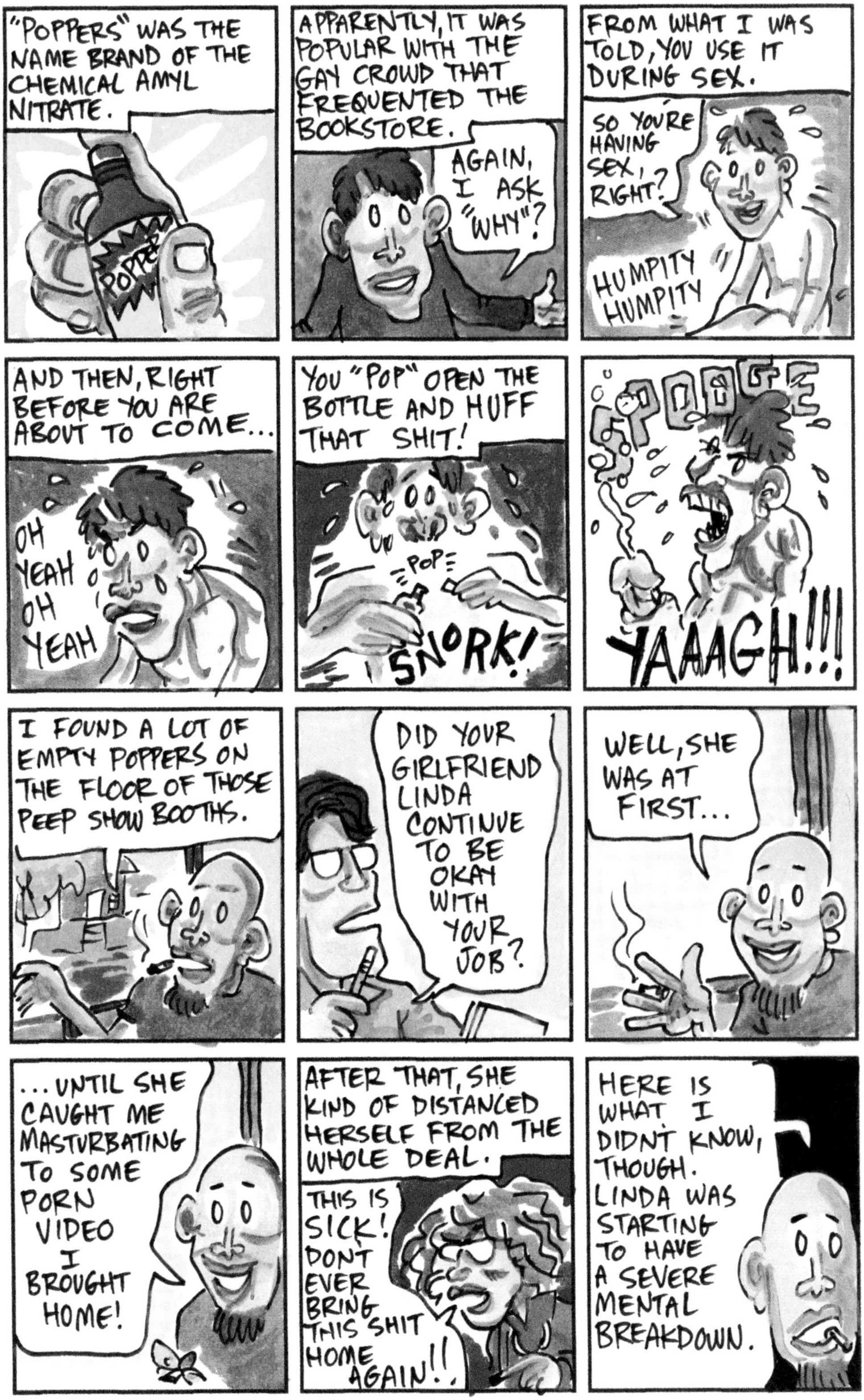
"POPPERS" WAS THE NAME BRAND OF THE CHEMICAL AMYL NITRATE.
POPPERS
APPARENTLY, IT WAS POPULAR WITH THE GAY CROWD THAT FREQUENTED THE BOOKSTORE.
AGAIN, I ASK "WHY"?
FROM WHAT I WAS TOLD, YOU USE IT DURING SEX.
SO YOU'RE HAVING SEX, RIGHT?
HUMPITY HUMPITY
AND THEN, RIGHT BEFORE YOU ARE ABOUT TO COME...
OH YEAH OH YEAH
YOU "POP" OPEN THE BOTTLE AND HUFF THAT SHIT!
POP
SNORK!
SPOOGE
YAAAGH!!!
I FOUND A LOT OF EMPTY POPPERS ON THE FLOOR OF THOSE PEEP SHOW BOOTHS.
DID YOUR GIRLFRIEND LINDA CONTINUE TO BE OKAY WITH YOUR JOB?
WELL, SHE WAS AT FIRST...
...UNTIL SHE CAUGHT ME MASTURBATING TO SOME PORN VIDEO I BROUGHT HOME!
AFTER THAT, SHE KIND OF DISTANCED HERSELF FROM THE WHOLE DEAL.
THIS IS SICK! DON'T EVER BRING THIS SHIT HOME AGAIN!!
HERE IS WHAT I DIDN'T KNOW, THOUGH. LINDA WAS STARTING TO HAVE A SEVERE MENTAL BREAKDOWN.

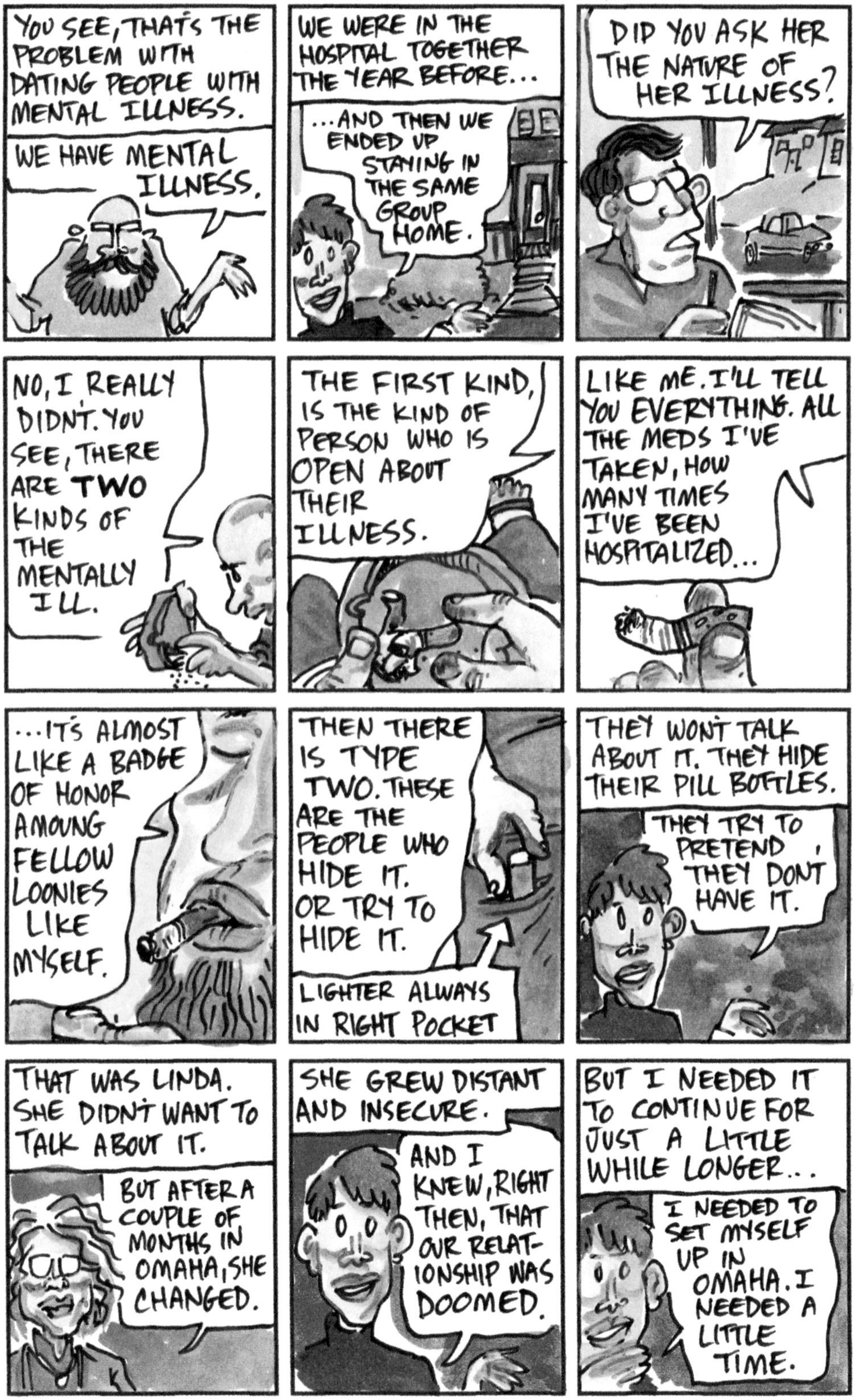
YOU SEE, THAT'S THE PROBLEM WITH DATING PEOPLE WITH MENTAL ILLNESS.
WE HAVE MENTAL ILLNESS.
WE WERE IN THE HOSPITAL TOGETHER THE YEAR BEFORE...
...AND THEN WE ENDED UP STAYING IN THE SAME GROUP HOME.
DID YOU ASK HER THE NATURE OF HER ILLNESS?
NO, I REALLY DIDN'T. YOU SEE, THERE ARE **TWO** KINDS OF THE MENTALLY ILL.
THE FIRST KIND, IS THE KIND OF PERSON WHO IS OPEN ABOUT THEIR ILLNESS.
LIKE ME. I'LL TELL YOU EVERYTHING. ALL THE MEDS I'VE TAKEN, HOW MANY TIMES I'VE BEEN HOSPITALIZED...
...IT'S ALMOST LIKE A BADGE OF HONOR AMOUNG FELLOW LOONIES LIKE MYSELF.
THEN THERE IS TYPE TWO. THESE ARE THE PEOPLE WHO HIDE IT. OR TRY TO HIDE IT.
LIGHTER ALWAYS IN RIGHT POCKET
THEY WON'T TALK ABOUT IT. THEY HIDE THEIR PILL BOTTLES.
THEY TRY TO PRETEND THEY DON'T HAVE IT.
THAT WAS LINDA. SHE DIDN'T WANT TO TALK ABOUT IT.
BUT AFTER A COUPLE OF MONTHS IN OMAHA, SHE CHANGED.
SHE GREW DISTANT AND INSECURE.
AND I KNEW, RIGHT THEN, THAT OUR RELAT-IONSHIP WAS DOOMED.
BUT I NEEDED IT TO CONTINUE FOR JUST A LITTLE WHILE LONGER...
I NEEDED TO SET MYSELF UP IN OMAHA. I NEEDED A LITTLE TIME.

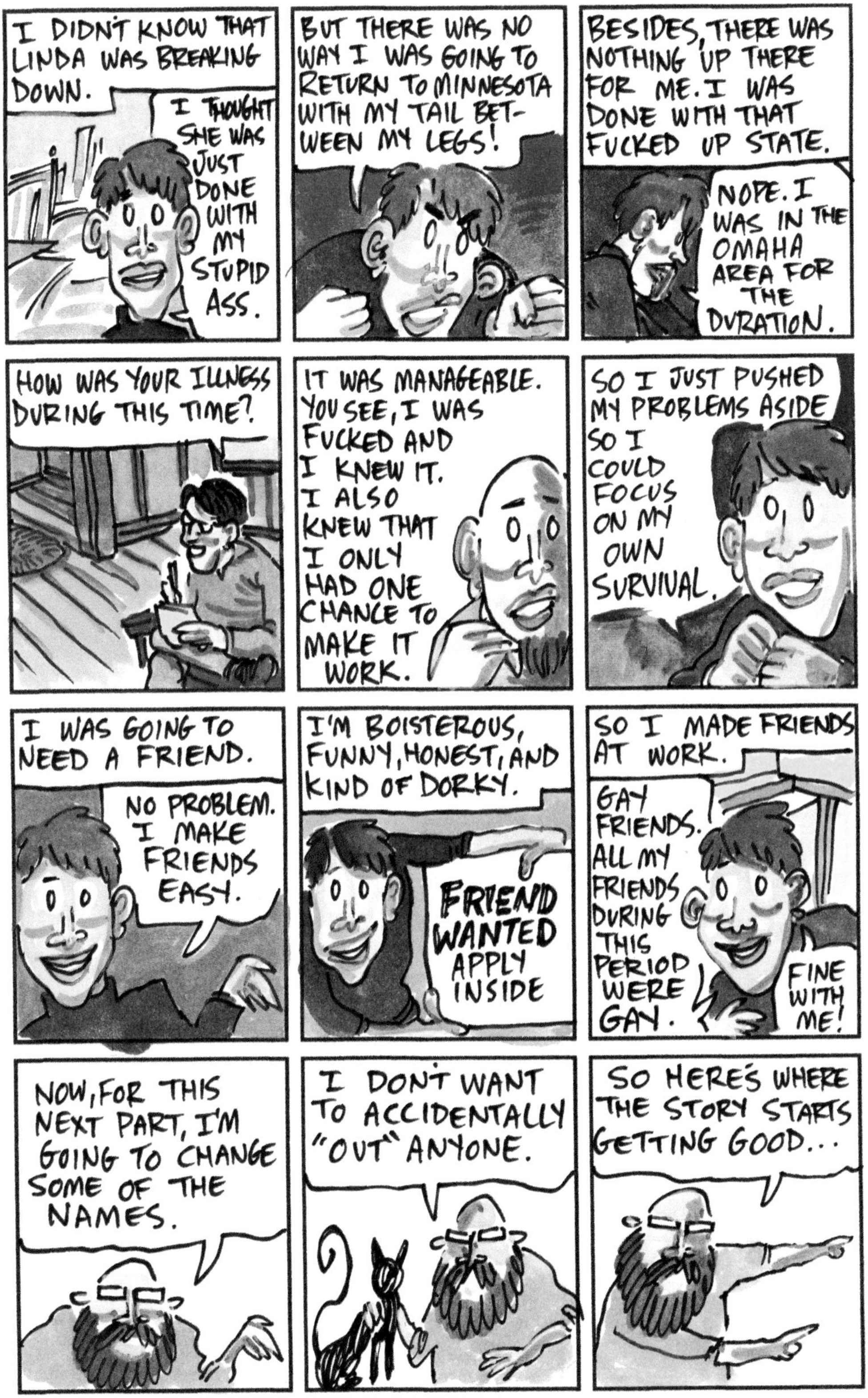
I DIDN'T KNOW THAT LINDA WAS BREAKING DOWN.
I THOUGHT SHE WAS JUST DONE WITH MY STUPID ASS.
BUT THERE WAS NO WAY I WAS GOING TO RETURN TO MINNESOTA WITH MY TAIL BETWEEN MY LEGS!
BESIDES, THERE WAS NOTHING UP THERE FOR ME. I WAS DONE WITH THAT FUCKED UP STATE.
NOPE. I WAS IN THE OMAHA AREA FOR THE DURATION.
HOW WAS YOUR ILLNESS DURING THIS TIME?
IT WAS MANAGEABLE. YOU SEE, I WAS FUCKED AND I KNEW IT. I ALSO KNEW THAT I ONLY HAD ONE CHANCE TO MAKE IT WORK.
SO I JUST PUSHED MY PROBLEMS ASIDE SO I COULD FOCUS ON MY OWN SURVIVAL.
I WAS GOING TO NEED A FRIEND.
NO PROBLEM. I MAKE FRIENDS EASY.
I'M BOISTEROUS, FUNNY, HONEST, AND KIND OF DORKY.
FRIEND WANTED APPLY INSIDE
SO I MADE FRIENDS AT WORK.
GAY FRIENDS. ALL MY FRIENDS DURING THIS PERIOD WERE GAY.
FINE WITH ME!
NOW, FOR THIS NEXT PART, I'M GOING TO CHANGE SOME OF THE NAMES.
I DON'T WANT TO ACCIDENTALLY "OUT" ANYONE.
SO HERE'S WHERE THE STORY STARTS GETTING GOOD...

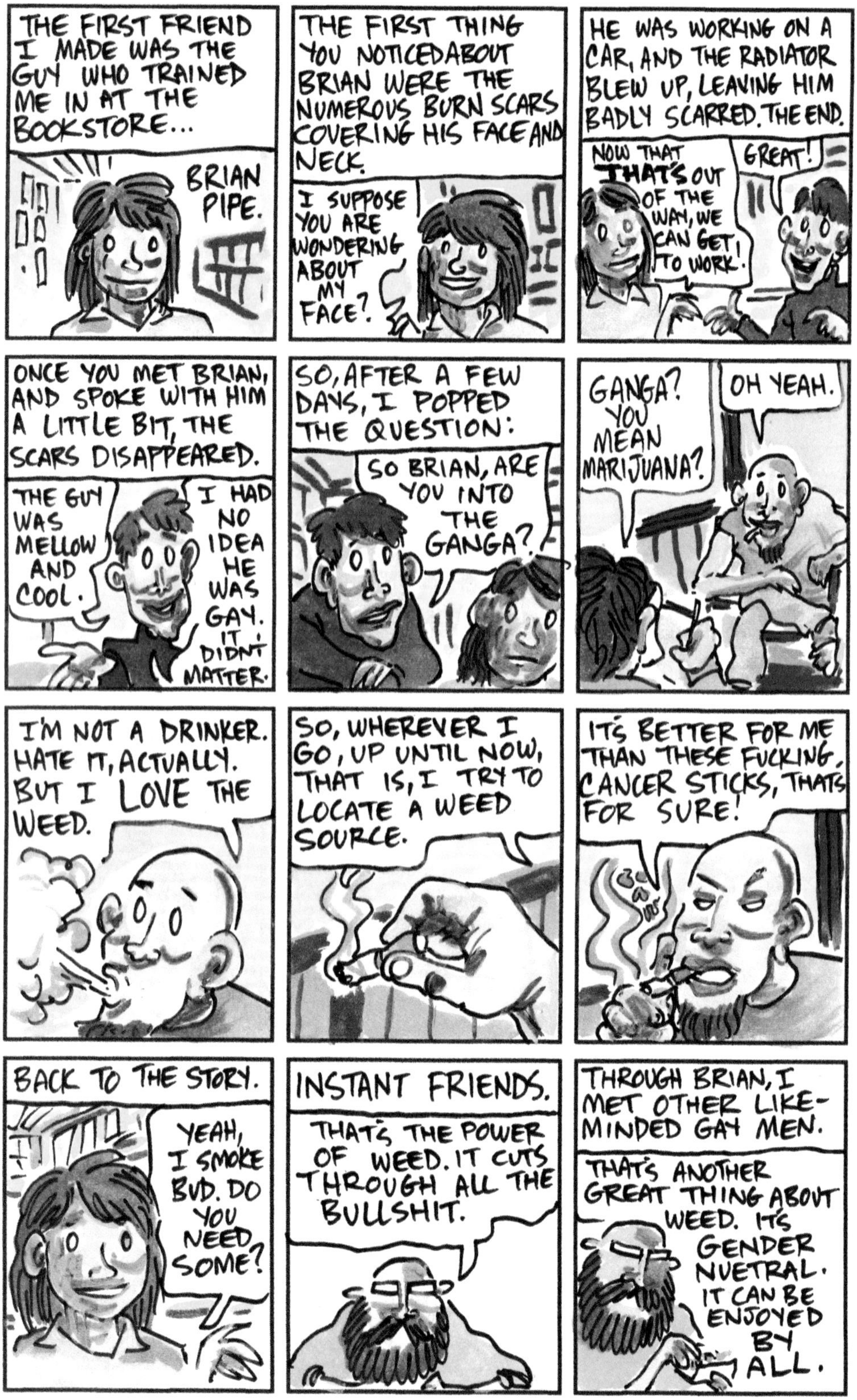
THE FIRST FRIEND I MADE WAS THE GUY WHO TRAINED ME IN AT THE BOOKSTORE...
BRIAN PIPE.
THE FIRST THING YOU NOTICED ABOUT BRIAN WERE THE NUMEROUS BURN SCARS COVERING HIS FACE AND NECK.
I SUPPOSE YOU ARE WONDERING ABOUT MY FACE?
HE WAS WORKING ON A CAR, AND THE RADIATOR BLEW UP, LEAVING HIM BADLY SCARRED. THE END.
NOW THAT THAT'S OUT OF THE WAY, WE CAN GET TO WORK!
GREAT!
ONCE YOU MET BRIAN, AND SPOKE WITH HIM A LITTLE BIT, THE SCARS DISAPPEARED.
THE GUY WAS MELLOW AND COOL.
I HAD NO IDEA HE WAS GAY. IT DIDN'T MATTER.
SO, AFTER A FEW DAYS, I POPPED THE QUESTION:
SO BRIAN, ARE YOU INTO THE GANGA?
GANGA? YOU MEAN MARIJUANA?
OH YEAH.
I'M NOT A DRINKER. HATE IT, ACTUALLY. BUT I LOVE THE WEED.
SO, WHEREVER I GO, UP UNTIL NOW, THAT IS, I TRY TO LOCATE A WEED SOURCE.
IT'S BETTER FOR ME THAN THESE FUCKING CANCER STICKS, THAT'S FOR SURE!
BACK TO THE STORY.
YEAH, I SMOKE BUD. DO YOU NEED SOME?
INSTANT FRIENDS.
THAT'S THE POWER OF WEED. IT CUTS THROUGH ALL THE BULLSHIT.
THROUGH BRIAN, I MET OTHER LIKE-MINDED GAY MEN.
THAT'S ANOTHER GREAT THING ABOUT WEED. IT'S GENDER NUETRAL. IT CAN BE ENJOYED BY ALL.

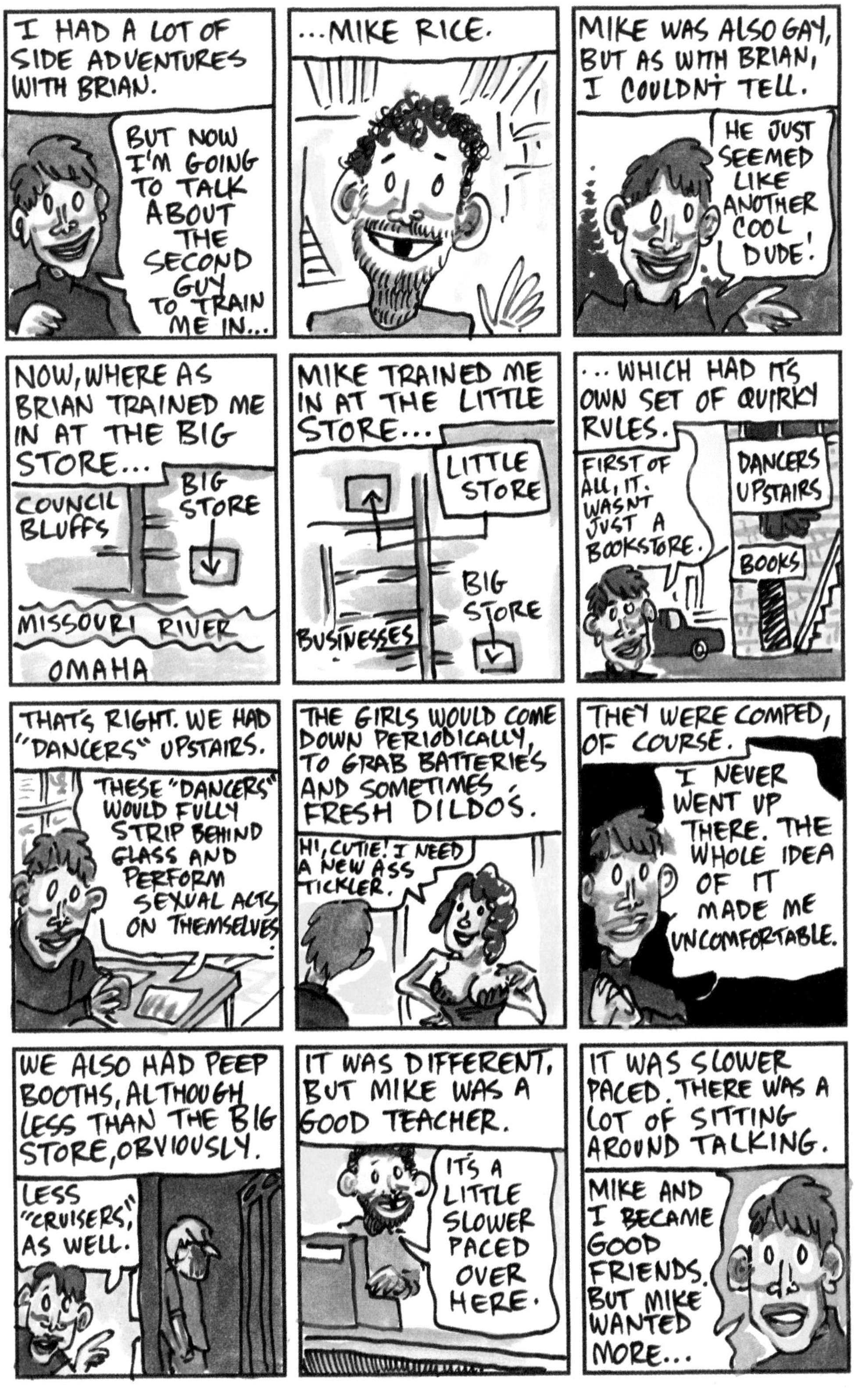
I HAD A LOT OF SIDE ADVENTURES WITH BRIAN.
BUT NOW I'M GOING TO TALK ABOUT THE SECOND GUY TO TRAIN ME IN...
...MIKE RICE.
MIKE WAS ALSO GAY, BUT AS WITH BRIAN, I COULDN'T TELL.
HE JUST SEEMED LIKE ANOTHER COOL DUDE!
NOW, WHERE AS BRIAN TRAINED ME IN AT THE BIG STORE...
COUNCIL BLUFFS
BIG STORE
MISSOURI RIVER
OMAHA
MIKE TRAINED ME IN AT THE LITTLE STORE...
LITTLE STORE
BIG STORE
BUSINESSES
...WHICH HAD IT'S OWN SET OF QUIRKY RULES.
FIRST OF ALL, IT WASN'T JUST A BOOKSTORE.
DANCERS UPSTAIRS
BOOKS
THAT'S RIGHT. WE HAD "DANCERS" UPSTAIRS.
THESE "DANCERS" WOULD FULLY STRIP BEHIND GLASS AND PERFORM SEXUAL ACTS ON THEMSELVES.
THE GIRLS WOULD COME DOWN PERIODICALLY, TO GRAB BATTERIE'S AND SOMETIMES, FRESH DILDO'S.
HI, CUTIE! I NEED A NEW ASS TICKLER.
THEY WERE COMPED, OF COURSE.
I NEVER WENT UP THERE. THE WHOLE IDEA OF IT MADE ME UNCOMFORTABLE.
WE ALSO HAD PEEP BOOTHS, ALTHOUGH LESS THAN THE BIG STORE, OBVIOUSLY.
LESS "CRUISERS," AS WELL.
IT WAS DIFFERENT, BUT MIKE WAS A GOOD TEACHER.
IT'S A LITTLE SLOWER PACED OVER HERE.
IT WAS SLOWER PACED. THERE WAS A LOT OF SITTING AROUND TALKING.
MIKE AND I BECAME GOOD FRIENDS. BUT MIKE WANTED MORE...

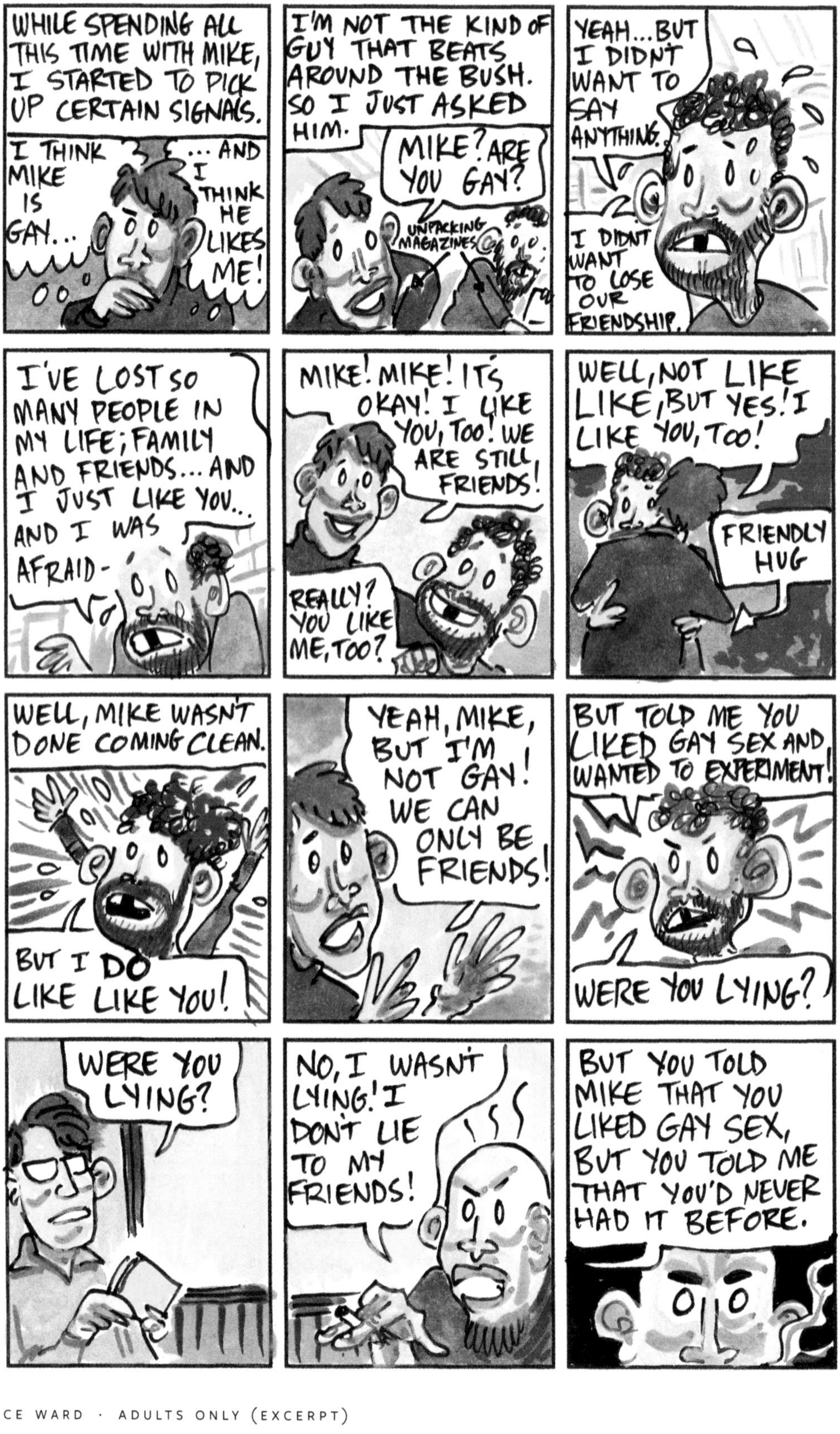
WHILE SPENDING ALL THIS TIME WITH MIKE, I STARTED TO PICK UP CERTAIN SIGNALS.
I THINK MIKE IS GAY...
...AND I THINK HE LIKES ME!
I'M NOT THE KIND OF GUY THAT BEATS AROUND THE BUSH. SO I JUST ASKED HIM.
MIKE? ARE YOU GAY?
UNPACKING MAGAZINES
YEAH...BUT I DIDN'T WANT TO SAY ANYTHING.
I DIDN'T WANT TO LOSE OUR FRIENDSHIP.
I'VE LOST SO MANY PEOPLE IN MY LIFE; FAMILY AND FRIENDS... AND I JUST LIKE YOU... AND I WAS AFRAID-
MIKE! MIKE! IT'S OKAY! I LIKE YOU, TOO! WE ARE STILL FRIENDS!
REALLY? YOU LIKE ME, TOO?
WELL, NOT LIKE LIKE, BUT YES! I LIKE YOU, TOO!
FRIENDLY HUG
WELL, MIKE WASN'T DONE COMING CLEAN.
BUT I DO LIKE LIKE YOU!
YEAH, MIKE, BUT I'M NOT GAY! WE CAN ONLY BE FRIENDS!
BUT TOLD ME YOU LIKED GAY SEX AND WANTED TO EXPERIMENT!
WERE YOU LYING?
WERE YOU LYING?
NO, I WASN'T LYING! I DON'T LIE TO MY FRIENDS!
BUT YOU TOLD MIKE THAT YOU LIKED GAY SEX, BUT YOU TOLD ME THAT YOU'D NEVER HAD IT BEFORE.

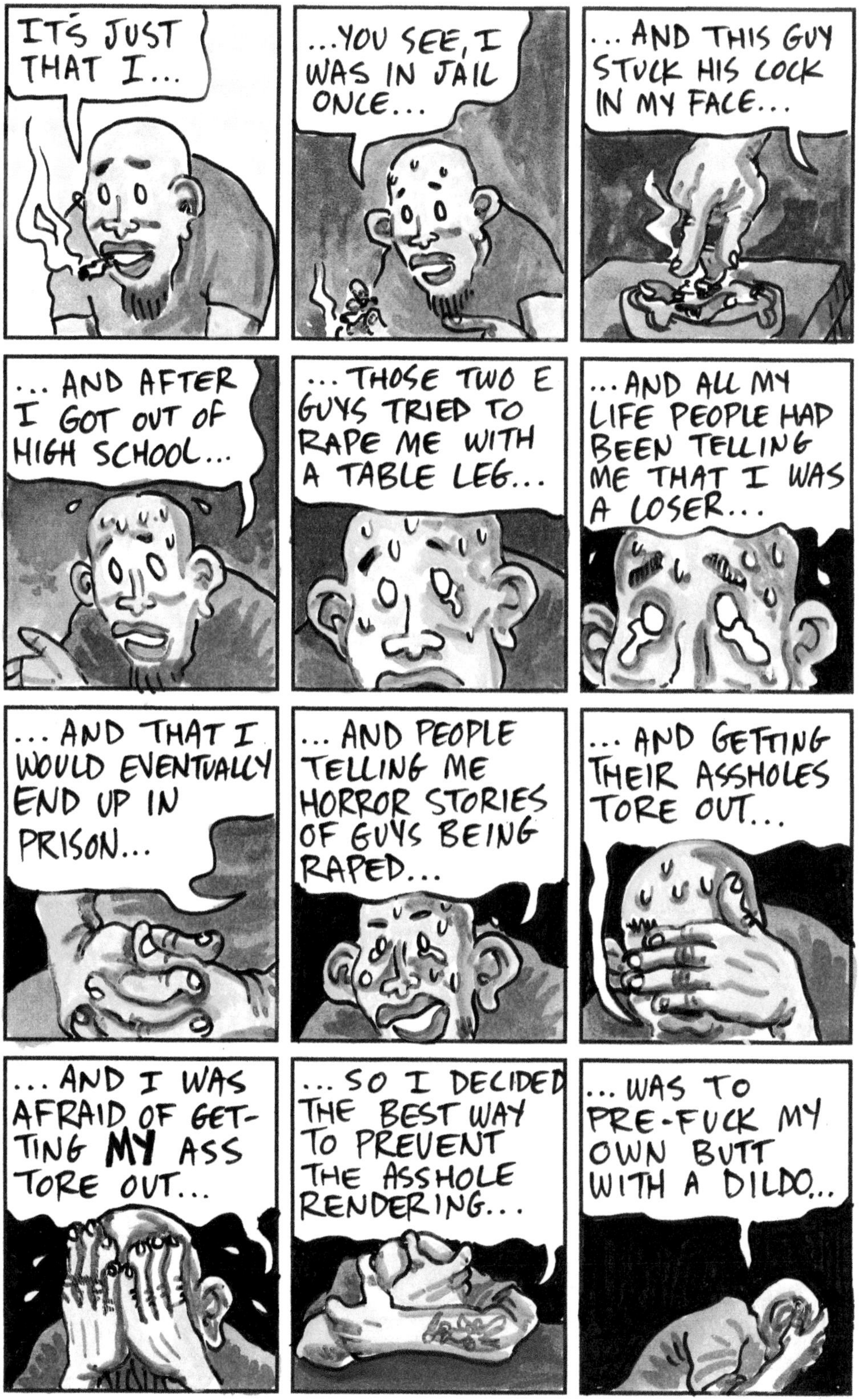
IT'S JUST THAT I...
...YOU SEE, I WAS IN JAIL ONCE...
...AND THIS GUY STUCK HIS COCK IN MY FACE...
...AND AFTER I GOT OUT OF HIGH SCHOOL...
...THOSE TWO E GUYS TRIED TO RAPE ME WITH A TABLE LEG...
...AND ALL MY LIFE PEOPLE HAD BEEN TELLING ME THAT I WAS A LOSER...
...AND THAT I WOULD EVENTUALLY END UP IN PRISON...
...AND PEOPLE TELLING ME HORROR STORIES OF GUYS BEING RAPED...
...AND GETTING THEIR ASSHOLES TORE OUT...
...AND I WAS AFRAID OF GETTING MY ASS TORE OUT...
...SO I DECIDED THE BEST WAY TO PREVENT THE ASSHOLE RENDERING...
...WAS TO PRE-FUCK MY OWN BUTT WITH A DILDO...

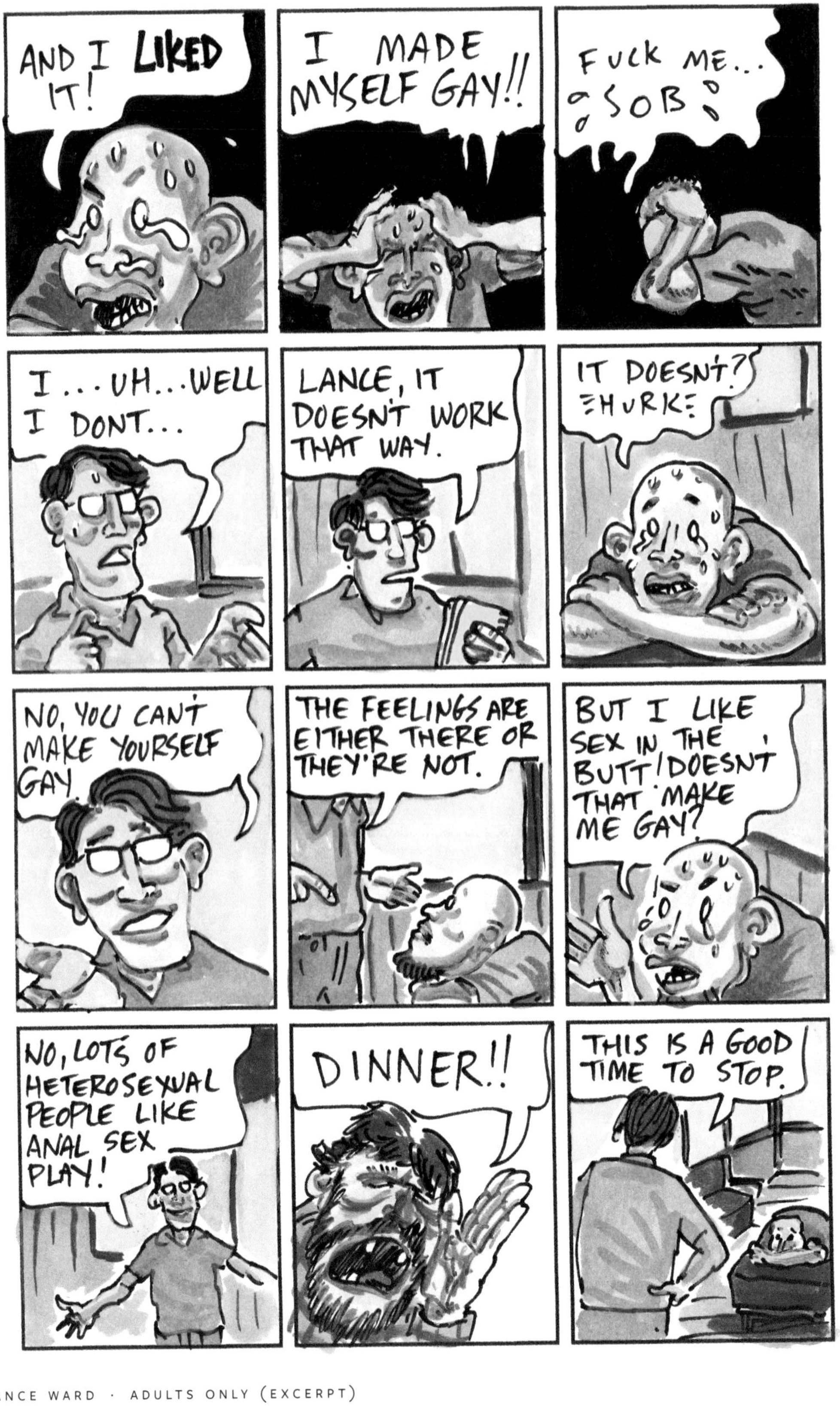

AND I LIKED IT!
I MADE MYSELF GAY!!
FUCK ME... SOB
I... UH... WELL I DONT...
LANCE, IT DOESN'T WORK THAT WAY.
IT DOESN'T? HURK
NO, YOU CAN'T MAKE YOURSELF GAY.
THE FEELINGS ARE EITHER THERE OR THEY'RE NOT.
BUT I LIKE SEX IN THE BUTT! DOESN'T THAT MAKE ME GAY?
NO, LOTS OF HETEROSEXUAL PEOPLE LIKE ANAL SEX PLAY!
DINNER!!
THIS IS A GOOD TIME TO STOP.

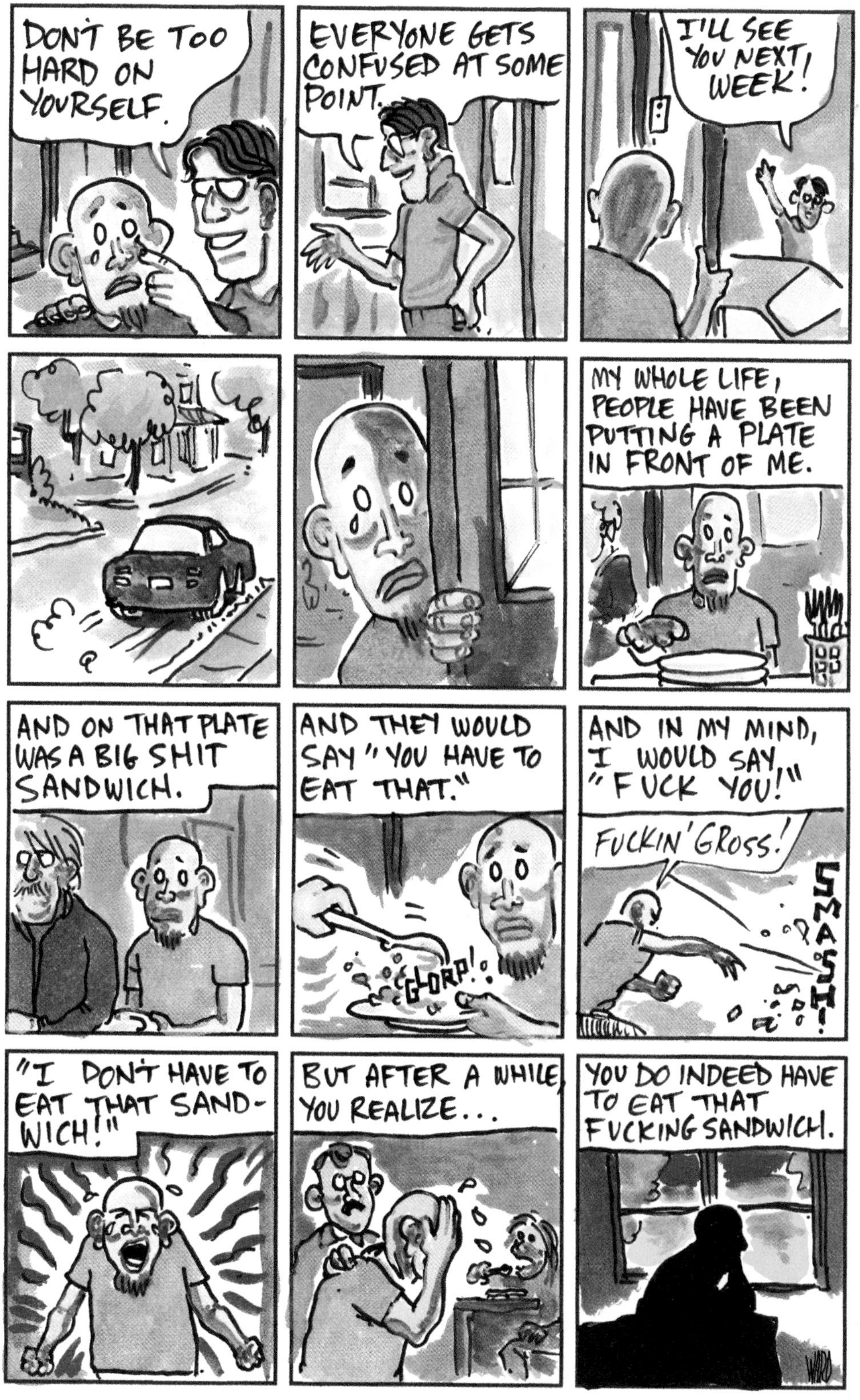
DON'T BE TOO HARD ON YOURSELF.
EVERYONE GETS CONFUSED AT SOME POINT.
I'LL SEE YOU NEXT WEEK!
MY WHOLE LIFE, PEOPLE HAVE BEEN PUTTING A PLATE IN FRONT OF ME.
AND ON THAT PLATE WAS A BIG SHIT SANDWICH.
AND THEY WOULD SAY "YOU HAVE TO EAT THAT."
GLORP!
AND IN MY MIND, I WOULD SAY, "FUCK YOU!"
FUCKIN' GROSS!
SMASH!
"I DON'T HAVE TO EAT THAT SANDWICH!"
BUT AFTER A WHILE, YOU REALIZE...
YOU DO INDEED HAVE TO EAT THAT FUCKING SANDWICH.
WARD

METROPOLIS
Is Everyone a Maker?

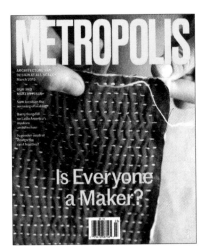

# The Danish Modern Borer, The Latest Laugh, The Needleless Garment Extruder, Illness in the Window, The Vontsel Institute, AND The Brazen Bull Corporation

BEN KATCHOR

*originally published in*

Metropolis

METROPOLIS

9 x 10.75 inches

## Biography

Ben Katchor's picture-stories appear in *Metropolis* magazine. His latest collection, *Hand-Drying in America and Other Stories*, was published by Pantheon Books in 2013. He's collaborated on five music-theater shows with Mark Mulcahy. He is the director of the Illustration program at Parsons The New School in New York City. katchor.com

## Statement

These are excerpts from a long-running series appearing on the back page of *Metropolis*. It is my hope that these strips will help bring about the end of the wage system along with the end of private ownership of the means of production on this planet.

## e Danish Modern Borer

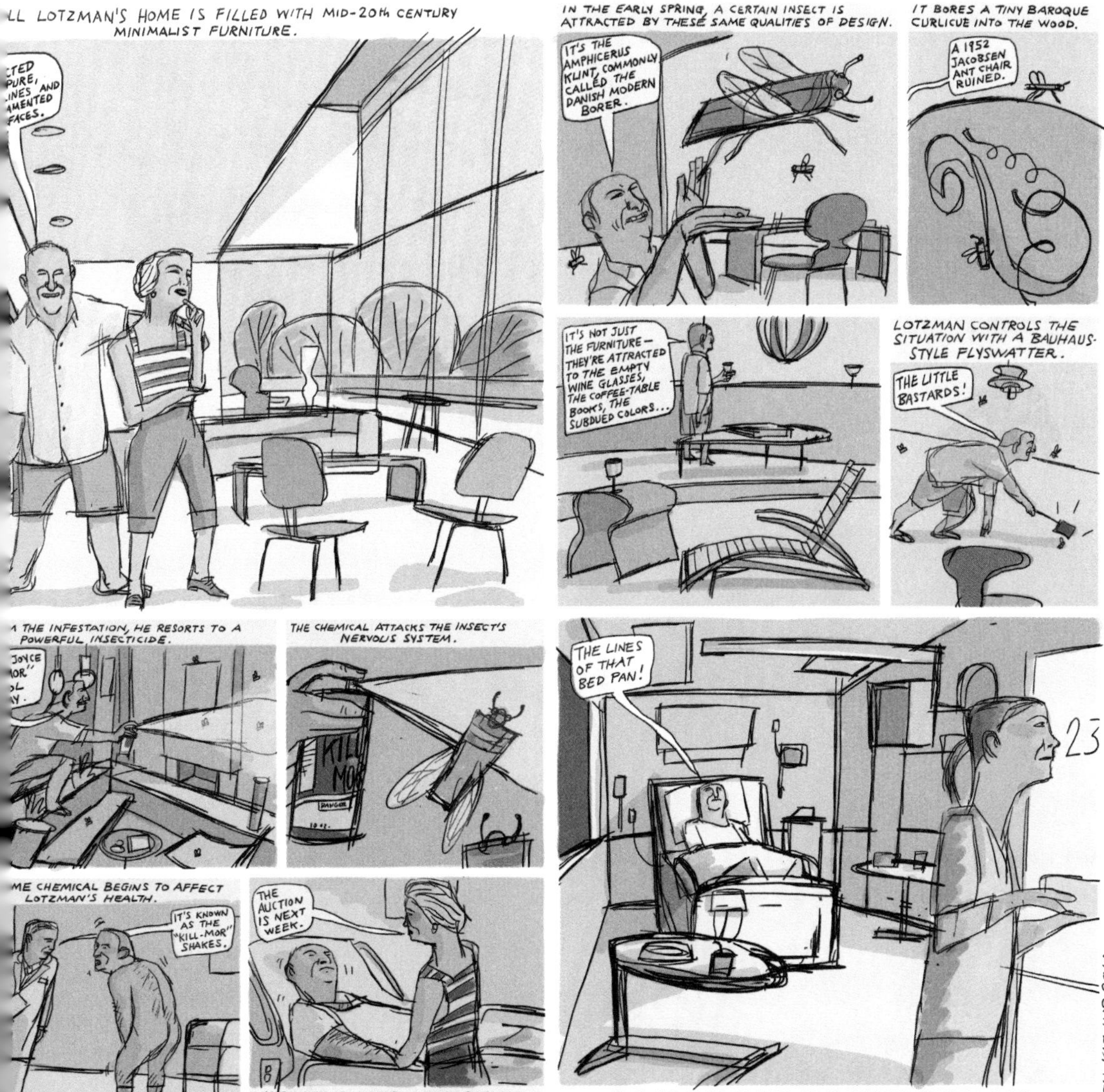
LL LOTZMAN'S HOME IS FILLED WITH MID-20th CENTURY MINIMALIST FURNITURE.
CTED PURE, LINES AND AMENTED FACES.
IN THE EARLY SPRING, A CERTAIN INSECT IS ATTRACTED BY THESE SAME QUALITIES OF DESIGN.
IT'S THE AMPHICERUS KLINT, COMMONLY CALLED THE DANISH MODERN BORER.
IT BORES A TINY BAROQUE CURLICUE INTO THE WOOD.
A 1952 JACOBSEN ANT CHAIR RUINED.
IT'S NOT JUST THE FURNITURE— THEY'RE ATTRACTED TO THE EMPTY WINE GLASSES, THE COFFEE-TABLE BOOKS, THE SUBDUED COLORS...
LOTZMAN CONTROLS THE SITUATION WITH A BAUHAUS-STYLE FLYSWATTER.
THE LITTLE BASTARDS!
A THE INFESTATION, HE RESORTS TO A POWERFUL INSECTICIDE.
JOYCE MOR" OL AY.
THE CHEMICAL ATTACKS THE INSECT'S NERVOUS SYSTEM.
KILL MOR
ME CHEMICAL BEGINS TO AFFECT LOTZMAN'S HEALTH.
IT'S KNOWN AS THE "KILL-MOR" SHAKES.
THE AUCTION IS NEXT WEEK.
HIS WIFE IS HEARTBROKEN TO SEE HIM CONFINED TO A HOSPITAL BED...
THE LINES OF THAT BED PAN!
23
BUT HE IS DELIGHTED BY THE SLEEK FUNCTIONALITY OF EVERYTHING AROUND HIM.

# The Latest Laugh

TWO YOUNG COUPLES CONVULSE WITH LAUGHTER OVER A NOVEL NAPKIN DESIGN.
IT LOOKS LIKE YOUR LAP IS ON FIRE!
IN A SHOP NEXT DOOR, A MAN CHOKES WITH MERRIMENT OVER A NEW EDIBLE SHOPPING BAG.
IT'S ALL SWEET RICE PAPER!
Parfum
CHANTAL
Dior
IN THE PRIVACY OF HER HOME, A WOM
GIGGLES UNCONTROLLABLY OVER A NEW BALLPOINT PEN.
IN THE SHAPE OF A CUCUMBER!
BY THESE INGENIOUSLY DEVISED OBJECTS, INDIVIDUALS ARE DISTRACTED FROM CONTEMPLATING THE NATURAL WORLD.
MY SORE THUMB.
THE VERY SIGHT OF A TREE FILLS THEM WITH BOREDOM AND DREAD.
THE FOUR SEASONS ...AGAIN?
THEY'RE REMINDED OF TH
LATE MOTHER'S ARTHRIT
KNEE...
LET'S STOP HERE.
AND THE INEVITABILITY OF BIOLOGICAL DECAY.
A SHOE MADE OF COW DUNG!
TWO FRIENDS LAUGH HYSTERICALLY OVER THE LATEST SHADE OF BULLET-PROOF NAIL POLISH.
ONLY THE ENDLESS NOVELTY OF PRODUCT DESIGN OFFERS A MOME
OF RELIEF.
A WRISTWATCH THAT READS YOUR FACE!
42 YEARS OLD.

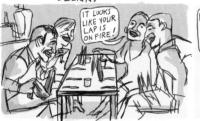

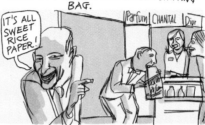

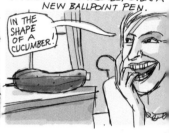

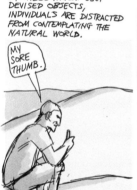

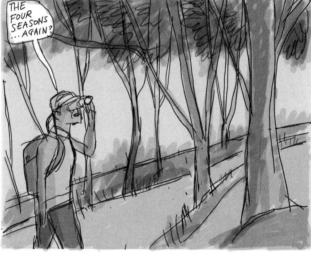

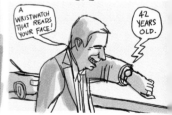

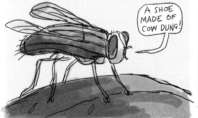

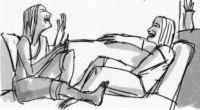

e Needleless Garment Extruder

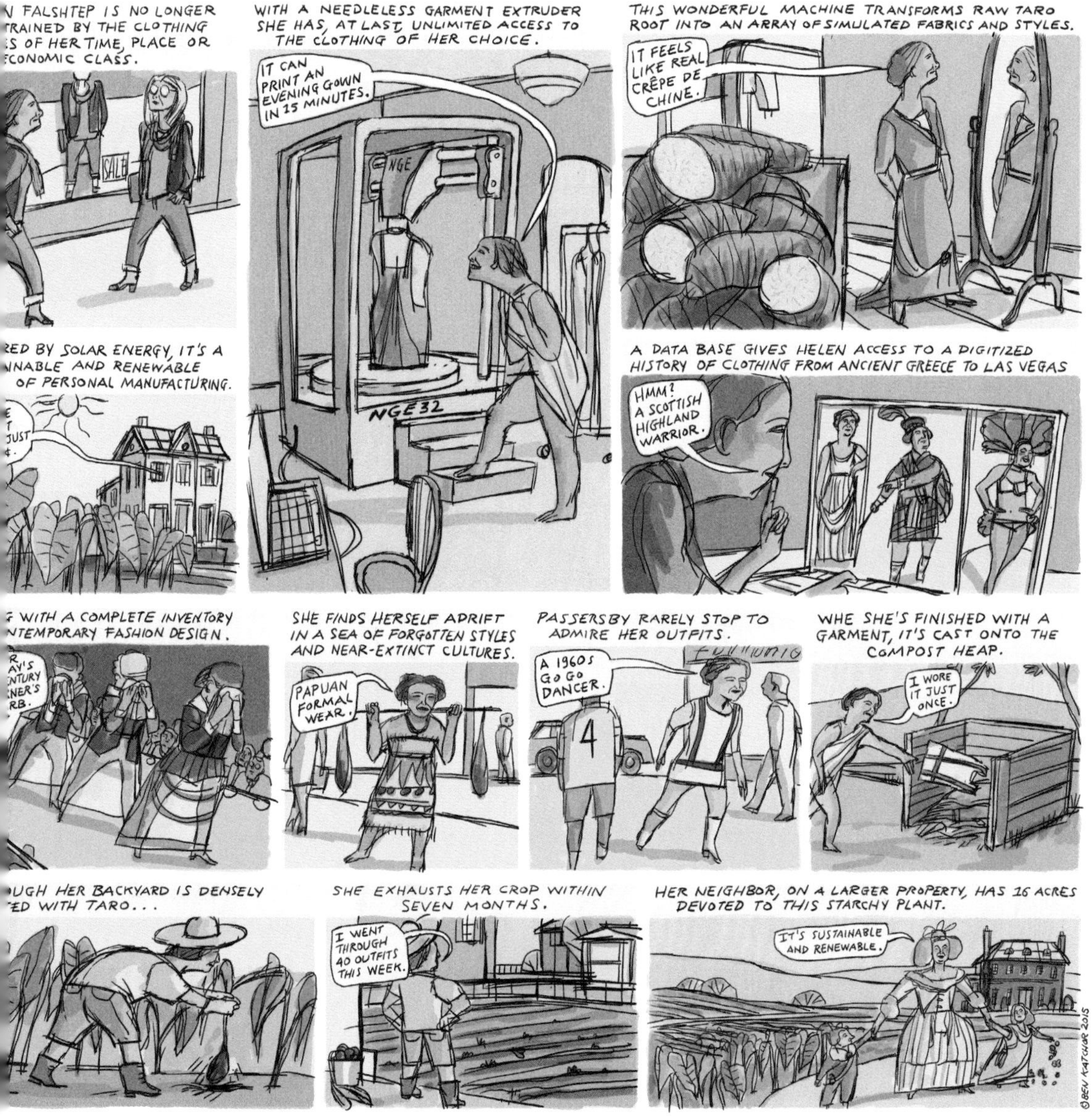
N FALSHTEP IS NO LONGER
TRAINED BY THE CLOTHING
S OF HER TIME, PLACE OR
ECONOMIC CLASS.
SALE
WITH A NEEDLELESS GARMENT EXTRUDER SHE HAS, AT LAST, UNLIMITED ACCESS TO THE CLOTHING OF HER CHOICE.
IT CAN PRINT AN EVENING GOWN IN 15 MINUTES.
NGE
NGE32
THIS WONDERFUL MACHINE TRANSFORMS RAW TARO ROOT INTO AN ARRAY OF SIMULATED FABRICS AND STYLES.
IT FEELS LIKE REAL CRÊPE DE CHINE.
RED BY SOLAR ENERGY, IT'S A
INABLE AND RENEWABLE
OF PERSONAL MANUFACTURING.
A DATA BASE GIVES HELEN ACCESS TO A DIGITIZED HISTORY OF CLOTHING FROM ANCIENT GREECE TO LAS VEGAS
HMM? A SCOTTISH HIGHLAND WARRIOR.
WITH A COMPLETE INVENTORY
NTEMPORARY FASHION DESIGN.
SHE FINDS HERSELF ADRIFT IN A SEA OF FORGOTTEN STYLES AND NEAR-EXTINCT CULTURES.
PAPUAN FORMAL WEAR.
PASSERSBY RARELY STOP TO ADMIRE HER OUTFITS.
A 1960s GO GO DANCER.
4
WHE SHE'S FINISHED WITH A GARMENT, IT'S CAST ONTO THE COMPOST HEAP.
I WORE IT JUST ONCE.
UGH HER BACKYARD IS DENSELY
ED WITH TARO...
SHE EXHAUSTS HER CROP WITHIN SEVEN MONTHS.
I WENT THROUGH 40 OUTFITS THIS WEEK.
HER NEIGHBOR, ON A LARGER PROPERTY, HAS 16 ACRES DEVOTED TO THIS STARCHY PLANT.
IT'S SUSTAINABLE AND RENEWABLE.
©BEN KATCHOR 2015

# Illness in the Window

BETWEEN THE PRIVACY OF A DOCTOR'S OFFICE...

AND THE SPECTACLE OF A HOSPITAL EMERGENCY ROOM...

THERE HAS ARISEN A NEW FORM OF MEDICAL SERVICE.

QUIK CURE URGENT CARE INS.
QUIK-CURE STROLL-IN MEDICAL CARE
NON STOP 24

OPERATING OUT OF STOREFRONTS ONCE OCCUPIED BY BANKS, CLOTHING STORES AND OTHER FAILED BUSINESSES.

CORDIAL BROTHERS
CAIN
RETAIL SPACE FOR RENT
241 MAIN

THESE WAITING ROOMS, OPEN TO VIEW FROM THE STREET, OFFER A PERVERSE FORM OF WINDOW-SHOPPING.

I FEEL FINE TODAY.
NON STOP 24
MEAT

INDIVIDUALS STRICKEN BY A VARIETY OF ILLNESSES, YET SHOWING NO OUTWARD SYMPTOMS, WAIT THEIR TURN.

A VICTIM OF A HOUSHOLD ACCIDENT BRAVELY STANCHES HIS WOUND.

A FRIGHTENED MOTHER COMFORTS HER SICK CHILD.

A LOVESICK TEENAGER HOLDS BACK HER TEARS.

AN UNEMPLOYED MAN WINCES AT THE THOUGHT OF THE PAYMENT DUE.

WE ACCEPT ALL MAJOR
NEWS

ALL ON DISPLAY FOR THE EDIFICATION OF HEALTHY PASSERSBY.

AND I HAVE A GOOD APPETITE.
STROLL-IN
42

OCCASIONALLY, A HAGGARD DOCTOR STEPS OUTSIDE FOR A SMOKE.

STROLL-IN MEDICAL CARE
OPEN

e Vontsel Institute

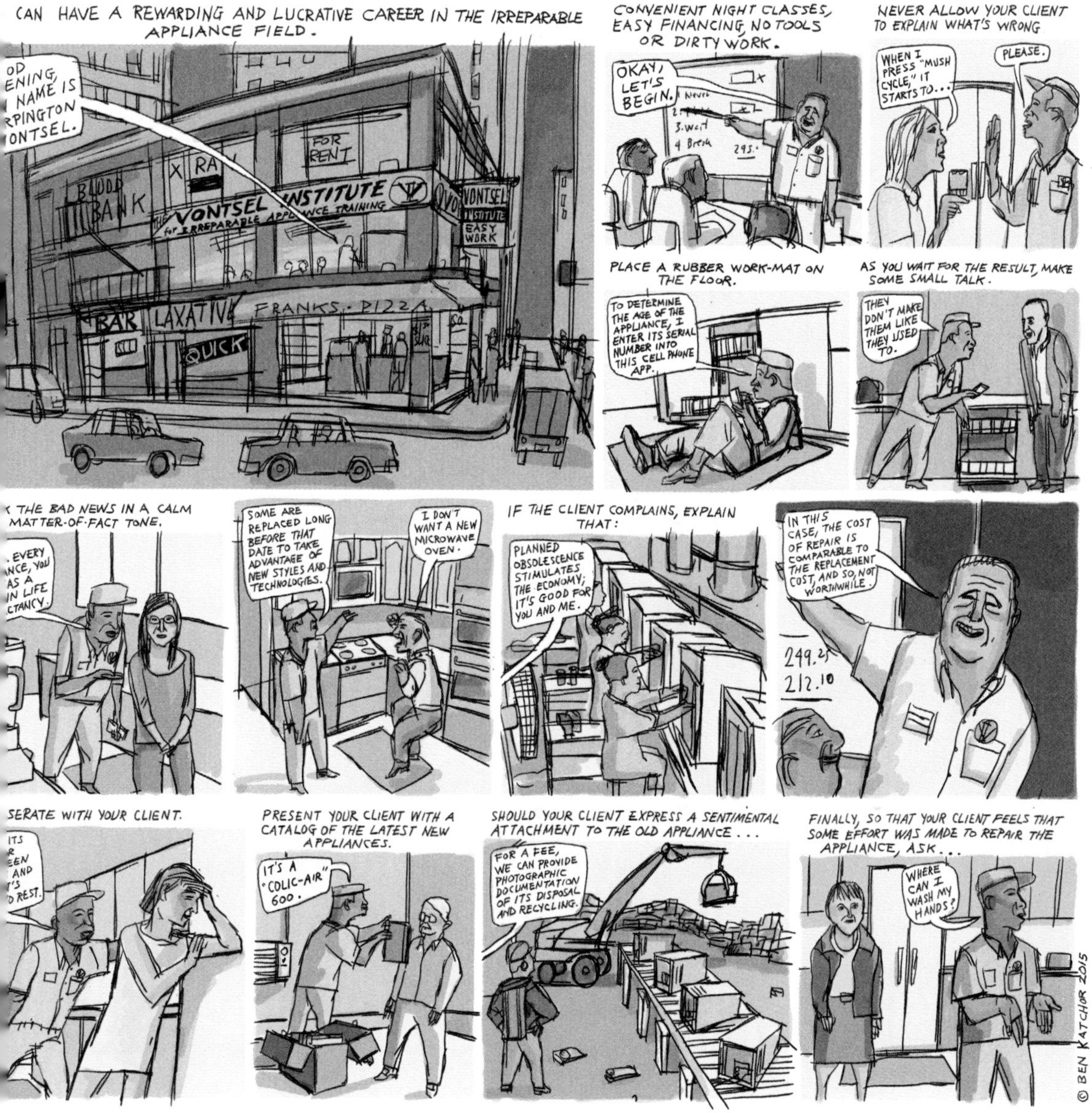
CAN HAVE A REWARDING AND LUCRATIVE CAREER IN THE IRREPARABLE APPLIANCE FIELD.
FOR RENT
VONTSEL INSTITUTE
VONTSEL INSTITUTE for IRREPARABLE APPLIANCE TRAINING
VONTSEL INSTITUTE EASY WORK
BANK
BAR
LAXATIVE
QUICK
FRANKS PIZZA
CONVENIENT NIGHT CLASSES, EASY FINANCING, NO TOOLS OR DIRTY WORK.
OKAY, LET'S BEGIN.
NEVER ALLOW YOUR CLIENT TO EXPLAIN WHAT'S WRONG
WHEN I PRESS "MUSH CYCLE," IT STARTS TO...
PLEASE.
PLACE A RUBBER WORK-MAT ON THE FLOOR.
TO DETERMINE THE AGE OF THE APPLIANCE, I ENTER ITS SERIAL NUMBER INTO THIS CELL PHONE APP.
AS YOU WAIT FOR THE RESULT, MAKE SOME SMALL TALK.
THEY DON'T MAKE THEM LIKE THEY USED TO.
THE BAD NEWS IN A CALM MATTER-OF-FACT TONE.
SOME ARE REPLACED LONG BEFORE THAT DATE TO TAKE ADVANTAGE OF NEW STYLES AND TECHNOLOGIES.
I DON'T WANT A NEW MICROWAVE OVEN.
IF THE CLIENT COMPLAINS, EXPLAIN THAT:
PLANNED OBSOLESCENCE STIMULATES THE ECONOMY; IT'S GOOD FOR YOU AND ME.
IN THIS CASE, THE COST OF REPAIR IS COMPARABLE TO THE REPLACEMENT COST, AND SO, NOT WORTHWHILE.
249.25
212.10
SERATE WITH YOUR CLIENT.
PRESENT YOUR CLIENT WITH A CATALOG OF THE LATEST NEW APPLIANCES.
IT'S A "COLIC-AIR" 600.
SHOULD YOUR CLIENT EXPRESS A SENTIMENTAL ATTACHMENT TO THE OLD APPLIANCE...
FOR A FEE, WE CAN PROVIDE PHOTOGRAPHIC DOCUMENTATION OF ITS DISPOSAL AND RECYCLING.
FINALLY, SO THAT YOUR CLIENT FEELS THAT SOME EFFORT WAS MADE TO REPAIR THE APPLIANCE, ASK...
WHERE CAN I WASH MY HANDS?
© BEN KATCHOR 2015

# The Brazen Bull Corporation

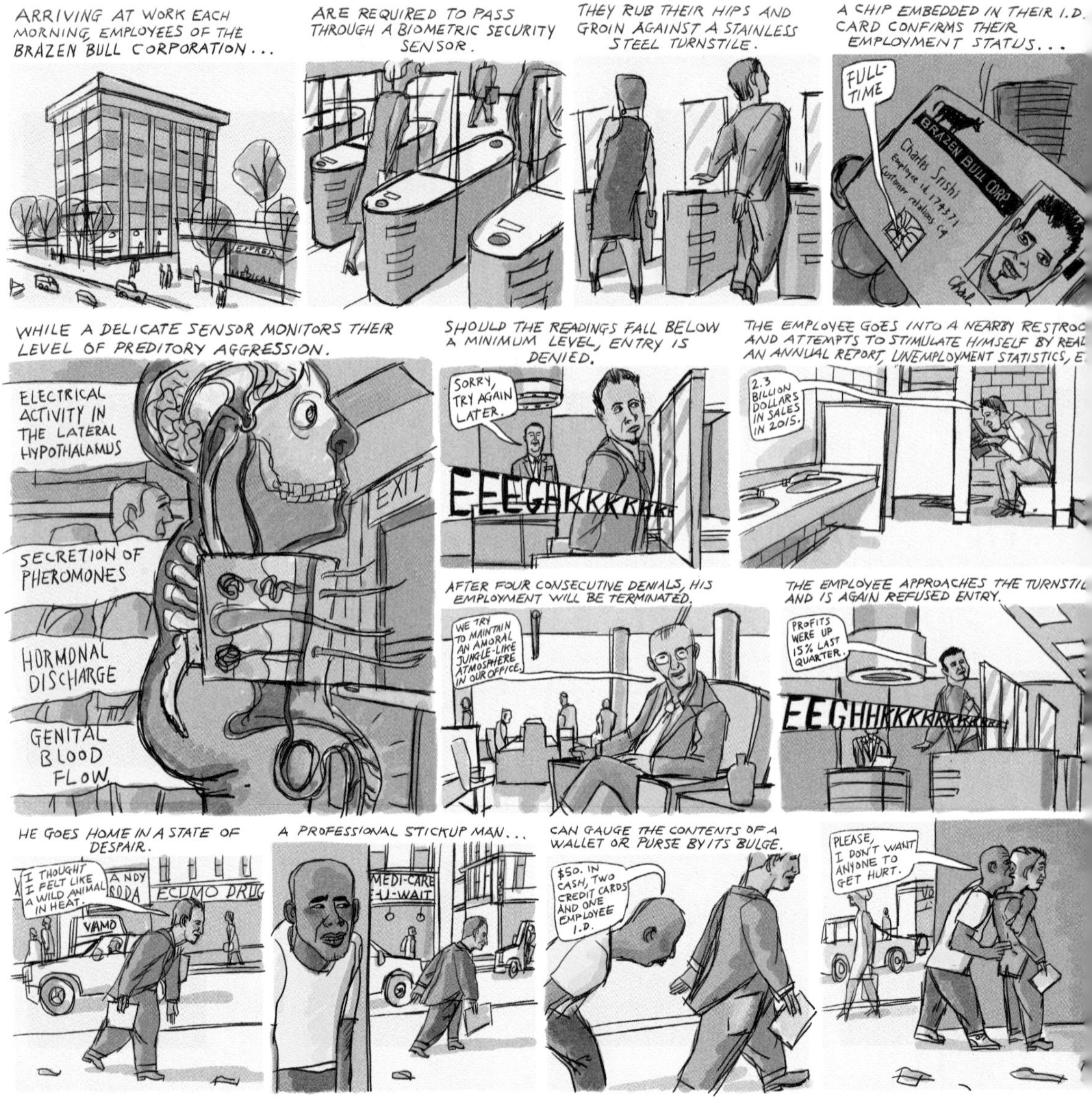
ARRIVING AT WORK EACH MORNING, EMPLOYEES OF THE BRAZEN BULL CORPORATION...
ARE REQUIRED TO PASS THROUGH A BIOMETRIC SECURITY SENSOR.
THEY RUB THEIR HIPS AND GROIN AGAINST A STAINLESS STEEL TURNSTILE.
A CHIP EMBEDDED IN THEIR I.D. CARD CONFIRMS THEIR EMPLOYMENT STATUS...
FULL-TIME
BRAZEN BULL CORP.
Charles Srishi
WHILE A DELICATE SENSOR MONITORS THEIR LEVEL OF PREDITORY AGGRESSION.
ELECTRICAL ACTIVITY IN THE LATERAL HYPOTHALAMUS
SECRETION OF PHEROMONES
HORMONAL DISCHARGE
GENITAL BLOOD FLOW
EXIT
SHOULD THE READINGS FALL BELOW A MINIMUM LEVEL, ENTRY IS DENIED.
SORRY, TRY AGAIN LATER.
EEEGHKKKKRRR
THE EMPLOYEE GOES INTO A NEARBY RESTROC
AND ATTEMPTS TO STIMULATE HIMSELF BY REAL
AN ANNUAL REPORT, UNEMPLOYMENT STATISTICS, E
2.3 BILLION DOLLARS IN SALES IN 2015.
AFTER FOUR CONSECUTIVE DENIALS, HIS EMPLOYMENT WILL BE TERMINATED.
WE TRY TO MAINTAIN AN AMORAL JUNGLE-LIKE ATMOSPHERE IN OUR OFFICE.
THE EMPLOYEE APPROACHES THE TURNSTIL
AND IS AGAIN REFUSED ENTRY.
PROFITS WERE UP 15% LAST QUARTER.
EEGHHKKKKRRR
HE GOES HOME IN A STATE OF DESPAIR.
I THOUGHT I FELT LIKE A WILD ANIMAL IN HEAT.
ANDY SODA
ECUMO DRUG
VAMO
A PROFESSIONAL STICKUP MAN...
MEDI-CARE
E-U-WAIT
CAN GAUGE THE CONTENTS OF A WALLET OR PURSE BY ITS BULGE.
$50. IN CASH, TWO CREDIT CARDS AND ONE EMPLOYEE I.D.
PLEASE, I DON'T WANT ANYONE TO GET HURT.

# Blanket Portraits

GENEVIÈVE ELVERUM

*originally published in*

Drawn and Quarterly: Twenty-Five Years of Contemporary Cartooning, Comics, and Graphic Novels

DRAWN AND QUARTERLY

7 × 9 inches • 776 pages

DRAWN
AND
QUARTERLY
TWENTY-FIVE YEARS OF CONTEMPORARY
CARTOONING, COMICS, AND GRAPHIC NOVELS

## Biography

Geneviève Elverum (AKA Castrée) is a Canadian-born cartoonist and musician who lives with her husband and daughter in Washington State. genevievecastree.com

## Statement

I collect wool blankets; comfort and coziness are important to me. I like to wrap my loved ones and myself in warmth whenever I can.

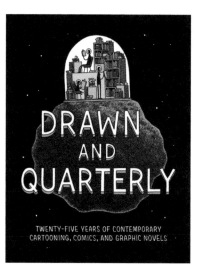

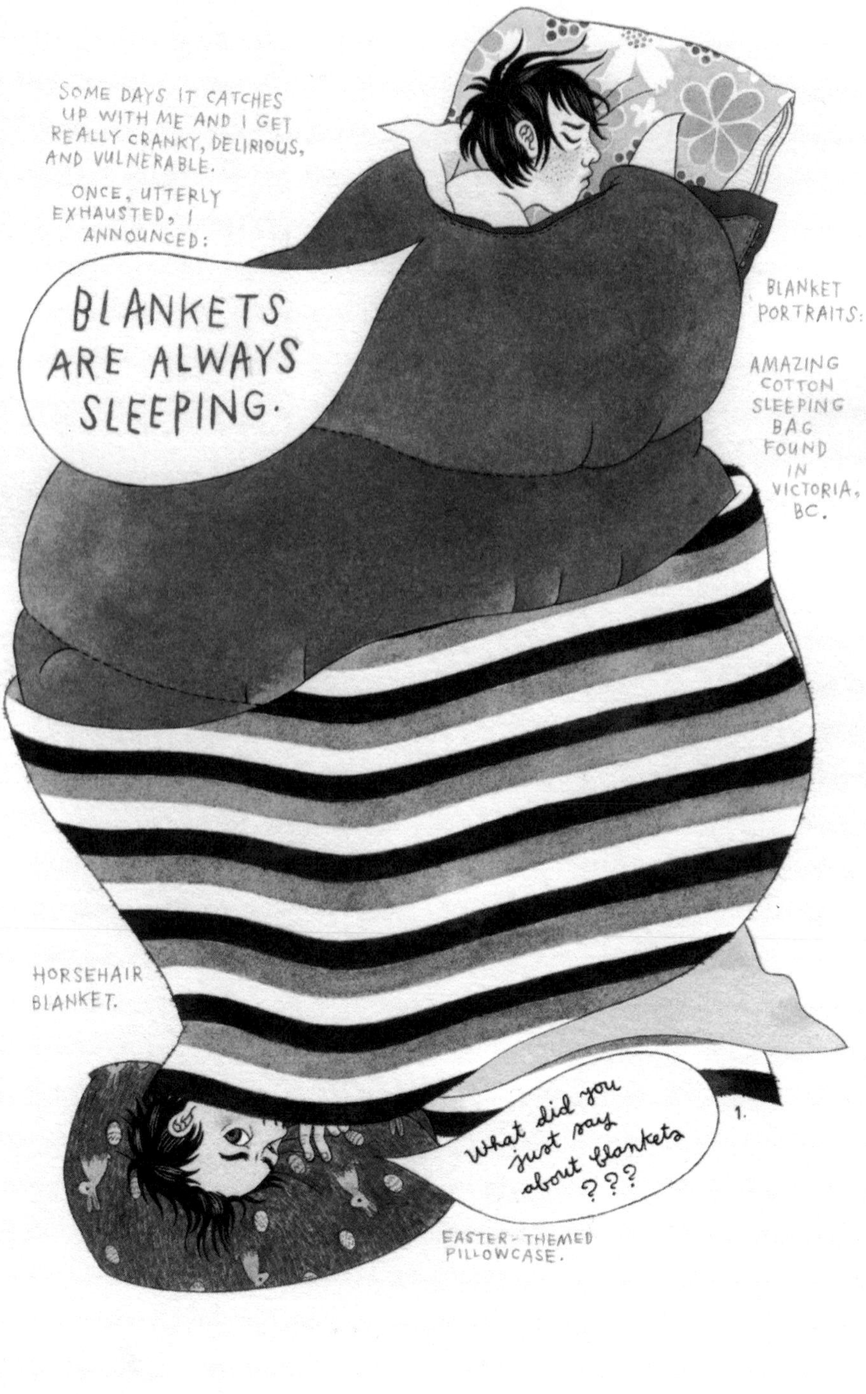
SOME DAYS IT CATCHES UP WITH ME AND I GET REALLY CRANKY, DELIRIOUS, AND VULNERABLE.
ONCE, UTTERLY EXHAUSTED, I ANNOUNCED:
BLANKETS ARE ALWAYS SLEEPING.
BLANKET PORTRAITS:
AMAZING COTTON SLEEPING BAG FOUND IN VICTORIA, BC.
HORSEHAIR BLANKET.
What did you just say about blankets ???
1.
EASTER-THEMED PILLOWCASE.

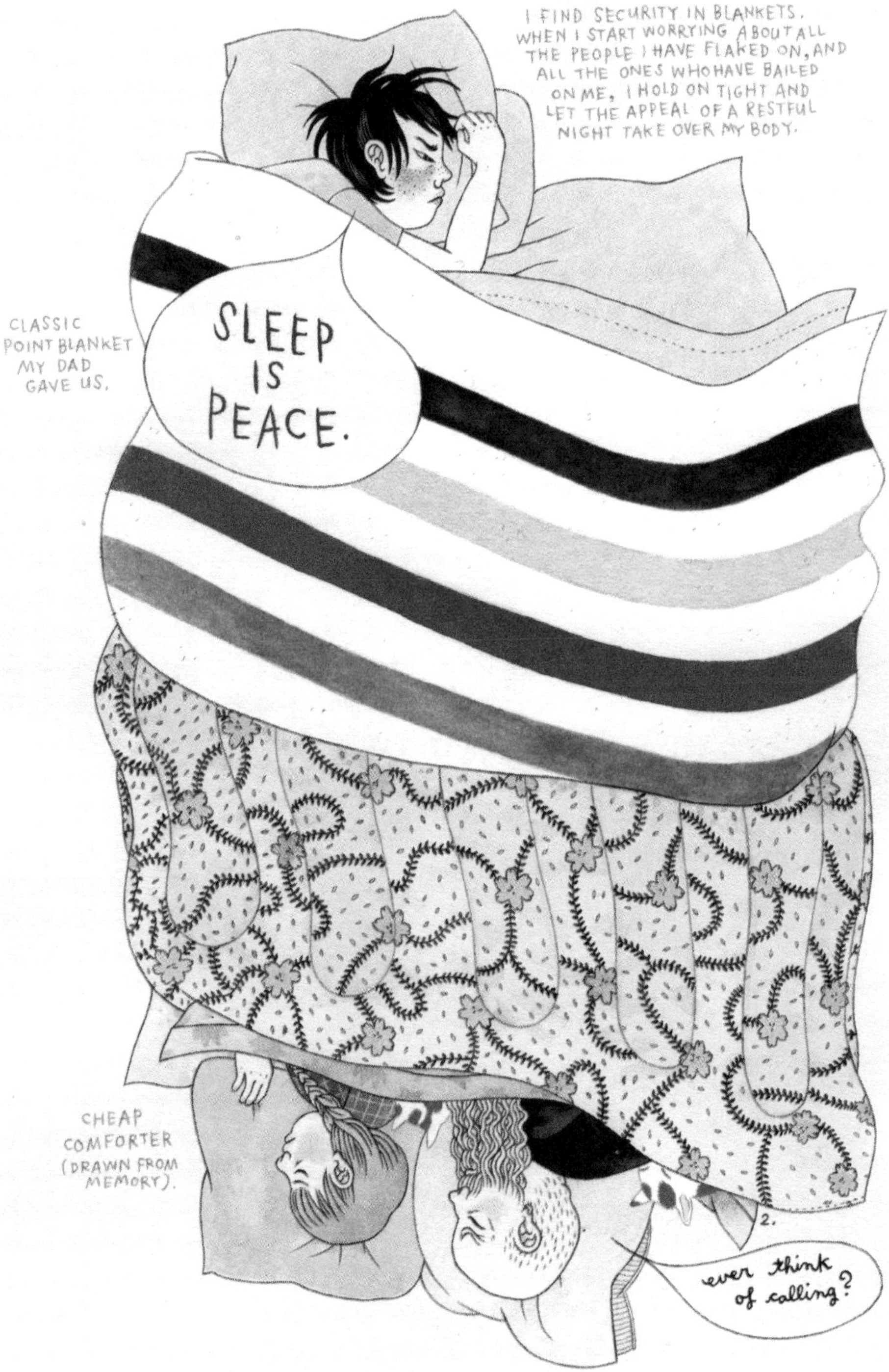
I FIND SECURITY IN BLANKETS. WHEN I START WORRYING ABOUT ALL THE PEOPLE I HAVE FLAKED ON, AND ALL THE ONES WHO HAVE BAILED ON ME, I HOLD ON TIGHT AND LET THE APPEAL OF A RESTFUL NIGHT TAKE OVER MY BODY.
CLASSIC POINT BLANKET MY DAD GAVE US.
SLEEP IS PEACE.
CHEAP COMFORTER (DRAWN FROM MEMORY).
2.
ever think of calling?

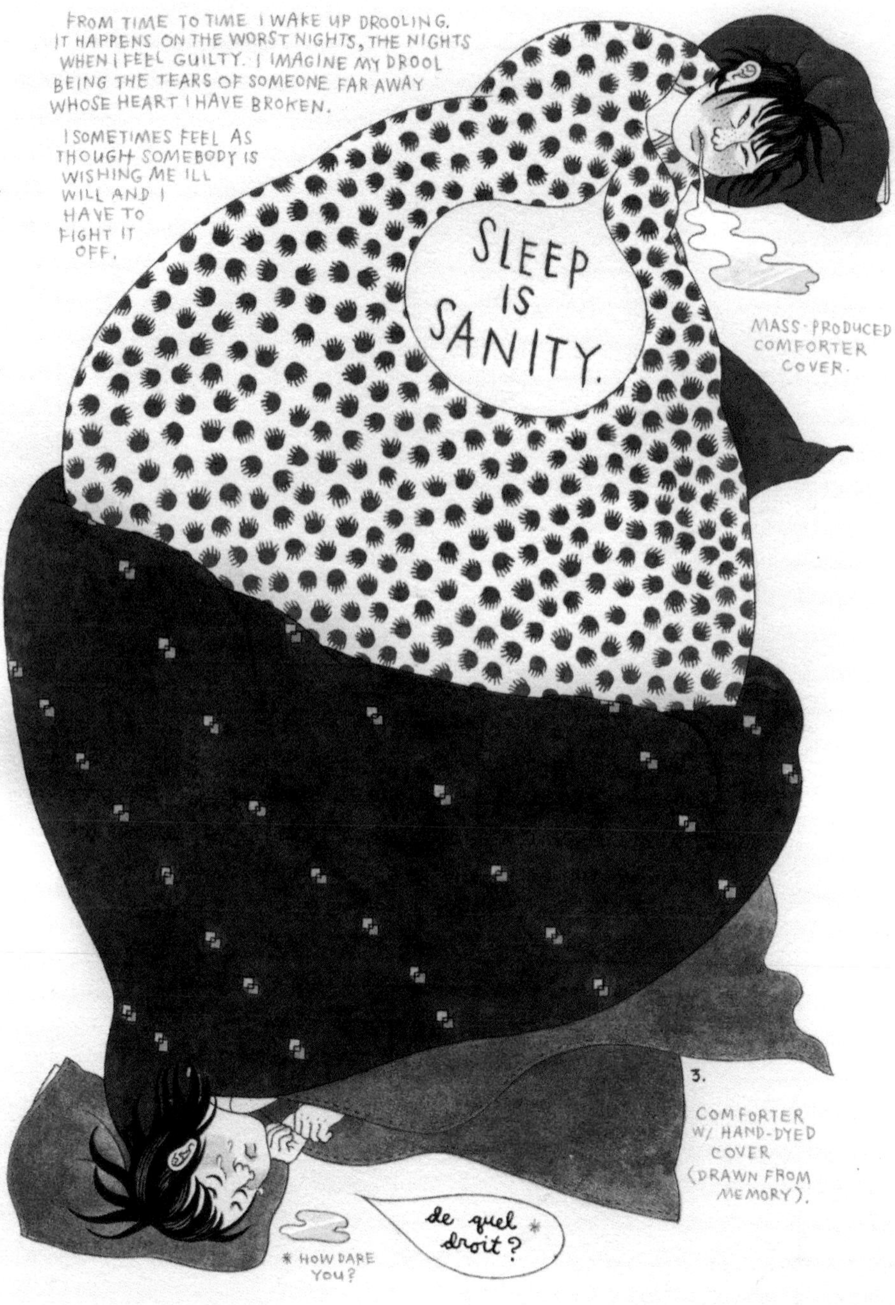
FROM TIME TO TIME I WAKE UP DROOLING. IT HAPPENS ON THE WORST NIGHTS, THE NIGHTS WHEN I FEEL GUILTY. I IMAGINE MY DROOL BEING THE TEARS OF SOMEONE FAR AWAY WHOSE HEART I HAVE BROKEN.
I SOMETIMES FEEL AS THOUGH SOMEBODY IS WISHING ME ILL WILL AND I HAVE TO FIGHT IT OFF.
SLEEP IS SANITY.
MASS-PRODUCED COMFORTER COVER.
3.
COMFORTER W/ HAND-DYED COVER (DRAWN FROM MEMORY).
de quel droit? *
* HOW DARE YOU?

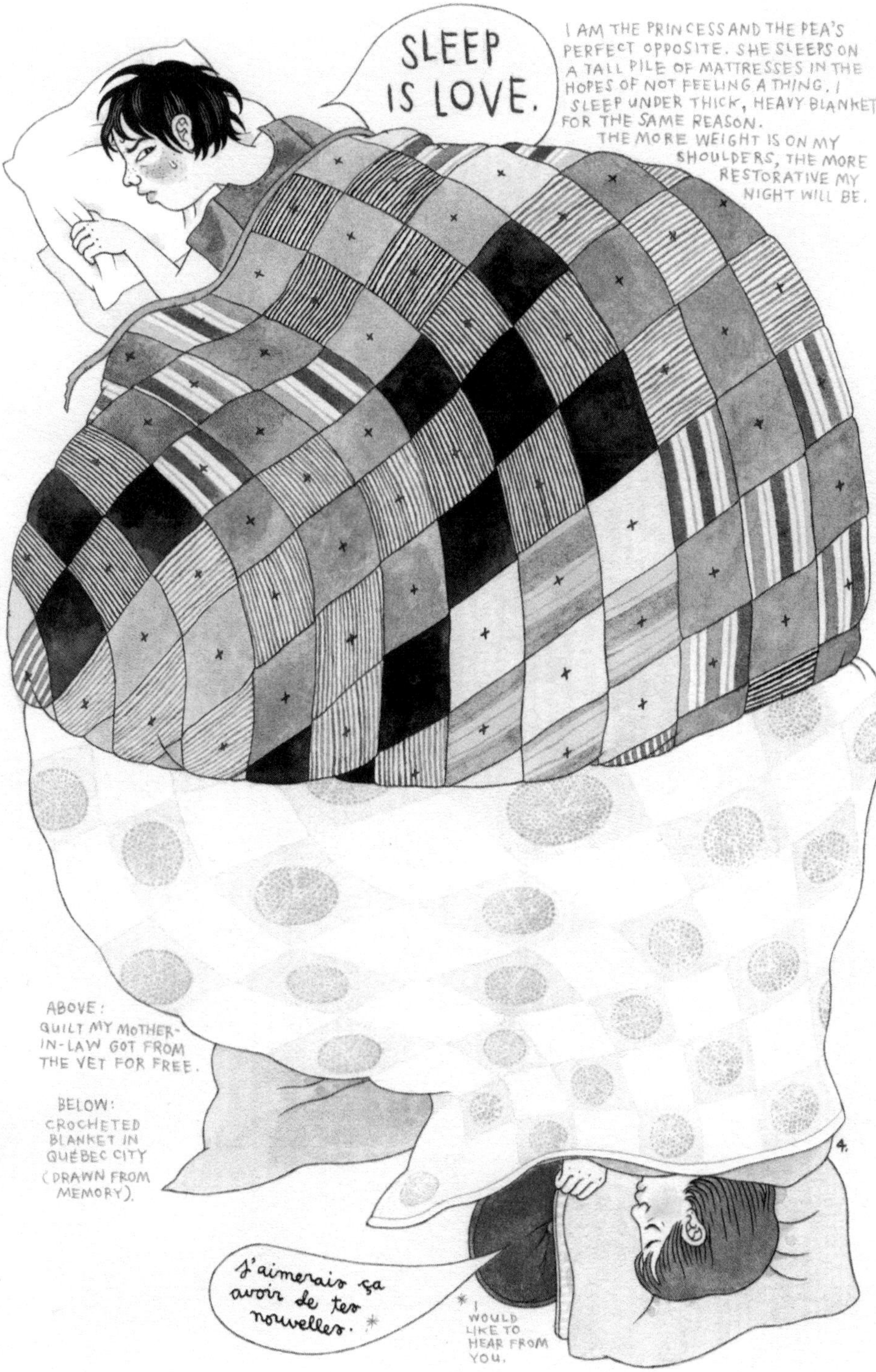
SLEEP IS LOVE.
I AM THE PRINCESS AND THE PEA'S PERFECT OPPOSITE. SHE SLEEPS ON A TALL PILE OF MATTRESSES IN THE HOPES OF NOT FEELING A THING. I SLEEP UNDER THICK, HEAVY BLANKETS FOR THE SAME REASON. THE MORE WEIGHT IS ON MY SHOULDERS, THE MORE RESTORATIVE MY NIGHT WILL BE.
ABOVE: QUILT MY MOTHER-IN-LAW GOT FROM THE VET FOR FREE.
BELOW: CROCHETED BLANKET IN QUÉBEC CITY (DRAWN FROM MEMORY).
4.
J'aimerais ça avoir de tes nouvelles.*
* I WOULD LIKE TO HEAR FROM YOU.

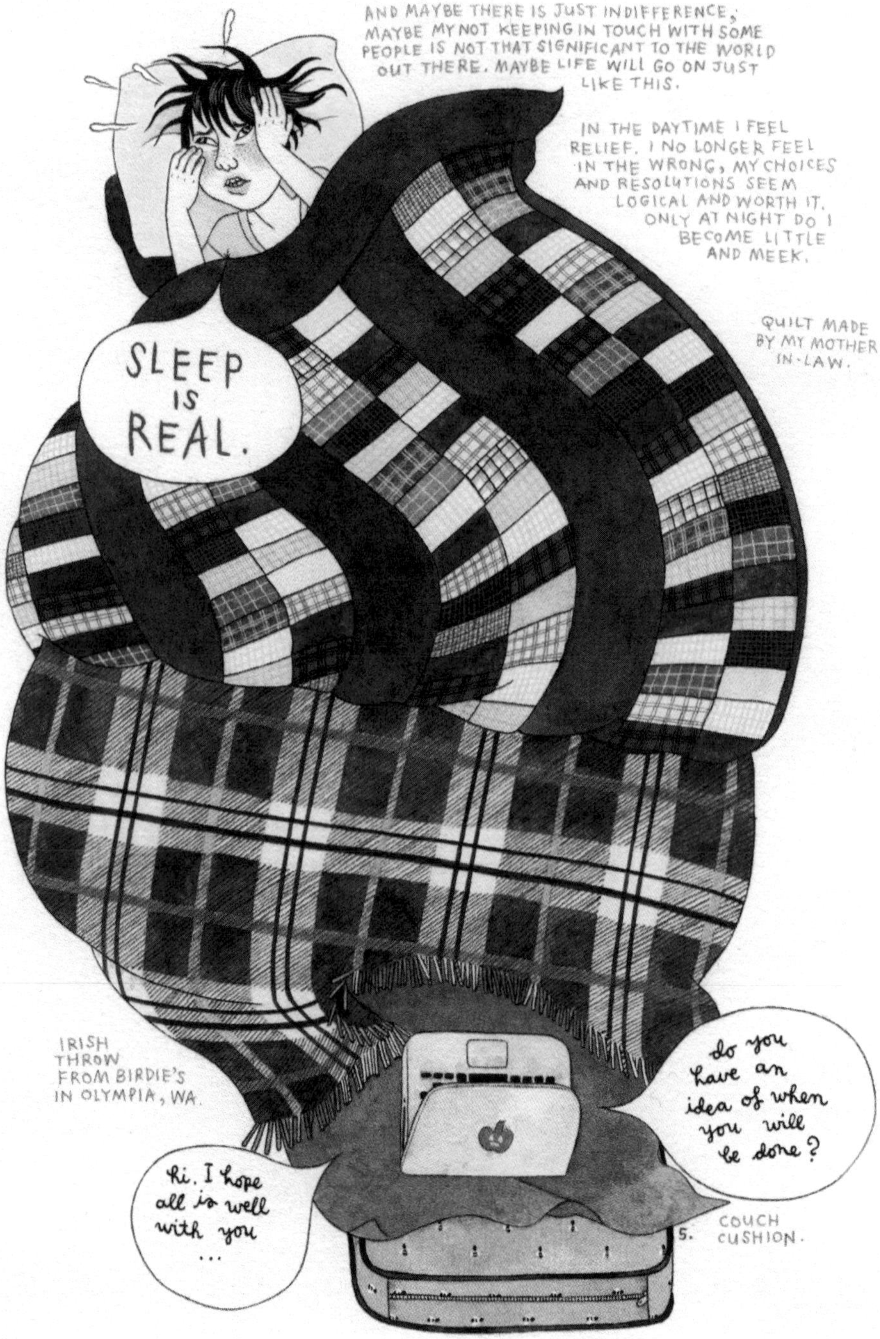
AND MAYBE THERE IS JUST INDIFFERENCE; MAYBE MY NOT KEEPING IN TOUCH WITH SOME PEOPLE IS NOT THAT SIGNIFICANT TO THE WORLD OUT THERE. MAYBE LIFE WILL GO ON JUST LIKE THIS.
IN THE DAYTIME I FEEL RELIEF. I NO LONGER FEEL IN THE WRONG, MY CHOICES AND RESOLUTIONS SEEM LOGICAL AND WORTH IT. ONLY AT NIGHT DO I BECOME LITTLE AND MEEK.
SLEEP IS REAL.
QUILT MADE BY MY MOTHER-IN-LAW.
IRISH THROW FROM BIRDIE'S IN OLYMPIA, WA.
do you have an idea of when you will be done?
hi. I hope all is well with you ...
5. COUCH CUSHION.

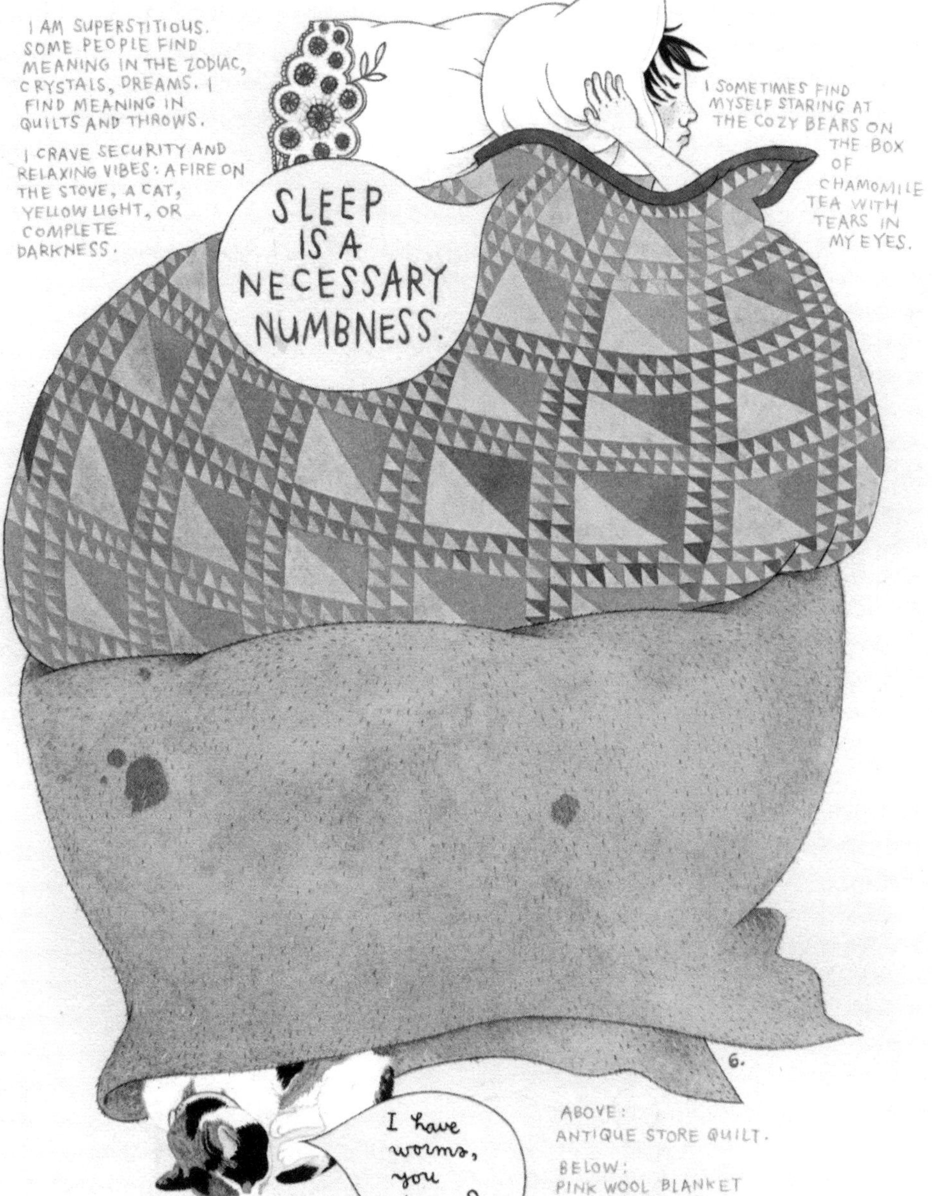
I AM SUPERSTITIOUS. SOME PEOPLE FIND MEANING IN THE ZODIAC, CRYSTALS, DREAMS. I FIND MEANING IN QUILTS AND THROWS.
I CRAVE SECURITY AND RELAXING VIBES: A FIRE ON THE STOVE, A CAT, YELLOW LIGHT, OR COMPLETE DARKNESS.
SLEEP IS A NECESSARY NUMBNESS.
I SOMETIMES FIND MYSELF STARING AT THE COZY BEARS ON THE BOX OF CHAMOMILE TEA WITH TEARS IN MY EYES.
6.
I have worms, you know?
ABOVE: ANTIQUE STORE QUILT.
BELOW: PINK WOOL BLANKET W/ CAT VOMIT.

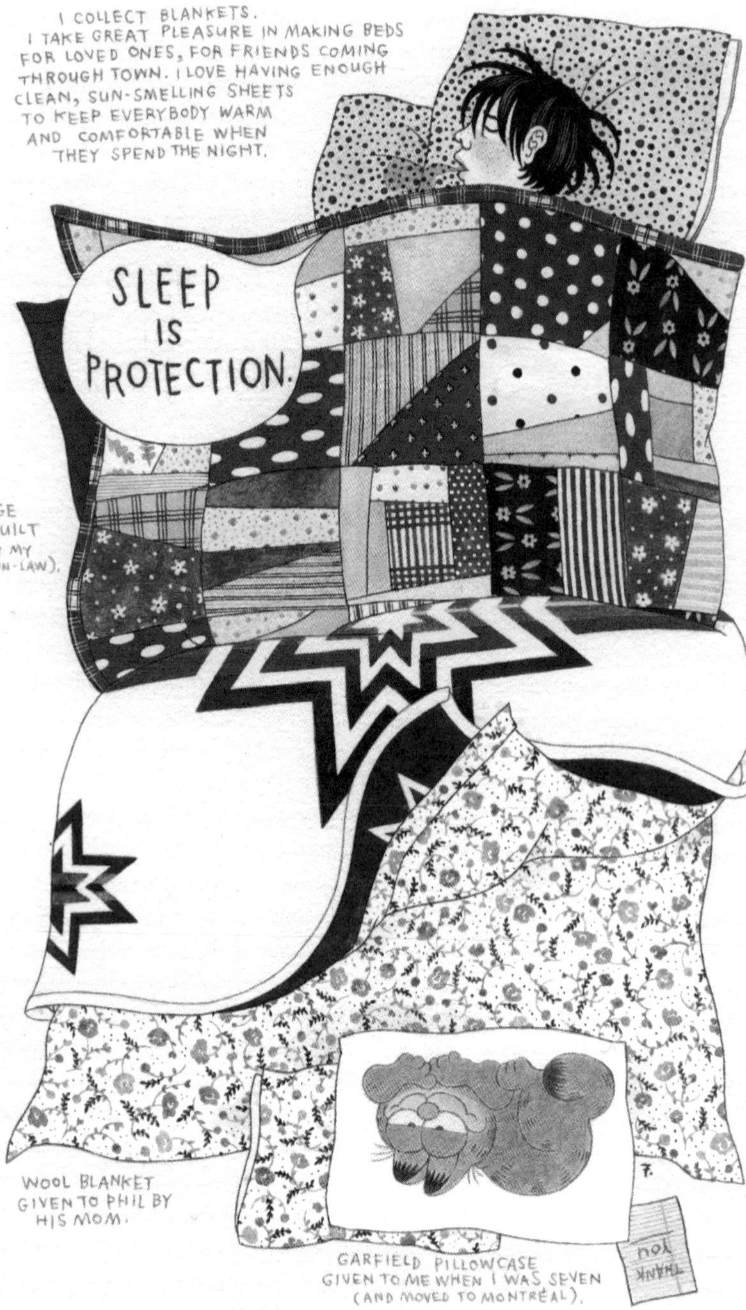
I COLLECT BLANKETS.
I TAKE GREAT PLEASURE IN MAKING BEDS FOR LOVED ONES, FOR FRIENDS COMING THROUGH TOWN. I LOVE HAVING ENOUGH CLEAN, SUN-SMELLING SHEETS TO KEEP EVERYBODY WARM AND COMFORTABLE WHEN THEY SPEND THE NIGHT.
SLEEP IS PROTECTION.
GARAGE SALE QUILT (FIXED BY MY MOTHER-IN-LAW).
WOOL BLANKET GIVEN TO PHIL BY HIS MOM.
GARFIELD PILLOWCASE GIVEN TO ME WHEN I WAS SEVEN (AND MOVED TO MONTRÉAL).
THANK YOU
F.

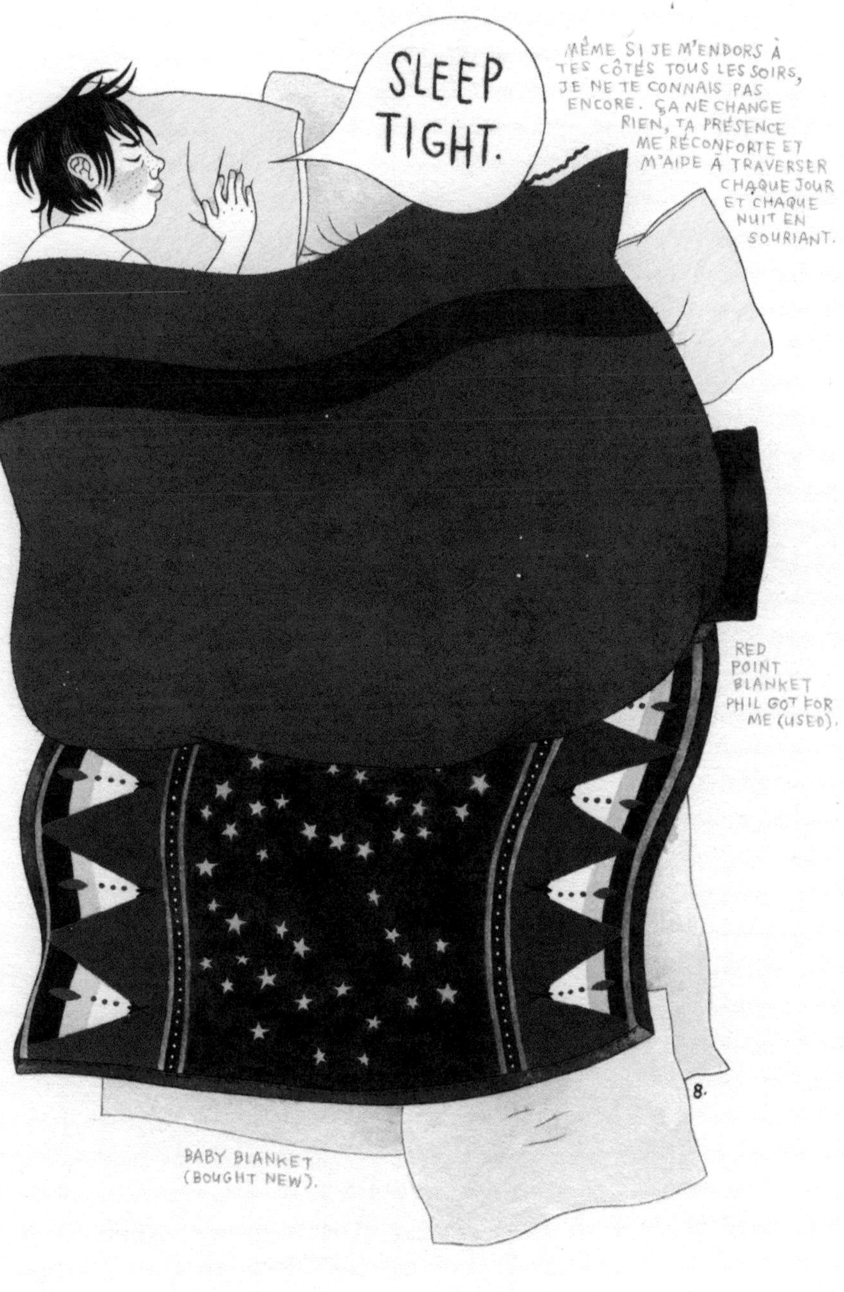
SLEEP TIGHT.
MÊME SI JE M'ENDORS À TES CÔTÉS TOUS LES SOIRS, JE NE TE CONNAIS PAS ENCORE. ÇA NE CHANGE RIEN, TA PRÉSENCE ME RÉCONFORTE ET M'AIDE À TRAVERSER CHAQUE JOUR ET CHAQUE NUIT EN SOURIANT.
RED POINT BLANKET PHIL GOT FOR ME (USED).
8.
BABY BLANKET (BOUGHT NEW).

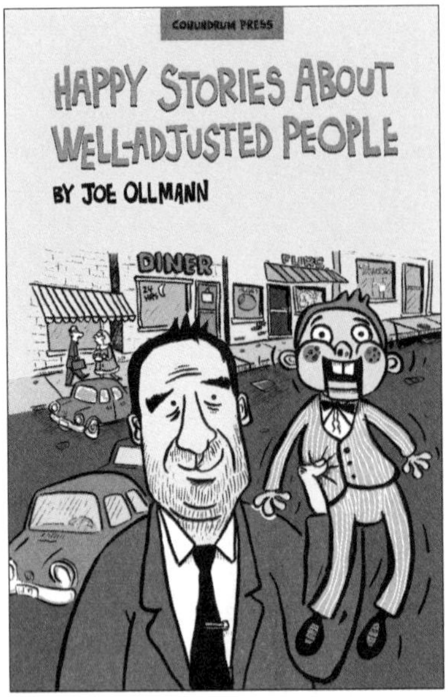
CONUNDRUM PRESS
HAPPY STORIES ABOUT WELL-ADJUSTED PEOPLE
BY JOE OLLMANN
DINER

# Shut Your Pie Hole, Johnny Pinetop

JOE OLLMANN

*originally published in*

Happy Stories About Well-Adjusted People
CONUNDRUM PRESS
6 × 9 inches • 260 pages

## Biography

Joe Ollmann lives in Hamilton, the Riviera of Southern Ontario. He is the winner of the Doug Wright Award for Best Book in 2007 and loser of the same award many other times. He is author of seven books, including the upcoming comics biography of writer-adventurer William Seabrook. wagpress.net

## Statement

While in the middle of a long, biographical work about the life of William Seabrook, I took a break to return to good old short fiction comics, just to reassure myself I could still do nonbiographical comics that didn't require elaborate research and technical veracity and that was, you know, just for fun. I didn't use panel borders for the first time in my life. This was the result, and I'm gratified to have it included in this publication.

# SHUT YOUR PIE HOLE, JOHNNY PINETOP!

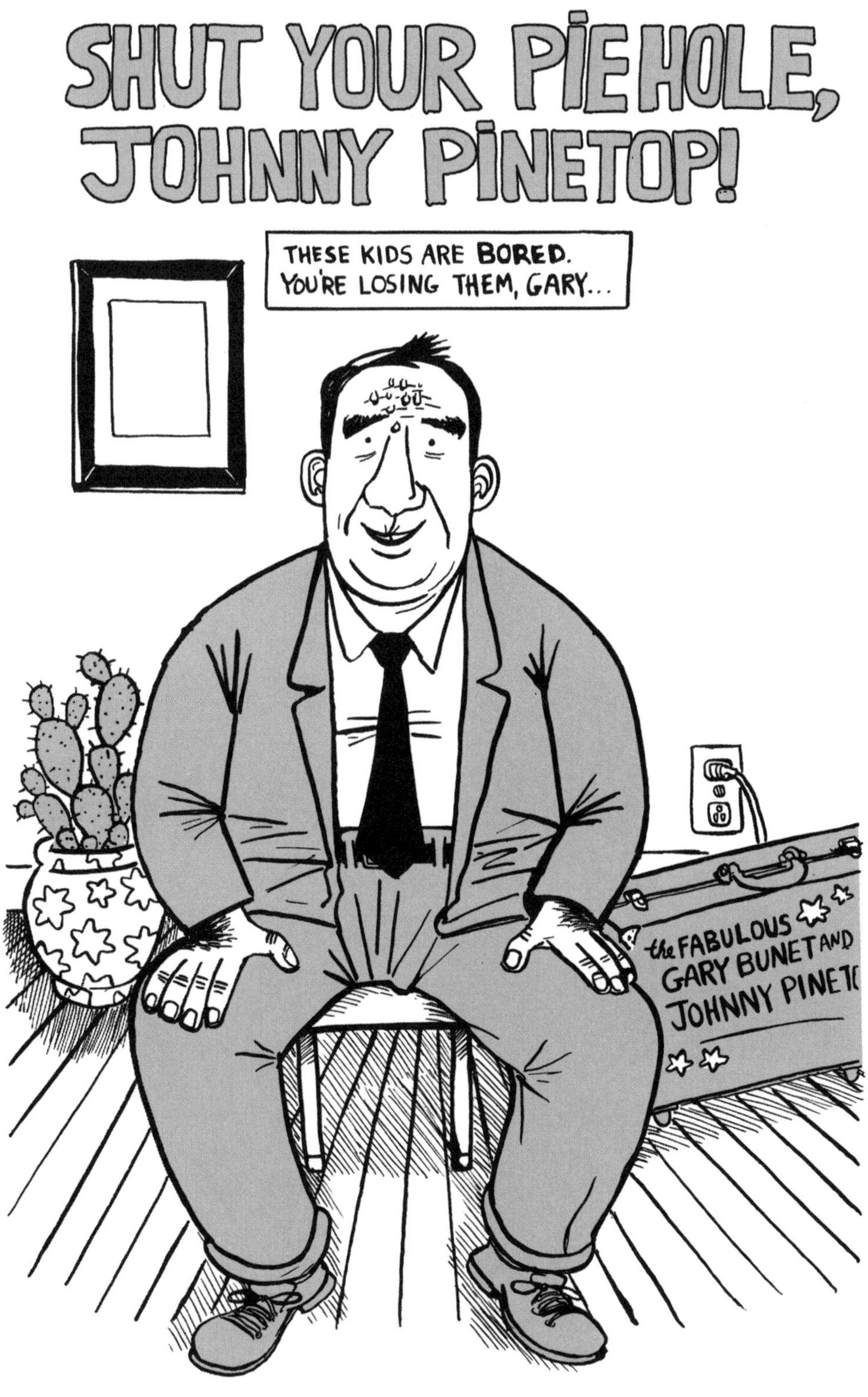
THESE KIDS ARE BORED. YOU'RE LOSING THEM, GARY...
the FABULOUS GARY BUNET AND JOHNNY PINET

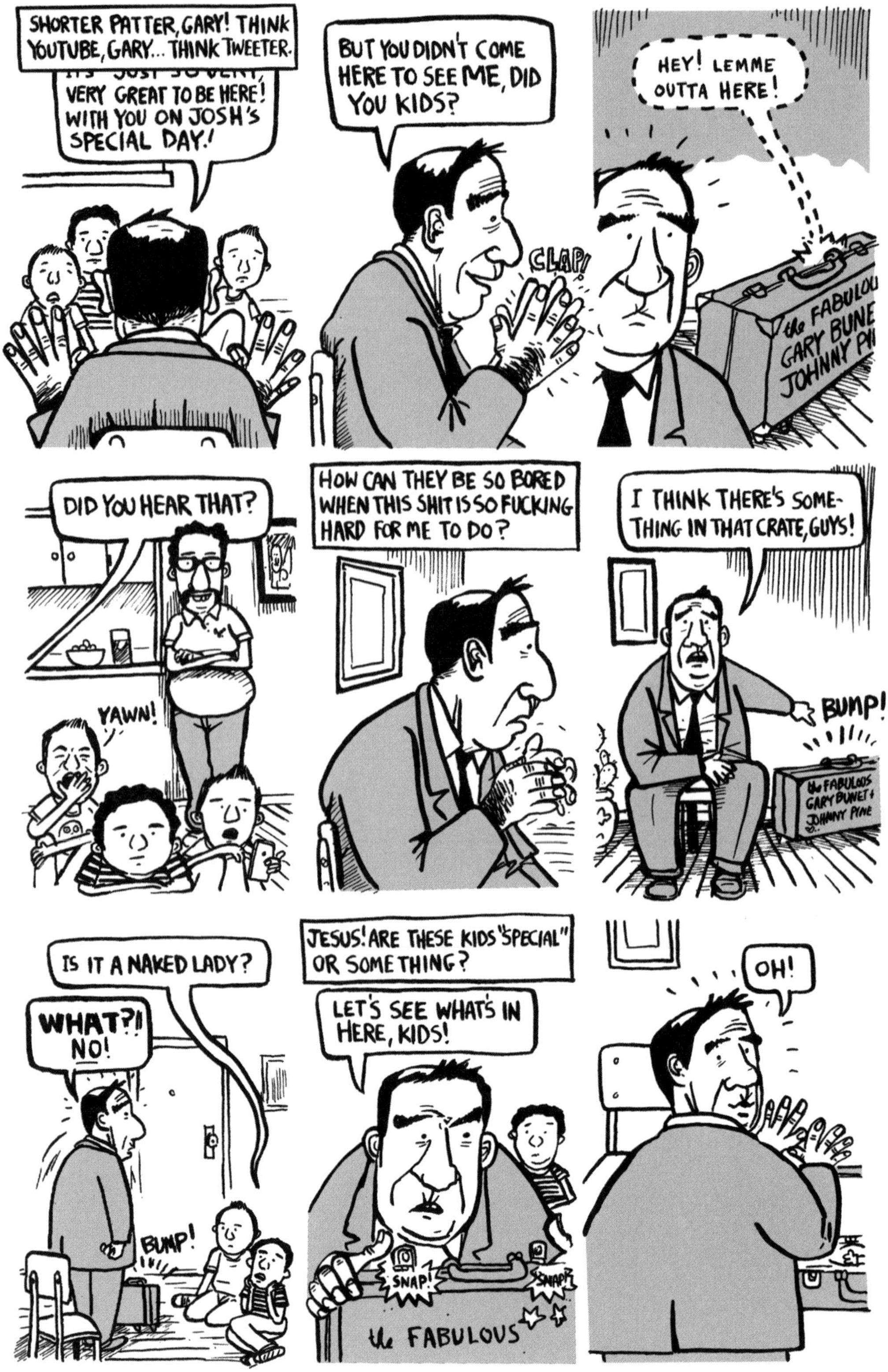
SHORTER PATTER, GARY! THINK YOUTUBE, GARY... THINK TWEETER.
VERY GREAT TO BE HERE! WITH YOU ON JOSH'S SPECIAL DAY!
BUT YOU DIDN'T COME HERE TO SEE ME, DID YOU KIDS?
CLAP!
HEY! LEMME OUTTA HERE!
DID YOU HEAR THAT?
YAWN!
HOW CAN THEY BE SO BORED WHEN THIS SHIT IS SO FUCKING HARD FOR ME TO DO?
I THINK THERE'S SOME-THING IN THAT CRATE, GUYS!
BUMP!
IS IT A NAKED LADY?
WHAT?! NO!
BUMP!
JESUS! ARE THESE KIDS "SPECIAL" OR SOMETHING?
LET'S SEE WHAT'S IN HERE, KIDS!
SNAP!
SNAP!
the FABULOUS
OH!

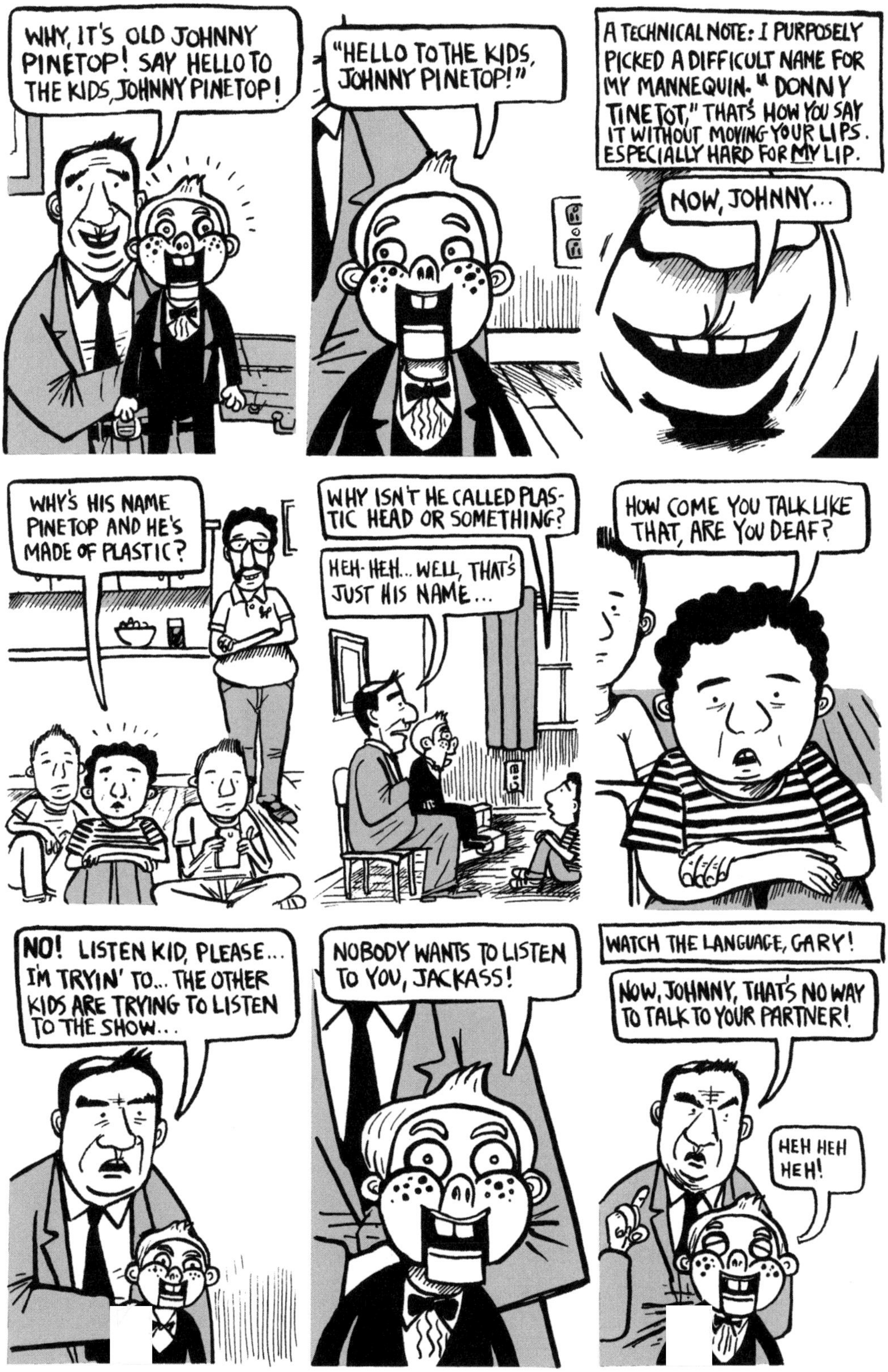
WHY, IT'S OLD JOHNNY PINETOP! SAY HELLO TO THE KIDS, JOHNNY PINETOP!
"HELLO TO THE KIDS, JOHNNY PINETOP!"
A TECHNICAL NOTE: I PURPOSELY PICKED A DIFFICULT NAME FOR MY MANNEQUIN. "DONNY TINETOT," THAT'S HOW YOU SAY IT WITHOUT MOVING YOUR LIPS. ESPECIALLY HARD FOR MY LIP.
NOW, JOHNNY...
WHY'S HIS NAME PINETOP AND HE'S MADE OF PLASTIC?
WHY ISN'T HE CALLED PLAS-TIC HEAD OR SOMETHING?
HEH-HEH... WELL, THAT'S JUST HIS NAME...
HOW COME YOU TALK LIKE THAT, ARE YOU DEAF?
NO! LISTEN KID, PLEASE... I'M TRYIN' TO... THE OTHER KIDS ARE TRYING TO LISTEN TO THE SHOW...
NOBODY WANTS TO LISTEN TO YOU, JACKASS!
WATCH THE LANGUAGE, GARY!
NOW, JOHNNY, THAT'S NO WAY TO TALK TO YOUR PARTNER!
HEH HEH HEH!

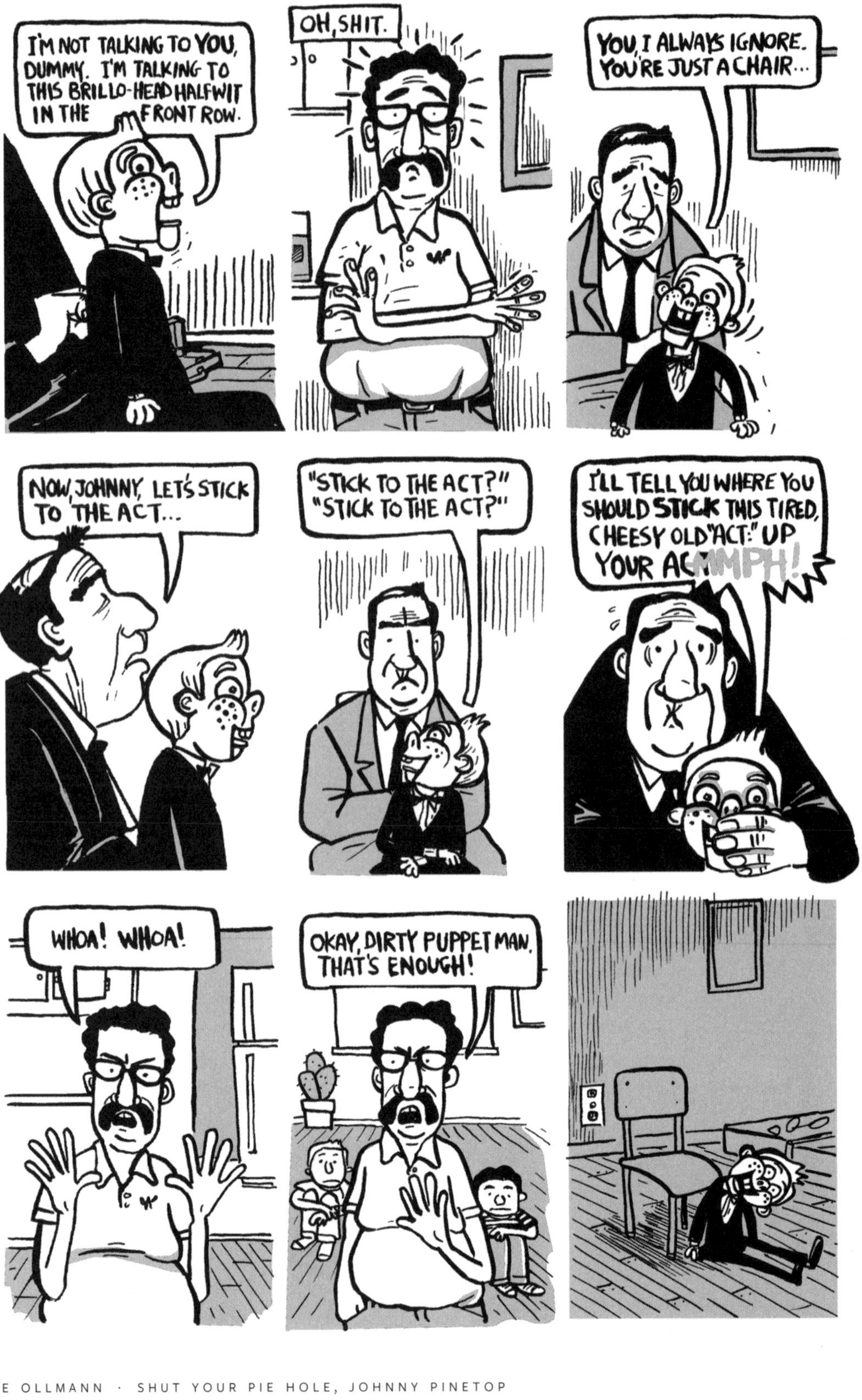

I'M NOT TALKING TO YOU, DUMMY. I'M TALKING TO THIS BRILLO-HEAD HALFWIT IN THE FRONT ROW.
OH, SHIT.
YOU, I ALWAYS IGNORE. YOU'RE JUST A CHAIR...
NOW, JOHNNY, LET'S STICK TO THE ACT...
"STICK TO THE ACT?" "STICK TO THE ACT?"
I'LL TELL YOU WHERE YOU SHOULD STICK THIS TIRED, CHEESY OLD "ACT:" UP YOUR ACMMPH!
WHOA! WHOA!
OKAY, DIRTY PUPPET MAN. THAT'S ENOUGH!

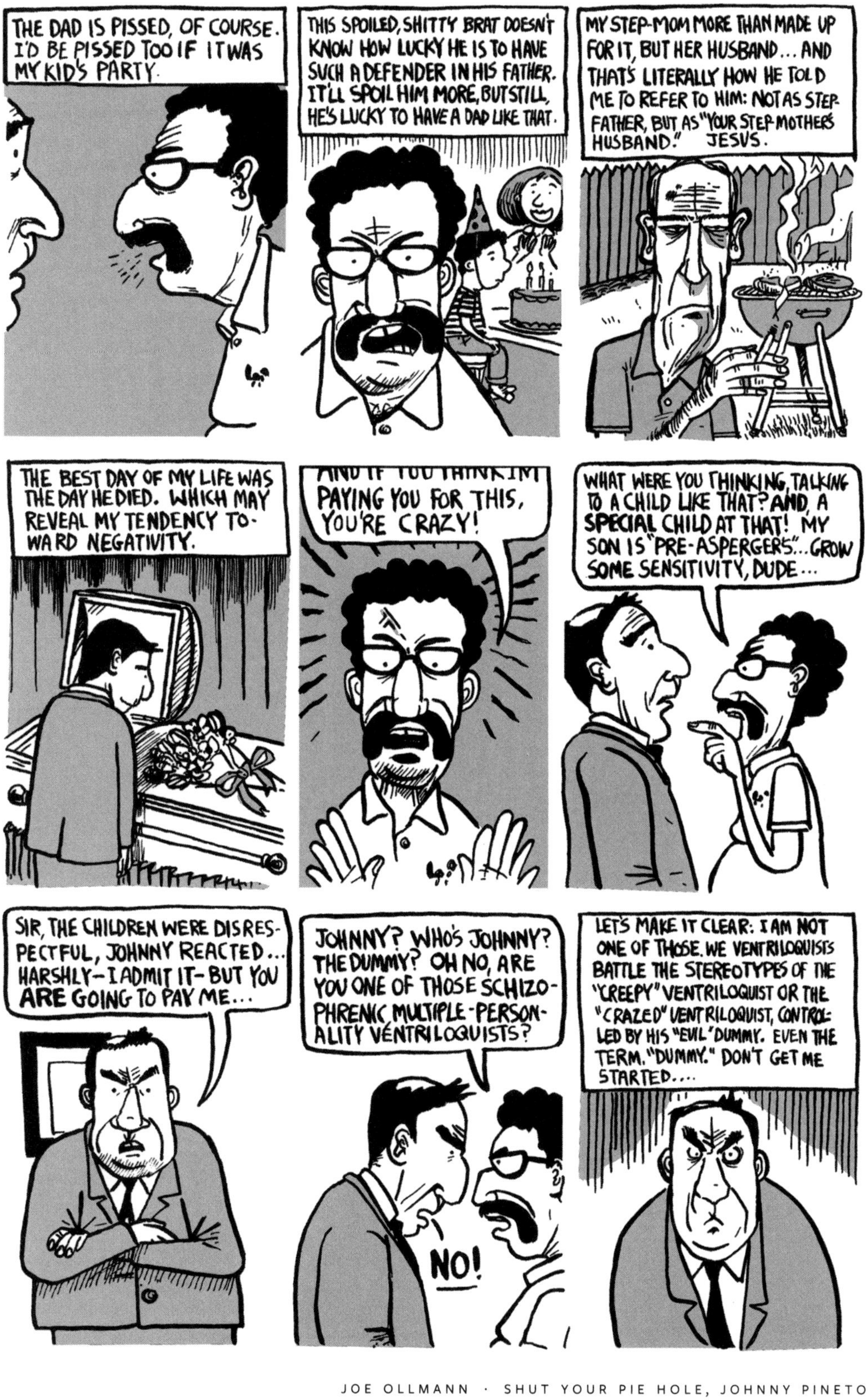
THE DAD IS PISSED, OF COURSE. I'D BE PISSED TOO IF IT WAS MY KID'S PARTY.
THIS SPOILED, SHITTY BRAT DOESN'T KNOW HOW LUCKY HE IS TO HAVE SUCH A DEFENDER IN HIS FATHER. IT'LL SPOIL HIM MORE, BUT STILL, HE'S LUCKY TO HAVE A DAD LIKE THAT.
MY STEP-MOM MORE THAN MADE UP FOR IT, BUT HER HUSBAND... AND THAT'S LITERALLY HOW HE TOLD ME TO REFER TO HIM: NOT AS STEP-FATHER, BUT AS "YOUR STEP-MOTHER'S HUSBAND." JESUS.
THE BEST DAY OF MY LIFE WAS THE DAY HE DIED. WHICH MAY REVEAL MY TENDENCY TO-WARD NEGATIVITY.
PAYING YOU FOR THIS, YOU'RE CRAZY!
WHAT WERE YOU THINKING, TALKING TO A CHILD LIKE THAT? AND, A SPECIAL CHILD AT THAT! MY SON IS "PRE-ASPERGER'S"... GROW SOME SENSITIVITY, DUDE...
SIR, THE CHILDREN WERE DISRES-PECTFUL, JOHNNY REACTED... HARSHLY—I ADMIT IT—BUT YOU ARE GOING TO PAY ME...
JOHNNY? WHO'S JOHNNY? THE DUMMY? OH NO, ARE YOU ONE OF THOSE SCHIZO-PHRENIC MULTIPLE-PERSON-ALITY VENTRILOQUISTS?
NO!
LET'S MAKE IT CLEAR: I AM NOT ONE OF THOSE. WE VENTRILOQUISTS BATTLE THE STEREOTYPES OF THE "CREEPY" VENTRILOQUIST OR THE "CRAZED" VENTRILOQUIST, CONTROL-LED BY HIS "EVIL" DUMMY. EVEN THE TERM "DUMMY." DON'T GET ME STARTED....

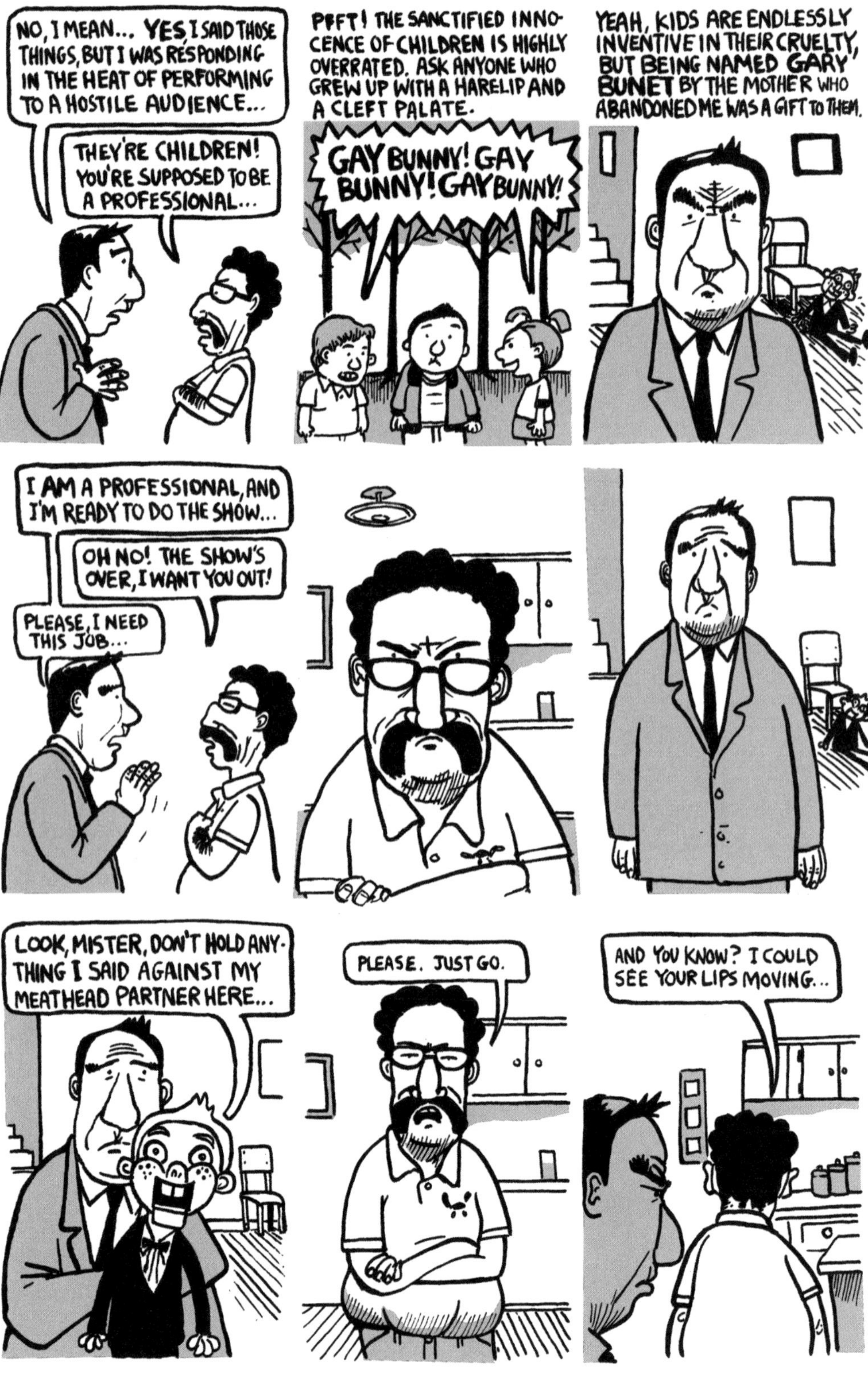
NO, I MEAN... YES, I SAID THOSE THINGS, BUT I WAS RESPONDING IN THE HEAT OF PERFORMING TO A HOSTILE AUDIENCE...
THEY'RE CHILDREN! YOU'RE SUPPOSED TO BE A PROFESSIONAL...
PFFT! THE SANCTIFIED INNOCENCE OF CHILDREN IS HIGHLY OVERRATED. ASK ANYONE WHO GREW UP WITH A HARELIP AND A CLEFT PALATE.
GAY BUNNY! GAY BUNNY! GAY BUNNY!
YEAH, KIDS ARE ENDLESSLY INVENTIVE IN THEIR CRUELTY, BUT BEING NAMED GARY BUNET BY THE MOTHER WHO ABANDONED ME WAS A GIFT TO THEM.
I AM A PROFESSIONAL, AND I'M READY TO DO THE SHOW...
OH NO! THE SHOW'S OVER, I WANT YOU OUT!
PLEASE, I NEED THIS JOB...
LOOK, MISTER, DON'T HOLD ANYTHING I SAID AGAINST MY MEATHEAD PARTNER HERE...
PLEASE. JUST GO.
AND YOU KNOW? I COULD SEE YOUR LIPS MOVING...

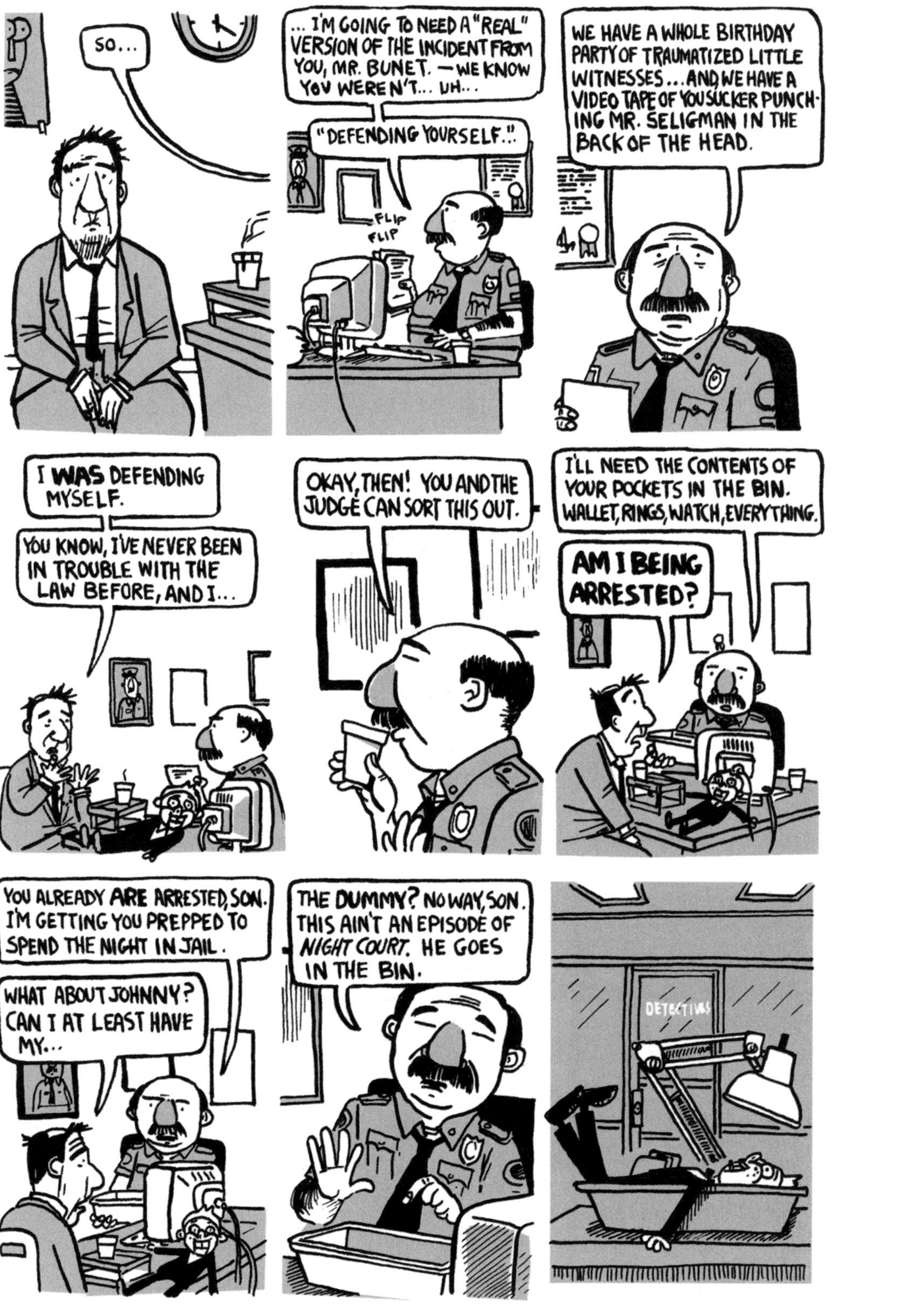
SO...
... I'M GOING TO NEED A "REAL" VERSION OF THE INCIDENT FROM YOU, MR. BUNET. — WE KNOW YOU WEREN'T... UH...
"DEFENDING YOURSELF."
FLIP FLIP
WE HAVE A WHOLE BIRTHDAY PARTY OF TRAUMATIZED LITTLE WITNESSES... AND WE HAVE A VIDEO TAPE OF YOU SUCKER PUNCHING MR. SELIGMAN IN THE BACK OF THE HEAD.
I WAS DEFENDING MYSELF.
YOU KNOW, I'VE NEVER BEEN IN TROUBLE WITH THE LAW BEFORE, AND I...
OKAY, THEN! YOU AND THE JUDGE CAN SORT THIS OUT.
I'LL NEED THE CONTENTS OF YOUR POCKETS IN THE BIN. WALLET, RINGS, WATCH, EVERYTHING.
AM I BEING ARRESTED?
YOU ALREADY ARE ARRESTED, SON. I'M GETTING YOU PREPPED TO SPEND THE NIGHT IN JAIL.
WHAT ABOUT JOHNNY? CAN I AT LEAST HAVE MY...
THE DUMMY? NO WAY, SON. THIS AIN'T AN EPISODE OF NIGHT COURT. HE GOES IN THE BIN.
DETECTIVES

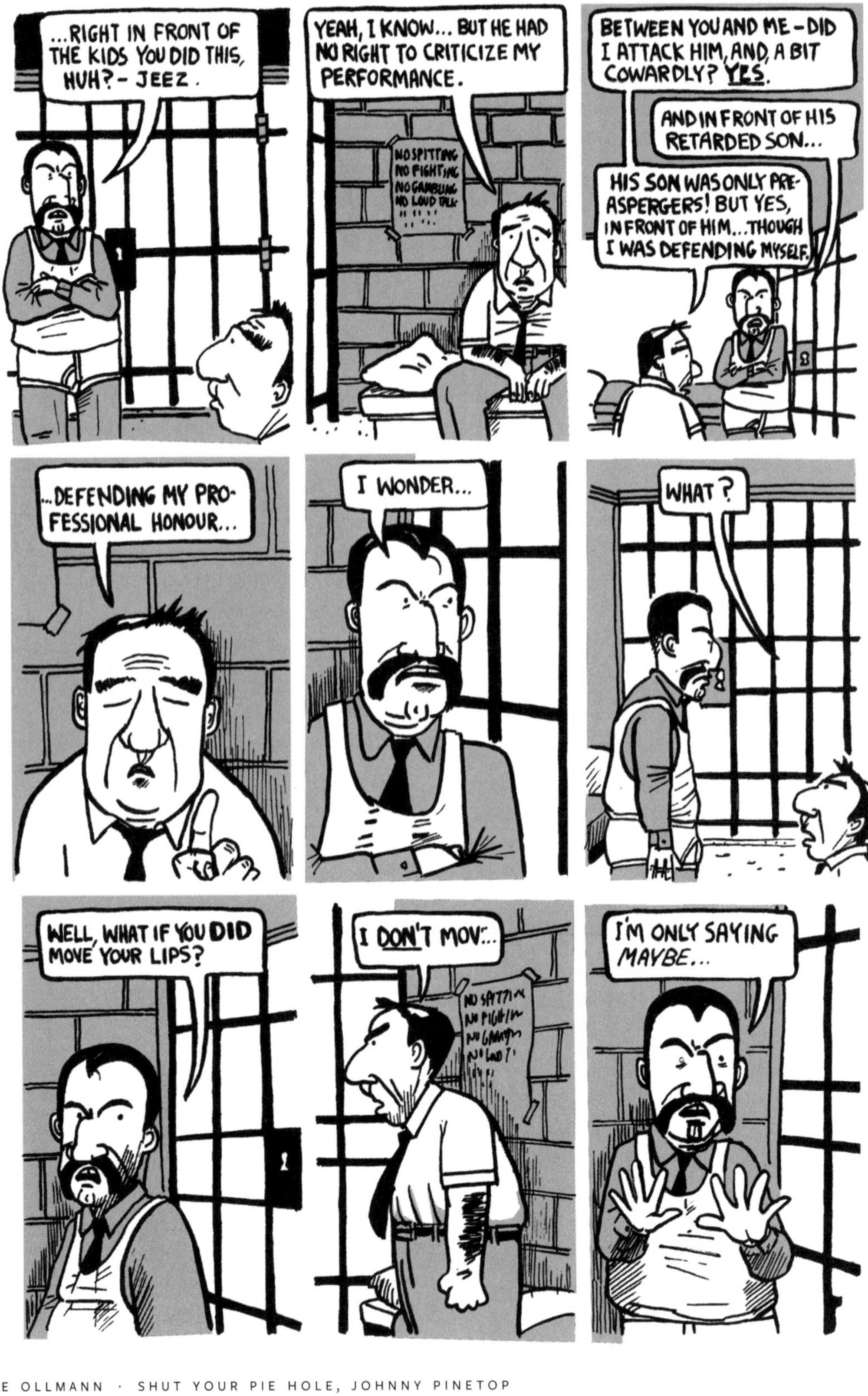
...RIGHT IN FRONT OF THE KIDS YOU DID THIS, HUH? - JEEZ.
YEAH, I KNOW... BUT HE HAD NO RIGHT TO CRITICIZE MY PERFORMANCE.
NO SPITTING
NO FIGHTING
NO GAMBLING
NO LOUD TALK
BETWEEN YOU AND ME - DID I ATTACK HIM, AND, A BIT COWARDLY? YES.
AND IN FRONT OF HIS RETARDED SON...
HIS SON WAS ONLY PRE-ASPERGERS! BUT YES, IN FRONT OF HIM... THOUGH I WAS DEFENDING MYSELF.
...DEFENDING MY PROFESSIONAL HONOUR...
I WONDER...
WHAT?
WELL, WHAT IF YOU DID MOVE YOUR LIPS?
I DON'T MOV...
I'M ONLY SAYING MAYBE...

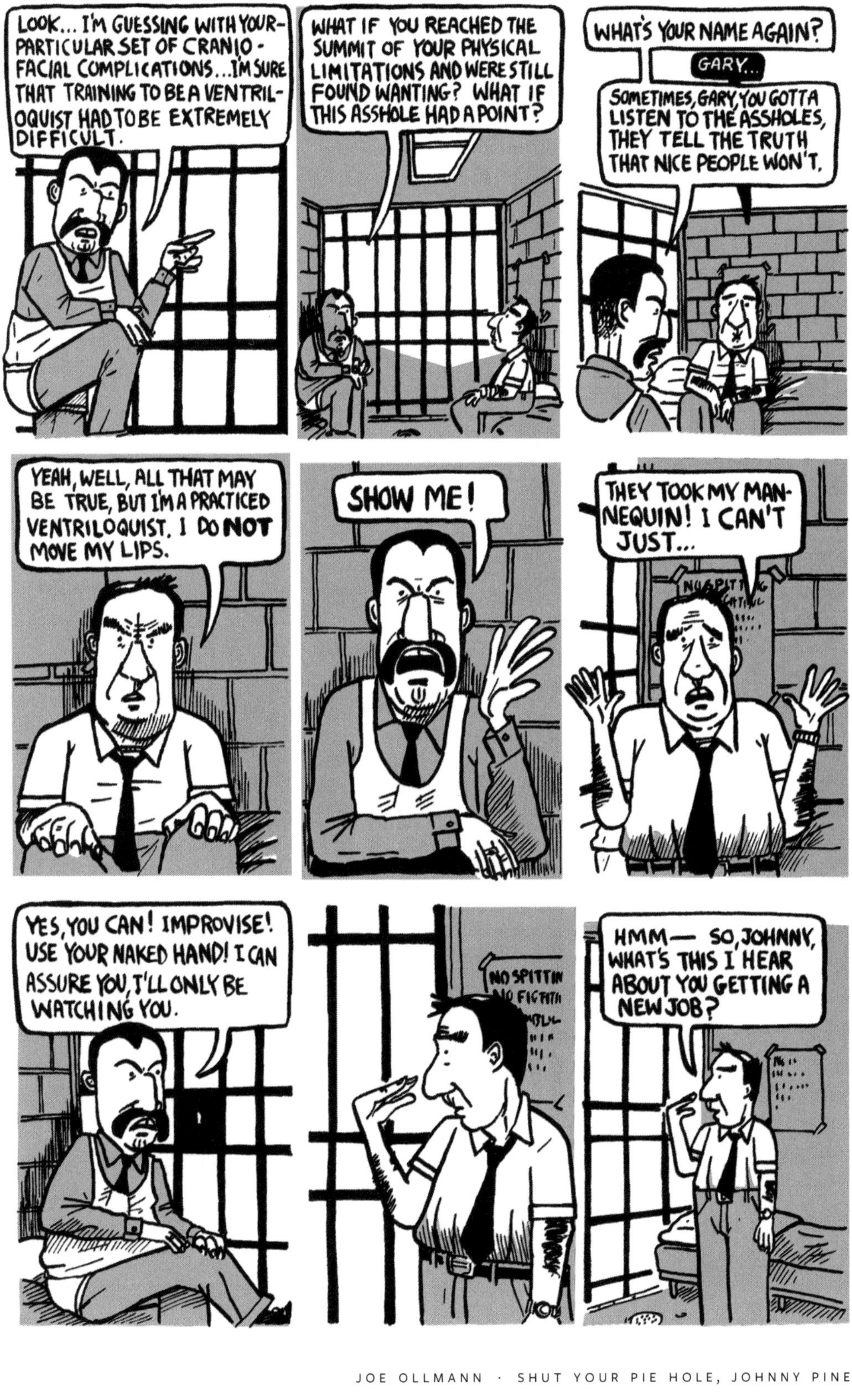
LOOK... I'M GUESSING WITH YOUR PARTICULAR SET OF CRANIO-FACIAL COMPLICATIONS... I'M SURE THAT TRAINING TO BE A VENTRILOQUIST HAD TO BE EXTREMELY DIFFICULT.
WHAT IF YOU REACHED THE SUMMIT OF YOUR PHYSICAL LIMITATIONS AND WERE STILL FOUND WANTING? WHAT IF THIS ASSHOLE HAD A POINT?
WHAT'S YOUR NAME AGAIN?
GARY...
SOMETIMES, GARY, YOU GOTTA LISTEN TO THE ASSHOLES, THEY TELL THE TRUTH THAT NICE PEOPLE WON'T.
YEAH, WELL, ALL THAT MAY BE TRUE, BUT I'M A PRACTICED VENTRILOQUIST. I DO **NOT** MOVE MY LIPS.
SHOW ME!
THEY TOOK MY MANNEQUIN! I CAN'T JUST...
YES, YOU CAN! IMPROVISE! USE YOUR NAKED HAND! I CAN ASSURE YOU, I'LL ONLY BE WATCHING YOU.
NO SPITTIN
HMM— SO, JOHNNY, WHAT'S THIS I HEAR ABOUT YOU GETTING A NEW JOB?

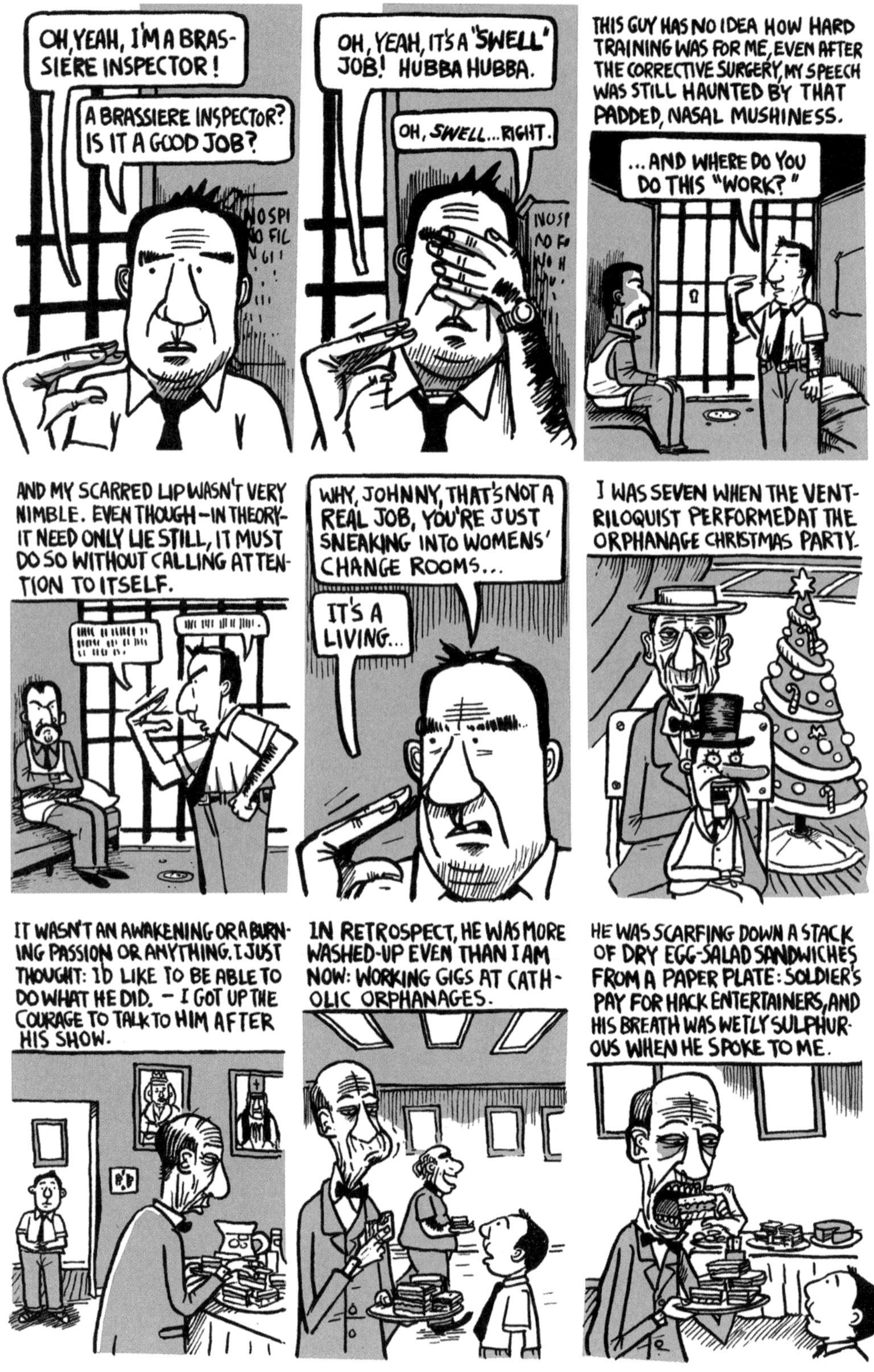
OH, YEAH, I'M A BRASSIERE INSPECTOR!
A BRASSIERE INSPECTOR? IS IT A GOOD JOB?
OH, YEAH, IT'S A "SWELL" JOB! HUBBA HUBBA.
OH, SWELL... RIGHT.
THIS GUY HAS NO IDEA HOW HARD TRAINING WAS FOR ME, EVEN AFTER THE CORRECTIVE SURGERY, MY SPEECH WAS STILL HAUNTED BY THAT PADDED, NASAL MUSHINESS.
...AND WHERE DO YOU DO THIS "WORK?"
AND MY SCARRED LIP WASN'T VERY NIMBLE. EVEN THOUGH—IN THEORY—IT NEED ONLY LIE STILL, IT MUST DO SO WITHOUT CALLING ATTENTION TO ITSELF.
WHY, JOHNNY, THAT'S NOT A REAL JOB, YOU'RE JUST SNEAKING INTO WOMENS' CHANGE ROOMS...
IT'S A LIVING...
I WAS SEVEN WHEN THE VENTRILOQUIST PERFORMED AT THE ORPHANAGE CHRISTMAS PARTY.
IT WASN'T AN AWAKENING OR A BURNING PASSION OR ANYTHING. I JUST THOUGHT: I'D LIKE TO BE ABLE TO DO WHAT HE DID. — I GOT UP THE COURAGE TO TALK TO HIM AFTER HIS SHOW.
IN RETROSPECT, HE WAS MORE WASHED-UP EVEN THAN I AM NOW: WORKING GIGS AT CATHOLIC ORPHANAGES.
HE WAS SCARFING DOWN A STACK OF DRY EGG-SALAD SANDWICHES FROM A PAPER PLATE: SOLDIER'S PAY FOR HACK ENTERTAINERS, AND HIS BREATH WAS WETLY SULPHUROUS WHEN HE SPOKE TO ME.

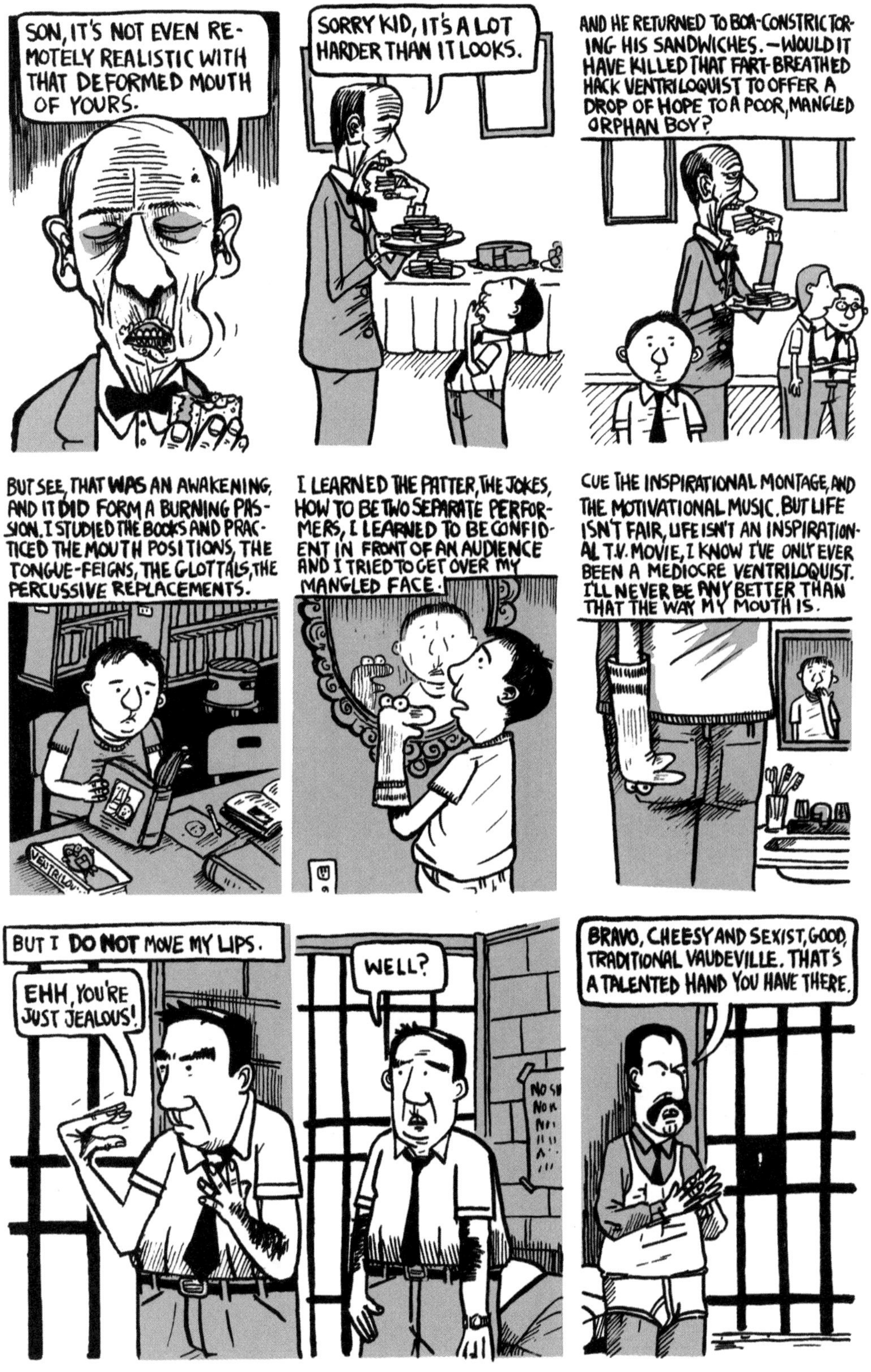
SON, IT'S NOT EVEN REMOTELY REALISTIC WITH THAT DEFORMED MOUTH OF YOURS.
SORRY KID, IT'S A LOT HARDER THAN IT LOOKS.
AND HE RETURNED TO BOA-CONSTRICTORING HIS SANDWICHES. —WOULD IT HAVE KILLED THAT FART-BREATHED HACK VENTRILOQUIST TO OFFER A DROP OF HOPE TO A POOR, MANGLED ORPHAN BOY?
BUT SEE, THAT WAS AN AWAKENING, AND IT DID FORM A BURNING PASSION. I STUDIED THE BOOKS AND PRACTICED THE MOUTH POSITIONS, THE TONGUE-FEIGNS, THE GLOTTALS, THE PERCUSSIVE REPLACEMENTS.
I LEARNED THE PATTER, THE JOKES, HOW TO BE TWO SEPARATE PERFORMERS, I LEARNED TO BE CONFIDENT IN FRONT OF AN AUDIENCE AND I TRIED TO GET OVER MY MANGLED FACE.
CUE THE INSPIRATIONAL MONTAGE, AND THE MOTIVATIONAL MUSIC. BUT LIFE ISN'T FAIR, LIFE ISN'T AN INSPIRATIONAL T.V. MOVIE, I KNOW I'VE ONLY EVER BEEN A MEDIOCRE VENTRILOQUIST. I'LL NEVER BE ANY BETTER THAN THAT THE WAY MY MOUTH IS.
BUT I DO NOT MOVE MY LIPS.
EHH, YOU'RE JUST JEALOUS!
WELL?
BRAVO, CHEESY AND SEXIST, GOOD, TRADITIONAL VAUDEVILLE. THAT'S A TALENTED HAND YOU HAVE THERE.

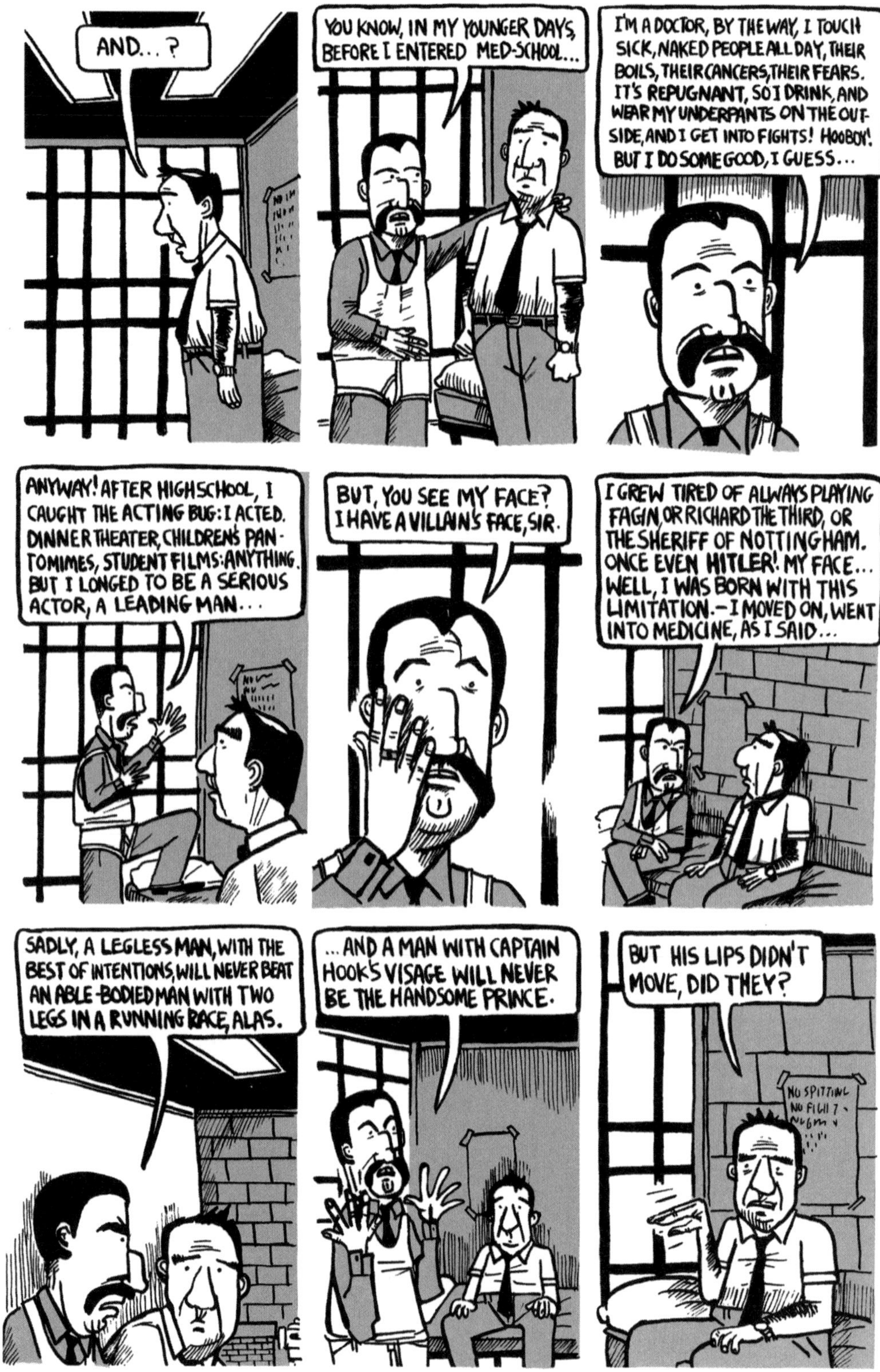
AND...?
YOU KNOW, IN MY YOUNGER DAYS, BEFORE I ENTERED MED-SCHOOL...
I'M A DOCTOR, BY THE WAY, I TOUCH SICK, NAKED PEOPLE ALL DAY, THEIR BOILS, THEIR CANCERS, THEIR FEARS. IT'S REPUGNANT, SO I DRINK, AND WEAR MY UNDERPANTS ON THE OUTSIDE, AND I GET INTO FIGHTS! HOOBOY! BUT I DO SOME GOOD, I GUESS...
ANYWAY! AFTER HIGHSCHOOL, I CAUGHT THE ACTING BUG: I ACTED. DINNER THEATER, CHILDREN'S PANTOMIMES, STUDENT FILMS: ANYTHING. BUT I LONGED TO BE A SERIOUS ACTOR, A LEADING MAN...
BUT, YOU SEE MY FACE? I HAVE A VILLAIN'S FACE, SIR.
I GREW TIRED OF ALWAYS PLAYING FAGIN, OR RICHARD THE THIRD, OR THE SHERIFF OF NOTTINGHAM. ONCE EVEN HITLER! MY FACE... WELL, I WAS BORN WITH THIS LIMITATION.—I MOVED ON, WENT INTO MEDICINE, AS I SAID...
SADLY, A LEGLESS MAN, WITH THE BEST OF INTENTIONS, WILL NEVER BEAT AN ABLE-BODIED MAN WITH TWO LEGS IN A RUNNING RACE, ALAS.
...AND A MAN WITH CAPTAIN HOOK'S VISAGE WILL NEVER BE THE HANDSOME PRINCE.
BUT HIS LIPS DIDN'T MOVE, DID THEY?
NO SPITTING

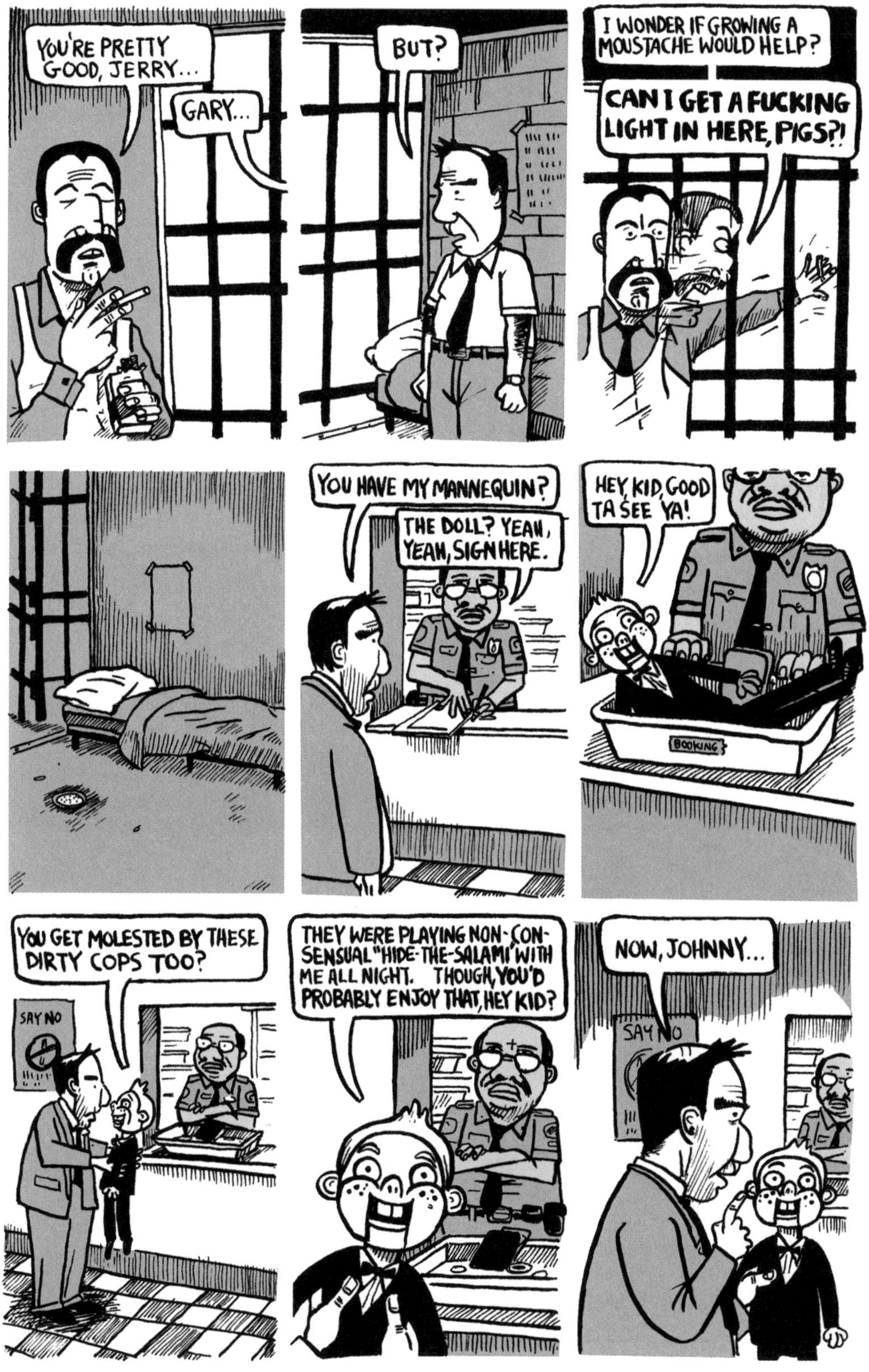
YOU'RE PRETTY GOOD, JERRY...
GARY...
BUT?
I WONDER IF GROWING A MOUSTACHE WOULD HELP?
CAN I GET A FUCKING LIGHT IN HERE, PIGS?!
YOU HAVE MY MANNEQUIN?
THE DOLL? YEAH, YEAH, SIGN HERE.
HEY, KID, GOOD TA SEE YA!
BOOKING
YOU GET MOLESTED BY THESE DIRTY COPS TOO?
SAY NO
THEY WERE PLAYING NON-CONSENSUAL "HIDE-THE-SALAMI" WITH ME ALL NIGHT. THOUGH, YOU'D PROBABLY ENJOY THAT, HEY KID?
NOW, JOHNNY...
SAY NO

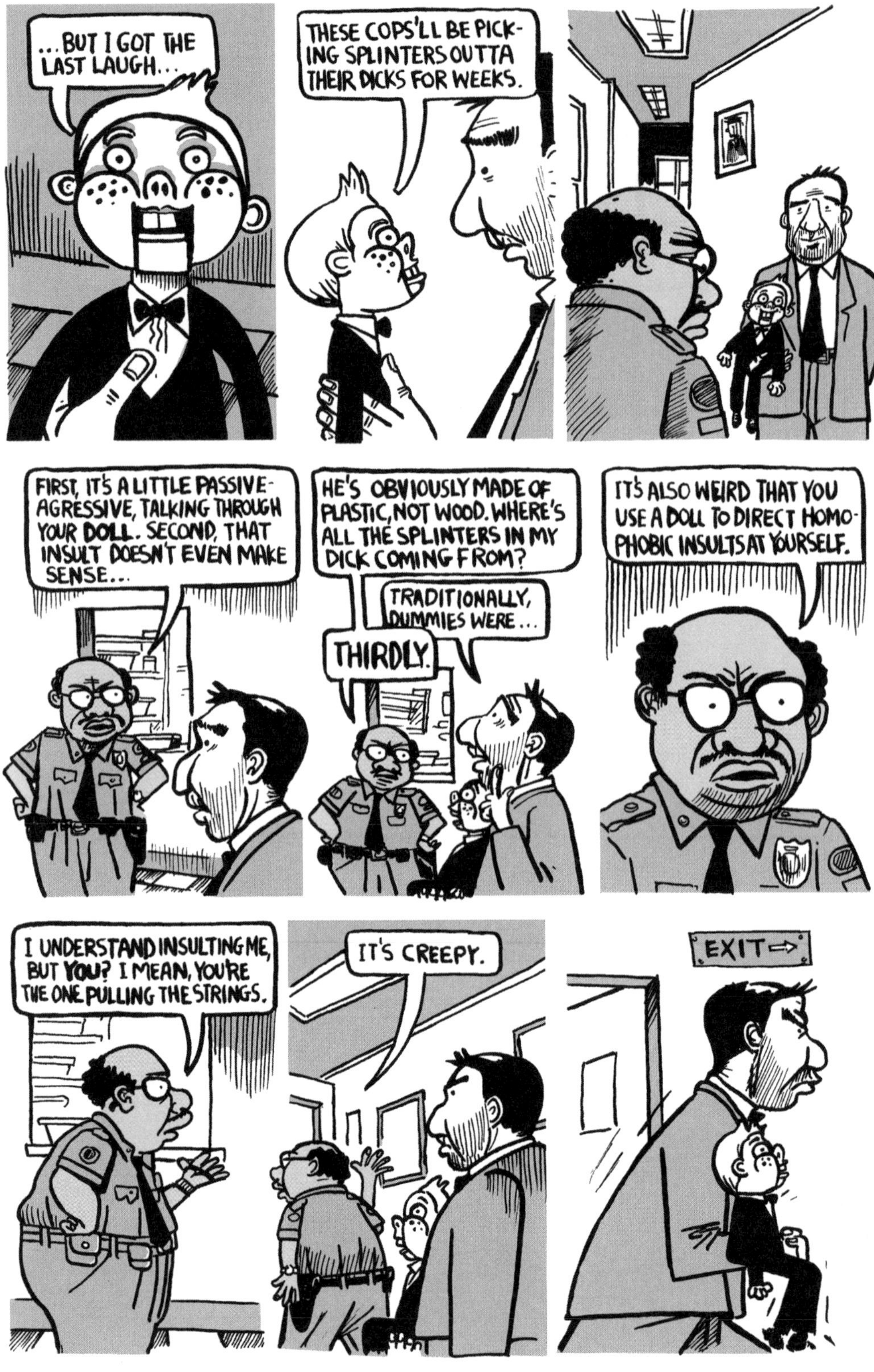
...BUT I GOT THE LAST LAUGH...
THESE COPS'LL BE PICKING SPLINTERS OUTTA THEIR DICKS FOR WEEKS.
FIRST, IT'S A LITTLE PASSIVE-AGRESSIVE, TALKING THROUGH YOUR DOLL. SECOND, THAT INSULT DOESN'T EVEN MAKE SENSE...
HE'S OBVIOUSLY MADE OF PLASTIC, NOT WOOD. WHERE'S ALL THE SPLINTERS IN MY DICK COMING FROM?
TRADITIONALLY, DUMMIES WERE...
THIRDLY.
IT'S ALSO WEIRD THAT YOU USE A DOLL TO DIRECT HOMOPHOBIC INSULTS AT YOURSELF.
I UNDERSTAND INSULTING ME, BUT YOU? I MEAN, YOU'RE THE ONE PULLING THE STRINGS.
IT'S CREEPY.
EXIT

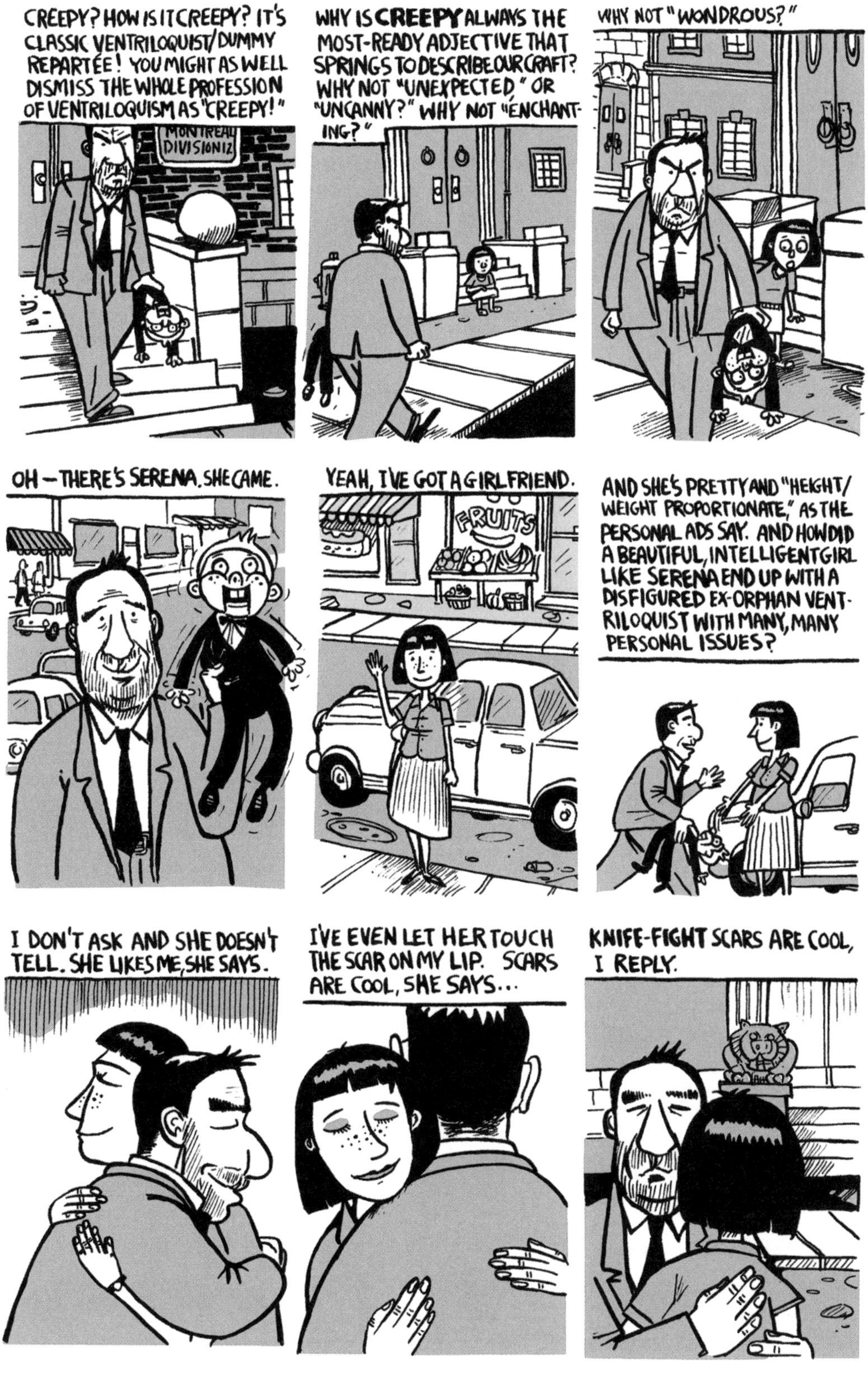
CREEPY? HOW IS IT CREEPY? IT'S CLASSIC VENTRILOQUIST/DUMMY REPARTÉE! YOU MIGHT AS WELL DISMISS THE WHOLE PROFESSION OF VENTRILOQUISM AS "CREEPY!"
MONTREAL DIVISION 12
WHY IS CREEPY ALWAYS THE MOST-READY ADJECTIVE THAT SPRINGS TO DESCRIBE OUR CRAFT? WHY NOT "UNEXPECTED," OR "UNCANNY?" WHY NOT "ENCHANTING?"
WHY NOT "WONDROUS?"
OH — THERE'S SERENA. SHE CAME.
YEAH, I'VE GOT A GIRLFRIEND.
FRUITS
AND SHE'S PRETTY AND "HEIGHT/WEIGHT PROPORTIONATE," AS THE PERSONAL ADS SAY. AND HOW DID A BEAUTIFUL, INTELLIGENT GIRL LIKE SERENA END UP WITH A DISFIGURED EX-ORPHAN VENTRILOQUIST WITH MANY, MANY PERSONAL ISSUES?
I DON'T ASK AND SHE DOESN'T TELL. SHE LIKES ME, SHE SAYS.
I'VE EVEN LET HER TOUCH THE SCAR ON MY LIP. SCARS ARE COOL, SHE SAYS...
KNIFE-FIGHT SCARS ARE COOL, I REPLY.

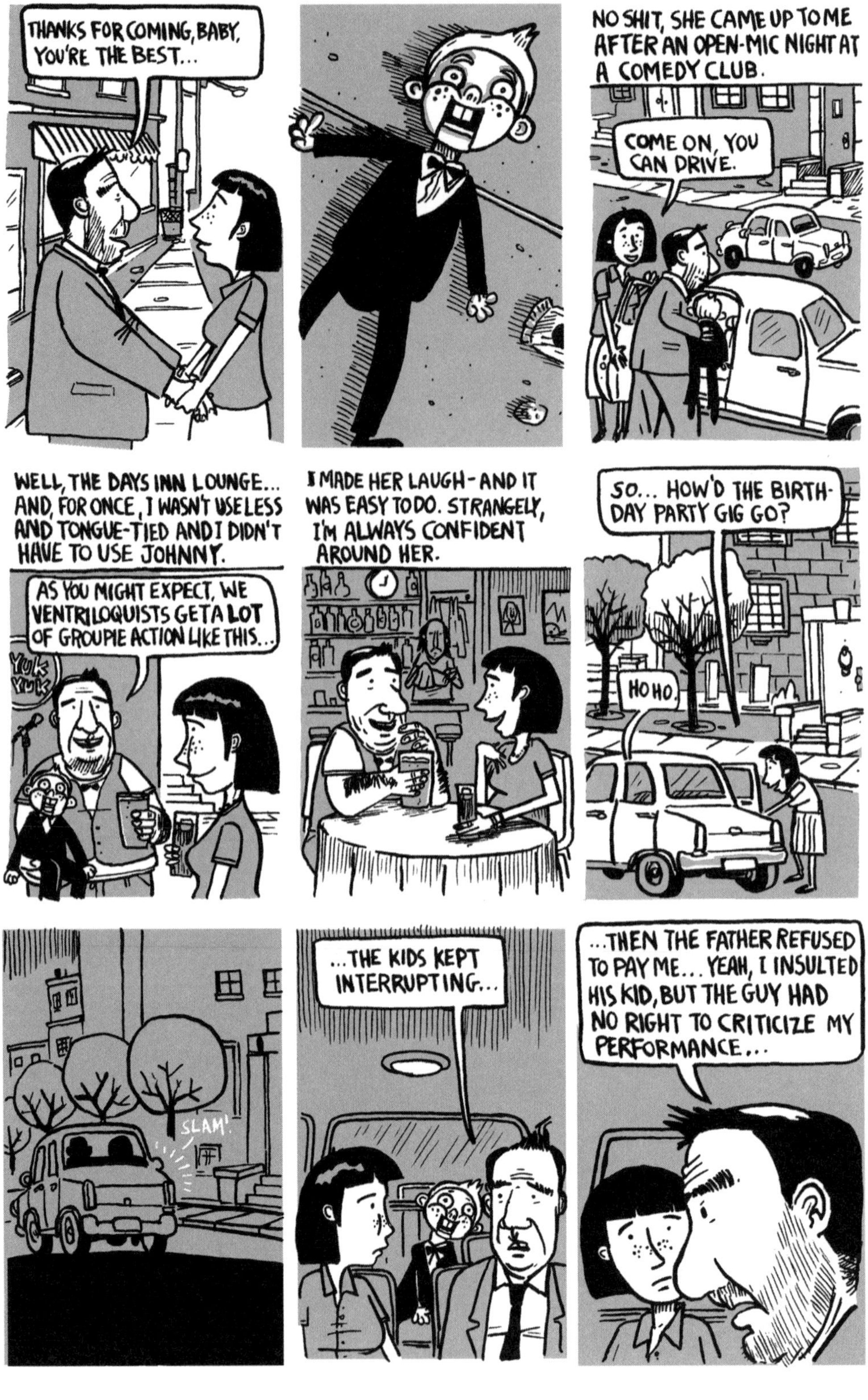
THANKS FOR COMING, BABY, YOU'RE THE BEST...
NO SHIT, SHE CAME UP TO ME AFTER AN OPEN-MIC NIGHT AT A COMEDY CLUB.
COME ON, YOU CAN DRIVE.
WELL, THE DAYS INN LOUNGE... AND, FOR ONCE, I WASN'T USELESS AND TONGUE-TIED AND I DIDN'T HAVE TO USE JOHNNY.
AS YOU MIGHT EXPECT, WE VENTRILOQUISTS GET A LOT OF GROUPIE ACTION LIKE THIS...
YUK YUK
I MADE HER LAUGH - AND IT WAS EASY TO DO. STRANGELY, I'M ALWAYS CONFIDENT AROUND HER.
SO... HOW'D THE BIRTHDAY PARTY GIG GO?
HO HO.
SLAM!
...THE KIDS KEPT INTERRUPTING...
...THEN THE FATHER REFUSED TO PAY ME... YEAH, I INSULTED HIS KID, BUT THE GUY HAD NO RIGHT TO CRITICIZE MY PERFORMANCE...

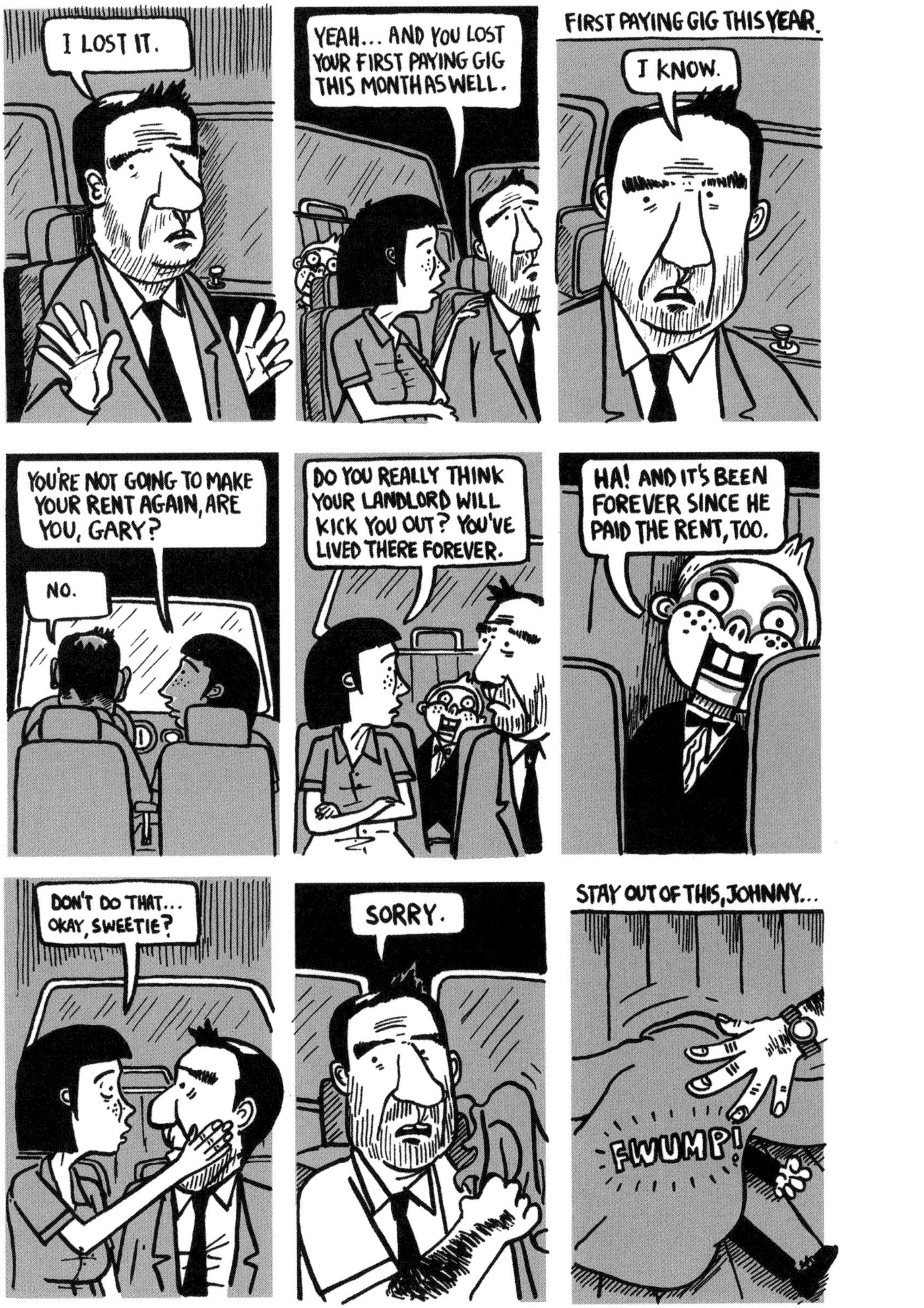
I LOST IT.
YEAH... AND YOU LOST YOUR FIRST PAYING GIG THIS MONTH AS WELL.
FIRST PAYING GIG THIS YEAR.
I KNOW.
YOU'RE NOT GOING TO MAKE YOUR RENT AGAIN, ARE YOU, GARY?
NO.
DO YOU REALLY THINK YOUR LANDLORD WILL KICK YOU OUT? YOU'VE LIVED THERE FOREVER.
HA! AND IT'S BEEN FOREVER SINCE HE PAID THE RENT, TOO.
DON'T DO THAT... OKAY, SWEETIE?
SORRY.
STAY OUT OF THIS, JOHNNY...
FWUMP!

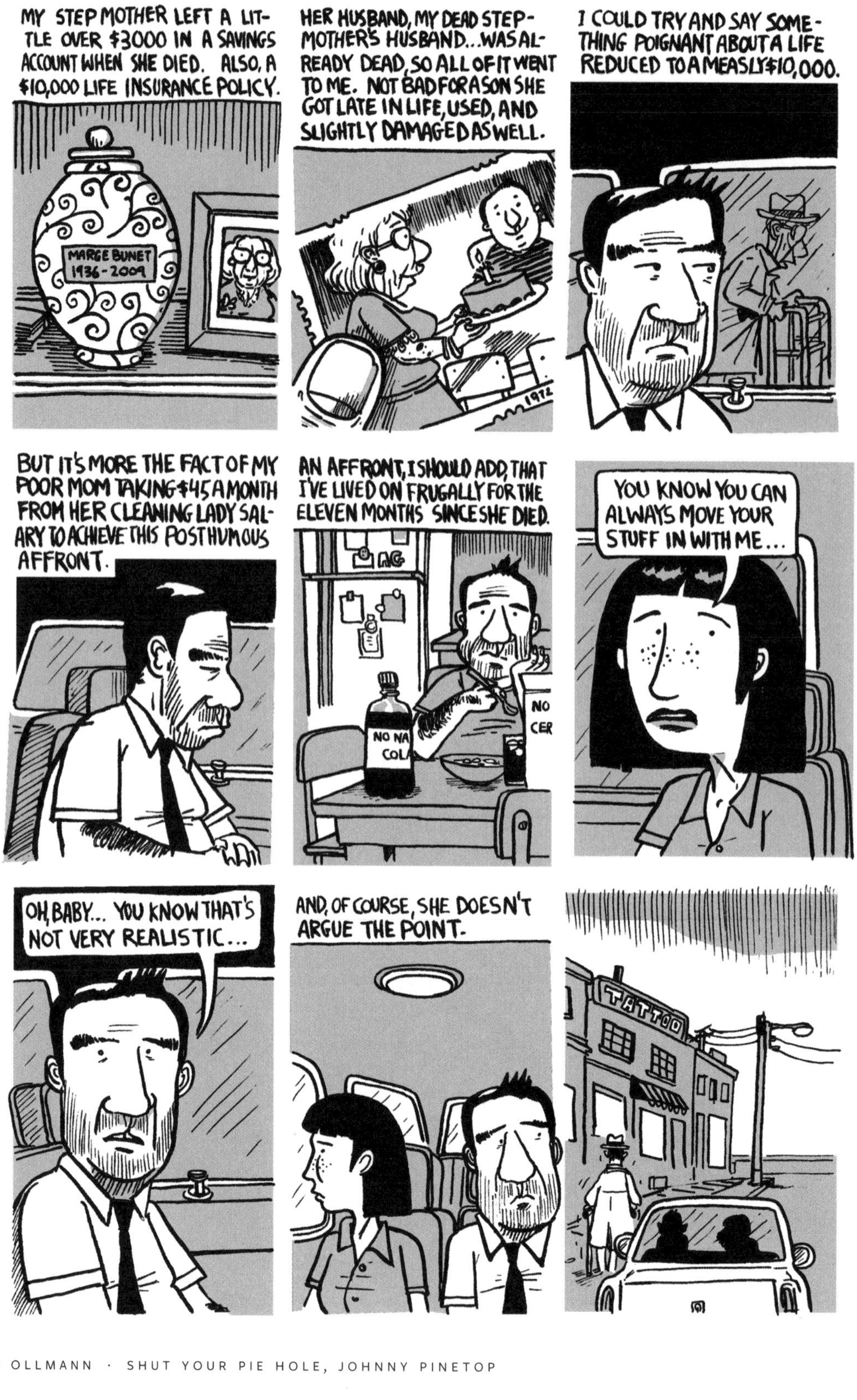

MY STEP MOTHER LEFT A LITTLE OVER $3000 IN A SAVINGS ACCOUNT WHEN SHE DIED. ALSO, A $10,000 LIFE INSURANCE POLICY.
MARGE BUNET 1936 - 2009
HER HUSBAND, MY DEAD STEPMOTHER'S HUSBAND...WAS ALREADY DEAD, SO ALL OF IT WENT TO ME. NOT BAD FOR A SON SHE GOT LATE IN LIFE, USED, AND SLIGHTLY DAMAGED AS WELL.
1972
I COULD TRY AND SAY SOMETHING POIGNANT ABOUT A LIFE REDUCED TO A MEASLY $10,000.
BUT IT'S MORE THE FACT OF MY POOR MOM TAKING $45 A MONTH FROM HER CLEANING LADY SALARY TO ACHIEVE THIS POSTHUMOUS AFFRONT.
AN AFFRONT, I SHOULD ADD, THAT I'VE LIVED ON FRUGALLY FOR THE ELEVEN MONTHS SINCE SHE DIED.
NO NA
COL
NO
CER
YOU KNOW YOU CAN ALWAYS MOVE YOUR STUFF IN WITH ME...
OH, BABY... YOU KNOW THAT'S NOT VERY REALISTIC...
AND, OF COURSE, SHE DOESN'T ARGUE THE POINT.
TATTOO

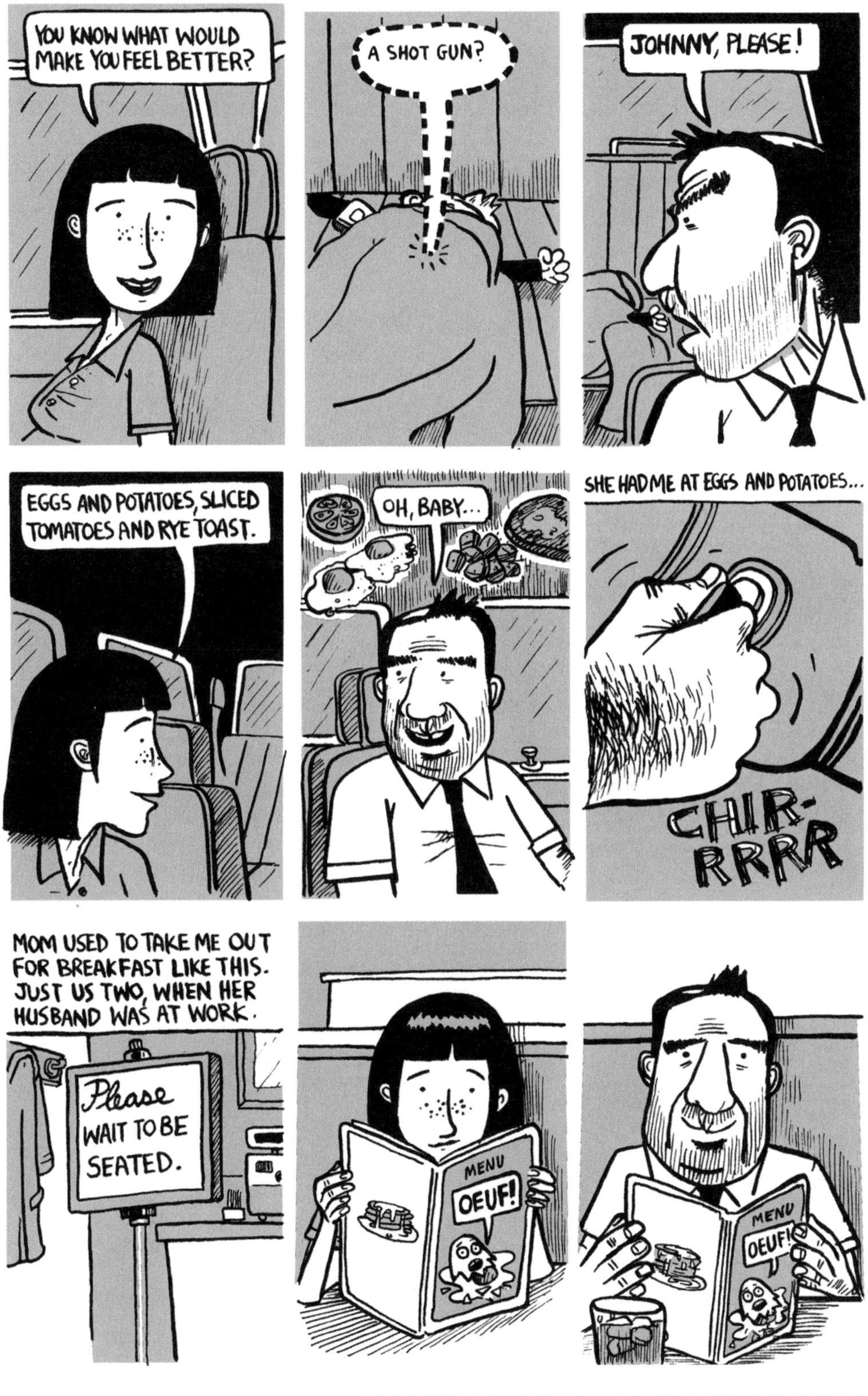
YOU KNOW WHAT WOULD MAKE YOU FEEL BETTER?
A SHOT GUN?
JOHNNY, PLEASE!
EGGS AND POTATOES, SLICED TOMATOES AND RYE TOAST.
OH, BABY...
SHE HAD ME AT EGGS AND POTATOES...
CHIR-RRRR
MOM USED TO TAKE ME OUT FOR BREAKFAST LIKE THIS. JUST US TWO, WHEN HER HUSBAND WAS AT WORK.
Please WAIT TO BE SEATED.
MENU
OEUF!
MENU
OEUF!

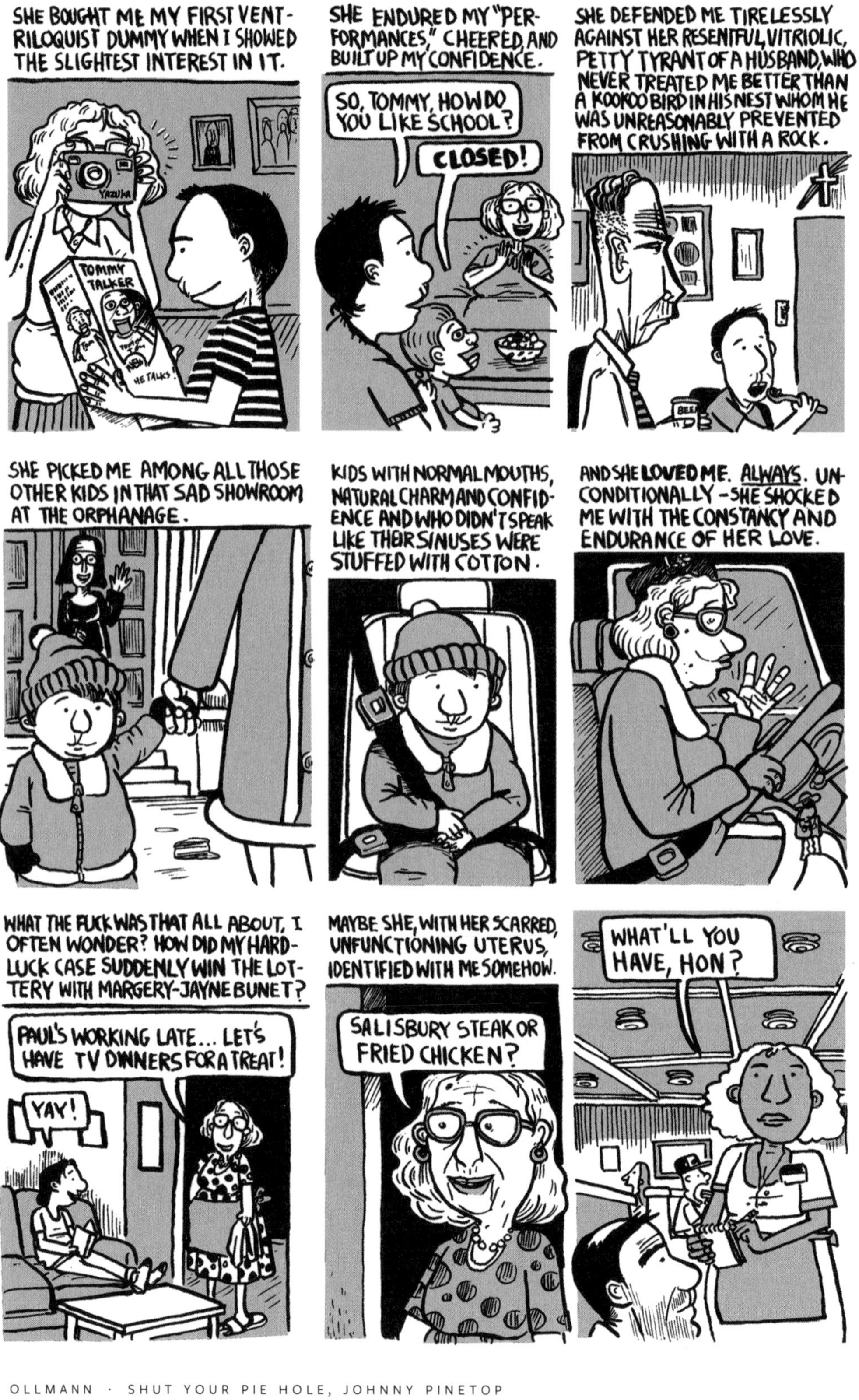
SHE BOUGHT ME MY FIRST VENTRILOQUIST DUMMY WHEN I SHOWED THE SLIGHTEST INTEREST IN IT.
YAZUKA
TOMMY TALKER
HE TALKS!
SHE ENDURED MY "PERFORMANCES," CHEERED, AND BUILT UP MY CONFIDENCE.
SO, TOMMY, HOW DO YOU LIKE SCHOOL?
CLOSED!
SHE DEFENDED ME TIRELESSLY AGAINST HER RESENTFUL, VITRIOLIC, PETTY TYRANT OF A HUSBAND, WHO NEVER TREATED ME BETTER THAN A KOOKOO BIRD IN HIS NEST WHOM HE WAS UNREASONABLY PREVENTED FROM CRUSHING WITH A ROCK.
SHE PICKED ME AMONG ALL THOSE OTHER KIDS IN THAT SAD SHOWROOM AT THE ORPHANAGE.
KIDS WITH NORMAL MOUTHS, NATURAL CHARM AND CONFIDENCE AND WHO DIDN'T SPEAK LIKE THEIR SINUSES WERE STUFFED WITH COTTON.
AND SHE LOVED ME. ALWAYS. UNCONDITIONALLY - SHE SHOCKED ME WITH THE CONSTANCY AND ENDURANCE OF HER LOVE.
WHAT THE FUCK WAS THAT ALL ABOUT, I OFTEN WONDER? HOW DID MY HARD-LUCK CASE SUDDENLY WIN THE LOTTERY WITH MARGERY-JAYNE BUNET?
PAUL'S WORKING LATE... LET'S HAVE TV DINNERS FOR A TREAT!
YAY!
MAYBE SHE, WITH HER SCARRED, UNFUNCTIONING UTERUS, IDENTIFIED WITH ME SOMEHOW.
SALISBURY STEAK OR FRIED CHICKEN?
WHAT'LL YOU HAVE, HON?

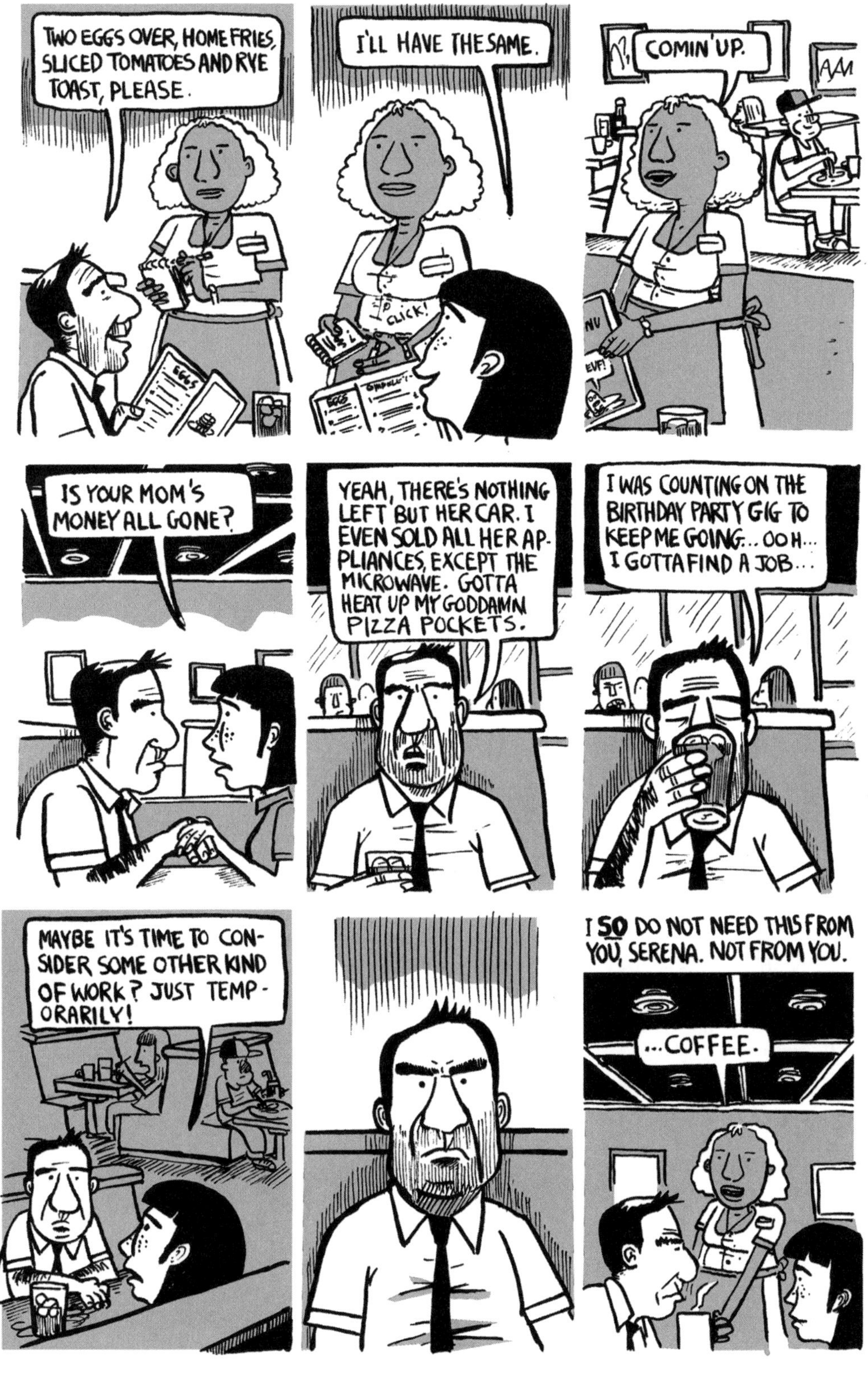
TWO EGGS OVER, HOME FRIES, SLICED TOMATOES AND RYE TOAST, PLEASE.
I'LL HAVE THE SAME.
CLICK!
COMIN' UP.
IS YOUR MOM'S MONEY ALL GONE?
YEAH, THERE'S NOTHING LEFT BUT HER CAR. I EVEN SOLD ALL HER APPLIANCES, EXCEPT THE MICROWAVE. GOTTA HEAT UP MY GODDAMN PIZZA POCKETS.
I WAS COUNTING ON THE BIRTHDAY PARTY GIG TO KEEP ME GOING... OOH... I GOTTA FIND A JOB...
MAYBE IT'S TIME TO CONSIDER SOME OTHER KIND OF WORK? JUST TEMPORARILY!
I SO DO NOT NEED THIS FROM YOU, SERENA. NOT FROM YOU.
...COFFEE.

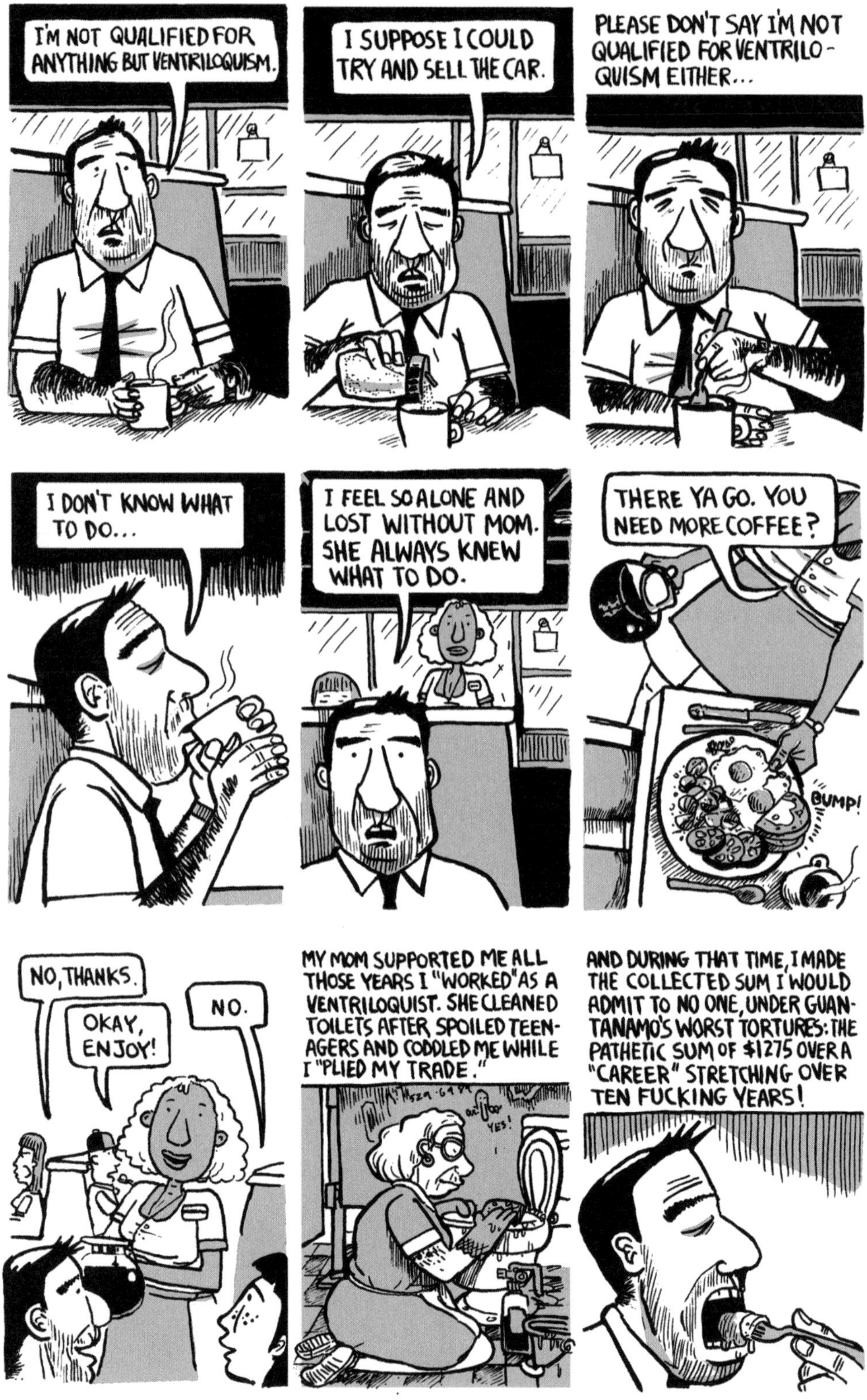
I'M NOT QUALIFIED FOR ANYTHING BUT VENTRILOQUISM.
I SUPPOSE I COULD TRY AND SELL THE CAR.
PLEASE DON'T SAY I'M NOT QUALIFIED FOR VENTRILO-QUISM EITHER...
I DON'T KNOW WHAT TO DO...
I FEEL SO ALONE AND LOST WITHOUT MOM. SHE ALWAYS KNEW WHAT TO DO.
THERE YA GO. YOU NEED MORE COFFEE?
BUMP!
NO, THANKS.
OKAY, ENJOY!
NO.
MY MOM SUPPORTED ME ALL THOSE YEARS I "WORKED" AS A VENTRILOQUIST. SHE CLEANED TOILETS AFTER SPOILED TEEN-AGERS AND CODDLED ME WHILE I "PLIED MY TRADE."
AND DURING THAT TIME, I MADE THE COLLECTED SUM I WOULD ADMIT TO NO ONE, UNDER GUAN-TANAMO'S WORST TORTURES: THE PATHETIC SUM OF $1275 OVER A "CAREER" STRETCHING OVER TEN FUCKING YEARS!

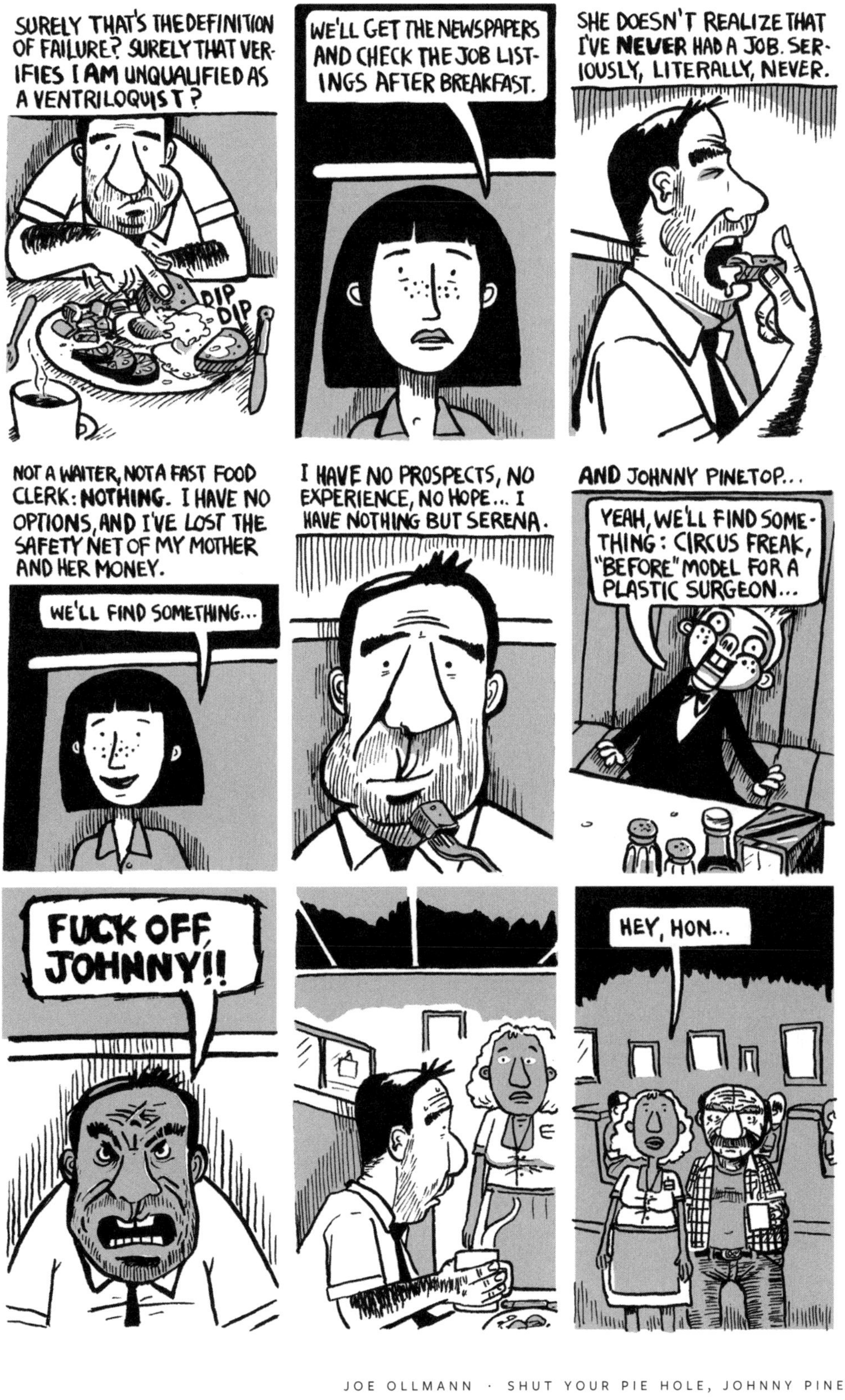

SURELY THAT'S THE DEFINITION OF FAILURE? SURELY THAT VERIFIES I AM UNQUALIFIED AS A VENTRILOQUIST?
DIP DIP
WE'LL GET THE NEWSPAPERS AND CHECK THE JOB LISTINGS AFTER BREAKFAST.
SHE DOESN'T REALIZE THAT I'VE NEVER HAD A JOB. SERIOUSLY, LITERALLY, NEVER.
NOT A WAITER, NOT A FAST FOOD CLERK: NOTHING. I HAVE NO OPTIONS, AND I'VE LOST THE SAFETY NET OF MY MOTHER AND HER MONEY.
WE'LL FIND SOMETHING...
I HAVE NO PROSPECTS, NO EXPERIENCE, NO HOPE... I HAVE NOTHING BUT SERENA.
AND JOHNNY PINETOP...
YEAH, WE'LL FIND SOMETHING: CIRCUS FREAK, "BEFORE" MODEL FOR A PLASTIC SURGEON...
FUCK OFF JOHNNY!!
HEY, HON...

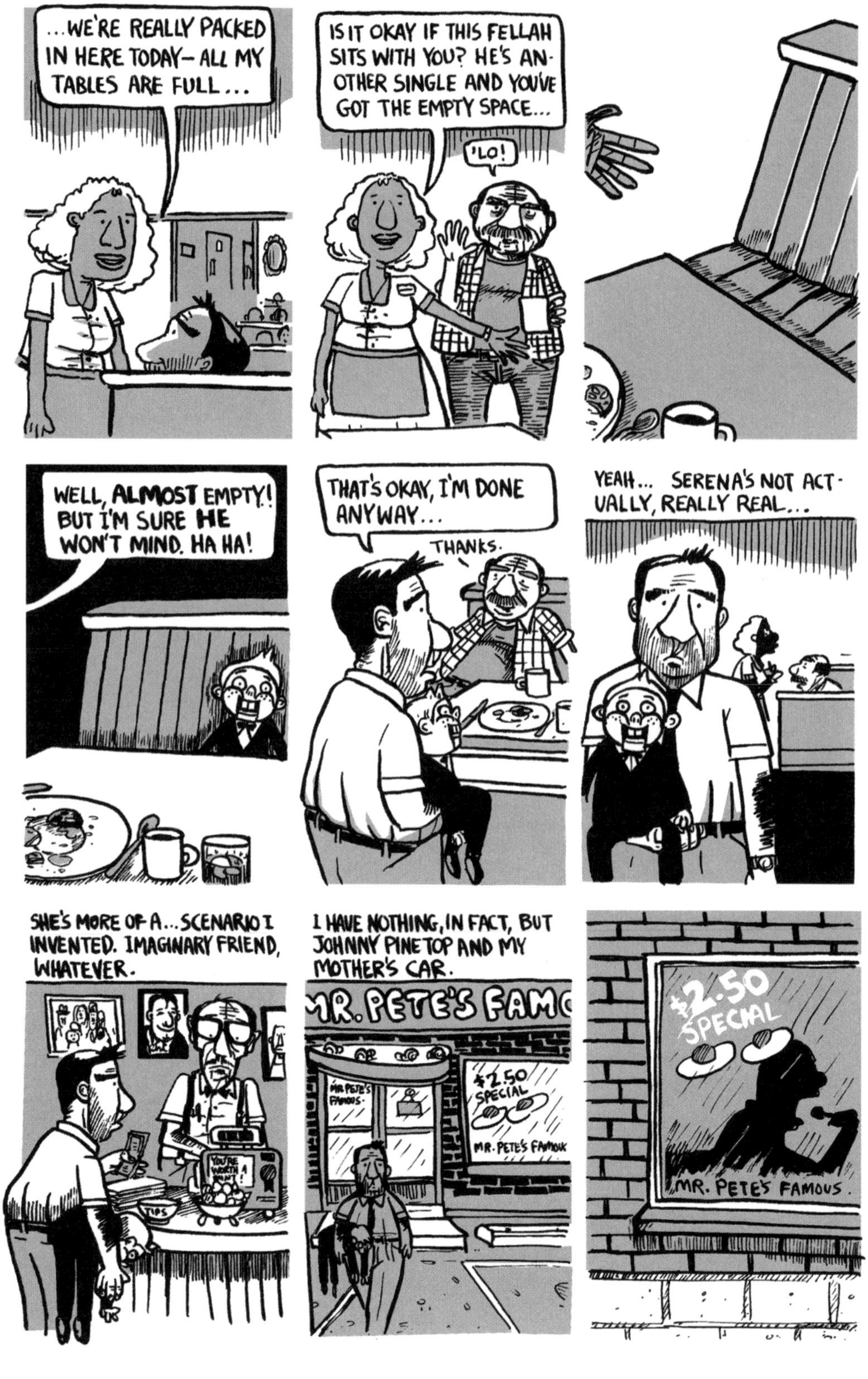
...WE'RE REALLY PACKED IN HERE TODAY— ALL MY TABLES ARE FULL...
IS IT OKAY IF THIS FELLAH SITS WITH YOU? HE'S AN-OTHER SINGLE AND YOU'VE GOT THE EMPTY SPACE...
'LO!
WELL, ALMOST EMPTY! BUT I'M SURE HE WON'T MIND. HA HA!
THAT'S OKAY, I'M DONE ANYWAY...
THANKS.
YEAH... SERENA'S NOT ACT-UALLY, REALLY REAL...
SHE'S MORE OF A...SCENARIO I INVENTED. IMAGINARY FRIEND, WHATEVER.
YOU'RE WORTH A MINT!
TIPS
I HAVE NOTHING, IN FACT, BUT JOHNNY PINETOP AND MY MOTHER'S CAR.
MR. PETE'S FAMO
MR PETE'S FAMOUS.
$2.50 SPECIAL
MR. PETE'S FAMOUS
$2.50 SPECIAL
MR. PETE'S FAMOUS.

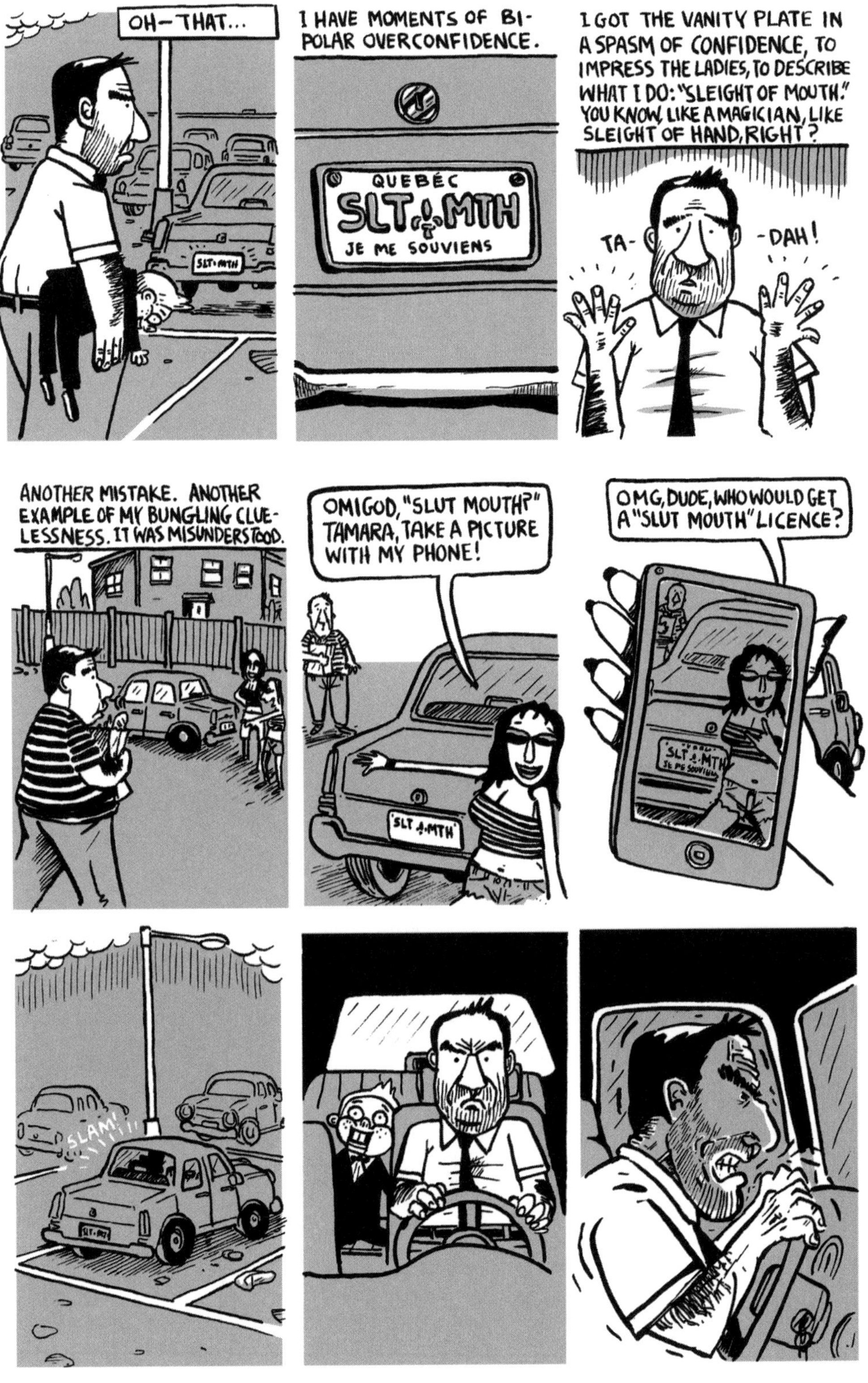
OH—THAT...
I HAVE MOMENTS OF BI-POLAR OVERCONFIDENCE.
QUEBÉC
SLT MTH
JE ME SOUVIENS
I GOT THE VANITY PLATE IN A SPASM OF CONFIDENCE, TO IMPRESS THE LADIES, TO DESCRIBE WHAT I DO: "SLEIGHT OF MOUTH." YOU KNOW, LIKE A MAGICIAN, LIKE SLEIGHT OF HAND, RIGHT?
TA-
-DAH!
ANOTHER MISTAKE. ANOTHER EXAMPLE OF MY BUNGLING CLUE-LESSNESS. IT WAS MISUNDERSTOOD.
OMIGOD, "SLUT MOUTH?" TAMARA, TAKE A PICTURE WITH MY PHONE!
SLT MTH
OMG, DUDE, WHO WOULD GET A "SLUT MOUTH" LICENCE?
SLAM!

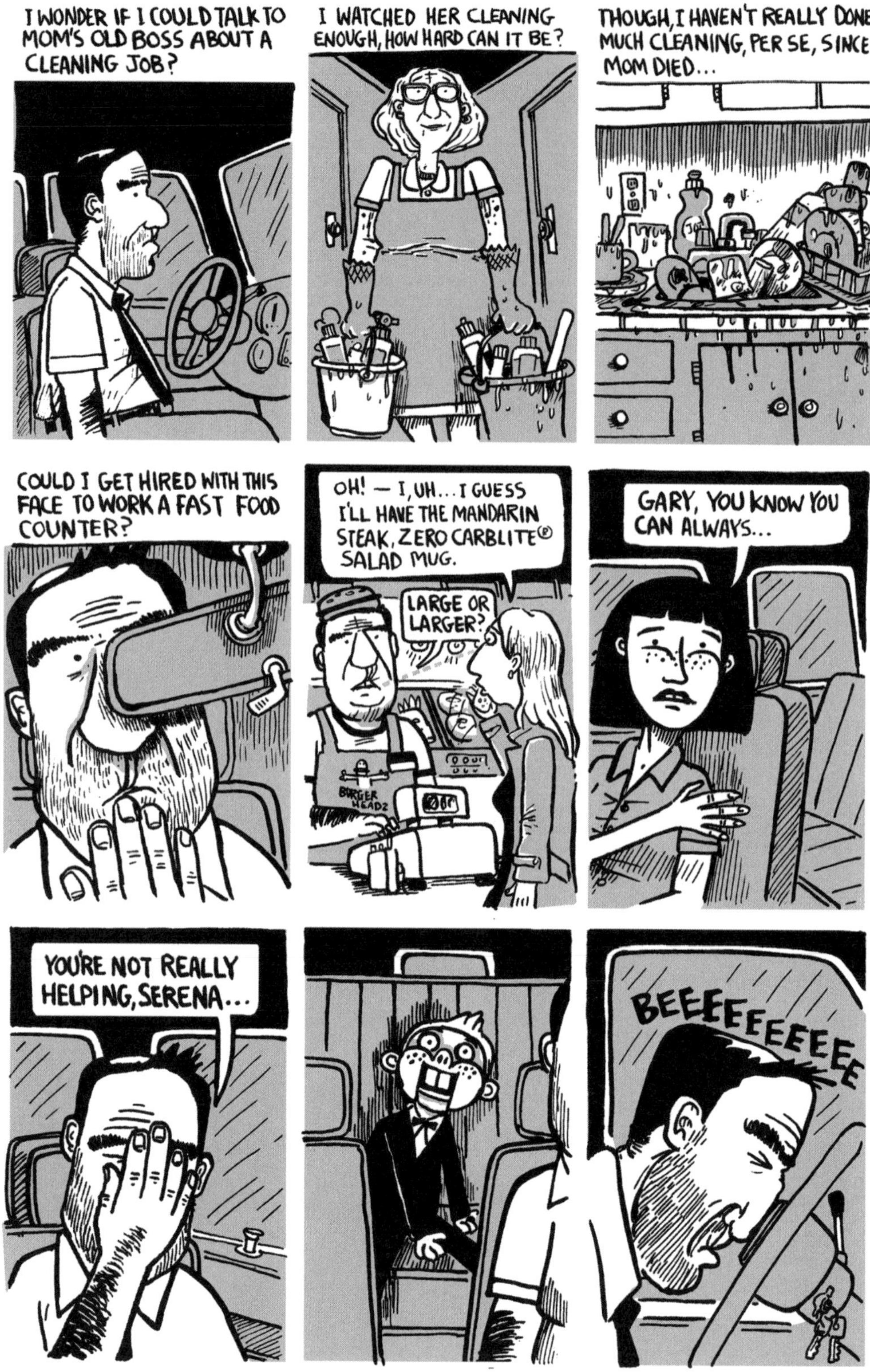
I WONDER IF I COULD TALK TO MOM'S OLD BOSS ABOUT A CLEANING JOB?
I WATCHED HER CLEANING ENOUGH, HOW HARD CAN IT BE?
THOUGH, I HAVEN'T REALLY DONE MUCH CLEANING, PER SE, SINCE MOM DIED...
COULD I GET HIRED WITH THIS FACE TO WORK A FAST FOOD COUNTER?
OH! — I, UH... I GUESS I'LL HAVE THE MANDARIN STEAK, ZERO CARBLITE® SALAD MUG.
LARGE OR LARGER?
BURGER HEADZ
GARY, YOU KNOW YOU CAN ALWAYS...
YOU'RE NOT REALLY HELPING, SERENA...
BEEEEEEEEEEE

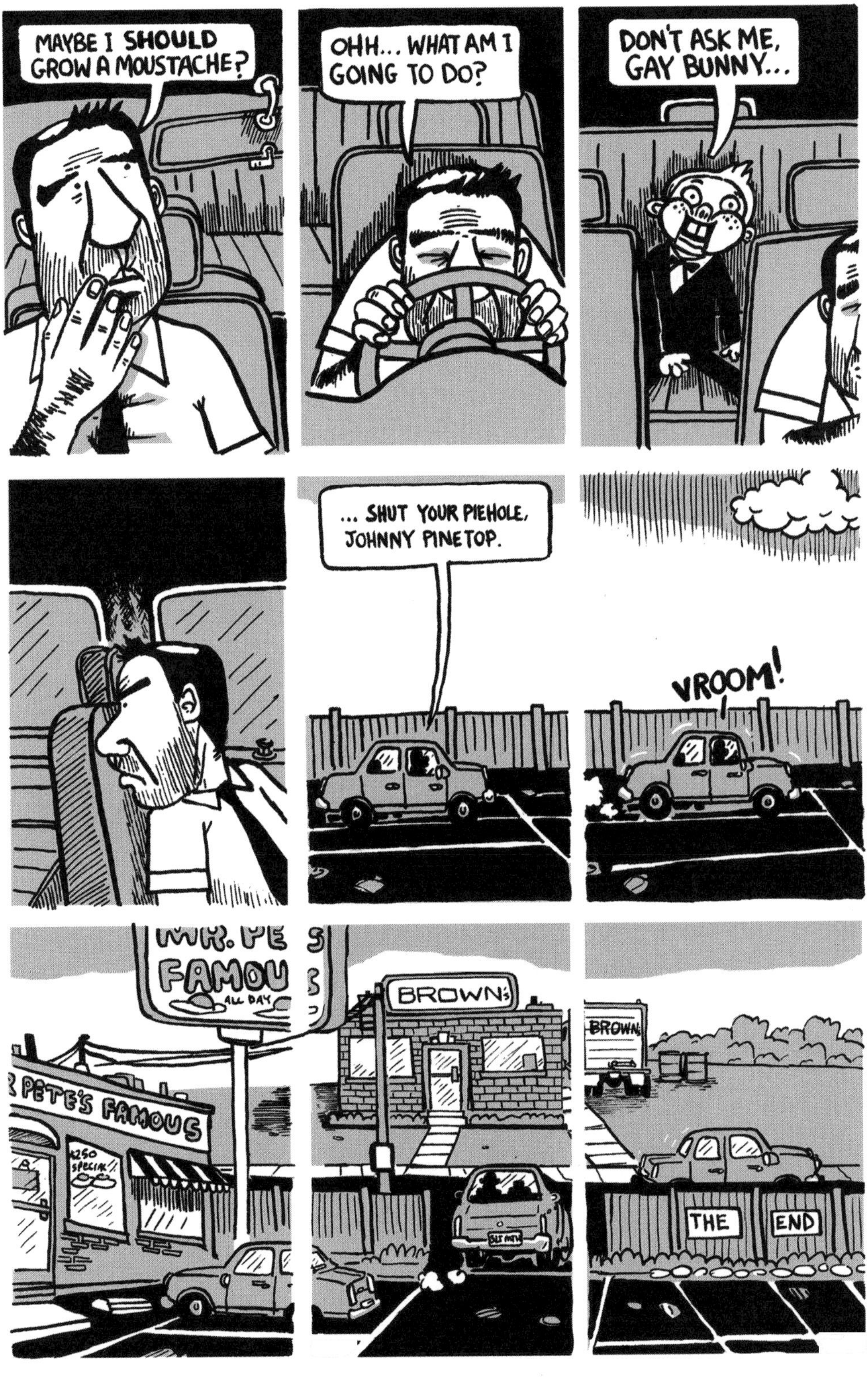
MAYBE I SHOULD GROW A MOUSTACHE?
OHH... WHAT AM I GOING TO DO?
DON'T ASK ME, GAY BUNNY...
... SHUT YOUR PIEHOLE, JOHNNY PINETOP.
VROOM!
MR. PETE'S FAMOUS
PETE'S FAMOUS
BROWN'S
THE
END

# Blinky-Jinks Playhouse

CHAR ESMÉ

# Big Rudy's Cowgirls Club

CHAR ESMÉ AND LAUREN POOR

*originally published in*

## Square Dance at Palms Promenade
DESERT ISLAND
8.5 × 11 inches • 64 pages

## Biographies

Cher Esmé is a multimedia artist and an editor of the *Spider's Pee Paw* anthologies and *Square Dance at Palms Promenade*. She is the author of the comic *Secret of the Saucers* (based on the autobiographies of Orfeo Angelucci) and coauthor of *Queasy's Smileybean Emporium*. Her work has been shown at various galleries, including Space 1026. She is interested in art and media functioning as a window to the unconscious and how both advertising and therapy can exploit this function.   charesme.info

Lauren Poor is an artist person forever inspired by fairies and witchcraft. laurenpoor.biz

## Statements

FROM CHAR ESMÉ: Both of these false flyers are very nostalgic to my childhood and finding my small self consumed by both wonder and horror twisted together upon encountering—for example—the Burger King kid's playhouse. Here are two attempts to construct a dream environment through false advertising, from the book *Square Dance*, a collaborative collection of comics all taking place in Palms Promenade.

FROM LAUREN POOR: Big Rudy's Cowgirls Club is supported and sponsored by so many Palms Promenade shops. We are so lucky. The two Cowgirls taking place in the ad know how to pass along the true aura of feeling associated with Big Rudy herself. Their fashions which I have culled together from the most soft fabric-ed internet stock photo providers hint at the sort of style and atmosphere you can imagine hearing all the pictured Juke and Jive titles in. With their lassos, empty gun and horseshoe these ladies will enforce Big Rudy's rules and look damn good doing so. All colors, outfits, styles and text have been chosen with these attributes in mind. Thank you.

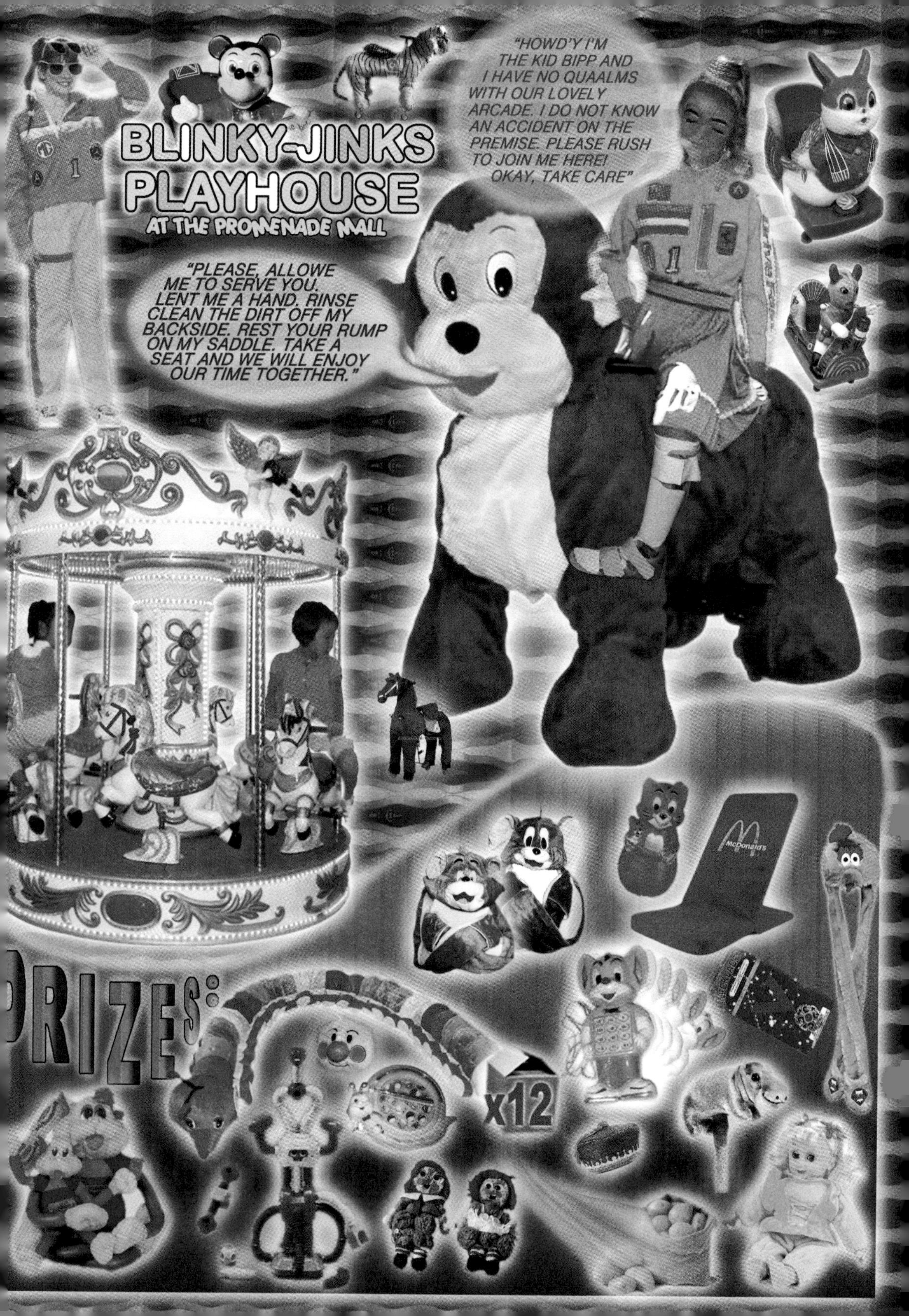
BLINKY-JINKS PLAYHOUSE
AT THE PROMENADE MALL
"HOWD'Y I'M THE KID BIPP AND I HAVE NO QUAALMS WITH OUR LOVELY ARCADE. I DO NOT KNOW AN ACCIDENT ON THE PREMISE. PLEASE RUSH TO JOIN ME HERE! OKAY, TAKE CARE"
"PLEASE, ALLOWE ME TO SERVE YOU. LENT ME A HAND. RINSE CLEAN THE DIRT OFF MY BACKSIDE. REST YOUR RUMP ON MY SADDLE. TAKE A SEAT AND WE WILL ENJOY OUR TIME TOGETHER."
McDonald's
PRIZES:
x12

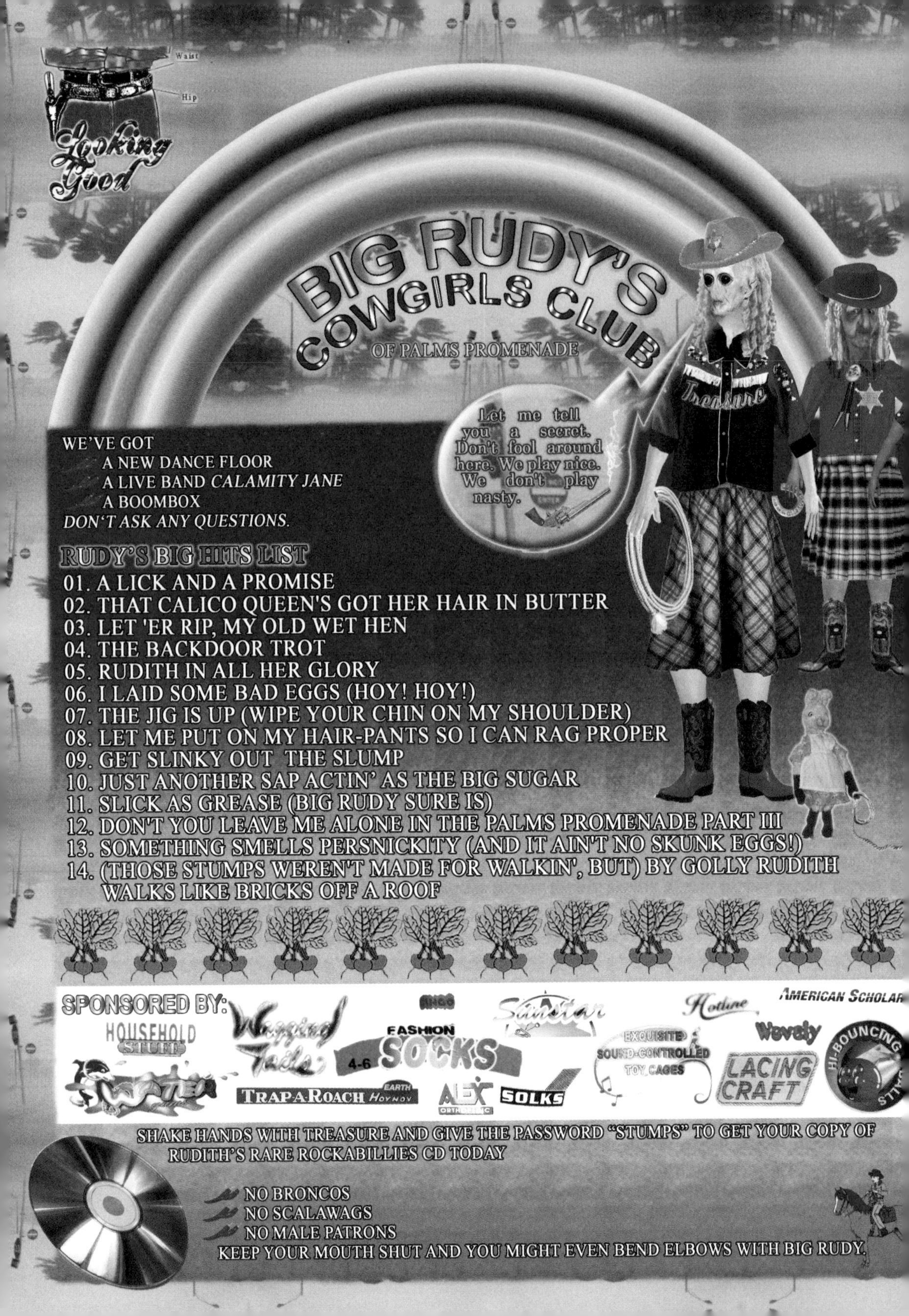

Waist
Hip
Looking Good
BIG RUDY'S COWGIRLS CLUB
OF PALMS PROMENADE
Let me tell you a secret. Don't fool around here. We play nice. We don't play nasty.
Treasure
WE'VE GOT
A NEW DANCE FLOOR
A LIVE BAND *CALAMITY JANE*
A BOOMBOX
*DON'T ASK ANY QUESTIONS.*
RUDY'S BIG HITS LIST
01. A LICK AND A PROMISE
02. THAT CALICO QUEEN'S GOT HER HAIR IN BUTTER
03. LET 'ER RIP, MY OLD WET HEN
04. THE BACKDOOR TROT
05. RUDITH IN ALL HER GLORY
06. I LAID SOME BAD EGGS (HOY! HOY!)
07. THE JIG IS UP (WIPE YOUR CHIN ON MY SHOULDER)
08. LET ME PUT ON MY HAIR-PANTS SO I CAN RAG PROPER
09. GET SLINKY OUT THE SLUMP
10. JUST ANOTHER SAP ACTIN' AS THE BIG SUGAR
11. SLICK AS GREASE (BIG RUDY SURE IS)
12. DON'T YOU LEAVE ME ALONE IN THE PALMS PROMENADE PART III
13. SOMETHING SMELLS PERSNICKITY (AND IT AIN'T NO SKUNK EGGS!)
14. (THOSE STUMPS WEREN'T MADE FOR WALKIN', BUT) BY GOLLY RUDITH WALKS LIKE BRICKS OFF A ROOF
SPONSORED BY:
HOUSEHOLD STUFF
Wagging Tails
FASHION SOCKS 4-6
Hotline
AMERICAN SCHOLAR
Wavely
EXQUISITE SOUND-CONTROLLED TOY CAGES
LACING CRAFT
HI-BOUNCING
TRAP-A-ROACH
EARTH HOYNOY
ALEX ORTHOPEDIC
SOLKS
SHAKE HANDS WITH TREASURE AND GIVE THE PASSWORD "STUMPS" TO GET YOUR COPY OF RUDITH'S RARE ROCKABILLIES CD TODAY
NO BRONCOS
NO SCALAWAGS
NO MALE PATRONS
KEEP YOUR MOUTH SHUT AND YOU MIGHT EVEN BEND ELBOWS WITH BIG RUDY.

# Untitled

TAYLOR-RUTH BALDWIN

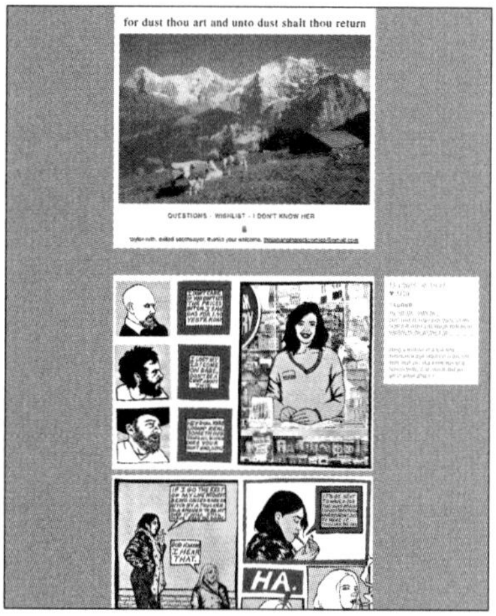
for dust thou art and unto dust shalt thou return
QUESTIONS - WISHLIST - I DON'T KNOW HER
I HEAR THAT.
HA.

*originally published at*

thisishangingrockcomics.tumblr.com

SELF-PUBLISHED

digital

## Biography

Taylor-Ruth, 21, Indianapolis, Indiana. Holy light, exiled soothsayer, the shape of satisfactory girl experience. thisishangingrockcomics.tumblr.com

## Statement

being a woman in a low end minimum wage retail job is fun cos men treat you like even less of a human being than usual and you get to smile about it

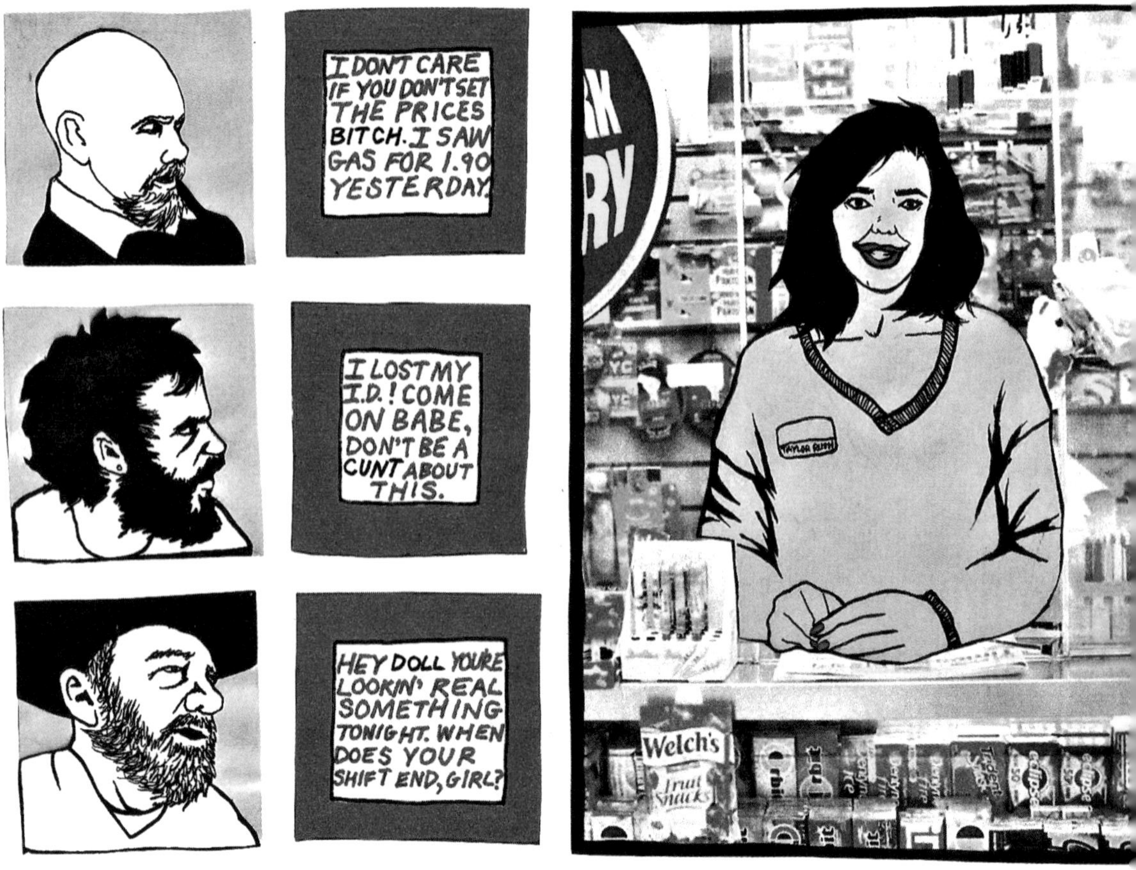
I DON'T CARE IF YOU DON'T SET THE PRICES BITCH. I SAW GAS FOR 1.90 YESTERDAY.
I LOST MY I.D.! COME ON BABE, DON'T BE A CUNT ABOUT THIS.
HEY DOLL YOU'RE LOOKIN' REAL SOMETHING TONIGHT. WHEN DOES YOUR SHIFT END, GIRL?
Welch's

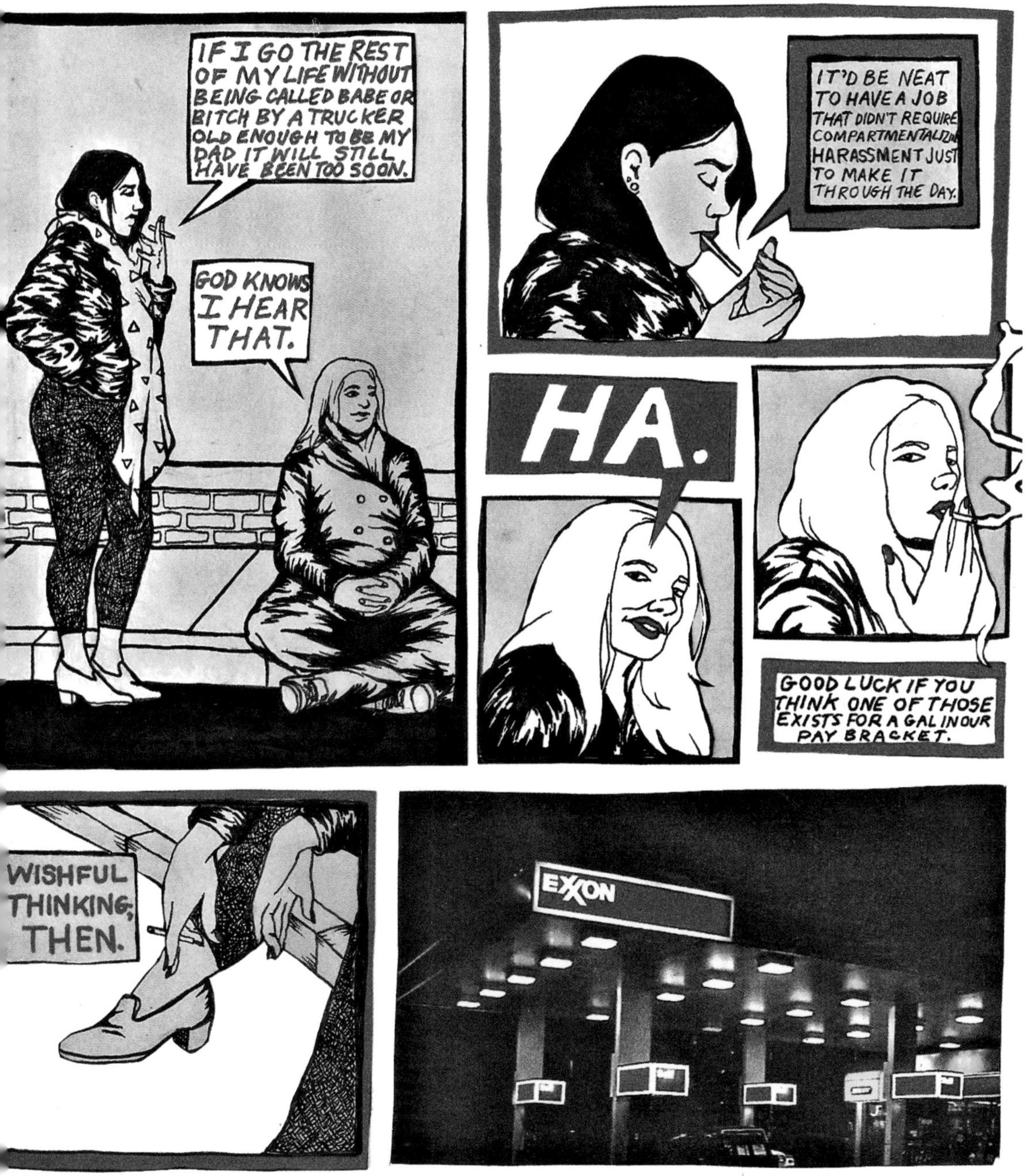
IF I GO THE REST OF MY LIFE WITHOUT BEING CALLED BABE OR BITCH BY A TRUCKER OLD ENOUGH TO BE MY DAD IT WILL STILL HAVE BEEN TOO SOON.
GOD KNOWS I HEAR THAT.
IT'D BE NEAT TO HAVE A JOB THAT DIDN'T REQUIRE COMPARTMENTALIZING HARASSMENT JUST TO MAKE IT THROUGH THE DAY.
HA.
GOOD LUCK IF YOU THINK ONE OF THOSE EXISTS FOR A GAL IN OUR PAY BRACKET.
WISHFUL THINKING, THEN.
EXXON

BUMPERHEAD
GILBERT
HERNANDEZ
X

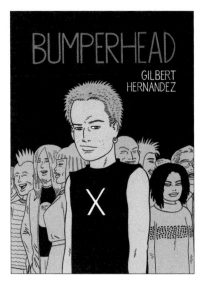

# Bumps in the Night (*Excerpt*)

GILBERT HERNANDEZ

*excerpted from*

Bumperhead

DRAWN AND QUARTERLY

8 × 10 inches • 142 pages

## Biography

Gilbert Hernandez was born in Oxnard, California, in 1957, with a comic book in his hand. As long as he can remember, there were comics in the house. He grew up on the comics of the 1960s; it was the greatest boom in comics history because of its lasting effects on comics today. The Marvel age began, and at the end of the decade the underground scene kick-started what we know now as the indie comics world. Gilbert is part of both and will always have inspiration to make new comics because of these influences.

## Statement

The lead character in *Bumperhead*/"Bumps in the Night" is slightly autobiographical because I wanted to show a rough example of what being a teen in the 1970s was like for me. It's specific to my experience and in turn reflects a universal expression. At least that's what I've been told.

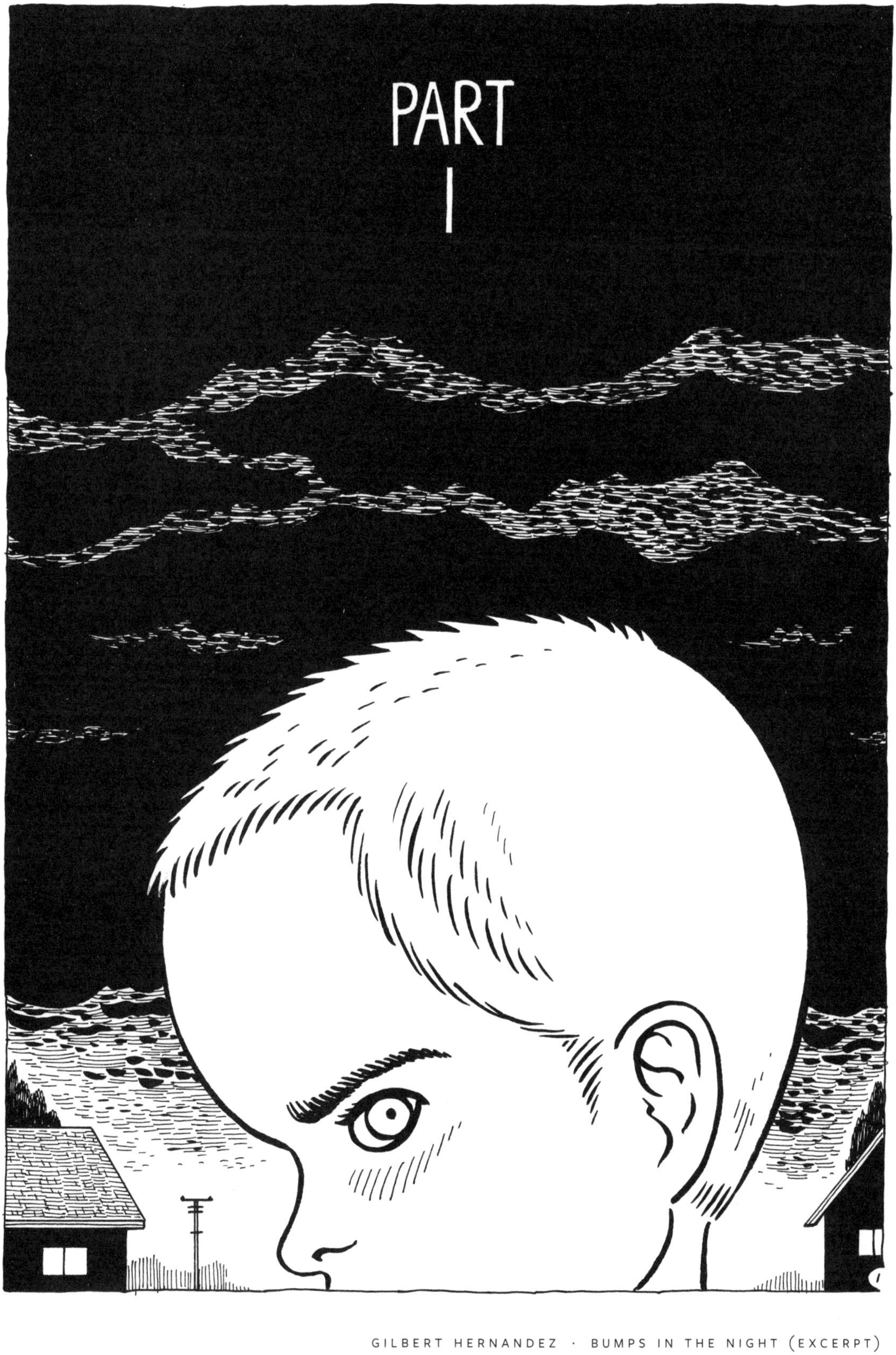
PART
I

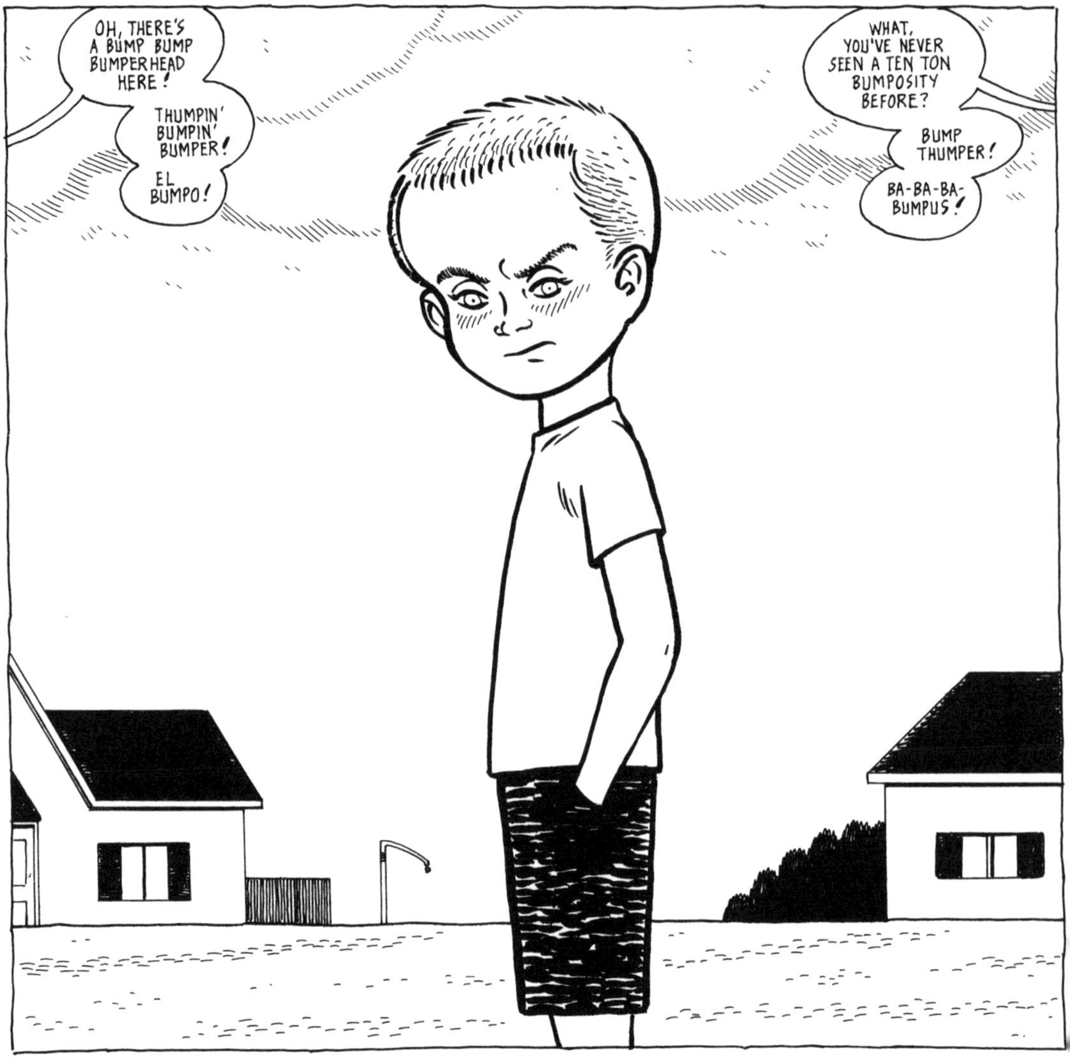
OH, THERE'S A BUMP BUMP BUMPERHEAD HERE!
THUMPIN' BUMPIN' BUMPER!
EL BUMPO!
WHAT, YOU'VE NEVER SEEN A TEN TON BUMPOSITY BEFORE?
BUMP THUMPER!
BA-BA-BA-BUMPUS!

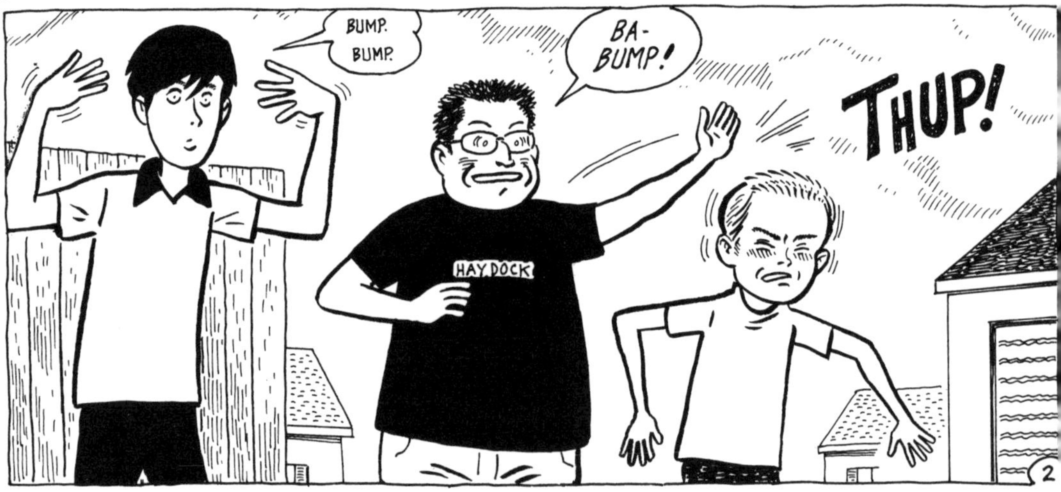
BUMP. BUMP.
BA-BUMP!
THUP!
HAYDOCK
2

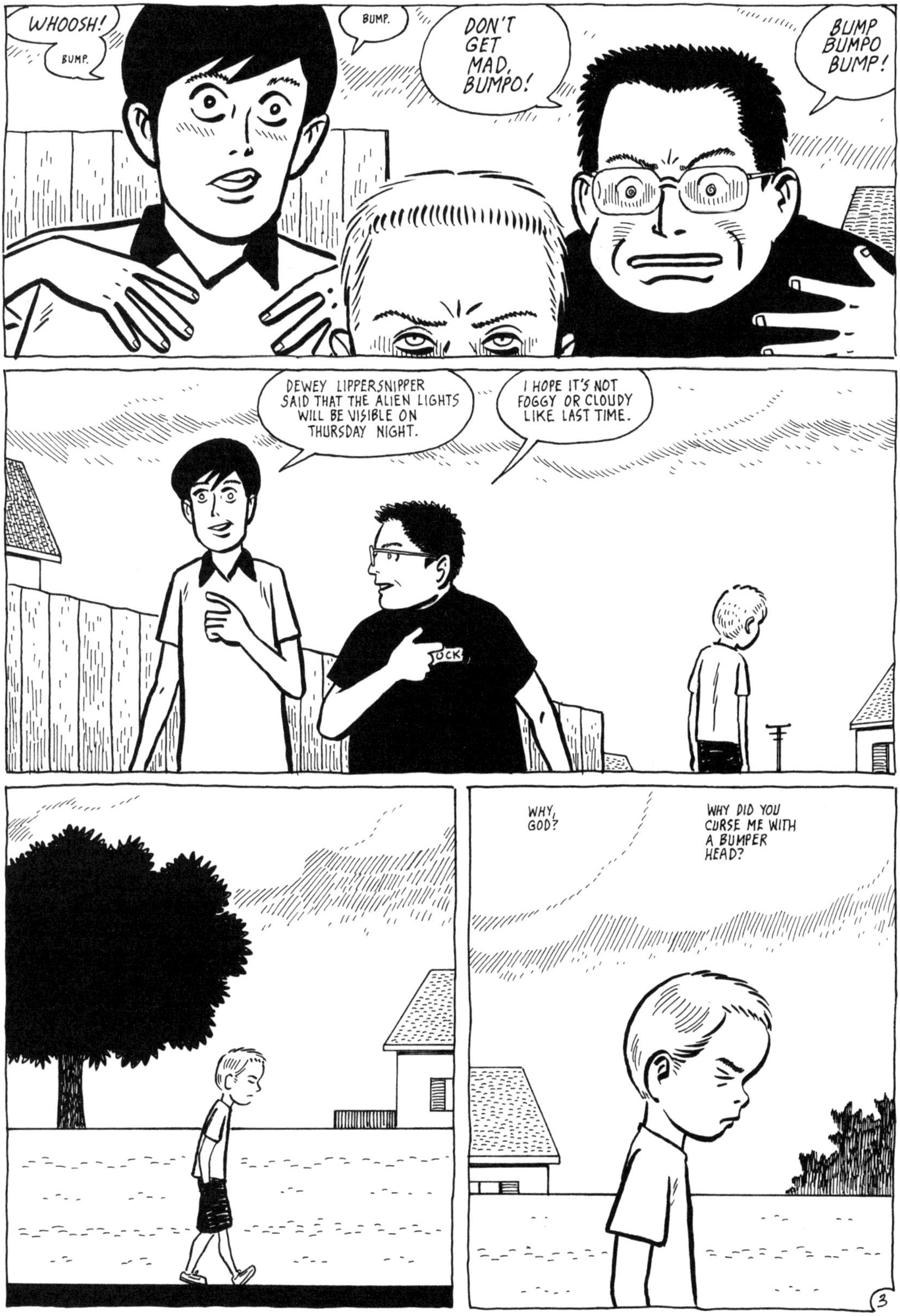
WHOOSH!
BUMP.
BUMP.
DON'T GET MAD, BUMPO!
BUMP BUMPO BUMP!
DEWEY LIPPERSNIPPER SAID THAT THE ALIEN LIGHTS WILL BE VISIBLE ON THURSDAY NIGHT.
I HOPE IT'S NOT FOGGY OR CLOUDY LIKE LAST TIME.
WHY, GOD?
WHY DID YOU CURSE ME WITH A BUMPER HEAD?
3

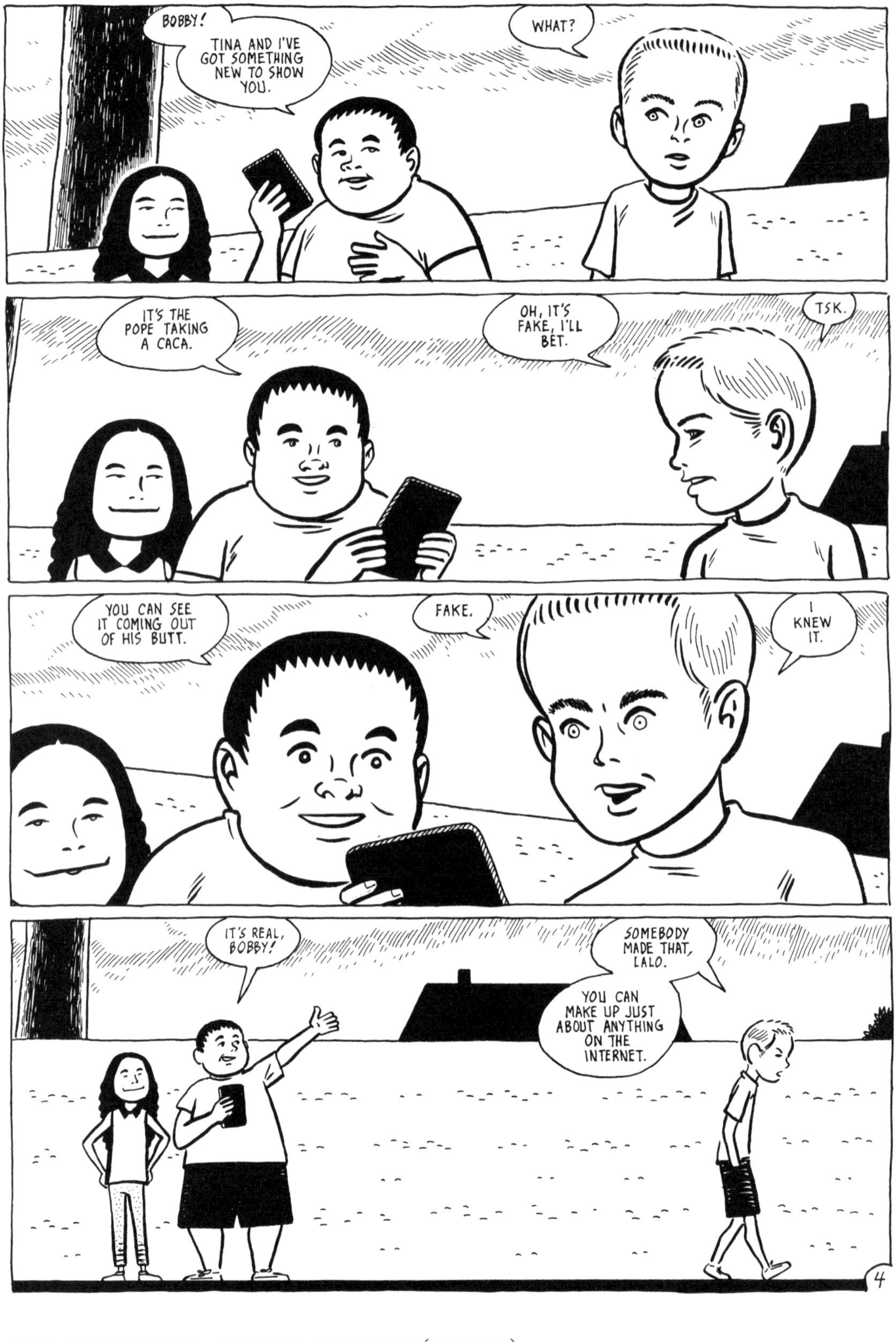
BOBBY!
TINA AND I'VE GOT SOMETHING NEW TO SHOW YOU.
WHAT?
IT'S THE POPE TAKING A CACA.
OH, IT'S FAKE, I'LL BET.
TSK.
YOU CAN SEE IT COMING OUT OF HIS BUTT.
FAKE.
I KNEW IT.
IT'S REAL, BOBBY!
SOMEBODY MADE THAT, LALO.
YOU CAN MAKE UP JUST ABOUT ANYTHING ON THE INTERNET.
4

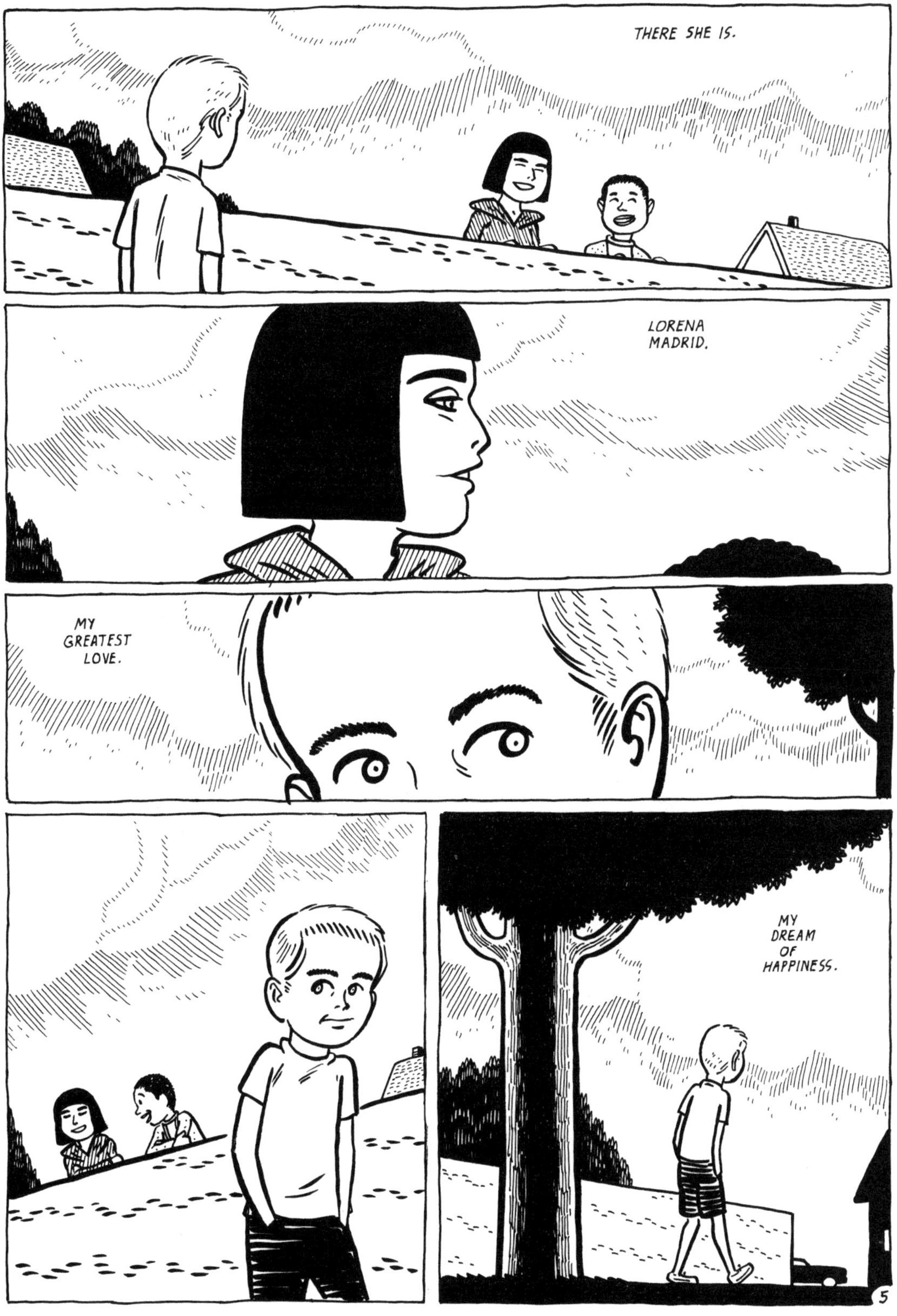
THERE SHE IS.
LORENA MADRID.
MY GREATEST LOVE.
MY DREAM OF HAPPINESS.
5

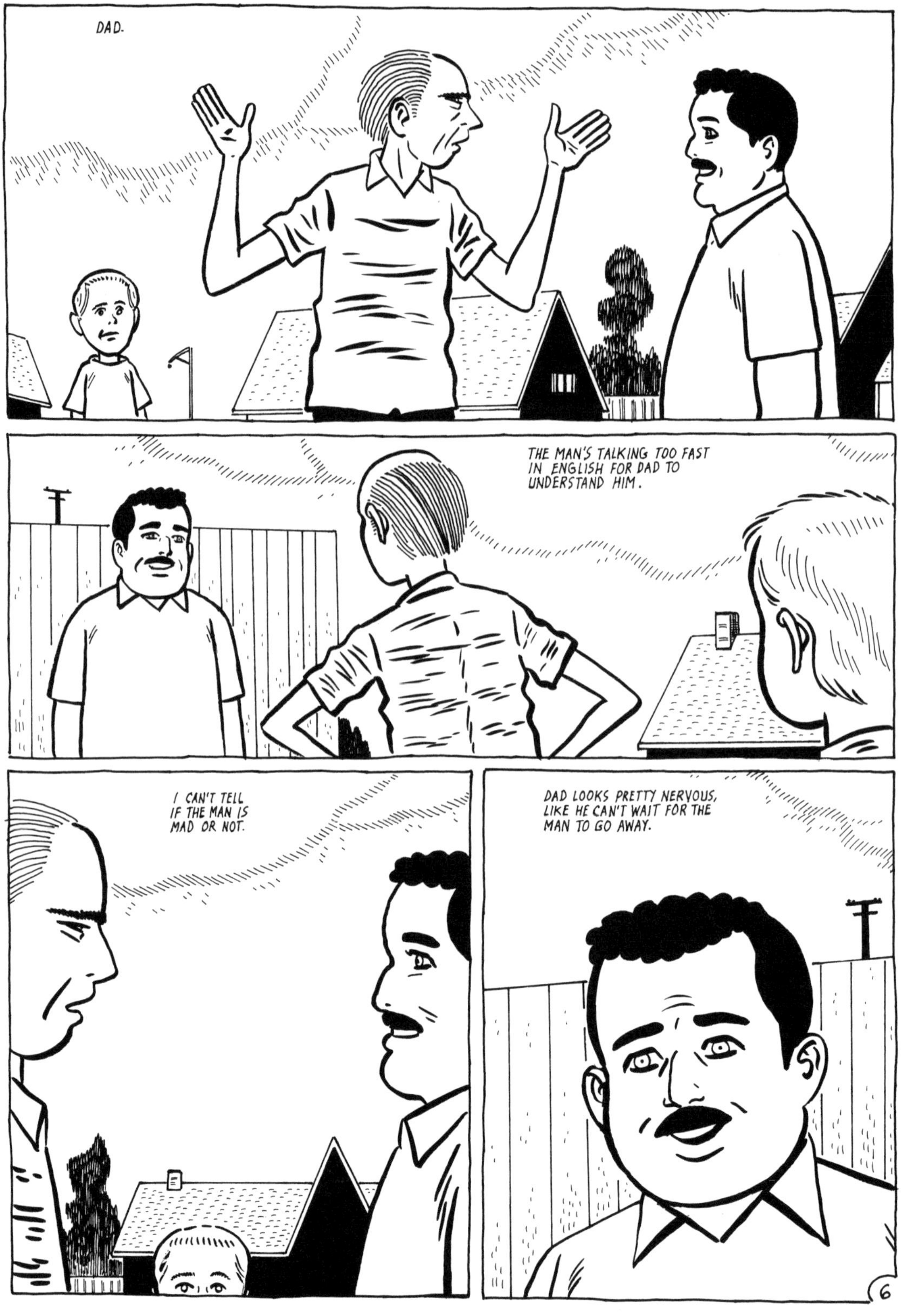
DAD.
THE MAN'S TALKING TOO FAST IN ENGLISH FOR DAD TO UNDERSTAND HIM.
I CAN'T TELL IF THE MAN IS MAD OR NOT.
DAD LOOKS PRETTY NERVOUS, LIKE HE CAN'T WAIT FOR THE MAN TO GO AWAY.
6

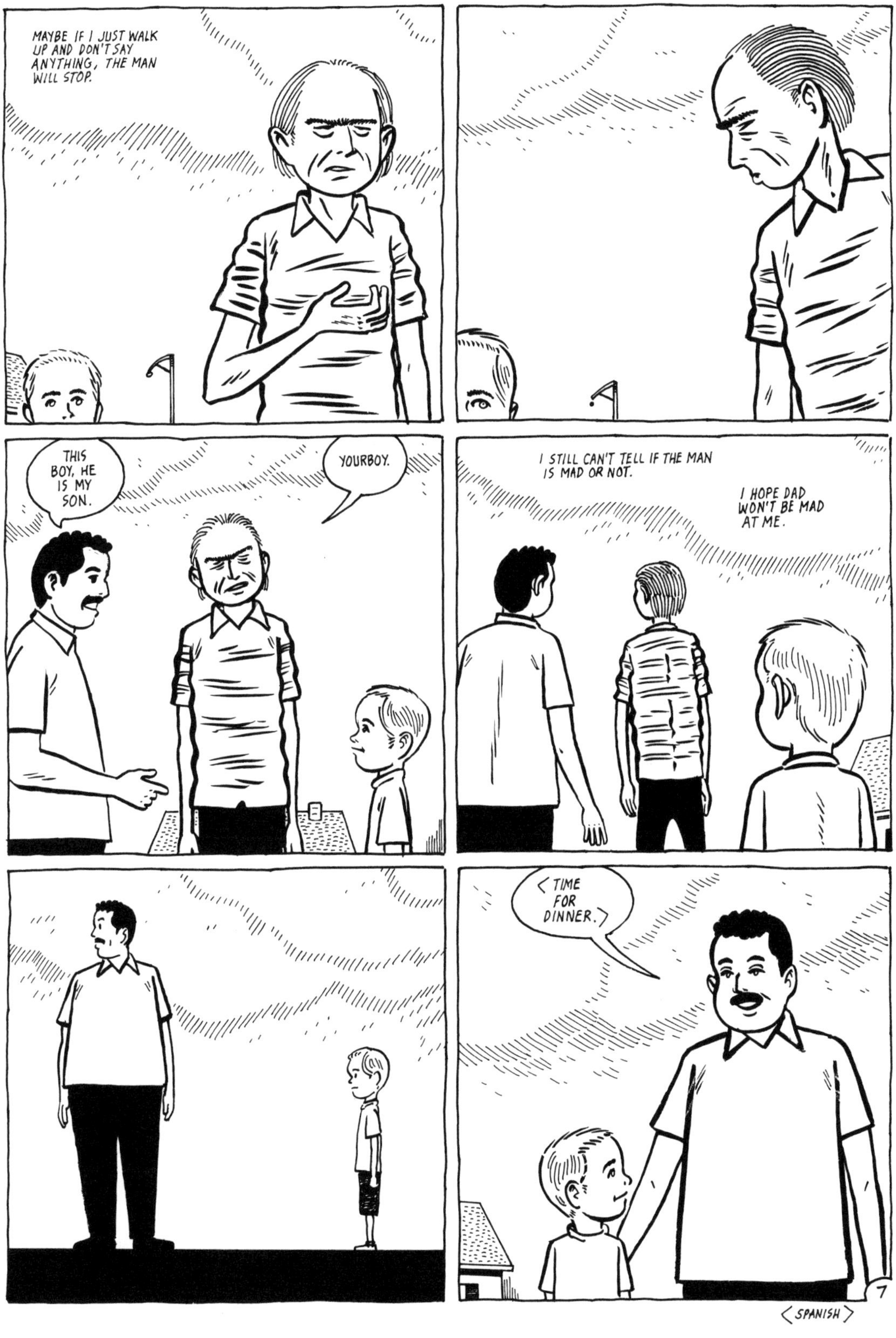
MAYBE IF I JUST WALK UP AND DON'T SAY ANYTHING, THE MAN WILL STOP.
THIS BOY, HE IS MY SON.
YOURBOY.
I STILL CAN'T TELL IF THE MAN IS MAD OR NOT.
I HOPE DAD WON'T BE MAD AT ME.
< TIME FOR DINNER. >
7
< SPANISH >

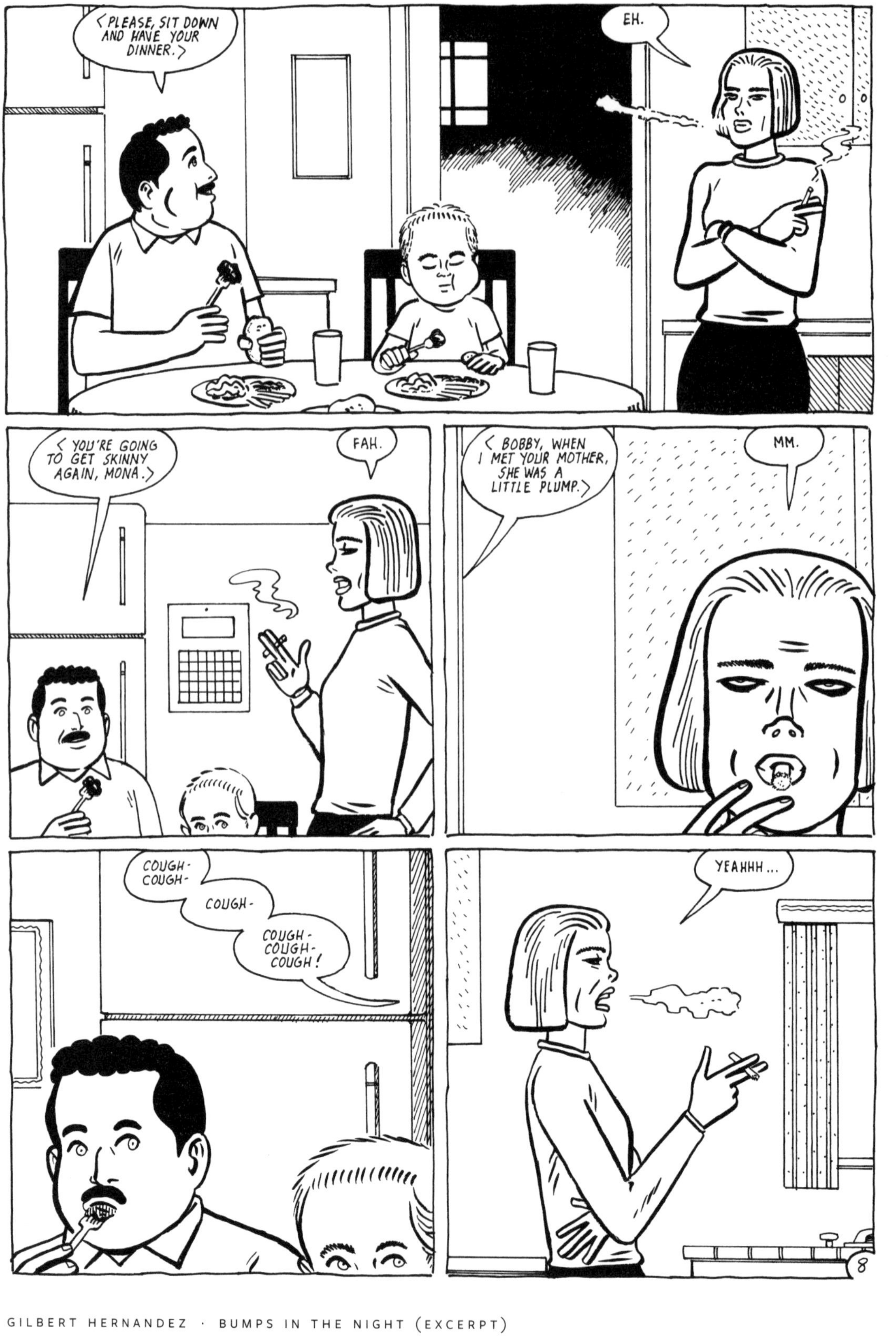

<PLEASE, SIT DOWN AND HAVE YOUR DINNER.>
EH.
<YOU'RE GOING TO GET SKINNY AGAIN, MONA.>
FAH.
<BOBBY, WHEN I MET YOUR MOTHER, SHE WAS A LITTLE PLUMP.>
MM.
COUGH-COUGH-
COUGH-
COUGH-COUGH-COUGH!
YEAHHH...
8

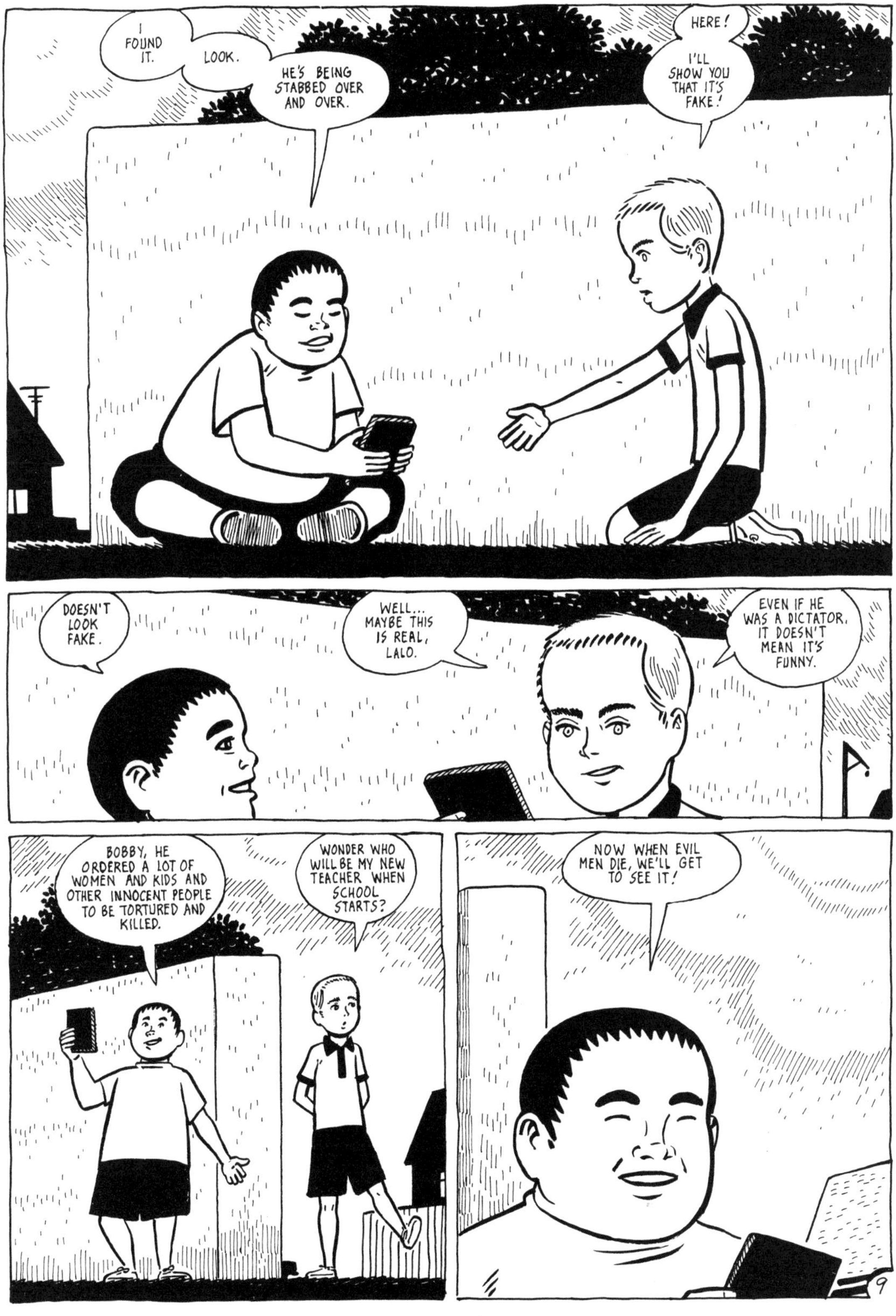
I FOUND IT.
LOOK.
HE'S BEING STABBED OVER AND OVER.
HERE!
I'LL SHOW YOU THAT IT'S FAKE!
DOESN'T LOOK FAKE.
WELL... MAYBE THIS IS REAL, LALO.
EVEN IF HE WAS A DICTATOR, IT DOESN'T MEAN IT'S FUNNY.
BOBBY, HE ORDERED A LOT OF WOMEN AND KIDS AND OTHER INNOCENT PEOPLE TO BE TORTURED AND KILLED.
WONDER WHO WILL BE MY NEW TEACHER WHEN SCHOOL STARTS?
NOW WHEN EVIL MEN DIE, WE'LL GET TO SEE IT!
9

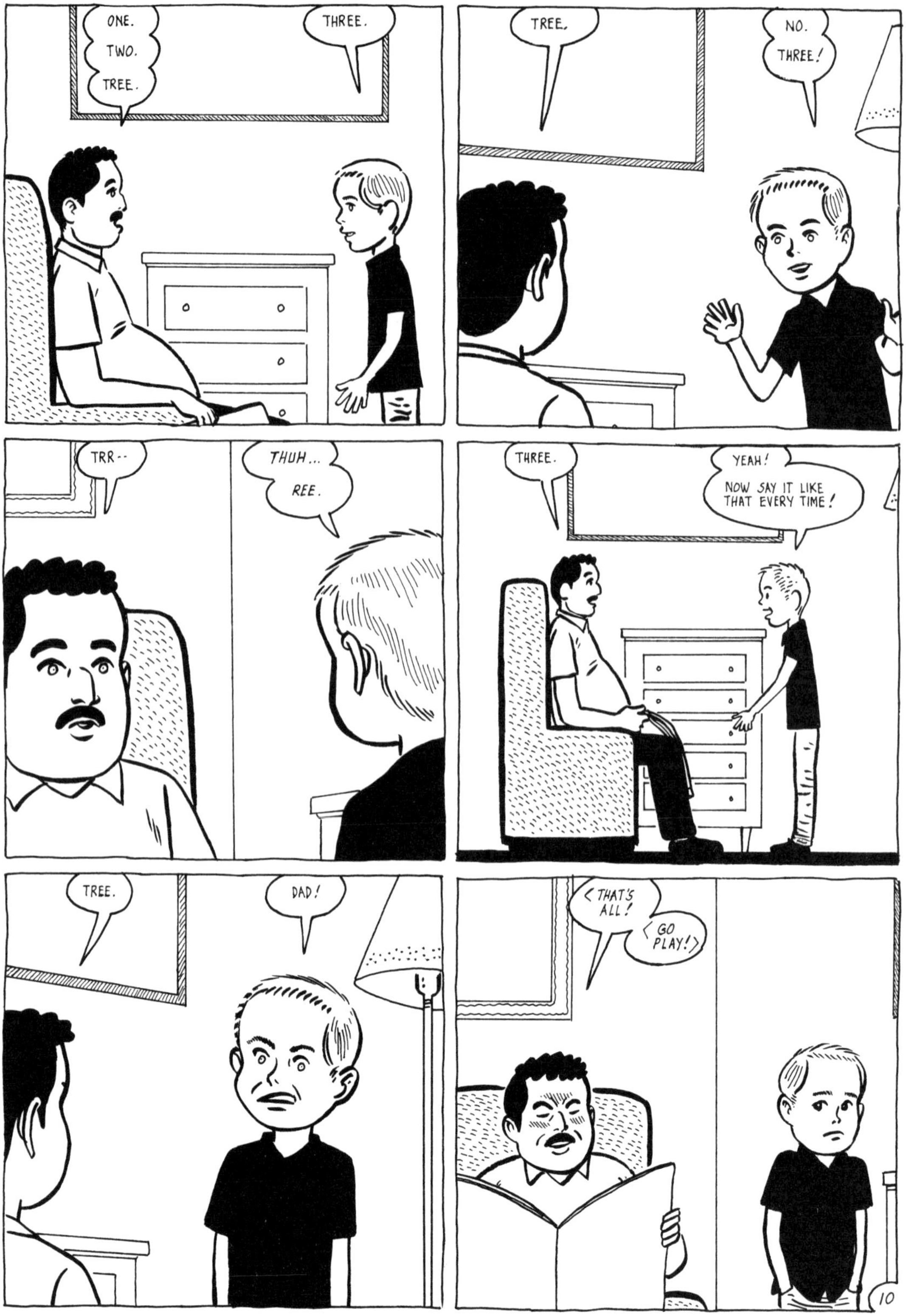
ONE.
TWO.
TREE.
THREE.
TREE.
NO.
THREE!
TRR--
THUH...
REE.
THREE.
YEAH!
NOW SAY IT LIKE THAT EVERY TIME!
TREE.
DAD!
<THAT'S ALL!
GO PLAY!>
10

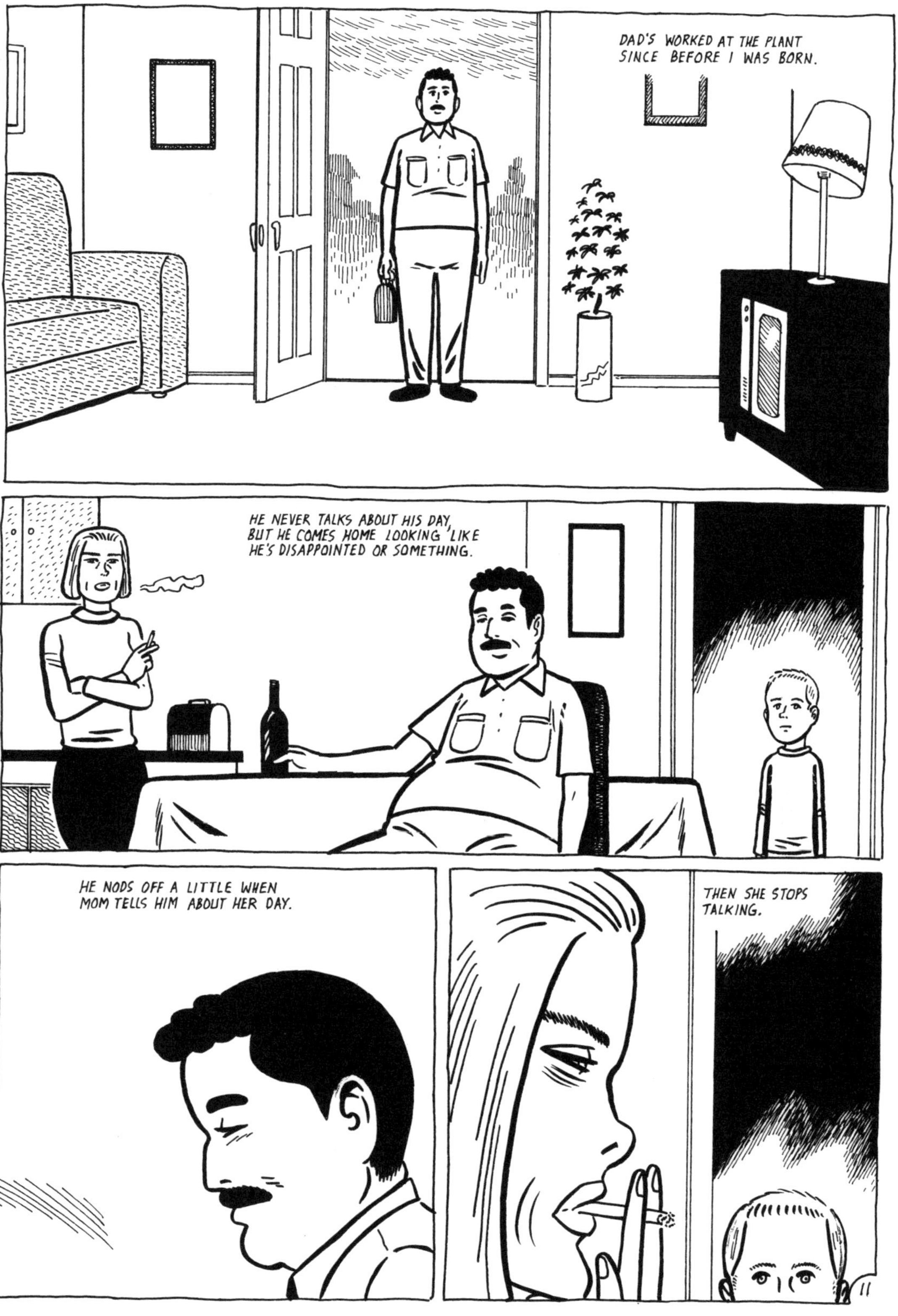
DAD'S WORKED AT THE PLANT SINCE BEFORE I WAS BORN.
HE NEVER TALKS ABOUT HIS DAY, BUT HE COMES HOME LOOKING LIKE HE'S DISAPPOINTED OR SOMETHING.
HE NODS OFF A LITTLE WHEN MOM TELLS HIM ABOUT HER DAY.
THEN SHE STOPS TALKING.

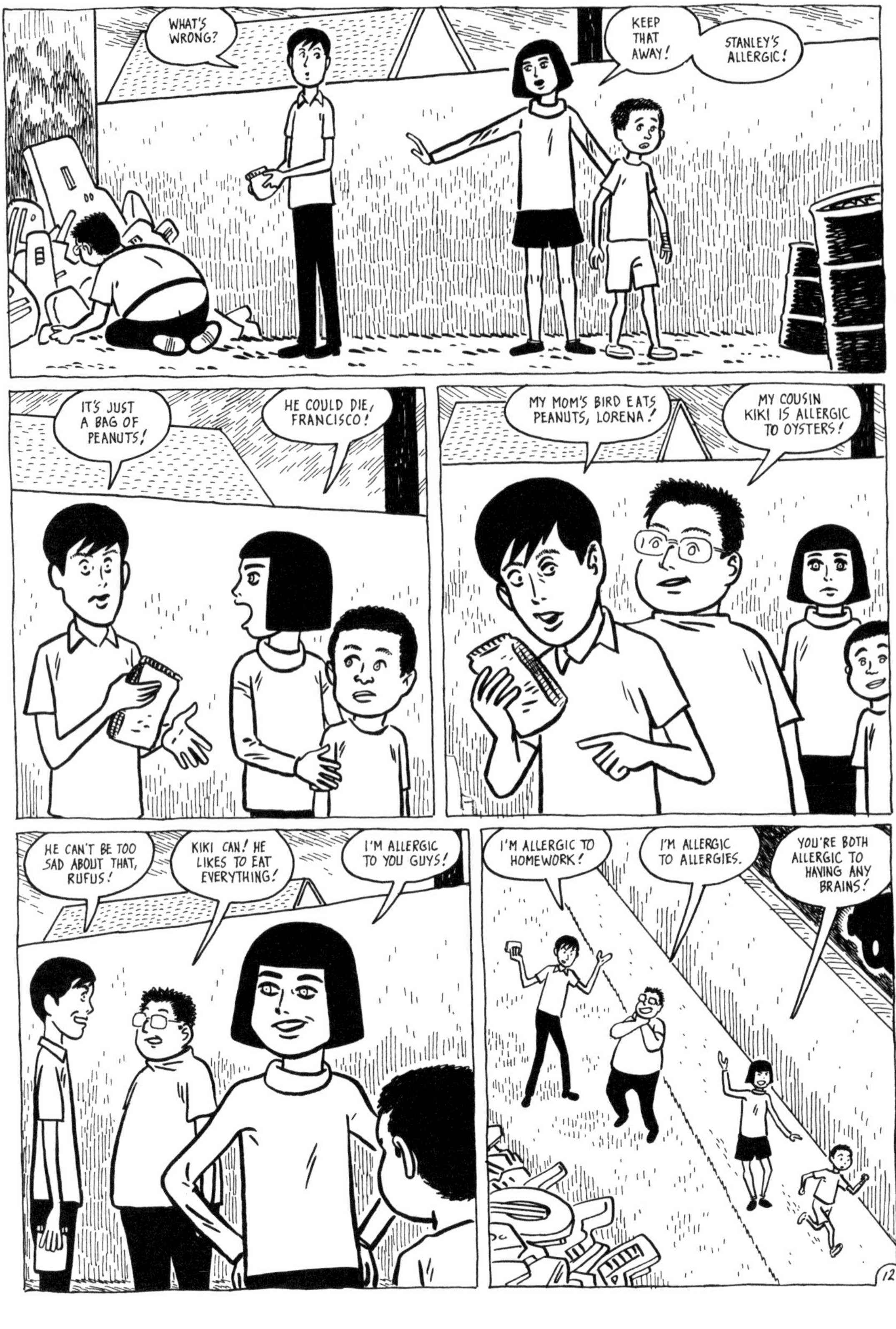
WHAT'S WRONG?
KEEP THAT AWAY!
STANLEY'S ALLERGIC!
IT'S JUST A BAG OF PEANUTS!
HE COULD DIE, FRANCISCO!
MY MOM'S BIRD EATS PEANUTS, LORENA!
MY COUSIN KIKI IS ALLERGIC TO OYSTERS!
HE CAN'T BE TOO SAD ABOUT THAT, RUFUS!
KIKI CAN! HE LIKES TO EAT EVERYTHING!
I'M ALLERGIC TO YOU GUYS!
I'M ALLERGIC TO HOMEWORK!
I'M ALLERGIC TO ALLERGIES.
YOU'RE BOTH ALLERGIC TO HAVING ANY BRAINS!
12

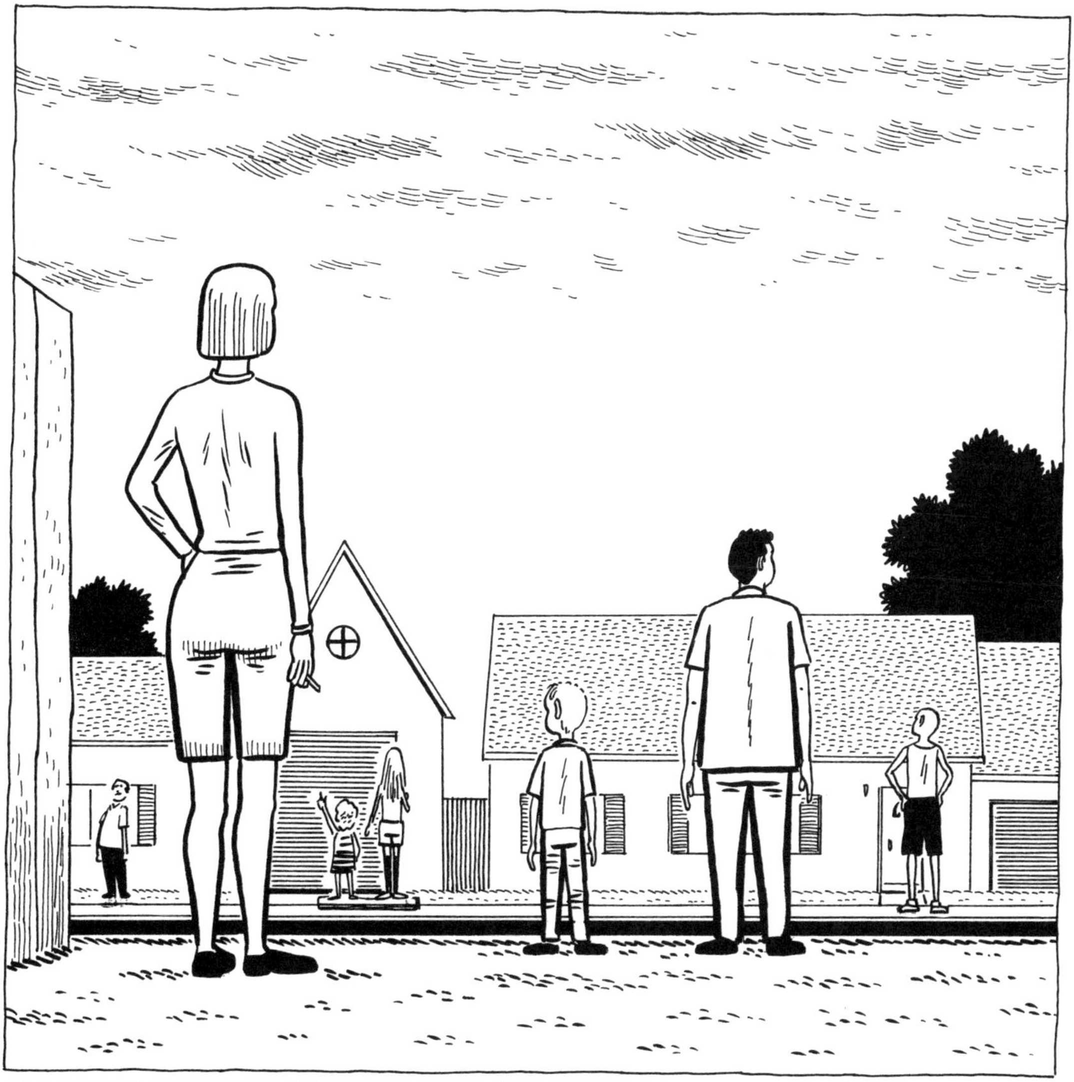

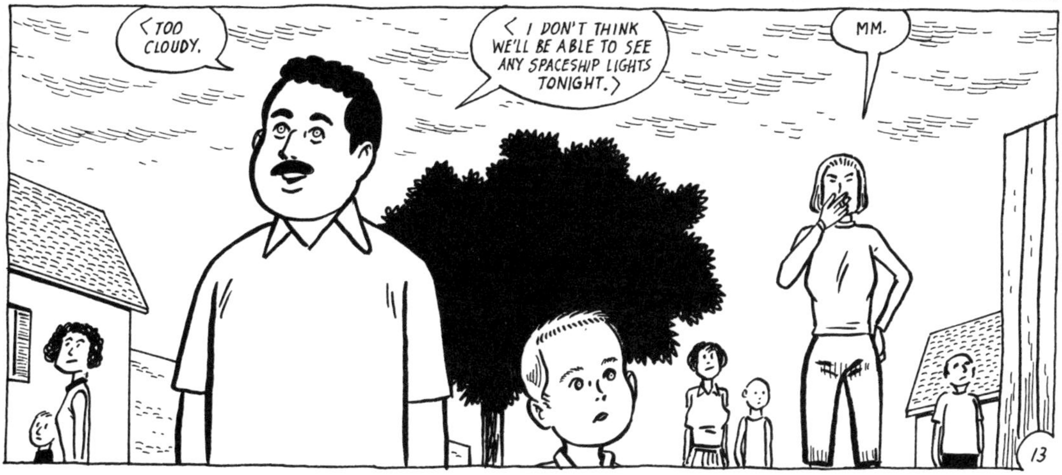

<TOO CLOUDY.
< I DON'T THINK WE'LL BE ABLE TO SEE ANY SPACESHIP LIGHTS TONIGHT.>
MM.
13

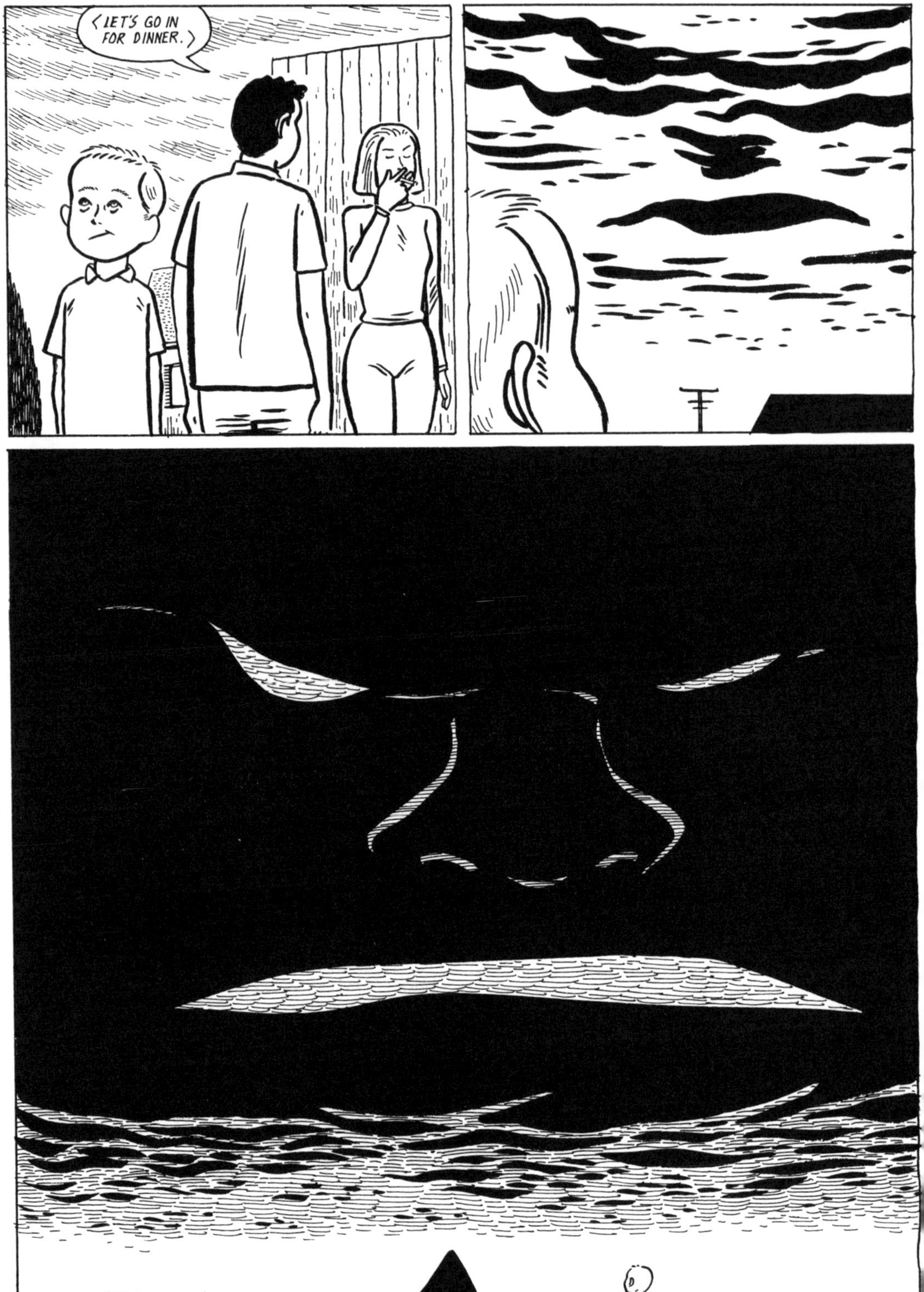
<LET'S GO IN FOR DINNER.>
14

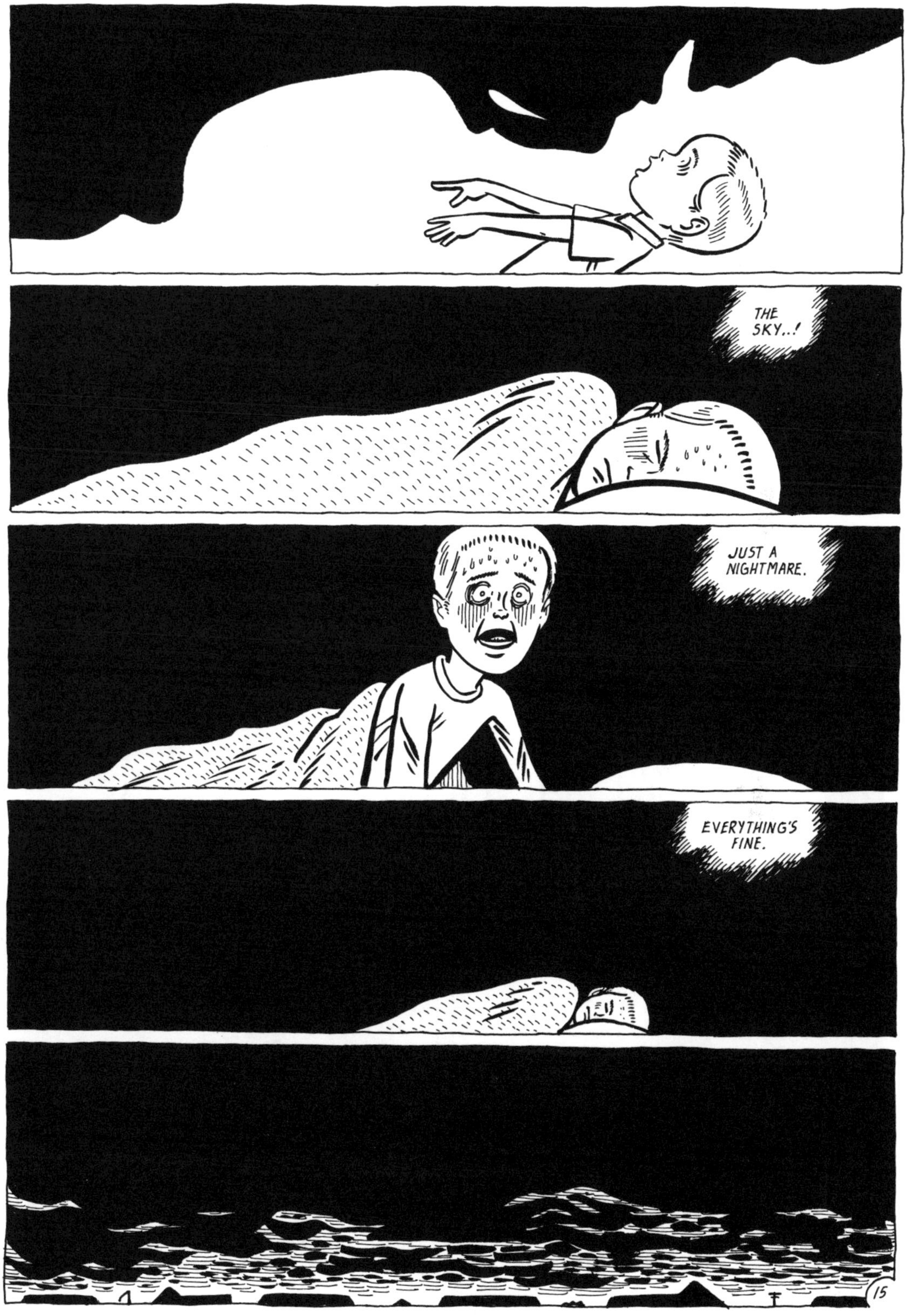
THE SKY..!
JUST A NIGHTMARE.
EVERYTHING'S FINE.
15

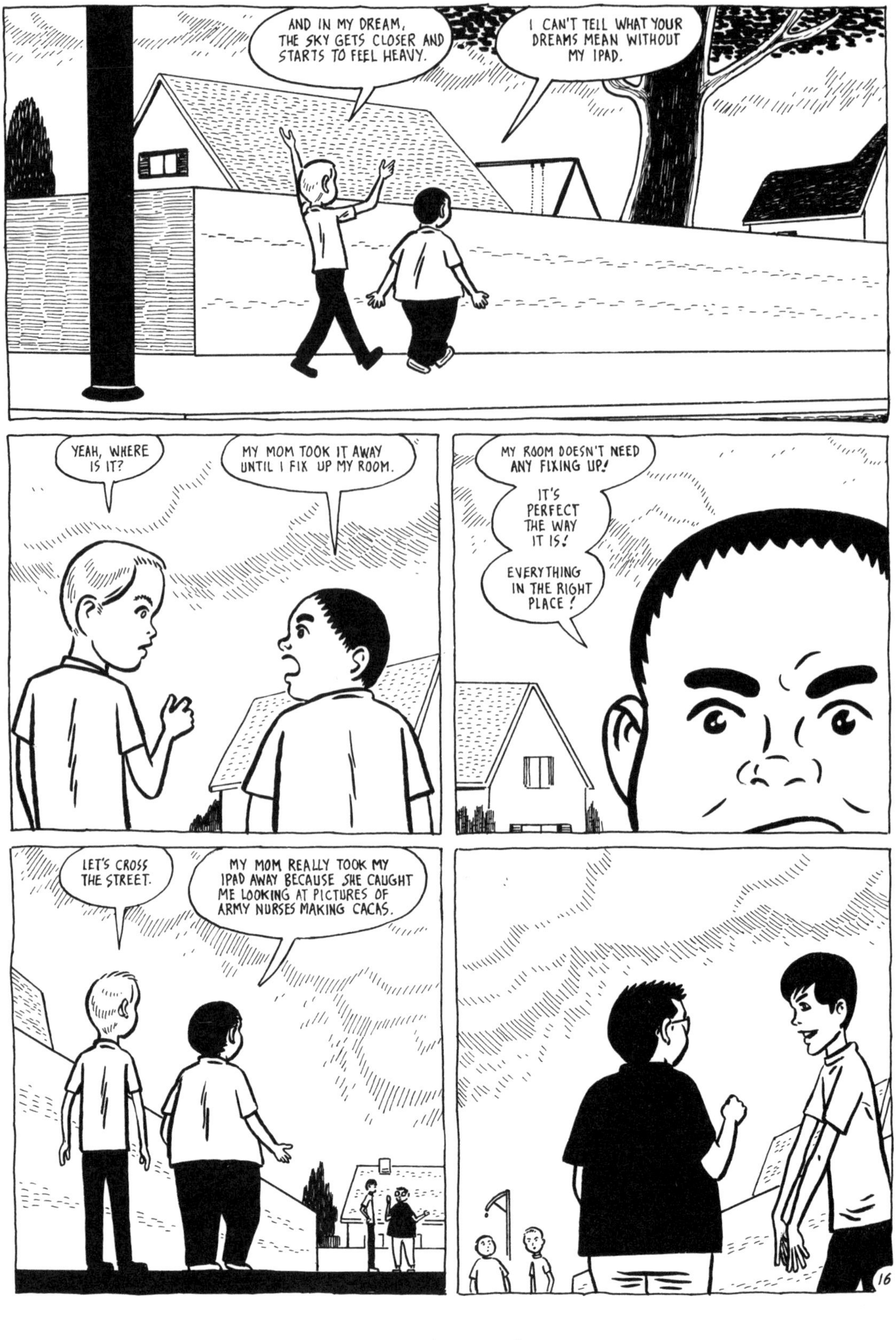
AND IN MY DREAM, THE SKY GETS CLOSER AND STARTS TO FEEL HEAVY.
I CAN'T TELL WHAT YOUR DREAMS MEAN WITHOUT MY IPAD.
YEAH, WHERE IS IT?
MY MOM TOOK IT AWAY UNTIL I FIX UP MY ROOM.
MY ROOM DOESN'T NEED ANY FIXING UP!
IT'S PERFECT THE WAY IT IS!
EVERYTHING IN THE RIGHT PLACE!
LET'S CROSS THE STREET.
MY MOM REALLY TOOK MY IPAD AWAY BECAUSE SHE CAUGHT ME LOOKING AT PICTURES OF ARMY NURSES MAKING CACAS.
16

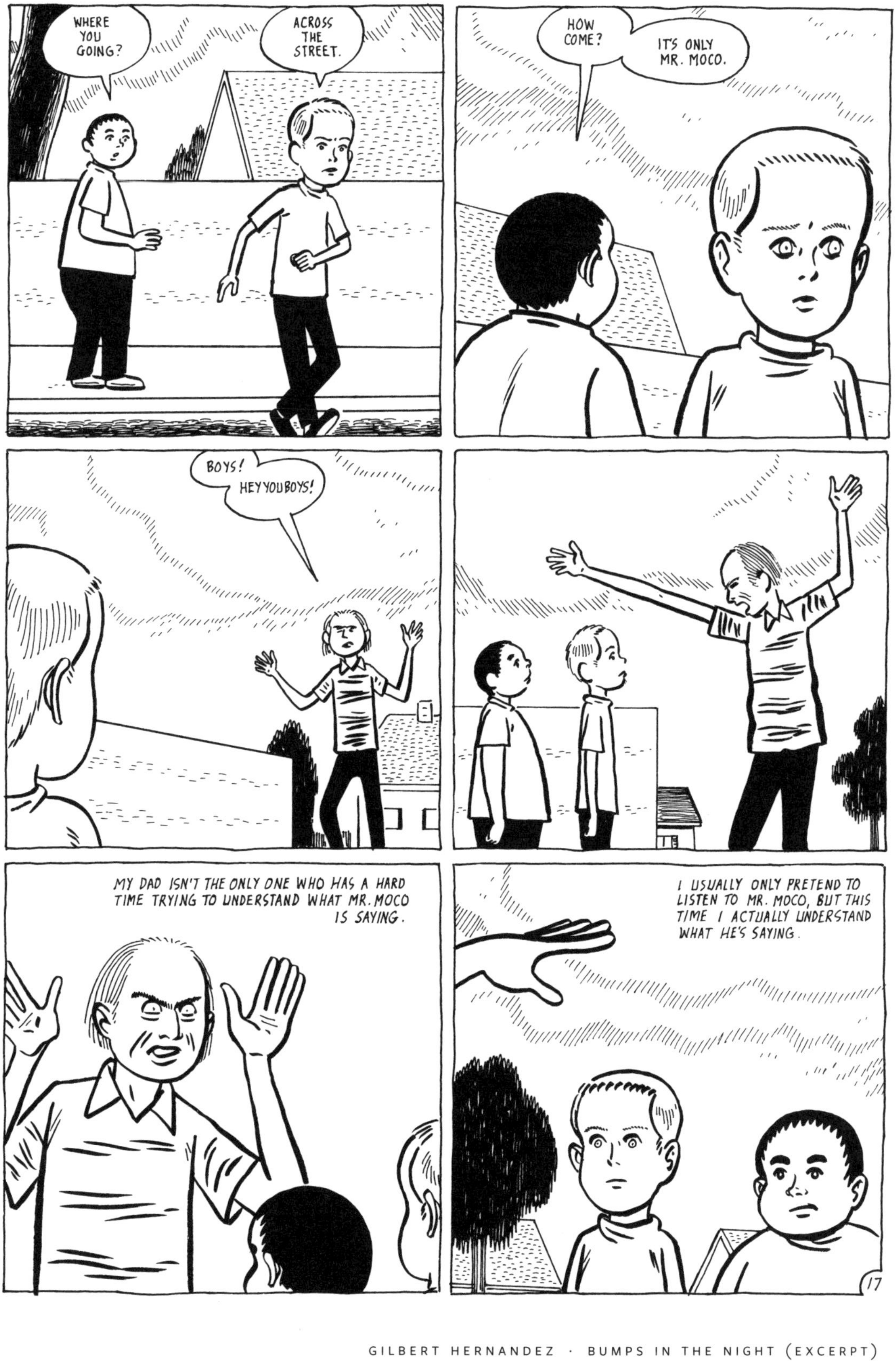
WHERE YOU GOING?
ACROSS THE STREET.
HOW COME?
IT'S ONLY MR. MOCO.
BOYS!
HEY YOU BOYS!
MY DAD ISN'T THE ONLY ONE WHO HAS A HARD TIME TRYING TO UNDERSTAND WHAT MR. MOCO IS SAYING.
I USUALLY ONLY PRETEND TO LISTEN TO MR. MOCO, BUT THIS TIME I ACTUALLY UNDERSTAND WHAT HE'S SAYING.
17

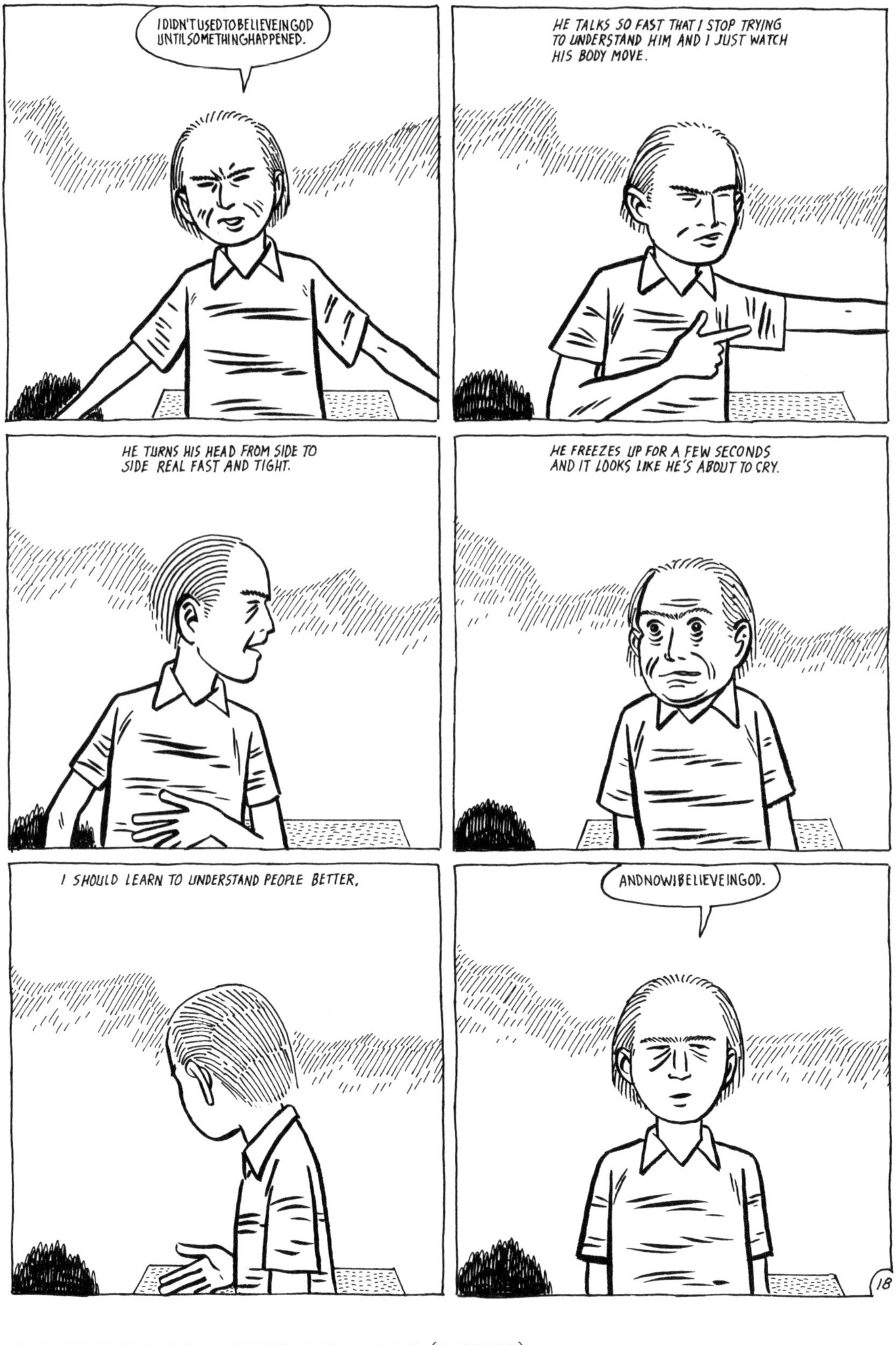
IDIDN'TUSEDTOBELIEVEINGOD UNTILSOMETHINGHAPPENED.
HE TALKS SO FAST THAT I STOP TRYING TO UNDERSTAND HIM AND I JUST WATCH HIS BODY MOVE.
HE TURNS HIS HEAD FROM SIDE TO SIDE REAL FAST AND TIGHT.
HE FREEZES UP FOR A FEW SECONDS AND IT LOOKS LIKE HE'S ABOUT TO CRY.
I SHOULD LEARN TO UNDERSTAND PEOPLE BETTER.
ANDNOWIBELIEVEINGOD.
18

# Don't Leave Me Alone

GG

*originally published as*

Don't Leave Me Alone

SELF-PUBLISHED

7 × 9 inches • 20 pages

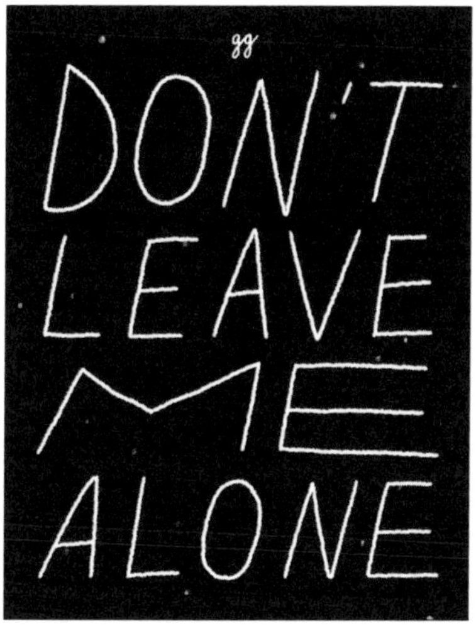
gg
DON'T
LEAVE
ME
ALONE

## Biography

GG grew up during the 1980s in a small Canadian prairie city. In this pre-Internet era, isolated geographically and culturally, drawing and making up stories was the means to connect to something more. It was romantic and lonely. ohgigue.com

## Statement

*Don't Leave Me Alone* takes some of my personal experiences of growing up and combines them with the general feeling of being helpless and scared and confused in a world where things don't always make sense. I originally made this story for the Comics Workbook Composition Competition 2014 and then self-published it as a Risograph printed book. The version included here has been redrawn and enhanced for aesthetic reasons and higher quality reproduction.

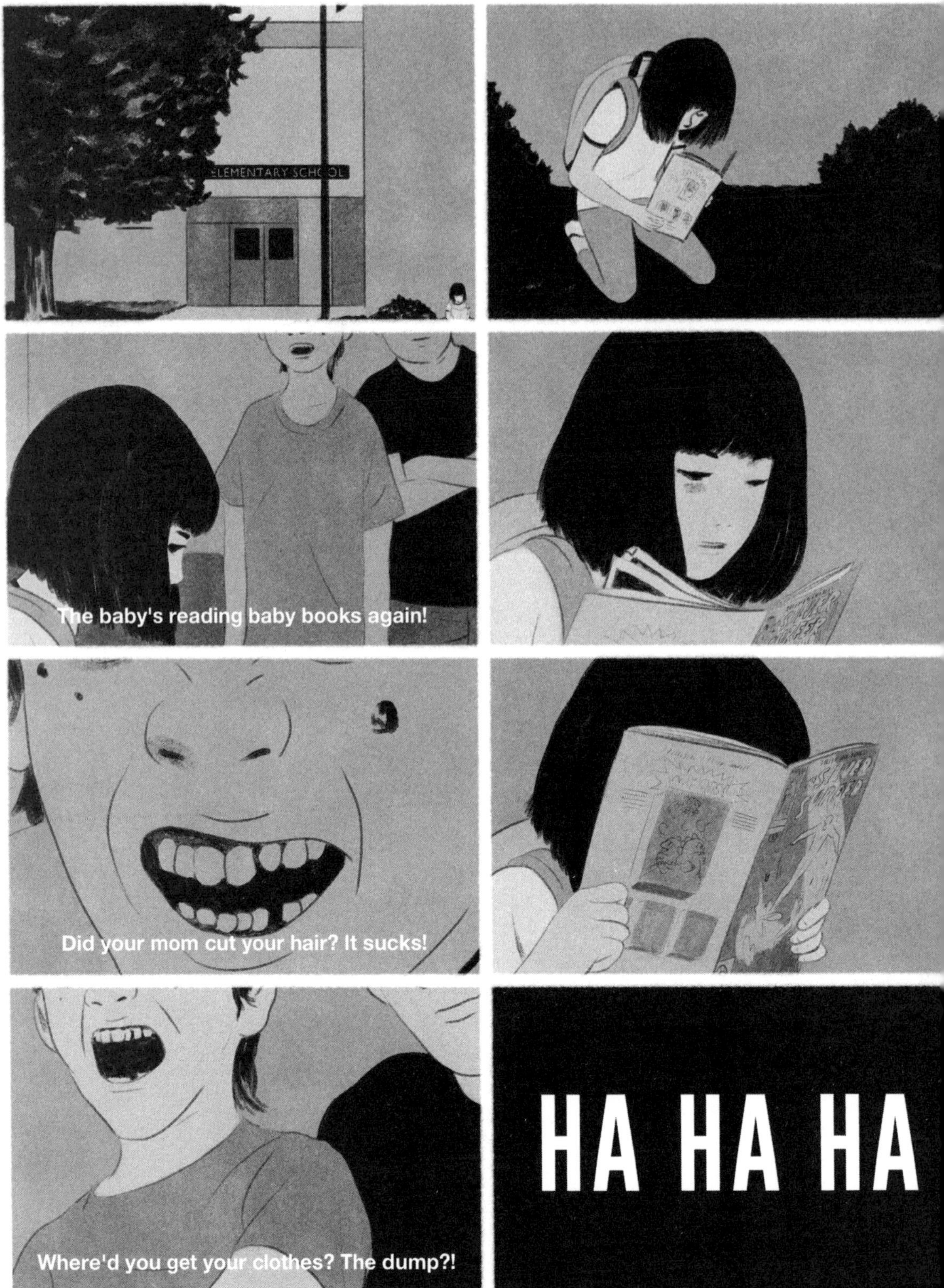
ELEMENTARY SCHOOL
The baby's reading baby books again!
Did your mom cut your hair? It sucks!
Where'd you get your clothes? The dump?!
HA HA HA

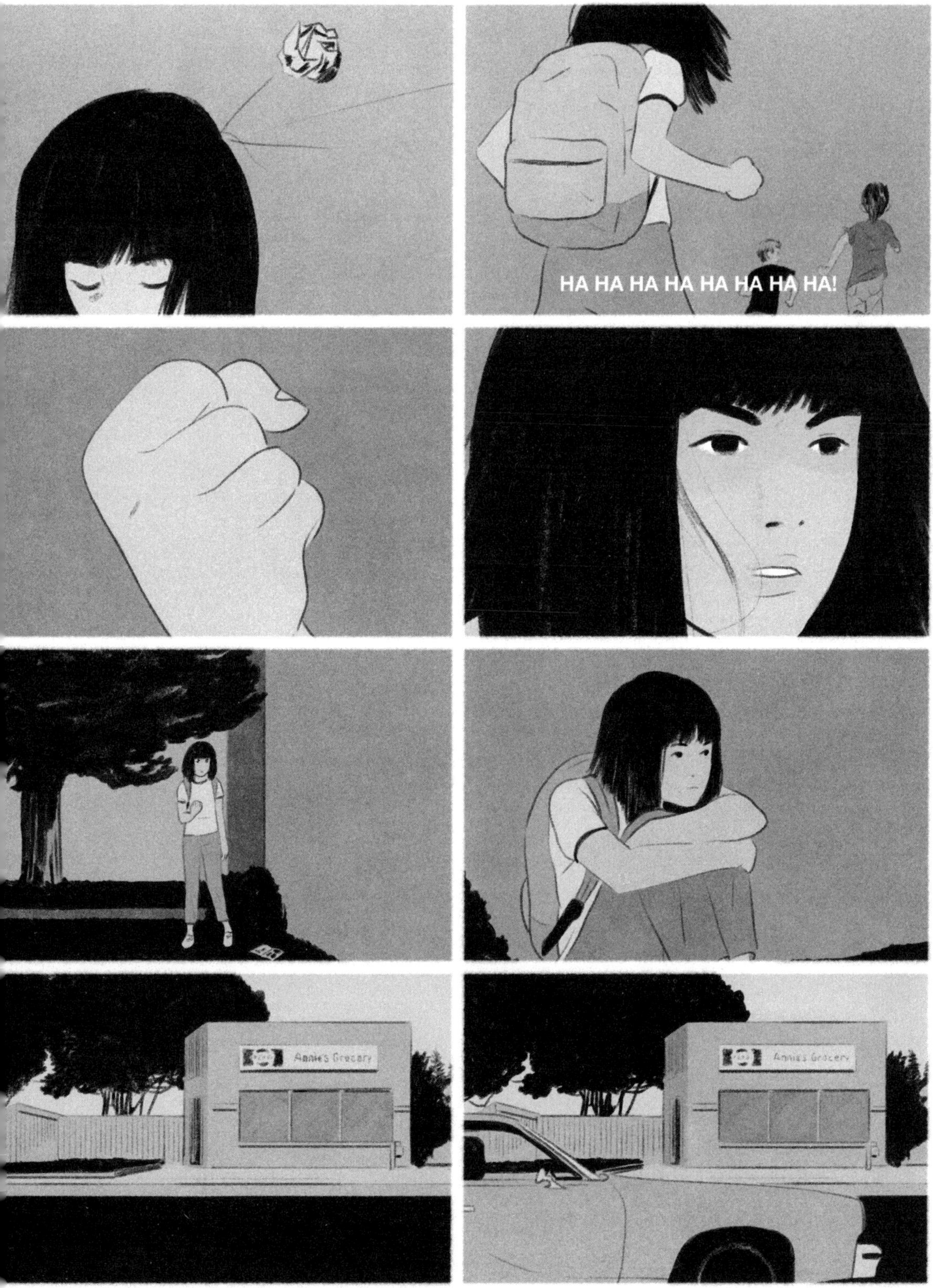
HA HA HA HA HA HA HA HA!
Annie's Grocery
Annie's Grocery

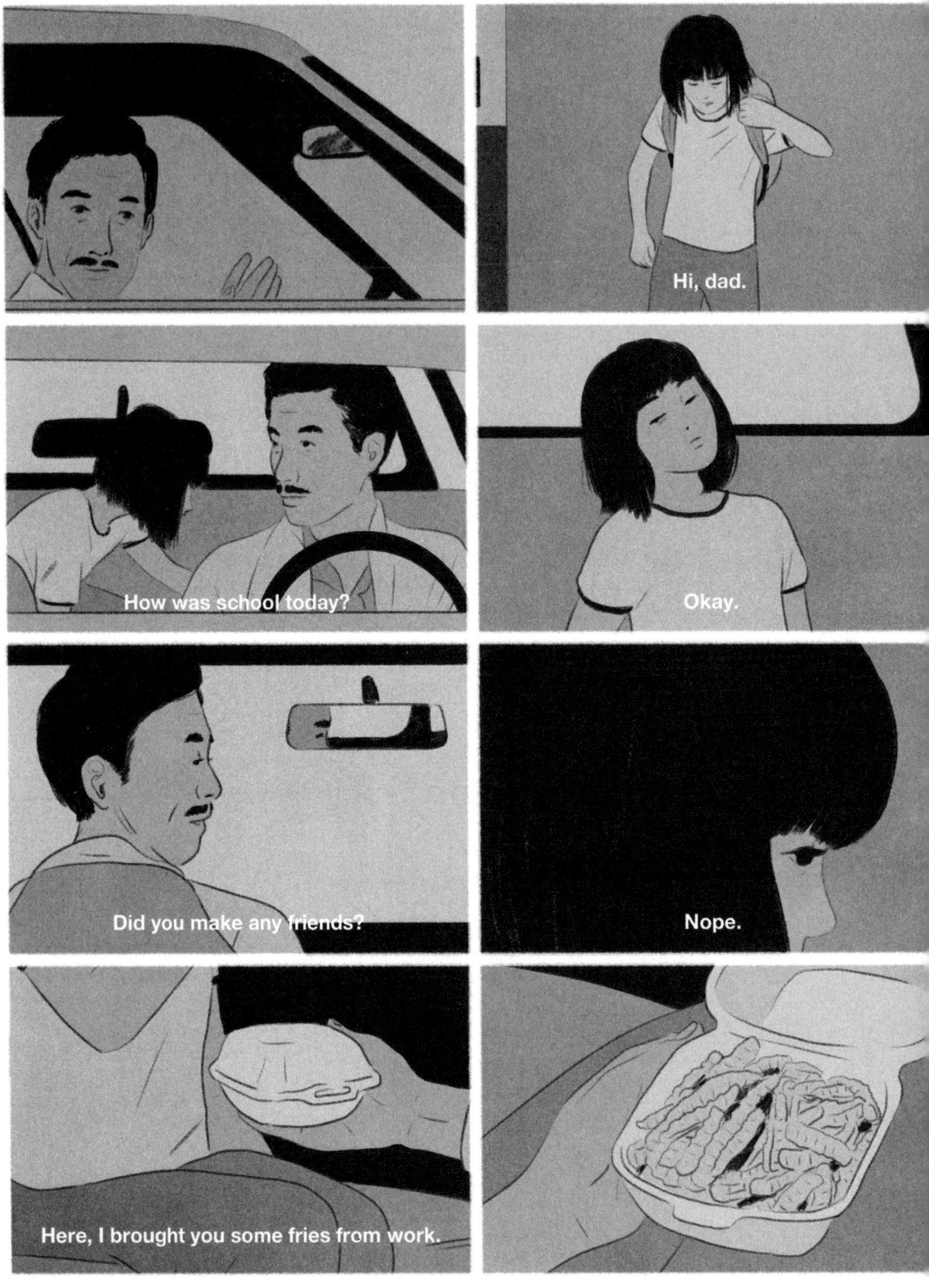
Hi, dad.
How was school today?
Okay.
Did you make any friends?
Nope.
Here, I brought you some fries from work.

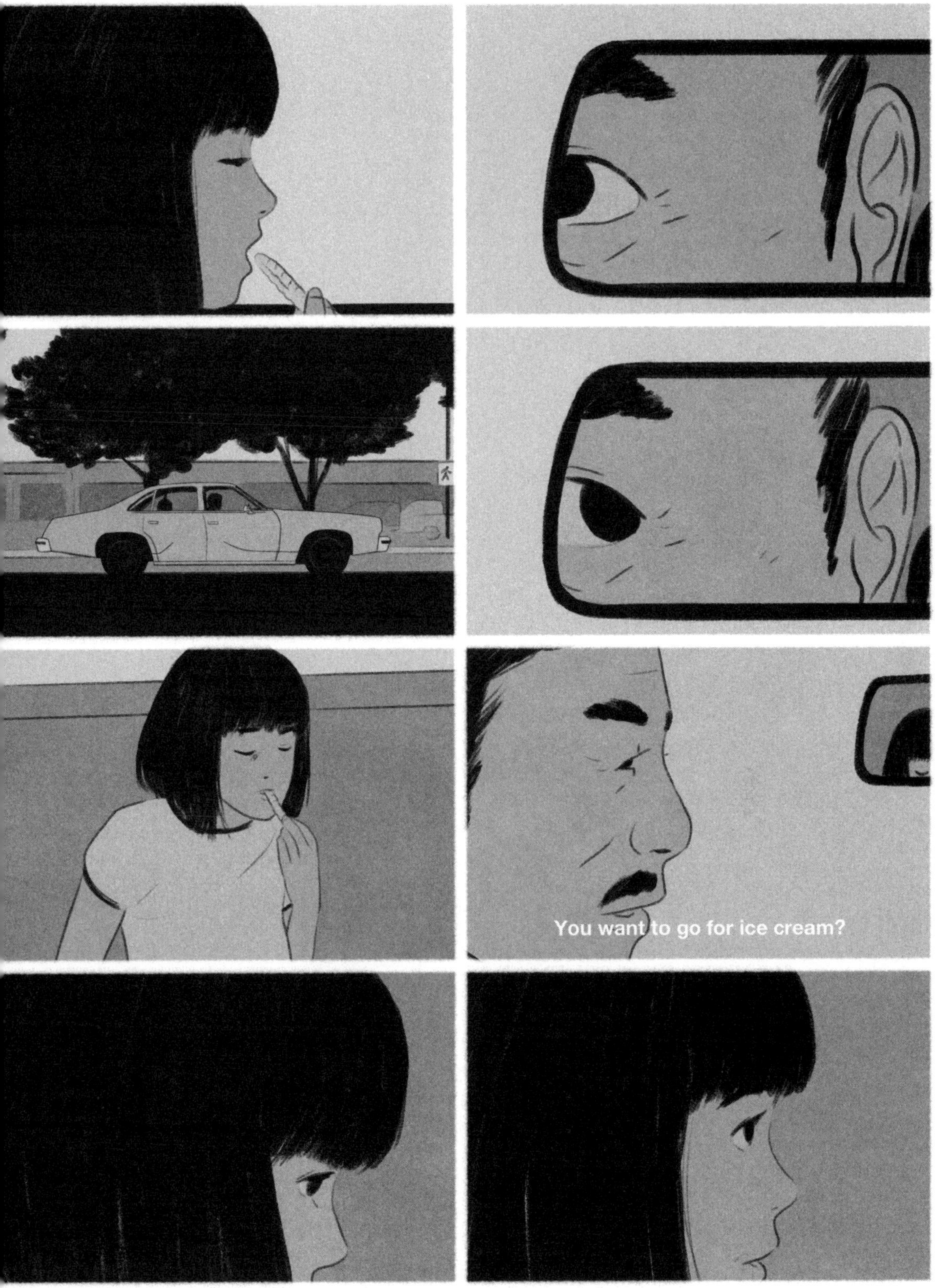
You want to go for ice cream?

Can I look in here for a second?

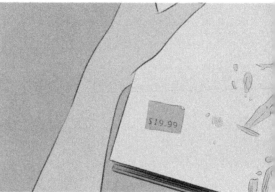

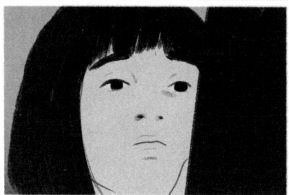

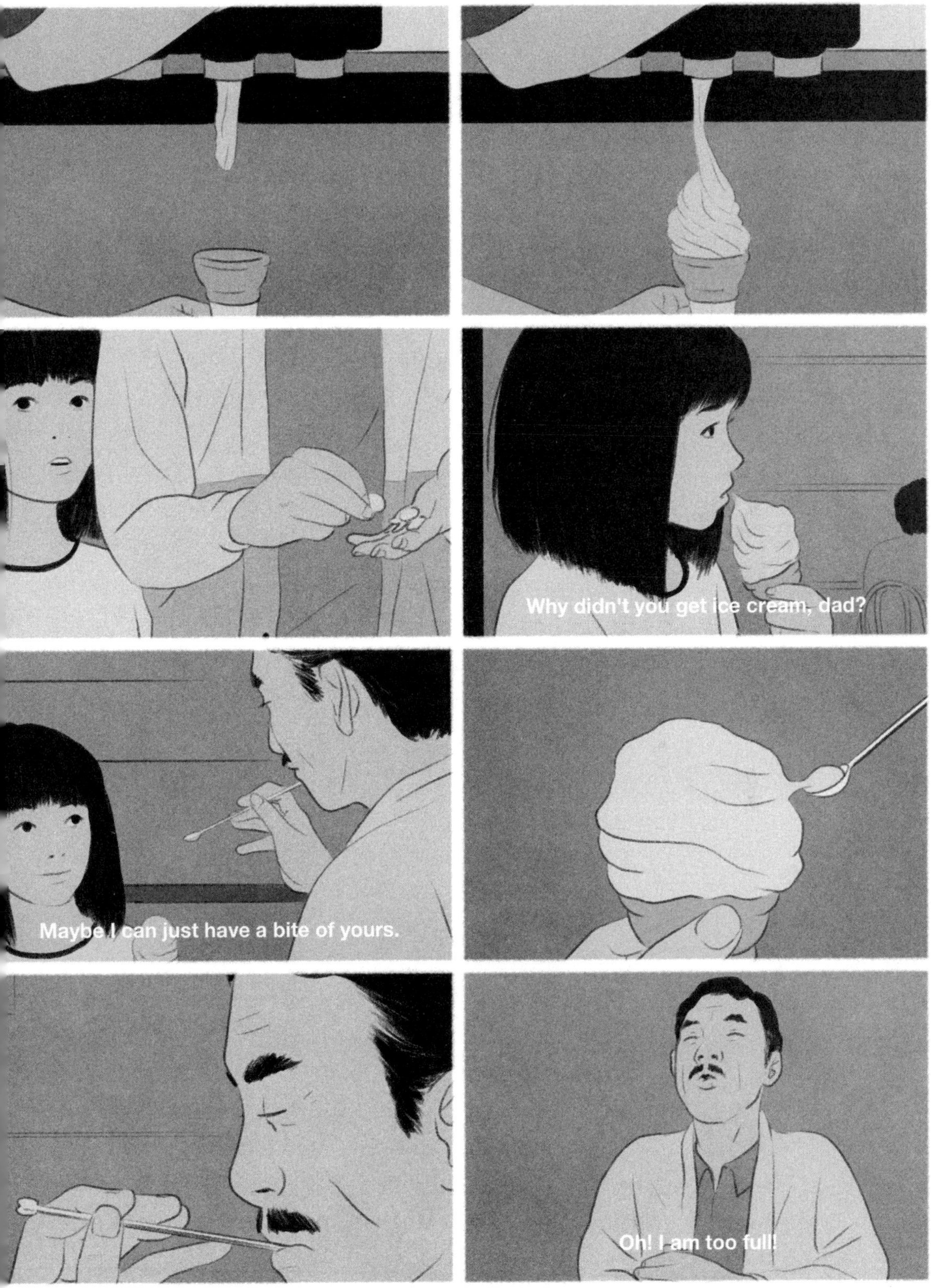
Why didn't you get ice cream, dad?
Maybe I can just have a bite of yours.
Oh! I am too full!

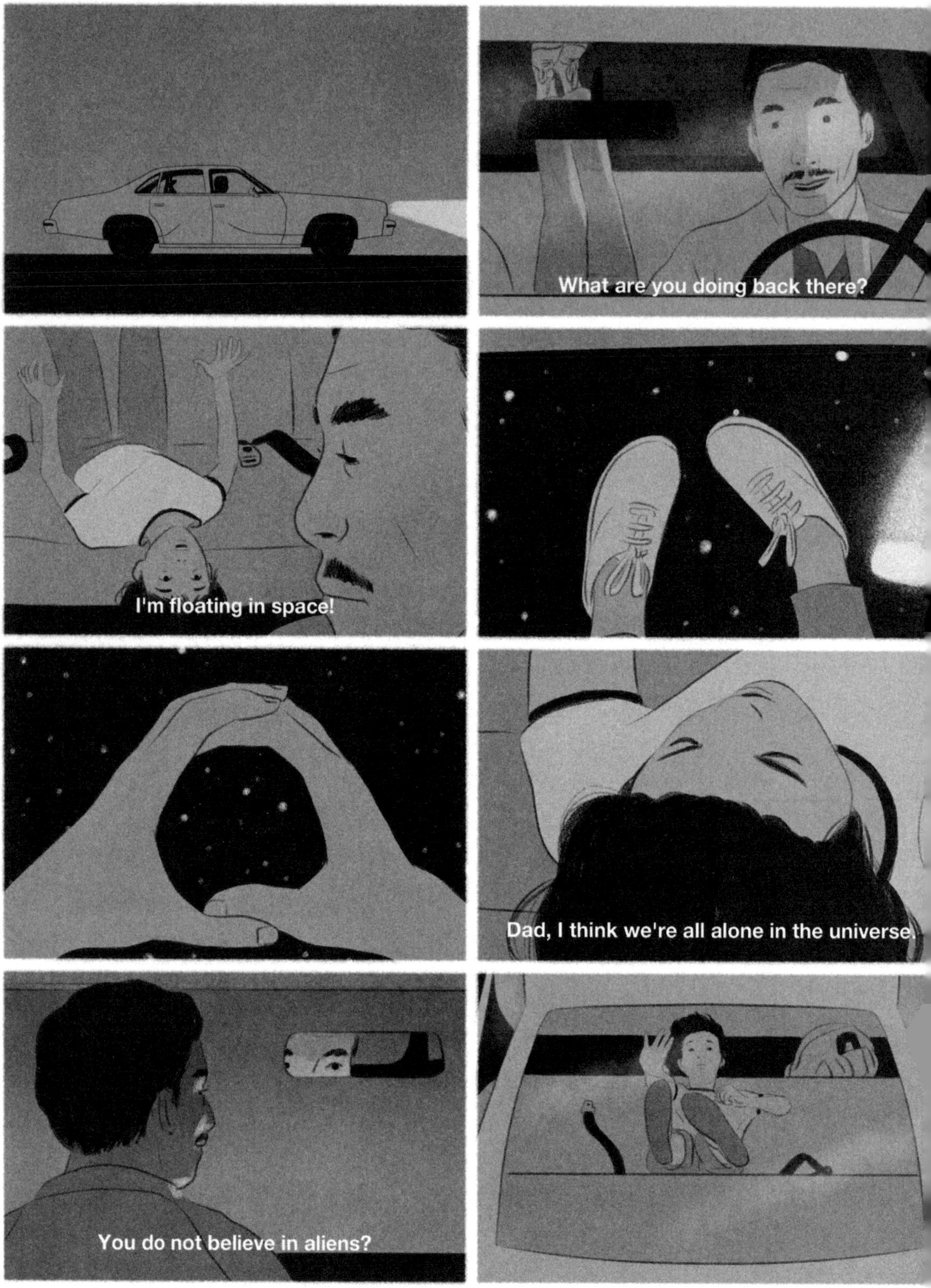
What are you doing back there?
I'm floating in space!
Dad, I think we're all alone in the universe.
You do not believe in aliens?

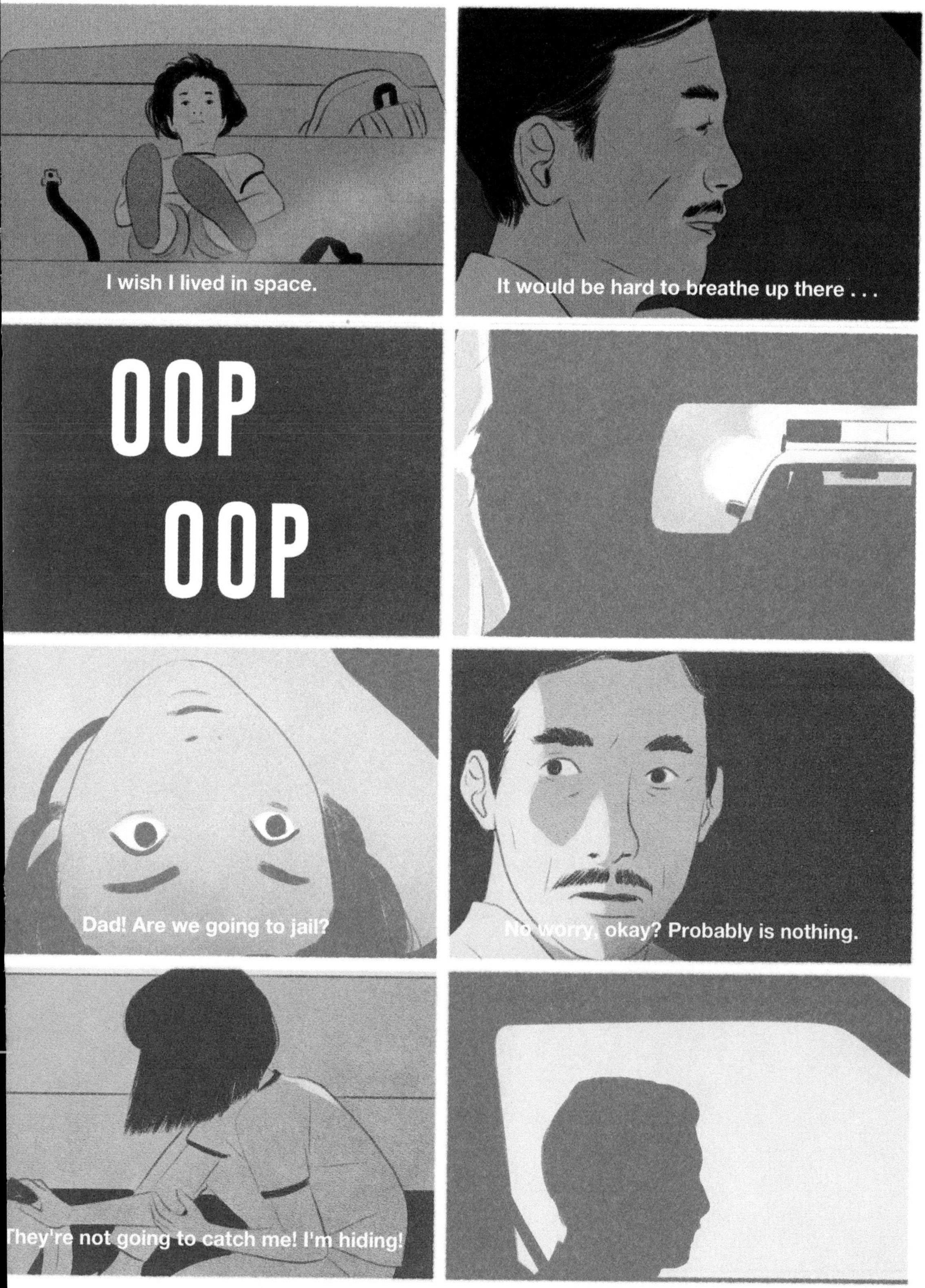
I wish I lived in space.
It would be hard to breathe up there . . .
OOP
OOP
Dad! Are we going to jail?
No worry, okay? Probably is nothing.
They're not going to catch me! I'm hiding!

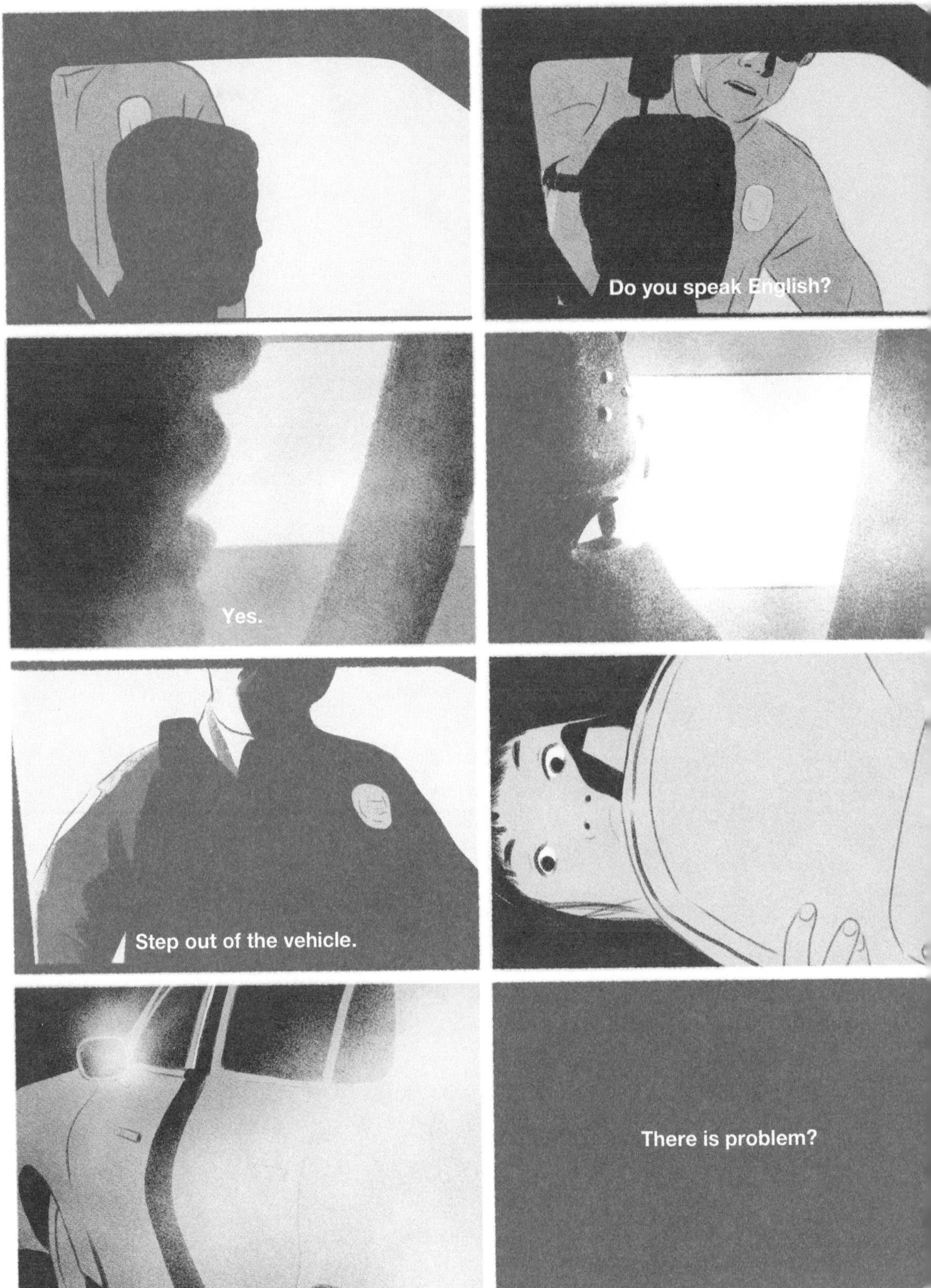
Do you speak English?
Yes.
Step out of the vehicle.
There is problem?

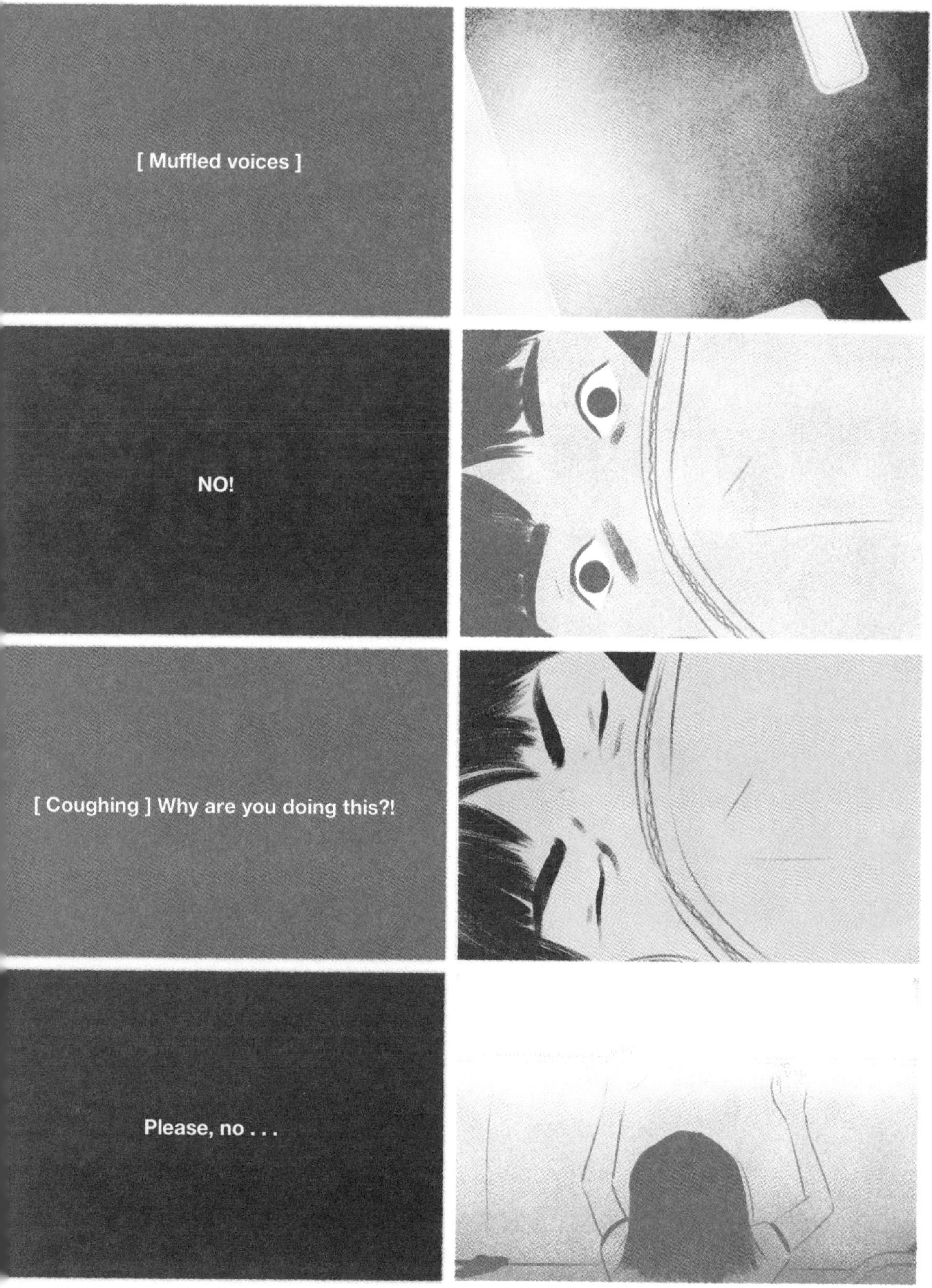
[ Muffled voices ]
NO!
[ Coughing ] Why are you doing this?!
Please, no . . .

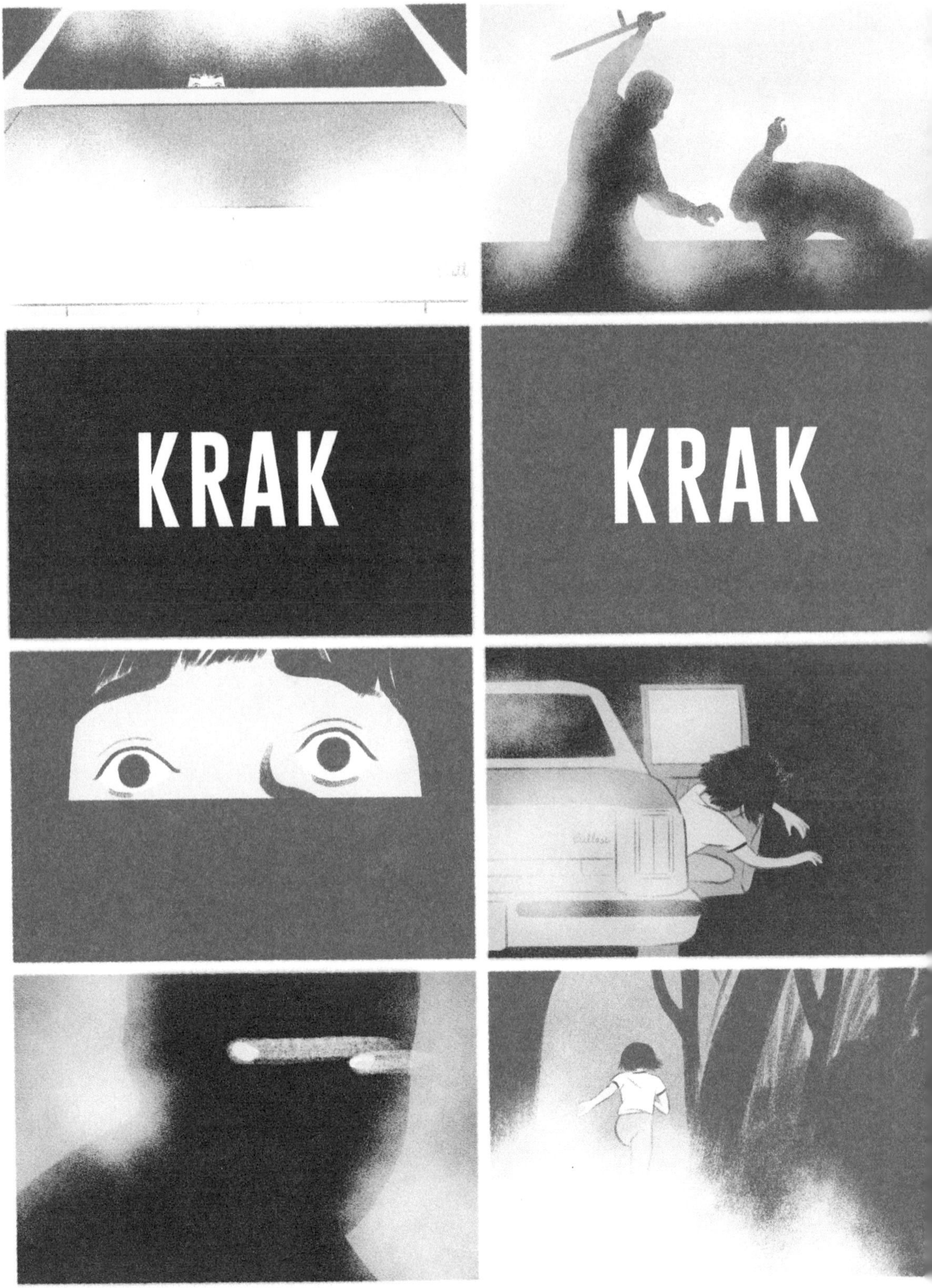
KRAK
KRAK

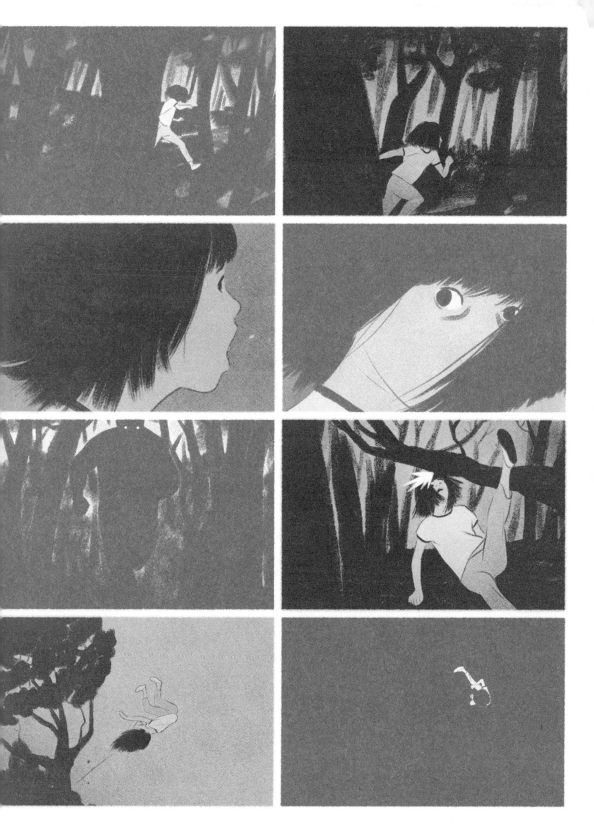

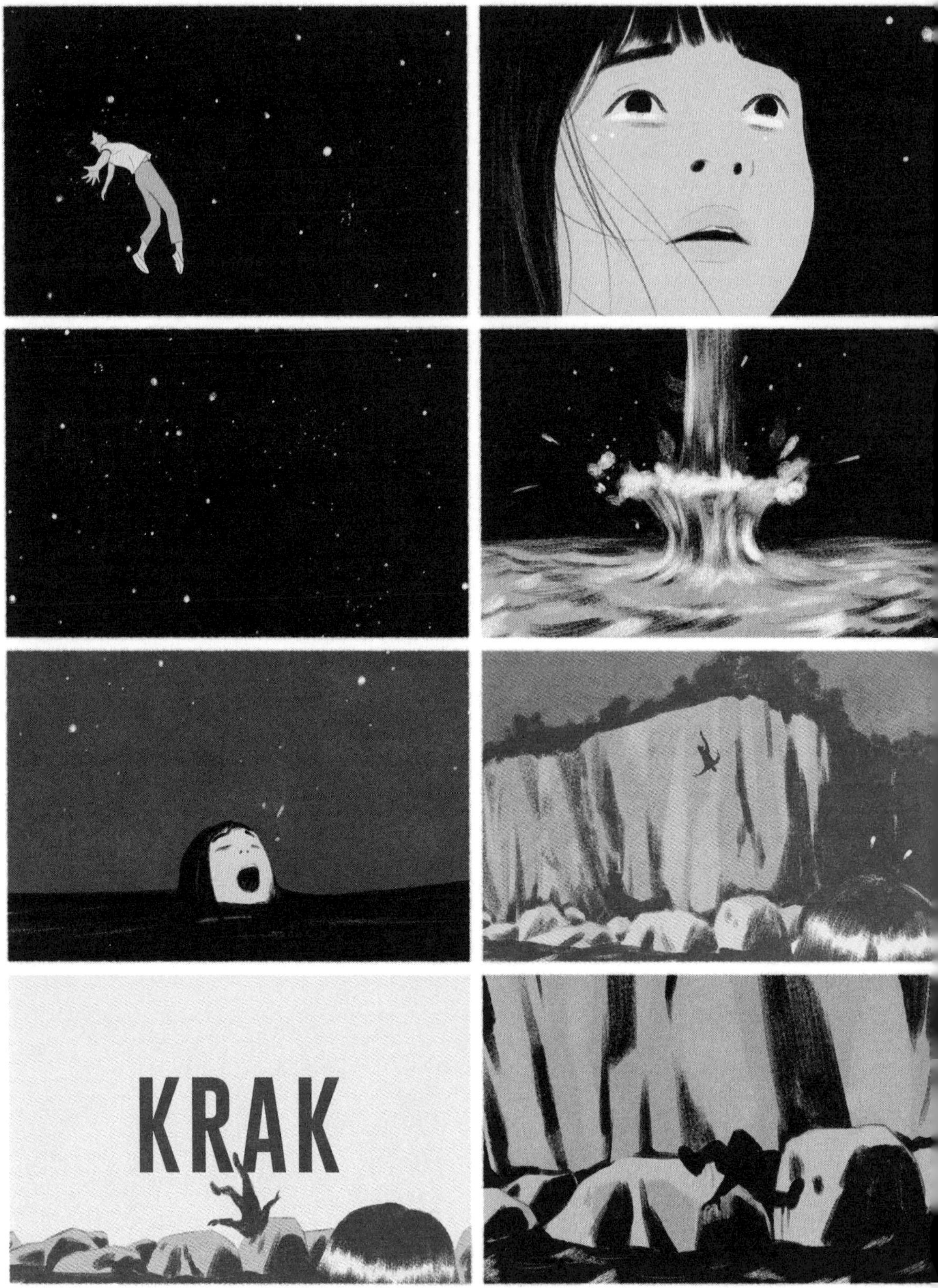
KRAK

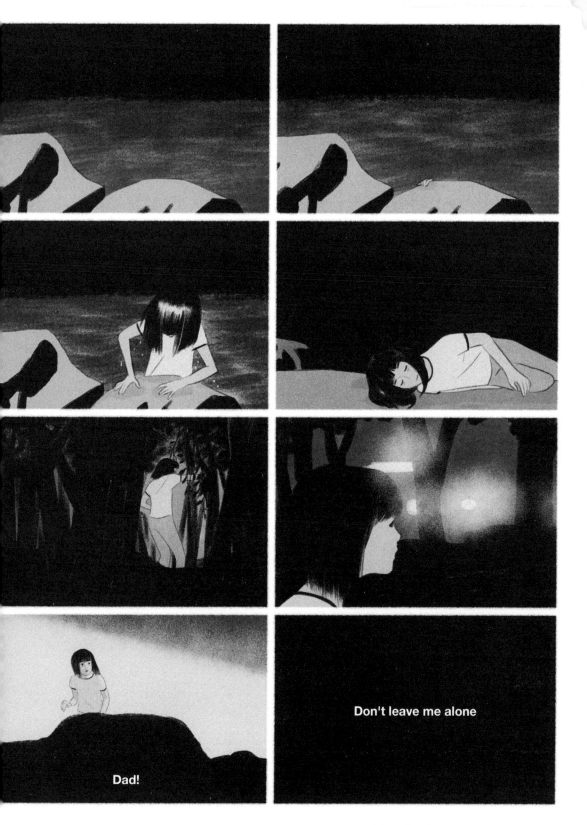

Dad!

Don't leave me alone

# Notable Comics

*from September 1, 2014, to August 31, 2015*

Selected by Bill Kartalopoulos

LALA ALBERT
Janus.

RICHARD ALEXANDER
Richy Vegas Comics #8.

TRACY AUCH
The Necrophilic Landscape.

RINA AYUYANG
A Cartoonist's Diary.
*tcj.com/author/rina-ayuyang/*

JOSH BAYER
Mr. Incompleto.

GEOFF BERNER AND TIN CAN FOREST
We Are Going to Bremen to Be Musicians.

BRIAN BLOMERTH
Understanding Nicotine.

MAT BRINKMAN
Cretin: Keep on Creep'n Creek, Episode 2.
*U.D.W.F.G.*, vol. 2.

ELIJAH BRUBAKER
Reich #12.

TESSA BRUNTON
Domestic Times.

ANDY BURKHOLDER
The Lower Style.

CHARLES BURNS
Sugar Skull.

TINGS CHAK
Undocumented.

CHRIS CILLA
Laybrinthectomy/Luncheonette.

MAX CLOTFELTER
The Elements of Rough, Volume One.

WARREN CRAGHEAD
Golden Smoke.

FAREL DALRYMPLE
It Will All Hurt #3.

ANYA DAVIDSON
Head Shrinka.

ELEANOR DAVIS
Love Story.
*hazlitt.net/comics/love-story*

MICHAEL DEFORGE
Lose #6.

KRYSTAL DIFRONZO
The Good Hodgkins.

STEVE DITKO
#200w1, #22, and #20ww30ww.

EVAN DORKIN
The Eltingville Club #2.

DW
Mountebank, Pages 1AIa+ to 26XVb+.
*Irene 5.*

DENNIS P. EICHHORN AND VARIOUS
Extra Good Stuff

THEO ELLSWORTH
The Understanding Monster, Book Two.

INÉS ESTRADA
Lapsos.

DEVIN FLYNN
Hawd Tales #1.

SOPHIA FOSTER-DIMINO
Sex Fantasy #4.

NOEL FREIBERT
Old Ground.

JASON FULFORD AND TAMARA SHOPSIN
This Equals That.

MARNIE GALLOWAY
In the Sounds and Seas vol. 2.

JULIAN GLANDER
Please Look at Me.
*vice.com/series/please-look-at-me*

CARLOS GONZALEZ
Scab County.

BILL GRIFFITH
Zippy the Pinhead.

NICHOLAS GUREWITCH
The Perry Bible Fellowship.
*pbfcomics.com*

TRENTON DOYLE HANCOCK
Step and Screw. *Nat. Brut* #5.

JOHN HANKIEWICZ
Education.

SAMMY HARKHAM
Crickets #4.

LEAH HAYES
Not Funny Ha-Ha.

JAIME HERNANDEZ
Stories from *Love and Rockets: New Stories,* vol. 7.

KEVIN HOOYMAN
Conditions on the Ground #11.

LAWRENCE HUBBARD
Real Deal #7.

EMILY HUTCHINGS
Boring Comics.

JESSE JACOBS
Mathematical Solutions for a Global Crisis.

CATHY G. JOHNSON
Dear Amanda.

KEN JOHNSON
Ball and Cone. *ballandcone.tumblr.com*

JUNE AND PAULA
Water. *World War 3 Illustrated* #46.

LAURA KNETZGER
Sea Urchin.

AIDAN KOCH
Impressions.

JAMES KOCHALKA
Fungus.

ALINE KOMINSKY-CRUMB AND ROBERT CRUMB
"Aline & Bob" comics. *Zap* #16.

RICHARD KRAFT
Here Comes Kitty.

PATRICK KYLE
New Comics #5 and 6.

KATE LACOUR
Eye Sees Eye.

AARON LANGE
Trim #3.

BLAISE LARMEE
3 Books.

SCOTT MCCLOUD
The Sculptor.

BEN MENDELEWICZ
The Lonely One Home.
*When the Joggers Run the Town.*

MELISSA MENDES
The Weight #1-3.

JASON T. MILES
How It Happened.

TONY MILLIONAIRE
Maakies.

TALYA MODLIN
Circling the Pomeroy Abyss.

VICTOR MOSCOSO
The Card Game AND Untitled. *Zap* #16.

CORINNE MUCHA
Fixated.

KRIS MUKAI
Weeping Flower, Grows in Darkness.

ROMAN MURADOV
(In a Sense) Lost and Found.

JASON MURPHY
Me Nut Nut Nut #3.

ERIK NEBEL
Well Come.
eriknebel.tumblr.com

MARK NEWGARDEN AND MEGAN MONTAGUE CASH
Bow-Wow's Nightmare Neighbors.

MOLLY COLLEEN O'CONNELL
Stripp Mall #1.

JOHN PHAM
Epoxy #5.

DAVID PLUNKERT
Heroical 2.

RICHARD SALA
Super-Enigmatix. *In a Glass Grotesquely.*

ZAK SALLY
Recidivist IV.

SETH SCRIVER
Blob Top #2.

DARYL SEITCHIK
Flag Day. *SubCultures.*

ROBERT SERGEL
Eschew #4.

SETH
Palookaville #22.

DASH SHAW
Doctors.

GILBERT SHELTON
The Fabulous Furry Freak Brothers in Phineas Becomes a Suicide Bomber. *Zap #16.*

JASON SHIGA
Demon, Chapters 6 through 14. *shigabooks.com*

JOSH SIMMONS
Black River.

ART SPIEGELMAN
Notes from a First Amendment Fundamentalist. *The Nation*, March 23, 2015.

CONOR STECHSCHULTE
Generous Bosom, Part One.

LESLIE STEIN
Bright-Eyed at Midnight.

JILLIAN TAMAKI
SexCoven. *Frontier #7.*

WALKER TATE
Waiting Room.

MATTHEW THURBER
Art Comic #1 & 2.

PETE TOMS
The Red Swan. *Felony Comics #2.*

PAUL K. TUNIS
Juniper. *Ink Brick #3.*

MARGUERITE VAN COOK AND JAMES ROMBERGER
The Late Child and Other Animals.

MICKEY ZACCHILLI
Untitled. *Lovers Only.*

TILLIE WALDEN
The End of Summer.

KIM WAYMAN
Special Intelligence. *Chlorophilia.*

LAUREN WEINSTEIN
Flower Voyeur. *www.theparisreview.org/blog/2015/07/28/flower-voyeur-a-comic/*

LALE WESTVIND
Hot Dog Beach #3.

LISA WILDE
Yo, Miss.

RON WIMBERLY
Ten Years After. *The New Yorker*, August 24, 2015.

GINA WYNBRANDT
Big Pussy.

CREDITS

Untitled by Taylor-Ruth Baldwin. First published at This Is Hanging Rock Comics (thisishangingrockcomics.tumblr.com). Copyright © 2016 by Taylor-Ruth Baldwin. Reprinted by permission of Taylor-Ruth Baldwin.

Excerpt from "Syllabus" by Lynda Barry. First published in *Syllabus,* October 21, 2014. Copyright © 2015 by Lynda Barry. Reprinted by permission of *Drawn & Quarterly.*

"Broadside Ballads" by Kate Beaton. First published at harkavagrant.com. Copyright © 2015 by Kate Beaton. Reprinted by permission of *Drawn & Quarterly.*

*El Deafo* by Cece Bell. Copyright © 2014 Cece Bell. Used by permission of Amulet, an imprint of Harry N. Abrams, Inc., New York. All rights reserved.

"The Dishrack" by Gabrielle Bell. First published at gabriellebell.com. Copyright © 2015 by Gabrielle Bell. Reprinted by permission of Gabrielle Bell.

"Stroppy" by Marc Bell. First published in *Stroppy.* Copyright © 2015 by Marc Bell. Reprinted by permission of Marc Bell/ *Drawn & Quarterly.*

Excerpt from "Dissident Years" by Nina Bunjevac. First published in *Fatherland: A Family History* by Nina Bunjevac. Copyright © 2014 by Nina Bunjevac. Used by permission of Liveright Publishing Company. Published by Jonathan Cape in the UK and reprinted by permission of The Random House Group Limited. This selection may not be reproduced, stored in a retrieval system, or transmitted in any form or by any means without the prior written permission of the publisher.

"The Swim" and "Today" by Anne Emond. "The Swim" was first published at Okey-Panky.com. "Today" was first published at comiques.tumblr.com. Copyright © 2015 by Anne Emond. Reprinted by permission of Anne Emond.

"All the Paintings Here Agree" by Liana Finck. First published in *The Toast.* Copyright © 2015 by Liana Finck. Reprinted by permission of Liana Finck.

Excerpt from "The Corpse, the Ghost and the Hollow-Weenie" by Casanova Frankenstein. First published in *The Adventures of TAD MARTIN #6.* Copyright © 2015 by Casanova Frankenstein. Reprinted by permission of Casanova Frankenstein.

"R. Crumb and Me" by Drew Friedman. First published in *Masterful Marks: Cartoonists Who Changed the World,* Simon & Schuster. Copyright © 2015 by Drew Friedman. Reprinted by permission of Drew Friedman.

"Blinky-Jinks Playhouse" by Char Esmé. First published in *Square Dance at Palms Promenade.* Copyright © 2015 by Charlotte Esmé Glauberman. Reprinted by permission of Charlotte Esmé Glauberman.

"Big Rudy's Cowgirls Club" by Char Esmé and Lauren Poor. First published in *Square Dance At Palms Promenade.* Copyright © 2015 by Charlotte Esmé Glauberman and Lauren Poor. Reprinted by permission of Charlotte Esmé Glauberman and Lauren Poor.

"Blanket Portraits" by Genevieve Gosselin. From *Drawn & Quarterly: Twenty-five Years of Contemporary Cartooning, Comics, and Graphic Novels.* Copyright © 2015 by Genevieve Gosselin. Reprinted by permission of *Drawn & Quarterly.*

"Bumps in the Night" by Gilbert Hernandez. First published in *Bumperhead.* Copyright © 2015 by Gilbert Hernandez. Reprinted by permission of *Drawn & Quarterly.*

# THE BEST AMERICAN SERIES®

*FIRST, BEST, AND BEST-SELLING*

*The Best American Comics*

*The Best American Essays*

*The Best American Infographics*

*The Best American Mystery Stories*

*The Best American Nonrequired Reading*

*The Best American Science and Nature Writing*

*The Best American Science Fiction and Fantasy*

*The Best American Short Stories*

*The Best American Sports Writing*

*The Best American Travel Writing*

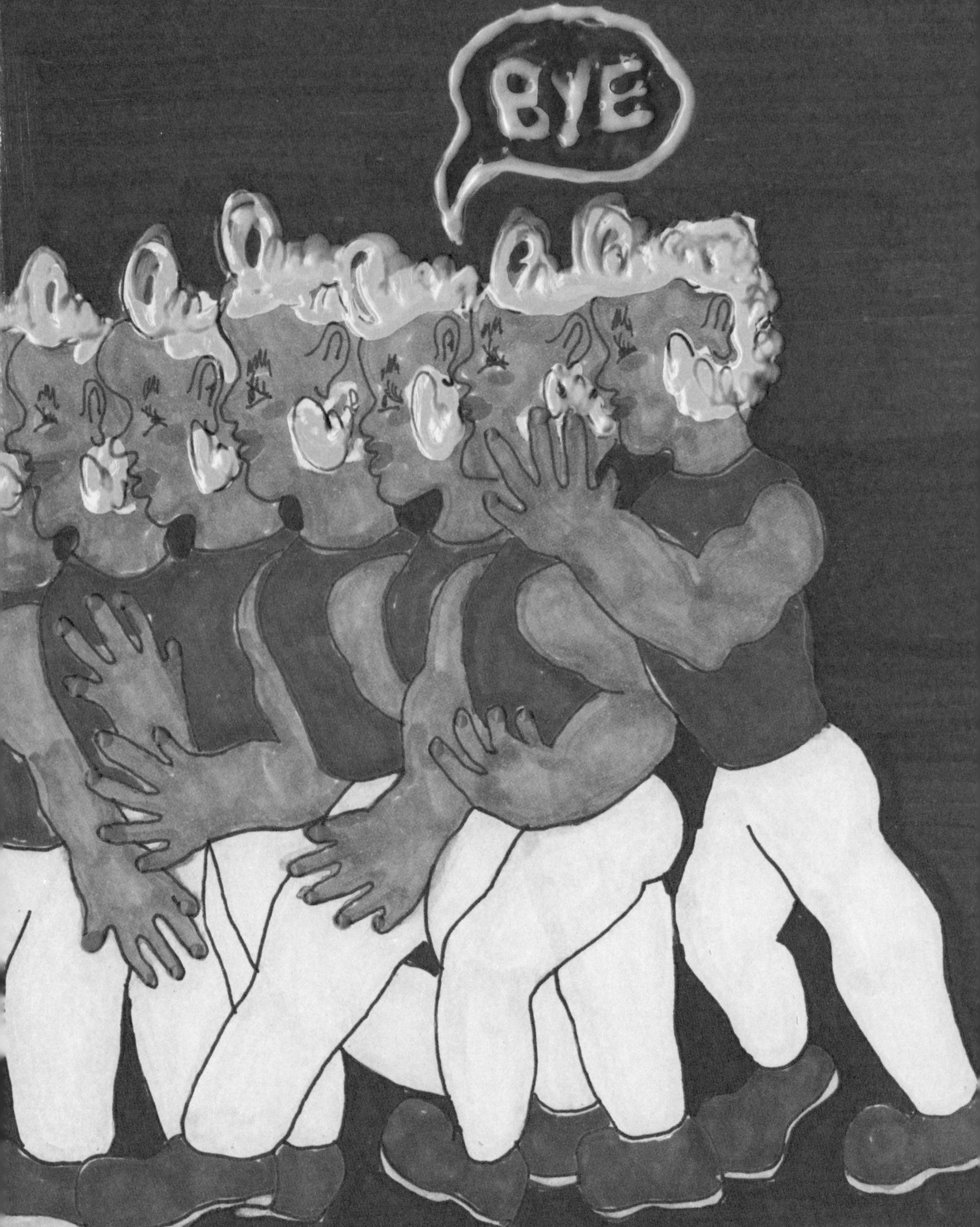
BYE